# THE BLACK FAMILY

## Essays and Studies

# OTHER TITLES OF RELATED INTEREST

Christopher Carlson, *Perspectives on the Family: History, Class, and Feminism*

John Crosby, *Illusion and Disillusion: The Self in Love and Marriage*, Fourth Edition

Norval Glenn/Marion Tolbert Coleman, *Family Relations: A Reader*

Mary Ann Lamanna/Agnes Riedmann, *Marriages and Families*, Fourth Edition

Thomas Lasswell/Marcia Lasswell, *Marriage and the Family*, Third Edition

E. E. LeMasters/John DeFrain, *Parents in Contemporary America: A Sympathetic View*, Fifth Edition

Lloyd Saxton, *The Individual, Marriage, and the Family*, Seventh Edition

# THE BLACK FAMILY

## Essays and Studies

### FOURTH EDITION

## Robert Staples

University of California, San Francisco

**Wadsworth Publishing Company,** Belmont, California
A Division of Wadsworth, Inc.

Sociology Editor   *Serina Beauparlant*
Editorial Assistant   *Marla Nowick*
Production   *Mary Douglas*
Print Buyer   *Randy Hurst*
Designer   *Merle Sanderson*
Copy Editor   *Toni Haskell*
Technical Illustrator   *John Foster, Reese Thornton*
Compositor   *Thompson Type*
Cover   *Vargas/Williams/Design*

Printed in the United States of America

1 2 3 4 5 6 7 8 9 10—95 94 93 92 91

**Library of Congress Cataloging-in-Publication Data**

Staples, Robert.
    The Black family : essays and studies / Robert Staples. — 4th ed.
        p.    cm.
    Includes bibliographical references.
    ISBN 0-534-15378-x
    1. Afro-Americans—Families.    I. Title.
E185.86.S7    1991
306.85′08996073—dc20                         90-44027
                                                CIP

# CONTENTS

## 4 · Sex Roles 101

## 5 · Male/Female Relationships: Single and Married 124

# PART THREE: THE FAMILY 155

## 6 · Childbearing and Parental Roles 160

## 7 · The Extended Family 192

# DEDICATION

---

To my nieces and nephews—

*Amber*

*Charles*

*Corliss*

*Darryl*

*Denise*

*Melvena*

*Mia*

*Orin*

*Shameka*

*Tanya*

*Toni*

# PREFACE

At the time of this writing, the *Moynihan Report* is observing its twenty-fifth anniversary. Daniel Patrick Moynihan, now the senior senator from the state of New York, is being hailed as a prophet for his prediction in 1965 that "At the root of the deterioration of the Negro community is the deterioration of the Negro family." Certainly, it has become increasingly difficult to refute the statistical indices of Black family disruption. However, it is instructive to note that the statistical indices Moynihan applied to define family "pathology" among Black Americans in 1965 (such as female-headed households, out-of-wedlock birth rates, and fertility rates) are very similar to statistical indices of the same phenomena among White Americans in 1990. Obviously, this fact suggests that the direction of social change was the same for all racial groups in the United States over that twenty-five year period.

The Black American community has its share of problems, and considerable controversy exists over the cause and nature of those problems. Some students of the subject assert that misguided liberal social policies have been the force behind Black family disruption. Other theorists claim that society's failure to provide relevant education, meaningful employment, and equal opportunities for Black Americans has adversely affected their family system. Both views are represented in this fourth edition of *The Black Family: Essays and Studies*. Moreover, we address as many dimensions of the Black family as possible in this new edition. A majority of the articles in this edition are new and thus represent recent information, theories, and statistics.

Also in this fourth edition, we have expanded the sections on history and public policy—two vital areas that explain much about the past and future of Black American families. We have included new articles on women's issues, family violence, and the Black gay experience. In addition, a new section on health issues that impact the Black family, such as AIDS and substance abuse has been added. Every dimension and segment of the Black American family is represented in this new edition. This coverage of topics maintains the tradition that has been established over the last twenty years that this text is the most comprehensive work available on the Black American family.

As always, this new edition is a collective effort, and I am indebted to a number of people for their assistance. Even though he is now Editor-in-Chief, Steve Rutter continues to support all efforts to produce, update, and promote this book. Serina Beauparlant came on board as Sociology Editor at Wadsworth and was not content to be a passive agent for this revision. Instead, she gave me the benefit of her work in the field and filled me in on the latest ideas and trends in family studies. Marla Nowick, Senior Editorial Assistant, was the anchor for all the tasks that must be done to put together a new manuscript. She is an excellent coordinator and maintained morale in the face of the tricky problems that beset any effort involving forty different authors. I am also grateful to the manuscript reviewers for their invaluable suggestions. They are Rose Brewer, University of Minnesota; Terry Jones, California State University, Hayward; and Teresa Labov, University of Pennsylvania. Others who played crucial roles in the production process were Mary Douglas, Production Coordinator, Toni Haskell, Copy Editor, and Robert Kauser, Permissions Editor whose tasks included quiet diplomacy and some detective work. Finally, I thank Professor Talmadge Anderson, the editor of the *Western Journal of Black Studies*, who was kind enough to give me permission to reprint articles from his journal. Moreover, he has been a good friend and source of support since he first met me as a young graduate student many years ago. Erma Lawson and Lawrence Gary were also helpful in my efforts to organize this book. Because only my name appears on the front of this book, I remain responsible for any omissions and flaws.

Robert Staples

# PART ONE

## The Setting

Many changes have occurred in this country since 1954, covering a wide array of personalities, values, and institutions and bringing about a marked change in the functioning of society as a whole. These changes have been most dramatic within the institution of the family where they have had a most telling effect on our personal lives. We are all, to some degree, affected by increasing sexual permissiveness, changes in sex role expectations, a declining fertility rate, altered attitudes toward childbearing and childrearing, a continuing increase in the divorce rate, and the like.

One would not expect Black families to be immune to the forces modifying our family forms. There is ample evidence that they are not. At the same time, their special status as a racial minority with a singular history continues to give the Black marital and family patterns a unique character. Despite what many allege to be the positive gains of the sixties and seventies, the problems of poverty and racial oppression continue to plague large numbers of Afro-Americans. Black Americans are still spatially segregated from the majority of the more affluent white citizenry, and certain cultural values distinguish their family life in form and content from that of the middle-class, white, Anglo-Saxon model.

Nevertheless, the commonality of the two may be greater than the differences. We lose nothing by admitting this. Moreover, the variations within the Black population may be greater than the differences between the two racial groups. Therefore, it becomes even more important to view the Black family from the widest possible perspective, from its peculiar history to the alternate family life-styles now emerging.

## The Changing Black Family

It is generally accepted that the precursor of contemporary sociological research and theories on the Black family is the work of the late Black sociologist E. Franklin Frazier. Although Frazier's investigations of the Black family began in the twenties, his works are still considered the definitive findings on Black family life in the United States (Frazier, 1939). As a sociologist, Frazier was primarily interested in race relations as a social process, and he sought to explain that process through the study of the Black family. Through his training in the University of Chicago's social ecology school under the tutelage of Park, Wirth, Burgess, and others, Frazier came to believe that race relations proceeded through different stages of development to the final stage of assimilation.

Since it is through the family that the culture of a group is transmitted, Frazier chose this group as the object of his sociological study. Using the natural history approach, he explained the present condition of the Black family as the culmination of an evolutionary process, its structure strongly affected by the vestiges of slavery, racism, and economic exploitation. The institution of enslavement and slavery virtually destroyed the cultural moorings of Blacks and prevented any perpetuation of African kinship and family relations. Consequently, the Black family developed various forms according to the different situations it encountered (Frazier, 1939).

Variations in sex and marital practices, according to Frazier, grew out of the social heritage of slavery; and what slavery began—the pattern of racism and economic deprivation—continued to impinge on the family life of Afro-Americans. The variations Frazier spoke of are: (1) the matriarchal character of the Black family whereby Black males are marginal, ineffective figures in the family constellation; (2) the instability of marital life resulting from the lack of a legal basis for marriage during the period of slavery, which meant that marriage never acquired the position of a strong institution in Black life and casual sex relations were the prevailing norm; and (3) the dissolution—caused by the process of urbanization—of the stability of family life that had existed among Black peasants in an agrarian society (Frazier, 1939).

Most of Frazier's studies were limited to pre–World War II Black family life. His research method was the use of case studies and documents whose content he analyzed and from which he attempted to deduce a pattern of Black family life. The next large-scale theory of the Black family was developed by Daniel Moynihan (1965); it was based largely on census data and pertained to Black family life as it existed in the sixties. In a sense, Moynihan attempted to confirm statistically Frazier's theory that the Black family was disorganized as a result of slavery, urbanization, and economic deprivation. But he added a new dimension to Frazier's theory: "At the heart of the deterioration of the fabric of Negro society is the deterioration of the Negro family" (Moynihan, 1965:5). Moynihan attempted to document his major hypothesis by citing statistics on the dissolution of Black marriages, the high rate of Black illegitimate births, the prevalence of female-headed households in the Black community, and how the deterioration of the Black family had led to a shocking increase in welfare dependency (Moynihan, 1965).

This study of the Black family, commonly referred to as the Moynihan Report, generated a largely critical response from members of the Black community. It drew a mixed response from members of the white academic community, some critically supporting most of Moynihan's contentions, others imputing no validity to his assertions (Rainwater and Yancy, 1967; Staples and Mirande, 1980). The reasons for the negative reaction to Moynihan's study are manifest. In effect, he made a generalized indictment of all Black families. And, although he cited the antecedents of slavery and high unemployment as historically important variables, he shifted the burden of Black deprivation onto the Black family rather than the social structure of the United States.

The Moynihan Report assumed a greater importance than other studies on the Black family for several reasons. As an official government publication, it implied a shift in the government's position in dealing with the effects of racism and economic deprivation on the Black community. However, the Moynihan Report did not spell out a plan for action. The conclusion drawn by most people was that whatever his solution, it would focus on strengthening the Black family rather than dealing with the more relevant problems of segregation and discrimination.

## Historical Background

The most ground-breaking research on Black families has been conducted by historians. For years the work of Frazier (1939), together with that of Stanley Elkins, had been accepted as the definitive history of Black families and posited as a causal explanation of their contemporary condition. Using traditional historical methods based on plantation records and slave owner testimony, both historians reached the conclusion that slavery destroyed the Black family and decimated Black culture. The first historian to challenge this thesis was Blassingame (1972), whose use of slave narratives indicated that in the slave quarters Black families did exist as functioning institutions and role models for others. Moreover, strong family ties persisted in face of the frequent breakups deriving from the slave trade. To further counteract the Frazier–Elkins thesis, Fogel and Engerman (1974) used elaborate quantitative methods to document that slave owners did not separate a majority of the slave families. Their contention, also controversial, was that capitalistic efficiency of the slave system meant it was more practical to keep slave families intact.

Continuing in the vein of revisionist historical research, Genovese used a mix of slave holders' papers and slave testimony. Still, he concluded that Black culture, through compromise and negotiation between slaves and slave owners, did flourish during the era of slavery. Within that cultural vortex there was a variety of socially approved and sanctioned relationships between slave men and women. The alleged female matriarchy extant during that era was described by Genovese as a closer approximation to a healthy sexual equality than was possible for whites. Finally, the landmark study by Gutman (1976) put to rest one of the most common and enduring myths about Black families. Using census data for a number of cities between 1880 and 1925, Gutman found that the majority of Blacks of all social classes were lodged in nuclear families. Through the use of plantation birth records and marriage applications, he concluded that the biparental household was the dominant form during slavery. More important than Gutman's compelling evidence that slavery did not destroy the Black family was his contention that their family form in the past era had evolved from family and kinship patterns that had originated under slavery. This contention gives credence to the Africanity model, which assumes African origins for Afro-American family values, traits, and behavior.

Using a classical theory of slave family life, Stanley Elkins made a comparative analysis of the effect of slavery on the bondsman's family life in North and South America. His thesis was that the principal differences between the two regions was the manumission process and the legal basis of marriage between slaves. That is, slaves could become free citizens more easily in South America and those who remained in bondage were permitted to have legal marriage ceremonies. The sanctity of the family was sanctioned in both law and the canons of the Catholic church. The reverse was true, he asserted, in the slave system of the United States. One should view the Elkins research critically since other historians contend that the slave code of which he speaks was not only unenforced but never promulgated in any of the South American countries. In fact, it is claimed, some of the measures encouraging marriage among slaves were designed to bind the slaves to the estates via family ties (Hall, 1970).

However, these historical studies demonstrate that the Black family was a stable unit during slavery and in the immediate postslavery years. The rise in out-of-wedlock births and female-headed households are concomitants of twentieth-century urban ghettos. A doubling of those phenomena is a function of the economic contingencies of industrial America. Unlike the European immigrants before them, U.S. Blacks were disadvantaged by the hard lines of Northern segregation along racial lines. Moreover, families in cities were more vulnerable to disruptions due to the traumatizing experiences of urbanization, the reduction of family functions, and the loss of extended family supports. In order to understand the modern Black family, it is necessary to look at how its structure is affected by socioeconomic forces.

# References

Blassingame, J.

1972    *The Slave Community*. New York: Oxford University Press.

Fogel, W., and S. Engerman

1974    *Time on the Cross*. Boston: Little, Brown.

Frazier, E. F.

1939    *The Negro Family in the United States*. Chicago: University of Chicago Press.

Gutman, H.

1976    *The Black Family in Slavery and Freedom, 1750–1925*. New York: Pantheon.

Hall, G. Midlo

1970    "The Myth of Benevolent Spanish Slave Law." *Negro Digest* 19:31–39.

Moynihan, Daniel P.

1965    *The Negro Family: The Case for National Action*. Washington, D.C.: U.S. Government Printing Office.

Rainwater, L., and W. Yancy

1967    *The Moynihan Report and the Politics of Controversy*. Cambridge, Mass.: M.I.T. Press.

Staples, R., and A. Mirande

1980    "Racial and Cultural Variations among American Families: A Decennial Review of the Literature on Minority Families." *Journal of Marriage and the Family* 42:887–903.

# 1 / The Changing Black Family

## THE GROWING RACIAL DIFFERENCE IN MARRIAGE AND FAMILY PATTERNS

*Reynolds Farley · Suzanne M. Bianchi*

*Since 1960, major changes have taken place in marital status and family structure, but their magnitude has been greater among blacks. In this paper, Farley and Bianchi review those changes and then consider two possible explanations for the growing racial difference. They find some empirical support for the explanation that the economic utility of marriage has declined more for black than for white women, but do not find support for the argument that the marriage market has become relatively worse for black than for white women.*

## Introduction

If one were to characterize changes in the marriage patterns of women between 1960 and the present, one would point to the delayed age at which first marriages occur resulting in an increased number of years spent single prior to marriage. Women also have become more likely to end their first marriage with divorce and so the average duration of first marriages has declined while the time women spent divorced between marriages has increased. With the rise in divorce and separation we now see an increase in the proportion of women who remarry and experience a second period of separation, followed by divorce.

These trends characterize black as well as white women but during this period, particularly between 1970 and the present, changes have been much more substantial for blacks than for whites. The result has been increasingly divergent marital and family experiences. In this paper, we describe the nature of the divergence and explore two possible explanations. While much is known about the differences between the races in marital and family living arrangements, there has been little systematic exploration of why those differences have widened over the past twenty-five years.

University of Michigan, Population Studies Center. Research Report No. 87-107, April 1987. Reprinted by permission of the authors. (This is a revised version of a paper presented at the 1986 meetings of the American Statistical Association, Social Statistics Section, Chicago, August 1986.)

TABLE 1   Indicators of Racial Differences in Marital and Family Status, 1960 to Mid-1980s

| YEAR | WHITE | BLACK | RACIAL DIFFERENCE |
|------|-------|-------|-------------------|
| | Percent of Women 15 to 44 Living with Husband | | |
| 1960[a] | 69% | 52% | 17 |
| 1970 | 61 | 42 | 19 |
| 1980 | 55 | 30 | 25 |
| 1984 | 55 | 28 | 27 |
| | Percent of Births Delivered to Unmarried Women | | |
| 1960[a] | 2% | 22% | 20 |
| 1970 | 6 | 35 | 29 |
| 1980 | 11 | 55 | 44 |
| 1984 | 13 | 59 | 46 |
| | Percent of Families with Children under 18 Maintained by a Woman | | |
| 1960[a] | 6% | 24% | 18 |
| 1970 | 9 | 33 | 24 |
| 1980 | 14 | 48 | 34 |
| 1984 | 15 | 50 | 35 |
| | Percent of Children under Age 18 in Mother-Only Families | | |
| 1960[a] | 6% | 20% | 14 |
| 1970 | 8 | 29 | 21 |
| 1980 | 14 | 44 | 30 |
| 1984 | 15 | 50 | 35 |

[a]Data for 1960 refer to whites and non-whites.
Sources: U.S. Bureau of the Census, *Census of Population: 1960*, PC(1)-1D, Table 176; PC(2)-4A, Table 2; *Census of Population: 1970*, PC(1)-D1, Table 203; *Census of Population: 1980*, PB80-1-D1-A, Table 264; *Current Population Reports*, Series P-20, No. 212, Table 4; No. 218, Table 1; No. 365, Table 4; No. 366, Table 1; No. 398, Table 1; No. 399, Table 4; U.S. National Center for Health Statistics, *Vital Statistics of the United States: 1970*, Vol. 1—Natality, Table 1–29, *Monthly Vital Statistics Reports*, Vol. 31, No. 8 (Supplement), November 30, 1982, Table 15; Vol. 35, No. 4 (Supplement), July 18, 1986, Table 18.

# Trends in Marital Status of Blacks and Whites

In 1960, 52 percent of black and 69 percent of white women 15 to 44 lived with a husband. By 1984, this proportion declined to 28 percent for black women, and 55 percent for white (U.S. Bureau of the Census, 1963: Table 176; 1985b: Table 1). Two major changes produced this shift in marital status. First, young people increasingly delayed their marriage, resulting in a sharp rise in the proportion of young adults who were single. Second, an increasing proportion of marriages ended in separation or divorce.

Traditionally, blacks married at younger ages than whites but this was reversed in the 1950s and whites now marry at much younger ages than blacks (Cherlin, 1981: Figure 4-1; Rodgers and Thornton, 1985; Michael and Tuma, 1985). An indication of these shifts is given in Figure 1 which shows the proportion of 20- to 24-year-old women and 25- to 29-year-old men who have married. The proportion for women peaked for both races at around 70 percent in the mid-to-late 1950s. By 1984, the proportion who had married fell to 20 percent for blacks and 40 percent for whites. A similar shift away from earlier marriage is evident among men and by the 1980s, fewer than one-half of black men aged 25 to 29 had married.

In addition to marrying at later ages, black and white women are spending less time in their first marriages. Demographic models suggest that as many as one-half of marriages contracted in the late

Proportion of women ever-married by 20–24

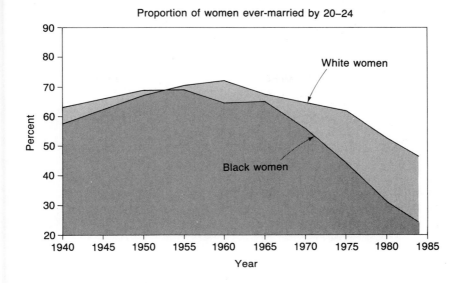

Proportion of men ever-married by 25–29

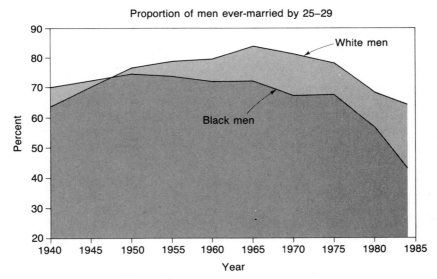

**FIGURE 1** Proportion of Women Ever Married by 20–24 and Men by 25–29, by Race, 1940–1984[a]

[a]Data prior to 1965 refer to non-whites.
Sources: U.S. Bureau of the Census, *Census of Population: 1960*, PC(1)-10, Table 177; *Current Population Reports*, Series P-20, Nos. 56, 62, 72, 105, 144, 212, 287, 365, and 399.

1970s will end in divorce. Among marriages contracted in the early 1940s, about one in four ended in divorce (Preston and McDonald, 1979; McCarthy, 1978; Plateris, 1978; Weed, 1980; Schoen et al., 1985).

The rate of marital dissolution due to separation or divorce is much higher for blacks than for whites. For example, among black women first marrying in 1960, approximately 48 percent separated

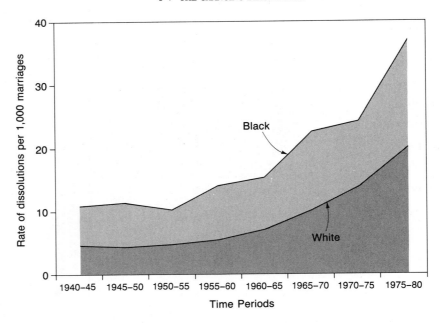

**FIGURE 2** Rates of Separation or Divorce per 1,000
Marriages for Five-Year Periods from 1940 to 1980 for
Black and White Women

Source: Thomas J. Espenshade, "Black-White Differences in Marriage, Separation,
Divorce, and Remarriage," paper presented at the annual meetings of the
Population Association of America, Pittsburgh, Penn., April 16, 1983.

from their husband within twenty years and 34 percent ended the marriage by divorce. For white
women first marrying in 1960, the comparable proportions were 30 percent separating and 27 percent
divorced (Thornton and Rodgers, 1983: Table 3-2).

As can be seen in Figure 2, the divorce/sepa-
ration rates of black and white women have become
more divergent since the early 1940s. Data shown in
this figure are based on the work of Thomas Espenshade and describe rates of marital dissolution in
different five-year intervals. In the early 1940s, the
divorce/separation rate (per thousand marriages)
was 11 for black women compared with 5 for white
women. Over the next four decades, rates increased
for both groups and by the late 1970s, black women
had a divorce/separation rate of 38 compared with
21 for white women (Espenshade, 1985: Tables 3
and 4).

Blacks and whites differ substantially in what
they do following marital discord. Data from the

1973 National Survey of Family Growth indicate that
about nine out of ten white couples who separated
obtained a divorce within five years but only one-
half of the black couples divorced this rapidly
(Thornton, 1977: Tables 1, 3, and 4; McCarthy, 1978:
Table 2). Espenshade (1985: Table 6) has also shown
that black women spend an average of 11 years separated between their first marriage and divorce
compared with 2 years for white women.

Finally, black women are much less likely to
remarry following divorce than are white women.
Whereas remarriage rates have risen along with divorce rates for white women since the mid-1960s,
remarriage probabilities have declined since the
early 1960s for black women (Espenshade, 1985:
207–208).

Figure 3 is based upon the rates of marriage,
divorce, and remarriage observed in five-year periods between 1940 and 1980, and shows the percent of a woman's lifetime which would be spent in

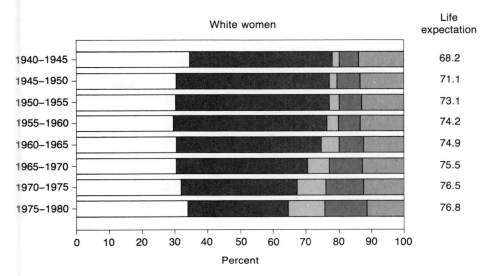

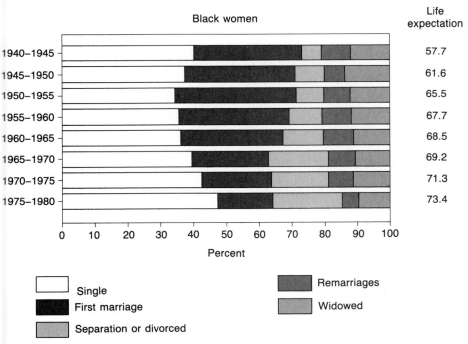

**FIGURE 3** Percent of the Life Span Spent in Each of Five Marital Statuses for Black and White Women According to the Rates Observed in Five-Year Periods, 1940–1980

Source: Thomas J. Espenshade, "Marriage Trends in America: Estimates, Implications, and Underlying Causes," *Population and Development Review*, Vol. 11, No. 2 (June, 1985): Tables 2 and 3.

each of five marital statuses if the rates of that period operated indefinitely. For both races, there has been a decline—especially since 1960—in the time women spend with their first husband and a corresponding increase in the interval of separation and divorce spent between marriages. Among black women, there has also been a sharp rise in the proportion of the life span spent as a single woman and a decline in the length of the remarriage period. According to the rates of the 1975–1980 period, white women can expect to spend 33 of their 77-year life span as a wife, while black women will spend only 16 of their 73 years with a husband. The result of these marital status changes is depicted in Table 1. A much lower percentage of black than white women of childbearing age are living with a spouse.

Given this, it is perhaps not surprising that the majority of black children are currently born to unmarried mothers. As shown in the second panel of Table 1, 59 percent of black births in 1984 were to unmarried women compared to 13 percent of white births. Even though the actual birth rates of unmarried black women have declined in recent years, rates are so much higher than for white unmarried women (whose rates of childbearing continue to increase, it should be noted) and the proportion of women unmarried is so much higher among blacks than among whites, that the racial difference in the percent of children born out of wedlock is now much greater than in previous decades.

The fact that young black women are delaying marriage but not motherhood and that married black women are separating and divorcing but not remarrying is reflected in the two other statistics reported in Table 1, the proportion of families with children that are maintained by a woman and the proportion of children under 18 who live in mother-only families.

Currently, one-half of all black children live with their mother but not their father, whereas 15 percent of white children are in these mother-only families. These percentages, based on cross-sectional data, underestimate the proportion of children who spend some time in a single-parent family. Combining estimates of the number of children born out of wedlock (such children usually begin life in a mother-only family) with estimates of children who will experience the marital separation or divorce of their parents before age 18, Bumpass (1984: Table 2) projects that 42 percent of white and 86 percent of black children are likely to spend some time in a single-parent household, usually a mother-only family.[1]

Between 1960 and 1984, the percent of families with children that were maintained by a woman increased from 24 to 50 among blacks. The proportion of such white families also increased between 1960 and 1984 but the change was from 6 to 15 percent. In fact, the trends in all the indicators shown in Table 1 are parallel for white and black women but they have been so much more accentuated for blacks that the marital and family experiences of the two races have grown increasingly dissimilar.

# Explanations for Growing Racial Differences

Why have marital and family living patterns of black and white women and their children become so divergent? If marriage has become a less desirable—or achievable—living arrangement for women, why has it become so much less so for black than for white women?

## *Women's Economic Independence*

The theoretical models of Gary Becker (1974; 1981) view marriage as involving an exchange of domestic services for financial security. In the past, women faced limited economic opportunities in the labor market so they found marriage desirable since they could exchange their time and efforts in the home for the economic security provided by a husband. Typically, women specialized in homemaking and childbearing while men specialized in breadwinning in the labor market.

As economic opportunities for women expand, more of them assume breadwinner roles, and they are increasingly able to maintain an adequate

TABLE 2    Median Earnings or Income of Women as a Percent of that of Men, by Race, 1947–1984

| | BLACK OR NONWHITE | WHITE |
|---|---|---|
| Median Wage and Salary Earnings for All Adults[a] Reporting Earnings | | |
| 1947[b] | 34% | 54% |
| 1954[b] | 43 | 55 |
| 1959[b] | 45 | 49 |
| 1964[b] | 48 | 49 |
| 1969 | 46 | 46 |
| 1974 | 55 | 45 |
| 1979 | 65 | 45 |
| 1984 | 80 | 50 |
| Median Wage and Salary Earnings for Full-Time, Year-Round Employees | | |
| 1954[b] | 58% | 64% |
| 1959[b] | 66 | 61 |
| 1964[b] | 62 | 59 |
| 1969[b] | 69 | 58 |
| 1974[b] | 73 | 57 |
| 1979[c] | 74 | 59 |
| 1984[c] | 86 | 62 |
| Median Income for Total Persons Receiving Income | | |
| 1948[b] | 36% | 45% |
| 1954[b] | 42 | 38 |
| 1959[b] | 41 | 31 |
| 1964[b] | 38 | 31 |
| 1969 | 47 | 32 |
| 1974 | 52 | 35 |
| 1979 | 52 | 36 |
| 1984 | 65 | 42 |

[a]Adults were defined as persons 14 and over from 1947 through 1974; age 15 and over at later dates.
[b]Data for these years refer to nonwhites.
[c]These data refer to total earnings, not just wage and salary earnings.

Sources: U.S. Bureau of the Census, *Current Population Reports*, Series P-60, No. 5, Table 22; No. 19, Tables 8 and 11; No. 23, Table 11; No. 35, Tables 23, 34, and 37; No. 47, Tables 30 and 33; No. 75, Tables 45, 61, and 62; No. 101, Tables 51, 68, and 72; No. 129, Tables 51, 54, and 64; No. 151, Tables 30, 35, and 39.

life-style apart from a husband. In some circumstances, they may have the resources to bear and raise children without engaging in the traditional exchange of domestic service for economic security. The financial independence of women decreases the "economic utility" of being married and may lead young women to delay their nuptials while also encouraging women to end marriages they find unsatisfactory.

A number of important trends are consistent with this hypothesis. Particularly in the last decade and a half, the educational attainment of women has increased, their labor force participation rates have risen sharply, and there has been upgrading of the occupational distribution of employed women (Bianchi and Spain, 1986: Chapters 4 and 5; Reskin and Hartmann, 1986: Chapter 2; Blau and Ferber, 1985; Bianchi and Rytina, 1986).

Have black women, in some sense, become economically independent at a faster rate than white women and does this explain the growing racial gap in marital status and family living arrangements? It is extremely difficult to test hypotheses about the declining economic utility of marriage to women because it is not easy to determine whether the increase in the economic independence of women is a *cause* or a *consequence* of changes in marital and family status.

Some evidence implies that, relative to men, women have become more independent in an economic sense and that this change has occurred more rapidly for blacks than for whites. Table 2 presents trend data about the earnings and income of women as a percent of those of men of the same race in the post–World War II era. The top panel, which shows median earnings for those reporting any earnings, illustrates that those of black women rose faster than those of black men. In 1947, black women had earnings only 34 percent of black men but by 1984, they earned 80 percent as much. The earnings of white women, relative to those of white men, on the other hand, deteriorated between 1947 and the mid-1970s and improved only slightly since that time. Ratios for full-time, year-round workers (shown in the second panel of Table 2) are higher but the trends are essentially the same: black women are "catching up" with black men more rapidly than white women are "catching up" with white men.

The final panel presents data on the median income of those persons who received any income during the year. Income differs from earnings since it includes money received from dividends, interest, or investments, as well as transfer payments such as Social Security, AFDC, or veteran's benefits (U.S. Bureau of the Census, 1985a: Appendix A). For the last two decades, the income of women has risen faster than that of men. Again, a substantial racial difference is evident since the sexual disparity in income is much smaller among blacks than among whites.

Although the evidence is indirect, it is likely that women now have fewer economic incentives to marry or remain married than in the past. The racial differences in women's independence, as measured by earnings or income, are consistent with the hypothesis that black women gain less economically from marriage than white women. The other aspect of financial independence of women that deserves mention is their access to federal and state transfer payments. During the 1960s and early 1970s, new governmental programs to aid the poor were established and existing ones expanded. Federal funding

for the Aid to Families with Dependent Children increased, eligibility rules eased and benefit levels rose more rapidly than inflation (S. A. Levitan, 1980: Chapter 2; C. Murray, 1984: Table 4; J. T. Patterson, 1986: Chapters 10 and 11). The Food Stamp program developed rapidly and by 1984, 25 percent of the nation's black and 6 percent of the white households received benefits (U.S. Bureau of the Census, 1985a: Tables 1 and 5).

George Gilder (1981), Martin Anderson (1978), and Charles Murray (1984) argue that this expansion of welfare is the key reason for changes in marital and family status. These programs, they assume, have little impact upon the affluent, but have great consequences for those at or near the poverty line and, for this reason, they would be expected to produce more dramatic effects among blacks.

This welfare hypothesis is a different version of the idea that the economic independence of women produces changes in marital and family status. Welfare, similar to any other income a woman receives, lessens her economic gain from marriage.

The empirical evidence concerning the destabilizing effects of welfare is mixed. The availability of cash benefits apparently does not lead women to bear additional children but it may reduce the likelihood that a premaritally pregnant woman marries in haste (K. A. Moore and M. R. Burt, 1982:108–113). It may also lessen the likelihood that she obtains an abortion and, hence, increase the proportion of unmarried women who maintain their own households (Ellwood and Bane, 1985:167). The availability of more generous welfare payments apparently reduces the likelihood that a mother remarries rapidly after termination of her previous marriage (Hutchins, 1979). The income maintenance experiments conducted in Denver and Seattle found that guaranteeing incomes to families at or near the poverty line increased the rate of marital dissolution (Bishop, 1980; Hannan, Tuma, and Groeneveld, 1978; Groeneveld, Tuma, and Hannan, 1980; also see Ellwood and Bane, 1985:175–178).

Although this evidence supports an economic interpretation of the growing racial disparity in marital patterns, we observe at least two discordant notes to the explanation that attributes family change to the increased economic independence of women. First, while the labor force participation rates of both black and white women have risen in recent decades, those of white women have been rising faster than those of black women. Hence, the *increase* in the percentage of white women who had access to their own earned income was greater in the 1970s than was the case for black women. For example, between 1972 and 1985, the labor force participation rate rose from 52 to 72 percent among white women 20 to 44 and from 59 to 71 percent among black women (U.S. Department of Labor, 1973, Table 2; 1986: Table 4). White women may not have been gaining on white men in terms of earnings as was the case for black women, but proportionately more white than black women were gaining access to labor market income during the period. Hence, focusing on the earnings of women relative to men presents only a partial picture.

Second, while it is true that as women's earnings rise, they have more choice and greater economic independence, it remains the case that if they combine their earnings with those of a husband, the level of economic well-being they enjoy far outpaces that which they can achieve on their own. As shown in Figure 4, among both whites and blacks, the level of per capita income in married-couple families has grown more rapidly than that of female-maintained families. Hence, it may be economically more rational for women to stay married and use their higher income to bargain for power within a marital relationship than to separate.

## The "Too Many Women" Hypothesis

Some investigators have suggested that it has become increasingly difficult for black women to find suitable mates, especially at income levels where marriage is an attractive alternative to relying on transfer income. The implication is that changes in black family structure result not so much from the economic independence of black women as from the shortage of appropriate black men. Guttentag and Secord (1983: Chapter 8), for example, examined the ratio of men to women and observed that

it is uniquely low among blacks. Indeed, they suggest that it is difficult to find other populations that have sex ratios as low as those of blacks in the United States.

Are there too few men for black women, as Guttentag and Secord argue? The marriage squeeze was a prominent demographic issue in the past because of the post–World War II baby boom. Women frequently marry men who are two or three years older than themselves. In 1947, about 1.85 million women were born but in 1945, there were only 1.36 million male births (U.S. National Center for Health Statistics, 1983: Table 1-2). Presumably, women born around 1947 faced a tight marriage market because of this shortage of men.

As a first step to investigate this hypothesis, Figure 5 shows ratios of unmarried men, 20 to 26 years of age, to unmarried women, 18 to 24 years of age, for dates between 1940 and 1985. The unmarried category includes all single, widowed, divorced, and currently separated persons, including those who reported themselves as married-spouse-absent.

Trend lines show the effects of the post–World War II baby boom since women who reached marriageable ages in the 1960s or early 1970s found themselves competing for relatively few men. The situation for women seeking marriage has improved since then, reflecting the slower rate of population growth. At all dates, there was a large racial difference and black women seemingly faced a much tighter marriage market than white women. According to these data, the sex ratio for these young unmarried persons in 1985 was 102 for whites but only 85 for blacks.

The lower panel of Figure 5 presents data adjusted for net census undercount (Passel and Robinson, 1984: Table 3; Siegel, 1974: Table 6; Coale, 1955: Tables 2 and 7). This correction has a modest effect upon the sex ratio of whites, but since enumerations missed more men than women, it leads to the conclusion that the marriage market women faced was not quite so tight. The correction produces a dramatic change for blacks and greatly reduces the racial discrepancy with regard to the "shortage of men." Clearly, estimates of the marriage market for blacks must correct for undercount.

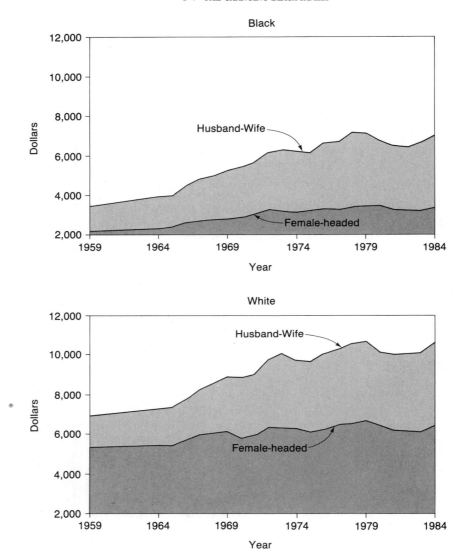

**FIGURE 4** Per Capita Income in Black and White
Husband-Wife and Female-Maintained Families,
1959–1984 (Amounts in 1984 Dollars)

Sources: U.S. Bureau of the Census, *Census of Population: 1960*, PC(1)-ID, Table 224; PC(2)-4B, Table 48; *Current Population Reports*, Series P-20, Nos. 139, 153, 164, 173, 191, 200, 218, 223, 246, 258, 276, 291, 311, 326, 340, 352, 366, 381, 388, and 398; Series P-60, Nos. 47, 51, 53, 59, 66, 75, 80, 85, 90, 97, 101, 105, 114, 118, 123, 129, 140, 145, and 149.

Ratios of unmarried men to unmarried women are crude indicators of the composition of a marriage market. Women may exclude from their consideration men who are too old, too young, who are incarcerated, or who have an educational attainment deemed too little or too extensive. Marital availability ratios that take these factors into account have been developed by Goldman, Westoff, and

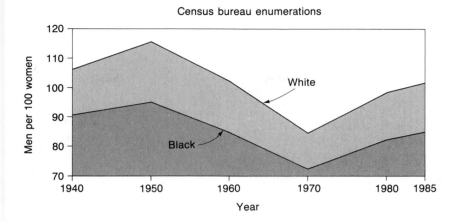

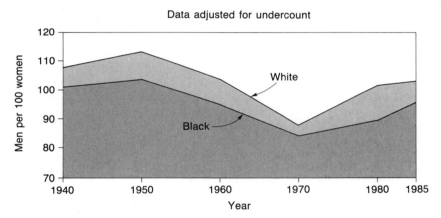

**FIGURE 5** Unmarried Men 20 to 26 per 100
Unmarried Women 18 to 24 by Race, 1940–1985

Sources: U.S. Bureau of the Census, *Census of Population: 1980*, PC80-1-D1-A, Table 264; *Census of Population: 1970*, PC(1)-D1, Table 203; *Census of Population: 1960*, PC(1)-D1, Table 176; *Census of Population: 1950*, P-C1, Table 104; *Sixteenth Census of the United States: 1940*, Vol. IV, Part 1, Tables 6, 7, 8, and 9; A. J. Coale, "The Population of the United States in 1950 Classified by Age, Sex, and Color—A Revision of Census Figures," *Journal of the American Statistical Association* (March 1955), Tables 2 and 7; J. S. Siegel, "Estimates of Coverage of the Population by Sex, Race, and Age in the 1970 Census," *Demography*, Vol. 11, No. 1, (February 1974), Table 6; Jeffery S. Passel and J. Gregory Robinson, "Revised Estimates of the Coverage of the Population in the 1980 Census Based on Demographic Analysis: A Report on Work in Progress," *Proceedings of the Social Statistics Section*, American Statistical Association (1984), pp. 160–165.

Hammerslough (1984:7–8). We use their methods to refine our measure of the marriage pools of black and white women.

To make these calculations, we determined the pool of eligible men from which an unmarried woman might select a husband. We assumed that women placed considerable emphasis upon a man's age and his earnings potential or social class as indexed by his educational attainment. We determined the age range that included 90 percent of the husbands actually selected by women of a given age who married in 1980 and used this to establish the age criteria for the eligibility pool. For example, 90 percent of the husbands married by 22-year-old women in 1980 were between the ages of 20 to 31 inclusively. To deal with educational homogeneity, we classified persons into one of three educational groups: less than twelve years of schooling, twelve years of education, and thirteen or more years of education. We assumed that women who had a completed high school education would marry men of any educational level, but that women who completed at least one year of college would not marry men who dropped out of high school. Similarly, women with less than twelve years of education were assumed to select from the pool of unmarried men who did not complete one or more years of college. These marital availability ratios were computed from data adjusted for undercount and exclude the institutionalized population.[2]

Table 3 shows availability ratios, that is, unmarried men per 100 unmarried women, for the 1960 to 1985 span. The figures in this table are a weighted average of ratios for women in the three educational groups so they incorporate the assumption of educational selectivity.

Data are shown by single year of age for women 18 to 34. For both races, the number of available men decreases with a woman's age. That is, the longer a woman delays her marriage, the smaller will be the pool of unmarried men from which she can select a husband. The decline with age was more precipitous in the 1980s than in 1960 reflecting, in part, the much larger fluctuations in the size of birth cohorts.

It is also clear from Table 3 that black women faced a much tighter marriage market at each point than did white women. In 1985, among black women in their late teens and early twenties, the number of available men per 100 unmarried women ranged between 92 and 100, whereas among whites, the comparable range was from 109 to 120. After age 28, availability ratios in 1985 fell into the 80s and 70s among white women but into the 70s and 60s for black women.

The last three columns of Table 3 show the percent change in availability ratios for the 1960s, 1970s, and early 1980s. As was indicated by the trend in the sex ratio for unmarried persons in Figure 5, the marriage market for women tightened between 1960 and 1970 as the number of available men per 100 women declined. During this decade, the percent decline among women in their early-to-mid twenties was much greater for blacks than for

whites. Between 1960 and 1970, the change in availability ratios was in line with a widening of racial differences in the marriage rates of women.

After 1970, as the marriage market began to improve for women, the percent increase was greater for black than for white women. If the trend in the availability of men is the major cause of changing racial differences, the marriage patterns of black and white women should have begun to converge after 1970. Instead, they widened even further than during the 1960s.

While racial differences in the pool of potential marriage partners for women may partially explain the large difference in the family patterns of black and white women, it is less clear how this factor can explain the growing racial divergence. That is, even when we refine our measure of marriage pools and take the age and educational attainment of potential spouses into account, the trend data do not suggest that the growing racial difference in marriage patterns results from changes in the marriage pool. In fact, the problem with the sex ratio explanation for both races is that the trend is not in the direction necessary to explain declining probabilities of marriage among women. Since 1970, the availability of suitable mates has increased for both white and black women. Nevertheless, fewer, not more, women have married and stayed married.

Before totally dismissing the sex ratio explanation of racial divergence in marriage patterns, we should note that we have only taken into account age and educational attainment in defining marriage pools. Another factor that may bear on the desirability of the available marriage pool is the employment status of prospective mates (Wilson and Neckerman, 1986). Educational attainment, we believe, indexes a man's future earnings, but women may look for men who have both a good earnings potential and a history of stable employment. Figure 6 shows that there has been a growing racial difference in the proportion of working-age males who are employed. Both at ages 16 to 24 and 25 to 54, the proportion of black men with jobs has declined more rapidly than among white men. This trend suggests that the pool of desirable marriage partners may have grown

TABLE 3   Trends in Marital Availability Ratios: Unmarried Men per 100 Unmarried Women

| AGE OF WOMEN | 1960 | 1970 | 1980 | 1985 | PERCENT CHANGE | | |
|---|---|---|---|---|---|---|---|
| | | | | | 1960–1970 | 1970–1980 | 1980–1985 |
| | | | | Black Women | | | |
| 18 | 85 | 71 | 94 | 95 | −16% | 32% | 1% |
| 19 | 83 | 70 | 95 | 100 | −16 | 35 | 5 |
| 20 | 86 | 73 | 95 | 97 | −16 | 31 | 2 |
| 21 | 75 | 62 | 88 | 95 | −18 | 42 | 9 |
| 22 | 68 | 55 | 82 | 92 | −20 | 50 | 13 |
| 23 | 73 | 58 | 83 | 95 | −21 | 45 | 14 |
| 24 | 77 | 61 | 89 | 97 | −22 | 47 | 9 |
| 25 | 71 | 53 | 78 | 92 | −24 | 45 | 19 |
| 26 | 76 | 57 | 81 | 94 | −26 | 44 | 16 |
| 27 | 68 | 53 | 72 | 87 | −23 | 37 | 21 |
| 28 | 68 | 54 | 69 | 83 | −20 | 28 | 20 |
| 29 | 66 | 52 | 64 | 77 | −21 | 24 | 20 |
| 30 | 66 | 52 | 59 | 74 | −22 | 14 | 26 |
| 31 | 66 | 53 | 56 | 68 | −21 | 6 | 22 |
| 32 | 66 | 55 | 55 | 67 | −16 | −1 | 23 |
| 33 | 66 | 56 | 53 | 63 | −16 | −5 | 20 |
| 34 | 68 | 58 | 53 | 64 | −15 | −8 | 21 |
| | | | | White Women | | | |
| 18 | 116 | 91 | 105 | 109 | −21% | 15% | 3% |
| 19 | 113 | 103 | 115 | 118 | −9 | 12 | 3 |
| 20 | 116 | 105 | 114 | 120 | −9 | 9 | 5 |
| 21 | 110 | 96 | 108 | 117 | −13 | 12 | 8 |
| 22 | 87 | 83 | 98 | 110 | −5 | 19 | 12 |
| 23 | 91 | 86 | 102 | 116 | −6 | 19 | 14 |
| 24 | 100 | 85 | 108 | 120 | −15 | 27 | 12 |
| 25 | 86 | 71 | 95 | 109 | −18 | 33 | 15 |
| 26 | 88 | 78 | 99 | 113 | −11 | 27 | 14 |
| 27 | 81 | 65 | 88 | 101 | −19 | 34 | 15 |
| 28 | 82 | 59 | 81 | 97 | −28 | 37 | 20 |
| 29 | 84 | 55 | 73 | 88 | −35 | 34 | 20 |
| 30 | 84 | 56 | 68 | 83 | −34 | 23 | 21 |
| 31 | 88 | 58 | 66 | 78 | −34 | 13 | 19 |
| 32 | 96 | 60 | 64 | 78 | −37 | 7 | 21 |
| 33 | 90 | 65 | 62 | 75 | −28 | −5 | 21 |
| 34 | 96 | 71 | 61 | 74 | −27 | −14 | 22 |

Note: Weighted by educational attainment.

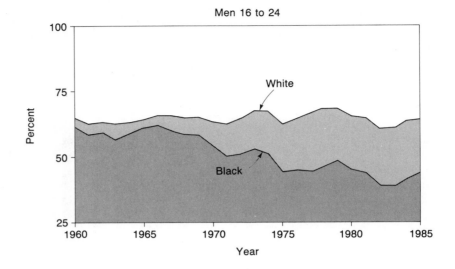

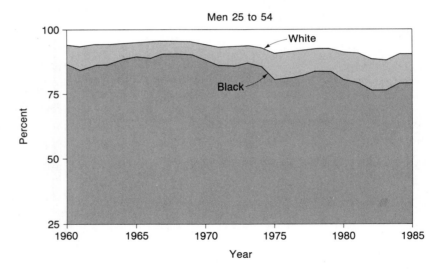

**FIGURE 6** Average Annual Proportions of Men
Employed for Whites and Non-Whites, 16 to 24 and
25 to 54: 1960–1985[a]

[a]These data have been standardized for age within each of the age groups. They pertain to whites and non-whites in all years.
Sources: U.S. Bureau of Labor Statistics, *Handbook of Labor Statistics*, Bulletin 2070: Tables 4 and 32; Bulletin 2175: Table 15; *Employment and Earnings*, Vol. 31, No. 1, Table 3; Vol. 32, No. 1, Table 3; Vol. 33, No. 1, Table 3.

more slowly for black than white women in recent years if factors beyond educational attainment and age are considered.

## Conclusion

Since 1960, major changes have taken place in the marital status and family structure of both blacks and whites, but the shift away from marriage and two-parent families has been much greater among blacks. No satisfactory explanation for this increasing racial difference exists.

We have explored two alternative explanations of the marriage patterns—one an economic interpretation having to do with the financial independence of women, the other a demographic argument concerning the relative size of the pool of potential spouses—to see if either accounts for the growing divergence in marriage patterns between black and white women. We show that black women's earnings vis-à-vis black men's have increased dramatically, whereas white women's earnings relative to white men's have not. To the extent that marriage becomes less attractive to women as their financial independence increases, the greater relative improvement in black women's earnings is in line with the more dramatic decline in the proportion married among black than white women. While this economic interpretation may not be the whole story, trends in the earnings of men and women are at least consistent with the growing racial difference in marriage patterns.

An alternative demographic argument contends that the marriage pool for black women is much more limited than that for white women. We have shown that availability ratios are lower for black than white women. However, in order for this to explain the growing racial difference, the marriage market should have worsened more (or, in the 1970s, improved less rapidly) for black than for white women. During the 1960s, when marriage pools were shrinking for women, they may have shrunk more rapidly for black women but since 1970, as marriage markets have improved greatly for women, the relative improvement has been greater for black than for white women. Hence, the sex ratio explanation of racial differences seems unsatisfactory.

In defining the pool of potential spouses, we considered educational attainment but not the actual employment of available mates. The percentage of black men who are employed has declined at a more rapid rate in recent years than for white men. However, such an explanation moves away from a sheer demographic argument and back to an economic interpretation: The employment prospects of males as a factor in the growing racial difference in the marriage patterns of females is, in some sense, the reverse of an explanation based on the growing economic independence of women. Increasingly, black women can take care of themselves financially and they are faced with a marriage pool in which men do not offer stable, high incomes.

Understanding the causes of the growing racial difference in marriage and family patterns would not be of more than passing interest if it were not so important to the economic well-being of the next generation. Children who live with their mothers fare much worse economically than children in two-parent homes. The noneconomic consequences of family disruption are not as easily demonstrated, but there is a growing body of evidence of detrimental consequences in areas such as academic achievement and psychological adjustment as well. McLanahan (1985), for example, reports that the absence of a father significantly truncates a child's educational attainment independent of the economic status of the family of origin. Both white and black children are more likely to experience family disruption and separation from one parent, usually the father, today than in the past, but the growing racial difference in family patterns translates into an increasingly dissimilar family experience for black and white children. The question that arises is, How significant is the growing difference in family patterns between the races for the future economic inequality of black and white Americans?

[1]*Hofferth's (1985) estimates are even more extreme and suggest that 70 percent of white and 94 percent of black children will spend at least some time in a single-parent household. These estimates appear too high, however. See Bumpass (1985) for a critique of Hofferth's estimates and Hofferth's (1986) response. Norton and Glick (1986) provide a third set of projections with figures intermediate to those of Bumpass and Hofferth.*
[2]*These ratios also assume that marriages are racially homogeneous. This is somewhat unrealistic since, in recent years, 3 to 5* *percent of the black men married white women, but only 2 percent of the black women married white men, (U.S. National Center for Health Statistics, 1985: Table 1-42; U.S. Bureau of the Census, 1985b: Table 16). If black men marry white women more frequently than black women marry white men, then the availability ratios are artificially high for black women and too low for black men. The calculations presented here also assume that the rate of undercount varies by age but not by educational attainment.*

# References

**Anderson, Martin**

1978   *Welfare*. Palo Alto: Hoover Institution, Stanford University.

**Becker, Gary S.**

1974   "A Theory of Marriage." In *Economics of the Family*, Theodore W. Schultz, ed. Chicago: University of Chicago Press.

1981   *A Treatise on the Family*. Cambridge, Mass.: Harvard University Press.

**Bianchi, Suzanne M., and Nancy Rytina**

1986   "The Decline in Occupational Sex Segregation during the 1970s: Census and CPS Comparisons." *Demography* 23(1):79–88.

**Bianchi, Suzanne M., and Daphne Spain**

1986   *American Women*. New York: Russell Sage.

**Bishop, John H.**

1980   "Jobs, Cash Transfers and Marital Instability: A Review and Synthesis of the Evidence." *Journal of Human Resources* XV(3):301–334.

**Blau, Francine D., and Marianne A. Ferber**

1985   "Women in the Labor Market: The Last Twenty Years." In *Women and Work, An Annual Review*, Laurie Larwood, Ann H. Stromberg, and Barbara A. Gutek, eds., Vol. 1, pp. 19–49. Beverly Hills, Calif.: Sage.

**Bumpass, Larry L.**

1984   "Children and Marital Disruption: A Replication and Update." *Demography* 21(1) (February): 71–82.

1985   "Bigger Isn't Necessarily Better." *Journal of Marriage and the Family* 47 (August):797–798.

**Cherlin, Andrew J.**

1981   *Marriage, Divorce, Remarriage*. Cambridge, Mass.: Harvard University Press.

**Coale, Ansley J.**

1955   "The Population of the United States in 1950 Classified by Age, Sex, and Color—a Revision of Census Figures." *Journal of the American Statistical Association* (March).

**Ellwood, David T., and Mary Jo Bane**

1985   "The Impact of AFDC on Family Structure and Living Arrangements." *Research in Labor Economics* 7:132–207.

**Espenshade, Thomas J.**

1985   "Marriage Trends in America: Estimates, Implications, and Underlying Causes." *Population and Development Review* 11(2) (June):193–245.

**Farley, Reynolds**

1986   "The Black Family: Recent Trends in the Marital and Family Status of Blacks and Whites." Report submitted to the National Research Council, Committee on the Status of Black Americans.

**Gilder, George**

1981   *Wealth and Poverty*. New York: Basic Books.

**Goldman, Noreen, Charles F. Westoff, and Charles Hammerslough**

1984   "Demography of the Marriage Market in the United States." *Population Index* 50(1) (Spring): 5–25.

**Groeneveld, Lyle P., Nancy Brandon Tuma, and Michael T. Hannan**

1980   "Marital Dissolution and Remarriage." In *A Guaranteed Annual Income: Evidence from a Social Experiment*, Philip K. Robins, Robert G.

Spiegelman, Samuel Weiner, and Joseph G. Bell, eds., New York: Academic Press.

Guttentag, Marcia, and Paul F. Secord
1983   *Too Many Women? The Sex Ratio Question*, Beverly Hills, Calif.: Sage.

Hannan, Michael T., Nancy Brandon Tuma, and Lyle P. Groeneveld
1978   "Income and Independence Effects on Marital Dissolution: Results from the Seattle-Denver Income Maintenance Experiments." *American Journal of Sociology* 84(3) (November):611–633.

Hofferth, Sandra L.
1985   "Updating Children's Life Course." *Journal of Marriage and the Family* 47 (February):93–115.
1986   "Response to a Comment by Bumpass on 'Updating Children's Life Course.'" *Journal of Marriage and the Family* 48 (August):680–682.

Hutchins, Robert M.
1979   "Welfare, Remarriage, and Marital Search." *American Economic Review* 69(3):369–379.

Levitan, Sar A.
1980   *Programs in Aid of the Poor for the 1980s*. Baltimore: Johns Hopkins University Press.

McCarthy, James
1978   "A Comparison of the Probability of the Dissolution of First and Second Marriages." *Demography* 15(3) (August):345–359.

McLanahan, Sara
1985   "Family Structure and the Reproduction of Poverty." *American Journal of Sociology* 90(4) (January):873–901.

Michael, Robert T., and Nancy Brandon Tuma
1985   "Entry into Marriage and Parenthood by Young Men and Women: The Influence of Family Background." *Demography* 22(4) (November):515–544.

Moore, Kristin A., and Martha R. Burt
1982   *Private Crisis, Public Cost: Policy Perspectives on Teenage Childbearing*. Washington, D.C.: Urban Institute Press.

Murray, Charles
1984   *Losing Ground*. New York: Basic Books.

Norton, Arthur J., and Paul C. Glick
1986   "One Parent Families: A Social and Demographic Profile." *Family Relations* 35 (February):9–17.

Passell, Jeffery S., and J. Gregory Robinson
1984   "Revised Estimates of Coverage of the Population in the 1980 Census, Based on Demographic Analysis: A Report on Work in Progress." *Proceedings of the Social Statistics Section*, American Statistical Association, pp. 160–165.

Patterson, James T.
1986   *America's Struggle Against Poverty*. Cambridge, Mass.: Harvard University Press.

Plateris, Alexander A.
1978   *Divorces and Divorce Rates: United States*. U.S. National Center for Health Statistics. Data from the National Vital Statistics System, Series 21, No. 29 (March).

Preston, Samuel H., and James McDonald
1979   "The Incidence of Divorce within Cohorts of American Marriage Contracted since the Civil War." *Demography* 16(1) (February):1–25.

Reskin, Barbara F., and Heidi I. Hartmann (Eds.)
1986   *Women's Work, Men's Work*. Washington, D.C.: National Academy Press.

Rodgers, Willard L., and Arland Thornton
1985   "Changing Patterns of First Marriage in the United States." *Demography* 22(2) (May):265–279.

Schoen, Robert, William Urton, Karen Woodrow, and John Baj
1985   "Marriage and Divorce in Twentieth Century American Cohorts." *Demography* 22(1) (February):101–114.

Siegel, Jacob S.
1974   "Estimates of Coverage of the Population by Sex, Race and Age in the 1970 Census." *Demography* 11(1) (February).

Thornton, Arland
1977   "Decomposing the Re-marriage Process." *Population Studies* 31(2) (July):572–595.
1978   "Marital Instability Differentials and Interaction: Insights from Multivariate Contingency Table Analysis." *Sociology and Social Research* 62(4):572–595.

Thornton, Arland, and Willard L. Rodgers
1983   *Changing Patterns of Marriage and Divorce in the United States*. Final Report Prepared for the National Institute for Child Health and Human Development, Ann Arbor: University of Michigan, Institute for Social Research.

U.S. Bureau of the Census

1963    *Census of Population: 1960*, PC(11)-1D.

1984    *Current Population Reports*, Series P-20, No. 398, Table 15.

1985a   *Current Population Reports*, Series P-60, No. 150, (November).

1985b   *Current Population Reports*, Series P-20, No. 398, (April).

U.S. Department of Labor

1973    *Employment and Earnings*, Vol. 19, No. 7 (January).

1986    *Employment and Earnings*, Vol. 33, No. 1 (January).

U.S. Department of Labor, Bureau of Labor Statistics

1985    *Handbook of Labor Statistics*. Bulletin 2217. Washington, D.C.: U.S. Government Printing Office.

U.S. National Center for Health Statistics

1983    *Vital Statistics of the United States: 1981*, Vol. I.

1985    *Vital Statistics of the United States: 1980*, Vol. III.

Weed, James A.

1980    "National Estimates of Marriage Dissolution and Survivorship: United States." U.S. National Center for Health Statistics, *Vital and Health Statistics*, Analytic Series, Series 3, No. 19 (November).

Wilson, William Julius, and Kathryn M. Neckerman

1986    "Poverty and Family Structure: The Widening Gap between Evidence and Public Policy Issues." In *Fighting Poverty: What Works and What Doesn't*, Sheldon H. Danziger and Daniel H. Weinberg, eds., Cambridge, Mass.: Harvard University Press.

# SINCE THE MOYNIHAN REPORT...

## Blanche Bernstein

*The Moynihan Report, issued in 1965, called for national action to increase the stability of the family structure of lower-class blacks. Since the report was written the instability of black families has increased: 40 percent of black families are now headed by women and an increasing number of teenagers give birth to children and become trapped in a life of poverty. The author discusses recent efforts to combat increases in teenage pregnancy.*

In March 1965, Daniel Patrick Moynihan, then head of the Office of Planning and Research in the U.S. Department of Labor, authored a report entitled *The Negro Family: The Case for National Action.*[1] It is fascinating to reread it almost 20 years later; it is also instructive to review its major thesis, the reaction to it, developments since its publication, and consider again the case for national action.

Moynihan warmly welcomed the establishment of the President's Committee on Equal Opportunity, the Manpower Development and Training Act of 1962, the Economic Opportunity Act of 1964, and the Civil Rights Act of 1964, all efforts to improve the economic position of blacks, abolish poverty, and eliminate legal and formal discrimination against blacks. The report also eloquently and sympathetically describes in the chapter on the "Roots of the Problem" the ill effects of the period of slavery, the frequently high levels of unemployment and low wages, and inferior education on the structure and well-being of the black family.

But as Moynihan studied the economic and demographic trends evident in available data for 1940–1963, he foresaw a serious clash between the newly enunciated black goals of achieving not just equal opportunity but equal results—in the sense of a comparable distribution of income, education etc., as between whites and nonwhites—and what he referred to as the crumbling of the black family. He noted that the white family "has achieved a high degree of stability" and is maintaining it, but in contrast, "the family structure of lower class Negroes is highly unstable, and in many urban centers is approaching complete breakdown." He added that "so long as this situation persists, the cycle of poverty and disadvantage will continue to repeat itself" and he called for national action "directed to a new kind of national goal: the establishment of a stable Negro family structure."

Did the report bring about a widespread public recognition of the role of family stability in improving the economic and social situation of blacks and a plan for national action? Quite the contrary: it elicited a sustained, vociferous attack from black leaders and many liberal white opinion makers. Moynihan was labeled racist and reactionary, as was anyone else who argued similarly in the ensuing years. And this despite the fact that some outstanding blacks had already written, or were to write in a similar vein: among others, E. Franklin Frazier in 1939 and Andrew Brimmer, then a member of the Federal Reserve Board, who in 1970, while noting the significant economic progress made by blacks during the 1960s, pointed out the deepening schism

From *New Perspectives* 16 (2, Fall 1984):3–7. Figures have been deleted.

in the black community evident "above all in the dramatic deterioration in the position of Negro families headed by a female." Despite those and some other voices raised in defense of the Moynihan thesis, the overwhelming reaction in terms of its influence on public policy was one of rejection. Some defended early child bearing on the grounds that black girls were more mature than whites and even plans to expand family planning services to blacks were labeled genocide.

As in the period prior to the passage of equal opportunity and civil rights legislation, the focus of attention of black leaders and others remained on denial of civil rights, discrimination, unemployment, and low wages. At the 1980 White House Conference on Families and Children, though President Carter began with the notion of strengthening the intact family, an HEW task force urged a more "neutral" model as the liberal goal; the task force won. As a result, the White House Conference degenerated into a conference on ways of aiding any and all types of families rather than focussing on the intact family. Indeed, the intact family got short shrift in the proceedings, and little consideration, if any, was given to possible programs for the prevention of family break-up or the nonformation of families.

During the almost 20 years since the publication of the Moynihan Report, has the economic and social situation of blacks improved and what do the data which became available in this period tell us about the current situation of the black family and its impact on their well-being?

Between 1940 and 1960–64 (the period examined in the Report), Moynihan found that the rate of black births out-of-wedlock had risen from 17 to 24 percent of all live births; the comparable figures for whites was from two to three percent. Between 1950 and 1960 the ratio of female-headed black families rose from 18 to 21 percent; among whites the figure was unchanged at about nine percent. The big increase in the indices of the deterioration of the black family were yet to come. At the beginning of the 1980s, the proportion of black families headed by women had reached 41 percent, almost a doubling of the ratio in two decades. It should be noted that the increase in families headed by a woman as a result of divorce, desertion, or nonfor-

mation of a family is evident among all income and ethnic groups, but among whites it reached 12 percent and among Hispanics, 20 percent, as compared to 41 percent among blacks.

Does family structure make a difference in terms of the family's standard of living? Indeed it does. In general, it takes about 1.3 wage earners per four-person family to achieve the Bureau of Labor Statistics lower-level standard of living ($15,323 in 1981 prices—later figures have not yet been published), 1.7 for the moderate level ($24,407) and two wage earners for the higher level ($38,060). The female-headed family is clearly at a serious disadvantage with limited opportunities for moving up the economic ladder. The data on the family characteristics of those in poverty are even more compelling. In 1982, only eight percent of two-parent families were poor compared to 36 percent of female-headed families. Among intact families with two wage earners, only five percent of white families, nine percent of black families, and 12 percent of Hispanic families were poor.

During the 1960s, the black/white income ratio improved—from 54 percent in 1959 to 63 percent in 1968—though the differential remained substantial. But the differential widened again in the 1970s. According to an analysis published in 1981, "a fundamental reason for the deterioration of the black/white income ratio between 1970 and 1976 is the substantially faster rate of growth of female-headed families among blacks than among whites. In fact, if the patterns of family composition that existed in 1970 had been present in 1978, the black/white income gap would have been narrowed in that period by five percentage points. If one went back to 1960, the gain would have been greater" (Sandell, 1981). And it was Dr. Robert Hill of the National Urban League who pointed out that the number of poor black families rose by 19 percent between 1969 and 1975 due to the sharp rise of black families headed by women. While the number of poor black families headed by men fell by 34 percent—the number of poor black families headed by women soared by 64 percent, accounting for all the increase in the number of poor black families.

Perhaps the most vulnerable of the female-headed families are those headed by a teenager or a mother who was a teenager when she had her first child. A study published by the Urban Institute found that women who were teenagers at the birth of their first child account for more than half of total AFDC expenditures in the country and comprise an astounding 71 percent of all AFDC mothers under 30 years of age (Moore and Burt, 1981).

Teenage mothers under 16 incur the most long-term disadvantages. They exhibit a high drop-out rate from school, have larger families, less opportunity for employment, and lower earnings when they do work. Further, they are more likely to find themselves and their children trapped in long-term poverty with its harmful consequences for health, housing, learning, and social development.

Reviewing trends from 1940 to 1960, Moynihan already expressed concern about the fact that black women were having babies at younger ages, but the problem then was still of modest dimension. It was not until the '60s and '70s that teenage pregnancy grew to enormous proportions and became the single most important cause of long-term poverty.

A few figures are necessary to delineate the growth and size of the problem, as well as its impact on the well-being of the major ethnic communities. The number of teenage out-of-wedlock births rose from 91,700 in 1960 to 262,500 in 1979; if one counts only those under 17, the increase is from 48,300 to 129,500. While out-of-wedlock teenage births have increased more rapidly among whites than among blacks, the rate of 15 births to unmarried teenagers per 1,000 white births is still far below the rate of 87 for blacks. In 1971, of all females 15–19 years old, eight percent conceived a child; by 1979 the figure had risen to 12 percent, or one out of nine teenagers. Births have also increased among children 13–15 years old. Some 1.3 million children in this country live with teenage mothers; an additional 1.6 million children under five years of age live with mothers who were teenagers when they gave birth.

Perhaps even more revealing than the data on births to teenagers are the trends in teenage sexual activity and its outcome. Between 1971 and 1979, while the number of teenagers 15 to 19 rose by six

percent, the number who were sexually active almost doubled; from 2.5 to 4.7 million. Among whites the figure went from 41 percent to 65 percent; among blacks, from 78 percent to 89 percent. Further, the number of teenagers who conceived a child was about double the number who gave birth out-of-wedlock. In other words, about half the conceptions terminated in an abortion or miscarriage, mainly the former.

The acceleration of family breakup and teenage pregnancy was reflected not only in a tripling of the welfare caseload during the 1960s and further substantial increases until the mid-1970s, but in the increase in crime, juvenile delinquency, and drug use, with the youngsters on welfare disproportionately represented in all those areas as well as among school dropouts. The "tangle of pathology" has become ever more tangled.

One cannot put all the blame for this dismaying picture on unemployment, or even on discrimination, though racial discrimination has not yet been eliminated from our society. Moynihan traced a positive correlation between black unemployment rates and family instability for the two decades he studied, but he noted that this connection appeared to have been broken in 1962–3; at that time he could only wonder whether it was the beginning of a trend. It was. From the early '60s to the early '70s unemployment declined from an overall rate of about six percent to three to four percent, and though unemployment for blacks remained higher than that for whites, it too declined. We were in fact in a tight labor market.

And yet, these were the very years of the explosion in the welfare caseload and the increasing evidence of social pathology. What was overlooked during this period of turbulence—when there was concern about the continued existence of poverty within the country; evidence of continuing though diminishing discrimination against blacks and other minorities; and violent reaction, as reflected in riots in many cities, to what was perceived as past and current injustices—was the enormous growth in female-headed families because of family breakup mainly as a result of teenage child-bearing. For more than two decades, the problem was largely ignored by the black community. In *A Statistical*

*Overview of Black America* published by the National Urban League in December, 1982, the family structure explanation of the economic disorder which had befallen blacks was discounted with the statement that "People are not poor because they are female and household heads; they are poor because they do not have jobs or adequate income." And the subject of black family structure was taboo among a significant section of the white community as well. Only recently has this changed.

At first only individual black voices were heard—William Raspberry in the *Washington Post*, Robert Curvin in the *New York Times*, William Haskins of the National Urban League, among others. They were saying publicly that in effect the blacks needed to concern themselves about the structure of the black family and particularly with teenage pregnancy. The major breakthrough came with the publication of a pamphlet in June, 1983, entitled *A Policy Framework for Racial Justice*, issued by 30 liberal black leaders (known as The Tarrytown Group) and members of the Black Leadership Forum. These leaders list the following as the most urgent problems to be tackled to bring poor blacks into the mainstream: progress in the economy, *the condition of the black family* (my emphasis), and educational opportunity. They add that unless major efforts are made quickly "The condition of a large portion of the black population will deteriorate beyond the point where any program of action can be effective." On the subject of teenagers they say "Teenagers and young men and women need to be encouraged to pursue training, work, and personal development while they delay pregnancy and family formation" and further that "For young people, there is a special need for sex education and education about the importance of *delaying sex, pregnancy, and marriage* (my emphasis)."

The issuance of *A Policy Framework for Racial Justice* served to galvanize the black community to action on a national scale. It was followed within a year by a Black Family Summit Conference called by the National Association for the Advancement of Colored People and the National Urban League. The news release issued at the end of the conference, May 5, 1984, contains language not heard for many years; for example John Jacobs, President of NUL,

warned that "some of our problems may be self-inflicted, that we may have allowed our just anger at what America has done to obscure our own need for self-discipline and strengthened community values."

If one reads through the summary recommendations of each of the ten task forces established at the conference, it is not difficult to be critical of its laundry list aspect or the lack of specificity of many of the recommendations. What is more important, however, is the recognition of the nature of the problem and the beginning effort to outline a strategy for dealing with it, a strategy which clearly must stress the economic and social advantages of family stability and the behavior necessary to achieve it and not rest solely on an appeal to morality.

The public recognition by black leaders of the responsibility of the black community for improvement in the structure of the black family and for persuading teenagers and young people, boys and girls alike, to postpone sexual activity and pregnancy has also made it easier for the white-sponsored foundations and other philanthropic organizations to assist in developing and funding necessary programs, and also to evaluate the effectiveness of different approaches. Hitherto, the foundations approached these issues very cautiously, concerned that they might be considered racist.

The importance of evaluation of the effectiveness of programs cannot be overemphasized. The belated recognition of the causes of poverty among blacks in the 1960s and onward—not to be confused with the causes of poverty in the 1930s or earlier—have resulted in a problem of enormous size and complexity. No one knows exactly how to promote family stability and persuade teenage boys and girls to postpone sexual activity after two decades of permissiveness and the erosion of earlier held values. Efforts to develop programs of any major scope are no more than two years old and some remain statements of intention rather than programs which can be implemented beginning next month. One of the early ones—Teaching Teens to Say No—begun on a demonstration basis in Cleveland and Atlanta and now being carried out on a large scale in the schools in Atlanta, is being evaluated by the Ford Foundation. Governor Mario Cuomo of New York has initiated a program on adolescent pregnancy which is, however, still largely on the drawing board, and the New York City public school system has within recent months initiated an updated sex education curriculum dealing with teenage pregnancy among other issues. Other efforts are underway in various cities sponsored by various foundations. What is needed is a national central repository of information on what programs are being tried, and which show promise of success under what circumstances, so that scarce resources are not wasted on reinventing the wheel, especially wheels that don't turn.

Government at all levels should join in the effort to strengthen the black family in appropriate ways. The federal government might well fund the national depository of information suggested above. Washington and the states should focus more attention and resources on advancing the educational achievement of the children in welfare fami-

lies since there is a positive correlation between progress in schools and delaying sexual activity. The names and addresses of the roughly 8 million children in the nation on welfare are known to local welfare departments. But little is done to provide extra assistance to them in the early years of schooling though it is known that they are disproportionately represented among school dropouts. If the effort is not made in the early grades we will continue to face a costly remediation effort—as we are now—in the high schools and even the colleges, as we seek with only limited success to prepare them for the existing opportunities in the world of work.

It is urgent that the effort to postpone teenage sexual activity succeed if we are to avoid the heavy costs to society of teenage child bearing and the even heavier costs to the teenager, her child, and the black community, as well as the costs of continuing conflict between blacks, whites, and other ethnic groups over the distribution of the nation's product. Moynihan was right.

---

[1]*The report itself does not indicate any individual authorship, only the government agency which issued it, but is well known as the Moynihan Report and he took the brunt of the attack against it. Beginning with the second half of the 1960s the word "Negro" became a term of opprobrium and "black" came into use. In this article, I follow current usage, unless I am quoting.*

---

# References

**Moore, Kristin A., and Martha F. Burt**
1981   *Private Crisis, Public Cost: Policy Perspective on Teen Age Child Bearing*. Washington, D.C.: Urban Institute.

**Sandell, Steven H.**
1981   *Family Income in the 1970's; The Demographics of Black/White Differences*, Technical Analysis Paper No. 23, U.S. Dept. of Health and Human Services, December, Office of Planning and Evaluation, Office of Income Security Policy Evaluation.

# CHANGES IN BLACK FAMILY STRUCTURE:
## The Conflict between Family Ideology and Structural Conditions

### Robert Staples

*This article compares the family ideology of Black Americans with actual family arrangements and life-styles. Dissonance between the two is explained by the intervention of structural conditions that prevent the fulfillment of normative familial roles by Black males. Exchange theory is presented to explain the conflict between family ideology and structural conditions. In general, the author argues, Black women fail to marry or remain married when the costs of such an arrangement outweigh the benefits.*

Historically, family theorists have argued that family structure and achievement interact with one another (Goode, 1963; Parson and Bales, 1955). While that may have some validity for certain ethnic groups in America, none of those groups share the history and current social conditions of the Black population in the United States. The peculiar history of Black Americans, combined with structural conditions inimical to family formation and maintenance, have precipitated a crisis in the Black family.

The basic theoretical perspective that informs the present analysis of Black family life is that of exchange theory. This theory focuses on the reinforcement patterns, the history of rewards and costs, that lead people to do what they do. Essentially it argues that people will continue to do what they have found rewarding in the past. The basic premise here is that certain kinds of family structures exist when there is an exchange of rewards; on the other hand, family arrangements that are costly to one or both parties are much less likely to continue (Blau, 1964; Homans, 1961).

We assume, first, that being married is important to the majority of Blacks, especially women. The fact that a near majority of Black Americans are not married and living in traditional nuclear family units is not a result of any devaluation of marriage qua institution but rather a function of limited choices to find individuals in a restricted and small pool of potential partners who can successfully fulfill the normatively prescribed familial roles. While many blacks fail to marry, the history of Black marriages shows only a minority surviving a lifetime with the same people. Exchange theory suggests that a person will not remain in a relationship where the services provided seem relatively meager compared with what the person knows about other relationships. It appears, then, that Blacks do not marry because the perceived outcome, derived from knowledge of past rewards and costs, is one where alternative sources of goal mediation are preferred risks (Thibaut and Kelley, 1959). This

From *Journal of Marriage and the Family* 47 (November 1985):1005–1015. © 1985 by the National Council on Family Relations. Reprinted by permission. The author is grateful to Paul Rosenblatt for his comments on an earlier draft of this paper.

cost-benefit analysis is mediated by structural conditions among the Black male population that give rise to dissonance between Black family ideology and actual family arrangements.

# Black Family Ideology

The popular image of Blacks as a group pressing for change in the area of race relations and economic opportunities often is translated into the image of a radical group in the forefront of social change. Other than being opposed to unfair discrimination against any group and favoring liberal social and economic policies, Blacks often hold very traditional, even conservative, attitudes on other social issues—attitudes that place them in the mainstream of American mores and folkways. Some years ago Robert Hill (1972) noted that Blacks have a strong work, achievement, and religious orientation. In particular, they believe strongly in the institution of the family. Gary and his associates (1983) found that the greatest source of life satisfaction among their Black subjects was family life.

Their unconventional family arrangements and lifestyles easily can mislead outsiders to assume the Blacks are strongly in accord with newly emerging alternative family lifestyles. While they are tolerant of people—especially Blacks—who live in other than nuclear families, the family ideology of most Blacks is in the direction of traditional family forms. Several studies, for instance, show that Black women wish to marry and maintain traditional roles in the conjugal relationship (Broderick, 1965; Kulesky and Obordo, 1972). One indication of the Black value of marriage is the fact that in the past more Black women entered into a marital union than their white counterparts. In 1973, among Black women 65 years and over, only 3.5% had never married, compared with 6.9% of white women (U.S. Bureau of the Census, 1978).

Among the most traditional of values is that of motherhood and childrearing. Except for college-educated Black women, almost all Black women bear children unless infertile. The role of mother is regarded as more important than any other role, including that of wife (Bell, 1971). While respectful of a woman's right to control her body, Blacks tend to have a more negative attitude towards abortion. The Zelnik and Kantner (1974) study revealed that 35% of white teenagers terminated their first pregnancy by abortion compared with only 4% of Black teenagers. However, some of this racial variation may reflect differential access to abortion rather than differential inclination. The Black mother's childrearing techniques are also more traditional. She is more likely than the white mother to use physical, rather than verbal, punishment to enforce child discipline. Threatening the child with withdrawal of the mother's love, used by some white mothers, is uncommon among Black women, which is one reason that the Black mother–child bond remains strong throughout adult life (Nolle, 1972; Scanzoni, 1971).

Although there has been a noticeable increase in feminist ideology among women in the last 20 years, Black women are greatly underrepresented in the women's liberation movement. Many Black women continue to perceive racism—not sexism—as the biggest obstacle to their career and family goals. They are relatively uninvolved in such prominent feminist issues as pornography, sexual harassment, abortion, comparable pay, rape, etc. Moreover, they are more traditional in their definition of the roles that men and women should play in society and the family (Hershey, 1978). While their attitudes remain very traditional, the family lifestyles and arrangements of Blacks are definitely unconventional. . . . We explain it as a conflict between family ideology and structural conditions. . . .

Some 20 years since the publication of the Moynihan Report (1965), the figures he cited as evidence that the Black family was deteriorating have doubled, almost tripled in some areas. How is it that a group that regards family life as its most important source of satisfaction finds a majority of its women unmarried? Why does a group with more traditional sexual values than its white peers have a majority of its children born out-of-wedlock? Finally, we must ask how a group that places such importance on the traditional nuclear family finds a near majority of its members living in single-parent households. While a number of reasons have been cited by theorists, we suggest that the dominant force can be found in structural conditions of the Black population.

# Family Ideology vs. Structural Conditions

The basis of a stable family rests on the willingness, and ability, of men and women to marry, bear and rear children, and fulfill socially prescribed familial roles. In the case of women, those roles have been defined traditionally as the carrying out of domestic functions such as cooking and cleaning; giving birth to children and socializing them; providing sexual gratification, companionship, and emotional support to their husbands. There is abundant evidence that Black women are willing and able to fulfill those roles (Staples, 1973). Conversely, the roles of men in the family are more narrowly confined to economic provider and family leader, but there are indications that a majority of Black American males cannot implement those roles. When it comes to a choice between remaining single or getting married, individuals often do a cost-benefit analysis. Marriage is frequently a quid pro quo arrangement. The desire to enter and maintain a conjugal relationship is contingent on their perception of the benefits that can be acquired and, conversely, of the anticipated costs (Blau, 1964). . . .

The major problem for Black women, however, is not the quantity of the available supply of potential mates, but the quality. Whereas Black women may select a mate on the basis of a number of attributes, a minimum prerequisite is that he be gainfully and regularly employed. According to a study by Joe and Yu (1984), almost a majority of working-age Black males fail to meet those minimum prerequisites. After an analysis of the economic and census data, they concluded that 46% of the 8.8 million Black men of working age were not in the labor force. Based on 1982 statistics, they found that 1.2 million Black men were unemployed, 1.8 million had dropped out of the labor force, 186,000 were in prison, and 925,000 were classified as "missing" because the Census Bureau said it could not locate them.

Furthermore, their study overstates the number of "desirable" and available Black males in the marriage pool. Even with the census undercount, there are still a half million more Black women over the age of 14 than Black men. Also, we must subtract from the marriage pool Black men with certain characteristics by which they substantially outnumber Black women. Among those characteristics would be Blacks serving in the Armed Forces. Approximately 90% of them will be male. The U.S. Bureau of the Census (1983) reports that there were 415,000 Blacks under arms in 1982, representing 20% of all United States military personnel. It can be stated reliably that a large number of those Black males had poor prospects for employment in the civilian labor force (Stewart and Scott, 1978). While the salaries and other benefits of military personnel have improved in recent years and a number of Black soldiers are currently married, the military does take out of circulation a number of marriage-age Black males by stationing them in foreign posts and isolated military stations. Furthermore, once their period of enlistment ends, Black veterans experience a higher rate of unemployment, even in relation to Black civilian males with no military service (Stewart and Scott, 1978). Hence, military service only postpones the entry of Black males into the ranks of the unemployed, one reason Black males have a higher rate of re-enlistment than their white counterparts. . . .

Another group of Black males regarded as undesirable or unavailable are those confined to mental institutions or who are otherwise mentally unstable. While their exact number is unknown, Black males are more likely to be committed to mental institutions than are Black women, and the strictures of racism are such that Blacks are more likely to suffer from mental distress. In 1970, 240 nonwhites per 100,000 population were confined to mental institutions, compared with 162 whites per 100,000 population. Blacks also used community mental health centers at a rate almost twice their proportion in the general population. The rate of drug and alcohol abuse is much greater among the Black population—especially males—based on their overrepresentation among patients receiving treatment services (U.S. Dept. of Health, Education and Welfare, 1979:163–183). It is estimated that as many as one-third of the young Black males in the inner city have serious drug problems (Staples, 1982). Many of the mentally unstable, drug and alcohol abusers will have been included in the figures on Black males who have dropped out of the labor force or are incarcerated in prison. The magnitude of the problem simply reinforces the fact that Black women are seriously disadvantaged in choosing from the eligible and desirable males in the marriage pool.

A large category of Black males who fit into the desirable group must also be considered not available. By all reliable estimates, the Black male homosexual population is considerably larger than the Black female homosexual population (Bell and Weinberg, 1978). Based on the often-quoted Kinsey estimate (Kinsey et al., 1948) that 10% of the adult male population is homosexual, that would mean about 800,000 Black men are not available to heterosexual Black women. Of course, many of these gay males do marry, for a variety of reasons, and serve well in the roles of husband and father; but, due to the increasing public tolerance of overt male homosexuality, it is reasonable to expect that fewer gay males will choose to enter into heterosexual marriages in the future. Finally, it should be noted that Black men marry outside their race at a rate twice as great as that of Black women (Heer, 1974; Staples, 1982).

Although the shortage and desirability of Black males in the marriage pool largely affects the non-college-educated Black woman's marriage chances, the college-educated Black female is not spared the problem if she desires to marry within her race and socioeconomic level. In 1980 there were 133,000 more Black women enrolled in college than Black men—about 57% of all Black college students. Moreover, Black male students have a much higher attrition rate than their female peers. In the University of California system, for instance, only 12 of every 100 Black male students graduate within four years. Thus, in 1981, 36,200 of 60,700 bachelor's degrees awarded to Blacks went to women (60%); and between the years 1976 and 1981, Black women receiving bachelor's degrees increased by 9%, and comparable Black males declined by 9%. These same trends existed for graduate degrees during the years 1976–1981: Black women declined by 12% and Black men by 21% in the receipt of the master's degree; in the receipt of the first professional degree, Black women increased by 71% while Black men declined by 21%; and the doctoral level, Black men declined by 10%,

while Black women increased at a rate of 29% (National Center for Education Statistics, 1983).

College-educated Black women do have the option of marrying men with less education and making a viable choice. In the past as many as 50% of college-educated Black women married men of a lower socioeconomic level (Noble, 1956), but increasingly there is resistance among these women to marrying down. Almost one-third of college-educated Black women remain unmarried past the age of 30 (Bayer, 1972; Staples, 1981). Of course, they face a similar shortage in the marriage pool of male high school graduates and must compete with lesser educated Black women for these same men. Also, such middle-level men tend to marry early and have the most stable marriages in the Black community (Glick and Mills, 1974). The marriage patterns of college-educated Black males tend to put college-educated Black women at a disadvantage. Many of these men marry women of a lower educational level, and the interracial marriage rate is highest in this group of Black men (Heer, 1974; Staples, 1981).

## Structural Conditions and the Changing Black Family

There is no great mystery as to what has happened to the Black family in the last 20 years: it is an acceleration of trends set in motion during the 1960s. A highly sexualized culture—via media, clothing, and example—has conveyed to American youth the notion that nonmarital sexual relations are not only acceptable but required for individual fulfillment. Women are reaching puberty earlier and emotional maturity later. Furthermore, the consequences of teenage sexual behavior are counteracted somewhat by easier access to effective contraceptives and abortion; and the number of pregnant teenagers has not really increased—only the proportion of births to that group of women as a result of the rapid decline in births to older married women.

While the nonmarital sexual activity rate of Black and white teenage women is converging, the Black female is more likely to be engaged in unprotected intercourse and less likely to marry or have an abortion if she becomes pregnant. According to Zelnik and Kantner (1974) only 8.5% of their Black sample (15–19 years) entered into marriage as an outcome of premarital pregnancy, compared with 50.8% of comparable white women. In addition, 35.5% of white women had their premarital pregnancies terminated by abortion, in contrast to 4.9% of similar Black women.

While it is reasonable to question the wisdom of young Black women attaining motherhood at such an early age, their decision to bear the children and raise them alone reflects their traditional values and limited options in life. Among Black males their age, the official unemployment rate is 52%, and as many as 75% of young Black men remain outside the work force (Malabre, 1980). While employment may be easier for Black women to obtain, it often will be in dead-end jobs that pay only half the wages earned by white males. Rather than remain childless and husbandless, these women choose to have the children and raise them alone. A good explanation of these life choices is given by Hortense Canady, President of Delta Sigma Theta Sorority (1984:40): "Having a child is probably the best thing that's ever going to happen to them in their whole lifetime and the only thing they can contribute—this is not true in most other countries in the world. But if you belong to a class or a group of people who have no educational opportunities stretching out before them, no other goals, that's probably the single, best thing that's ever going to happen to you in your life."

Having limited educational and career options ... is not the only reason for the increase in female-headed households. A welfare system that often requires men to be absent from the home is part of the problem; and Black women realize that the meager welfare payments are more reliable than a class of men who may never know gainful employment in their entire lives. In general, unemployed men do not make good husbands and fathers. Since employment and income are the measure of a man's masculinity in this society, men who have neither do not tend to feel good about themselves or act very positively toward their wives and children. In the Hampton (1980) study, for example, husbands who were not satisfied with themselves had a fairly high level of marital disruption.

However, the major reason for the increase in Black female-headed households is the lack of "desirable" men with whom to form monogamous marriages. According to Joe and Yu (1984), between 1976 and 1983 the number of Black families headed by women rose by 700,000, and the ranks of Black men out of the labor force or unemployed increased by the same number. The same trend has existed for the last 25 years: almost 75% of Black men were working in 1960, and Black families headed by women accounted for 21% of all Black families in the same year; but by 1982 only 54% of all Black men were in the labor force, and 42% of all Black families were headed by women (Joe and Yu, 1984).

Having a child out-of-wedlock and failing to marry accounts for 41% of all Black households headed by women. Another 51% are divorced or separated from their spouses (U.S. Bureau of the Census, 1983). These marriage disruptions are generally susceptible to the same structural conditions that plague never-married Black women. Unemployment and underemployment, the public assistance complex, the educational system, and the health care system all produce economic and psychological alienation in the Black male. As Hampton (1980) found, the pressures that push many Black males out of other social institutions within society also work to push them out of marital relationships. For every 1,000 Black married persons with spouses present, the number of divorces increased from 92 in 1971 to 233 in 1981; the comparable increase for whites was from 48 to 100. Black separations increased from 172 to 225 per 1,000 married persons in the same period; white separations rose from 21 to 29 (U.S. Bureau of the Census, 1983).

A number of social characteristics place Blacks at risk for divorce. They have a higher rate of urbanization, greater independence of women, earlier age at marriage, earlier fertility, a higher education and income levels for the wife and lower income status for the husband (Cherlin, 1981). Most Black marriages involve a wife who is more highly educated than her husband (Spanier and Glick, 1980). In one out of five Black marriages, the wife earns a higher income than her husband (U.S. Bureau of the Census, 1983). This incongruity between the socially assigned roles of the male as the primary provider and the wife as a subordinate member of the marital dyad may undermine the husband's self-esteem, frustrate the wife, and create marital dissatisfaction for both partners. In Hampton's (1980) study, the highest percentage of disrupted marriages (27.4%) was observed among wives with incomes accounting for 40% or more of the family's income. His explanation is that, when women have other means of support in the form of welfare or their own earnings, they may be less constrained to remain in a personally unsatisfying relationship. Alternatively, the wife may be satisfied with the husband's role; but her high income may threaten the husband's authority and status, undermining his self-concept so that *he* becomes unhappy.

These problems of the Black family are only variations of the general problems of American families. The direction of change in the family structure is basically the same for all racial groups in the United States and for the same reasons. Guttentag and Secord (1983) demonstrated that unbalanced sex ratios have certain predictable consequences for relationships between men and women. They give rise to higher rates of singlehood, divorce, out-of-wedlock births, and female-headed households in different historical epochs and across different societies. According to Ehrenreich (1983) the breakdown of the family began in the 1950s when men began a flight from commitment to the husband and father role. In the case of the Black family, it stems from the institutional decimation of Black males.

## Discussion

The basic thesis here is that the dissonance between Black family ideology and actual family arrangements is caused by the intervention of structural conditions that impede the actualization of Black aspirations for a traditional family life and roles. The central factor in this situation is the inability of Black males to meet the normative responsibilities of husband and father. Questions may be raised as to how the problem has reached its present magnitude and why it is so pronounced among the Black population. The answer appears to involve a combination of cultural and economic forces which have been ascendant in the last 20 years.

A basic cause of Black male unemployment has been the change in the economy and composition of the work force: automation and foreign competition have eliminated large numbers of jobs in manufacturing industries in the United States over the last couple of decades. Because Black males were disproportionately concentrated in these industries, Black males with years of seniority were displaced, and there were no high-paying unionized occupations for younger and newer workers to enter. Even low-paying menial jobs were automated or taken over by new immigrants, both legal and illegal. The expansion of the economy was in the private sector's high technology and service industries, which brought Black males into competition (or noncompetition) with the burgeoning numbers of white women entering and reentering the labor force.

Women, both Black and white, were better prepared to deal with the educational qualifications of an economy based on high technology and service industries. They require basic reading and writing skills precisely at the time when the public school system began to decline in its ability to produce students with those attributes. During this period Black and Hispanic males had the highest rate of functional illiteracy among the 23 million Americans so classified; estimates are that as many as 40% of the Black male population is not able to read and write well enough to function in a technological society (Staples, 1982). Moreover, the Black male's functional illiteracy can be traced to problems in America's urban school system. One explanation is that when a Black male perceives the opportunity structure as not allowing for his upward mobility through education, he is more likely to divert his energy into sports, music, or hustling. On the other hand, Black females—with fewer opportunities—continue to progress in the same educational system, possibly because, as Hale (1983) has noted, traditional classrooms are generally oriented toward feminine values; teachers are disproportionately female, and the behaviors tolerated and most encouraged are those that are more natural for girls.

The same general trends also occur to varying degrees among whites, but they affect their family structure differently. White male teenagers have an unemployment rate half that of the officially recorded rate for similar Black males. Moreover, the white male teenager ultimately uses his kinship and friend-of-the-family networks more effectively to secure employment, while many Black male teenagers who lack such networks drop out or never join the work force. The poor employment prospects for young Black males is illustrated by the fact that some employers refused to hire them for jobs that were totally subsidized by federal funds (Malabre, 1980). Lack of steady employment largely accounts for the Black male's high enlistment in the military, drug and alcohol abuse, and participation in criminal activities, ultimately leaving less than half the Black male population as rational husband and father candidates (Glasgow, 1979).

One other distinguishing characteristic of the Black population is the early age at which Black women give birth to their first children. More than 40% of Black women have given birth at least once by the time they reach 20 years of age. Estimates are that only one-sixth of the Black males in that age range have jobs (Cummings, 1983). Should they marry before age 20, more than 7 out of 10 such marriages fail (Cherlin, 1981). Exacerbating this situation is the fact that even gainfully employed Black men earn significantly less than white men. In 1982 the median income of Black men was $10,510, compared with $15,964 for white men (U.S. Bureau of the Census, 1983).

Under positive conditions there are good indications that the Black family is strong. College-educated Black women, for example, have their children later and in smaller numbers than any other socioeconomic or racial group in the United States. While probably as sexually active as lower income Black women, they are more effective in the use of birth control and more likely to resort to abortion if pregnancy occurs (Gebhard et al., 1958). Although college-educated Black males earn less income than white male high school dropouts, approximately 90% of them are married and living with their spouses (U.S. Bureau of the Census, 1978). Where negative social conditions are absent, family ideology prevails.

A central question that remains is why Black family ideology has not changed or adjusted to changing conditions. One answer is that it *has*

changed among one stratum of the Black population: the middle class. Within that segment of the Black community, mainstream values—even changing ones—are stronger because they have a higher level of acculturation into those norms due to their greater participation in the majority group's institutions (Staples, 1981). Even among this group, however, traditional values are still strong and exert an influence on their ideological posture toward the family. In part, that is a function of their recent entry into the middle class and the retention of values from their class of origin. Another factor, however, is that their participation in mainstream institutions and embrace of normative ideologies are still marginal, keeping traditional values attractive to many. Gary and his associates (1983) found that their middle-class Black subjects cited their family life as the source of most satisfaction, while the source of least satisfaction was their job. Hence, traditional family life remains the one viable option for Black Americans of all socioeconomic strata because it is less subject to the vagaries of race than any other institution in American life.

Similarly, lower income Blacks sustain traditional beliefs about marriage and the family because the many traumas experienced by this group have cultivated a stronger belief in the value of the family as a resource for their survival in a society not always hospitable to their aspirations. Other than the church, the family has been the only institution to serve as a vehicle for resisting oppression and facilitating their movement toward social and economic equality. Another factor may be the continued physical and social isolation of Blacks—especially lower income Blacks—from members of the majority group who are in the forefront of social and cultural change. In any context of social change, there is a gap between the ideal statements of a culture and the reality in which people live out their lives—a time lag between the emergence of new cultural forms and their internalization by the individuals who must act upon them. Thus, it would appear that Black family ideologies will change only as their social and economic isolation diminishes.

In many ways this situation is nothing new for the Black population. Social scientists continue to view the deterioration of the family as the problem when, in reality, the raison d'être of Black family structure is the structural conditions that prevent the fulfillment of Black family ideology. Given the present political and economic trends, there is little reason to expect an abatement of these trends in the Black family. In fact, female-headed families are projected to be 59% of all Black families with children by the year 1990 (Joe and Yu, 1984). Almost 75% of Black children will live in such families, and 70% of Blacks with incomes below the poverty level will belong to these families. The problem of the Black family cannot be solved without resolving the economic predicament of Black men. They are one and the same.

# References

Bayer, A.
1972   "College Impact on Marriage." *Journal of Marriage and the Family* 34 (November):600–610.

Bell, A., and M. Weinberg
1978   *Homosexualities*. New York: Simon & Schuster.

Bell, R.
1971   "The Related Importance of Mother and Wife Roles among Black Lower Class Women." In *The Black Family: Essays and Studies* (2nd ed.), R. Staples, ed., pp. 248–255. Belmont, Calif.: Wadsworth.

Blau, P.
1964   *Exchange and Power in Social Life*. New York: John Wiley.

Broderick, C.
1965   "Social Heterosexual Development among Urban Negroes and Whites." *Journal of Marriage and the Family* 27 (May):200–203.

Canady, H.
1984   Quoted in "Words of the Week." *Jet Magazine* (March 19):40.

Cherlin, H.
1981   *Marriage, Divorce, Remarriage*. Cambridge, Mass.: Harvard University Press.

Cummings, J.
1983   "Breakup of the Black Family Imperils Gains of Decades." *The New York Times* (November 20):1, 36.

Ehrenreich, B.
1983   *The Hearts of Men: American Dreams and the Flight from Commitment*. Garden City, N.Y.: Doubleday.

Gary, L., L. Beatty, G. Berry, and M. Price
1983   "Stable Black Families." Final Report, Institute for Urban Affairs and Research. Washington, D.C.: Howard University.

Gebhard, P., W. Pomeroy, C. Martin, and C. Christenson
1958   *Pregnancy, Birth and Abortion*. New York: Harper.

Glasgow, D.
1979   *The Black Underclass*. San Francisco: Jossey-Bass.

Glick, P., and K. Mills
1974   "Black Families: Marriage Patterns and Living Arrangements." Paper presented at the W.E.B. DuBois Conference on American Blacks, Atlanta.

Goode, W.
1963   *World Revolution and Changing Family Patterns*. Glencoe, Ill.: The Free Press.

Guttentag, M., and P. Secord
1983   *Too Many Women: The Sex Ratio Question*. Beverly Hills, Calif.: Sage.

Hale, J.
1983   *Black Children*. Provo, Utah: Brigham University Press.

Hampton, R.
1980   "Institutional Decimation, Marital Exchange and Disruption in Black Families." *Western Journal of Black Studies* 4 (Summer):132–139.

Heer, D.
1974   "The Prevalence of Black-White Marriages in the United States 1960 and 1970." *Journal of Marriage and the Family* 35 (February):246–258.

Hershey, M.
1978   "Racial Differences in Sex Role Identities and Sex Stereotyping: Evidence against a Common Assumption." *Social Science Quarterly* 58 (March):583–596.

Hill, R.

1972    *The Strengths of Black Families*. New York: Emerson Hall.

Homans, G.

1961    *Social Behavior: Its Elementary Forms*. New York: Harcourt, Brace and World.

Joe, T., and P. Yu

1984    *The "Flip-Side" of Black Families Headed by Women: The Economic Status of Black Men*. Washington, D.C.: The Center for the Study of Social Policy.

Kinsey, A., W. Pomeroy, and C. Martin

1948    *Sexual Behavior in the Human Male*. Philadelphia: W. B. Saunders.

Kulesky, W., and A. Obordo

1972    "A Racial Comparison of Teenage Girls' Projections for Marriage and Procreation." *Journal of Marriage and the Family* 34 (February):75–84.

Malabre, A., Jr.

1980    "Recession Hits Blacks Harder than Whites." *The Wall Street Journal* (August 21):1.

Moynihan, D. P.

1965    *The Negro Family: The Case for National Action*. Washington, D.C.: U.S. Government Printing Office.

National Center for Education Statistics

1983    *Participation of Black Students in Higher Education: A Statistical Profile from 1970–71 to 1980–81*. Washington, D.C.: U.S. Department of Education.

Noble, J.

1956    *The Negro Woman College Graduate*. New York: Columbia University Press.

Nolle, D.

1972    "Changes in Black Sons and Daughters: A Panel Analysis of Black Adolescents' Orientation toward Their Parents." *Journal of Marriage and the Family* 34 (August):443–447.

Parson, R., and R. Bales

1955    *Family, Socialization and Interaction Process*. Glencoe, Ill.: The Free Press.

Scanzoni, J.

1971    *The Black Family in Modern Society*. Boston: Allyn & Bacon.

Spanier, G., and P. Glick

1980    "Mate Selection Differentials between Blacks and Whites in the United States." *Social Forces* 58 (March):707–725.

Staples, R.

1973    *The Black Woman in America: Sex, Marriage and the Family*. Chicago: Nelson-Hall.

1981    *The World of Black Singles: Changing Patterns of Male-Female Relations*. Westport, Conn.: Greenwood Press.

1982    *Black Masculinity: The Black Male's Role in American Society*. San Francisco: The Black Scholar Press.

Stewart, J., and J. Scott

1978    "The Institutional Decimation of Black Males." Western Journal of Black Studies 2 (Summer):82–92.

Thibaut, J. W., and H. W. Kelley

1959    *The Social Psychology of Groups*. New York: John Wiley.

U.S. Bureau of the Census

1978    Current Population Reports. March 1977, Series P-20, No. 314. Washington, D.C.: U.S. Government Printing Office.

1983    *America's Black Population, 1970 to 1982: A Statistical View*. July 1983, Series P10/POP83. Washington, D.C.: U.S. Government Printing Office.

U.S. Dept. of Health, Education and Welfare

1979    *Health Status of Minorities and Low-Income Groups*. Washington, D.C.: Government Printing Office.

Zelnik, M., and J. F. Kantner

1974    "The Resolution of Teenage First Pregnancies." *Family Planning Perspectives* (Spring):74–80.

# 2 / Historical Background

## THE MYTH OF THE ABSENT FAMILY

*Eugene D. Genovese*

*This article examines some common myths about the Black family during the period of slavery. Genovese finds that despite considerable constraints on their ability to carry out normative family roles and functions, the bondsmen created impressive norms of family life and entered the post-emancipation era with a strong respect for the family and a comparatively stable family base.*

The recent controversy over the ill-fated Moynihan Report has brought the question of the black family in general and the slave family in particular into full review. Largely following the pioneering work of E. Franklin Frazier, the report summarized the conventional wisdom according to which slavery had emasculated black men, created a matriarchy, and prevented the emergence of a strong sense of family.[1] Historians and sociologists, black and white, have been led astray in two ways. First, they have read the story of the twentieth-century black ghettos backward in time and have assumed a historical continuity with slavery days. Second, they have looked too closely at slave law and at the externals of family life and not closely enough at the actual temper of the quarters.

During the twentieth century blacks went north in great waves and faced enormous hardship. The women often could find work as domestics; the men found themselves shut out of employment not so much by their lack of skills as by fierce racial discrimination. Some disorientation of the black family apparently followed; evaluation of its extent and social content must be left to others who can get beyond simple statistical reports to an examination of the quality of life.[2] But those inclined to read the presumed present record back into the past have always had a special problem, for by any standard of judgment the southern rural black family, which remained closer to the antebellum experience, always appeared to be much stronger than the northern urban family.[3]

The evidence from the war years and Reconstruction, now emerging in more systematic studies than were previously available, long ago should have given us pause.[4] Every student of the Union occupation and early Reconstruction has known of the rush of the freedmen to legalize their marriages; of the widespread desertion of the plantations by whole families; of the demands by men and women for a division of labor that would send the women out of the fields and into the homes; of the militancy of parents seeking to keep their children from apprenticeship to whites even when it would have been to their economic advantage; and especially of the heart-rending effort of thousands of freedmen to find long-lost loved ones all over the South. These events were prefigured in antebellum times. Almost every study of runaway slaves uncovers the importance of the family motive: thousands of slaves ran away to find children, parents, wives, or husbands from whom they had been separated by sale. Next to resentment over punishment, the attempt to find relatives was the most prevalent cause of flight.[5]

These data demand a reassessment of slave family life as having had much greater power than generally believed. But a word of warning: the pressures on the family, as E. Franklin Frazier, W. E. B. DuBois, Kenneth M. Stampp, Stanley M. Elkins, and other scholars have pointed out, were extraordinary and took a terrible toll. My claims must be read within limits—as a record of the countervailing forces even within the slavocracy but especially within the slave community. I suggest only that the slaves created impressive norms of family life, including as much of a nuclear family norm as conditions permitted, and that they entered the postwar social system with a remarkably stable base. Many families became indifferent or demoralized, but those with a strong desire for family stability were able to set norms for life in freedom that could serve their own interests and function reasonably well within the wider social system of white-dominated America.

The masters understood the strength of the marital and family ties among their slaves well enough to see in them a powerful means of social control. As a Dutch slaveholder wrote from Louisiana in the 1750s: "It is necessary that the Negroes have wives, and you ought to know that nothing attaches them so much to a plantation as children."[6] No threat carried such force as a threat to sell the children, except the threat to separate husband and wife. The consequences for the children loomed large in the actions of their parents. When—to take an extreme example—a group of slaves planned a mass suicide, concern for their children provided the ground for sober second thoughts.[7]

Evidence of the slaveholders' awareness of the importance of family to the slaves may be found in almost any well-kept set of plantation records. Masters and overseers normally listed their slaves by households and shaped disciplinary procedures to take full account of family relationships. The sale of a recalcitrant slave might be delayed or avoided because it would cause resentment among his family of normally good workers. Conversely, a slave might be sold as the only way to break his influence over valuable relatives.[8] Could whites possibly have missed the content of their slaves' marital relationships when faced with such incidents as the one reported by James W. Melvin, an overseer, to his employer, Audley Clark Britton?

> *[Old Bill] breathed his last on Saturday the 31st, Jan. about 8-1/2 o'clock in the morning. He appeared prepared for Death and said he was going to heaven and wanted his wife to meet him there. When he took sick he told all it would be his last sickness—I was very sorry to lose him.*[9]

The pretensions of racist propagandists that slaves did not value the marriage relation fell apart in the courts, which in a variety of ways wrestled with the problems caused by the lack of legal sanction for slave marriages. However much they insisted on treating the slaves' marriages as mere concubinage, they rarely if ever denied the moral content of the relationship or the common devotion of the parties to each other. Thus, Georgia and Texas illogically and humanely would not permit slave wives to testify against their husbands while continuing to insist that their relationship had no standing at law. The high courts of South Carolina and other states took a more consistent stand on the question of testimony but repeatedly acknowledged the painful problems caused by the lack of legal sanction for relationships everyone knew to be meaningful and worthy of respect.[10]

Many slaveholders went to impressive lengths to keep families together even at the price of considerable pecuniary loss, although, as Kenneth Stampp forcefully insists, the great majority of slaveholders chose business over sentiment and broke up families when under financial pressure. But the choice did not rest easy on their conscience. The kernel of truth in the notion that the slaveholders felt guilty about owning human beings resides largely in this issue. They did feel guilty about their inability to live up to their own paternalistic justification for slavery in the face of market pressure.[11]

The more paternalistic masters betrayed evidence of considerable emotional strain. In 1858, William Massie of Virginia, forced to decrease his debts, chose to sell a beloved and newly improved homestead rather than his slaves. "To know," he explained, "that my little family, white and *black*, [is] to be fixed permanently together would be as near that thing happiness as I ever expect to get. . . . Elizabeth has raised and taught most of them, and having no children, like every other woman under like circumstances, has tender feelings toward them."[12] An impressive number of slaveholders took losses they could ill afford in an effort to keep families together.[13] For the great families, from colonial times to the fall of the regime, the maintenance of family units was a matter of honor.[14] Foreign travelers not easily taken in by appearances testified to the lengths to which slaveholders went at auctions to compel the callous among them to keep family units together.[15] Finally, many ex-slaves testified about masters who steadfastly refused to separate families; who, if they could not avoid separations, sold the children within visiting distance of their parents; and who took losses to buy wives or husbands in order to prevent permanent separations.[16] Stampp's insistence that such evidence revealed the exception rather than the rule is probably true, although I think that exceptions occurred more frequently than he seems to allow for. But it does demonstrate how well the whites understood the strength of the slaves' family ties and the devastating consequences of their own brutal disregard of the sensibilities of those they were selling.

Masters could not afford to be wholly indifferent to slave sensibilities. "Who buys me must buy my son too," a slave defiantly shouted from an auction block. Better to buy in Virginia than Louisiana, wrote J. W. Metcalfe to St. John R. Liddell, for we stand a better chance of buying whole families, whose attachments will make them better and less troublesome workers. Enough slaves risked severe punishment in demanding that their families be kept intact to make masters thoughtful of their own self-interest.[17] So far as circumstances permitted, the slaves tried to stay close to brothers and sisters, aunts and uncles.[18] A woman with a husband who struck her too freely might turn to her brother for protection. A widowed or abandoned aunt could expect to live in a cabin with an affectionate niece and her husband. An old slave without spouse or children could expect attention and comfort from nieces, nephews, and cousins when facing illness and death.[19] Brothers looked after their sisters or at least tried to. An overseer killed a slave girl in Kentucky and paid with his own life at the hands of her brother, who then made a successful escape. In Virginia terrible whippings could not prevent a young man from sneaking off to visit a cherished sister on another plantation.[20]

The more humane masters took full account of their slaves' affection for and sense of responsibility toward relatives. Charles West wrote to the Reverend John Jones of Georgia to ask if a certain Clarissa was alive and about, for her sister, Hannah, in Alabama wanted to visit her during the summer. Dr. Bradford, a slaveholder in Florida, hired out three sisters at a lower price than he could have gotten because he would not separate them even for a year.[21] Few slaveholders took such pains to respect the strong ties of brothers and sisters, but fewer still could claim as excuse that they did not have evidence of the slaves' feelings. Three-quarters of a century after slavery, Anne Harris of Virginia, at age ninety-two, told her interviewer that no white person had ever set foot in her house.

> *Don't 'low it. Dey sole my sister Kate. I saw it wid dese here eyes. Sole her in 1860, and I ain't seed nor heard of her since. Folks say white folks is all right dese days. Maybe dey is, maybe dey isn't. But I can't stand to see 'em. Not on my place.*[22]

In the late antebellum period several states moved to forbid the sale of children away from their mother, but only Louisiana's law appears to have been effective. At that, Governor Hammond of South Carolina had the audacity to argue that the slaveholders deserved credit for efforts to hold slave families together and that the slaves themselves cared little.[23]

Masters not only saw the bonds between husbands and wives, parents and children, they saw the bonds between nieces and nephews and aunts and uncles and especially between brothers and sisters. Nowhere did the slaveholders' willful blindness, not to say hypocrisy, concerning the strength of their slaves' family ties appear so baldly as in their reaction to separations attendant upon sales. They told themselves and anyone who would listen that husbands and wives, despite momentary distress, did not mind separations and would quickly adjust to new mates. Not content with this fabrication, some slaveholders went so far as to assert that separation of mothers from children caused only minimal hardship. Most slaveholders knew this claim to be nonsense, but they nevertheless argued that the separation of fathers from their children was of little consequence.

From time to time a slave did prefer to stay with a good master or mistress rather than follow a spouse who was being sold away. In these cases and in many others in which slaves displayed indifference, the marriage had probably already been weakened, and sale provided the most convenient and painless form of divorce. Such incidents reveal nothing about the depth of grief aroused by the sale of cherished wives and husbands. The slaveholders knew that many slave marriages rested on solid foundations of affection. Slaves on all except the most entrenched and stable plantations lived in constant fear of such separations and steeled themselves against them. When the blow came, the slaves often took it with outward calm. A discernible decline in a master's fortune or growing trouble with the overseer or master might have given warning of what was coming. If the slaves suffered quietly and cried alone, their masters had an excuse to declare them indifferent.

No such excuses, frail as they were, could explain the slaveholders' frequent assertions that mothers and children adjusted easily to separations. The slaveholders saw the depth of the anguish constantly, and only the most crass tried to deny it. John A. Quitman said that he had witnessed the separation of a family only once. It was enough: "I never saw such profound grief as the poor creatures manifested." Mary Boykin Chesnut remarked to a visiting Englishwoman as they passed a slave auction, "If you can stand that, no other Southern thing need choke you."[24]

John S. Wise's testimony may stand for many others. An apologist who put the best face he could on the old regime, he described an auction in which a crippled man of limited use was in danger of being separated from his wife and children. Israel, the man, spoke up in his own behalf:

> *"Yes, sir, I kin do as much ez ennybody; and marsters, ef you'll only buy me and de chillum with Martha Ann, Gord knows I'll wuk myself to deth for you." The poor little darkeys, Cephas and Melinda, sat there frightened and silent, their white eyes dancing like monkey-eyes, and gleaming in the shadows. As her husband's voice broke on her ear, Martha Ann, who had been looking sadly out of the window in a pose of quiet dignity, turned her face with an expression of exquisite love and gratitude towards Israel. She gazed for a moment at her husband and at her children, and then looked away once more, her eyes brimming with tears.[25]*

Wise's story—of course—ended happily when a slaveholder accepted a loss he could not easily afford in order to buy the family as a unit. But Wise, a man of the world, had to know, as Brecht later reminded us, "In real life, the ending is not so fine/ Victoria's Messenger does not come riding often."

John Randolph of Roanoke, a slaveholder himself, who had known Patrick Henry, Henry Clay, and all the great political orators of the day and who himself ranked at the top, was asked whom he thought to have pride of place. "The greatest orator I ever heard," he replied, "was a woman. She was a slave and a mother and her rostrum was an auction block."[26]

All except the most dehumanized slaveholders knew of the attachments that the slaves had to their more extended families, to their friends, and to most of those who made up their little communities and called each other "brother" and "sister." Kate Stone wrote in 1862: "Separating the old family

Negroes who have lived and worked together for so many years is a great grief to them and a distress to us."[27] Those who pretended that the separations came easy never explained why so many ruses had to be used to keep men and women occupied while one or another of their children was being whisked off. Robert Applegarth, an Englishman, described a common scene in which slaves suffered threats and punishments at auctions in response to their wailing and pleading to be kept together.[28] So well did the slaveholders understand the strength of these family ties that the more humane among them found it useful to argue against separations on the grounds of economic expediency by pointing out that the slaves worked much better when kept together.[29]

The extent of separation of wives from husbands and children from parents will probably remain in dispute. The impressive econometric work by Robert Fogel and Stanley Engerman suggests that separations occurred less frequently than has generally been believed, but the data do not permit precise measurement.[30] The nostalgic son of an antebellum planter did not fear contradiction when he recalled long after emancipation: "Were families separated by sale, etc.? Yes, quite often."[31] The potential for forced separation—whatever the ultimate measure of its realization—struck fear into the quarters, especially in the slave-exporting states of the Upper South. If the rich and powerful Pierce Butler of the Sea Islands had to sell hundreds of slaves to cover debts in the 1850s, was anyone safe? Even planters willing to take financial losses to keep families intact could not always control events. Once slaves passed out of the hands of their old masters, their fate depended upon the willingness of professional traders to honor commitments to keep families together or upon the attitude of new masters. And many masters did not respect their slaves' family feelings and did not hesitate to sell them as individuals.

Frederick Douglass referred to "that painful uncertainty which in one form or another was ever obtruding itself in the pathway of the slave."[32] Perhaps no single hardship or danger, not even the ever-present whip, struck such terror into the slaves and accounted for so much of that "fatalism" often attributed to them. If the spirit of many did crack and if many did become numb, nothing weighs so heavily among the reasons as the constant fear of losing loved ones. In the weakest slaves it instilled reckless irresponsibility and a fear of risking attachments—of feeling anything—and in the strongest, a heroic stoicism in the face of unbearable pain. A majority of the slaves probably suffered from some effects of these fears, but their vibrant love of life and of each other checked the slide into despair.

But the pain remained, and the slaveholders knew as much. Is it possible that no slaveholder noticed the grief of the woman who told Fredrika Bremer that she had had six children, three of whom had died and three of whom had been sold: "When they took from me the last little girl, oh, I believed I never should have got over it! It almost broke my heart!"[33] Could any white southerner pretend not to know from direct observation the meaning of Sojourner Truth's statement: "I have borne thirteen chillun and seen 'em mos' all sold off into slavery, and when I cried out with a mother's grief, none but Jesus heard. . . ."[34] Whatever the whites admitted to others or even themselves, they knew what they wrought. And the slaves knew that they knew. A black woman, speaking to Lucy Chase, recalled her first husband's being sold away from her: "White folks got a heap to answer for the way they've done to colored folks! So much they won't never pray it away!"[35]

---

[1] *Lee Rainwater and William L. Yancey,* The Moynihan Report and the Politics of Controversy *(Cambridge, Mass., 1967), which includes the text of the report; Frazier,* Negro in the United States *and* Negro Family; *Elkins,* Slavery.

[2] *For a brief general critique of prevailing notions of family disorganization see Charles V. Willie, "The Black Family in America,"* Dissent, *Feb., 1971, pp. 80–83. The specialized literature is growing rapidly. For one of the most careful and responsible of the older studies see Drake and Cayton,* Black Metropolis, *II, 582–583.*

[3] *See, e.g., Myrdal,* American Dilemma, *p. 935; Jessie Bernard,* Marriage and Family among Negroes *(Englewood Cliffs, N.J., 1966), p. 21; Powdermaker,* After Freedom, *p. 143.*

[4] *See esp. Peter Kolchin,* First Freedom: The Responses of Alabama's Blacks to Emancipation and Reconstruction *(Westport, Conn., 1972), Ch. 3.; Herbert G. Gutman, "Le Phénomène in-*

visible: La Composition de la famille et du foyer noirs après la Guerre de Sécession," Annales: Économies, Sociétés, Civilisations, XXVII (July–Oct., 1972), 1197–1218. Of special interest in these studies are the data from marriage certificates in the Union archives, which show an impressive number of cases in which slaves had lived together for ten years and longer, sometimes much longer.

5Mullin, Flight and Rebellion, p. 109; Sydnor, Slavery in Mississippi, p. 103; Bancroft, Slave Trading, p. 206.

6Quoted in M. Le Page Du Pratz, History of Louisiana or of the Western Parts of Virginia and Carolina (London, 1924), p. 365.

7WPA, Negro in Virginia, p. 74; Fisk University, Unwritten History of Slavery, p. 136.

8See, e.g., Agnew Diary, Aug. 19, 1862 (II, 124a–124b); Sitterson, Sugar Country, pp. 103–104; the correspondence of Charles C. Jones, Jr., and C. C. Jones, Oct., 1856, in Myers, ed., Children of Pride.

9James W. Melvin to A. C. Britton, Feb. 11, 1863, in the Britton Papers.

10Catterall, ed., Judicial Cases, I, passim; III, 89–90, 160; V, 182; also C. P. Patterson, Negro in Tennessee, pp. 57, 154.

11Kenneth Stampp, having studied the wills of a large number of slaveholders, concludes that the financial return to the heirs constitutes the overriding consideration; see Peculiar Institution, p. 204. But see also J. B. Sellers, Slavery in Alabama, p. 168, for a somewhat different reading.

12Quoted in Phillips, Life and Labor, p. 243.

13For some evidence of masters who went to great lengths to keep the families of even recalcitrant slaves together, or who took financial losses to avoid separations, see the Witherspoon–McDowall Correspondence for 1852; Richard Whitaker to A. H. Boykin, Nov. 17, 1843, in the Boykin Papers; J. B. Hawkins to Charles Alston, Nov. 28, 1847, in the Alston Papers; William Otey to Octavia A. Otey, Nov. 20, 1855, in the Wyche–Otey Papers; Ernest Haywood Correspondence, 1856–1857; Lewis Stirling to his son, Jan. 10, 1843; Henry A. Tayloe to B. O. Tayloe, Jan. 5, 1835; Correspondence of Joseph Bryan of Savannah, Ga., a slave trader, in the Slave Papers, Library of Congress; Gavin Diary, July 2, 1857; George W. Clement to Capt. John P. Wright, Oct. 28, 1849, in the Pocket Plantation Record. For evidence and analyses in secondary works see esp. R. H. Taylor, Slaveholding in North Carolina, p. 85; Phillips, Life and Labor, pp. 274–275; McColley, Slavery and Jeffersonian Virginia, pp. 66–68.

14See, e.g., Morton, Robert Carter of Nomini Hall, p. 111; Joseph Clay to Edward Telfair, Dec. 6, 1785, in the Telfair Papers; Heyward, Seed from Madagascar, p. 88; W. T. Jordan, Hugh Davis, passim; Myers, ed., Children of Pride, passim; John Lynch to Ralph Smith, Oct. 13, 1826, in Pocket Plantation Record; J. B. Grimball Diary, June 20, 1835, Jan. 11, 1860, July 17, 1863; C. C. Mercer to John and William Mercer, July 28, 1860; wills dated Dec. 12, 1849, July 9, 1857, Feb. 2, 1862, in the Lawton Papers; A.G.G. to Thomas W. Harriss, Oct. 28, 1848, in the Harriss Papers; Gavin Diary, Sept. 9, 1856; William McKean to James Dunlop, April 4, 1812, in the McKean Letterbook; Eaton, Henry

Clay, pp. 120–121; John Kirkland to his son, Sept. 15, 1858, in the Wyche–Otey Papers.

15See, e.g., Lyell, Second Visit, I, 209–210; Stirling, Letters from the Slave States, p. 260.

16Fisk University, Unwritten History of Slavery, pp. 1, 33; Rawick, ed.,S. C. Narr., II (1), 206; III (3), 2; Texas Narr., IV (2), 110; Indiana Narr., VI (2), 10; George Teamoh Journal, Pts. 1–2, p. 31, in the Woodson Papers.

17Schoepf, Travels in the Confederation, II, 148; Metcalfe to Liddell, June 24, 1848, in the Liddell Papers. Also Charles M. Manigault to Louis Manigault, Jan. 8, 1857; John W. Pittman invoice and note, in the Slave Papers, Library of Congress.

18In general see Rawick, Sundown to Sunup, p. 90.

19For illustrations of each of these cases see Fisk University, Unwritten History of Slavery, pp. 140, 143; Phillips, Life and Labor, p. 270; Henry [the Driver] to William S. Pettigrew, July 1, 1857, in the Pettigrew Papers; Eliza G. Roberts to Mrs. C. C. Jones, May 20, 1861, and Mary Jones to Mary S. Mallard, Nov. 7, 1865, in Myers, ed., Children of Pride.

20Rawick, ed., Kansas Narr., XVI, 71; Ohio Narr., XVI, 12.

21Charles West to John Jones, July 23, 1855, in the John Jones Papers; Chatham, "Plantation Slavery in Middle Florida," unpubl. M.A. thesis, University of North Carolina, 1938, p. 80. See also Father Henson's Story of His Own Life, pp. 147–148, 157; Fisk University, Unwritten History of Slavery, p. 78.

22WPA, Negro in Virginia, p. 34.

23DBR, VIII (Feb., 1850), 122. For a discussion of the state laws designed to protect families from separation see Bancroft, Slave Trading, pp. 197–199.

24Quitman as quoted in Bancroft, Slave Trading, p. 308; Chesnut, Diary from Dixie, p. 18.

25Wise, End of an Era, p. 84; also pp. 85–86.

26As quoted by R. E. Park in his introduction to Doyle, Etiquette of Race Relations, p. xxvii.

27Kate Stone, Brokenburn, p. 84. Or see the remarks of the court in Nowell v. O'Hara (S.C.), 1833, in Catterall, ed., Judicial Cases, II, 352.

28See Applegarth's statement in the Slave Papers, Library of Congress.

29See, e.g., Judge DeSaussure of South Carolina in Gayle v. Cunningham, 1846, in Catterall, ed., Judicial Cases, II, 314; or Judge Slidell of Louisiana in Bertrand v. Arcueil, Ibid., III, 599–600.

30Fogel and Engerman, Time on the Cross, pp. 126–144. See also the suggestive article by William Calderhead, "How Extensive Was the Border State Slave Trade: A New Look," CWH, XVIII (March, 1972), 42–55.

31J. A. McKinstry to H. C. Nixon, Feb. 11, 1913, in Correspondence: Slavery, Tennessee State Library and Archives. In general see Bancroft, Slave Trading, esp. Chs. 2 and 10.

32Life and Times of Frederick Douglass, p. 96.

33Bremer, Homes of the New World, II, 93.

34Quoted in Du Bois, Gift of Black Folk, p. 143.

35Swint, ed., Dear Ones at Home, p. 124.

# WOMEN AND SLAVERY IN THE AFRICAN DIASPORA:
## A Cross-Cultural Approach to Historical Analysis

*Rosalyn Terborg-Penn*

*In this comparative review of the study of women and slavery in the African diaspora, the author begins with an assessment of the demographic impact of slavery upon African females. She raises several questions about the relationship of enslaved women to men of the master-class. Among the other factors considered are the role of free women in the master-class, the extent to which female slaves assimilated into the society of the master-class, and how they fitted into the kinship structure of the society.*

## African Diaspora Women's History

The subject is Black women and slavery, a topic of growing interest among scholars, but one which is rarely studied cross-culturally by historians. As a result, theoretical models for examining the historical impact of enslaving women of African descent are in the pioneering stages. A cross-cultural analysis of slavery and Black women belongs in the realm of African Diaspora Studies, an interdisciplinary area of scholarship. Whether to use interdisciplinary approaches to historical analysis or not is a debate that reemerges periodically among historians. A theory for African Diaspora Women's History which in-

cludes the use of interdisciplinary methods will stimulate this debate even further. Nonetheless, such an approach seems quite viable, and anthropologist Filomina Chioma Steady's concept, which she calls African feminism, lends itself to an historically based theoretical framework.[1]

In essence, the theory is used to approach the study of Black women's lives through an analysis of their own networks and to view Black women's plight and goals to overcome their problems cross-culturally. Beginning with an examination of the values which foster the customs of free women in traditional African societies, historians can plot how these traits have changed, yet the values remained somewhat the same, as women of African descent were forcibly transported throughout Africa, Europe and the Western hemisphere. Perhaps the two most dominant values in African feminist theory, traceable through a time perspective, are developing survival strategies and encouraging self-reliance through female networks. Historically, this combination has not been present among females in the Western world, but can be traced among women of African descent in New World societies as well as in Africa.[2]

The dispersal of Africans through the slave trade is the process by which the African diaspora phenomenon was created. Before we look at the role of African women in this process, it is important

---

From *SAGE: A Scholarly Journal on Black Women* 3 (Fall 1986): 11–15. © 1986 by the SAGE Women's Educational Press, Inc. Reprinted by permission.

to define the term "African diaspora." Traditionally, scholars refer to Africans sent away from the continent as those who become part of the diaspora. At times these people of African descent are called "Africans abroad."[3] It seems that to limit the diaspora to areas outside of the continent of Africa is valid for the study of African men, but not for African women, because during the height of the transatlantic slave trade—from the 17th century into the first decade of the 19th century—the majority of African women enslaved were sent throughout the continent of Africa. African women were removed from their local areas and taken to other regions or to nearby areas in Africa, but usually to places outside of their kinship network, often to societies foreign to them in language, customs and environment. As a result, the majority of men enslaved during this period were dispersed throughout the Western hemisphere or New World societies, while the majority of women enslaved were dispersed throughout Africa. Consequently, the disruption and alienation that most men experienced with enslavement throughout the diaspora, women experienced on the continent of Africa.

The enslavement of African women has been a topic of limited interest to scholars of the past, be they Africanists, Americanists or Caribbeanists. Only in the 1980s has the trend to analyze enslaved women of African descent developed to the point where anthologies and monographs written in English have been published. Scholars in African history have taken the lead, notably Claire Robertson and Martin A. Klein.[4] Scholars in Afro-American history have followed, notably Deborah Gray White.[5] However, those in Latin-American and the Caribbean histories fall behind. Nonetheless, there are limited data that can be used to look at Latin America and the Caribbean to determine why African Diaspora women's history has developed more slowly than that of other regions. In addition, we can begin to make some assumptions about women enslaved in the southern regions of the Western hemisphere.

Before beginning this introduction to a cross-cultural view of enslaved Black women, it is important to look at the term "Black," because not all women of African descent identify equally with this term. In the United States, for example, by law, people with any "measurable" degree of African ancestry are considered to be Black. As a result, since slavery, women of African descent, regardless of skin color, have been perceived as and often have perceived themselves as "colored," or as "Negro," or as "Black." In this sense, "Black" becomes a manifestation of a cultural milieu, more than a color. On the other hand, in many Caribbean and South American societies, women of African descent vary in colors that determine legal status as well as cultural association. Hence, a mulatto woman in the British-speaking West Indies, for example, does not identify as Black, whereas the same woman born in the United States may choose to or is forced by the society to do so. Differences in legal and cultural identification by race cause barriers to reconstructing the past, especially for researchers studying countries such as Argentina and Brazil, where Black as a racial category has not been enumerated in the population census for several generations.

The key to historical reconstruction of slavery or any other institution must then rest first upon how women perceive themselves and second on how they are perceived by the society in which they live. In the cross-cultural historical reconstruction of enslaved Black women's lives, color and cultural perception should be taken into consideration and questions relating to these factors raised for each society under study. Likewise, questions about the master-class and the female slaves' relationship to it must be considered: What was the numerical relationship between slaves and masters in a given society? What was the role of free women in the master-class? What determined kinship and how did slaves fit into the kinship structure of the society? To what extent did female slaves assimilate into the society of the master-class? To what extent did female slaves resist their status as slaves? Finally, time must be considered in any comparative study. Comparing colonial slavery in the British Caribbean with early 19th-century slavery in the United States and with late 19th-century slavery in West Africa may result in misleading conclusions, if time periods and changes in the various institutions of slavery are not taken into consideration.

# Enslaving Women of African Descent

To begin this comparative review of the study of women and slavery in the African diaspora, let us look at the demographic impact of slavery upon African females. Women of African descent had been transported for sale from the mid-7th century through the early 20th century. The slave trade began as the Trans-Saharan trade on the African continent in about 650. It was supplemented by trade routes to the Red Sea and to East Africa by 800, creating a trade which shipped Africans away from the continent. With the colonization of the Western hemisphere by Europeans in the 16th century, the Atlantic slave trade became dominant, pulling Africans from Central and West Africa to the west African coast. The Atlantic trade peaked in the mid-18th century, declining by the early 19th century and ending in the late 1800s.[6] By the turn of the 20th century, vestiges of the trade remained on the African continent, where the largest number of slaves traded remained, and where the largest number of slaves traded throughout the history of slaving had been women. There is evidence that African women were still exchanged as pawns as late as the 1930s. Surprising as it may seem, the demographics of the slave trade in African women reveal a continuous demand for nearly 1300 years, mainly among Africans themselves, who paid more for adult female slaves than for adult male slaves.[7]

Recent studies about the role of women in the African slave trade astonish Americanists who have assumed that since the majority of slaves brought to New World societies were male, fewer African women were enslaved. Refocusing research about slavery toward women paints a new picture about the dynamics of slavery and the role of African women in the diaspora. Subsequent studies of slavery and women in the Western hemisphere should surely revise preconceived notions about African women transplanted into the New World.

Africanists have speculated about why more men than women were slated for the Atlantic slave trade, concluding that women were more valuable as slaves in African societies for both their productive and their reproductive functions. In most traditional African societies, women produced most of the food consumed by the community. Food producers included free and enslaved women, whose labor freed men to participate in war, long-distance trade, hunting and fishing. In addition, slave women were often used as rewards to free and enslaved males who sought wives to reproduce and to care for children, expanding the lineage of masters. Because slaves were considered to be kinless people, they remained loyal to their master's lineage. Masters who married slave women did not fear accountability to their slave wives' kin as they would if they had married free women. Slave women had no kin to protect them from spousal abuse and no kin to demand a bride-price. In addition, it was believed that women could be more easily assimilated into the society of the master-class. Furthermore, in many African societies, free women also benefited from enslaving women because slaves could increase food production and create a greater surplus, profits from which free wives often kept for themselves. In the case of secluded Muslim women, female slaves traded goods in public markets in behalf of their secluded mistresses. All of these factors made the demand for African women on the continent of Africa greater than the demand for men throughout most of the slave trading period.[8]

The high demand for enslaved women resulted in a lower price for enslaved men, many of whom would have been executed after being captured in wars if there had not been an outlet for their sale to European traders in the Atlantic slave trade. At first Europeans acquired more male slaves because they believed a strong, young male would work harder than a female. Ironically, when women were enslaved on plantations in both North America and in the Caribbean, the gender division of labor common throughout Africa broke down. New World masters worked many female slaves in the fields alongside of males and worked the females as hard as they worked male slaves.[9]

Here we see differences in work patterns among African women enslaved on the continent and those enslaved in the Western hemisphere. Gender determined work assignments in African societies, but less so in New World societies. Nonetheless, preconceived Western notions about women's work prevented European slave masters from seeking women during the first 200 years of the Atlantic trade. One common factor shared among enslaved women in African as well as in New World societies was work associated with childrearing and domestic duties. Slave women's daily chores included work for the master as well as domestic activities for the family unit wherein the woman functioned. Male slaves who lived in family units did not have this universal double work load forced upon women.

Reproducing the slave population is another topic that can be viewed comparatively. In the Caribbean, masters' attempts to reproduce the slave population did not become universal until the last century of the slave trade, as European abolitionists successfully limited access to a continuous, inexpensive stream of fresh slaves to replace those who died, usually within seven years. In North America, the slave trade developed about 100 years later, yet the preference for males remained until the early 17th century. Then Amerian masters sought men and women and encouraged slaves to reproduce themselves in family units.[10]

Reproduction as a function of enslaved women remains a controversy, especially among African-Americanists, when it comes to the issue of enslaved women resisting reproductive functions imposed upon them by masters. Some scholars of African-American history, who look to the prestigious role of the African woman as mother, argue that deliberate attempts to limit reproduction or to abort fetuses by enslaved women appear contrary to African values. Nonetheless, the literature about Africa and the United States indicates evidence of abortive practices among slave women.[11]

Although African-Americanists debate about whether abortion was atypical of women enslaved in the United States because African women brought their beliefs about the value of children and motherhood with them, we can now presume that there were two statuses for traditional African women during the height of the African slave trade—free and non-free women who were slaves or pawns. The evidence has yet to reveal how many of the women who were brought to the Western hemisphere were captured as free women or were previously slaves before being shipped to the Americas. Values about motherhood would have been influenced by previous status.

Enslaved women in both Africa and in the Americas had no control over their offspring. In Zaire and in the western Sudan, the birthrate among slave women was considerably lower than the birthrate among free women.[12] In the plantation South of the United States, however, slave women bore more children than free white women. Nonetheless, slaves appeared to have limited conception to a later time than hoped for by their masters. Black women were often able to restrict pregnancy for several years after reaching puberty, despite masters' attempts to have them breed earlier as their life cycle enabled them.[13]

Several issues still remain: Did overwork, disease and poor diet—conditions prevalent among enslaved women universally—lead to miscarriages and spontaneous abortions, or did some slaves practice abortion by use of herbs and roots? Similarly, did victimization leave women little control over their bodies, or did some enslaved women make rebellious choices about bringing children into the master's world, a world which the women could not otherwise control?

# Comparative Historical Reconstruction

Earlier in this discussion we looked at several questions about enslaved women and about their relationship to the master-class. Answers to these questions are essential for establishing a framework for the historical reconstructive process cross-culturally. The published data about female slavery in Africa, in the United States, and in Latin America/the Caribbean can give us only partial answers to these reconstruction processes. Nonetheless, these factors can provide clues to the direction future research about Black women and slavery should take.

Perceptions about race and color have been established as factors to consider in reconstructing women's attitudes and responses to slavery. The numerical relationship between Black slaves and white masters often influenced these perceptions. Data about these numerical relationships are available for New World societies, where, unlike Africa, racial differences were significant, thus influencing self-perception as well as culture. In the Caribbean, during most of the Atlantic slave trade period, Africans and their descendants outnumbered white masters. A population survey of the British West Indies in 1791 reveals that in ten of the twelve British-held islands, Blacks outnumbered whites by almost ninety percent. In Jamaica, for example, the white population estimate was 30,000, while Blacks numbered about 250,000. Of the Blacks, 10,000 were believed to be free, leaving a slave population of about 240,000. During this period, masters and the colonial government encouraged the slave women to reproduce; therefore imports of African women increased. Although at this point it is difficult to estimate the numbers of female slaves in Jamaica, it is clear that Blacks were in the majority and that most of them lived on plantations where their interaction with whites was minimal. As a result, the impact of the master-class culture was less significant than it would be for women enslaved in Bermuda, where whites comprised fifty-two percent of the population.[14]

In turning to another English-speaking slave society of the time, the United States represented what Graham Irwin calls the "white settler society of the temperate zones."[15] In societies such as this, whites outnumbered Africans significantly and European culture was re-created with modifications. Most of North America and the Spanish-speaking slave societies of Argentina and Chile fell into this category. In these areas, the white population overwhelmed the Black; hence, the impact of the master-class culture was significant. Even in areas like the plantation South in the United States during the antebellum period, where Blacks comprised somewhat more than fifty percent of the population, Euro-American culture could not be ignored by slaves. In comparing the culture and self-perception of enslaved Black women in New World societies, the impact of the master-class culture must be considered, for mainstream standards of beauty, family organization, and women's worth often clashed with African standards. Influence variables include not only the percentage of whites and Blacks, but the degree to which the master-class attempted to assimilate slaves into the mainstream. In the United States, as in most English-speaking societies, the effort was discouraged, whereas in Spanish-speaking countries such as Argentina and Chile, assimilation was ultimately encouraged. The assimilation of Blacks makes it difficult to reconstruct the culture of female slaves, because retaining elements of the African past was not rewarded by the mainstream society.

Other related factors for comparative consideration are the role of free women in the master-class, the extent to which female slaves assimilated into the society of the master-class, and how female slaves fit into the kinship structure of the society. For these comparisons we can look first to Africa, where free African women often owned and usually supervised the work, the rewards and the punishment of slave women. The available studies, however, dwell more upon the ways in which mistresses victimized their slaves rather than upon the socialization and assimilation process of slave women by free women.[16] Since female slaves were valued for their ability to become more assimilated into their master's society than male slaves, the process must have been initiated with the free women who supervised the slave women. In addition, as wives and concubines, slaves were part of the master's compound, as were his free wives. Networking for survival was essential to these food producers and childrearers, who may have established fictive kinship relationships. Even if the free wives did not establish support systems with enslaved women, female slaves probably did. Just because a slave woman was considered kinless in the eyes of the master's lineage does not mean that she did not relate to other female slaves, especially those enslaved at the same time as she was, thus experiencing the same initiation into the community of the master.[17]

For the United States, free women of the master-class may have worked closely with slave women if the master owned a small farm and one or two slaves, who contributed to the upkeep of the household, including family and surplus food production. However, if the mistress was the wife of a plantation owner, she did no manual labor, but probably supervised household slaves. Nonetheless, white slaveholding masters held the final word about the treatment of slaves. Assimilation and socialization on plantations were left to the individuals in the slave community, not to the mistresses, who rarely had contact with field slaves who worked in agricultural production.

On many plantations young female slaves entering puberty often worked in squads of slave women in the fields. The squads were called "trash gangs," and were comprised also of pregnant women and older women who could not do the intensive labor other female slaves and male slaves performed. In the "trash gangs" younger slave women learned from the elders about work, plantation survival, male-female relations, motherhood and networking.[18] Kinship included blood relations and fictive kin—all providing the extended kinship relationships, the concept of which originated for African-Americans in Africa, but practices were adapted and transformed by the realities of New World slavery. The studies about plantation slavery in the United States, however, deal with the antebellum period or the first half of the 19th century, when the sex ratio among the slaves was nearly equal. Here the use of a time perspective is important to determine what types of kinship and assimilation practices occurred during the 18th century and earlier.

The emphasis upon lineage among Africans, who distinguished slaves as kinless people, appears totally different from family structure in New World societies. Yet slaves throughout the diaspora, whether in alien environments on the African continent or in the Western hemisphere, constructed survival mechanisms, including modified kinship structures, which retained values and elements of African family life.[19]

The final factor is female resistance to slavery or slave status. Both on the African continent and in New World societies there is evidence of both covert and overt female resistance. Abortion and the refusal to conceive children are covert forms previously discussed. Overt resistance took the form of running away or open revolt. African women enslaved on the continent escaped and protested slave status to higher authorities. On slave ships crossing the

Atlantic from Africa, African women were known to assist in slave revolts. In the Caribbean, slave women participated in Maroon communities of runaways, where resistance to re-enslavement was an ever-present threat. In the United States slave women participated in the Underground Railroad and in open rebellion. Women such as these were revered for their wisdom, leadership and courage. The memory of their deeds has been passed down by women during slavery and in the post-slavery eras. Studies about female slave resistance and protest against slave status provide views of women's choices about the acceptance or the rejection of victimization.[20]

# Future Research

Much has to be done to prepare the theoretical framework, to select the factors for historical reconstruction, but most importantly, to collect the data needed for the various diaspora societies to be studied. For some areas, much of the groundwork has been established, but for others, especially key countries like Brazil, very little scholarly work about female slaves has been published by historians in either Portuguese or English.

Scholars have choices about using a female perspective or not. Hopefully, those who consider African diaspora women's history will choose a female perspective. Writing about women does not guarantee a feminist interpretation, especially in this case if the focus avoids the interaction among slave women themselves, or the survival mechanisms female slaves adopted and implemented. For the United States and Africa, the use of slave testimony by women, though infrequent, is producing data banks that can be used for cross-cultural analysis.[21] Sources of this kind are not readily available for Latin America/the Caribbean, but should be sought out.[22] Finally, challenges that re-define or reverse previous interpretations about women in African, Latin America/Caribbean, and African-American histories are important when the research has been carefully and thoroughly conducted and evaluated.

[1] *Filomina Chioma Steady, ed.,* The Black Woman Cross-Culturally *(Cambridge: Schenkman Publishers, 1981).*

[2] *Steady, Introduction and Overview, pp. 1–41.*

[3] *Joseph E. Harris, ed.,* Global Dimensions of the African Diaspora *(Washington: Howard University Press, 1982), pp. 3–5.*

[4] *Claire Robertson and Martin A. Klein, eds.,* Women and Slavery in Africa *(Madison: The University of Wisconsin Press, 1983).*

[5] *Deborah Gray White,* A'rn't I A Woman? Female Slaves in the Plantation South *(New York: W.W. Norton and Co., 1985).*

[6] *Paul E. Lovejoy,* Transformations in Slavery: A History of Slavery in Africa *(Cambridge: Cambridge University Press, 1983), pp. 25–27.*

[7] *Herbert S. Klein, "African Women in the Atlantic Slave Trade," in* Women and Slavery in Africa, *pp. 29–39.*

[8] *Klein, pp. 34–37; John Thornton, "Sexual Demography: The Impact of the Slave Trade on Family Structure," in* Women and Slavery in Africa, *pp. 45–46; Martin A. Klein, "Women in Slavery in the Western Sudan," in* Women and Slavery in Africa, *pp. 68–77.*

[9] *Claire C. Robertson and Martin A. Klein, "Women's Importance in African Slave Systems," in* Women and Slavery in Africa, *p. 10.*

[10] *White, pp. 67–69.*

[11] *Herbert G. Gutman,* The Black Family in Slavery and Freedom, 1750–1925 *(New York: Pantheon Books, 1976), p. 60, fn1; Darlene Clark Hine and Kate Wittenstein, "Female Slave Resistance: The Economics of Sex," in* The Black Woman Cross-Culturally, *pp. 292–95; Robert Harms, "Sustaining the System: Trading Towns Along the Middle Zaire," in* Women and Slavery in Africa, *pp. 105–7; White, pp. 85–88.*

[12] *Klein, "Women in Slavery in the Western Sudan," p. 73; Harms, p. 105.*

[13] *White, pp. 97–99.*

[14] *"Population of the British West Indies, 1791," in* Africans Abroad: A Documentary History of the Black Diaspora in Asia, Latin America, and the Caribbean During the Age of Slavery, *ed. Graham W. Irwin (New York: Columbia University Press, 1977), pp. 202–203.*

[15] *"The Experience of Slavery," in* Africans Abroad, *p. 185.*

[16] *Klein, pp. 84–86; Harms, pp. 100–102.*

[17] *Marcia Wright, "Bwanikwa: Consciousness and Protest among Slave Women in Central Africa, 1886–1911," in* Women and Slavery in Africa, *pp. 255–58.*

[18] *White, p. 95.*

[19] *Niara Sudarkasa, "Interpreting the African Heritage in Afro-American Family Organization," in* Black Families, *ed. Harriette Pipes McAdoo (Beverly Hills: Sage Publications, 1981), pp. 44–48.*

[20] *Wright, pp. 250–66; White, pp. 62–64; Kenneth Bilby and Filomina Chioma Steady, "Black Women and Survival: A Maroon Case," in* The Black Woman Cross-Culturally, *pp. 451–65; Rosalyn Terborg-Penn, "Black Women in Resistance: A Cross-Cultural Perspective," in* In Resistance: Studies in African, Caribbean, and Afro-American History, *ed. Gary Y. Okihiro (Amherst: University of Massachusetts Press, 1986), pp. 250–55.*

[21] *Edward A. Alpers, "The Story of Swema: Female Vulnerability in Nineteenth Century East Africa," in* Women and Slavery in Africa, *pp. 185–200; Sojourner Truth,* Narrative of Sojourner Truth: A Bondwoman of Olden Time *(Chicago: Johnson Publishing Co., Inc., 1970); Elizabeth Keckley,* Behind the Scenes: Thirty Years a Slave and Four Years in the White House *(New York: Arno Press and the New York Times, 1968); Linda Brent,* Incidents in the Life of a Slave Girl *(New York: Harcourt Brace Jovanovich, 1973).*

[22] *For a study published outside the US, see (political economist) Rhoda Reddock, "Women and Slavery in the Caribbean: A Feminist Perspective,* Latin American Perspective *12 (Winter 1985).*

# THE PAPER TRAIL:
# A Historical Exploration of the Black Family

*Barnetta McGhee White*

*In this genealogical history of her own family, developed through the use of primary sources and oral history, the author cites examples of how the paper trail led to the verification of a direct line ancestor. By following the steps and carefully documenting each event, she hopes to capture the essence of Black family life and history.*

*Who controls the past, controls the future: Who controls the present controls the past.*[1]

These lines from George Orwell's futuristic novel, *1984*, are as true in this very real world as they were in his world of make-believe. The knowledge of history has been controlled primarily by those who wrote it. Future behavior is driven by present behavior, and both have origins in one's beliefs about one's past. In the wide expanse of time, only recently have Blacks, as African-Americans, been permitted to read and write, and more recently still have they become secure enough to write with some objectivity about their early lives in America, without anger or shame clouding the story they tell. It is important that Blacks put aside the anger, the discomfort and strive for the ideal objectivity that is needed to tell the story, knowing that complete objectivity can never be possible, yet remaining aware that their own point of view is just as valid as any other. Blacks must tell their story themselves, as the control of the story of their past is too important a task to be left entirely to others.

Robert Harris, in a recent issue of *The Journal of Negro History*, identified three major areas of concentration which historians have used as vehicles for their writings about African-Americans. They are (1) the African background, (2) slavery, and (3) reconstruction. While writing on these broad topics, historians' methodologies generally fell into the categories of *revisionist*—used to correct misconceptions; *hidden hand*—the work of God in human affairs; *contributionist*—using an extraordinary person to demonstrate participation in American development; *cyclical*—successes and failures are the inevitable rhythms of nature; and *liberal*—a rather idealized and glorified perception of the march to freedom and equality.[2] These writings sought to reveal, explain, and help the reader understand the experiences of Black folk in America.

One of the major areas, slavery, is a very broad one, and one in which many writers of history have invested enormous amounts of emotion, intellect, time, and energy. Even among respected scholars, there is often disagreement about the cultural, economic, and social significance resulting from it.[3] The great diversity among writers on this topic has resulted in conscious and unconscious biases, omissions, and distortions. These writers tried with varying successes to overcome the limitations of

From the *Western Journal of Black Studies* 12 (Spring 1988):1–7. © 1988 by the Washington State University Press. Reprinted by permission.

their own perspectives, assumptions, predictions, and moral dilemmas.[4]

All of the areas, as outlined by Harris, are of continuing importance, but there is another area, *genealogy*, which has been neglected and ignored by most historians. Although research is often driven by perceptions of the public interest and hopes of heightened prestige, perhaps it is now time for a different, more systematic approach in search of accuracy. This systematic examination of our ancestors and relatives causes the investigator not only to be a skillful researcher, but also to possess or acquire knowledge of geography, sociology, religion, history, anthropology, law, and language as it has evolved over time. Genealogy, as an area of study, especially, needs an understanding of the psychology of the human nature of the slaveholder and the slave.

Growing up during the 40s and 50s as Black and female in the South, this writer found little in the historical literature during her childhood public school education which touched a responsive chord of recognition. This lack of information paired with a burning "need to know," spurred effort decades later to investigate the concrete and specific experiences of ordinary Black people by using one family (the writer's) as a vehicle through which these experiences could be revealed.

Such a study is, admittedly, by its very nature personalized, individualized, and in spite of knowing the pitfalls of prior work in this field, it cannot be completely value-free. The author's background is of common stock, one of the masses of ordinary people, and having grown up and being nurtured in a large, extended family, she decided to analyze her family's structure, its origin, development, and duration, and attempt to discover the events that stabilized it, gave it a sense of purpose, preserved it, and permitted it to remain functional. These beginnings occurred during that time and place known in history as American slavery. Writing in *Phylon*, Clarence Mohr stated,

> *Available evidence indicates that . . . blacks were bought and sold on a purely pragmatic basis, with little or no regard for family ties . . . were most often treated simply as a portion of the chattel property in an estate and disposed of accordingly . . .*[5]

Although Mohr was reporting of conditions in Oglethorpe County, Georgia, historians closer to home told the same story. Bobby Frank Jones determined that in North Carolina

> *. . . since family groups sold for less than individuals, husbands were frequently separated from wives, and parents from children. They could be divided out [and] would belong to a group of relatives . . . [These] crazy quilt separations are characteristic of estate divisions—children and parents scattered all over a county or a state.*[6]

There was little hope that one individual, working alone, conducting research using primary sources that had been written in antiquated handwriting, could find and trace just one family of slaves through such a maze of business dealings. And there was even less possibility that the tracing of the movements of this one family could be documented as they lived out their lives under the most trying of circumstances, all the while maintaining and communicating to future generations a strong sense of family. It was important, nevertheless, to retrace their steps, and by remembering *them*, pay homage to all of those countless others who were the true builders of this country . . . who cleared the land, dug the canals, planted and reaped the harvest, all the while rearing the children of all races. From their story, that of the common man who survived a most uncommon experience, generalizations could be made of the journey that many others took along beside them.

The first problem encountered was deciding where to start. The solution was to start with the present and work back—year by year—into the past, knowing that one false lead, or one skipped generation, would lead to a dead end and the loss of months of work. Concurrent with this problem was the effort to learn the generations of rich oral history. Oral history served as a guidepost along this journey from the present to the past, and was consequently validated in doing so.

Each person has two parents, four grandparents, eight great-grandparents, etc. yet the various problems encountered in documenting Black genealogy and the solutions found to the problems are best understood by the following three illustrations. Each example shows how the paper trail led to the verification of a direct line ancestor. Each is responsible for the writer being here. The writer is ever mindful that the essence of her being is directly related to who they were. Recognition and revival is owed to them.

The first story is of Creasy. Born a slave in the eighteenth century, she lived to experience freedom and to see her many descendants reap part of the harvest of her ordeals. It is also the story of how oral history can be documented, thereby, affirming its accuracy.

Creasy was only five years old when she left Virginia to come to the strange and different place called North Carolina.[7] Born in 1799 into slavery, she learned at an early age that she must do as the white folks bid, so she moved as told, leaving many relatives and friends behind. The sorrow was somewhat lessened because other relatives and friends came along with her to this new plantation and new home. Work was steady and hard. She even got married one day to Claiborne and had several children who lived and worked on the same plantation. Although there was always the possibility that her children could be taken away from her, her paternalistic master did not deal in buying and selling slaves, therefore, a slave was seldom sold from this plantation.[8]

One day when she was quite old, everything changed. Her master died, and his wife died shortly after. The fear was real and very great as all the slaves speculated on their fate. It was months before the estate was settled and the final disposition of her master's property was made known. There was talk in the cabins about a will in which some slaves were mentioned by name. As it turned out, many slaves were evaluated and placed in lots of equal value and the lots were then drawn by the heirs to her dead master's property. Creasy and old Claiborne remained together in the same lot, along with her daughter Lucinda and granddaughter Rose, who was

---

**CHART #1    Norman Surname for Slaves**

CREASY NORMAN (slave)
  (1799–1879)  Mortality schedule of the 1880 Census
LUCINDA NORMAN (her daughter, a slave)
  (1827–1914)  Slaveholder Bible record, death certificate

      (Lucinda's four children, all born slaves)
ROSE NORMAN
  (1852–1943)  Death and marriage certificates
CHARLES NORMAN
  (1858–1924)  Same as above
SANDY NORMAN
  (1861–1906)  Same as above
RICHARD JOHNSON NORMAN
  (1864–1929)  Same as above
OTHER DOCUMENTATION
1853 division of the Estate of Thomas W. Norman, slaveholder

| Lot #1 | Claiborne | $50 |
| | Creasy | $100 |
| | Lucinda & child | $1,000 |

—drawn by son-in-law of deceased slaveholder, Richard P. Taylor for his wife, Martha.

---

The widow of Armistead Burwell, Elizabeth *Norman* Burwell, another daughter of the deceased Thomas W. Norman, sold Bob McGehee his farmland in 1880. Bob's son David had married the above named Rose in 1871.

---

not yet weaned.[9] The fear that her dead master's children would not hesitate to break up her family never left her, and it was that fear that guided her every action and determined the nature and context of her training of her own children and grandchildren. She survived to taste freedom and to hold her great-grandchildren before she died in 1879. The reason given for her death was paralysis.[10]

Documentation for the Norman surname and the relationship was supplied by a slaveholder's Bible entry, estate division papers of 1853, all Census records, the Mortality Schedule of 1880, nineteenth century marriage records, and death certificates after 1913. Although she and her children changed slaveholders, contrary to popular opinion, there is no evidence that they changed surnames.

This Creasy was the mother of Lucinda who was the mother of Rose, who was the mother of Benjamin, who was the father of this writer.

The second story is about another great-great grandmother, Franky.

CHART #2    Littlejohn Surname for Slaves

slave:              FRANKY LITTLEJOHN
                         (1795–1870/80)
slaveholder:  Thomas B. Littlejohn, died 1854
1815  Bill of Sale: From Roger Atkinson (son-in-law of
          the above)
1827  Deed of Trust: From T. B. Littlejohn to John Nuttall
          and Willis Lewis named "Franky and her
          children, Caroline & Isabella."
1840  Deed of Trust: From T. B. Littlejohn to John R.
          Hicks named "Franky and her children Caroline,
          Isabella, William, Frederick & Alexander."
slave:              CAROLINE LITTLEJOHN
                         (1822–1912)

Shortly after the beginning of the nineteenth century in Danville, Virginia, the sale of a slave woman named Franky took place. Although both the buyer and seller were business men, they were also connected to each other by the marriage of the buyer's daughter to the seller's son. Franky fetched four hundred and twenty-five dollars ($425) that year of 1815 and she too moved across the border to live in North Carolina.[11] She survived slavery and was alive in 1870. Although the census for that year is notoriously inaccurate in many respects, the information given there showed that she had been born around 1795.[12]

Her stability and very existence were tenuous from the beginning as she was used repeatedly, along with her children as they arrived, as collateral to secure loans and to cover the debts that her master incurred. First with her daughters, Caroline and Isabella,[13] then thirteen years later with these two daughters and sons William, Frederick, and Alexander, she was transferred, at least on paper, to the servitude of another master.[14] When her master died she was an old woman and a grandmother many times over and logically of little use to the slave economy.[15] It is believed that during the ten years between the death of her master and the end of the war, Franky changed hands many times.[16]

Documentation for the Littlejohn surname and the familial relationship was supplied by a Bill of Sale dated 1815, 1827 and 1840 Deeds of Trust,

and the 1870 Census. There is no evidence to suggest that Franky or her children changed surnames when they changed owners.

Franky was the mother of Caroline, who was the mother of David, who was the father of Benjamin, who was the father of the writer.

The third story is of Robert McGehee who married Franky's oldest daughter, Caroline. One of their sons, David, married Creasy's granddaughter, Rose.

Caroline, the oldest daughter of Franky, was a teenager when she became enamored of Robert who lived on the next plantation.[17] Bob was only a teenager himself and his ownership was very much in question. Nevertheless, they were able to get the permission of their respective masters to marry.

To identify Bob McGehee among the many slaves named Bob involved making judgments based upon the preponderance of the evidence found and using sound deductive reasoning. It appears that the surname, *Hester*, was used for him just after the war. Nevertheless, at least eight different points of evidence confirm his identity.

1.  In 1842, a seventeen year old slave named "Bob" was named in the will and inventory of a Mary D. Hester. Bob McGehee's year of birth was given consistently as 1824 in the 1880 and 1900 Census and he would have been seventeen years old in 1842.

2.  This Mary D. Hester's husband, Benjamin, had died in 1829. His plantation on the North Fork of the Tar River was close to one of the plantations of Caroline's slaveholder, Thomas B. Littlejohn, on Hatchers Run.

3.  Robert and Caroline had to live near each other to parent the children born between 1841 and 1865.

4.  There is no doubt that these were Bob's children because he named each of them in his will written in 1900.

5.  Of nearly 1,400 extant 1866–7 marriage records of Granville County's freed people, only one couple fit their description—"Robert Hester and Caroline Hester, married twenty-seven years."

6.  After the war, there were at least four persons with the surname of Hester who were known by

## CHART #3    Franky Littlejohn (1795–1870/80)

| ROBERT McGEHEE (McGhee) (1824–1900/03) | CAROLINE LITTLEJOHN (1822–1912) | # OF CHILDREN |
|---|---|---|
| FRANK (1841–1946) | Ida Hicks | 4 |
|  | Anna Johnson | 1 |
| FANNIE (Frances?) (1843–1920) | Lee Pool(e) | 4 |
| AMANDA (Mandy) (1845–1915) | Orchon Faison | 8 |
| DAVID (1848–1914) | Rose Norman | 14 |
| ISABELLA (1853–1934) | Isaac Hicks | 10 |
| FREDERICK (1856–1939) | Fannie Hicks | 10 |
| ALEXANDER (1858–1928) | Virginia Royster | 7 |
|  | Delia Kittrell | 4 |
| ROSA (died after 1870) (1861–?) |  |  |
| THOMAS (1863–1947) | Lucy Hunt | 12 |
| MOLLIE (Mary) (1865–1942) | Otis Hicks | 8 |

### DOCUMENTATION

Deeds of Trust, 1827 & 1840 naming "Franky & her children
1866 Cohabitation record of Robert & Caroline; Fannie & Lee Pool(e)
Marriage licenses of Frank, David, Isabella, Frederick, Thomas & Mollie
Population and Agricultural Schedules, 1870–1910
1900 will of Robert McGhee
Death records after 1913

Bob's children and grandchildren as their close relatives.

7. There is a strong family oral tradition that Bob always knew that his name was McGehee and "when he got the chance he *went back* to his original name." This leads one to believe that he was called by some other name before he was in a position to attest to his own identity.

8. This Robert McGehee/Robert Hester dichotomy supports the theory advanced by others that the last names recorded by scribes directly after the war were not necessarily the last names slaves chose or knew for themselves.

Bob, his ownership uncertain, moved from place to place in the county because he was "hired out" for many years to different members of a large, extended, slaveholding family. A paper trail of annual "hire-outs" and court transcripts was followed from 1830 to 1844 until the contested will of his master was finally settled in the State Supreme Court.[18] By that time Bob and Caroline had at least one child with another on the way.

It was very difficult to maintain family ties while Caroline and the children had one master and Bob another.[19] The cost was high, and Bob paid it, literally, when he offered up his meager cache saved from cultivating cash crops at night by pine-torch to assist a buyer in buying his wife and children when they were due to be sold away from the county.[20] He saw some of his children taken away from him, yet at war's end, he shepherded them back around the family hearth. He heard of a daughter in a distant county who had been left a widow with several small children to raise alone.[21] He sent his now grown sons, my grandfather David and great-uncle Frank, to get her and bring her back home to the family.

After the war, Bob and his sons farmed, sharecropping at first, then he bought his own small farm.[22] Within two decades at least two of his sons had bought individual farms, also.[23]

To follow this one family in the post war years as they struggled to earn a living is a study in land owned and land lost by Black farmers throughout the South. Beginning in the 1870s, time and again they borrowed the money to buy seeds and plant the crops. These legal, agricultural contracts were sometimes for as little as five or ten dollars—with the farmer putting up a cow and calf, or as one lien read, "one gray horse, 'Charlie'."[24] Then when the livestock was gone, they used the land for collateral. In many cases it can be assumed that they lost all, including the land for nonpayment of these meager loans.

Documentation for this story was supplied by the eight points of evidence just mentioned, 1866 cohabitation records, nineteenth century marriage licenses for Bob and Caroline's children, land deeds, Population and Agricultural Schedules 1870–1910, and the 1900 will of Robert McGehee.

This Robert McGehee was the father of David, who was the father of Benjamin, who was the father of the writer.

When searching for an individual ancestor who lived as a slave, seldom is there available a collected and sorted body of material from one large plantation. Absence of correspondence, bills of sale, account books with names and ages of slaves, etc., is remedied by perusing all records of deeds for that locality, and many wills, hoping to find one specific, familiar name. This disadvantage becomes an advantage because looking for the movements of a specific slave makes one keenly aware of the movements of many slaves. Reading deeds, court minutes and trial transcripts helps one view a wide range of slaveholding behavior upon which to make assumptions regarding prevalent attitudes of the antebellum era. The search for one slave becomes much broader as the story unfolds for hundreds of slaves. In the final analysis, the problem of not having a catalogued group of papers becomes an advantage if one wishes to make statements about the wider range of behavior evident during the antebellum era.

These stories are true and the facts, as presented, have been documented. Starting with the *present* generation and *moving back* through time with each generation, using public records and all types of empirical data such as census, marriage licenses, church baptisms, birth and death records, the writer was able to reconstruct the movements and lives of this one family. As the story unfolded back to 1865, the task became more difficult because the controllers of the history of this family recorded them as chattel and refused to record last names for them. At that juncture, it was discovered that the researcher must adopt different methodology and retrace the slaveholders' movements and study their lives, attitudes, perceptions and business dealings. It was from the readings of their wills, deeds, court minutes, estate settlements and the like that made it possible to piece together the antebellum part of the story.

The greatest, most disabling problem encountered was the common custom of the slaveholding society of not recording surnames for slaves. The solution to this problem was multifaceted in that it involved understanding naming patterns and practices, determining the geographic location to include the specific plantation of the ancestor, matching the ages given for slaves in ancient documents with ages listed in post civil war population census records, and then using sound deductive reasoning to draw conclusions from the preponderance of the available evidence.

Of course there were other clues to follow and patterns did emerge along the way. Naming practices of slaves and slaveholders, specifically that of giving their children the names of mothers and fathers, aunts, uncles and grandparents, provided clues. A notable example of this was that Caroline gave her children the names of three of her brothers and sisters; Isabella, Frederick, and Alexander. The greatest hindrance was the prevailing custom of slaveholders not recording the surnames for slaves.

Slaves did have surnames which they themselves knew and used, even if the recorders of history seldom recorded them when they put pen to paper. Herbert G. Gutman, in his study of a group of eighteenth century slaves stated, "... most slaves had surnames, and most with surnames in 1783 had surnames different from their last owners." He then concluded that it appeared that the last name was adopted by slaves from "the slaveholder of origin."[25] It would seem that the surname could be passed to successive generations through either the mother or the father, but most often the father. The writer's own research tends to support this concept.

Much has been written from a historical perspective about the stability, or lack of stability, of the African-American family. Not all agree with Fogel and Engerman that slaveholders encouraged and supported slave marriage and stable slave families during the antebellum period.[26] James D. Anderson, as one of the scholars responding to Blassingame's *The Slave Community*, reported that as recently as 1951 Kardiver and Oversey asserted that slavery "prevented Blacks from forming permanent familial ties" without a necessary qualifying "most," or "many," or even "some."[27] The wide publicity given by social scientists in the 1960s to the characterization of the African-American family as being historically pathological and deficient has been disputed vigorously by more recent scholars.

The examples presented here are some of the highlights from the writer's book, *In Search of Kith and Kin: The History of a Southern Black Family*. By following each of Robert's and Caroline's 1500 + descendants to the present day, the story of a strong family emerged. That greatly expanded study was done to compare how closely the history of one family fits the picture of what is generally known about the African-American family. When time permits examination of antebellum Virginia papers, that study will reach further in the past.

To document Black genealogy during the antebellum era is difficult, but not impossible. There are myriad problems but they are not insoluble if one takes care not to skip generations, nor leap to premature, unsupported conclusions. The key turns through investigation of the slaveholder, which assists in determining what is possible and probable. The reward for such sustained, persistent effort is to capture the essence of Black family life and history by discovering the specific events and circumstances which impacted upon it for many generations. It is from such essence that Blacks as a people derive their strength and sense of rootedness.

Despite the many problems encountered in doing so, the stories must be carefully documented for each of the events related. For

> ... *without citation of sources for assumptions made it is difficult to examine the records supposedly used in order to scrutinize the findings and arguments presented in support of the assumptions.*[28]

To write the story and not document it, to embellish it or enlarge upon it, is to discredit it and to cause it to be discounted. The story, if carefully researched and accurately told, speaks for itself.

Winston's and O'Brien's conversation from the novel *1984* continues:

> *Is it your opinion, Winston, that the past has real existence?*
> *No.*
> *Then where does the past exist, if at all?*
> *In records. It is written down.*
> *In records. And—?*
> *In the mind. In human memories.*[29]

---

[1] *George Orwell, 1984 (New York, 1949), p. 251.*

[2] *Robert L. Harris, "Coming of Age: The Transformation of Afro-American Historiography,"* The Journal of Negro History, *(Summer, 1982), pp. 107–121.*

[3] *John W. Blassingame,* The Slave Community: Plantation Life in the

Antebellum South *(New York, 1979); Paul A. David, Herbert G. Gutman, Richard Sutch, Peter Temin & Gavin Wright,* Reckoning With Slavery: A Critical Study in the Quantitative History of American Negro Slavery *(New York, 1976); John Hope Franklin,* From Slavery to Freedom: A History of Negro Americans, *5th* ed. *(New York, 1980); George P. Rawick,* From Sundown to Sunup: The Making of the Black Community (Westport, Connecticut, 1973).

[4]*Robert W. Fogel & Stanley Engerman,* Time on the Cross: The Economics of American Negro Slavery *(Boston, 1974); Herbert G. Gutman,* Slavery and the Numbers Game: A Critique of Time on the Cross *(Chicago, 1975); Abram Kardiner & Lional Oversey,* The Mark of Oppression: A Psychosocial Study of the American Negro *(New York, 1951), pp. 384–87.*

[5]*Clarence L. Mohr, "Slavery in Oglethorpe County, Georgia,"* Phylon: The Atlanta University Review of Race and Culture, *33:1 (Spring, 1972), pp. 11–12.*

[6]*Bobby Frank Jones,* A Cultural Middle Passage: Slave Marriages and Family in the Antebellum South, *(unpublished dissertation, University of North Carolina, 1965), pp. 189–195.*

[7]*All Census records refer to the Population, Mortality, and Agricultural Census of the United States. All other records are North Carolina records and those of Granville County, North Carolina.*

*The information for this statement was taken from the Mortality Schedule for 1880 showing persons who had died during the year ending 31 May 1880, Supervisor District (SD)2, Enumerator District (ED)107, page 2. Her place of birth, as well as that of her father and mother, was given as Virginia.*

[8]*Deed books and Will books for Granville County, NC, from ca 1775 to ca 1865 were read, and although identification of slave traders and the transfers of hundreds of slaves could be made, there is no indication that this particular family was thus engaged. Documentation for these statements is also found in the Burwell Family Papers, #112, in the Southern Historical Collection, University of North Carolina, Chapel Hill.*

[9]*The will of Thomas W. Norman was written 16 November 1852 (he died 6 December 1852) and proven in the February Court of 1853 (Granville County Will Book 19, p. 199). In it were the names of 59 slaves who were willed to his wife, three daughters and one granddaughter. After his wife died in 1853, the slaves that she had held were divided again among the heirs. A February, 1853 petition to the Court of Pleas and Quarter Sessions was filed among Miscellaneous Records of Slaves and Free Person of Color, 1755–1871 in the North Carolina State Archives. One share, or lot, of the division contained Claiborne, Creasy, her daughter Lucinda, and Lucinda's daughter, Rose. It was beyond December of 1855 before this estate was finally settled.*

[10]*The 1880 Mortality Schedule of the U.S. Population Census for Granville County, North Carolina, Supervisors District 2, Enumerator District 107, page 2. (Henceforth, this will be shown as SD and ED.)*

[11]*N.C. State Archives, Bills of Sale for Slaves and Personal Property, Granville County. Although it is doubtful that this receipt, which shows the transfer of the slave Franky from Thomas P. Atkinson to Thomas B. Littlejohn, is the latter's original acquisition of Franky, it was the first piece of hard evidence discovered regarding her location during slavery.*

[12]*1870 Census, Granville County, Oxford Township, page 24, household 212.*

[13]*Deed Book 3, pp. 312–313 dated 30 October 1827. Thomas B. Littlejohn placed six slaves, including "Franky & her two children Caroline and Isabella" in a special trust to his friends John Nuttall and Willis Lewis "to sell as many of said slaves at public auction to the highest bidder for ready money."*

*Deeds of Trust were not the same as deeds of sale. If creditors could be satisfied prior to the due date of the obligation, the owner retained possession of his property which had been used as collateral to secure the loan.*

[14]*Deed Book 10, pp. 85–86. This document, dated 29 July 1840, showed that Thomas B. Littlejohn was deeply in debt to at least twelve named creditors for thousands of dollars. He placed in trust to his friend, Dr. John R. Hicks, several town lots, farm acreage, five slaves in addition to "Franky & her children Caroline, Isabella, William, Frederick & Alexander," livestock, grow-*

ing crops, ". . . and all his household furniture of every description—to have & to hold the said Negro slaves, and the said several lots & parcels of land, . . ." etc. . . . and "proceed to sell the said slaves, lands . . . after due advertisement . . . pay off any amount of money . . . the said Thomas B. by consent of the parties is to remain in possession of the said lands, slaves & other property until such sale shall be made . . ."

*Records of the land sales have been discovered but no record has been found of the sale of the slaves.*

[15]*The will of Thomas B. Littlejohn, dated 18 October 1850, with two codicils dated 23 November 1850 and 29 September 1852, was probated during the August Court of 1854 (Warren County Will Book 43, p. 185). No slaves were named in this will but reference was made to the 1840 Deed of Trust, which in turn led to the 1827 Deed of Trust. Although the Slave Schedule lists him as holding 65 slaves in 1820 and 20 slaves in 1830, no complete listing of the names of his holdings has been found. The names of many of these numbers have been learned by reading and abstracting them from the Granville County Deed Books from 1800 until his death.*

[16]*The 1870 Population Census lists Franky as a 75 year old female head of a household which also contained a Henry Wilson and Julia, Susan, Eliza, and Robert Potter. Next door were more Potters and David Clark. Although the 1870 Census does not indicate the relationship of household members to each other, it is likely that this former slave, who had lived in this county and township for most of her life, was living with children and/or grandchildren at that time. The different last names provided a clue as to who her slaveholders might have been after Littlejohn died (1870 Census, Granville County, Oxford Township, page 24, household 212).*

[17]*To identify Bob McGehee among the many slaves named Bob involved making judgments using deductive reasoning. There is no evidence to indicate how he got the surname McGehee. However, the greater weight of the evidence appears to tip the scales toward the surname Hester being used in referring to him in 1866. This conclusion is supported in these documents: early maps of Granville County showing rivers, creeks and other waterways which were compared with plantation boundaries in early deeds; Will Book 15, pp. 299 & 356; Will Book 16, p. 63; Granville County Marriages of Freed People, Reel #133, NC State Archives; Will Book 25, pp. 515–516.*

[18]Supreme Court Case #4049. *Each year from 1830 until 1844, the 53 slaves of this estate were "hired out" throughout the county to different Hester relatives as the Courts decided the legal heirs.*

[19]Ibid.

[20]*This story was told by Frank, the oldest son of this couple. It was included in a feature article in the* Durham Sun *Newspaper on October 9, 1939. Frank also said that the master he remembered was James Littlejohn, son of Thomas B. Littlejohn.*

[21]*This bit of oral history is supported by the 1870 Census for Johnston County, One Moiety of Smithfield Township, p. 488, dwelling 56. In 1880, Mandy and her family lived in the Wilson's Mills area of the county (SD 2, ED 164, p. 19). By 1900 Mandy had moved back to Granville County with her children (SD 5, ED 59, Sheet 5).*

[22]*Granville County Deed Book 33, p. 335; Agricultural Schedule for 1870, Oxford Township, p. 5; Agricultural Schedule for 1880, SD 2, ED 107, pp. 21–23.*

[23]*Deed Book 38, pp. 82–84; Deed Book 39, p. 361.*

[24]*Many of these mortgage liens read "under the provisions of the Act of the General Assembly of this state in such cases." Some of the supporting documentation is found in the following Mortgage Books: Book 4, p. 429; 5, p. 496; 5, p. 536; 6, p. 206; 9, p. 500; 10, p. 388; 12, p. 536; 13, p. 366; 16, p. 46; 17, p. 140; 21, p. 73; 39, p. 456; 46, p. 204.*

*This Act to Secure Advances for Agricultural Purposes was ratified March 1, 1867, by which ". . . if any person . . . shall make any advance . . . to any person . . . who [is] engaged . . .*

in the cultivation of the soil . . . [he] shall be entitled to a lien on the crops which may be made during the year upon the land . . . in preference to all other liens existing . . ." Other acts were made, amended, and expanded during the years 1870 through 1889 to include personal property and the land itself. (North Carolina State Library, Public Laws of the State of North Carolina passed by the General Assembly, published by authority of the State.)

[25] Herbert G. Gutman, The Black Family in Slavery and Freedom, 1750–1925 (New York, 1976), pp. 239–250.

[26] Robert W. Fogel & Stanley Engerman, Time on the Cross; The Economics of American Negro Slavery (Boston, 1974), pp. 84–85.

[27] A. T. Gilmore (Ed), Revisiting Blassingame's The Slave Community: The Scholars Respond, (Westport, Connecticut, 1978), p. 127.

[28] Herbert G. Gutman, Slavery and the Numbers Game: A Critique of Time on the Cross (Chicago, 1975), p. 133.

[29] George Orwell, 1984, (New York, 1949), pp. 251–252.

# PART TWO

## The Dyad

### Dating and Sexual Patterns

Each unit of the family begins as a dyad, usually two members of the opposite sex who occupy a range of roles based on the stage of their relationship. Historically, the first stage in the process of forming a family has been dating and courtship. Changes in attitudes toward the family have brought about variations in the practice of these behaviors. Among the most marked changes in the dating and courtship system are the differing characteristics of its participants, the changing purpose of dating, and variations in its form. Dating, for instance, now involves not only the very young; the increasing numbers of individuals who remain unmarried until fairly advanced ages means that a dating partner could as easily be 38 as 18. Spiraling divorce and low remarriage rates create another large pool of dating partners. Dating has also become time contained, often existing only for the moment for sexual or recreational purposes, and is no longer automatically presumed to be a prelude to courtship or marriage. Even the concept of dating has been modified as men and women get together without making formal arrangements for an evening out in a public setting.

Much of this description is relevant to the white middle class, which has developed a new ideology about the nature and content of the dating system. There are limitations to the generalizations we can make about Black dating because there is less literature on the subject. The practice of Black dating varies by region, epoch, and social class. In the past, when Blacks formed a small, cohesive community in the rural and urban South, what might be called dating behavior centered on the neighborhood, church, and school. In general it was a casual process where men and women met, formed emotional attachments, and later married. Most of the participants were members of larger social units whose members or reputation were generally known to the community. As Blacks moved into urban areas outside of the South, the anonymity of individuals in these settings modified dating patterns. The school and house party became centers for fraternizing between the sexes, particularly among the lower class. In the middle-class group, dating habits took on the characteristics of mainstream culture as they included more activities like movies, dances, or bowling.

Black sexuality is another area of Black family life neglected in the literature. This is particularly difficult to understand in light of the special role accorded to Blacks—that of a peculiarly desirable or essentially different sexual object. Yet, although we have witnessed a full-blown sexual revolution, at least in the media, a reliable study of Black sexuality is hard to find. Blacks rarely are included in the many studies on white sexual attitudes and behavior. The paucity of past research on Black sexuality makes it difficult to assess what, if any, changes have occurred as a result of the fundamental transformation of sexual attitudes and practices occurring among the general population.

We do know that historically Black sexuality differed from its white counterpart in a number of ways. This difference began with the African and European conceptions of the nature of human sexuality. While Europeans traditionally have viewed sex as inherently sinful, Africans have viewed it as a natural function that should be enjoyed. These contrasting views may suggest a dichotomy of permissiveness versus puritanism. However, within the African continent a wide range of sexual codes and practices coexisted, differing from the European sexual traditions in the secular basis for the code as well as in the belief that sex is a natural function for humans.

Slavery exercised another influence on Afro-American sexuality. Women in bondage, unlike their white counterparts, had no way to protect their sexual purity. This fact has led to the assumption that because Black women could not be accorded any respect for, or defense of, their sexual integrity, it failed to have any strong value for them. Although such an assumption might be logical, it ignores the existence of moral codes related to sex in the Black community that, while different from mainstream norms, do regulate sexual activity for both men and women.

## Sex Roles

In recent years the issue of sex roles and their definition has received much attention. The debate has centered on the issue of female subordination and male dominance and privilege, but Blacks have considerably different problems in terms of their sex role identities. They must first overcome certain disabilities based on racial membership, not gender affiliation. However, this does not mean that sex role identities within the Black community do not carry with them advantages and disadvantages. In many ways they do, but instead of fighting over the

question of who is the poorest of the poor, Blacks must contend with the plaguing problems of an unemployment rate that is as high as 45 percent among Black men. Correlates of that central problem are the declining life expectancy rate of Black men and rises in drug abuse, suicide, crime, and educational failures. These facts do not warrant much support for a movement to equalize the condition of men and women in the Black community.

Along with the economic conditions that impinge on their role performance, Black men are saddled with a number of stereotypes that label them as irresponsible, criminalistic, hypersexual, and lacking in masculine traits. Some of these stereotypes become self-fulfilling prophecies because the structure of the dominant society prevents many Black men from achieving the goals of manhood. At the same time, the notion of the castrated Black male is largely a myth. While mainstream culture has deprived many Black men of the economic wherewithal for normal masculine functions, most of them function in such a way as to gain the respect of their mates, children, and communities.

Along with all the dynamic changes occurring in U.S. society are slow but perceptible alterations in the role of Black women. The implications of these changes are profound in light of the fact that women are central figures in the family life of Black people. Historically, the Black woman has been a bulwark of strength in the Black community. From the time of slavery onward, she has resisted the destructive forces she has encountered in American society. During the period of slavery she fought and survived the attacks on her dignity by the slave system, relinquished the passive role ascribed to members of her gender to ensure the survival of her people, and tolerated the culturally induced irresponsibility of her man in recognition of this country's relentless attempts to castrate him.

Too often the only result of her sacrifices and suffering has been the invidious and inaccurate labeling of her as a matriarch, a figure deserving respect but not love. The objective reality of the Black woman in America is that she occupies the lowest rung of the socioeconomic ladder of all sex–race groups and has the least prestige. The double burden of gender and race has put her in the category of a super-oppressed entity. Considering the opprobrium to which she is subjected, one would expect her to be well represented in the woman's liberation movement. Yet that movement remains primarily white and middle class. This is due in part to the class-bound character of the women's movement, which is middle class while most Black women are poor or working class. Their low profile in that movement also stems from the fact that many of the objectives of white feminists relate to psychological and cultural factors such as language and sexist behavior, while the Black woman's concerns are economic.

There is a common ground on which Black and women can and do meet: on issues like equal pay for equal work, child care facilities, and female parity in the work force. Instead of joining the predominantly white and middle-class women's movement, many Black women have formed their own organizations such as the Welfare Rights Organization, Black Women Organized for Action, and the Black Feminist Alliance. There is little question that there is a heightened awareness among Black women of the problems they face based on their sex roles alone. Whether the struggle of Black women for equal rights will come in conflict with the movement for Black liberation remains to be seen. It is fairly clear that Black women have to be freed from the disabilities of both race and sex.

# Male/Female Relationships: Singles and Married

Relationships between Black men and Black women have had a peculiar evolution. Unlike the white family, which was a patriarchy and was sustained by the economic dependence of women, the Black dyad in North America has been characterized by more equalitarian roles and economic parity. The system of slavery did not permit the Black male to assume the superordinate role in the family constellation because the female was not economically dependent on him. Hence relationships between the sexes were based on sociopsychological factors rather than on economic compulsion to marry

and remain married. This fact, in part, explains the unique trajectory of Black male/female relationships.

Finding and keeping a mate is complicated by a number of sociopsychological factors as well as structural restraints. Social structure and individual attitudes interface to make male/female relationships ephemeral rather than permanent. The imbalance in the sex ratio will continue to deny large numbers of professional Black women a comparable mate, and there are only a limited number of ways to deal with that irreversible fact of life. At the same time there exists a pool of professional Black males who are available to this group of women, and the tension between them builds barriers to communicating and mating. This is a complex problem and there is no easy solution.

Although there are some Black men who are threatened by the successful Black woman, further investigation reveals other underlying forces. Men are torn between the need for security and the desire for freedom, the quest for a special person to call their own and the temptation of sexual variety. They see marriage as a way of establishing roots but are seduced by the enticement of all the attractive, possibly "better," women in their midst. Given the advantage they have as males in a sexist society, and a high prestige (which is in short supply in the Black community), Black males have little incentive to undertake the actions needed to meet the needs of women. Consequently, women who feel that their emotional needs are not being met begin to recoil and to adopt their own agenda based on a concept of self-interest.

Some recognition must be made of the changing relations between men and women. The old exchange of feminine sexual appeal for male financial support is declining. Women increasingly are able to define their own status and to be economically independent. What they seek now is the satisfaction of emotional needs, not an economic cushion. While men must confront this new reality, women must realize that emotional needs can be taken care of by men in all social classes. Although similar education and income can mean greater compatibility in values and interests, they are no guarantee of this compatibility nor of personal happiness. Common needs, interests, and values are more a function of gender than of class.

We should not be deluded by the ostensible reluctance of many Black singles to enter the conjugal state. People who have not been able to develop a lasting permanent relationship with a member of the opposite sex must make the best of whatever circumstances they have at the moment. The industrial and urban revolution has made singlehood more viable as a way of life, but it has also made the need for belonging more imperative. The tensions of work and the impersonality of the city have created a need to escape depersonalization by retreating into an intimate sanctum. This is especially imperative for Blacks in the middle class who have their personhood tested daily by a racist society and who often must work and live in isolation. In modern society individuals are required to depend on each other for permanence and stability. That function was previously served by a large familial and social network.

It is the fear that even marriage no longer provides permanence and stability that causes people to enter and exit relationships quickly. It is the fear of failure that comes from failure. Until Black singles develop the tenacity to work at relationships as they did at schooling and jobs, we will continue to see this vicious cycle repeated again and again. Marriage and the family continue to be the most important buffer for Blacks against racism and depersonalization. When we look at the strongest predictors of happiness in the United States, they are inevitably social factors such as marriage, family, friends, and children. Across the board, married people tend to be happier than unmarrieds. The best confirmation of this fact is that most people who divorce eventually remarry. Before people can find happiness in a marriage, they have to form a strong basis for marriage. That task continues to perplex Black singles.

We are all aware that marriages are very fragile nowadays. Fewer people are getting married and the divorce rate in the United States is at an all-time high. It is estimated that the majority of marriages no longer will last a lifetime. Many forces are responsible for this changing pattern, including changing attitudes and laws on divorce, changing and conflicting definitions of sex roles and their functions in the family, economic problems, and personality conflicts. The increase in divorce cuts across racial and class lines, but divorce is still more pronounced among Blacks. Only one out of every three Black couples will remain married longer than ten years.

It is not easy to pinpoint unique causes of Black marital dissolution because they are similar to those for their white counterparts. In some cases it is the severity of the problems they face. Economic problems are a major factor in marital conflicts and there are three times as many Blacks with incomes below the poverty level as whites. The tensions Blacks experience in coping with the pervasive incidents of racism often have their ramifications in the marital arena. A peculiar problem Blacks face is the imbalanced sex ratio, which places many women in competition for the available males. Too often the males they compete for are not available, and this places serious pressure on many Black marriages.

At the same time, many Blacks are involved in functional marriages. Many adult Blacks are married and have positive and loving relationships with their spouses. Unfortunately, practically no research exists on marital adjustment and satisfaction among Blacks. What little research we have does indicate that Black wives are generally less satisfied with their marriages than are white wives. But the source of their dissatisfaction is often associated with the problems of poverty and racism.

The 1970s witnessed a significant increase in interracial dating and marriage. Among the reasons for this change in Black/white dating and marriage was the desegregation of the public school system, the work force, and other social settings. In those integrated settings Blacks and whites met as equals, which facilitated heterogeneous matings. There were, of course, other factors such as the liberation of many white youth from parental control and the racist values conveyed to them.

Not only has the incidence of interracial relations increased but their character has also changed. In the 1960s, the most typical interracial pairing was a Black male and a white female, with the male partner generally of a higher status. This pattern was so common that social theorists even developed a theory of racial hypergamy. In essence, it was assumed that the high-status Black male was exchanging his socioeconomic status for the privilege of marrying a woman who belonged to a racial group that was considered superior to all members of the Black race. Contemporary interracial relations are much more likely to involve persons with similar educational backgrounds and occupational statuses.

Although no research studies have yet yielded any data on the subject, there appears to be a change in interracial unions toward a decline in Black male/ white female couples and an increase in Black female/white male pairings. Several factors seem to account for this modification of the typical pattern. Many Black women are gravitating toward white men because of the shortage of Black males and their disenchantment with those to whom they have access. Similarly some white men are dissatisfied with white females and their increasingly vociferous demands for sex role parity. At the same time, there is a slight but noticeable decrease in Black male/ white female unions. A possible reason is that these are no longer as fashionable as they were many years ago. Also, much of the attraction of the members of both races to each other was based on the historic lack of access to each other and the stereotypes of Black men as superstuds and white women as forbidden fruit. Once there was extensive interaction the myths were exploded and the attraction consequently diminished.

It should be fairly clear that there are relatively normal reasons for interracial attractions and matings. At the same time it would be naive to assume that special factors are not behind them in a society that is stratified by race. Given the persistence of racism as a very pervasive force, many interracial marriages face rough sledding. In addition to the normal problems of working out a satisfactory marital relationship, interracial couples must cope with social ostracism and isolation. A recent phenomenon has been the increasing hostility toward such unions by the Black community, which has forced some interracial couples into a marginal existence. It is such pressures that cause the interracial marriage rate to remain at a very low level. Less than 5 percent of all marriages involving a Black person are interracial.

# 3 / Dating and Sexual Patterns

## SEXUAL DEVELOPMENT AND BEHAVIOR IN BLACK PREADOLESCENTS

*Ouida E. Westney · Renee R. Jenkins*
*June Dobbs Butts · Irving Williams*

*In this article the authors report results of a study of sexual development in Black preadolescents. They examined both sexual maturation and heterosexual behavior. There was considerable variation in sexual maturation for chronological age. Heterosexual activities were generally at the lower end of the scale. For girls there was no association between heterosexual activities and degree of biological maturation. For boys, genital development was related to sexual behavior.*

There is considerable concern in this country regarding the decreasing age of first sexual intercourse and the increasing rate of premarital pregnancy among very young teenagers. In their study of sexual behavior among teenagers, one of the strongest associations reported by Zelnik, Kantner, and Ford (1980) was between the age at menarche and age of first intercourse. This finding is of particular concern given that black teenage girls have reported earlier ages both for menarche and first intercourse as compared to white girls.

Afro-American girls are among the earliest maturing girls in the world. Harlan, Harlan, and Grillo (1980) reported that black girls were ahead of white girls in the development of breasts and pubic hair. Further, although adolescence is commonly considered as beginning at age 12, many black girls have developed early signs of pubertal changes by age 9, with menarche (a late-stage pubertal marker) coming on the average at 12.5 years of age (MacMahon, 1973). The implication of this early sexual development during the preadolescent period (age 9 through 12) and its impact on sexual behavior, in the broadest sense, has not received much attention in the research literature.

With respect to black boys, Harlan, Grillo,

From *Adolescence* 19 (75, Fall 1984):557–568. © Libra Publishers, 1984. Reprinted by permission. This research was supported by the Behavioral Science Branch, National Institute of Child Health and Human Development through Contract No. 1–HD–82840.

Cornoni-Huntley, and Leaverton (1979) reported that they are similar to their 12- to 17-year-old white counterparts in the timing of development of their secondary sex characteristics. However, with regard to sexual behavior at the preadolescent level, black boys have been reported to be ahead of white boys and girls, as well as ahead of black girls in heterosexual behaviors (Broderick, 1965). Research which examines biological sequencing in boys in relation to sexual behaviors has not been reported. This report focuses on relationships between maturational sequencing and sexual behavior in black preadolescent girls and boys.

## Background Theory and Research

Classic psychoanalytic theory views preadolescence as a period of psychosexual quiescence (S. Freud, 1938). Neopsychoanalytic investigations, however, suggest that during this period there is renewed psychosexual struggle to avert fixation to preoedipal levels (Blos, 1962; Peller, 1958). For boys, this struggle is manifested by "despising" girls while simultaneously experiencing heterosexual curiosity and covert heterosexual strivings. Girls deal with the struggle by manifesting pseudo-mature behaviors including display of feminine charms, subtle "seducing strategies," as well as the imitation of masculine traits and activities (Kohen-Raz, 1971).

Although preadolescent boys and girls are often described as being hostile toward each other, it is possible that this apparent mutual hostility may instead be a mechanism for coping with their psychosexual concerns. Actually, in the Broderick (1965) study, preadolescent boys and girls were reported generally as being friendly toward each other. Some preadolescents reported having boy/girl friends, kissing, dating, and going steady.

In attempting to explain the psychology underlying individual behaviors in adolescents, Petersen and Taylor (1980) utilized a biopsychosocial model. They proposed interacting biological, sociocultural, and self-perception pathways leading to the psychological adaptations of developing adolescents. The biological factors include genetic potentials, endocrine changes, secondary characteristics, and time of pubertal onset. Sociocultural factors encompass attractiveness standards, peer and parental responses, and stereotypes of early and late maturers. Self-perception factors include body-image, self-image, self-esteem, and gender identity. Although the authors were tracing pathways to personal responses during adolescence, it is not unreasonable to apply this model to preadolescence. Our larger study addresses variables in each of the categories outlined by Petersen and Taylor. At this time, however, we are dealing with the biological aspect of the model—specifically the relationships between the development of secondary characteristics and sexual behaviors.

It is known that there is a causal relationship between the elaboration of sex hormones and the development of secondary sex characteristics. There is growing evidence from cross-sectional data correlating increasing levels of sex hormones with the progression in maturational staging. Gupta, Attanasio, and Raaf (1975) in their cross-sectional study demonstrated stage-related (Tanner, 1955) increases in dihydrotestosterone and testosterone for males and in estradiol and estrogen for females. Other cross-sectional studies (Angsusingha, Kenny, Nankin, and Taylor, 1974; Korth-Schultz, Levine, and New, 1976) also report similar increases in hormones which are related to maturational staging. Longitudinal studies to support these findings have not yet been reported.

Since there is growing empirical evidence linking progression in the elaboration of certain sex hormones to stages of biological maturation, two related questions may be asked: (1) What is the relationship between increase in sex hormones and sexual behavior during the process of maturation? and, (2) What is the relationship between biological maturation (staging) and sexual behavior during the maturational process? Regarding the relationship between increasing sex hormone levels and sexual behavior, Katchadourian (1980) indicated that there was a more consistent correlation between testosterone levels and sexual interest levels and behavior in maturing males than between estrogen levels and sexual behavior in maturing females. It is to the substance of the second question, the relationship between maturational staging and heterosexual behavior, that this report addresses itself.

# Method

## Subjects

The 101 preadolescent participants in this study were 46 boys and 55 girls living in a metropolitan area and its suburbs in the eastern United States. This volunteer sample was obtained through several sources including the Well-Child Clinics of a university hospital which serves a predominantly black clientele, independent schools, churches, and other agencies. The ages of the boys ranged from 8.5 to 11.4 years, with a mean age of 10.0 years. The girls ranged in age from 8.3 to 11.2 years with a mean age of 10.1 years. Sixty-two of the participants were from middle-income families and 37 from low-income families. Socioeconomic status was defined in terms of parental income and education.

## Procedure

A medical assessment was completed on all participants by two pediatricians with formal training in adolescent medicine. A standard age-appropriate history was obtained and physical examination conducted. From this assessment, data on sociosexual behaviors and physical maturation characteristics were obtained. Most of the historical information was elicited through an open-ended interview rather than a questionnaire format. Sexual maturation was assessed according to Tanner's (1955) criteria on a scale from I through V, with I representing the prepubertal stage, and progressing through pubescence to V, the adult stage. Except for two boys, each individual was examined by a pediatrician of the same sex as the participant.

Reported heterosexual behaviors as heterosexual physical activities (HPA) ranging from game playing to intercourse were quantified on a weighted scale which utilized the following designations: game playing = 1 point; holding hands, or hugging, or kissing = 2 points; light petting = 3 points; heavy petting = 4 points; and intercourse = 5 points. Thus, an HPA score was obtained by transforming each heterosexual activity into the appropriate code and summing the responses. This score represented the composite sexual behavior variable. For example, if a preadolescent reported participation in game playing, hugging, and kissing, the HPA score was 5.

Frequencies for all data were expressed in the form of percentages. Relationships between the HPA score, biological, and other variables were assessed using Spearman correlations. Significance was established at .05 level.

# Findings

## Sexual Maturation

Complete Tanner staging data were obtained on 43 boys and 50 girls. Staging data on breast development in girls and genital development in boys can be seen in Table 1. Most of the boys (67%) were prepubertal with respect to genital development. The remainder were at Stages II and III with mean ages of 10.7 and 10.8 years, respectively. Thirty-six percent of the girls showed no signs of breast development. The others were at various stages of development from Stage II through Stage IV. For these stages of breast development, their mean ages were 10.2, 10.6, and 10.9 years, respectively. There were marked overlaps in the age ranges for Stages I through III in the boys, and Stages I through IV in the girls.

Data regarding pubic hair development for both sexes appear in Table 2. Girls were more advanced than boys in pubic hair maturation. Again, the most advanced stage of pubic hair development attained by the boys was Stage III, while some girls had progressed to Stage IV. As with breast and genital development, wide variations in the ages of Tanner staging were observed in pubic hair growth. Among the sample, 33% of the boys and 76% of the girls had begun pubertal development.

**TABLE 1    Genital Development of Boys and Breast Development of Girls**

| Tanner stages | BOYS (n = 43) | | | | GIRLS (n = 50) | | |
|---|---|---|---|---|---|---|---|
| | Mean age | Age range | n | | Mean age | Age range | n |
| I | 10.0 | 8.5–11.3 | 29 | | 10.0 | 8.9–11.2 | 18 |
| II | 10.7 | 9.6–11.8 | 12 | | 10.2 | 8.3–10.9 | 9 |
| III | 10.8 | 10.4–11.1 | 2 | | 10.6 | 10.0–11.3 | 18 |
| IV | — | — | — | | 10.9 | 10.2–11.6 | 5 |
| V | — | — | — | | — | — | — |

**TABLE 2    Pubic Hair Development of Boys and Girls**

| Tanner stages | BOYS (n = 43) | | | | GIRLS (n = 50) | | |
|---|---|---|---|---|---|---|---|
| | Mean age | Age range | n | | Mean age | Age range | n |
| I | 10.0 | 8.5–11.3 | 33 | | 10.0 | 8.3–10.9 | 16 |
| II | 10.7 | 9.6–11.3 | 7 | | 10.6 | 9.3–11.6 | 17 |
| III | 11.1 | 10.4–11.9 | 3 | | 10.6 | 10.2–11.3 | 14 |
| IV | — | — | — | | 10.9 | 10.5–11.4 | 3 |
| V | — | — | — | | — | — | — |

Figure 1 shows the Tanner staging concordance of genital and pubic hair development in boys and breast and pubic hair development in girls at 9, 10, and 11 years. It is evident that at each age level, an increasing percentage of both boys and girls were pubescents. Although there was considerable variability in the progression of development in the pubescent boys and girls with regard to their respective secondary sex characteristics, there was complete Tanner staging concordance in many cases. This was more true for the boys than for the girls (57% and 32%, respectively).

For boys, the correlation between genital development and pubic hair development was significant at the .001 level; and for girls, the correlation between breast development and the development of pubic hair was also significant at the .001 level.

## Sociosexual Behavior

When asked whether they had a special boy or girl friend of the opposite sex, 60.9% of the boys and 56.4% of the girls responded affirmatively. The places where heterosexual activity occurred are reported in Table 3. The school was the most common location for interaction. Although the telephone cannot be strictly categorized as a place of heterosexual interaction, so many children (particularly girls) gave this as an answer that it is included in

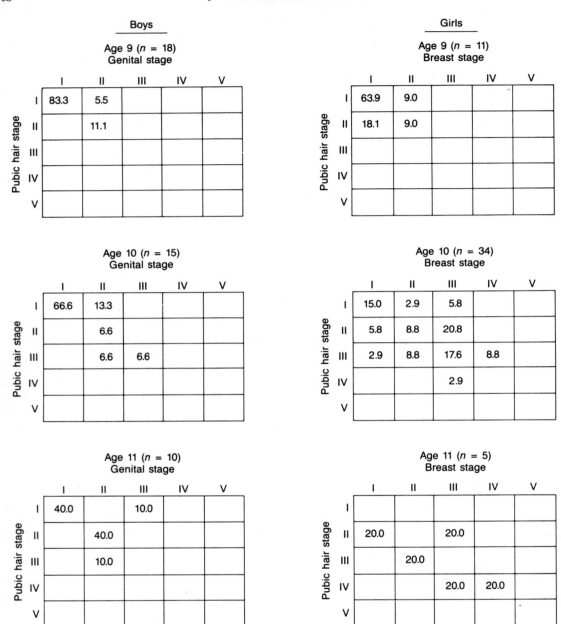

FIGURE 1

Table 3. Table 4 presents reported heterosexual physical activities of the participants. For both boys and girls, the number who reported having special opposite-sex friends was greater than those claiming involvement in heterosexual physical activities. Although comparatively more girls were involved in heterosexual activities than boys, these involvements were at the lower end of the HPA scale. The girls reported no behaviors beyond level 2 on the HPA scale (holding hands, kissing, and hugging). In addition to level 1 and level 2 behaviors, a small percentage of the boys reported involvement in heavy petting, and coitus, levels 4 and 5 behaviors on the HPA scale.

The games in which the boys and girls were involved were chiefly heterosexual chasing and tagging. Behaviors reported as possibilities when, for example, a boy chased a girl and caught her ranged from hitting her, to kissing her, to performing "humping" actions toward her.

## Relationships between HPA and Biological Maturation

The occurrence of heterosexual behaviors as represented by the HPA score was correlated with the maturational and other relevant variables; the results appear in Table 5. For both boys and girls,

**TABLE 4    Reported Heterosexual Activities**

| HPA | PERCENTAGES | |
| --- | --- | --- |
| | Boys ($n = 46$) | Girls ($n = 55$) |
| Any activity | 30.4 | 47.2 |
| Playing games | 17.4 | 29.1 |
| Holding hands | 10.9 | 5.5 |
| Kissing | 13.0 | 16.4 |
| Hugging | 8.7 | 7.3 |
| Light petting | — | — |
| Heavy petting | 4.3 | — |
| Intercourse | 2.2 | — |

there was no significant relationship between age and involvement in heterosexual activities. The 9-, 10-, and 11-year-old girls who reported heterosexual activities generally participated in level 1 and level 2 activities without respect to age. Regarding the boys, those who reported heavy petting and coitus were exclusively in the 9-year-old age group. In boys there was a significant relationship between the HPA score and genital staging ($r = .404$; $p < .005$), but no clear relationship existed between pubic hair staging and the HPA score. In the case of the girls, both breast and pubic hair development bore no significant relationship to the HPA score.

The relationship between the HPA score and reports of having a girlfriend or boyfriend was significant beyond the .001 level for boys and beyond the .05 level for girls. However, for both boys and girls, there were no significant relationships between having a girl/boy friend and the maturational variables. The small degree of relationship that existed was positive for the boys but inverse for the girls. Socioeconomic status for both boys and girls had no relationship of importance to the HPA score.

## Discussion

Our data indicate that chronologically, the girls are ahead of the boys in biological development, a finding which is consistent with earlier research

**TABLE 3    Places of Heterosexual Activity**

| Places | PERCENTAGES | |
| --- | --- | --- |
| | Boys ($n = 46$) | Girls ($n = 55$) |
| School | 23.9 | 36.4 |
| His home | 8.7 | 9.1 |
| Her home | 6.5 | 12.7 |
| Recreation center | 4.3 | 1.8 |
| Church | 0 | 1.8 |
| Telephone* | 2.2 | 36.4 |
| Other | 2.2 | 3.6 |

*Technically, the telephone is not a place, but it was included in the table because of the frequency with which it was reported as an interacting medium.

TABLE 5    Correlates of Heterosexual Physical Activities

|                         | BOYS (n = 43) | | GIRLS (n = 50) | |
|-------------------------|------|-------|------|-------|
|                         | r    | p     | r    | p     |
| Age in months           | .091 | .274  | .166 | .122  |
| Having a girl/boy friend | .550 | .001* | .311 | .020* |
| Genital stage           | .404 | .005* | —    | —     |
| Breast stage            | —    | —     | .004 | .488  |
| Pubic hair stage        | .143 | .195  | .056 | .354  |
| Socioeconomic status    | .173 | .146  | .150 | .158  |

*Significant beyond .05 level.

(Tanner, 1978). Staging progressions of genital development among boys and breast development in girls are within the age spans provided by Tanner. However, placed in Tanner's frame of reference, it appears that our sample is weighted toward the younger portion of these age spans. According to Tanner, the average age for acceleration of penis growth is about age 12½, but sometimes as early as 10½, and sometimes as late as 14½ years. In our sample, 16.6%, 33.1%, and 60%, respectively, of the 9-, 10-, and 11-year-old boys were at or beyond the beginning of penile growth. For girls, Tanner's mean age for breast development is 11 years with a range of 9.0 to 13.0 years. Eighteen percent of the 9-year-old girls were at or beyond Stage II of breast development; so were 73.8% of these who were 10, and 80% of those who were 11 years old. Of course, one limitation in comparing this sample with these normative standards is evidenced by the absence of blacks in Tanner's sample.

The National Health Survey data analyzed by Harlan and his associates (1979, 1980) contain staging information on black children, but the exclusion of children younger than 12 from the sample precludes meaningful comparisons. These researchers noted that 80% of the 12-year-old girls (actually, 87% of the black 12-year-old girls) had progressed beyond Stage II of breast development. In our younger sample of girls, 76% and 80% of the 10- and 11-year-old girls, respectively, were at or

beyond Stage II of breast development. The absence of large representative preadolescent samples with which to compare the onset of maturation in smaller samples indicates the need for further research to establish norms for pubertal development in black children.

Boys showed greater agreement in the progression of their staging characteristics than girls. The greater concordance between genital and pubic hair development in boys than between breast and pubic hair development in girls may be explained by the hormonal sources which stimulate the growth of these structures. Androgens influence both genital development and pubic hair development in boys, while breast development is controlled by estrogen, and pubic hair by androgen in girls (Root, 1973).

Regarding heterosexual interaction, more than half of the boys and girls (boys more frequently than girls) stated that they had special opposite-sex friends. In this period of emerging sociosexual interaction, it is difficult to ascertain the quality of sexual content of the boyfriend/girlfriend relationship reported by these participants. A larger portion of the heterosexual relationships may be platonic.

The significant relationships between the occurrence of HPA and having a girlfriend and a boyfriend are noteworthy. One researcher (Furstenberg, 1976) reported that young adolescents who had opposite-sex friends and dated, compared with others, were more likely to be involved in advanced levels of sexual behavior as late adolescents.

The representation of the girls in the lower levels of HPA may imply somewhat of a developmental progression in these activities, as compared with the boys during the pubescent period. Even in the case of the boys, however, advanced behaviors were by no means generalized. Actually, taking all reported activities into consideration, girls were more involved in HPA than boys, most of the activity being at the game-playing level. Preadolescent girls characteristically have been identified as demonstrating prominent behavior features including, among others, activeness, zest, and initiative (Deutsch, 1945; Kohen-Raz, 1971). It is possible that preadolescent girls, as well as boys, view game-playing as a benign yet satisfying means of having fun while at the same time associating with persons of the other sex.

More advanced levels of heterosexual interaction among black preadolescent boys, as compared with girls, have been reported by Broderick (1965). From samples of teenagers, Udry (1981) and Sorensen (1973) suggest that black teenagers report less mid-range behaviors preceding intercourse than do white teenagers. These studies also portray females as being less involved in sexual activity than males. In this preadolescent group, patterns of heterosexual activity are just beginning to emerge. However, among the boys in the sample, none reported light petting, but 4.3% reported heavy petting, and 2.2% reported coitus.

With respect to relationships between biological maturation and heterosexual activities, for girls the data revealed no significant association between the prevalence of HPA and maturation in terms of the development of the breasts and the development of pubic hair. It appears that for females at this level of development, involvement in sociosexual behaviors does not vary with staging. However, most of the girls are at Stages II and III of breast development, and none have yet achieved Stage V. The breasts, as easily observable secondary sex characteristics, may show greater relationships to sexual behavior as maturation progresses.

For boys, there was a significant relationship between genital development and the HPA score. Further research is needed to ascertain whether degree of genital development could emerge as a possible predictor of heterosexual behavior during preadolescence. It appears that this finding regarding the significant correlation of HPA with genital development, but not with breast development, is akin to findings regarding a stronger correlation between male hormone levels and sexual behavior in developing boys than between female hormone levels and sexual behaviors in developing girls (Katchadourian, 1980).

## Summary

The findings in this aspect of the study have indicated that biologically, this 9- to 11-year-old sample of black boys and girls is essentially in the pre- and early pubertal stages of development. Although the maturation of the participants is dispersed through Stages I to IV, confirming the considerable variability in sexual maturation as it related to chronological age, the sample is predominantly early maturational. The sociosexual behaviors are distributed most heavily in the less intimate categories, but are more advanced for the boys than the girls. At this stage, no significant association exists between sociosexual behavior and maturational staging for the girls, but in the boys genital staging is positively and significantly related to sexual behavior.

As stated earlier, these are findings from the baseline data of a longitudinal study. Further assessments will chart advancement in sexual maturation and sociosexual behavior among these developing young people. Research on these variables using larger samples of preadolescents would be of great value.

# References

Angsusingha, K., F. M. Kenny, H. R. Nankin, and F. H. Taylor
1974    "Unconjugated Estrone, Estradiol, and FSH and LH in Prepubertal and Pubertal Males and Females." *Journal of Clinical Endocrinology and Metabolism* 39:63–68.

Blos, P.
1962    *On Adolescence*. New York: Free Press.

Broderick, C. B.
1965    "Social Heterosexual Development among Urban Negroes and Whites." *Journal of Marriage and the Family* 27:200–203.

Deutsch, H.
1945    *The Psychology of Women*. New York: Grune & Stratton.

Freud, S.

1938    *The Basic Writings of Sigmund Freud* (A. A. Brill, ed.). New York: Random House.

Furstenberg, F. F.

1976    *Unplanned Parenthood: The Social Consequences of Teenage Childbearing.* New York: Free Press.

Gupta, D., A. Attanasio, and S. Raaf

1975    "Plasma Estrogen and Androgen Concentrations in Children during Adolescence." *Journal of Clinical Endocrinology and Metabolism* 40: 636–643.

Harlan, W. R., G. P. Grillo, J. Cornoni-Huntley, and P. E. Leaverton

1979    "Secondary Sex Characteristics of Boys 12 to 17 Years of Age: The U.S. Health Examination Survey." *The Journal of Pediatrics* 95:293–297.

Harlan, W. R., E. A. Harlan, and G. Grillo

1980    "Secondary Sex Characteristics of Girls 12 to 17 Years of Age: The U.S. Health Examination Survey." *The Journal of Pediatrics* 96:1074–1078.

Katchadourian, H.

1980    "Adolescent Sexuality." *Pediatric Clinics of America* 27:17–28.

Kohen-Raz, R.

1971    *The Child from 9 to 13: The Psychology of Preadolescence and Early Puberty.* New York: Atherton.

Korth-Schultz, S., L. S. Levine, and M. I. New

1976    "Serum Androgens in Normal Prepubertal and Pubertal Children with Precocious Andrenarche." *Journal of Clinical Endocrinology and Metabolism* 42:117–124.

MacMahon, B.

1973    *Age at Menarche.* United States Department of Health, Education and Welfare Publication No. (HRA) 74–1615, NHS Series 11, No. 133. Rockville, Md.: National Center for Health Statistics.

Peller, L.

1958    "Reading and Day Dreaming in Latency." *Journal of the American Psychoanalytic Association* 6:57–60.

Petersen, A. C., and B. Taylor

1980    "The Biological Approach to Adolescence: Biological and Psychological Adaptation." In *Handbook of Adolescent Psychology,* J. Adelson, ed. New York: Wiley.

Root, A. W.

1973    "Endocrinology of Puberty." *Medical Progress* (83 [1] July):1–19.

Sorensen, R.

1973    *Adolescent Sexuality in Contemporary Society: Personal Values and Sexual Behavior, 13–19.* New York: World.

Tanner, J. M.

1955    *Growth at Adolescence.* Springfield, Ill.: Thomas.

1978    *Fetus to Man.* Cambridge, Mass.: Harvard University Press.

Udry, J. R.

1981    "A Biosocial Model of Adolescent Sexual Behavior." Paper presented at the National Institute of Child Health and Human Development. Bethesda, Maryland, June.

Zelnick, M., J. F. Kantner, and K. Ford

1980    *Determinants of Fertility Behavior among U.S. Females Aged 15–19, 1971 and 1976.* Final Report, Contract No. 1–HD–28248.

# SOCIO-HISTORICAL STUDY OF BLACK FEMALE SEXUALITY:
## Transition to First Coitus

### Velma McBride Murry

*Using data from the 1982 National Survey of Family Growth Cycle (III), the author takes a life course perspective approach to examine those aspects of Black adolescent females' personal, family, and community life circumstances that facilitate or inhibit the initiation of early coital experiences. Data analyses were limited to Black females who entered and completed adolescence during the 1950s, 1960s, or 1970s. Results from the multivariate discriminant analyses indicate that certain personal, family, and community life circumstances consistently distinguished early coital initiators from late coital initiators. More specifically, these data strongly suggest that over the years Black females have tended to delay the onset of first coitus when life circumstances have provided opportunities for them to achieve adult status through more socially acceptable roles.*

## Introduction

The sexual behavior pattern of Black females has received considerable attention over the last two decades. Researchers have primarily focused on describing racial differences in the timing of first coitus and subsequent sexual activities. For example, a national study conducted in 1979 revealed that Black unmarried 15 to 17 year old females are one and a half times more likely to be sexually active as their White counterparts in the same age grouping (Zelnik and Kanter, 1980). Another study indicated that unmarried Black females aged 15 to 19 years had 71.4 births per 1,000 women in this age category compared to 20.1 births per 1,000 White women of the same age (U.S. Bureau of the Census, 1986). Available data also suggest that Black females become sexually active about two years earlier than their White counterparts (Zelnik, Kantner, and Ford, 1981).

A plethora of studies have been devoted to identifying the source of racial differences in the timing of first sexual intercourse and the proportion of adolescents who are sexually active. Some trace the differences to subcultural factors (that is, peer group influence, mother's and siblings' sexual and fertility experience as adolescents, family size, and community's acceptance of early sexual activity) (Hogan and Kitagawa, 1985; Newcomer and Udry, 1987). Others suggest that racial differences are related to socioeconomic factors (Abrahamse, Morrison, and Waite, 1985; Moore, Peterson, and Furstenberg, 1985; Zelnik, Kantner, and Ford, 1981). Several researchers, however, argue that these generalizations should be cautiously interpreted because the majority of comparative studies have not included a representative sample of Blacks (Chilman, 1980; McKenry et al., 1989; Weddle, McKenry, and Leigh, 1988). Further, many of these findings are based on stereotypes and myths about Black

Previously unpublished paper, 1990. Printed by permission of the author.

sexuality and sexual practices (Staples, 1971). One frequently cited stereotype, "that blacks are more sexually permissive than are whites" (Reiss, 1967:51), has resulted in limited efforts in examining changes in the sexual behavior patterns of Black females. The present study was an attempt to overcome some of these methodological weaknesses by testing previously identified factors associated with the timing of first coitus on a nationally representative sample of Black adolescent females.

## Theoretical Perspective

Because much of previous research on adolescent sexuality has been either descriptive or evaluative, researchers have recognized the need for theory to guide research questions on Black adolescence (Bell-Scott, 1987; McKenry et al., 1989). The life course perspective was selected for this study because it allows one to study adolescent sexuality through a social environmental framework. This perspective focuses on specific aspects of personal, family, and community circumstances that facilitate or inhibit the onset of first intercourse, contraceptive use, and early motherhood among adolescent females and has been utilized in previous sociological investigations. For example, Hogan and Kitagawa (1985), using the life course approach identified aspects of Black adolescent females life circumstances—personal, family, and community—that appear to encourage early sexual coitus and early pregnancy as pathways to adult status. The work of Hogan and Kitagawa (1985) provides a useful framework for a socio-historical examination of how life circumstances of Black adolescent females over three decades facilitate or inhibit the female's decision to initiate first sexual coitus.

## Review of Variables

In this study pubertal development, religiosity, and educational attainment were categorized as *personal* life circumstances; family structure, socioeconomic status, and parental socialization in sexuality

were classified as *family* life circumstances. *Community* life circumstance was labeled geographic residence. The significance of each of these factors in explaining the timing of first coitus among Black adolescent females will be discussed below. It should be noted that, as in most secondary analysis, not all factors necessary to understanding the context of sexual behavior were available in the data set used. However, several significant factors frequently identified as correlates of the transition to first coitus were identified and have been included to begin to ascertain salient variables that distinguish those adolescents who are at risk of initiating sexual coitus at an early age from those who delay the onset of first coitus until late adolescence and beyond.

## *Personal Life Circumstances*

**Pubertal Development**   Data from several studies indicate that improvements in health care and living conditions have resulted in females reaching puberty earlier today than in former generations, with physical maturation occurring earlier in Blacks than Whites (Frisch, 1983; Harlan, Harlan, and Grillo, 1980). A substantial body of research indicates a strong relationship between pubertal development, hormonal levels, and sexual activity (Udry and Billy, 1987). These data are based primarily on White youth; consequently, the significance of physical maturity on the sexual activity of Black adolescents has received limited attention. However, those studies that are available indicate that pubertal development, the onset of menarche, was not independently related to the onset of sexual intercourse among Black adolescent females (Leigh, Weddle, and Loewen, 1988; Westney, Jenkins, and Benjamin, 1983). Conversely, one study conducted in 1981 revealed a direct, but weak, relationship between early physical maturation and the onset of early sexual intercourse among Black adolescent females (Zelnik and Kantner, 1980). However, the relationship was stronger for White than Black females. As pointed out by Hayes (1987) and others (Udry, Talbert, and Morris, 1985), the weak relationship between physical maturation and the initiation of early sexual coitus among Black adolescent females may be related to the intervening effect of their social environment. Moreover, results from Hogan and Kitagawa's (1985) study of fertility of Black adolescents revealed that females from high-risk social environments (low income, resident in ghetto neighborhoods, living in nonintact family, and lax parental control of dating) are at greater risk of initiating sexual activity at an early age.

**Religiosity** For centuries, religious organizations have been considered symbolic of morality and values. These institutions have historically restricted and even repressed, in many stances, sexuality for females and males. Empirically, the impact of religion on the sexual behavior of adolescents has not been well substantiated. Some researchers report minimal correlations between frequency of church attendance and the acceptance of premarital sexual intercourse among Blacks (Christenson and Johnson, 1978). On the other hand, several researchers (Brown, 1985; Fox and Inazu, 1980; Thornton and Camburn, 1986; Zelnik, Kantner, and Ford 1981) report that sexual permissiveness occurs less frequently among Black females who are frequent church attenders. As pointed out by Hayes (1987), religious adolescents may have stronger social supports to enforce more conservative behavioral norms. Moreover, results reported by Lewis and Looney (1983) indicated that Black families who attend church frequently expressed the significance of religion in assisting them in rearing their children, providing moral guidelines, and augmenting the cohesiveness of the family unit. There is a need to further illuminate the interrelation between religiosity and other personal and family characteristics thought to predict the onset of first coitus among adolescent females.

**Educational Attainment** Results from numerous studies have shown that intellectual ability, academic achievement, and career aspirations are inversely related to initiating sexual intercourse at an early age by adolescent females (Devaney & Hubley, 1981; Hogan and Kitagawa, 1985; Murry, 1988). Although there is strong evidence of these associations,

it is also important to consider the interactional effect of social, economic, familial, and community circumstances on the relationship between timing of first coitus and academic achievement and aspiration (Hayes, 1987).

# Family Life Circumstances

**Family Structure** The role of family structure (that is, living in one-parent versus two-parent families) in predicting the sexual behavior pattern of adolescents has received considerable attention in recent years. Several researchers suggest that adolescents, particularly females, living in female-headed families become sexually active earlier than those living in two-parent families (Hogan and Kitagawa, 1985; Murry, 1988; Robbins, Kaplan, and Martin, 1985). It is thought that the socialization of adolescent females in one-parent, female-headed families may enhance the acceptability of sex outside of marriage because their parents are not involved in or tied to traditional family or marital forms (Fox, 1980). This may be communicated directly or indirectly to daughters in these families (Inazu and Fox, 1980; Newcomer and Udry, 1987; Zelnik, Kantner, and Ford, 1981). It should be noted that the majority of studies investigating the role of family structure on the sexual activity of adolescents are primarily based on cross-sectional data. In an era of high divorce and increased cohabitation rates, few studies have examined the significance of change in family structure over time on trends of premarital sexual intercourse among Black adolescent females.

**Socioeconomic Status** The social and economic status of families appear to be fundamentally related to changing attitudes about sexual behavior. For example, early works by Reiss (1965) suggest that one's social status influences the degree to which the individual has liberal or conservative views about sex outside of marriage. Other explanations concede that being economically disadvantaged may cause adolescents to have different outlooks on marriage and family formation. More specifically, some investigators report that adolescent females of low social status may engage in premarital sexual intercourse because of the lack of educational and occupational alternatives to achieve adulthood through more socially acceptable roles, such as obtaining gainful employment (Bowerman, Irish, and Pope, 1966; Hogan and Kitagawa, 1985).

Existing research findings concerning the association of socioeconomic status and early sexual intercourse continue to show that the incidence of premarital sexual intercourse remains higher among Black adolescents, even with controlling for socioeconomic status (as measured by mother's educational attainment). As Hayes (1987) reports, data on the relationship of race, socioeconomic status, and onset of sexual intercourse among adolescents should be cautiously interpreted given the economic gap between Blacks and Whites, the various ways in which socioeconomic status is measured, and the failure of researchers to recognize the length of time individuals have been in a particular social strata.

Recognizing the significance of socioeconomic status on adolescent sexual behavior, some researchers have begun to consider this issue using social stratification analysis on samples of Blacks (Brown, 1985; Hogan and Kitagawa, 1985; Murry, 1988). However, disagreement exists over the significance of socioeconomic status in predicting the sexual behavior of Black adolescents. For example, some researchers report no association between socioeconomic status and sexual permissiveness among Black adolescent females (Brown, 1985). On the other hand, results from local (Hogan and Kitagawa, 1985) and national studies (Murry, 1988) show that Black adolescent females from families of high and middle socioeconomic status become sexually active later than those from families of low socioeconomic status. Further, findings from Zelnik and Kantner's (1981) examination of data from two national surveys, conducted in 1971 and 1976, show a decline in prevalence of premarital sexual intercourse with increasing socioeconomic status for Blacks. How socioeconomic status influences the sexual behavior of Black youth appears to be an important yet not fully explored issue.

**Parental Socialization in Sexuality**   Some family scholars report that greater parent-child communication about sexuality does not reduce the probability of early sexual activity (Kahn, Smith, and Roberts, 1984). Others have illustrated that receiving socialization in sexuality from parents is negatively related to early transition to sexual activity. For example, Abrahamse, Morrison, and Waite (1985) and others (Darling and Hicks, 1982; Fox and Inazu, 1980) report that mother-daughter communicating about sexuality appears to lower the risk of their adolescent daughters becoming pregnant. Further, Hogan and Kitagawa (1985) and Murry (1988) report that parental socialization in sexuality appears to determine when Black adolescent females will experience first coitus. It is not clear, however, why or how parental socialization in sexuality affects their offspring's sexual behavior (Fox, 1980).

## Community Life Circumstances

**Geographic Residence**   A few studies have focused on the relationship between geographic residence and the incidence of early sexual activity among adolescents. Most of the studies have compared the sexual activity of adolescents residing in urban (inner city) to those living in suburb or rural areas. There is strong evidence that adolescents living in metropolitan areas are at risk of becoming sexually active at an early age (Hogan and Kitagawa, 1985; Murry, 1988; Zelnik, Kantner, and Ford, 1981). Limited attention has been given to determining if the onset of sexual activity occurs early among adolescents living in certain regions of the United States. Coles and Stokes (1985), however, found no difference in the initiation of sexual activity among adolescents living in southern, western, northeastern, or northcentral regions of the United States. However, given that childbearing among adolescents living in southern and western regions of the United States is higher than among their counterparts living in other regions of the United States (U.S. Bureau of the Census, 1987), it seems reasonable to assume that the onset of first coitus among adolescents may also differ by regions. Further, results from a recent study indicate that Black adolescent females of low socioeconomic status living in metropolitan areas of southern states are at greater risk of initiating coitus at an early age than their counterparts living in other regions of the United States (Murry, 1988).

# Statement of the Problem

Although research continues to show strong Black-White differences in adolescent sexual activity, these findings should be cautiously interpreted. Results from an extensive review of the literature on adolescent sexuality revealed that the data tend not to include representative samples of Blacks (Chilman, 1980). More specifically, when Blacks are included they tend to be of low-income or undifferentiated status, obtained from clinical or convenient populations, or researchers fail to include the demographic characteristics of Blacks (McKenry et al., 1989; Weddle, McKenry, and Leigh, 1988).

Another concern is that much of the research on trends in premarital sex over the past decades is based primarily on White high school (Reiss, 1967; Roebuck and McGee, 1977) and college students (Belcastro, 1985; Jessor and Jessor, 1975). Because it is often assumed that Blacks are already highly sexually permissive, social scientists have largely ignored the impact of social and economic changes on the sexual attitudes and behavior of Blacks. However, in order to understand behavior one has to examine it in socio-historical context. This present study contributes to the field of research on Black adolescents by utilizing data obtained from a nationally representative sample to address the following questions: (1) Has the proportion of Black adolescent females initiating sexual intercourse at an early age changed over time? (2) If so, what personal, family, and community life circumstances accurately predict whether an adolescent will initiate first coitus during early or late adolescence? and, (3) Which of these factors have been consistent predictors of the timing of first coitus among Black adolescent females over three decades?

# Methods

## *Data*

Data for this present study were obtained from the 1982 National Survey of Family Growth Cycle (III) (NSFG). NSFG data were collected by the National Center for Health Statistics and include information on a nationally representative cross-section sample of women of childbearing age (15–44 years) living in the continental United States. Blacks and adolescent females were oversampled in order to provide more reliable data for these subgroups. The survey focused on the contraception and pregnancy history, reproductive knowledge and sex education, sexual activity patterns, and a wide range of social, economic, and family characteristics of American women.

## *Sample*

The subsample for this secondary analysis consists of 3,468 Black women who experienced first coitus before marriage and were born between the years of 1938 and 1962. The sample was then stratified into three cohorts representing decades in which the respondents were adolescents (that is, 442 respondents born 1938 through 1943 were adolescents during the 1950s; 975 respondents born 1944 through 1952 were adolescents during the 1960s; and, 1,323 respondents were born 1953 through 1962 and were adolescents during the 1970s). All percentages reported in this article were appropriately weighted to make them representative of a national cross-section of youth aged 12 to 20 during the three decades under investigation. A more complete description of the NSFG sample can be found in the work of Bachrach et al. (1985).

## *Codification of Measures*

The dependent variable for this analysis, age at first coitus, was measured by a direct question asking the respondents when, after their first menstrual period, did they have sexual intercourse for the first time.

Ten independent variables were included in this analysis.

Pubertal development was measured by respondents indicating in both month and year when they had their first menstrual period.

Religiosity was measured by respondents indicating how often they attend religious services. The responses ranged from never to five times a week or more.

Educational attainment was measured by the respondents indicating the number of completed years of schooling.

Family structure reflects the respondents' living arrangements at age 14 years.

Socioeconomic status was measured using mothers' educational attainment. This variable was selected for two reasons. First, mothers' educational attainment is comparable across family structure. In addition, the amount of missing data in the variable family income would not permit one to successfully use it to calculate family socioeconomic status.

Parental socialization in sexuality included three variables that assessed whether the respondents had received human sexuality information from parents about menstruation, sexually transmitted diseases (STDs), and conception.

Geographic residence represents the respondents' place of residence by geographic *region* (southern or nonsouthern) and *area* (metropolitan and nonmetropolitan). Region was categorized as southern and nonsouthern (that is, northeast, northcentral, and western regions of the United States), because the majority of respondents included in this study lived in the South. (See Table 1.)

## Analyses

Because the purpose of the study was to identify factors associated with the timing of first coitus and to determine the extent to which those factors accurately classified subjects into early or late coital initiators, multivariate discriminant analysis was se-

lected. The stepwise procedure was included in the equation, and Wilk's Lambda was selected as the test statistic.

## Results

Data reflecting demographic characteristic of the respondents are presented in Table 1. Results from that table provide evidence of increased educational attainment among Black females over time. For example, 24 percent of the females had completed one to six years of college during the 1950s; 35.5 percent in the 1960s; and 38.6 percent during the 1970s. Further, there was an increase of 16.7 percent more of the respondents' mothers completing twelve years or more of education during the 1960s than in the 1950s. This trend toward increased educational attainment among the respondents' mothers continued during the 1970s. Most of the respondents lived in two-parent families at age 14 years and resided in southern metropolitan areas of the United States. Findings in Table 1 also revealed that most of the respondents were frequent church attenders.

The percentage distributions of the timing of first coitus age pattern among Black adolescent females from three cohorts are presented in Table 2. These data indicate that a higher proportion of Black adolescent females of the 1950s initiated first coitus during preadolescence compared to those who were in the same age category during the 1960s and 1970s (4.3 percent, 3.1 percent, and 3.7 percent, respectively). Results also reveal that for each age category, excluding preadolescence (aged 12 years or less), a greater proportion of Black females became sexually active during the 1970s compared to their counterparts in either of the other two cohorts. It is also interesting to note that the proportion of 1960s adolescent females initiating sexual intercourse during early adolescence was less than those initiating sexual intercourse at age 15 years or younger during the 1950s or the 1970s. A closer examination of the incidence of early coital initiation, preadolescence through age 15, revealed that 28.7 percent of the 1960s cohort had initiated sexual intercourse, compared to 30.3 percent of those who were adoles-

TABLE 1    Descriptive Statistics for Black Adolescent Females by Cohort

| | COHORT | | |
| --- | --- | --- | --- |
| | 1950s (N = 773) (%) | 1960s (N = 1,536) (%) | 1970s (N = 2,259) (%) |
| **Individual** | | | |
| Religiosity | | | |
| Never | 9.8 | 4.7 | 5.9 |
| Once a year | 4.6 | 9.5 | 13.1 |
| Several times a year | 14.3 | 16.2 | 15.7 |
| Once or twice a month | 29.8 | 30.0 | 33.2 |
| Once or more per week | 41.4 | 39.6 | 32.2 |
| Educational attainment | | | |
| Less than twelve years | 43.0 | 25.0 | 20.0 |
| Twelve years | 35.5 | 38.4 | 41.7 |
| College (one to six years) | 24.0 | 35.5 | 38.6 |
| **Family** | | | |
| Family structure | | | |
| Two-parent | 65.0 | 57.2 | 57.4 |
| Socioeconomic status | | | |
| Mother's education | | | |
| Twelve years or more | 31.4 | 48.1 | 52.3 |
| Mother's occupation | | | |
| White-collar | 6.9 | 15.6 | 33.4 |
| Blue-collar | 21.4 | 20.2 | 19.0 |
| Service | 71.7 | 64.2 | 47.6 |
| Parental sexuality socialization | | | |
| Menstruation | 49.7 | 57.1 | 65.8 |
| STDs | 31.2 | 23.0 | 32.9 |
| Birth control | 22.5 | 20.3 | 47.0 |
| Conception | 39.9 | 39.5 | 50.8 |
| **Community** | | | |
| Geographic residence | | | |
| Southern region | 43.2 | 48.6 | 53.0 |
| Metropolitan | 86.7 | 82.3 | 81.1 |

cents during the 1950s, and 35.4 percent who were adolescents during the 1970s. From ages 16 to 17 years, 29.6 percent of the 1960s adolescent females had initiated first coitus, compared to 33.6 percent and 38.8 percent for their 1950s and 1970s counterparts, respectively. Finally, 25.5 percent of the 1960s had experienced their first coitus between the ages of 18 to 20 (late coital initiators), compared to 27.4 percent and 23.2 percent of those who were adolescents during the 1950s and the 1970s, respectively.

Results also provide evidence of declining age of pubertal development among Black adolescent females for the three periods under consideration. (See Table 2.) For instance, 39.3 percent of the 1950s

**TABLE 2    Age Pattern of First Coitus and Pubertal Development of Black Adolescent Females by Cohort**

| | | | COHORT | | |
|---|---|---|---|---|---|
| | 1950s (N = 773) (%) | (%) | 1960s (N = 1,536) (%) | (%) | 1970s (N = 2,259) (%) |
| **First coitus (age in years)** | | | | | |
| 12 or less | 4.3 | | 3.1 | | 3.7 |
| 13–14 | 11.6 | (14.8) | 12.9 | (16.0) | 14.9 | (18.7) |
| 15 | 15.4 | (30.3) | 12.7 | (28.7) | 16.7 | (35.4) |
| 16–17 | 33.6 | (63.9) | 29.6 | (58.3) | 38.8 | (74.3) |
| 18–20 | 27.4 | (91.3) | 25.5 | (93.7) | 23.2 | (97.4) |
| $\overline{X}$ | 16.8 | | 16.95 | | 16.28 |
| **Pubertal development (age in years)** | | | | | |
| Less than 12 | 17.5 | | 22.2 | | 30.6 |
| 12 | 21.8 | (39.3) | 26.1 | (48.4) | 23.9 | (54.5) |
| 13–14 | 40.1 | (79.4) | 37.3 | (85.7) | 33.6 | (88.0) |
| 15 | 9.5 | (88.9) | 8.4 | (94.1) | 7.0 | (95.0) |
| 16 or more | 11.1 | (100) | 13.9 | (100) | 5.0 | (100) |
| $\overline{X}$ | 13.0 | | 12.66 | | 12.4 |

Note: Calculated cumulative percentages are presented in parentheses.

adolescent females had their first menstrual cycle by age 12 years, compared to 48.4 percent of the 1960s, and 54.5 percent of those in the same age category during the 1970s. Moreover, over 30 percent of the 1970s adolescents indicated that they had reached puberty before age 12 years.

In order to evaluate group differences in factors that distinguish early coital initiators from late coital initiators, discriminant function analysis was conducted with ten variables. After all data are transformed into standard scores, discriminant function analysis computes a discriminant equation that produces the greatest statistically derivable distance between the two groups for each cohort (for example, early coital initiators versus late coital initiators). The larger the discriminant coefficient of a variable, the more powerful it is as a group discriminant. The variables submitted to discriminant function analyses and their summary statistic are presented in Table 3. Canonical correlation, another statistic included in the table, is a measure of the association between the single discriminant function and the set of variables that defines the two group memberships for each cohort (Huberty, 1975). Analysis demonstrates that across the three cohorts early coital initiators can be significantly distinguished from late coital initiators ($p < .001$). (See Table 3.) Next, attention was given to identifying variables that make the most significant contribution to the discriminant equation for each cohort. As indicated in Table 3, variables providing the greatest contribution to the discriminant equation for the 1950s cohort included pubertal development, educational attainment, and parental socialization in sexuality about STDs and birth control. The remaining variables, religiosity, geographic residence, and receiving parental socialization in sexuality about conception were significant, but contributions were of less magnitude. The limited contributions of these variables may be reflective of little variation between the groups in church attendance, geographic residence, and parental socialization in sexuality.

TABLE 3 Summary of Standardized Discriminant Function Coefficients for Age at First Coitus by Cohort

| | COHORT | | |
| --- | --- | --- | --- |
| | 1950s | 1960s | 1970s |
| **Individual** | | | |
| Pubertal development | .546 | .383 | .542 |
| Religiosity | −.115 | .312 | .212 |
| Educational attainment | .790 | .791 | .814 |
| **Family** | | | |
| Family structure[a] | — | — | .207 |
| Socioeconomic status | — | .277 | −.120 |
| Parental sexuality socialization[b] | | | |
| Menstruation | — | −.112 | — |
| STDs | −.411 | −.118 | −.282 |
| Birth control | .269 | .308 | — |
| Conception | .151 | — | — |
| **Community** | | | |
| Geographic residence | | | |
| Southern region | −.131 | — | — |
| Metropolitan | −.150 | −.124 | — |
| Canonical correlation | .499 | .483 | .486 |
| Wilk's Lambda | .751 | .767 | .766 |
| df | 8 | 8 | 6 |
| p | <.001 | <.001 | <.001 |
| Percentage of cases correctly classified | | | |
| | 73.09% | 68.55% | 71.57% |

[a]Dummy coded 1 = two-parent household, 0 = one parent-household.
[b]Dummy coded 1 = yes, 0 = no.

The most powerful distinguishing variables for the 1960s cohort included pubertal development, religiosity, educational attainment, socioeconomic status, parental socialization in sexuality about birth control, and geographic residence. Receiving parental socialization in sexuality about menstruation and STDs, although significant, provided less discriminating power. Variables included in the discriminant equation for the 1970s cohort were pubertal development, educational attainment, religiosity, family structure, and receiving parental sexuality socialization about STDs. Socioeconomic status was significant but had the least contributing power to the discriminant equation.

These data analyses also identify factors that accurately distinguish subjects at risk of early coital experiences from those who initiated coitus at age 18 years or older. For example, during the 1950s pubertal development, educational attainment, and receiving parental socialization in sexuality about birth control were regarded as good discriminators of late coital initiators. Receiving parental socialization in sexuality about STDs, religiosity, and geographic residence were better discriminators of early coital initiators than of late coital initiators.

For the 1960s cohort, pubertal development, religiosity, socioeconomic status, and parental socialization in sexuality about birth control were better distinguishing factors of late coital initiators than of early coital initiators; receiving parental socialization in sexuality about menstruation and geographic residence (that is, living in metropolitan areas) were good discriminators of early coital initiators. Factors associated with late coital initiators for the 1970s cohort included pubertal development, religiosity, educational attainment, and family structure; socioeconomic status and receiving parental socialization in sexuality about STDs were associated with early coital initiators.

Finally, examination of the stability of the selected variables across the three decades in distinguishing early coital initiators from late coital initiators illustrated that of the ten variables selected, four were consistent discriminating factors. Across cohorts, pubertal development, religiosity, educational attainment, and receiving parental socialization in sexuality about STDs distinguish early coital initiators from late coital initiators. The number of cases correctly classified using the selected variables are presented in Table 3. Applying the unstandardized versions of the discriminant function coefficients to the raw scores used to derive the function, 73 percent of the cases were correctly classified for the 1950s cohort (77 percent of the early coital initiators and 69 percent of the late coital initiators), 69 percent of the cases were correctly classified for the 1960s cohort (65 percent of the early coital initiators and 72 percent of the late coital initiators), and 72 percent of the cases were correctly classified for the 1970s cohort (80 percent of the early coital initiators and 58 percent of the late coital initiators).

The final analysis was devoted to determining the unique contribution of each variable to the discriminant function. For this procedure, the correlations between the values of the function and the values of the variables were examined. (See Table 4.)

Across each cohort, educational attainment had the highest correlation with the discriminant function, with the greatest association evidenced for the 1960s cohort. The contributions of the remaining variables were unique to each cohort with some similarity existing between the 1950s and 1970s cohorts. For example, pubertal development had the

second highest correlation with the discriminant function for the 1950s and 1970s cohort, with pubertal development having greater association with the discriminant function for the 1950s cohort ($r = .52$ and $r = .42$, respectively); the second highest correlate for the 1960s adolescents was socioeconomic status. The third variable having the highest level of association with the discriminant function for each cohort included receiving parental socialization in sexuality about STDs for adolescents of the 1950s, pubertal development for adolescents of the 1960s, and family structure for their counterparts of the 1970s.

# Discussion and Conclusions

Data gathered in a nationwide survey made in 1982 provide an opportunity to examine the impact of social and economic change on the initiation of first coitus among Black females who were adolescents during the 1950s, 1960s, and 1970s. Admittedly, there are salient personal, family, and community life experiences of adolescents that have not been considered in this study, but major predictions identified in past research were examined. The study does indicate that there is a relationship between some aspects of life circumstances and the timing of first coitus among Black adolescent females. One of the major findings of this investigation was the lower incidence of early coitus initiation among adolescents of the 1960s, compared to their counterparts of the 1950s and 1970s. This result is opposite of the pattern commonly associated with the "sexual revolution" (that is, increased incidence of premarital sex among females). The decline in incidence of early sexual intercourse among Black adolescent females of the 1960s may be related to the religious and political climate of this era. For example, Eshleman (1988) points out that conservative religion and political orientation may have led to more restrictive sexual behavior. Also, improved racial and ethnic pride, as well as increased federal commitment to economic and social reform in the 1960s may have motivated Black youth toward adult goals. Moreover, increased educational and occupational opportunities experienced by many Blacks may have provided alternatives for youth to achieve adult status through

TABLE 4    Within Group Correlations between Discriminating Variables and Canonical Discriminating Functions for Each Cohort

| | COHORT | | |
|---|---|---|---|
| | 1950s | 1960s | 1970s |
| **Individual** | | | |
| Pubertal development | .520 | .306 | .419 |
| Religiosity | −.136 | .234 | .198 |
| Educational attainment | .736 | .812 | .732 |
| **Family** | | | |
| Family structure[a] | .043 | .114 | .343 |
| Socioeconomic status | .175 | .429 | .064 |
| Parental sexuality socialization[b] | | | |
| Menstruation | −.243 | −.203 | −.157 |
| STDs | −.282 | −.020 | −.256 |
| Birth control | −.007 | .073 | −.061 |
| Conception | −.004 | −.147 | −.167 |
| **Community** | | | |
| Geographic residence | | | |
| Southern region | −.037 | −.022 | .016 |
| Metropolitan | −.007 | −.007 | .010 |

[a]Dummy coded 1 = two-parent household, 0 = one-parent household.
[b]Dummy coded 1 = yes, 0 = no.

more socially acceptable roles, instead of early sexual activity (Bowerman, Irish, and Pope, 1966).

Unfortunately, the trend toward delayed onset of first coitus evidenced in the 1960s did not continue during the 1970s. Increased incidence of early coitus among the 1970s Black adolescent females may be attributed to the social and economic hardships experienced by Americans during this decade. Economic stagnation and decline and dwindling social programs from the federal government affected the life-styles of Americans in general, and Black Americans specifically (U.S. Bureau of the Census, 1983a). Moreover, during a period of increased poverty and bleak prospects, Black adolescent females were more likely to initiate sexual intercourse at an early age. This finding substantiates previous studies that show a relationship between early sexual activity among adolescent females of low socioeconomic status (Hogan and Kitagawa, 1985; Murry, 1988; Zelnik, Kantner, and Ford, 1981).

A second possible explanation for increased incidence of early sexual intercourse among adolescents during the 1970s may be related to the dramatic change in Black family structure during the 1970s. Data from the U.S. Bureau of the Census (1983a) show that Black families headed by women doubled during the 1970s. Because of high divorce rates and feminization of poverty more women with children, especially minority families, became dependent on public assistance. According to Chilmon (1980) youth in poverty have pessimistic attitudes about the possibility of obtaining adult status through education and employment. Thus, with limited life options early sexual activity and motherhood provide pathways to adulthood (Hogan and Kitagawa, 1985).

Researchers also conclude that adolescent females in single-parent families initiate sexual intercourse early because they may have weaker social supports to enforce socially acceptable behavioral norms (Hayes, 1987). Results from several studies indicate that the socialization of adolescents in female-headed families may enhance the acceptability of premarital sexual intercourse because their parents are least involved in or tied to traditional family or marital forms (Fox, 1980; Murry, 1988; Robbins, Kaplan, and Martin, 1985). In addition, such families may also provide inadequate adult supervision.

Data from this present study also document the significance and consistency, over three decades, of the ability of several factors to distinguish early coital initiators from late coital initiators. Consistent with Udry and Billy (1987), but unlike other studies (Leigh, Weddle, and Loewen, 1988; Westney, Jenkins, and Benjamin, 1984), pubertal development within this sample was related to the timing of first sexual intercourse. Similar to findings from previous studies (Fox and Inazu, 1980; Thornton and Camburn, 1986), results from this study indicate also that across cohorts Black adolescent females who attended church frequently were less likely to initiate sexual intercourse at an early age. Perhaps, adolescents who participate in church have stronger social supports to enforce premarital sexual abstinence. However, some caution must be used with the interpretation of the data on church attendance and initiation of first coitus. Because data on both variables were collected at the same time, the NFSG data do not permit one to determine whether adolescents decreased church attendance just before or at the time of initiating first coitus. However, the consistent association between religiosity and timing of first coitus across cohorts supports Brown's conclusion that the "influence of Black religious institutions on the sexual activity of Black adolescents may be more important than previously assumed" (1985:385).

These data substantiate the significant role of parental socialization in sexuality and educational attainment in predicting the timing of first sexual intercourse among Black adolescent females. Similar studies also report that mother-daughter communication about sex, as well as increased academic performance and aspiration, appear to lower the risk of early sexual experiences among adolescent females (Darling and Hicks, 1982; Devaney and Hubley, 1981; Hogan and Kitagawa, 1985; Murry,

1988). However, the dynamics of the relationship between parental socialization in sexuality and the timing of first intercourse among adolescents remains unclear (Fox, 1980).

Although living in metropolitan areas of the United States was associated with the timing of first coitus for adolescent females of the 1970s, this finding was not consistent across cohorts. Several researchers have noted an association between living in urban settings and early sexual activity among adolescents (Zelnik, Kantner, and Ford, 1981). According to Hogan and Kitagawa (1985) this relationship is a result of loosely defined and enforced norms of sexual behavior. It also seems reasonable to assume that adolescents living in neighborhoods with limited social and recreational outlets will initiate sexual coitus earlier than those who do not. Results from this study also substantiate previous findings which suggest that living in certain geographic regions does not put youth at greater risk of early sexual intercourse (Coles and Stokes, 1985). Finally, the relationship between socioeconomic status and the timing of first coitus was associated with late coital initiation for Black adolescent females of the 1960s and early coital initiation for their counterparts of the 1970s, but did not affect the timing of first coitus for Black adolescent females of the 1950s.

This study does not present a causal model; however, findings do support an interpretation that change in social and economic patterns of families appears to significantly affect the timing of first coitus among Black adolescents. This finding is of some significance as one begins to reflect upon the possible association between rate of early parenting among adolescent females and the current economic and social conditions of Black Americans.

In conclusion, results from this study revealed that, over three decades, change in social and economic conditions of America affected the life circumstances and subsequently the timing of first sexual intercourse among Black adolescent females. Evidence of delayed onset of first coitus occurred during the 1960s, a time of increased federal commitment to social and economic reform and improved racial and ethnic pride. Moreover, across cohorts early coital initiation was associated with early pubertal development, infrequent church attendance, and inadequate parental socialization in sexuality. Results from this study also show that across cohorts, educational attainment was the most significant factor discriminating early coital initiators from late coital initiators. Finally, findings from this study substantiate the significance of increased educational and opportunities in providing alternatives for youth to achieve adult status through more acceptable roles. For example, during times of decreased life options (socially and economically) there was evidence of increased incidence of early sexual intercourse among Black adolescent females.

It is hoped that further research will expand the socio-historical ideas supported by this study in order to continue to clarify the extent to which social and economic conditions influence life circumstances and subsequently sexual career paths of adolescents (that is, transition to dating, onset of first coitus, age at first pregnancy, and age at first birth). Given the current labor market position and employment problems of Black adolescent males, it may be useful to examine Black male sexuality from a socio-historical, life course perspective. For example, have Black males, over time, initiated sexual activity and entered fatherhood early during eras of decreased life options? Further, it is hoped that researchers will expand the socio-historical ideas supported by this study to include additional personal, family, and community life circumstances not considered here. Finally, because Americans have experienced enormous social and economic change during the last decade, this study could be expanded to include Black females who were adolescents during the 1980s.

# References

Abrahamse, Allen F., Peter A. Morrison, and Linda J. Waite
1985 "How Family Characteristics Deter Early Unwed Motherhood." Paper presented at the annual meeting of the Population Association of America.

Bachrach, Christine A., Majorie C. Horn, William D. Mosher, and I. Shimizu
1985 "The National Survey of Family Growth, Cycle III: Sample Design, Weighting, and Variance Estimation." *Vital and Health Statistics*, NCHS, Series 2.

Belcastro, Philip A.
1985 "Sexual Behavior Differences between Black and White Students." *Journal of Sex Research* 21:56–67.

Bell-Scott, Patricia
1987 "Introduction." In *Consortium for Research on Black Adolescence, Black Adolescence: Topical Summaries and Bibliographies of Research*, pp. 5–9. Storrs: University of Connecticut, School of Family Studies, Author. (ERIC Document Reproduction Service No. ED 285 924).

Bowerman, C. E., D. D. Irish, and A. Pope
1966 *Unwed Motherhood: Personal and Social Con-*
*sequences*. Chapel Hill, N.C.: Institute for Research in the Social Sciences.

Brown, Shirley Vining
1985 "Premarital Sexual Permissiveness among Black Adolescent Females." *Social Psychology Quarterly* 48:381–387.

Bumpass, Larry L., and Sara McLanahan
1987 Social Background, not Race, Conditions for Black Premarital Childbearing." *Family Planning Perspective* 19:219–220.

Chilman, Catherine S.
1980 "Social and Psychological Research concerning Adolescent Childbearing: 1970–1980." *Journal of Marriage and the Family* 42:793–805.

Christensen, Harold, and Leanor B. Johnson
1978 "Premarital Coitus among the Southern Black: A Comparative View." *Journal of Marriage and the Family* 40:721–731.

Coles, R., and G. Stokes
1985 *Sex and the American Teenager*. New York: Harper & Row.

Darling, Carol A., and Mary W. Hicks
1982 "Parental Influence on Adolescent Sexuality: Im-

plications for Parents as Educators." *Journal of Youth and Adolescence* 11:231–245.

Devaney, B. L., and K. S. Hubley
1981   "The Determinants of Adolescent Pregnancy and Childbearing." Final report to the National Institute of Child Health and Human Development. Washington, D.C.: Mathematica Policy Research.

Eshelmann, J. Ross
1988   "Sexual Relationships in Premarital and Nonmarital Contexts." In *The Family*, pp. 333–361. Needham Heights, Mass.: Allyn & Bacon.

Fox, Greer Litton
1980   "The Mother–Adolescent Daughter Relationship as a Sexual Socialization Structure: A Research Review." *Family Relations* 29:21–28.

Fox, Greer Litton, and Judith K. Inazu
1980   "Patterns and Outcomes of Mother-Daughter Communication about Sex." *Journal of Social Issues* 36:7–29.

Frisch, R. E.
1983   "Fatness, Menarche, and Fertility: The Effects of Nutrition and Physical Training on Menarche and Ovulation." In *Girls at Puberty: Biological and Psychological Perspectives*, J. Brooks-Gunn and A. C. Peterson, eds., 273–300. New York: Plenum.

Harlan, W. R., E. A. Harland, and G. Grillo
1980   "Secondary Sex Characteristics of Girls 12 to 17 Years of Age: The U.S. Health Examination Survey." *Journal of Pediatrics* 96:1074–1078.

Hayes, Cheryl D.
1987   *Risking the Future: Adolescent Sexuality, Pregnancy, and Childbearing*. Volume 1. Washington, D.C.: National Academy Press.

Hogan, Dennis P., and Evelyn M. Kitagawa
1985   "The Impact of Social Status, Family Structure, and Neighborhood on the Fertility of Black Adolescents." *American Journal of Sociology* 90:825–855.

Hogan, Dennis P., and M. Pazul
1982   "The Occupational and Earning Return to Education among Black Men in the North." *American Journal of Sociology* 87:905–920.

Inazu, J. K., and Greer L. Fox
1980   "Patterns and Outcomes of Mother Daughter Communication and Sexuality." *Journal of Social Issues* 36:7–13.

Huberty, C. J.
1975   "Discriminant Analysis." *Review of Educational Research* 45:543–598.

Jessor, S., and R. Jessor
1975   "Transition from Virginity among Youth: A Social-Psychological Study over Time." *Developmental Psychology* 11:473–484.

Leigh, Geoffrey K., Karen D. Weddle, and Irene R. Loewen
1988   "Analysis of the Timing Transition to Sexual Intercourse for Black Adolescent Females." *Journal of Adolescent Research* 3:333–334.

Lewis, Jerry M., and John G. Looney
1983   *The Long Struggle: Well-functioning Working-class Black Families*. New York: Brunner/Mazel.

Kahn, Janet, Kevin W. Smith, and Elizabeth J. Roberts
1984   *Family Communication and Adolescent Sexual Behavior*. Cambridge, Mass.: American Institute for Research.

McClendon, McKee J.
1976   "The Occupational Status Attainment Process of Males and Females." *American Sociological Review* 41:52–64.

McKenry, Patrick C., Joyce E. Everett, Howard P. Ramseur, and Carol J. Carter
1989   "Research on Black Adolescents: A Legacy of Cultural Biases." *Journal of Adolescent Research* 4:254–264.

Moore, Kristin A., James L. Peterson, and Frank F. Furstenberg, Jr.
1985   "Parental Attitudes and the Occurrence of Early Sexual Activity." *Journal of Marriage and the Family* 48:777–782.

Murry, Velma McBride
1988   "Sexual Career Paths of Black Females: A Social Stratification Analysis." Paper presented at National Council on Family Relations, Philadelphia, Pa., November, 1988.

Newcomer, Susan F., and J. Richard Udry
1987   "Parental Marital Status Effects on Adolescent Sexual Behavior." *Journal of Marriage and the Family* 49:235–240.

Reiss, Ira
1965   "Social Class and Premarital Sexual Permissiveness: A Reexamination." *American Sociological Review* 30:747–756.

1967   *The Social Context of Premarital Sexual Permissiveness*. New York: Holt, Rinehart & Winston.

Robbins, Cynthia, Howard Kaplan, and Steven S. Martin
1985 "Antecedents of Pregnancy among Unmarried Adolescents." *Journal of Marriage and the Family* 47:567–583.

Roebuck, J., and M. G. McGee
1977 "Attitudes toward Premarital Sex and Sexual Behavior among Black High School Girls." *Journal of Sex Research* 13:104–114.

SPSS, Inc.
1986 *SPSS-X User's Guide* Chicago: SPSS Inc.

Staples, Robert
1971 "Toward a Sociology of the Black Family: A Theoretical and Methodological Assessment." *Journal of Marriage and the Family* 33:119–138.

Thornton, Arland, and Donald Camburn
1986 "Religious Commitment and Adolescent Sexual Behavior and Attitudes." Unpublished paper of the Survey Research Center, University of Michigan.

Udry, J. Richard, and John O. G. Billy
1987 "Initiation of Coitus in Early Adolescence." *American Sociological Review* 52:841–855.

Udry, J. Richard, L. Talbert, and N. M. Morris
1985 "Biosocial Foundations for Adolescent Female Sexuality." Paper presented at the annual meeting of the American Sociological Association, Washington, D.C.

United States Bureau of the Census
1983a "America's Black Population. 1970 to 1982. A Statistical Review." Special Publication, P10/POP 83-1. Washington, D.C.: Government Printing Office.

1983b "Money, Income, and Poverty Status of Families and Persons in the United States: 1982." Advance data from the March 1983 Current Population of Commerce, P-60, no. 140. Washington, D.C.: Government Printing Office.

1986 "Marital status and living arrangements: March 1985." *Current Population Reports*, Series P-20, no. 410. Washington, D.C.: Government Printing Office.

1987 "Statistical Abstract of the United States: 1987." 107th ed. no. 84. Washington, D.C.: Government Printing Office.

Weddle, Karen D., Patrick C. McKenry, and Geoffrey K. Leigh
1988 "Adolescent Sexual Behavior: Trends and Issues in Research." *Journal of Adolescent Research* 3:245–257.

Westney, O. E., R. R. Jenkins, and C. M. Benjamin
1983 "Sociosexual Development of Preadolescents." In *Girls at Puberty: Biological and Psychological Perspectives*, J. Brooks-Gunn and A. C. Peterson, eds. 273–300. New York: Plenum.

Zelnik, Melvin, and John F. Kantner
1980 "Sexual Experiences of Young Unmarried Women in the United States." *Family Planning Perspectives* 4:4–17.

Zelnik, Melvin, John F. Kantner, and Kathleen Ford
1981 *Sex and Pregnancy in Adolescence*. Beverly Hills, Calif.: Sage.

Zelnik, Melvin, and Farida K. Shah
1983 "First Intercourse among Young Americans." *Family Planning Perspectives* 15:64–70.

# THE SEXUAL REVOLUTION AND THE BLACK MIDDLE CLASS

## Robert Staples

*In this essay on the current sexual life-styles among middle-class Black Americans, the author reports that the age-old problem of the male shortage is now compounded by the fear of the sexually transmitted disease— AIDS. Mating and dating are taking on new forms to facilitate the meeting of compatible members of the opposite sex. The author suggests that some unconventional methods may be needed to cope with the problems of middle-class Black singles in the 1990s.*

Caution, conservatism and commitment have generally typified the sexual attitudes and behavior of the Black middle class. E. Franklin Frazier once wrote, "There is much irregularity in this class. The importance of sex to this class is indicated by their extreme sensitivity to any charge that Blacks are more free or easy in their sexual behavior than Whites." For example, rules that had been abolished in White colleges long ago persisted in a number of Black colleges well into the 20th century. In the 1920s, some Black colleges had printed regulations that it was forbidden for two students of the opposite sex to meet each other without the presence and permission of the dean of women or of a teacher. A girl and boy could be sent home for walking together in broad daylight.

As the sexual revolution hit American society in the 1960s, middle-class Blacks were slow to adapt to it and never participated, in any significant numbers, in certain aspects of it. By the 1970s, premarital sexual activity had become the norm for the formerly conservative and chaste middle-class Black female. It is impossible to address any issue in Black male/female relationships without taking note of the shortage of eligible and "desirable" Black men. Not only are there about 1.5 million more Black females than Black males in general, the sex ratio is extremely imbalanced among Black college graduates. For a long time Black women have outnumbered Black men among college graduates and the gap is widening. Between 1976 and 1981, the number of Black men receiving baccalaureates declined by nine percent and that of Black women increased by the same percentage. Black women outnumber Black men in colleges, three to one. For example, for Black women who are between 35 and 54 years old, divorced and with five years or more of college, the ratio of comparable men is 38 to 1.

Consequently, sexually conservative and college-educated Black women met the sexual demands of their male peers, fully realizing that if they did not, the men could always find women who would. Once liberated, voluntarily or not, middle-class Black women indulged in a full range of sexual expression. No longer confined to the outdated notions that "nice" women did not enjoy sex (and were limited to the husband and conventional sexual practices), traditional taboos among Blacks were violated. Oral sex, for instance, became something that a majority of Blacks engaged in. A Black woman's magazine survey revealed that more than 90 percent of their readers had been exposed to oral sex (as recipients and providers). Much to the surprise of Black men, the women even initiated, or eagerly complied with male requests for, sexual relations. Some of the excesses of the sexual revolution never took hold among Blacks. Few middle-class Black women willingly engaged in one-night stands or changed sexual partners indiscriminately. Some sexual practices such as group sex, sado-masochism and father/child incest were rarely observed among Blacks. Homosexuality, at least among Black males, was more open and tolerated although lesbianism among Black women received a mixed and often hostile reception.

Around the 1980s, the news media was reporting the end of the sexual revolution, that men and women were looking for commitment and marriage chances instead of casual sex. This new sexual conservatism coincided with the aging of baby boom women (those born between 1945 and 1960) and the election of a conservative president who supported the traditional sexual ideals. Because women were getting older and facing biological deadlines for bearing a child, they started looking for fathers instead of sexual partners. Their anxiety over their marriage chances were only reinforced by a highly publicized study which proclaimed that college-educated women over age 40 had a better chance of being kidnapped by a terrorist than finding a husband.

The male shortage has traditionally meant limited options for Black women seeking a monogamous marriage. Now, it seems to be restricting the pool of sexual partners. A 38-year-old social worker/divorcee from Kansas City says, "In a place with a small town atmosphere like Kansas City, even finding a man to go to bed with is a problem. There's only certain types of men still available. One of them is the perennial playboy who's been had by everybody. The desirable men are all married and I would be barred from most social circles if it became known I was sleeping with one of their husbands. Married women are already threatened by single women and I am frozen out of a lot of social events that involve married people."

Adding to the rising tide of conservatism has been the massive amount of media publicity around the largely sexual disease known as AIDS. Although originally thought of as a White male's disease, the Center for Disease Control reports that Blacks constitute 25 percent of those diagnosed with AIDS, 50 percent of the heterosexual cases, 51 percent of the female cases and 60 percent of all pediatric cases. In talking to middle-class Blacks, most of them heterosexual, that was the topic always mentioned whenever the subject of sex was raised. However, it seemed to be women who appeared to be most frightened of aquiring the disease. Such a fear is disproportionate to the risks they face. About 93 percent of the AIDS victims are men. When the other high risk group of intravenous drug users are excluded, the Center for Disease Control found that fewer than 200 heterosexual Americans have acquired the AIDS disease by intercourse with others who do not belong to one of the high risk groups.

Nonetheless, if people believe something is real, it becomes real in its consequences for them. A 36-year-old single nurse in Washington claims, "Ever since this AIDS stuff emerged, I just quit having sex—cold turkey. It's just too risky and I was not enjoying sex enough to take chances with my life. As for sexual enjoyment, I don't mind admitting that I use masturbation and just plain old fantasizing." Such an extreme reaction was not typical of most Blacks. One woman, a 39-year-old vice-principal in Detroit, says, "I am concerned enough about AIDS to be cautious but not enough to give up sex. After all, I don't know anyone personally who has AIDS and doubt that the men I know are using heroin. I prefer to have sex with men that I have known for a while or those who are just coming out of a divorce or a steady relationship. The one type I avoid is the man who's sleeping around. There's no telling what he's caught and is passing along."

A combination of AIDS fear and the shortage of eligible Black men has led some single Black women into liaisons with married men. A school teacher in a Midwest city admits that she currently prefers married men. According to her, "The last couple of men I have been sexually involved with were married and I have come to desire them over single men. In either case it was not likely that the single or married men were going to marry me. But, the married men treated me better. They had time to listen to my problems and didn't always expect me to listen to theirs while ignoring mine. Besides, in this era of sexually transmitted diseases, I feel safer with married men. Generally, the only other woman they are sexually involved with is their wife, and most wives are not fooling around."

The sexual habits of middle-class Blacks often vary according to gender and age. A 46-year-old Black male divorcee, a government employee, told us, "I am not having any trouble finding a sexual partner. AIDS has made it more difficult and you have to wait longer before getting a woman into bed. But, there's plenty out there to choose from; old women, young women, White, Asian and Hispanic women. I am a little more careful about the women I date. Generally, I stay away from women who date men doing heavy drugs and I would definitely be suspicious of a woman I just met who's ready to hop in the bed with me."

Among the most sexually active Black women are those between 20 to 35 years of age. These women still harbor hopes of marriage and children. Unlike the women past the age of 40, there are still some single males in their age and socio-economic category. Moreover, these women often extend the age ranges of their dating partners by consorting with men considerably younger or older than they are. Unrestricted by some of the traditional norms, they grew up in the sexual revolution and believe that sexual gratification is their right. A 30-year-old accountant in Los Angeles says, "I am not ready to get married and settle down with a bunch of kids at this point in my life. There are a number of career opportunities available that I want to take advantage of. And, I don't want to deny myself the pleasures of sex until I am ready to get married, especially when that might be never."

Even the younger women who entertain aspirations for a marriage and children realize that sexual interaction generally precedes marriage. In the 1960s the male might make the commitment to marriage and sexual relations ensued before the wedding ceremony. During the 1970s, sexual relations occurred between the first and third date for most Black couples. Some serious relationships evolved out of the sexual interaction but many people, for a variety of reasons, went on to other things and people. What the sexual revolution did was establish

sexual relationships as the basis for entering into a mutually defined romantic relationship. As a 32-year-old Internal Revenue official in Detroit says, "This professional man, really nice looking, had asked me out on six or seven dates, always on Friday or Saturday night. The chemistry was so thick you could cut it with a knife. But, he hadn't initiated sex and I realized that, at the rate we were going, we could just be good friends forever. My feeling is that it was up to him to make the first move. If I did it he would consider me too aggressive, even desperate. Eventually, I stopped accepting dates with him."

Despite the old adage that it was easier for a woman to find a sexual partner than a drink of water, middle-class Black women find it necessary to be innovative in the 1980s to meet and bed the Black men of their choice. Making it somewhat easier has been the proliferation of singles clubs and dating services aimed at the Black urban professional. Increasingly, Blacks are using personal ads in Black and general singles magazines to meet members of the opposite sex. The singles bars that were prevalent among Whites never developed in the same form among Blacks. Restaurants and bars catering to Blacks always had a mixed clientele consisting of married and single Blacks. A common method for meeting Black singles is the happy hour at favorite bars frequented by Black professionals. There, men and women on a fast career track meet over drinks, exchange business cards and connect later.

A favorite meeting place for Black urban professionals is an old staple of the Black community—the church. In large numbers many young Black professionals have rejoined the church. Usually these Buppy churches hire an educated minister with a strong commitment to social programs to aid Black causes. These churches also sponsor special events for singles which will bring members and outside individuals together for fun and relaxation. Some Black churches have even organized a singles auxiliary and published a singles newsletter. Otherwise, a number of diverse avenues are utilized to meet members of the opposite sex. This is necessary because the Black middle class is more likely to be scattered in racially integrated job settings and residences. Thus, they have to match up at Black-oriented plays, concerts, film festivals and similar social events. Nowadays, few places are off limits for meeting singles and laundromats, health clubs, tennis courts, jogging tracks are all legitimate places for finding sexual partners or potential mates.

However, this active search for a sexual partner does seem to be confined to Blacks under the age of 35. A 45-year-old female urban planner in New York laments, "I have pretty much given up on meeting Mr. Wonderful and so have most of my friends. Occasionally, married friends will match me up with a single man by inviting us both to dinner. Otherwise, I go out with my female friends to social functions such as a Luther Vandross concert or a Broadway play. Very few Black women my age are actively dating. There are no men out there for us. The few left are dating younger or White women."

Ironically, the AIDS fear has only worsened the plight of those women. It intensified the desire of women to elicit a commitment to marriage or monogamy from their current boyfriends. Some men, on their own, decided to confine their sexual relations to one woman. Previously, some women had "benefitted" by the multiple sexual partners Black men kept as part of their social life. While not an ideal situation for many women, it provided them with some semblance of male companionship. As men become more monogamous, it lays bare the real shortage of "desirable" Black men available to Black women.

The present situation may demand more innovative approaches and techniques than previously used by Black women. In reality, the male shortage is a function of the standards they use to evaluate male prospects. There are Black men available who only need a job, alcohol or drug rehabilitation programs, to be released from prison and to regain their self-esteem, to be viable sexual partners and mates. Perhaps our attention should be directed toward resolving the problems of those men instead of finding mates for women with odds of 10 to 1. From the resolution of that problem will come the solution of many of the other problems faced by the Black community.

# THE BLACK WOMEN'S RELATIONSHIPS PROJECT:
## A National Survey of Black Lesbians

*Vickie M. Mays • Susan D. Cochran*

*This article is a study of sexual orientation as a salient social status characteristic shaping the experiences of a subgroup of Black women. The authors' sample included 530 self-identified Black lesbians and 66 bisexual women. Primarily a descriptive study, this article looks at how sociocultural factors influence the development, maintenance, and dissolution of lover, friend, and community relationships of Black lesbians.*

Black lesbians are relatively invisible in our society. Despite popular stereotypes, we actually know very little about their lives. Research on lesbians (see Peplau & Amaro, 1982 for review) has generally focused solely on Anglos. In a recent search of psychological research on lesbians using *Dialogues* and *Psych Info* databases, we found that only two of over 300 references contained "black women" in the title or abstract. Turning to the social science literature on black women also provides little assistance. In compiling a forthcoming bibliography on social science materials topically related to black women and mental health (Mays, forthcoming-a), there were over 2,100 references to black women, but not a single empirically-based article or review on black lesbians, other than those of the first author (Mays, 1985). Most written information on black lesbians is found (even here only rarely) in popular magazines, gay publications or in the form of published poetry, short stories or autobiographies.

Why is there so little psychological research on black lesbians? There are probably several reasons. First, social scientists have, for the most part, neglected sexual orientation as a variable of interest in psychological research in general. Psychology, while well developed in race relations research, particularly with black Americans, has not yet incorporated sexual orientation as a variable of interest to any great extent. Yet, like gender or ethnicity, sexual orientation represents a social status characteristic that may have important implications. Potentially, it can structure an individual's experiences of being in the world and expectations for social interactions (for a review see Webset and Driskoll, 1985).

A second possible reason for the dearth of black lesbian-related research is that much current research on the lives of lesbians arose out of feminist academic roots, which have been predominantly Anglo in focus. To address the topic of black lesbians adequately, one must meld both the issues of race and sexual orientation.

## Conceptual Issues

Psychological research from the areas of stereotyping, status expectations, the contact hypothesis or

From *A Sourcebook of Gay/Lesbian Health Care* (M. Shernoff and W. A. Scott, eds.) Washington, D.C.: National Gay and Lesbian Health Foundation, 2nd ed., 1988, pp. 54–62. Copyright 1988 by the National Gay and Lesbian Health Foundation. Reprinted by permission. An earlier version of this chapter was presented at the annual meeting of the American Psychological Association, Washington, D.C., August 25, 1986. The authors wish to acknowledge L. Anne Peplau's work on this project as well as her comments on an earlier version of this manuscript.

social cognition can give us some potential insight into what happens when a person has one salient status or characteristic, such as ethnicity, social class or gender. Only in recent years have researchers begun utilizing clearly formulated ideas about the conditional relationship between two or more statuses (e.g., gender and ethnicity) in behavior. The thrust of much of this research has been to approach these statuses from the perspective of an additive model rather than examining the simultaneous contribution of these statuses as interactive, interdependent or interrelated (Kessler and Neighbors, 1986; Mays, forthcoming-b). In the latter perspective, the goal is to investigate the complex web of hierarchical social arrangements generating different experiences (Zinn, Cannon and Dill, 1984), modified by combinations and salience of the status characteristics.

It is from this conceptual framework that the Black Lesbian's Relationship Project was begun. The survey is the first of four related studies that are now in progress. These include investigations of relationship issues among black heterosexual women; black heterosexual men, with a particular emphasis on their relationships with black women; black gay and bisexual men, with an emphasis on how AIDS has impacted upon their relationships; and the intimate relationships of black lesbians. This chapter will focus on the black lesbians we have surveyed.

Our black lesbian research adds the dimension of sexual orientation as a salient social status characteristic shaping the experiences of a subgroup of black women. Like gender and ethnicity, sexual orientation can be a status characteristic when it is an obvious or known factor about the person. Yet, it also differs from gender and ethnicity in that it can be, at times, a hidden characteristic. While we expect direct relationships between the various social statuses and women's life experiences (e.g., a direct relationship between race discrimination and mental health factors such as depression or drug problems), we are particularly interested in exploring the interactions among our status characteristics. For example, we believe that social support structures, so necessary to protect one from the psychological effects of discrimination, will be influenced by one's sexual orientation, and may differ depending upon the salience of the latter characteristic. Elsewhere it has been shown that we are most likely to receive help from similar others (Thoits, 1986).

# Methodological Concerns

Early research on homosexuality and lesbianism tends to formulate questions, collect data, and interpret results in ways reflecting ethnocentric, male, heterosexist or class biases (Morin, 1977; Suppe, 1981). Obviously, we hoped to avoid making similar mistakes. Since social scientists have never had access to scientifically valid or nationally representative data on the lives of black lesbians, we were especially concerned about capturing the diversity present in this group of women. Our aim was to gather data on black lesbian relationships that would be both scientifically valid and sensitive to ethnic and cultural contexts. In structuring our research, we focused on developing both instruments and recruitment methods that would accomplish our goals.

# Instrument Development

There are several special issues of concern in devising an appropriate survey instrument for black lesbians. First, research on black Americans has been hampered by the inapplicability of standard measures and procedures of survey data collection (Jackson, Gurin and Hatchett, 1979). The National Survey of Black Americans clearly demonstrated the need for specialized procedures across all aspects of research design, data collection and analysis. For example, in asking about health problems, it was important to use the term, "high blood pressure," rather than hypertension, a term unfamiliar to many participants.

Second, survey research methods developed for use with black Americans assumes a heterosexual orientation of respondents while research instruments developed for use with lesbians targets primarily Anglo populations. Neither captures the unique concerns of black lesbians. For example, previous research has documented that the family of origin plays a central role in the lives of black women (Brown and Gary, 1985; Vaux, 1985).

Black lesbians, in contrast to white lesbians, may be more likely to remain a part of the heterosexual community, maintaining relationships outside of the lesbian population. This may happen for several reasons. First, black community values emphasize ethnic commitment and participation by all members of the community. Second, the relatively smaller population of black lesbians (a minority within a minority) puts more pressure on these women to maintain their contacts with a black heterosexual community in order to satisfy some of their ethnically-related social support needs. Third, black lesbians may contribute much needed financial and informational resources to their families of origin. This assistance may be critical for the maintenance of a reasonable standard of living. In contrast, for white lesbians, there may be a sufficiently large lesbian population (a similar minority, but drawn from a larger population) from which to derive most ethnic/cultural, social and emotional needs. Also, distance from family of origin may be more achievable for a greater percentage of white lesbians due to greater financial resources within the family system. Thus, black lesbians may find that the need to juggle family of origin demands and their lives as lesbians is somewhat more complicated.

It was our goal to collect data that would allow for an exploration of how these sociocultural factors influence the development, maintenance and dissolution of lover, friend and community relationships of black lesbians. Most investigations of relationships have centered mainly on interpersonal or intrapersonal aspects. While this focus is important, our research team felt that other factors (such as availability of black lovers, perceptions of discrimination within the primarily Anglo lesbian community or perceived class discrimination within the black lesbian community) may be additional mediating factors in explaining relationship choices as well as overall psychological well-being.

Generally there is insufficient questioning in survey research whether or not underlying assumptions or universal applications of concepts, measures or procedures are appropriate (Schumann, 1966; Warwick and Lininger, 1975; Jackson et al.,

1979). It was our strong belief that development of an effective questionnaire necessitated initial field work to establish even the types of questions that we needed to ask of our participants.

Development of the questionnaire incorporated a variety of methodological techniques. These included the use of focus groups, employment of a modified back translation procedure (Jackson et al., 1979; Warwick and Oberson, 1973) and random probes (Schumann, 1966; Jackson et al., 1979).

## Collection of Qualitative Data

We began our research in 1984 by listening carefully to the experiences of black lesbians. A pilot study, using extensive individual interviews with black lesbians, gathered information on women's perceptions of how discrimination influenced their interpersonal relationships and participation in various community activities (Mays, 1988). Responses to open-ended questions were tape-recorded and later transcribed. These transcriptions served as one basis for development of the first pre-test instrument.

Next, we conducted two focus groups, one with single and one with coupled black lesbians, to help identify relevant issues in relationship values, social support, community participation and sources of discrimination. The focus groups were conducted in a relaxed atmosphere designed to encourage participants to talk openly about past and present relationship experiences. These focus groups supplied detailed information assisting us in decisions about appropriate language and meaningful concepts to be included in the questionnaire.

## Finalizing the Questionnaire

A pool of questions was then written, aided by previous research on Anglo lesbians (Aura, 1985; Peplau, Cochran, Rook and Pedesky, 1978), Anglo gay men (Peplau and Cochran, 1981), Anglo heterosexual college students (Cochran and Peplau, 1986) and heterosexual black men and women (Jackson et al., 1979; Mays, forthcoming-a). Many questions needed to be "translated" into culturally-relevant phrasing determined from the interview and focus group sessions. As an example, we found that the word, "lover," rather than the previously used terminology, "romantic/sexual partner" (Cochran and Peplau, 1986; Peplau and Cochran, 1981; Peplau et al., 1978), was important when referring to a woman's sexual significant other. Unlike Anglo lesbians, black lesbians often use "partner" to refer to a good friend one travels about with to various activities (social, family visits, business).

From this process, we developed a 28-page questionnaire. The questionnaire covered a wide range of topics including questions about participants' friendships and love relationships, perceptions of support and discrimination, openness about being lesbian and problems experienced. Included also was the Center for Epidemiological Studies Depression Scale, a standard measure of depressed mood with norms for the black population (Radloff, 1977).

After the initial questionnaire was developed, it was piloted with a small sample of black lesbians. Attempts were made to have this pretest group as heterogeneous as possible. Women varied in relationship status (single vs coupled), age (ranging from 18 to 52), class background and whether or not they had children. After the women completed the questionnaire, they were then interviewed extensively regarding the meaningfulness of the concepts and the completeness of the items. This was done to assure ourselves that the instrument was clear and functioned as intended. We used a variant of the random probe technique to determine the shared meaning of items. This use of the random probe parallels the procedures of the National Survey of Black Americans ( Jackson et al., 1979). It ensures the validity of questions. The questionnaire was then modified to arrive at our final version.

# Collection of Survey Data

## *Sampling*

Sampling our subjects also provided its own set of special concerns. Random probability sampling of a gay or lesbian population is impossible (Gatozzi,

1986; Morin, 1977) although the larger and more diverse the sample, the more likely results will be externally valid. Recruiting a diverse, large sample of black lesbians from across the country was not an easy task. The black lesbian community is small, isolated and relatively invisible. However, we developed a variety of techniques that proved successful in finding black lesbians.

Participants were recruited using a variant of the "snowball" technique. We started with large mailings to potential participants. Several organizations and social and political groups, including the National Coalition of Black Lesbians and Gays, mailed the questionnaire to their lesbian members. Participants who returned the questionnaire to us were also given the opportunity to separately return a postcard requesting additional questionnaires for friends. These were then mailed to the participant who personally recruited additional participants.

Distribution of the questionnaire also involved less focused tactics. The questionnaire was handed out by volunteers at several major lesbian events throughout the United States. In addition, press releases were periodically mailed to lesbian and gay newspapers, such as the *Gay Community News* in Boston, *Off Our Backs*, or the *Washington Blade*, all of which have a sizeable black lesbian readership, inviting participation. Flyers and questionnaires were sent to lesbian and gay bookstores and bars around the country where black gay men and lesbians might frequent. And finally, announcements of the study were distributed to gay and lesbian radio programs throughout the country.

Approximately every three months during the field phase of this project, the demographic characteristics of respondents were tabulated. Those aspects of the community or geographic region that appeared underrepresented were then targeted for more concentrated recruitment efforts. For example, based on the U.S. Census statistics on the number of black women in the Midwest, we decided that our response rate for the major midwest urban areas did not reflect expected percentages. To correct this, the field phase of our study was extended. We remained in the field for approximately 18 months distributing approximately 2,100 questionnaires. Our final sample consists of responses from 530 self-identified black lesbians and 66 bisexual women.

## Inclusionary and Exclusionary Criteria

Even after receiving the 612 completed questionnaires from potential study participants, decisions had to be made about whom to include and whom to exclude. At first, it may seem that the inclusion criteria for this study would be relatively easy. Yet, the measurement of ethnicity and sexual orientation is not always simple. We decided to include in the sample any woman who was black American, including two women from the Carribbean. Additionally, the participant also had to self-identify herself as a lesbian or bisexual woman and report at least one prior sexual experience with a woman. Thus, a few women who had not had a same-sex sexual experience were dropped from our sample. Notice that our definition of lesbian or bisexual status refers only to those individuals who are currently or have been sexually active with women. Obviously, it is possible to consider oneself a lesbian without ever having had a lesbian sexual experience (Peplau and Cochran, in press). However, for the purposes of our study, we felt that sexual experience was an important criterion; a lack of sexual experience might also indicate a relative inexperience with the lesbian lifestyle.

## Characteristics of the Sample

Turning now to a description of the sample, the focus will be on our lesbian respondents. Demographic characteristics of the 530 women are given in Table 1. The women ranged in age from 18 to 59 (mean age = 33.3 years). Most of the women were somewhat religious, although this varied considerably. They were also, by and large, fairly well educated. Nearly half reported having completed a college education or more. Most of the women held jobs, with approximately 84% employed at least half-time. Their median yearly income (1985–1986) was $17,500. On the average, respondents categorized themselves as coming from the middle class. Approximately a third of the sample had children. While one-third of the women lived alone, another

third lived with their partner or lover. Two-thirds of our sample were currently in a serious/committed relationship. Almost half of our sample came from the Western United States, primarily California; another 21.3 percent were drawn from the East Coast/Northeast, 14.3 percent from the Midwest and 14.3 percent from the South.

Clearly from our demographics, we have for the most part BLUPPIES (Black Lesbian Upwardly Mobile People); a group of black lesbians who are relatively well educated, have reasonable incomes and consider themselves as coming from class backgrounds considered middle class in the black community. While our sample is perhaps not representative of the black lesbian community as a whole, it does present us with an opportunity to examine in detail a particular segment of that community. One useful aspect of the sample is that these are women who, on the average, are in their thirties and have been lesbians for quite some time. Thus, their views and adjustments to life probably reflect those of women with a relatively committed lesbian lifestyle. On the negative side, we have too few respondents with lower incomes and less education. This could have resulted from several factors, including demand characteristics of the study instrument, such as reading level or sampling bias. Nonetheless, we do have a small group of this segment of the black lesbian community which will allow us to make some comparisons on the basis of income, education or class.

Looking at Table 2, we get a picture of the relationship experiences of the sample. The mean age at which they reported first being attracted to a women was 15.8 years (median = 14.0 years). Their first lesbian sexual experience occurred at approximately 19 years of age. Almost all of the participants had had a sexual relationship with a black woman, approximately two-thirds with an Anglo woman and 39 percent with other women of color. In general, particularly with the number of West Coast women completing our sample, we were surprised by the relatively low percentage of sexual and committed relationships with other women of color. The median number of sexual partners was nine, which is similar to research on other lesbian samples (Bell and Weinberg, 1978; Peplau et al, 1978).

TABLE 1    Demographic Characteristics of the Black Lesbian Sample

| | |
|---|---|
| Mean age | 33.3 years (range = 18 to 59) |
| Religious background (in percentages) | 33.3% Baptist |
| | 16.8% Protestant |
| | 16.3% Catholic |
| | 33.6% Other |
| Mean level of religiosity | 3.9 |
| (5-point scale where 3 = somewhat religious) | |
| Socioeconomic background | 3.0 (reflecting middle class) |
| Mean years of schooling | 15.4 (consistent with junior year in college) |
| Women possessing four-year college degree or more | 46.0% (in percentage) |
| Annual income (1985–1986) | |
| Less than $5,000 | 8.3% |
| $5,000 to $10,999 | 17.5% |
| $11,000 to 19,999 | 34.5% |
| $20,000 or more | 39.7% |
| Median yearly income | $17,500 |
| Women employed at least 20 hrs/week (in percentage) | 83.6% |
| Geographic location of respondent (in percentages): | |
| West/Northwest/Southwest | 49.7% |
| Northeast/East | 21.2% |
| Midwest | 14.3% |
| South/Southeast | 14.3% |
| Women who have given birth to at least one child | 33.1% |
| Women who: | |
| live alone | 32.1% |
| live with relationship partner | 35.1% |
| live with others | 32.8% |
| Women who are currently in a committed relationship | 65.7% |

Note: $N = 530$.

While the means and medians give you some insight into our sample, they do not really capture the richness of our data set. On each of the variables we have discussed, we have a wide range of responses. There are unique possibilities that derive from the fact that our data are based on a large national sample of black lesbians. In contrast, the largest previous sample of black lesbians consisted of 64 young women recruited from the San Francisco area (Bell and Weinberg, 1978). To date, knowledge of the black lesbian community has been limited by our lack of information. Therefore, some of our most straightforward analyses will involve the simple documentation of relationships and the heterogeneity of black lesbians themselves in relation to such characteristics as age, economic status, social support networks, friendship patterns, problems and levels of psychological distress and

openness of sexual orientation (Cochran and Mays, in press). For example, two manuscripts that are currently in preparation examine the mental health aspects of depressive symptomatology (Cochran and Mays, 1987) and drinking/drug use (Mays and Cochran, 1987) in this sample. Our focus in these manuscripts has been less on the documentation of pathology than the identification of subgroups of black lesbians that are at higher risk for depression and substance abuse. We know that our sample, as a whole, has levels of depressive symptomatology no different than the population of black women (as measured by the CES-D) (Cochran and Mays, 1987). However, some of our participants evidence considerable levels of depression. Preliminary analyses suggest that black lesbians who are isolated from other black lesbians and participate more extensively in the Anglo lesbian community are more

TABLE 2  Participants' Reports of Lesbian Sexual and Relationship Experiences

| | |
|---|---|
| Mean age of first attraction to women | 15.8 years<br>(Range = 4 to 52 years) |
| Mean age of first sexual experience | 19.5 years |
| Median number of sexual partners | 9.0 |
| Women reporting at least one sexual relationship with: | |
| a black woman | 93% |
| an Anglo woman | 65% |
| other women of color | 39% |
| Median number of lifestyle serious/<br>committed lesbian relationships | 3.0 |
| Women reporting at least one committed relationship with: | |
| a black woman | 83% |
| an Anglo woman | 40% |
| other women of color | 17% |
| Median length of longest relationship | 42.0 months<br>(range = 1 month to 20 years) |

Note: $N$ = 530.

likely to suffer from depression. In contrast, women who are more integrated into the black lesbian community (in terms of sources of support, ethnicity of sexual partners and lovers) than the average woman in our sample are more likely to have drug and alcohol problems. In future analyses, we will be able to use our large sample to explore factors that put particular segments of the black lesbian community at risk for emotional problems. Our data can help to identify strategies for intervening with these at risk women as well as assisting therapists and other helpers by better identifying the role of structural factors (i.e., discriminations) versus intrapersonal dynamics in the development and maintenance of emotional problems. The need to document this heterogeneity is particularly important to aid in eradicating the negative stereotypes that exist about black lesbians.

Other analyses will tackle more complex issues. Two major themes in our dataset are social support and discrimination—concepts of particular importance for black Americans. Much of the research on black Americans has discussed the impor-

tance of the black family and social networks to the psychological well-being and survival of this group. Our data allow us to investigate the relationship between social support and sexual orientation. This can take many forms from the particular stresses of an interracial relationship (where the interracial pairing may make the lesbian status more salient to others) (Mays and Cochran, 1986) to the relative importance of ethnicity versus sexual orientation in defining social support structures (Cochran and Mays, 1986).

A final area of interest is in the factors that predict achieving and maintaining a satisfying close relationship. As with Anglo lesbians (Peplau, Padesky and Hamilton, 1982), the black lesbians in our sample reported their relationships as generally satisfying and close (Peplau, Cochran and Mays, 1986). Further work in the area will seek to determine which factors are important in generating a positive relationship.

We are hopeful that this study will aid in bringing the lives of black lesbians out of the research closet they have inhabited for so many years.

# References

Aura, J.
1985    "Women's Social Support: A Comparison of Lesbians and Heterosexuals," doctoral dissertation. University of California, Los Angeles.

Bell, A. and Weinberg, M.
1978    *Homosexualities: A Study of Diversity in Men and Women.* New York: Simon and Schuster.

Brown, D. R. and Gary, L. E.
1985    "Social Support Network Differentials Among Married and Nonmarried Black Females." *Psychology of Women Quarterly, 9*, pp. 229–241.

Cochran, S. D. and Mays, V. M.
1987    "Correlates of Depression Among Black Lesbians." Paper presented at the annual meeting of the Association for Women in Psychology, Denver. Under revision.
        (in press) "Disclosure of Sexual Preference to Physicians by Black Lesbian and Bisexual Women," *Western Journal of Medicine.*

Cochran, S. D. and Peplau, L. A.
1985    "Value Orientations in Heterosexual Relationships," *Psychology of Women Quarterly, 9*, pp. 477–488.

Gatozzi, A.
1986    "Psychological and Social Aspects of the Acquired Immune Deficiency Syndrome: Early Findings of Research Supported by the National Institute of Mental Health." Unpublished working paper. Office of Scientific Information, National Institute of Mental Health.

Jackson, J. S.; Gurin, G. and Hatchett, S.
1979    "A Study of Black American Life and Mental Health." Proposal submitted to the National Institute of Mental Health.

Kessler, R. C. and Neighbors, H. W.
1986    "A New Perspective on the Relationships Among Race, Social Class, and Psychological Distress," *Journal of Health and Social Behavior*, 27, pp. 107–115.

Mays, V. M.
1985    "Black Women Working Together: Diversity in Same Sex Relationships," *Women's Studies International Forum*, 8, pp. 67–71.

1988    "Perceived Discrimination and Black Women's Relationships." Manuscript under review.
        (forthcoming-a) *A Bibliographic Guide to Research Materials on Black Women in the Social Science and Mental Health Area.* New York: Praeger Publications.
        (forthcoming-b) "The State of the Art of Research on Black Women." In Mays, V. M. (ed.) *A Bibliographic Guide to Research Materials on Black Women in the Social Science and Mental Health Area.* New York: Praeger Publications.

Mays, V. M. and Cochran, S. D.
1986    "Relationship Experiences and the Perception of Discrimination." Paper presented at the meetings of the American Psychological Association, Washington, D.C., August.

1987    "Alcohol and Drug Problems Among Black Lesbians." Paper presented at the meetings of the Association for Women in Psychology, Denver, Colorado, March. Under revision.

Morin, S. F.
1977    "Heterosexual Bias in Psychological Research on Lesbianism and Male Homosexuality." *American Psychologist, 32*, pp. 629–637.

Peplau, L. A. and Cochran, S. D.
1981    "Value Orientations in the Intimate Relationships of Gay Men," *Journal of Homosexuality, 6,* pp. 1–19.
        (in press) "A Relationship Perspective on Homosexuality," McWhirter, D. P.; Sanders, S. A. & Reinisch, J. M. (eds.) *Homosexuality/heterosexuality: The Kinsey Scale.* New York: Oxford University Press.

Peplau, L. A.; Cochran, S. D. and Mays, V. M.
1986    "Satisfaction in the Intimate Relationships of Black Lesbians." Paper presented at the annual meeting of the American Psychological Association, Washington, D.C., August.

Peplau, L. A.; Cochran, S.; Rook, K. and Padesky, C.
1978    "Loving Women: Attachment and Autonomy in Lesbian Relationships," *Journal of Social Issues, 34*, pp. 7–27.

Peplau, L. A.; Padesky, C. and Hamilton, M.

1982   "Satisfaction in Lesbian Relationships," *Journal of Homosexuality, 8,* pp. 23–35.

Radloff, L. S.

1977   "The CES-D Scale: A Self-Report Depression Scale for Research in the General Population." *Journal of Applied Psychological Measurement, 1,* pp. 385–401.

Schumann, H.

1966   "The Random Probe: A Technique for Evaluating the Validity of Closed Questions," *American Sociological Review, 32* (2), pp. 218–222.

Suppe, F.

1981   "The Bell and Weinberg Study: Future Priorities for Research on Homosexuality," *Journal of Homosexuality, 6,* pp. 69–97.

Thoits, P. A.

1986   "Social Support as Coping Assistance," *Journal of Consulting and Clinical Psychology, 54,* pp. 416–423.

Vaux, A.

1985   "Variations in Social Support Associated with Gender, Ethnicity and Age," *Journal of Social Issues, 41,* pp. 89–110.

Warwick, D. P. and Lininger, C. A.

1975   *The Sample Survey.* New York: McGraw Hill.

Warwick, D. P. and Osherson, D.

1973   *Comparative Research Methods.* Englewood Cliffs, N.J.: Prentice-Hall.

Webster, M. and Driskoll, J. E.

1985   "Status Generalization," Berger, J. & Zeditch, M. (eds.) *Status, Rewards, and Influence.* San Francisco: Jossey-Bass Publishers, 1985.

Zinn, M. B.; Cannon, L. W. and Dill, B. T.

1984   "The Costs of Exclusionary Practices in Women's Studies." Unpublished manuscript.

# 4 / Sex Roles

## THE BLACK MALE:
## Searching beyond Stereotypes

### *Manning Marable*

*Every socioeconomic and political indicator illustrates that the Black male in the United States is facing an unprecedented crisis. Despite singular examples of successful males in elected politics, business, labor unions, and the professions, the overwhelming majority of Black men find it difficult to acquire self-confidence and self-esteem in the chaos of modern economic and social life. Stereotypes imposed by white history and by their lack of knowledge of their own past have too often convinced younger Black men that their struggle is overwhelming.*

What is a black man? Husband and father. Son and brother. Lover and boyfriend. Uncle and grandfather. Construction worker and sharecropper. Minister and ghetto hustler. Doctor and mineworker. Automechanic and presidential candidate.

What is a black man in an institutionally racist society, in the social system of modern America? The essential tragedy of being black and male is our inability, as men and as people of African descent, to define ourselves without the stereotypes which the larger society imposes upon us, and through various institutional means perpetuates and permeates within our entire culture. Our relations with our sisters, our parents and children, and indeed across the entire spectrum of human relations, are imprisoned by images of the past, false distortions which seldom if ever capture the essence of our being. We cannot come to terms with black women until we understand the half hidden stereotypes which have crippled our development and social consciousness. We cannot challenge racial and sexual inequality, both within the black community and across the larger American society, unless we comprehend the critical difference between the myths about ourselves and the harsh reality of being black men.

## Confrontation with White History

The conflicts between black and white men in contemporary American culture can be traced directly through history to the earliest days of chattel slavery.

From *National Scene* 53 (6, 1984):5–6, 26–30. Reprinted by permission of the author. Figures have been deleted.

White males entering the New World were ill adapted to make the difficult transition from Europe to the American frontier. As recent historical research indicates, the development of what was to become the United States was accomplished largely, if not primarily, by African slaves, men and women alike. Africans were the first to cultivate wheat on the continent; they showed their illiterate masters how to grow indigo, rice and cotton; their extensive knowledge of herbs and roots provided colonists with medicines and preservatives for food supplies. It was the black man, wielding his sturdy ax, who cut down most of the virgin forest across the southern colonies. And in times of war, the white man reluctantly looked to his black slave to protect him and his property. As early as 1715, during the Yemassee Indian war, black troops led British regulars in a campaign to exterminate Indian tribes. After another such campaign in 1747, the all-white South Carolina legislature issued a public vote of gratitude to black men, who "in times of war, behaved themselves with great faithfulness and courage, in repelling the attacks of his Majesty's enemies." During the American Revolution, over two thousand black men volunteered to join the beleaguered Continental Army of George Washington, a slaveholder. A generation later, two thousand blacks from New York joined the state militia's segregated units during the War of 1812, and blacks fought bravely under Andrew Jackson at the battle of New Orleans. From Crispus Attucks to the 180,000 blacks who fought in the Union Army during the Civil War, black men gave their lives to preserve the liberties of their white male masters.

The response of white men to the many sacrifices of the sable counterparts was, in a word, contemptuous. Their point of view of black males was conditioned by three basic beliefs. Black men were only a step above the animals—possessing awesome physical powers, but lacking in intellectual ability. As such, their proper role in white society was as laborers, and not as the managers of labor. Second, the black male represented a potential political threat to the entire system of slavery. And third, but by no means last, the black male symbolized a lusty sexual potency which threatened white women. This uneven mixture of political fears and sexual anxieties were reinforced by the white

males' crimes committed against black women, the routine rape and sexual abuse which all slave societies permit between the oppressed and the oppressor. Another dilemma, seldom discussed publicly, was the historical fact that some white women of all social classes were not reluctant to request the sexual favors of their male slaves. These inherent tensions produced a racial mode of conduct and social control, which transcended the colonial period and embraced much of the twentieth century. The white male-dominated system dictated that the *only* acceptable social behavior of any black male was that of subservience—the loyal slave, the proverbial Uncle Tom, the ever-cheerful and infantile Sambo. It was not enough that black men must cringe before their white masters; they must express open devotion to the system of slavery itself. Politically, the black male was unfit to play even a minor role in the development of democracy. Supreme Court Chief Justice Roger B. Tawney spoke for his entire class in 1857: "Negroes [are] beings of an inferior order, and altogether unfit to associate with the white race, either in social or political relations; and so far inferior that they have no rights which the white man was bound to respect." Finally, black males disciplined for various crimes against white supremacy—such as escaping from the plantation, or murdering their masters—were often punished in a *sexual* manner. On this point, the historical record is clear. In the colonial era, castration of black males was required by the legislatures of North and South Carolina, Virginia, Pennsylvania, and New Jersey. Black men were castrated simply for striking a white man, or for attempting to learn to read and write. In the late nineteenth century, hundreds of black male victims of lynching were first sexually mutilated before being executed. The impulse to castrate black males was popularized in white literature and folklore, and even today, instances of such crimes are not entirely unknown in the rural South.

The relations between black males and white women were infinitely more complex. Generally, the vast majority of white females viewed black men through the eyes of their fathers and husbands. The black man was simply a beast of burden, a worker who gave his life to create a more comfortable environment for her and her children. And yet, in truth, he was still a man. Instances of interracial marriage were few, and were prohibited by law even as late as the 1960s. But the fear of sexual union did not prohibit many white females, particularly indentured servants and working class women, to solicit favors from black men. In the 1840s, however, a small group of white middle class women became actively involved in the campaign to abolish slavery. The founders of modern American feminism—Susan B. Anthony, Elizabeth Cady Stanton and Lucretia Mott—championed the cause of emancipation, and defended blacks' civil rights. In gratitude for their devotion of black freedom, the leading black abolitionist of the period, Frederick Douglass, actively promoted the rights of white women against the white male power structure. In 1848, at the Seneca Falls, New York women's rights convention, Douglass was the only man, black or white, to support the extension of voting rights to all women. White women looked to Douglass for leadership in the battle against sexual and racial discrimination. Yet curiously they were frequently hostile to the continued contributions of black women to the cause of freedom. When the brilliant orator Sojourner Truth, second only to Douglass as a leading figure in the abolitionist movement, rose to lecture before an 1851 women's convention in Akron, Ohio, white women cried out, "Don't let her speak!" For these white liberals, the destruction of slavery was simply a means to expand democratic rights to white women: the goal was defined in racist terms. Black men like Douglass were useful allies only so far as they promoted white middle class women's political interests.

The moment of truth came immediately following the Civil War, when Congress passed the Fifteenth Amendment, which gave black males the right to vote. For Douglass and most black leaders, both men and women, suffrage was absolutely essential to preserve their new freedoms. While the Fifteenth Amendment excluded females for the electoral franchise, it nevertheless represented a great democratic victory for all oppressed groups. For most white suffragists, however, it symbolized the political advancement of the black male over white middle class women. Quickly their liberal rhetoric gave way to racist diatribes. "So long as the Negro was lowest in the scale of being, we were

willing to press his claims," wrote Elizabeth Cady Stanton in 1865. "But now, as the celestial gate to civil rights is slowly moving on its hinges, it becomes a serious question whether we had better stand aside and see 'Sambo' walk into the kingdom first." Most white women reformists concluded that "it is better to be the slave of an educated white man, than of a degraded, ignorant black one." They warned whites that giving the vote to the black male would lead to the widespread rape and sexual assaults of white women of the upper classes. Susan B. Anthony vowed that "I will cut off this right arm of mine before I will ever work for or demand the ballot for the Negro and not the (white) woman." In contrast, black women leaders like Sojourner Truth and Frances E. Watkins Harper understood that the enfranchisement of black men was an essential initial step for the democratic rights of all people. The division between white middle class feminists and the civil rights movement of blacks, beginning over a century ago, has continued today in debates over affirmative action and job quotas. White liberal feminists frequently use the rhetoric of racial equality, but often find it difficult to support public policies that will advance black males over their own social group. Even in the 1970s, liberal women writers like Susan Brownmiller continued to resurrect the myth of the "black male-as-rapist," and sought to define the white women, in crudely racist terms. The weight of white history, from white women and men alike, has been an endless series of stereotypes used to frustrate the black man's images of himself, and to blunt his constant quest for freedom.

## Confronting the Black Woman

Images of our suffering—as slaves, sharecroppers, industrial workers, and standing in unemployment lines—have been intermingled in our relationship with the black woman. We have seen her straining under the hot Southern sun, chopping cotton row upon row, and nursing our children on the side. We have witnessed her come home, tired and weary after working as a nurse, cook, or a maid in white men's houses. We have seen her love of her children, her commitment to the church, her beauty and dignity in the face of political and economic exploitation. And yet, so much is left unsaid. All too often the black male, in his own silent suffering, fails to communicate his love and deep respect for the mother, sister, grandmother and wife who gave him the courage and commitment to strive for freedom. The veils of oppression and the illusions of racial stereotypes limit our ability to speak the inner truths about ourselves and our relationships to black women.

The black man's image of the past is, in most respects, a distortion of social reality. All of us can feel the anguish of our great-grandfathers as they witnessed their wives and daughters being raped by their white masters, or as they wept when their families were sold apart. But do we feel the double bondage of the black woman, trying desperately to keep her family together, and yet at times distrusted by her own black man? Less then a generation ago, most black male social scientists argued that the black family was effectively destroyed by slavery; that the black man was much less than a husband or father; and that a "black matriarchy" emerged which crippled the economic, social and political development of the black community. Back in 1965, black scholar C. Eric Lincoln declared that the slavery experience had "stripped the Negro male of his masculinity" and had "condemned him to a eunuch-like existence in a culture which venerates masculine primacy." The rigid rules of Jim Crow applied more to black men than to their women, according to Lincoln: "Because she was frequently the white man's mistress, the Negro woman occasionally flouted the rules of segregation.... The Negro [male] did not earn rewards for being manly, courageous, or assertive, but for being accommodating—for fulfilling the stereotype of what he has been forced to be." The social byproduct of black demasculinization, concluded Lincoln, was the rise of black matriarchs, who psychologically castrated their husbands and sons. "The Negro female has had the responsibility of the Negro family for so many generations that she accepts it, or assumes it, as second nature. Many older women have forgotten why the responsibility developed upon the Negro woman in the first place, or why it later became institutionalized," Lincoln argued. "And young Negro women do not think it absurd to reduce the relationship to a matter of money since many of

them probably grew up in families where the only income was earned by the mothers: the fathers may not have been in evidence at all." Other black male sociologists perpetuated these stereotypes, which only served to turn black women and men against each other instead of focusing their energies and talents in the struggle for freedom.

Today's social science research on black female–male relations tells us what our common sense should have indicated long ago—that the essence of black family and community life has been a positive, constructive and even heroic experience. Andrew Billingsley's *Black Families and the Struggle for Survival* illustrates that the black "extended family" is part of our African heritage which was never eradicated by slavery or segregation. The black tradition of racial cooperation, the collectivist rather than individualistic ethos, is an outgrowth of the unique African heritage which we still maintain. It is clear that the black woman was the primary transmitter and repositor of the cultural heritage of our people, and played a central role in the socialization and guidance of black male and female children. But this fact does not by any way justify the myth of a "black matriarchy." Black women suffered from the economic exploitation and racism which black males experienced—but they also were trapped by institutional sexism and all of the various means of violence that have been used to oppress all women, such as rape, "wife beating," and sterilization. The majority of the black poor throughout history have been overwhelmingly female; the lowest paid major group within the labor force in America is black women, not men.

In politics, the sense of the black man's relations with black women are again distorted by stereotypes. Most of us can cite the achievements of the great black men who contributed to the freedom of our people: Frederick Douglass, Dr. W. E. B. DuBois, Marcus Garvey, Martin Luther King, Jr., Malcolm X, Paul Robeson, Medgar Evers, A. Philip Randolph. Why then are we often forgetful of Harriet Tubman, the fearless conductor on the Underground Railroad, who spirited over 350 slaves into the North? What of Ida B. Wells, newspaper editor and anti-lynching activist; Mary Church Terrell, educator, member of the Washington, D.C. Board of Education from 1895–1906, and civil rights leader;

Mary McLeod Bethune, college president and Director of the Division of Negro Affairs for the National Youth Administration; and Fannie Lou Hamer, courageous desegregation leader in the South during the 1960s? In simple truth, the cause of black freedom has been pursued by black women and men equally. In black literature, the eloquent appeals to racial equality penned by Richard Wright, James Baldwin and DuBois are paralleled in the works of Zora Neale Hurston, Alice Walker, and Toni Morrison. Martin Luther King, Jr., may have expressed for all of us our collective vision of equality in his "I Have A Dream" speech at the 1963 March on Washington—but it was the solitary act of defiance by a black woman, Rosa Parks, that initiated the great Montgomery Bus Boycott in 1955, and gave birth to the modern civil rights movement. The struggle of our foremothers and forefathers transcend the barrier of gender, as black women have tried to tell their men for generations. Beyond the stereotypes, we find a common heritage of suffering, and a common will to be free.

## The Black Man Confronts Himself

The search for reality begins and ends with an assessment of the actual socioeconomic condition of black males within the general context of the larger society. Beginning in the economic sphere, one finds the illusion of black male achievement in the marketplace is undermined by statistical evidence. Of the thousands of small businesses initiated by black entrepreneurs each year, over ninety percent of them go bankrupt within thirty-six months. The black businessman suffers from redlining policies of banks, which keep capital outside his hands. Only one out of two hundred black businessmen have more than twenty paid employees and over 80 percent of all black men who start their own firms must hold a second job, working sixteen hours and more each day to provide greater opportunities for their families and communities. . . .

Advances in high technology leave black males particularly vulnerable to even higher unemployment rates over the next decades. Millions of black men are located either in the "old line" industries such as steel, automobiles, rubber, and textiles, or in the public sector—both of which have experienced severe job contractions. In agriculture, to cite one typical instance, the disappearance of black male workers is striking. As late as forty years ago, two out of every five black men were either farmers or farm workers. In 1960, roughly five percent of all black men were still employed in agriculture, and another three percent owned their own farms. By 1983, however, less than 130,000 black men worked in agriculture. From 1959 to 1974, the number of black-operated cotton farms in the South dropped from 87,074 to 1,569. Black tobacco farmers declined in number from 40,670 to barely 7,000 during the same period. About three out of four black men involved in farming today are not self-employed. From both rural and urban environments, the numbers of jobless black adult males have soared since the late 1960s. . . . These statistics fail to convey, however, the human dimensions of the economic chaos of black male joblessness. Thousands of jobless men are driven into petty crime annually, just to feed their families; others find temporary solace in drugs or alcohol. The collapse of thousands of black households and the steady proliferation of female-headed, single parent households is a social consequence of the systemic economic injustice which is inflicted upon black males.

Racism also underscores the plight of black males within the criminal justice system. Every year in this country there are over two million arrests of black males. About 300,000 black men are currently incarcerated in federal and state prisons or other penal institutions. At least half of the black prisoners are less than thirty years of age, and over one thousand are not even old enough to vote. Most black male prisoners were unemployed at the time of their arrests; the others averaged less than $8,000 annual incomes during the year before they were jailed. And about 45 percent of the 1,300 men currently awaiting capital punishment on death row are Afro-Americans. As Lennox S. Hinds, former National Director of the National Conference of Black Lawyers has stated, "someone black and poor tried for stealing a few hundred dollars has a 90 percent likelihood of being convicted of robbery with a sentence averaging between 94 to 138 months. A white business executive who embezzled hundreds of thousands of dollars has only a 20 percent likelihood of conviction with a sentence averaging about 20 to 48 months." Justice is not "color blind" when black males are the accused. . . .

Every socioeconomic and political indicator illustrates that the black male in America is facing an unprecedented crisis. Despite singular examples of successful males in electoral politics, business, labor unions, and the professions, the overwhelming majority of black men find it difficult to acquire self confidence and self esteem within the chaos of modern economic and social life. The stereotypes imposed by white history, by the lack of knowledge of our own past, often convince many younger black males that their struggle is too overwhelming. Black women have a responsibility to comprehend the forces which destroy the lives of thousands of their brothers, sons and husbands. But black men must understand that they, too, must overcome their own inherent and deeply ingrained sexism, recognizing that black women must be equal partners in the battle to uproot inequality at every level of the society. The strongest ally black men have in their battle to achieve black freedom is the black woman. Together, without illusions and false accusations, without racist and sexist stereotypes, they can achieve far more than they can ever accomplish alone.

# SEX ROLES AND SURVIVAL STRATEGIES IN AN URBAN BLACK COMMUNITY

## Carol B. Stack

*The existence of a viable network of relationships between the single Black parent and other persons is shown. The author finds that in spite of disruptive forces on the single parent family, a variety of creative solutions are available to the parent. She shows how these survival strategies help maximize the lone parent's independence.*

The power and authority ascribed to women in the Black ghettos of America, women whose families are locked into lifelong conditions of poverty and welfare, have their roots in the inexorable unemployment of Black males and the ensuing control of economic resources by females. These social-economic conditions have given rise to special features in the organization of family and kin networks in Black communities, features not unlike the patterns of domestic authority that emerge in matrilineal societies, or in cultures where men are away from home in wage labor (Gonzalez, 1969, 1970). The poor in Black urban communities have evolved, as the basic unit of their society, a core of kinsmen and non-kin who cooperate on a daily basis and who live near one another or co-reside. This core, or nucleus, has been characterized as the basis

From *Woman, Culture, and Society*, ed. Michelle Z. Rosaldo and Louise Lamphere (Stanford University Press, 1974). Adapted from *All Our Kin: Strategies for Survival in a Black Community* by Carol B. Stack (Harper & Row, 1974). Copyright 1974 by Carol B. Stack. Reprinted by permission. Tables have been renumbered.

of the consanguineal household (Gonzalez, 1965) and of matrifocality (Abrahams, 1963; Moynihan, 1965; Rainwater, 1966).

The concept of "matrifocality," however, has been criticized as inaccurate and inadequate. Recent studies (Ladner, 1971; Smith, 1970; Stack, 1970; Valentine, 1970) show convincingly that many of the negative features attributed to matrifocal families—that they are fatherless, unstable, and produce offspring that are "illegitimate" in the eyes of the folk culture—are not general characteristics of low-income Black families in urban America. Rather than imposing widely accepted definitions of the family, the nuclear family, or the matrifocal family on the ways in which the urban poor describe and order their world, we must seek a more appropriate theoretical framework. Elsewhere I have proposed an analysis based on the notion of a domestic network (Stack, 1974). In this view, the basis of familial structure and cooperation is not the nuclear family of the middle class, but an extended cluster of kinsmen related chiefly through children but also through marriage and friendship, who align to provide domestic functions. This cluster, or domestic network, is diffused over several kin-based households, and fluctuations in individual household composition do not significantly affect cooperative arrangements.

In this paper I shall analyze the domestic network and the relationships within it from a woman's perspective—from the perspective that the women in this study provided and from my own interpretations of the domestic and social scene. Many previous studies of the Black family (e.g., Liebow, 1967, and Hannerz, 1969) have taken a male perspective emphasizing the street-corner life of Black men and viewing men as peripheral to familial concerns. Though correctly stressing the economic difficulties that black males face in a racist society, these and other studies (Moynihan, 1965; Bernard, 1966) have fostered a stereotype of Black families as fatherless and subject to a domineering woman's matriarchal rule. From such simplistic accounts it is all too easy to come to blame juvenile delinquency, divorce, illegitimacy, and other social ills on the Black family, while ignoring the oppressive reality of our political and economic system and the adaptive resiliency and strength that Black families have shown.

My analysis will draw on life-history material as well as on personal comments from women in The Flats, the poorest section of a Black community in the Midwestern city of Jackson Harbor.[1] I shall view women as strategists—active agents who use resources to achieve goals and cope with the problems of everyday life. This framework has several advantages. First, because the focus is on women rather than men, women's views of family relations, often ignored or slighted, are given prominence. Second, since households form around women because of their role in child care, ties between women (including paternal aunts, cousins, etc.) often constitute the core of a network; data from women's lives, then, crucially illuminate the continuity in these networks. Finally, the life-history material, taken chiefly from women, also demonstrates the positive role that a man plays in Black family life, both as the father of a woman's children and as a contributor of valuable resources to her network and to the network of his own kin.

I shall begin by analyzing the history of residential arrangements during one woman's life, and the residential arrangements of this woman's kin network at two points in time, demonstrating that although household composition changes, members are selected or self-selected largely from a single nework that has continuity over time. Women and men, in response to joblessness, the possibility of welfare payments, the breakup of relationships, or the whims of a landlord, may move often. But the very calamities and crises that contribute to the constant shifts in residence tend to bring men, women, and children back into the households of close kin. Newly formed households are successive recombinations of the same domestic network of adults and children, quite often in the same dwellings. Residence histories, then, are an important reflection of the strategy of relying on and strengthening the domestic kin network, and also reveal the adaptiveness of households with "elastic boundaries." (It may be worth noting that middle-class whites are beginning to perceive certain values, for their own lives, in such households.)

In the remainder of the paper, the importance of maximizing network strength will be reemphasized and additional strategies will be isolated by examining two sets of relationships within kin networks—those between mothers and fathers and those between fathers and children. Women's own accounts of their situations show how they have developed a strong sense of independence from men, evolved social controls against the formation of conjugal relationships, and limited the role of the husband-father within the mother's domestic group. All of these strategies serve to strengthen the domestic network, often at the expense of any particular male–female tie. Kin regard any marriage as a risk to the woman and her children, and the loss of either male or female kin as a threat to the durability of the kin network. These two factors continually augment each other and dictate, as well, the range of socially accepted relationships between fathers and children.

## Residence and the Domestic Network

In The Flats, the material and cultural support needed to sustain and socialize community members is provided by cooperating kinsmen. The individual can draw upon a broad domestic web of kin and friends—some who reside together, others who do not. Residents in The Flats characterize household composition according to where people sleep, eat, and spend their time. Those who eat together may be considered part of a domestic unit. But an individual may eat in one household, sleep in another, contribute resources and services to yet another, and consider himself or herself a member of all three households. Children may fall asleep and remain through the night wherever the late-evening visiting patterns of the adult females take them, and they may remain in these households and share meals perhaps a week at a time. As R. T. Smith suggests in an article on Afro-American kinship (1970), it is sometimes difficult "to determine just which household a given individual belongs to at any particular moment." These facts of ghetto life are, of course, often disguised in the statistical reports of census takers, who record simply sleeping arrangements.

Households in The Flats, then, have shifting memberships, but they maintain for the most part a steady state of three generations of kin: males and females beyond child-bearing age; a middle gener-

ation of mothers raising their own children or children of close kin; and the children. This observation is supported in a recent study by Ladner (1971:60), who writes, "Many children normally grow up in a three-generation household and they absorb the influences of a grandmother and grandfather as well as a mother and father." A survey of eighty-three residence changes among welfare families, whereby adult females who are heads of their own households merged households with other kin, shows that the majority of moves created three-generation households. Consequently, it is difficult to pinpoint structural beginning or end to household cycles in poor Black urban communities (Buchler and Selby, 1968; Fortes, 1958; Otterbein, 1970). But it is clear that authority patterns within a kin network change with birth and death; with the death of the oldest member in a household, the next generation assumes authority.

Residence changes themselves are brought on by many factors, most related to the economic conditions in which poor families live. Women who have children have access to welfare, and thus more economic security than women who do not, and more than all men. Welfare regulations encourage mothers to set up separate households, and women actively seek independence, privacy, and improvement in their lives. But these ventures do not last long. Life histories of adults show that the attempts by women to set up separate households with their children are short-lived: houses are condemned; landlords evict tenants; and needs for services among kin arise. Household composition also expands or contracts with the loss of a job, the death of a relative, the beginning or end of a sexual partnership, or the end of a friendship. But fluctuations in household composition rarely affect the exchanges and daily dependencies of participants. The . . . chronology of residence changes made by Ruby Banks graphically illuminates these points [Table 1].

Ruby's residential changes, and the residences of her own children and kin, reveal that the same factors contributing to the high frequency of moving also bring men, women, and children back into the households of close kin. That one can repeatedly do so is a great source of security and dependence for those living in poverty.

## TABLE 1

| AGE | HOUSEHOLD COMPOSITION AND CONTEXT OF HOUSEHOLD FORMATION |
|---|---|
| Birth | Ruby lived with her mother, Magnolia, and her maternal grandparents. |
| 4 | To be eligible for welfare, Ruby and Magnolia were required to move out of Ruby's grandparents' house. They moved into a separate residence two houses away, but ate all meals at the grandparents' house. |
| 5 | Ruby and Magnolia returned to the grandparents' house and Magnolia gave birth to a son. Magnolia worked and the grandmother cared for her children. |
| 6 | Ruby's maternal grandparents separated. Magnolia remained living with her father and her (now) two sons. Ruby and her grandmother moved up the street and lived with her maternal aunt Augusta and maternal uncle. Ruby's grandmother took care of Ruby and her brothers, and Magnolia worked and cooked and cleaned for her father. |
| 7–16 | The household was now composed of Ruby, her grandmother, her grandmother's new husband, Augusta and her boyfriend, and Ruby's maternal uncle. At age sixteen Ruby gave birth to a daughter. |
| 17 | Ruby's grandmother died and Ruby had a second child, by Otis, the younger brother of Ruby's best friend, Willa Mae. Ruby remained living with Augusta, Augusta's boyfriend, Ruby's maternal uncle, and her daughters. |
| 18 | Ruby fought with Augusta and she and Otis moved into an apartment with her two daughters. Ruby's first daughter's father died. Otis stayed with Ruby and her daughters in the apartment. |
| 19 | Ruby broke up with Otis. Ruby and her two daughters joined Magnolia, Magnolia's "husband," and her ten half-siblings. Ruby had a miscarriage. |
| 19½ | Ruby left town and moved out of state with her new boyfriend, Earl. She left her daughters with Magnolia and remained out of state for a year. Magnolia then insisted she return home and take care of her children. |
| 20½ | Ruby and her daughters moved into a large house rented by Augusta and her mother's brother. It was located next door to Magnolia's house, where Ruby and her children ate. Ruby cleaned for her aunt and uncle, and gave birth to another child, by Otis, who had returned to the household. |
| 21 | Ruby and Otis broke up once again. She found a house and moved there with her daughters, Augusta, and Augusta's boyfriend. Ruby did the cleaning, and Augusta cooked. Ruby and Magnolia, who now lived across town, shared child care, and Ruby's cousin's daughter stayed with Ruby. |
| 21½ | Augusta and her boyfriend have moved out because they were all fighting, and the two of them wanted to get away from the noise of the children. Ruby has a new boyfriend. |

A look in detail at the domestic network of Ruby's parents, Magnolia and Calvin Waters, illustrates the complexity of the typical network and also shows kin constructs at work both in the recruitment of individuals to the network and in the changing composition of households within the network, over less than three months [Table 2].

These examples do indeed indicate the important role of the Black woman in the domestic structure. But the cooperation between male and female siblings who share the same household or live near one another has been underestimated by those who have isolated the female-headed household as the most significant domestic unit among the urban Black poor. The close cooperation of adult siblings arises from the residential patterns typical of young adults (Stack, 1970). Owing to pov-

erty, young women with or without children do not perceive any choice but to remain living at home with their mothers or other adult female relatives. Even when young women are collecting welfare for their children, they say that their resources go further when they share food and exchange goods and services daily. Likewise, the jobless man, or the man working at a part-time or seasonal job, often remains living at home with his mother—or, if she is dead, with his sisters and brothers. This pattern continues long after such a man becomes a father and establishes a series of sexual partnerships with women, who are in turn living with their own kin or friends or are alone with their children. A result of this pattern is the striking fact that households almost always have men around: male relatives, affines, and boyfriends. These men are often intermit-

## TABLE 2

| HOUSEHOLD | DOMESTIC ARRANGEMENTS, APRIL 1969 | DOMESTIC ARRANGEMENTS, JUNE 1969 |
|---|---|---|
| 1 | Magnolia, her husband Calvin, their eight children (4–18). | Unchanged. |
| 2 | Magnolia's sister Augusta, Augusta's boyfriend, Ruby, Ruby's children, Ruby's boyfriend Otis. | Augusta and boyfriend have moved to #3 after a quarrel with Ruby. Ruby and Otis remain in #2. |
| 3 | Billy (Augusta's closest friend), Billy's children, Lazar (Magnolia's sister Carrie's husband, living in the basement), Carrie (from time to time—she is an alcoholic). | Augusta and boyfriend have moved to a small, one-room apartment upstairs from Billy. |
| 4 | Magnolia's sister Lydia, Lydia's daughters Georgia and Lottie, Lydia's boyfriend, Lottie's daughter. | Lottie and her daughter have moved to an apartment down the street, joining Lottie's girl friend and child. Georgia has moved in with her boyfriend. Lydia's son has moved back into Lydia's home #4. |
| 5 | Ruby's friend Willa Mae, her husband and son, her sister, and her brother James (father of Ruby's daughter). | James has moved in with his girl friend, who lives with her sister; James keeps most of his clothes in household #5. James's brother has returned from the army and moved into #5. |
| 6 | Eloise (Magnolia's first son's father's sister), her husband, their four young children, their daughter and her son, Eloise's friend Jessie's brother's daughter and her child. | Unchanged. |
| 7 | Violet (wife of Calvin's closest friend Cecil, now dead several years), her two sons, her daughter Odessa, and Odessa's four children. | Odessa's son Raymond has fathered Clover's baby. Clover and baby have joined household #7. |

tent members of the households, boarders, or friends who come and go—men who usually eat, and sometimes sleep, in these households. Children have constant and close contact with these men, and especially in the case of male relatives, these relationships last over the years. The most predictable residential pattern in The Flats is that individuals reside in the households of their natal kin, or the households of those who raised them, long into their adult years.

Welfare workers, researchers, and landlords in Black ghetto communities have long known that the residence patterns of the poor change frequently and that females play a dominant domestic role. What is much less understood is the relationship between household composition and domestic organization in these communities. Household boundaries are elastic, and no one model of a household, such as the nuclear family, extended family, or matrifocal family, is the norm. What is

crucial and enduring is the strength of ties within a kin network; the maintenance of a strong network in turn has consequences for the relationships between the members themselves, as demonstrated in the following discussion of relationships between mothers and fathers and between fathers and their children.

## Mothers and Fathers

Notwithstanding the emptiness and hopelessness of the job experience in the Black community, men and women fall in love and wager buoyant new relationships against the inexorable forces of poverty and racism. At the same time, in dealing with everyday life, Black women and men have developed a number of attitudes and strategies that appear to militate against the formation of long-term relationships. Even when a man and woman set up temporary housekeeping arrangements, they both maintain primary social ties with their kin. If other members of a kin network view a particular relationship as a drain on the network's resources, they will act in various and subtle ways to break up the relationship. This is what happened in the life of Julia Ambrose, another resident of The Flats.

When I first met Julia, she was living with her baby, her cousin Teresa, and Teresa's "old man." After several fierce battles with Teresa over the bills, and because of Teresa's hostility toward Julia's boyfriends, Julia decided to move out. She told me she was head over heels in love with Elliot, her child's father, and they had decided to live together.

For several months Julia and Elliot shared a small apartment, and their relationship was strong. Elliot was very proud of his baby. On weekends he would spend an entire day carrying the baby around to his sister's home, where he would show it to his friends on the street. Julia, exhilarated by her independence in having her own place, took great care of the house and her baby. She told me, "Before Elliot came home from work I would have his dinner fixed and the house and kid clean. When he came home he would take his shower and then I'd bring his food to the bed. I'd put the kid to sleep and then get into bed with him. It was fine. We would get a little piece and then go to sleep. In the morning we'd do the same thing."

After five months, Elliot was laid off from his job at a factory that hires seasonal help. He couldn't find another job, except part-time work for a cab company. Elliot began spending more time away from the house with his friends at the local tavern, and less time with Julia and the baby. Julia finally had to get back "on aid" and Elliot put more of his things back in his sister's home so the social worker wouldn't know he was staying with Julia. Julia noticed changes in Elliot. "If you start necking and doing the same thing that you've been doing with your man, and he don't want it, you know for sure that he is messing with someone else, or don't want you anymore. Maybe Elliot didn't want me in the first place, but maybe he did 'cause he chased me a lot. He wanted me and he didn't want me. I really loved him, but I'm not in love with him now. My feelings just changed. I'm not in love with no man, really. Just out for what I can get from them."

Julia and Elliot stayed together, but she began to hear rumors about him. Her cousin, a woman who had often expressed jealousy toward Julia, followed Elliot in a car and told her that Elliot parked late at night outside the apartment house of his previous girl friend. Julia told me that her cousin was "nothing but a gossip, a newspaper who carried news back and forth," and that her cousin was envious of her having an "old man." Nevertheless, Julia believed the gossip.

After hearing other rumors and gossip about Elliot, Julia said, "I still really liked him, but I wasn't going to let him get the upper hand on me. After I found out that he was messing with someone else, I said to myself, I was doing it too, so what's the help in making a fuss. But after that, I made him pay for being with me!

"I was getting a check every month for rent from welfare and I would take the money and buy me clothes. I bought my own wardrobe and I gave my mother money for keeping the baby while I was working. I worked here and there while I was on aid and they were paying my rent. I didn't really need Elliot, but that was extra money for me. When he asked me what happened to my check I told him I got off and couldn't get back on. My mother knew. She didn't care what I did so long as I didn't let Elliot make an ass out of me. The point is a woman has to have her own pride. She can't let a man rule her. You can't let a man kick you in the tail and tell you what to do. Anytime I can make an ass out of a man, I'm going to do it. If he's doing the same to me, then I'll quit him and leave him alone."

After Elliot lost his job, and kin continued to bring gossip to Julia about how he was playing around with other women, Julia became embittered toward Elliot and was anxious to hurt him. There had been a young Black man making deliveries for a local store who would pass her house every day, and flirt with her. Charles would slow down his truck and honk for Julia when he passed the house. Soon she started running out to talk to him in his truck and decided to "go" with him. Charles liked Julia and brought nice things for her child.

"I put Elliot in a trick," Julia told me soon after she stopped going with Charles. "I knew that Elliot didn't care nothing for me, so I made him jealous.

He was nice to the kids, both of them, but he didn't do nothing to show me he was still in love with me. Me and Elliot fought a lot. One night Charles and me went to a motel room and stayed there all night. Mama had the babies. She got mad. But I was trying to hurt Elliot. When I got home, me and Elliot got into it. He called me all kinds of names. I said he might as well leave. But Elliot said he wasn't going nowhere. So he stayed and we'd sleep together, but we didn't do nothing. Then one night something happened. I got pregnant again by Elliot. After I got pregnant, me and Charles quit, and I moved in with a girl friend for a while. Elliot chased after me and we started going back together, but we stayed separate. In my sixth month I moved back in my mother's home with her husband and the kids."

Many young women like Julia feel strongly that they cannot let a man make a fool out of them, and they react quickly and boldly to rumor, gossip, and talk that hurts them. The power that gossip and information have in constraining the duration of sexual relationships is an important cultural phenomenon. But the most important single factor affecting interpersonal relationships between men and women in The Flats is unemployment. The futility of the job experience for street-corner men in a Black community is sensitively portrayed by Elliot Liebow in *Tally's Corner*. As Liebow (1967:63) writes, "The job fails the man and the man fails the job." Liebow's discussion (p. 142) of men and jobs leads directly to his analysis of the street-corner male's exploitive relationships with women: "Men not only present themselves as economic exploiters of women but they expect other men to do the same." Ghetto-specific male roles that men try to live up to at home and on the street, and their alleged round-the-clock involvement in peer groups, are interpreted in *Soulside* (Hannerz, 1969) as a threat to marital stability.

Losing a job, then, or being unemployed month after month debilitates one's self-importance and independence and, for men, necessitates sacrificing a role in the economic support of their families. Faced with these familiar patterns in the behavior and status of men, women call upon life experiences in The Flats to guide them. When a man loses his job, that is the time he is most likely to begin "messing around."

And so that no man appears to have made a fool of them, women respond with vengeance, out of pride and self-defense. Another young woman in The Flats, Ivy Rodgers, told me about the time she left her two children in The Flats with her mother and took off for Indiana with Jimmy River, a young man she had fallen in love with "the first sight I seen." Jimmy asked Ivy to go to Gary, Indiana, where his family lived. "I just left the kids with my mama. I didn't even tell her I was going. My checks kept coming so she had food for the kids, but I didn't know he let his people tell him what to do. While he was in Gary, Jimmy started messing with another woman. He said he wasn't, but I caught him. I quit him, but when he told me he wasn't messing, I loved him so much I took him back. Then I got to thinking about it. I had slipped somewhere. I had let myself go. Seems like I forgot that I wasn't going to let Jimmy or any man make an ass out of me. But he sure was doing it. I told Jimmy that if he loved me, he would go and see my people, take them things, and tell them we were getting married. Jimmy didn't want to go back to The Flats, but I tricked him and told him I really wanted to visit. I picked out my ring and Jimmy paid thirty dollars on it and I had him buy my outfit that we was getting married in. He went along with it. What's so funny was when we come here and he said to me, 'You ready to go back?' and I told him, 'No, I'm not going back. I never will marry you.'"

Forms of social control in the larger society also work against successful marriages in The Flats. In fact, couples rarely chance marriage unless a man has a job; often the job is temporary, low-paying, and insecure, and the worker is arbitrarily laid off whenever he is not needed. Women come to realize that welfare benefits and ties within kin networks provide greater security for them and their children. In addition, caretaker agencies such as public welfare are insensitive to individual attempts for social mobility. A woman may be immediately cut off the welfare rolls when a husband returns home from prison or the army, or if she gets married. Unless there is either a significant change in employment opportunities for the urban poor or a livable guaranteed minimum income, it is unlikely that urban low-income Blacks will form lasting conjugal units.

Marriage and its accompanying expectations of a home, a job, and a family built around the husband and wife have come to stand for an individual's desire to break out of poverty. It implies the willingness of an individual to remove himself from the daily obligations of his kin network. People in The Flats recognize that one cannot simultaneously meet kin expectations and the expectations of a spouse. Cooperating kinsmen continually attempt to draw new people into their personal network; but at the same time they fear the loss of a central, resourceful member in the network. The following passages are taken from the detailed residence life history of Ruby Banks. Details of her story were substantiated by discussions with her mother, her aunt, her daughter's father, and her sister.

"Me and Otis could be married, but they all ruined that. Aunt Augusta told Magnolia that he was no good. Magnolia was the fault of it, too. They don't want to see me married! Magnolia knows that it be money getting away from her. I couldn't spend the time with her and the kids and be giving her the money that I do now. I'd have my husband to look after. I couldn't go where she want me to go. I couldn't come every time she call me, like if Calvin took sick or the kids took sick, or if she took sick. That's all the running I do now. I couldn't do that. You think a man would put up with as many times as I go over her house in a cab, giving half my money to her all the time? That's the reason they don't want me married. You think a man would let Aunt Augusta come into the house and take food out of the icebox from his kids? They thought that way ever since I came up.

"They broke me and Otis up. They kept telling me that he didn't want me, and that he didn't want the responsibility. I put him out and I cried all night long. And I really did love him. But Aunt Augusta and others kept fussing and arguing so I went and quit him. I would have got married a long time ago to my first baby's daddy, but Aunt Augusta was the cause of that, telling Magnolia that he was too old for me. She's been jealous of me since the day I was born.

"Three years after Otis I met Earl. Earl said he was going to help pay for the utilities. He was going to get me some curtains and pay on my couch. While Earl was working he was so good to me and my children that Magnolia and them started worrying all over again. They sure don't want me married. The same thing that happened to Otis happened to many of my boyfriends. And I ain't had that many men. I'm tired of them bothering me with their problems when I'm trying to solve my own problems. They tell me that Earl's doing this and that, seeing some girl.

"They look for trouble to tell me every single day. If I ever marry, I ain't listening to what nobody say. I just listen to what he say. You have to get along the best way you know how, and forget about your people. If I got married they would talk, like they are doing now, saying, 'He ain't no good, he's been creeping on you. I told you once not to marry him. You'll end up right back on aid.' If I ever get married, I'm leaving town!"

Ruby's account reveals the strong conflict between kin-based domestic units and lasting ties between husbands and wives. When a mother in The Flats has a relationship with an economically nonproductive man, the relationship saps the resources of others in her domestic network. Participants in the network act to break up such relationships, to maintain kin-based household groupings over the life cycle, in order to maximize potential resources and the services they hope to exchange. Similarly, a man's participation is expected in his kin network, and it is understood that he should not dissipate his services and finances to a sexual or marital relationship. These forms of social control made Ruby afraid to take the risks necessary to break out of the cycle of poverty. Instead, she chose the security and stability of her kin group. Ruby, recognizing that to make a marriage last she would have to move far away from her kin, exclaimed, "If I ever get married, I'm leaving town!" While this study was in progress, Ruby did get married, and she left the state with her husband and her youngest child that very evening.

## Fathers and Children

People in The Flats show pride in all their kin, and particularly new babies born into their kinship networks. Mothers encourage sons to have babies, and even more important, men coax their "old ladies" to have their babies. The value placed on children, the love, attention, and affection children receive from women and men, and the web of social relationships spun from the birth of a child are all basic to the high birthrate among the poor.

The pride that kinsmen take in the children of their sons and brothers is seen best in the pleasure that the mothers and sisters of these men express. Such pride was apparent during a visit I made to Alberta Cox's home. She introduced me to her nineteen-year-old son Nate and added immediately, "He's a daddy and his baby is four months old." Then she pointed to her twenty-two-year-old son Mac and said, "He's a daddy three times over." Mac smiled and said, "I'm no daddy," and his friend in the kitchen said, "Maybe going on four times, Mac." Alberta said, "Yes you are. Admit it, boy!" At that point Mac's grandmother rolled back in her rocker and said, "I'm a grandmother many times over, and it make me proud." A friend of Alberta's told me later that Alberta wants her sons to have babies because she thinks it will make them more responsible. Although she usually dislikes the women her sons go with, claiming they are "no-good trash," Alberta accepts the babies and asks to care for them whenever she has a chance.

Although Blacks, like most Americans, acquire kin through their mothers and fathers, the economic insecurity of the Black male and the availability of welfare to the mother–child unit make it very difficult for an unemployed Black husband-father to compete with a woman's kin for authority and control over her children. As we have seen women seek to be independent, but also, in order to meet everyday needs, they act to strengthen their ties with their kin and within their domestic network. Though these two strategies, especially in the context of male joblessness, may lead to the breakup of a young couple, a father will maintain his ties with his children. The husband-father role may be limited, but, contrary to the stereotype of Black family life, it is not only viable but culturally significant.

Very few young couples enter into a legal marriage in The Flats, but a father and his kin can sustain a continuing relationship with the father's children if the father has acknowledged paternity, if his kin have activated their claims on the child, and if the mother has drawn these people into her personal network. Widely popularized and highly misleading statistics on female-headed households have contributed to the assumption that Black children derive nothing of sociological importance from their fathers. To the contrary, in my recent study of domestic life among the poor in a Black community in the Midwest (Stack, 1972), I found that 70 percent of the fathers of 1,000 children on welfare recognized their children and provided them with kinship affiliations. But because many of these men have little or no access to steady and productive employment, out of the 699 who acknowledged paternity, only 84 (12 percent) gave any substantial financial support to their children. People in The Flats believe a father should help his child, but they know that the mother cannot count on his help. Community expectations of fathers do not generally include the father's *duties* in relation to a child; they do, however, assume the responsibilities of the father's kin. Kinship through males in The Flats is reckoned through a chain of acknowledged genitors, but social fatherhood is shared by the genitor with his kin, and with the mother's husband or with her boyfriends.

Although the authority of a father over his genealogical children or his wife's other children is limited, neither the father's interest in his child nor the desire of his kin to help raise the child strains the stability of the domestic network. Otis's kin were drawn into Ruby's personal network through his claims on her children, and through the long, close friendship between Ruby and Otis's sister, Willa Mae. Like many fathers in The Flats, Otis maintained close contact with his children, and provided goods and care for them even when he and Ruby were not on speaking terms. One time when Otis and Ruby separated, Otis stayed in a room in Ruby's uncle's house next door to Ruby's mother's house. At that time Ruby's children were being kept by Magnolia each day while Ruby went to school to finish working toward her high school diploma. Otis was out of work, and he stayed with Ruby's uncle over six months helping Magnolia care for his children. Otis's kin were proud of the daddy he was, and at times suggested they should take over the raising of

Otis and Ruby's children. Ruby and other mothers know well that those people you count on to share in the care and nurturing of your children are also those who are rightfully in a position to judge and check upon how you carry out the duties of a mother. Shared responsibilities of motherhood in The Flats imply both a help and a check on how one assumes the parental role.

Fathers like Otis, dedicated to maintaining ties with their children, learn that the relationship they create with their child's mother largely determines the role they may assume in their child's life. Jealousy between men makes it extremely difficult for fathers to spend time with their children if the mother has a boyfriend, but as Otis said to me, "When Ruby doesn't have any old man then she starts calling on me, asking for help, and telling me to do something for my kids." Between such times, when a man or a woman does not have an ongoing sexual relationship, some mothers call upon the fathers of their children and temporarily "choke" these men with their personal needs and the needs of the children. At these times, men and women reinforce their fragile but continuing relationship, and find themselves empathetic friends who can be helpful to one another.

A mother generally regards her children's father as a friend of the family whom she can recruit for help, rather than as a father failing his parental duties. Although fathers voluntarily help out with their children, many fathers cannot be depended upon as a steady source of help. Claudia Williams talked to me about Harold, the father of her two children. "Some days he be coming over at night saying, 'I'll see to the babies and you can lay down and rest, honey,' treating me real nice. Then maybe I don't even see him for two or three months. There's no sense nagging Harold. I just treat him as some kind of friend even if he is the father of my babies." Since Claudia gave birth to Harold's children, both of them have been involved in other relationships. When either of them is involved with someone else, this effectively cuts Harold off from his children. Claudia says, "My kids don't need their daddy's help, but if he helps out then I help him out, too. My kids are well behaved, and I know they make Harold's kinfolk proud."

## Conclusions

The view of Black women as represented in their own words and life histories coincides with that presented by Joyce Ladner: "One of the chief characteristics defining the Black woman is her [realistic approach] to her [own] resources. Instead of becoming resigned to her fate, she has always sought creative solutions to her problems. The ability to utilize her existing resources and yet maintain a forthright determination to struggle against the racist society in whatever overt and subtle ways necessary is one of her major attributes" (Ladner, 1971:276–77).

I have particularly emphasized those strategies that women can employ to maximize their independence, acquire and maintain domestic authority, limit (but positively evaluate) the role of husband and father, and strengthen ties with kin. The last of these—maximizing relationships in the domestic network—helps to account for patterns of Black family life among the urban poor more adequately than the concepts of nuclear or matrifocal family. When economic resources are greatly limited, people need help from as many others as possible. This requires expanding their kin networks—increasing the number of people they hope to be able to count on. On the one hand, female members of a network may act to break up a relationship that has become a drain on their resources. On the other, a man is expected to contribute to his own kin network, and it is assumed that he should not dissipate his services and finances to a marital relationship. At the same time, a woman will continue to seek aid from the man who has fathered her children, thus building up her own network's resources. She also expects something of his kin, especially his mother and sisters. Women continually activate these lines to bring kin and friends into the network of exchange and obligation. Most often, the biological father's female relatives are also poor and also try to expand their network and increase the number of people they can depend on.

Clearly, economic pressures among cooperating kinsmen in the Black community work against the loss of either males or females—through marriage or other long-term relationships—from the kin network. The kin-based cooperative network represents the collective adaptations to poverty of the men, women, and children within the Black community. Loyalties and dependencies toward kinsmen offset the ordeal of unemployment and racism. To cope with the everyday demands of

ghetto life, these networks have evolved patterns of co-residence, elastic household boundaries; life-long, if intermittent, bonds to three-generation households; social constraints on the role of the husband-father within the mother's domestic group; and the domestic authority of women.

---

[1]*This work is based on a recent urban anthropological study of poverty and domestic life of urban-born Black Americans who were raised on public welfare and whose parents had migrated from the South to a single community in the urban North (Stack, 1972). Now adults in their twenties to forties, they are raising their own children on welfare in The Flats. All personal and place names in this paper are fictitious.*

---

# References

Abrahams, Roger
1963 *Deep Down in the Jungle*. Hatboro, Pa.

Bernard, Jessie
1966 *Marriage and Family among Negroes*. Englewood Cliffs, N.J.

Buchler, Ira R., and Henry A. Selby
1968 *Kinship and Social Organization: An Introduction to Theory and Method*. New York.

Fortes, Meyer
1958 "Introduction." In *The Developmental Cycle in Domestic Groups*, Jack Goody, ed. Cambridge, England.

Gonzalez, Nancie
1965 "The Consanguineal Household and Matrifocality." *American Anthropologist* 67:1541–1549.

1969 *Black Carib Household Structure: A Study of Migration and Modernization*. Seattle.

1970 "Toward a Definition of Matrifocality." In *Afro-American Anthropology: Contemporary Perspectives*, N. E. Whitten and J. F. Szwed, eds. New York.

Hannerz, Ulf
1969 *Soulside: Inquiries into Ghetto Culture and Community*. New York.

Ladner, Joyce
1971 *Tomorrow's Tomorrow: The Black Woman*. Garden City, N.Y.

Liebow, Elliot
1967 *Tally's Corner*. Boston.

Moynihan, Daniel Patrick
1965 *The Negro Family: The Case for National Action*. Washington, D.C.

Otterbein, Keith F.
1970 "The Development Cycle of the Andros Household: A Diachronic Analysis." *American Anthropologist* 72:1412–1419.

Rainwater, Lee
1966 "Crucible of Identity: The Negro Lower-Class Family." *Daedalus* 95 (2):172–216.

Smith, Raymond T.
1970 "The Nuclear Family in Afro-American Kinship." *Journal of Comparative Family Studies* 1 (1):55–70.

Stack, Carol B.
1970 "The Kindred of Viola Jackson: Residence and Family Organization of an Urban Black American Family." In *Afro-American Anthropology: Contemporary Perspectives*, N. E. Whitten and J. F. Szwed, eds. New York.

1972 "Black Kindreds: Parenthood and Personal Kindreds Among Blacks Supported by Welfare." *Journal of Comparative Family Studies* 3 (2): 194–206.

1974 *All Our Kin: Strategies for Survival in a Black Community*. New York.

Valentine, Charles
1970 "Blackston: Progress Report on a Community Study in Urban Afro-America." Mimeo. Washington University, St. Louis.

# THE "FLIP-SIDE" OF BLACK FAMILIES HEADED BY WOMEN:
## The Economic Status of Black Men

### *The Center for the Study of Social Policy*

*This paper notes that parallel with the increase in single-parent Black families has been a deterioration in the economic status of Black men. Recent figures show that only 55 percent of Black men are currently in the labor force; the remainder are unemployed, discouraged and not seeking work, in correctional facilities, or unaccounted for.*

In both 1960 and 1982, the median income of black families was 55 percent that of white families. One quick conclusion is that black Americans have made little or no relative economic progress in the past two decades. But such gross numbers mask a complex phenomenon: the changing structure of black families. The rising number of black families headed by women has hindered the economic progress of black Americans.

All this is fairly common knowledge. But still the numbers are worth recalling (see Table 1):

1. Since 1960, the number of black families headed by women has more than tripled.
2. 49 percent of all black families with children are headed by women (the comparable figure for whites is 15 percent).
3. The median income of black female-headed families is less than one-third the national median.
4. More than 60 percent of black female-headed families with children live in poverty.

The economic status of black Americans is perhaps best assessed as a dual phenomenon, divided by family type. For example, while the poverty rate among black married-couple families has dropped dramatically from more than 50 percent in 1959 to 20 percent in 1982, the poverty rate among black female-headed families has only dropped from 70 percent to 59 percent. Similarly, since 1968 the median income for black married-couple families has risen 11 percent (in constant dollars), while the median income for black female-headed families has fallen by 14 percent. This dichotomy is manifest in the changing composition of the poverty population. In 1959, less than 30 percent of all blacks in poverty lived in female-headed families; today, more than 67 percent of all poor blacks live in such families (see Figure 1).

The real victims in the erosion of the black family are children. Today, of the 4.6 million black children growing up without a father, 3.3 million live in poverty (see Figure 2). With poverty often comes poor nutrition, poor health, low academic achievement, and high unemployment.

Most commentators stop with the family composition explanation of the black/white income disparity. In doing so, however, they neglect a prior and equally perplexing question: why the boom in black female-headed families? In response to that question, this paper sketches a hypothesis: that the increase in black female-headed families is linked to equally noteworthy and startling trends in the

The Center for the Study of Social Policy, April 1984. Reprinted by permission. Footnotes and tables have been renumbered. This work was supported by the Field Foundation.

### TABLE 1    Black Female-Headed Families, 1960–1990

| | BLACK FEMALE-HEADED FAMILIES | | CHILDREN IN BLACK FEMALE-HEADED FAMILIES | |
| YEAR | Total (1,000's) | Percent of Black Families | Total (1,000's) | In Poverty (1,000's) |
|---|---|---|---|---|
| 1960 | 889 | 20.9 | 1,808 | 1,475 |
| 1965 | 1,125 | 23.7 | 2,751 | 2,107 |
| 1970 | 1,382 | 28.3 | 3,520 | 2,383 |
| 1975 | 1,940 | 35.3 | 4,127 | 2,724 |
| 1980 | 2,495 | 40.3 | 4,543 | 2,944 |
| 1983 | 2,734 | 41.9 | 4,624 | 3,269 |
| 1990 (projected) | 3,531 | 48.3 | 5,979 | — |

Source: U.S. Bureau of the Census. Projections based on percentage trends from 1960–1983 and Census projections of black population. Projections of children based on 1983 average family size.

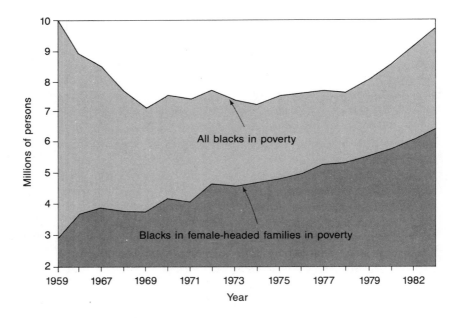

**FIGURE 1** Trends in Black Poverty, 1960–1982

economic and social status of black males. The plight of black men is the other, virtually unnoticed, side of the troubling increase in single-parent black families. Simply put, the economic status of many black men is deteriorating.

It is axiomatic that unemployment among blacks is twice the national rate. Moreover, in hard times, employed blacks are laid off earlier and rehired later. Thus, even in the midst of [the 1983] recovery when national unemployment was 9 percent, unemployment among blacks was 19 percent; 1.4 million black men could not find work.

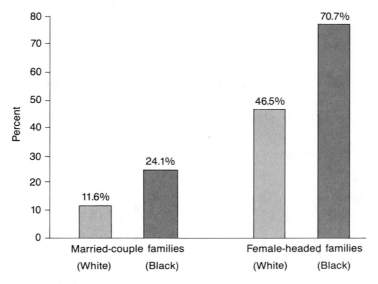

**FIGURE 2  Poverty Rates among Children, 1982
(by Race and Family Type)**

But unemployment is only part of the story. Unemployment rates reflect only the status of persons "in the labor force." In addition, there are millions of persons who, for various reasons, are not looking for work. Among black men, some are full-time students, some are physically disabled, a few are needed in the home, and some are simply discouraged workers who have stopped looking for work after repeated failures. Twenty percent of all working-age black men—nearly two million persons—were out of the labor force in 1982. For more detailed analysis of those out of the labor force and sources for these data, see Table 2. This dropout is a recent phenomenon: since 1960, the number of black men out of the labor force has more than tripled (see Table 3).

The combination of unemployment and labor force data more accurately reflects the status of black men than either gauge taken alone. In 1960, nearly three-quarters of all black men included in Census data were working; today, only 55 percent are working.

The picture gets even worse. There are an estimated 925,000 working-age black men whose labor force status cannot be determined because they are missed in the Census. This "undercount" in the Census is most severe among black men,

amounting to more than 10 percent among working-age black men, compared to less than one percent for working-age white men. (See Table 2 for a more detailed discussion of the undercount.)

The cumulative impact of these measures—unemployment, labor force participation, and the "missing" black men—is startling. For each black man we count as unemployed, another two are out of the labor force. Figure 3 shows the labor force status of black men age 16–64: 4 million out of the 8.8 million working-age black men, or 46 percent, are without jobs; i.e., they are either unemployed, out of the labor force, in correctional facilities, or unaccounted for. These data are even more noteworthy when juxtaposed with comparable data for white men. In 1982, while 78 percent of all working-age white men were employed, only 54 percent of all working-age black men had jobs.

Looking at this another way, the percent of working-age black men who are unemployed, discouraged workers, or unaccounted for is almost three times that for white men. Thirty percent of all working-age black men are in these categories, compared to only 11 percent of working-age white men.

The importance of these figures lies in the link between the economic alienation of black men and the erosion of the black family. Graphing the

## TABLE 2  Where Black and White Men Are (1982) (Sources for Figure 3)

### TOTAL WORKING-AGE MALE POPULATION

*Statistical Abstract of the United States, 1984*, Table 33, page 33. The 1982 figures for males 65–74 and 75 and over were subtracted from the number of males 16 years and over. There were 7,998,000 black men 16–64 in 1982 and 63,774,000 white men. In addition, the publication *Coverage of the National Population in the 1980 Census by Age, Sex, and Race*, U.S. Bureau of the Census, Current Population Reports (CPR), P-23, No. 115, Table 3, shows that there were an estimated 824,000 black men age 15–64 who were not counted in the 1980 Census and an "overcount" of 114,000 white males age 16–64. This brings the universe of black males 16–64 to 8.8 million (7,998,000 plus 824,000) and the universe of white males 16–64 to 63.7 million.

### ARMED FORCES

*Statistical Abstract of the United States, 1984*, Tables 574 and 577, pages 353 and 354. Because 25 percent of all armed service personnel are overseas, the number of military personnel on active duty was reduced by 25 percent to yield the number within the United States. Table 574, after this reduction, shows 273,000 black men and 1,033,000 white men. These figures are not broken down by age, but they, by definition, include few if any men under age 16 or over age 64.

### EMPLOYED, UNEMPLOYED, AND NOT IN LABOR FORCE

#### Employed

Data about the employed, unemployed, and those not in the labor force are annual averages of monthly figures for 1982. *Employment and Earnings, January 1982* (Bureau of Labor Statistics, U.S. Department of Labor) shows 4,515,000 black males age 16–64 and 48,663,000 white males ages 16–64 employed in the civilian labor force.

#### Unemployed

*Employment and Earnings* shows 1,155,000 black men age 16–64 and 4,793,000 white men age 16–64 unemployed in 1982.

#### Not in the Labor Force

*Employment and Earnings* shows 1,769,000 black men age 16–64 and 8,389,000 white men age 16–64 not in the labor force in 1982.

A further breakdown of the reasons black and white men 16–64 are out of the labor force is found in quarterly Bureau of Labor Statistics (BLS) data. The following detailed data are unpublished BLS data for the quarter January–March 1984:

| White Men 16–64 | | Reason Not in Labor Force | Black Men 16–64 | |
|---|---|---|---|---|
| 9,216,000 | | TOTAL | | 1,944,000 |
| 4,066,000 | (44%) | In school | (47%) | 908,000 |
| 1,495,000 | (16%) | Ill health | (15%) | 291,000 |
| 1,559,000 | (17%) | Retired | (8%) | 155,000 |
| 147,000 | (2%) | Needed at home | (2%) | 42,000 |
| 1,949,000 | (21%) | Other | (28%) | 548,000 |

It should be noted that the categories "in school" and "ill health" may actually include discouraged workers. In fact, 26 percent of black men and 17 percent of white men who were out of the labor force because they were in school wanted a job but did not have one. Similarly, of those out of the labor force because of ill health, 18 percent of black men and 17 percent of white men wanted a job.

### CORRECTIONAL INSTITUTIONS

*1980 Census of Population*, Detailed Population Characteristics, PC80–1–D1, Table 266 (forthcoming) shows 186,137 black men and 211,652 white men age 15–64 in correctional facilities in 1980.

### LABOR FORCE STATUS UNDETERMINED

This estimate is derived by the Census Bureau from the difference between an expected population taken from birth, death, immigration, and emigration records as well as other sources and the actual census counts obtained from the decennial census.

The omission rates were most severe for black men age 20–64. In 1980, the Census Bureau estimates that it undercounted the black male population age 35–54 by more than 15 percent, and those age 20–34 by 9.4 percent. In contrast, they undercounted white males age 35–54 by only 1.5 percent, and they actually overcounted white males age 20–34 by 1.3 percent.

Recognizing its high undercount among minority men between the ages of 20 and 50, the Census Bureau has conducted several special studies to determine some of the characteristics of these "missing" black males.[1]

One study used a "casual interview technique" in bars, restaurants, pool rooms, on street corners, park benches, and similar locations, and was concentrated in urban poverty areas since these were thought to be where the highest undercounts were. Some information was obtained in three central cities, but we still do not know where the unaccounted for men are nationwide.

In addition to the 824,000 black men not counted in the 1980 census, there are approximately another 101,000 black men not counted in the 1982 CPS data. This brings the total number of working-age black men whose labor force status cannot be determined to 925,000, or 10.5 percent of the total working age black male population. In addition to the 114,000 overcount of white men in the 1980 Census, there was an undercount of 684,000 white men in the 1982 CPS data, bringing the total undercount of white men 16–64 to 570,000, or less than one percent of the white male population age 16–64.

---

[1]See, for example, "Status of Men Missed in the Census," Special Labor Force Report 117, U.S. Department of Labor, Bureau of Labor Statistics, 1982.

TABLE 3   Selected Unemployment and Labor Force Data, 1960–1982[1]

| | MALE UNEMPLOYMENT | | Black Men Unemployed (in Millions) | Black Men Out of Labor Force (in Millions) | Black Men Unemployed Plus Out of Labor Force (in Millions) |
|---|---|---|---|---|---|
| Year | White Rate | Black Rate | | | |
| 1960 | 4.8% | 10.7% | 0.45 | 0.86 | 1.31 |
| 1965 | 3.6 | 7.4 | 0.32 | 1.13 | 1.45 |
| 1970 | 4.0 | 7.3 | 0.34 | 1.43 | 1.77 |
| 1975 | 7.2 | 13.6 | 0.74 | 2.04 | 2.78 |
| 1980 | 6.1 | 13.2 | 0.82 | 2.33 | 3.15 |
| 1982 | 8.8 | 20.1 | 1.17 | 2.48 | 3.65 |

[1]Data are for all men 16 and older (not only 16–64).
Source: Bureau of Labor Statistics. 1960, 1965, and 1970 data are
estimates based on data for black and other races.

percentage of black men out of the labor force or unemployed and the percentage of black families headed by women yields two roughly parallel lines (see Figure 4). [Just from 1977 to 1983,] the number of black families headed by women [rose] by 700,000 and the ranks of black men out of the labor force or unemployed . . . increased by the same number.

The rise in black families headed by women is the result of multiple forces, and these data suggest that the increase is due at least in part to the increasing economic anomie of black men. If 46 percent of all black men are jobless—either unemployed, not looking for work, in correctional facilities, or unaccounted for—it is little wonder that an increasing number of black women are raising families alone.

These data on black men suggest that researchers may be treating the symptoms of poverty rather than the ailment. Current research emphasizes unwed mothers and income programs for female-headed families. At the very least, one can neither fully understand nor slow the growth of female-headed families without first assessing the deteriorating status of black men.

These data support a hypothesis that the erosion of the black family is not necessarily a mystical cultural trend but a palpable economic event. The boom in black families headed by women is not the simple result of the "welfare curse," pervasive and invidious discrimination, or changing sexual mores. Instead, the problem lies in an intricate economic and social dynamic. The anomie of black men is the upshot of subtle social and economic cues which we have barely begun to decipher.

These brief data on the status of black men are far from sufficient to explain the economic differentials between blacks and whites. In fact, they provoke many more questions. The dimensions of the social attrition of black men demand a diagnostic study of their status: Where are these men: homeless? part of an underground economy? How have they dropped out of the mainstream economy? How does their attrition affect black women and children?

One area for more immediate action is employment policies. Detailed labor force data by age illustrate the process of economic alienation. High unemployment among black teenagers leads to decreased labor force participation among black men in their 20's which leads to high Census undercounts among black men in their 30's.

Clearly, new measures must be developed to encourage those out of the labor force to re-enter the economy. More importantly, youth training and employment programs must be strengthened and reshaped with a new urgency that recognizes this process of alienation. Youth employment is not only

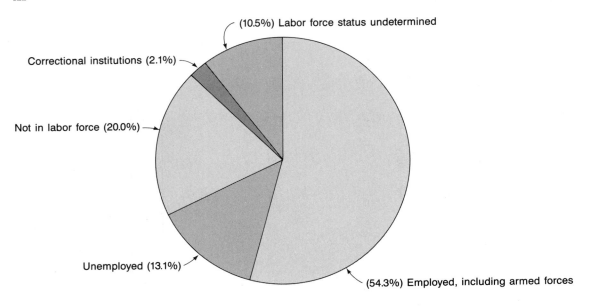

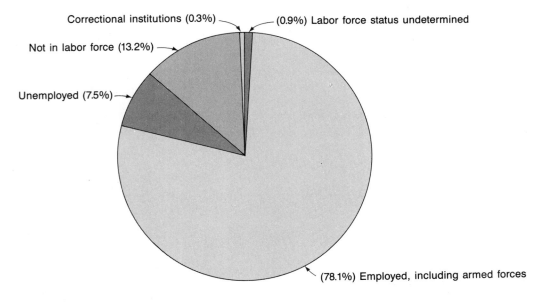

**FIGURE 3b  White Men: Where They Are (1982)**
**(Age 16–64; Total 63.7 Million)**

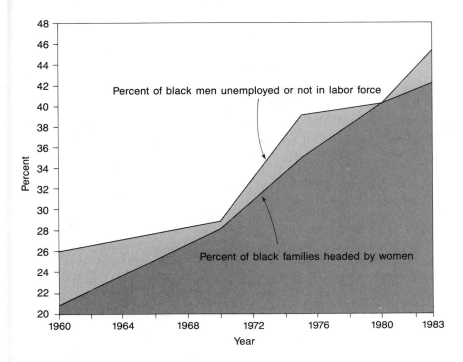

**FIGURE 4  Trends in Black Families, 1960–1983**
Source: U.S. Bureau of the Census, Bureau of Labor Statistics, 1983.

an end in itself but as well a means to preventing the economic attrition of black men and improving the structure and economic status of black families.

The plight of black men is of critical importance because of the enormous number of black children growing up in poverty today. If we are to stem the tide of female-headed families and the attendant rise of poverty, we must begin to investigate the social attrition of America's black men.

The persistent alienation and attrition of black men constitutes a formidable challenge to both researchers and policymakers, a challenge that is only now beginning to be recognized. How to study, understand, and eventually respond to this phenomenon are fresh and troubling issues. But they are, as well, critical issues, for the human costs of the continued erosion of the black family are socially, politically, and morally unacceptable.

Given the bleak prospects for narrowing the income gap between single-parent and two-parent families, questions surrounding the economic and social status of black men are at the heart of a fundamental social problem. Past efforts to remedy this problem have been entirely inadequate, and we are now witnessing the consequences of our failures. The attrition of black men from the labor force may be the result of institutional discrimination, weak affirmative action policies, ineffective youth employment programs, lack of quality education, changing sexual mores and many other economic and cultural forces.

Clearly, the problem pervades the fabric of our society and economy and requires an attack on all fronts. Neither a single commission nor a discrete piece of legislation will suffice as a response. The continued erosion of the black family should be a national priority that is addressed through decisive action initiated at all levels of government.

# 5 / Male/Female Relationships: Single and Married

## THE BLACK MALE'S ACCEPTANCE OF THE PRINCE CHARMING IDEAL

*Clyde W. Franklin II · Walter Pillow*

*The Prince Charming ideal is the other half of the Cinderella complex, which encourages women to repress full use of their minds and creativity and to become dependent upon others. The Prince Charming ideal holds that becoming a mature man means assuming a protective, condescending, patriarchal role toward one's female mate and toward women in general. The authors differentiate between internalization of the Prince Charming ideal and acting in accordance with it. They develop a model of these differences and discuss the implications for male–female relationships.*

Jeanne Noble's *Beautiful Also Are the Souls of My Black Sisters* and Colette Dowling's *The Cinderella Complex* serve as points of departure in this paper, which is devoted to an exploration of the Black male role and its effect on Black male–female social interaction (Dowling, 1981; Noble, 1978). The above books are provocative in that their theses propose two distinct, though related, empirical statements about male–female relationships in the United States. Of the two, Noble's book admittedly is more specific and more critical of Black men. She suggests that Black males have destructive, sexist attitudes. Dowling's work, which is oriented more toward sex role relationships in the United States generally, characterizes women as being engulfed in a destructive and debilitating fear of independence which is posited as the main reason for female subjugation in our society.

Noble's thesis implicitly blames Black men for negative social interaction between themselves and

From *Black Caucus* 13 (Spring 1982):3–7. © 1982 by the National Association of Black Social Workers. Reprinted by permission.

Black females. Dowling's thesis implies that a complex set of factors may be responsible for the state of Black male–female relationships. It is within the context of the latter thesis that we explore the role of the Black male and its effects on intersex social interaction.

Two important assumptions underlie our efforts. The first is that, despite Dowling's contention, which is based on Horner's studies indicating that Black females appear to be less fearful of independence than are white females *and* Black males, another observation might be more accurate. This is due to the fact that Horner's studies, which were conducted at the University of Michigan during the middle of the late 1960's, might be outdated. We suggest instead that present day Black women only *appear* to be more independent than are white women and Black men due to their historically imposed independent subsistence relative to the former. In actuality, Black females internalize values regarding not only their roles in society, but also those of Black males that are similar to the ones internalized by their white counterparts. The result is that Black females are just as emotionally dependent upon Black men as white women are on white men.

A second assumption is that Black men presently are socialized into the Prince Charming ideal *to the same extent* as are white males with one exception—they do not receive either the means or the societal support by which to approximate the ideal as do their white counterparts. Moreover, Black males oftentimes accede to the idea that Black females are independent, assertive, and so forth. Wallace's observations are instructive here:

> *Black men and women were separated, given conflicting roles, and the creation of various myths assured our nation would be disunified. One of the most harmful myths was . . . the idea of the Black matriarchy. The Black woman's role was defined in such an intentional manner as to emasculate our men and give them limited responsibility (Wallace, 1979:122).*

Because Black females actually *are* dependent upon Black males and many Black males' role responses are not congruent with Black female dependence, Black male–Black female social interaction suffers. The purpose of this paper, therefore, is *to explore factors within the Black male role which militate against fulfilling dependency needs in Black females*. These factors, we submit, are entrenched in *Black male responses to the "Prince Charming" ideal*—the role model for males to use in their relationships with females in the United States. This ideal, Black male responses to the ideal, and the implications of those responses to Black male–Black female relationships are the subject of this article.

## The Prince Charming Ideal

In the fairy tale, not only was there a Cinderella, but there was also a Prince Charming. Dowling's book concentrated on Cinderella; we focus our attention on Prince Charming—at least the "Prince Charming" ideal which is just as pervasive in the fantasies of Black men and Black women as it is in the fantasies of their white counterparts. Dowling defines the "Cinderella complex" as "a network of largely repressed attitudes toward the full use of their minds and creativity. . . . That psychological dependency—the deep wish to be taken care of by others—is the chief force holding women down today (Dowling, 1981:31).

While Dowling's thesis certainly is thought-provoking, we contend that more than the Cinderella complex holds women down today. More specifically, the Prince Charming ideal also contributes to the subordination of women in society. In fact, the authors contend that the Prince Charming ideal negatively affects the Black male in the performance of his role as he interacts with the Black female. The Prince Charming ideal may be defined as the *philosophical belief that being a responsible, mature male means the assumption of a protective, condescending, providing and generally patriarchal role regarding one's female mate and women in general*. Implicit in this definition is a denial of the ability of women to fend for themselves as well as all of the psychological implications of the philosophical stance. Goldberg describes the syndrome in detail in his book, although he does not refer to the "Prince Charming" labels (Goldberg, 1976). Instead, he refers to so-called masculine traits such as competition, internalization of the Protestant work ethic, domination, emphasis on independence, intellect, activity, and the like.

It is interesting to note that, prior to the Black male-led civil rights movement of the late '60's and early '70's, relatively few Black Prince Charmings existed in the Black subculture in America because few Black Cinderellas existed. We contend that this social movement had the latent function of producing Black Cinderellas and Black Charmings without a fairyland. Let us explore this contention further.

Antecedent to the modern day civil rights movement, Black women generally were taught to be much more assertive, competitive, and active than were Black men. Black parents, fearing for the safety of their male offspring, generally taught them to assume the deferential mask . . . to be submissive. In 1968, Grier and Cobbs wrote at length about how Black parents tended to curb aggression, competitiveness, and domination in their male offspring for fear that it was too dangerous for them to exhibit such traits in the United States (Grier and Cobbs, 1968:62). Because Black females were not perceived by white American society to be as threatening as were Black males, Black females generally were allowed greater access to the meager opportunities for social mobility available to Blacks. This resulted in widespread perceptions of the Black females as the more dominant, aggressive, and authoritarian figure in the Black race substructure. This perception was held not only by the larger American society, but also by many Black men at the outset, and during the course, of the Black movement. These "new" Black males who were leaders and supporters of the movement, viewed the Black male as a sexual victim of matriarchal tyranny (Porter, 1979). As a result, Black females were exhorted to assume supportive rather than leadership roles in the movement, to get behind Black men, to become less aggressive and domineering, and to become more submissive in social interaction with Black men. Succinctly stated, many Black men felt that for the first time in American history they were ready to become Black Prince Charmings. Of Black female response to the Black male and Black female sex-

role modification, Wallace states, "When she stood by silently as he (the Black male) became a man, she assumed that he would finally glorify and dignify Black womanhood just as the white man had done for white women" (Wallace, 1979:14). Wallace could have stated that Black females transformed themselves from self-reliant, independent, confident, and mature adults into Black Cinderellas waiting for their Black Prince Charmings. The length of the waiting period is what has troubled growing numbers of Black females and is the topic of our next section.

## Black Male Responses to the Prince Charming Ideal

Once Black males and Black females accepted the Prince Charming ideal for Black males, Black male role expectations changed appreciably. The responses to these changes are the focus of our attention in this section. In a sense, it is possible to say that Black males respond to the Prince Charming ideal on two levels: an *internalization level* and an *action level*. Let us consider the nature of these responses.

*Black male responses on an internalization level.* Black males learn the Prince Charming ideal (that is, the "appropriate" male role), both formally and informally. Sources for this instruction are both external and internal to the Black race subculture. Instruction on the appropriate role models for men in our society may result when Black men are exposed to formal socialization from educational institutions, religious institutions, the mass media, and other basic societal institutions. While such instruction historically has occurred, it was not until the civil rights movement that increasing numbers of Black males *adopted*, and numerous Black females submissively *accepted*, the Prince Charming ideal. As a result, the Black subculture as a whole began to accept this role model. This acceptance paved the way for subcultural support of the internalization of the Prince Charming ideal by young Black males who were being instructed in appropriate male sex roles. Morever, it is suggested that many older Black males similarly became re-socialized with respect to the appropriate male sex roles which Black men should internalize.

As a result of this change in Black male sex role socialization, we submit that a majority of Black males have internalized the Prince Charming ideal. This position places us diametrically opposite popular beliefs which posit that one reason for disharmony among increasing numbers of Black males and Black females is a failure of Black males to internalize a male sex role which emphasizes the assumption of responsibility, self-reliance, assertiveness, competitiveness, independence, and the like. Indeed, the myth of Black males' noninternalization of the normative male sex role probably persists because of the failure of many persons to distinguish between the two levels of Black male responses to the role ideal—that is, internalization and action. Internalizing the ideal does not automatically result in behavior congruent with the ideal, as will be shown below. Given the inordinate number of societal constraints Black males experience when they attempt to exhibit behavior congruent with their internalized values, it is not surprising that, on the whole, Black male actions are viewed as being divergent from the Prince Charming ideal. Such perceptions seemingly support the notion that a majority of Black males reject the ideal and, therefore, do not act in accordance with the ideal. The authors contend that this is not the case and, instead, offer an alternative explanation of Black male action on the ideal.

*Black male response on an action level.* For Black males, unlike counterparts in our society, there is not a linear relationship between internalization of the Prince Charming ideal and action congruent with the ideal. On the contrary, for Black males, numerous societal factors militate against their actualization of the Prince Charming ideal. Such factors are well known, and have been explored extensively. The important point to note is that a failure to act upon the ideal may not reflect a rejection of the ideal. Acting upon the ideal is some function of class status for Black males just as it is for white males. However, for Black males, unlike white males, it is also some function of actual and perceived opportunities for obtaining the means by which to act upon the ideal. This means that Black males continue to be inhibited in their efforts to act upon the Prince Charming ideal. The existence of this inhibition illuminates the need for social science scholars and practitioners to conduct research and respond to clients on the basis of a model of the Black male role as one that involves not only internalizing and acting upon the ideal, but also a failure to do so. The accompanying table shows the proposed model.

At a simple action response level, Black males either act or fail to act in accordance with the Prince Charming ideal. Because two levels of Black male responses are suggested, Black male responses always involve at least two variables *and* one of two subtypes of each variable. Thus, the Black male response to the Prince Charming ideal at the most simple level assumes one of four possible forms. First, some Black males (category one) internalize the ideal and exhibit behavior congruent with the ideal. Black males most likely to be characterized in this manner typically are middle class, although they can be found throughout the Black social stratification. When such males come from the lower socioeconomic classes, they have usually acquired the necessary means for actualizing the ideal. Entertainers and sports figures who, after years of poverty, suddenly acquire great wealth are highly visible examples of lower class Black males who become socially mobile and, therefore, are able to actualize the internalized Prince Charming ideal. Other less visible Black males in this category include those who become socially mobile through education, hard work, and rare opportunities.

Category two calls attention to those Black males who, for a variety of reasons related to their socialization experience (both formal and informal), *do not* internalize the Prince Charming ideal, but rather act in a ritualistic manner regarding the ideal. These males, then, act in accordance with the ideal and may superficially resemble those Black males in category one. The characteristic that distinguishes the Black male category two from all of the others is a tendency to actualize his resentment of the roles he performs. In addition, when the opportunity presents itself, such Black males are extremely likely to discard the "performing" role. We

### Black Male Responses to the Prince Charming Ideal

|  |  | BLACK MALE INTERNALIZATION RESPONSE RELATED TO THE PRINCE CHARMING IDEAL | |
| --- | --- | --- | --- |
|  |  | Internalize | Failure to Internalize |
| Black male action responses related to the Prince Charming ideal | Act in accordance with the ideal | 1 | 2 |
|  | Fail to act in accordance with the ideal | 3 | 4 |

contend that some unknown proportion of Black males who reject parental and spousal obligations fall into this category. However, not all Black men who initially act on the ideal but who do not subsequently continue to do so should be characterized as having failed to internalize the Prince Charming ideal, as we show later.

A third response category in which we feel a large number of poor Black males can be placed is category three. Black males in this category *do* internalize the Prince Charming ideal, but the behaviors which they exhibit are not congruent with the internalized values. Many of these Black males, we feel, come from the lower Black social stratum, while the remainder have experienced *downward social mobility.* The distinguishing feature of the males in this category is the high probability that they will engage in self-destructive behavior as well as anti-social behavior, that is, physically abusive behavior toward their mates. Such behavior, when viewed by the uninformed, is likely to be perceived as a failure to internalize the ideal. To the contrary, we believe that such behavior reflects feelings of poor self-esteem due to the lack of means by which to actualize the internalized and societally supported Prince Charming ideal. Additionally, such feelings and the resulting anti-social behavior may be increased when the Black female in such a rela-

tionship also holds expectations for the Black male that are congruent with the ideal.

The fourth Black male response category describes the Black male who does not internalize the ideal and who fails to act in accordance with the ideal. These Black males can include two types: (1) those who appear to be estranged from Black females (and females in general), often by exhibiting boorish behavior and an apparent lack of respect for women; and (2) those Black males who in the vernacular seemingly "have it all together," but who refuse to allow Black females to become emotionally dependent upon them or to act in a protective, condescending, and generally patriarchal manner toward Black females. Because of the influence and pervasiveness of the Prince Charming ideal, however, we believe that Black males falling into this category are relatively few in number in comparison to those in the other three categories.

## The Implications of Black Male Responses for Black Male–Black Female Relations

By now, the implications of Black male responses to the Prince Charming ideal for social interaction between Black males and Black females are probably apparent. Black males who interact with Black females from the vantage point of category one (internalization of the ideal and action in accordance with the ideal) usually do so with a minimum of difficulty. Both the male and the female generally experience a positive interaction. This is to be expected, since both individuals have similar expectations about the roles of Black males and Black females involved in social interaction. Moreover, hidden resentment is less likely to characterize the male involved in the interaction. In this case, Black Prince Charming is meeting his own expectations as well as the expectations of the Black Cinderella.

But, what happens to Black male–Black female relationships when Prince Charming does *not* internalize the Prince Charming ideal (category two)? Such relationships can superficially appear to be positive for years. This is true because the Black male's visible behavior under these circumstances may be no different from that of the true Black Prince Charming. However, the possible exception is that the Black male in category two strictly fulfills the overt behavioral requirements of his role and *demands* that Black Cinderella fulfill the requirements of her role. In such instances, the Black male is likely to be hypercritical of the Black female— making extreme demands on her and placing her in impossible situations (Goldberg, 1976). Her inability to meet these demands or to extricate herself from such situations provides the needed excuse for him not to *fulfill* his own and her expectations of his role. When this occurs, the Black male is inclined to leave the relationship. If he remains in the relationship, the situation usually becomes intolerable for the Black female and she is forced to flee the relationship. When both remain, the relationship becomes an overtly conflict-ridden one with both parties feeling that the expectations for the other are not being met.

Black male–Black female relationships are most visibly conflict-ridden when Black males fall into category three . . . (when they have internalized the Prince Charming ideal, but do not have the means by which to act on the ideal). Black males in these situations suffer from poor self-esteem *and* a loss of respect from Black females. These men are much more likely than are those in any other category to be physically abusive toward the Black female, who is perceived as demanding, nagging, domineering, and aggressive. On another level, however, such males feel that they are not adequately fulfilling their self-internalized roles. The Black female who also has accepted the definition of the Black male's role as that of "Prince Charming" and who exhibits behavior congruent with this acceptance is viewed by this Black male as a constant reminder of his failure to live up to his own ideals. Hostilities which Black males in this category direct toward these women may be construed as efforts to eradicate the "reminder."

Category four characterizes Black males who neither internalize nor act upon the Prince Charming ideal. The implications of this Black male response for Black male–Black female relationships take two diverse directions. One direction leads to unstable relationships between Black males in this category and Black females. The other direction, given modifications in the expectations for Black males held by many Black females, can lead to stable and positive relationships between these Black males and Black females.

With respect to the first direction, Black males who have neither internalized nor acted upon the ideal include those who visibly shirk all responsibility and act contrary to the male role ideal. Such men indicate verbally and by their actions that they have no intention of participating in a stable relationship with any Black female. Obviously, a proliferation of Black males who perform their roles in this manner foretells doom for Black male–Black female relationships.

Yet, there is a small and growing cadre of Black males who epitomize category four, but who believe that Black females should renounce many elements of the Cinderella complex and, therefore, modify their expectations of the role of Black men in Black male–Black female relationships. Such men *are* responsible and behave responsibly toward Black females, respecting Black females as mature adults. When these males form relationships with Black females who have modified their conceptions of the Black male's role in Black male–Black female relationships, stable relationships between the two may be obtained. Men and women who begin their relationship in this manner can be characterized in sex-role parlance as having an androgynous sex-role orientation. Moreover, we suggest that such relationships can be fulfilling to both parties. Given the fact that support exists in our society for less dependent, more assertive women and for less aggressive, less domineering men, those possessing an androgynous sex-role orientation may increase the probability that the relationships they form are both positive and powerful.

# Conclusion

A latent but persistent theme in our analysis of Black male responses to the Black male's role in Black male–Black female relationships has been that Black men may respond in several ways. In addition, we indicated that there may not be a linear relationship between internalization of the traditional male role and the exhibition of behavior which is congruent with that role. Societal constraints on acting upon the Prince Charming ideal, noninternalization of the ideal, and an inability to act upon the ideal, among the factors, may all be responsible for Black male behavior which appears to be contrary to the Prince Charming ideal.

An additional feature of our analysis is that both the Prince Charming ideal and the Cinderella complex lock persons into social roles, which may be difficult to fulfill in a modern society. The Black male role may be the most difficult of all to fulfill, given the complexities of, and the contradictions inherent in, his role in a society which is often diametrically opposed to his interests.

Given the above statements, social scientists (both theoreticians and practitioners) should begin to view Black male responses in terms of the multiplicity of possible meanings of the responses. Traditionally, Black male responses deemed to be inappropriate in Black male–Black female relationships have been defined as meaning noninternalization of what we call the "Prince Charming ideal." As we have seen, this perception may or may not be accurate. Morever, when disruptive responses are defined in this way, measures designed to alter the responses may be inadequate. Certainly, the model presented in this paper to represent possible meanings underlying Black male responses is simplistic. Some Black males, for example, may partially internalize the ideal, act upon the ideal only part of the time, and so forth. Yet, we believe that approaching a particular case from the framework presented—with whatever modifications may be required by that case—may improve the rate of problem resolution between Black males and Black females. This undoubtedly will contribute to the unification of Black men and Black women in America.

# References

Dowling, Colette
1981    *The Cinderella Complex*. New York: Summit Books.
Goldberg, Herb
1976    *The Hazards of Being Male*. New York: New American Library.
Grier, William H., and Price M. Cobbs
1968    *Black Rage*. New York: Basic Books.
Noble, Jeanne
1978    *Beautiful Also Are the Souls of My Black Sisters*. Englewood Cliffs, N.J.: Prentice-Hall.

Porter, John R.
1979    *Dating Habits of Young Black Americans*. Dubuque, Ia.: Kendall/Hunt.
Wallace, Michelle
1979    *Black Macho and the Myth of the Superwoman*. New York: Dial Press.

# BLACK SPOUSE ABUSE:
## A Focus on Relational Factors and Intervention Strategies

*Odell Uzzell · Wilma Peebles-Wilkins*

*The purpose of this article is to review the coverage of Black spouse abuse in the social science literature, to identify the relational factors and circumstances associated with Black spouse abuse, and to propose intervention strategies designed to reduce abusive behavior between Black spouses. The authors conclude that new research approaches are needed, and that research related to marital violence among Black spouses needs to consider factors that operate differently for Blacks.*

## Introduction

Family violence has increasingly claimed the attention of family sociologists and helping professionals. The growth of research in the area of family violence, particularly wife battering, is a phenomenon of the early 1970s. The *Journal of Marriage and the Family* (1971) devoted the entire issue to "Violence in the Family." Currently, an assortment of books on family violence is available. These include empirical studies on marital violence (Gelles, 1974) and family violence (Steinmetz, 1977); support systems for helping battered wives (Roy, 1977; Schuall, 1976) and personal experiences of battered women (Langley and Levy, 1977; Martin, 1976; Pizzey, 1974). An edited volume on violence (Madden and Lion, 1976) contains chapters on child abuse and family violence.

Black spouse abuse, as a form of family violence, is the major concern in this paper. Media coverage, court records and crime statistics suggest that a substantial proportion of the spousal violence which occurs in the general population involves Black spouses (Crime In The United States—Uniform Crime Reports, 1976; Demos, 1970; *Journal of Marriage and the Family*, 1976; Straus, 1977).

## Purpose

The major purpose of this paper is three-fold: (1) to review the coverage of Black spouse abuse in the social science literature; (2) to identify the relational factors and circumstances associated with Black spouse abuse, and (3) to propose intervention strategies designed to ameliorate abusive behavior between Black spouses.

## Method

The literature review focused on selective references published in the social sciences during the period 1977–1987. These included indexes to the major social science journals, books and book reviews, Dissertation Abstracts International, Masters Abstracts International, Sociological Abstracts, the Social Science Index, publications by the Department of Health, Education and Welfare, and the National Center for Mental Health Files. In addition to

From the *Western Journal of Black Studies* 13 (Spring 1989):10–16. © 1989 by the Washington State University Press. Reprinted by permission.

these sources, papers presented at a number of professional organization meetings and colleagues were consulted in an effort to identify unpublished articles.

In the literature, the term "spouse abuse," "spouse beating," and "spouse battering" are used interchangeably. An eight-item scale was developed (Straus, 1977) to measure the physical abuse which occurs among family members. The last five items in this scale comprise a wife-beating index. They include kicking, hitting, beating, threatening with a weapon and assaulting with a weapon. For the purpose of this paper, the five items constituting the wife-beating index will also be used to denote a spouse-beating index. Thus, "spouse abuse" is defined as any deliberate act of physical violence committed by *either* spouse which causes injury, or threatening act that involves a weapon.

The criteria employed in selecting the articles reviewed specified that: (1) the article's date of publication occur during the period 1977–1987; (2) the article include Black spouses in the sample population, if research or clinically oriented; (3) the article propose a theoretical explanation of Black spouse abuse, if theory is the emphasis. Either of the latter two criteria, or a combination of the latter two criteria, was perceived as an effort to address the topic of Black spouse abuse.

# Relational Factors and Circumstances Associated with Black Spouse Abuse

It is perhaps significant that in one of the most recent literature reviews of articles focusing upon changes that have occurred in social workers' perceptions of battered wives, none of those cited in the review dealt specifically with battered Black wives (Davis, 1987).

Utilizing the selection criteria cited, twelve articles and one thesis were identified on the basis of including Blacks and/or non-whites in the sample population. Of these, two presented analyses which dealt specifically with Black sub-samples, one with a non-white sample, and one which focused on

"causes" of Black spouse abuse. The articles appeared in seven different journals, three unpublished papers and one thesis. Journals in which the articles appeared were: *Journal of Marriage and the Family*, two; *Social Work*, two; *The Journal of Comparative Family Studies*, one; *Social Casework*, one; *The American Journal of Orthopsychiatry*, one; *Victimology—An International Journal*, one; and the *Journal of the National Medical Association*, one. These thirteen articles represented a very, very small percentage of the total number of articles which focused on spouse abuse.

The categorization and review of articles are based on the relational factors and circumstances associated with marital violence in articles that include Blacks in the sample populations, or theoretical articles which address causes of spousal violence among Blacks.

## *Structural Arrangements*

For small non-random samples of Black and white women who sought and utilized the services of social agencies, Babcock-Williams (1979) and Hilberman and Munson (1977–1978) found no significant relationship between the amount of abuse reported and wives who were employed and those who were not employed. Likewise, Babcock-Williams (1979) and Hilberman and Munson (1977–1978) noted no strong relationship between the educational level of abused wives, the occupational levels of husbands (blue-collar and white-collar), and the severity of abuse.

In a national probability study, Cazenave and Straus (1979) compared a sample of 147 Black respondents and a randomly selected sample of 427 white respondents. When the occupation of Black husbands was considered (white-collar and blue-collar), higher rates of hitting a spouse occurred for the blue-collar group than for the white-collar group. However, a Black/white comparison indicated that Blacks in both groups, white-collar and blue-collar, reported higher rates of hitting a spouse than their respective white counterparts.

A fairly positive relationship between abuse and income level was noted (Cazenave and Straus,

1979). Generally, the higher the level of family income, the lower the level of abuse reported. Aside from higher family income, the participation of Black wives in the labor market apparently affected how they were treated by their husbands and influenced their tolerance for or rejection of abuse. The rate of abuse was lower for employed wives in middle-income families than for unemployed wives in middle-income families.

Network embeddedness was related strongly to Black spouse abuse (Cazenave and Straus, 1979). A high level of spousal involvement in family kin, neighborhood and organizational networks was associated with a low level of reported spousal slapping. On the other hand, spouses who were isolated or minimally involved reported a high incident of spousal slapping.

Carlson (1977) maintained that financial and interpersonal stresses lead to domestic violence, not intrapsychic causes. In particular, environmental stress related to limited social and economic resources was considered the primary basis of spousal violence. Carlson further contended that within the environmental setting, violence tended to occur when the husband's role is not traditional (lower than wife's), and if accompanied by structural stress and a history of learned violence. Alcoholic and drug abuse are other behaviors associated with environmental stress.

## *The Incident and Effect of Parental Violence on Children*

Hilberman and Munson (1977–1978), Babcock-Williams (1979), and Pfouts (1977) observed that wives who use the services of public agencies were likely than not to have experienced a life-long pattern of violence and family discord. During childhood, this pattern included violence between parents, paternal alcoholism and physical and/or sexual abuse.

The prevalency and consequence of parental violence was explored by Ulbrich and Huber (1981). In a national stratified cluster probability sample of 1,092 women and 910 men, it was noted that 23 percent of the nonwhite and 16 percent of the white respondents reported the occurrence of parental hitting in their family of orientation. Race failed to affect attitudes about violence toward men, whereas witnessing parental hitting significantly influenced attitudes about violence toward women.

Forsstrom-Cohen and Rosenbaum (1985) noted that exposure to parental marital violence has negative effects on children who witness the violence and these effects are manifested in these children as young adults. Both males and females have a high level of anxiety as young adults. Only females exhibited a high level of depression and aggression (consistent with "learned helplessness").

The relationship between the perception of family power and the incident of spouse abuse was explored by Phillips and Rust (1983). Thirty-three percent of the subjects indicated some instance of spousal abuse while they were growing up. Abusive homes were perceived as having reflected a mother-centered distribution of power, while the non-abusive homes were perceived as having been egalitarian.

According to Star, et al. (1979), at least one-third of the respondents had been exposed to violence during their childhood. The forms of violence included witnessing parental abuse of one another (30 percent), enduring severe punishment (33 percent), and abuse/sexual assault by other men (33 percent). The abused wives displayed a number of psychological characteristics. In general, they had low self-esteem, little self-confidence, and displayed a tendency to withdraw and avoid interpersonal contact. They further noted that wives experienced situational stress from limited finance, household responsibilities, employment and childrearing.

## *Identification of Abuse and Potential Abuse Victims*

Lewis (1985) constructed a Wife Abuse Inventory designed to predict which women are at risk of being abused by their spouses. The inventory discriminates between abused/non-abused groups. The three predictor variables identified were:

husband's self-image, family isolation and family style of conflict resolution.

The refusal of abused victims to maximize the use of available resources may further impede the process of identifying existent problems and devising strategies to resolve them. Rounsaville (1978) categorized into two groups abused women who initially sought emergency services at a hospital facility. The categorization was based on whether or not the women attended counseling sessions to which the hospital invited them at no charge. The women who came for counseling were designated as the follow through (FT group), while those who did not come were designated as non-follow through (NFT group). Both groups were from the lower socio-economic level and the inner city. However, the two groups of women differed in other respects. The women who came for counseling demonstrated greater social resourcefulness, more of them worked, and fewer were financially dependent on their husbands. Those who did not come for counseling had fewer options and had taken less advantage of them. Thus, barriers to the identification, treatment and resolution of the problems confronting these women were posed.

## Cultural Ideology

In the search for "causes" of Black spouse abuse, Gullattee (1979) suggested several areas to investigate. These included, among others, the value system which placed males in more dominant roles and assigned higher evaluation to these roles and the selective sanction of violence in resolving disputes. These are viewed as the source of "sociopolitical" variables which interact with "intrapsychic" forces. Gullattee does not make clear what is meant by "sociopolitical" nor "intrapsychic" variables as they apply to spouse abuse except to say that they are superimposed "upon an ego matrix that is mosaic and amorphous" and linked in some way. In suggesting special areas of concern to behaviorists for research, Gullattee identified one research concern that was considered as having special relevancy for Blacks. This concern was: "The escalating nihil-

istic nature of the general population of the white Judeo-Christian world and the rebound impact on Blacks" (p. 335).

Again, Gullattee does not make clear a concern which is identified. Thus, it is difficult to determine what the "nihilistic trends" are and the nature of their presumed "rebound impact" on Blacks.

## Spouse Reaction to Abuse

In a literature review of areas of victimization for Black women, Scott (1978) concluded that spouse abuse is one of the two most prominent areas (rape is the other). Based upon the review, two assumptions relating to spousal (wife) abuse were derived: (1) Black women are more likely to strike back at their abusive husbands and (2) husbands are more likely to assault wives and cause bodily harm, but wives are more likely to kill abusive husbands after years of assault.

Hilberman and Munson (1977–1978) and Pfouts (1977) noted that responses to abuse varied. However, there were some responses which were fairly categoric. Many wives assumed self-blame if the abuse occurred while spouses were drinking or under stress because of unemployment. Likewise, abusive behavior was frequently justified if the wives perceived its occurrence as a response to their "nagging" or assertiveness. Aggressive reactions toward husbands in the form of physical confrontation occurred frequently. Wives used hands, fists, feet, rocks, bottles, iron bars, knives and guns in assaults. There were wives who did not become engaged in physical battle with their husbands. They simply absorbed the physical abuse. If there were abrasions, they often attempted to conceal them. Another pattern that characterized the reaction of a significant number of wives was early and late disengagement. If the wife were concerned with "saving" the marriage, disengagement tended to occur much later. Frequent deliberations relative to the cost/benefits perceived in continuing or terminating the marriage occurred. When disengagement occurred, wives were more likely to leave the residence than husbands.

# Discussion

Two observations seem appropriate at this point. First, the articles reviewed tended to focus on abused wives and their responses to abusive spouses. Secondly, with the exception of two articles (Cazenave and Straus, 1979; Scott, 1978), which provided analyses that dealt specifically with Blacks, one article (Gullattee, 1979) which considered "causes" of Black spouse abuse, and one article (Ulbrich and Huber, 1981) which provided for the non-white sample, Black spouse abuse in the remaining articles is not clearly delineated from white spouse abuse. Hence, findings in the latter are not generalizable to Blacks exclusively.

When the occupation of Black husbands is considered (Cazenave and Straus, 1979), higher rates of hitting a spouse occurred in the blue-collar group than in the white-collar groups. To the extent that the blue-collar and white-collar occupations can be broadly categorized as "working class" and "middle class" respectively, a relationship between social class and abuse seems evident. There is support in the literature for this relational pattern. Goode (1969) contended that members of the middle class are socialized to mediate conflict, thereby avoiding or minimizing the use of physical confrontation, and are more likely to rely on verbal skills to settle marital disputes than are members of the working and lower classes. Moreover, it has been noted that the inability to communicate is also highly related to physical violence between spouses (Steinmetz, 1977). A Black/white comparison (Cazenave and Straus, 1979) showed that Blacks in both groups (blue-collar and white-collar) reported higher rates of hitting a spouse than their respective white counterparts. This might suggest that there are factors independent of occupation which cause marital stress among Black couples and culminate in abusive behavior.

For Blacks, there was a fairly positive relationship between abuse and income level. Generally, the higher the level of family income, the lower the level of abuse reported. In addition to higher family income, the involvement of Black wives in the labor market seemed to have affected how they were treated by their husbands. The rate of abuse was lower for employed wives in middle-income families than for unemployed wives in middle-income families (Cazenave and Straus, 1979). An explanation for this variation might be that employed wives have access to resources which unemployed wives do not. These resources can enhance wives' position of power within the marital relationship. On the other hand, when both spouses work, there is the probability that the level of financial resources for the family in general is likely to be enhanced, thereby reducing much of the environmental stress that is often generated under the conditions of financial deprivation. There is implicit support for both of these patterns in the resource theory explanation of spouse abuse (*Journal of Marriage and the Family*, Volume 38, 1976).

Spouses who lack close personal relationships and who are minimally integrated into the community are more likely to experience violence for several reasons. First, they lack the friendship networks which could provide support and protection during times of extreme stress, and second, they are less likely perhaps to be influenced by the social expectations of their peers, friends, or community, or to modify their behavior according to their expectations.

The occurrence of violence in one's family of orientation is highly related to the occurrence of violence in one's family of procreation (Hilberman and Munson, 1977–1978; Babcock-Williams, 1979; Pfouts, 1977; Star *et al.*, 1979). A comparative non-white and white response rate regarding the occurrence of parental hitting indicated that 23 percent of the non-white and 16 percent of the white respondents reported the occurrence of parental hitting (Ulbrich and Huber, 1981).

While the reaction of respondents to abuse varied, there were some responses that were fairly categoric. Often, wives blamed themselves if the abuse occurred while the spouses were drinking or under stress because of unemployment. Abuse was frequently justified if the wives perceived its occurrence as a response to their "nagging." Another pattern that characterized a significant number of wives was early and late disengagement tended to occur much later (Hilberman and Munson, 1977–1978). In responding to abuse, Black women appear more likely to strike back at their abusive husbands than their white counterparts. A comparison of Black wives and Black husbands involved in an abusive relationship over a period of time indicated that husbands are more likely to continue to assault their wives and inflict bodily harm, while wives are more likely to kill their abusive husbands after years of assault (Scott, 1978).

Although the literature review was somewhat limited with regard to factors that are associated specifically with Black spouse abuse, there are a number of factors that appear to be relevant. These include occupation, income, embeddedness in family, neighborhood and organizational networks, unemployment and violence in one's family of orientation. An examination of these factors might lead one to conclude that they are quite similar to those that are associated with spouse abuse in the general population, and hence conclude that Black spouse abuse occurs for the same reasons that white spouse abuse occurs. A generalization of this order would be premature and inconclusive at this time. There is an urgent need for more definitive research.

# Implications for Intervention

Marital violence in the general population continues to represent a major challenge to helping professionals. Broadly focused programs have been designed to shelter women from abusive males. Efforts have concentrated on environmental circumstances and shifted away from focus on the individual female personality. As a rule, intervention programs have reflected changing social attitudes toward gender roles (Pfouts and Renz, 1984).

Previously, interventive strategies focused primarily on reducing relational power disparities by increasing resources or options available for wives. Little attention was given to the batterers. Recently, mental health efforts have attempted to respond to the treatment needs of the wife abusers. Counseling programs associated with court assault case referrals represent one avenue for treating abusers.

Although statistics suggest that Black families represent a significant portion of violent families identified and served by agencies, limited attention has been given to selective programming for Black families. Recognizing that the need for further research has been identified, tentative considerations for designing and implementing programs aimed at deterring Black spouse abuse can still be proposed. While current intervention trends need to be maintained, relational factors associated with marital violence in Black families have implications for additional planning of both macro and micro level intervention strategies.

The significance of network embeddedness for Black spouses has been identified in the research. Macro level intervention should be ecological in focus and designed to promote network development through community coordinated efforts. Such networks would include helping responses such as community supported resources for women, community education programs, policy advocacy, and the involvement of Black churches and organizations for economic and emotional support (Peebles, et al., 1982). Structural efforts to reduce unemployment continue to be tantamount. Reduction of stress through job-related mutual support groups and similar activities could spearhead opportunities for Blacks to gain a sense of accomplishment outside the employment arena.

At the micro-level, an individual and family-oriented focus for prevention would include programs and activities aimed at re-education of individuals and reinforcement of the concept of extended family bonds which has historically prevailed in the Black community. Research findings suggest the need to re-educate Black females out of the victim role through group and other activities designed to reduce self-blame. Services designed to help couples recognize alternatives to learned violent behavior and violent retaliation are also suggested by research findings. Helping professionals need to continue to foster and promote a climate that encourages Black males and females in developing positive images of each other, thereby reducing the conflict that may characterize their interpersonal relationships.

More extensive research on marital violence among Black couples may reveal findings with definitive implications for program development within the Black community and provide stronger directives for culturally sensitive interventions.

## Summary and Conclusion

The literature inquiry revealed that research on marital violence among Black spouses was very limited during the period 1977–1987. Aside from the limited research, a majority of the research reports involved small nonrandom populations of abused wives who had utilized the services of public agencies. Thus, the samples tended to be biased in the direction of poverty and, therefore, can tell one very little about the social class distribution of marital violence among Blacks in general. Generalizations and subsequent interventive planning which can be made concerning marital violence among Black spouses is, therefore, severely limited.

There is a need for research that utilizes random probability samples of Black spouse abusers as well as research that focuses on Blacks and other racial/ethnic groups on a comparative basis. The findings of such research hold a greater potential for effective intervention strategies.

While some of the factors identified tentatively as being associated with marital violence among spouses are also ones that are related to marital violence in the general population, there is the need not only to explore these factors further, but to consider other factors which might operate independently of these factors. For example, the higher rates noted for Blacks in white-collar and blue-collar occupations as compared with whites in these occupations suggest perhaps that there are factors independent of occupation which cause stress leading to marital violence among Black couples. One research approach which might be used to identify some of these factors would be to focus upon structural factors such as the denial of job entry, job discrimination, underemployment and social exclusion in general. The "carry home" effects of these deprivations and indignities are likely to have addictive consequences for violent behavior among Black couples.

## References

**Babcock-Williams, C.**

1979 "Abused Wives: Factors Contributing to Tolerance of Abuse Among Wives Seeking Advice From Wake Women's Aid." Unpublished master's thesis, North Carolina State University, Raleigh, NC.

**Carlson, Bonnie**

1977 "Battered Women and Their Assailants," *Social Work* 22(6):455–471.

**Cazenave, N. H. and M. A. Straus**

1979 "Race, Class, Network Embeddedness and Family Violence: A Search for Potent Support Systems," *The Journal of Comparative Family Studies*, 10:281–300.

——Crime in the United States—Uniform Crime Reports, 1976

1976 U.S. Government Printing Office, Washington, D.C.

**Davis, Liane V.**

1987 "Battered Women: The Transformation of a Social Problem," *Social Work* 32(4):306–311.

**Demo, J. A.**

1970 *A Little Commonwealth*. New York: Oxford University Press.

**Fersstrom-Cohen, Barbara and Alan Rosenbaum**

1985 "The Effects of Parental Marital Violence on Young Adults: An Explanatory Investigation," *Journal of Marriage and the Family* 47:467–472.

Gelles, R. J.

1974  *The Violent Home: A Study of Physical Aggression Between Husbands and Wives.* Beverly Hills, California: Sage Publications.

Goode, W. J.

1969  "Violence Among Inmates" (Report of the U.S. National Commission on the Causes and Prevention of Violence, Task Force on the Causes of Violence), *Crime and Violence* 13:941–977.

Gullattee, A. C.

1979  "Spousal Abuse," *Journal of the National Medical Association* 71(4):335–340.

Hilberman, E. and K. Munsen

1977– "Sixty Battered Women," *Victimology—An International Journal* (Special Issue on Spouse
1978   Abuse), 2(3–4):460–479.

——Journal of Marriage and the Family

1971  "Violence in the Family," vol. 33.

——Journal of Marriage and the Family

1976  "Abused Wives: Why Do They Stay?" 38:659–668.

Langley, R. and R. C. Leroy

1977  *Wife Beating: The Silent Crisis.* New York: E. P. Sutton.

Lewis, Bonnie Yegidis

1985  "The Wife Abuse Inventory: A Screening Device for the Identification of Abused Women," *Social Work* 30(1):32–35.

Madden, D. J. and J. R. Lion (eds.)

1976  *Rage, Hate, Assault and Other Forms of Violence.* New York: Spectrum Publishers, 1976.

Martin, D.

1976  *Battered Wives.* San Francisco, CA: Glide Press.

Newberger, E. H. and J. N. Hyde

1975  "Child Abuse: Principles and Implications of Current Pediatric Practices," *Pediatric Clinics of North America* 22:695–715.

Peebles, W. C., D. Hicks, E. Williams, et al.

1982  "Developing a Community-Wide Response to Family Violence: The Family Violence Service Network." Paper presented at the 59th Annual Meeting of the American Orthopsychiatric Association. San Francisco, California, March.

Pfouts, J. H.

1977  "Coping Responses of Abused Wives." Paper presented at the Annual Forum of the National Conference on Social Welfare. Chicago, Ill.

Pfouts, J. H. and C. Renz

1984  "The Future of Wife Abuse Programs," *Social Work* 26(6):451–456.

Phillips, Jonathan and James O. Rust

1983  "Spouse Abuse: How Family Power Is Shared." A paper presented at the Annual Meeting of the Southwestern Psychological Association, Atlanta, Georgia, March 23–26.

Pizzey, E.

1974  *Scream Quietly or the Neighbors Will Hear.* London, England: Penguin.

Rounsaville, Bruce J.

1978  "Battered Wives: Barriers to Identification and Treatment," *American Journal of Orthopsychiatry* 48(3):487–494.

Roy, M. (ed.)

1977  *Battered Women: A Psychosocial Study of Domestic Violence.* New York: Van Nostrand Reinhold Company.

Schnall, M.

1976  *Your Marriage.* New York: Pyramid Books.

Scott, Elsie L.

1978  "Black Women, Crime and Crime Prevention." A paper presented at the National Conference of Black Political Scientists, Jackson, Mississippi, April.

Star, Barbara, et al.

1979  "Psychosocial Aspects of Wife Battering," *Social Casework* 60(8):479–487.

Steinmetz, S. K.

1977  *The Cycle of Violence: Assertive, Aggressive and Abusive Family Interaction.* New York: Praeger.

Straus, M. A.

1977  "Normative and Behavioral Aspects of Violence Between Spouses: Preliminary Data on a Nationally Representative U.S.A. Sample." Paper presented at the Symposium on Violence in Canadian Society.

Ulbrich, Patricia and Joan Huber

1981  "Observing Parental Violence: Distribution and Effects," *Journal of Marriage and the Family* 43:623–631.

# MARITAL STATUS AND POVERTY AMONG WOMEN

*United States Commission on Civil Rights*

*This government report is a compendium of studies and statistical data on the relationship between poverty and marital status: Women with children and no husband have considerably lower incomes than married couples. For Black women, marital disruption virtually determines economic hardship. Fewer Black women remarry, and poverty is likely to be a permanent condition as long as they remain unmarried. Other problems of being a female household head are described.*

For American women, the correlation between marital status and economic well-being has become an increasingly harsh reality in the latter half of the 20th century. For some women, marital status matters more than labor market status as an indicator of financial well-being.[1] Mothers who do not marry and women who are separated, divorced, or widowed may face the prospect of financial insecurity more often than married women.

This chapter discusses the relationship between marital status and economic well-being for women. It examines trends in marital disruption (separation and divorce), child care, and the consequences of teenage childbearing. One of the principal Federal assistance programs that poor women rely on, aid to families with dependent children, is also reviewed.

## Trend toward Female-Headed Families

The increase in the number and proportion of women heading households was small between 1960 and 1970, but has changed markedly since then. In 1960 female-headed families were 10 percent of all families;[2] in 1970, 10.8 percent.[3] By 1981 female-headed families were 18.8 percent of all families with children under 18 years of age, and the number of female-headed families had increased by 2.8 million (97 percent) since 1970.[4]

Female-headed families continued to be a larger proportion of the black family population than in any other subgroup. By 1981, 47.5 percent of black families with children present were headed by women, a rise from an already high 30.6 percent in 1970.[5] Among Hispanics, women headed 21.8 percent of all families in 1981, an increase from the 16.9 percent figure of 1970.[6] For whites, the proportion was smallest and the increase greatest: Women headed 14.7 percent of white families with children present in 1981, compared to 7.8 percent in 1970.[7]

Women with children but no husbands may lack the economic resources of husband-wife families for various reasons that include inadequate child support, lack of marketable skills, or job discrimination. Table 1 depicts not only the low median income of female householders when compared to husband-wife families, but also the increasing disparities between the two since 1970.[8]

From the report *A Growing Crisis: Disadvantaged Women and Their Children* (Washington, D.C.: U.S. Government Printing Office, 1983), pp. 5–14. Tables and footnotes have been renumbered.

TABLE 1    Median Income by Race and Type of Family

|  | 1970 | 1981 | INCREASE, 1970–1981 |
|---|---|---|---|
| **Type of family** | | | |
| Husband-wife families[1] | $10,516 | $25,065 | 138% |
|   Wife in labor force | 12,276 | 29,247 | 138 |
| Female householder, no husband present | 5,093 | 10,960 | 115 |
| Male householder, no wife present | — | 19,889 | — |
| **White families** | | | |
| Husband-wife families | $10,723 | $25,474 | 138 |
|   Wife in labor force | 12,543 | 29,713 | 137 |
| Female householder, no husband present | 5,754 | 12,508 | 117 |
| Male householder, no wife present | — | 20,421 | — |
| **Black families** | | | |
| Husband-wife families | $ 7,816 | $19,624 | 151 |
|   Wife in labor force | 9,721 | 25,040 | 158 |
| Female householder, no husband present | 3,576 | 7,506 | 110 |
| Male householder, no wife present | — | 14,489 | — |

[1]This item may be read as follows: Median income earnings for female householder families with no husbands present rose from $5,093 to $10,960, an increase of 115 percent, between 1970 and 1981.

Sources: U.S., Department of Commerce, Bureau of the Census, *Consumer Income: Income in 1970 of Families and Persons in the United States*, series P–60, no. 80, pp. 33, 35, and 37; *Money Income and Poverty Status of Families and Persons in the United States: 1981* (Advance Data), series P–60, no. 134, pp. 6, 7, 8, and 10.

The distribution of family income has changed markedly since 1970. Median income differences between all female householder families and all husband-wife families widened over the decade. When median family income of female householders is compared with median income of couples with wives in the labor force, the disparities are even greater. Total female householder median income as a proportion of working couple income declined from 41.4 to 37.4 percent between 1970 and 1981.

Among black families, median income of female householders grew 110 percent between 1970 and 1981, but median income of husband-wife families grew 151 percent, a striking difference. Median income growth among black couples with wives in the labor force grew 158 percent. The decline in black female householder median income relative to black husband-wife median income was 7.5 percent between 1970 and 1981.

Among all Hispanic families, median family income rose from $7,348 to $16,401 between 1969 and 1981, an increase of 123 percent.[9] Median income among female-headed Hispanic families increased 107 percent, from $3,654 to $7,586, during this period.[10] Also between 1969 and 1981, Hispanic female householder median income as a percentage of all Hispanic median family income decreased from 49.7 percent to 46.2 percent. These data indicate that Hispanic female-headed families experienced income losses during the 1970s relative to all Hispanic families.

Much, if not all, of the income growth during this period was dissipated by an increase in the cost of living. For example, in 1981 median income for all families was $22,388. However, in 1970 median family income expressed in 1981 dollars was $23,111.[11] While inflation has eroded the value of all families' purchasing power by about 3.5 percent, female householders, being poorer, have suffered the most.

## Single Mothers

Whether by choice or circumstance, growing numbers of mothers have no husbands. Increased separation, divorce, and out-of-wedlock childbearing account for most of this trend. Between 1970 and 1981, for example, the divorce rate climbed from 47 to 109 finalized divorces per 1,000 married couples.[12] During the same period, families headed by never-married mothers climbed to 3.4 million, an increase of 356 percent.[13] As a result of this overall trend, 12.6 million children (20 percent of all children) lived with one parent; in 90 percent of these situations, that parent was the mother.[14] "In 1981, of the children who lived only with their mothers, 43 percent had a mother who was divorced, 27 percent had a separated mother and 16 percent had a mother who had never married."[15]

Regardless of why they are single parents, female householders earn less than male householders. For the categories shown in Table 2, female median earnings range between 52 and 74 percent of male householder earnings.

High poverty rates among female householders have not been changing much. Table 3 shows that about one-third of all female householders were poor in 1969, 1978, and 1981; slight declines in the poverty rate in 1978 were erased by 1981. Hardest hit were black and Hispanic female householders: Consistently more than half were poor.[16] Overall, women headed about half of all poor families in 1981.[17]

Poverty among male householders and husband-wife families was significantly less, ranging in 1981 from a low of 6.0 percent of white husband-wife families to highs of 19.1 and 19.2 percent of black and Hispanic male householders, respectively. These highs were still more than 8 percentage points below the lowest female householder poverty rate of 27.4 percent, for white female house-

| TABLE 2    Householder Median Income, 1981 | |
|---|---|
| MALE HOUSEHOLDERS: | |
| Married, wife absent | $14,582 |
| Widowed | 10,157 |
| Divorced | 18,806 |
| Single | 15,640 |
| FEMALE HOUSEHOLDERS: | |
| Married, husband absent[1] | $ 7,612 |
| Widowed | 7,324 |
| Divorced | 12,380 |
| Single | 11,496 |

[1]This item may be read as follows: Median income for female householders without husbands was $7,612 in 1981.

Source: U.S., Department of Commerce, Bureau of the Census, *Money Income and Poverty Status of Families and Persons in the United States: 1981* (Advance Data), series P–60, no. 134, pp. 6, 7, 8, and 10.

holders. In overall terms, the poverty rate for all female householders in 1981 was more than three times that for male householders (34.6 percent compared to 10.3 percent) and more than five times that for husband-wife families (6.8 percent).[18]

The apparent persistence of poverty among black female-headed families suggests to some a culture of poverty that recycles from one generation to another.[19] One writer who subscribes to this view noted recently: "Among the economically weakest segment of Afro-Americans—perhaps 35 percent of black households—there is ample evidence of structural and cultural ingredients that transmit poverty across generations."[20] The author argues that income and employment deficiencies of increasing numbers of black female-headed families usually result in bad housing and schooling, which "translate into cross-generational disadvantages for disproportionately larger numbers of black children."[21] This author, among others, uses a traditional research approach to studying the poverty population, namely, working with overall data on different groups collected at different points in time that show fluctuations in the numbers and types of impoverished persons, but cannot show whether the same individuals are affected.

TABLE 3    Female and Male Poverty Rates

|  | 1969 | 1978 | 1981 |
|---|---|---|---|
| All female householders[1] | 32.3 | 31.4 | 34.6 |
| White female householders | 25.4 | 23.5 | 27.4 |
| Black female householders | 53.2 | 50.6 | 52.9 |
| Hispanic female householders | — | 53.1 | 53.2 |
| All male householders | — | 5.3 | 10.3 |
| White male householders | — | 4.7 | 8.8 |
| Black male householders | — | 11.8 | 19.1 |
| Hispanic male householders | — | — | 19.2 |
| All husband-wife families[2] | 6.9 | 5.2 | 6.8 |
| White husband-wife families | 6.0 | 4.7 | 6.0 |
| Black husband-wife families | 17.8 | 11.3 | 15.4 |
| Hispanic husband-wife families | — | — | 15.1 |

[1]This item may be read as follows: The poverty rates for all women heading families with no husband present were 34.6 in 1981, 31.4 in 1978, and 32.3 in 1969.

[2]Data for husband-wife families in 1969 were collected as "families with male head" and include some male householders with no wives present.

Sources: U.S., Department of Commerce, Bureau of the Census, *Twenty-Four Million Americans, Poverty in the United States, 1969,* series P–60, no. 76 (1970), p. 46; *Characteristics of the Population below the Poverty Level: 1978,* series P–60, no. 124 (1980), pp. 83–86; *Families Maintained by Female Householders: 1970–1979,* series P–23, no. 107, p. 37; and *Money Income and Poverty Status of Persons in the United States: 1981* (Advanced Data), series P–60, no. 134, p. 21.

When examined from a longitudinal perspective, however, the poverty population, including blacks, has been shown to be dynamic, rather than static.[22] In other words, a significant segment of the poverty population in one year was not impoverished in subsequent years. Bearing in mind that individuals move into and out of poverty, one of the limitations of even longitudinal research is that young persons, after forming nonpoor households, may subsequently fall into poverty. The conclusion that increasing numbers of black female-headed families transmit poverty to their offspring when they attain adulthood is less certain, although this group appears to be more vulnerable to intergenerational transmission than any other.

## Divorced and Separated Mothers

The increase in divorce is one of the most significant social trends in America. In 1940 six marriages occurred for every divorce; by 1975 two marriages occurred for every divorce.[23] By 1981 the divorce ratio of 109 divorces per 1,000 active marriages was more than twice that of 1970.[24] Provisional reports from the National Center for Health Statistics suggest that the long-term increase in divorce may be leveling off or even falling slightly.[25] The higher divorce ratio among women (129 divorces versus 88 for men per 1,000 active marriages) indicates that divorced men generally remarry more quickly than divorced women.[26]

Divorce patterns among black, white, and Hispanic women differed between 1970 and 1981. During those 11 years, the black female divorce ratio increased from 104 to 289 divorced persons per 1,000 persons in active marriages.[27] In other words, by 1981 there were nearly 3 divorced black women to every 10 living with their husbands. The white female divorce ratio increased from 56 to 118 divorced persons per 1,000 persons in active marriages.[28] Hispanic women experienced the smallest rate of increase, from 81 to 146 divorced persons per 1,000 persons in active marriages between 1970 to 1981.[29] For women as a group, divorce occurred most frequently between the ages of 30 to 44, child-rearing years for perhaps the majority of American households.[30]

## *Income and Poverty*

Should marital disruption occur, women with children, regardless of their previous economic circumstances, are usually poorer after the marriage fails. One longitudinal study found that among middle-aged women with children whose marriages ended between 1967 and 1972, the proportion of families below the poverty level increased from about 10 percent to over 25 percent for whites and from 44 percent to almost 60 percent for blacks.[31]

In assessing the relationship between family composition change and economic well-being, one researcher concluded that marriages and remarriages have the most beneficial effects whereas marital disruptions are the most harmful for women and children.[32] More recent research found similarly that changes in family composition increased the number of families below the poverty level. Families maintained by women tended to have much higher poverty rates than those maintained by men.[33]

Marital disruption significantly increases white women's chances for being poor and virtually determines economic hardship for black women. Using the standard definition of poverty,[34] one researcher found that:

> *about one white family out of four became poor after marital disruption. . . . About 40 percent of all white women who did not remarry over the seven-year [study] period were poor at least once; probably 15 to 20 percent were continuously poor or close to poverty.*[35]

For black women, the economic results of marital disruption were more severe:

> *At any one time 55 to 60 percent of the sample studied were poor by the standard definition and 70 percent were poor or relatively poor. If they did not remarry [and that likeli-*

> *hood is greater for black women than for white], the probability that they would remain poor was high.*[36]

When marital disruption occurs to couples with children, the children typically remain with the mother.[37] The new female householder presumably can rely upon a variety of sources that include her own earnings, alimony, child support, public assistance, personal savings, and division of community property; but these sources may not mean much. . . .

## *Child Support*

Commitments to pay child support are frequently broken. In 1978 approximately 60 percent of the 7.1 million women with children from an absent father were awarded or had an agreement to receive child support payments.[38] The proportion of women awarded child support payments was higher for white women (71 percent) than for Hispanic women (44 percent) or for black women (29 percent).[39] Of the women awarded child support by a court, roughly one-quarter received no payments, another quarter received less than the full amount awarded, and one-half received the agreed-upon amount.

## *Alimony*

Divorced and separated women eligible for alimony or spousal support receive it infrequently. Only 14 percent of ever-divorced or separated women in 1979 were awarded or had an agreement to receive maintenance payments or alimony.[40] Nearly 70 percent of the women due payments actually received them, with the average annual payment being $2,850.[41] "The mean total money income for women receiving payments ($11,060) was higher than that for women due payments but not receiving them ($7,270)."[42]

## Child Care

In previous factfinding efforts in the area of sex discrimination, the Commission has recognized the relationship between child care and equal opportunity and the need for a revised Federal role.[43]

Educational and employment opportunities that women cannot pursue due to inadequate child care are opportunities effectively denied.

Women of different socioeconomic strata rely upon different resources for child care. Those with higher family incomes are more able to afford and, therefore, tend to utilize child care services.[44] Unmarried women of more meager means tend to rely upon the extended family as they have in the past. Mothers without mates, adequate income, or extended family support face a dilemma in finding affordable, reliable, and convenient child care, access to which may be the difference between supporting themselves partially, if not totally, or depending upon public assistance.

The increased number of mothers participating in the labor force provides some indication of the national need for child care. "Between 1950 and 1980, the labor force participation rates for wives with children under 18 increased from 18 to 54 percent, while the rate for other ever-married women with children increased from 55 to 69 percent."[45] "Among women with a child under 1 year old, 31 percent of currently married women and 40 percent of all other women were in the labor force" by 1980.[46]

Although many mothers of preschool children are working, still more would be in the labor force if they could find adequate child care. One study found that between 17 and 23 percent of mothers with preschool children who were neither employed nor looking for work would be working if work were available and if they had access to adequate child care facilities.[47] If already working, these mothers would be working more hours if suitable child care could be found.[48]

*Women who are most in need of employment are most likely to report that the unavailability of satisfactory child care at reasonable cost affects their labor force participation: the young mother (18–24), the*

*unmarried mother, the black mother, the woman who did not graduate from high school, and the woman whose family income is less than $5,000.*[49]

. . . . . . . . . . . . . . . . . . . . . . . . . . . . .

# Summary

During the last several decades, many women and their dependent children have experienced economic hardship. The phenomenal growth of female householder families, stemming in part from increasing marital disruption and out-of-wedlock births, has forced many women to be both chief parent and chief provider. The continuing trend in teenage childbearing out of wedlock is cause for concern. Teenage mothers often must interrupt or discontinue their education, thereby making the acquisition of marketable employment skills more difficult. If unable to find adequate and affordable child care, the teenage mother and those who experience marital disruption may be forced to rely upon public assistance for basic needs.

Female-headed families are disproportionately impoverished. Families headed by women with no husband present constituted 47 percent of all families below the poverty line in 1981. Minority female heads of household experience even higher levels of deprivation. More than half (53 percent) of all female-headed black and Spanish-origin families were below the poverty line. The vulnerability of female-headed families, particularly minorities, to economic adversity and the surprising number of households having some recent contact with welfare programs underline the importance of these programs.

Disproportionate numbers of America's poor in the early 1980s are women. The demographic data that reflect these trends suggest that more of the same may lie ahead.

[1]Isabel V. Sawhill, "Comments," in U.S., Department of Commerce, Bureau of the Census, conference on Issues in Federal Statistical Needs Relating to Women, series P–23, no. 83 (December 1979), p. 21.

[2]U.S., Department of Commerce, Bureau of the Census, Special Studies: Female Family Heads, series P–23, no. 50 (July 1974), p. 6 (hereafter cited as Special Studies: Female Family Heads). Data for 1960 were not collected in terms of families with children under 18.

[3]U.S., Department of Commerce, Bureau of the Census, Families Maintained by Female Householders, 1970–1979, series P–23, no. 107, p. 7 (hereafter cited as Families Maintained by Female Householders, 1970–1979). Data for 1970 were not collected in terms of families with children under 18.

[4]U.S., Department of Commerce, Bureau of the Census, Household and Family Characteristics: March 1981, series P–20, no. 371, p. 7 (hereafter cited as Household and Family Characteristics: March 1981).

[5]Ibid., p. 7.

[6]Special Studies: Female Family Heads, p. 6; Household and Family Characteristics: March 1981, p. 12.

[7]Household and Family Characteristics: March 1981, p. 7.

[8]In this report, "female householder families" refers to those families headed by women with no husbands present. Hence, female-headed households and female householder families are used interchangeably. Male householders are men heading households without wives present.

[9]U.S., Department of Commerce, Bureau of the Census, 1970 Census of the Population: Persons of Spanish Origin, PC(2)–IC, p. 121 (hereafter cited as Persons of Spanish Origin: 1970); and Money Income and Poverty Status of Families and Persons in the United States: 1981 (Advance Data), series P–60, no. 134, p. 8 (hereafter cited as Money Income: 1981).

[10]Persons of Spanish Origin: 1970, p. 121; and Money Income: 1981, p. 9.

[11]Money Income: 1981, p. 10.

[12]U.S., Department of Commerce, Bureau of the Census, Marital Status and Living Arrangements: March 1981, series P–20, no. 372 (June 1982), p. 1 (hereafter cited as Marital Status and Living Arrangements: March 1981).

[13]Household and Family Characteristics: March 1981, p. 7.

[14]Marital Status and Living Arrangements: March 1981, p. 5.

[15]Ibid.

[16]Money Income: 1981, p. 21.

[17]Ibid., p. 4.

[18]Ibid., p. 21.

[19]Daniel P. Moynihan and Oscar Lewis, among others, have hypothesized about the culture of poverty and its hold on minority female-headed families.

[20]Martin Kilson, "Black Social Classes and Intergenerational Poverty," The Public Interest, no. 64 (Summer 1981), p. 68.

[21]Ibid., p. 62.

[22]Greg Duncan and James Morgan, eds., "Introduction, Overview, Summary, and Conclusions," in Five Thousand American Families—Patterns of Economic Progress (Ann Arbor: Institute for Social Research, Univ. of Michigan, 1976), vol. IV, pp. 1–22.

[23]U.S. Department of Health, Education, and Welfare, Social Security and the Changing Roles of Men and Women (1978), p. 2.

[24]Marital Status and Living Arrangements: March 1981, pp. 3–4.

[25]The divorce rate declined from 5.3 per 1,000 population to 5.1 from January through August 1982, as compared to the same period in 1981 (94,000 and 100,000 divorces, respectively). U.S., Department of Health and Human Services, Public Health Service, "Births, Marriages, Divorces, and Deaths for August 1982," Monthly Vital Statistics Report, vol. 31, no. 8 (Nov. 15, 1982), p. 3.

[26]Marital Status and Living Arrangements: March 1981, p. 4.

[27]Ibid., p. 3.

[28]Ibid.

[29]Ibid.

[30]Ibid.

[31]Lois Shaw, "Economic Consequences of Marital Disruption," National Longitudinal Study of Mature Women (contract paper for U.S. Department of Labor, June 1978), p. 8.

[32]James N. Morgan, "Family Composition," in Duncan and Morgan, eds., Five Thousand American Families—Patterns of Economic Progress (1974), vol. I, pp. 99–121.

[33]U.S., Department of Commerce, Bureau of the Census, Changing Family Composition and Income Differentials, by Edward Welniak and Gordon Green (August 1982), p. 13.

[34]See chap. 1 for standard definition of poverty.

[35]L. Shaw, "Economic Consequences of Marital Disruption," p. 18.

[36]Ibid.

[37]Male householders increased by 95 percent to 666,000 between 1970 and 1981. Female householders with children under 18 years old increased by 97 percent to 5,634,000, although divorces alone do not account for all of this increase.

[38]U.S., Department of Commerce, Bureau of the Census, Child Support and Alimony: 1978 (Advance Report), series P–23, no. 106, p. 1.

[39]Ibid.

[40]Ibid.

[41]Ibid.

[42]Ibid.

[43]Ibid.

[44]Ibid.

[45]See U.S. Commission on Civil Rights reports: Women and Poverty, staff report (1974); Women—Still in Poverty (1979); and Child Care and Equal Opportunity for Women (1981) (hereafter cited as Child Care and Equal Opportunity).

[46]U.S., Department of Commerce, Bureau of the Census, Trends in Child Care Arrangements of Working Mothers, series P–25, no. 117 (June 1982), p. 3 (hereafter cited as Trends).

[47]Ibid. U.S., Department of Labor, Children of Working Mothers, Special Labor Force Report 217 (March 1977), p. A–30.

[48]Trends, p. 3.

[49]Harriet Presser and Wendy Baldwin, "Child Care as a Constraint on Employment: Prevalence, Correlates, and Bearing on the Work and Fertility Nexus," American Journal of Sociology, vol. 85, no. 5 (March 1980), p. 1205.

# Marriage: Conducive to Greater Life Satisfaction for American Black Women?

## Richard E. Ball

*Objective differences between Black and white families (such as median income and illegitimacy rate) are well documented. It has been argued that because of social and economic pressures faced by Black families, such objective indicators are not appropriate measures of their functioning; rather, subjective impressions should be used. This study examines the life satisfaction of a sample of 373 Black women. Satisfaction was highest for the currently married, the widowed, and the divorced—and was significantly lower for the single and the separated.*

## Introduction

Differences between black and white families in the United States are well documented. Median family income for blacks is only 57 percent of that of whites, and the illegitimacy rate for blacks has reached 50 percent, as opposed to 8 percent for whites. Whereas 12 percent of white children reside in families headed by their mothers, 42 percent of black children are similarly situated (Bianchi and Farley, 1979; U.S. Bureau of the Census, 1980).

Disparities in objective indicators such as these have been viewed by some social scientists as

well as by the general public as reflecting weaknesses in the structure and functioning of the black family. In response, other writers have attacked this perspective as having reversed the relationship between economic and social handicap and the structure and functioning of black families (Billingsley, 1968, 1970; Rainwater and Yancey, 1967; Staples 1969, 1971a, 1971b, among others). In fact, the entire approach of using objective indicators to compare the functioning of black families vis-à-vis those of whites has been criticized strongly.

One of the most articulate of these critics has been Robert Staples, who has indicated that comparing black families with those of whites inevitably has resulted in the minority being seen as inferior. Other writers such as Andrew Billingsley and Robert B. Hill have pointed out that because of their disadvantaged place in society, black families have developed alternative family forms as mechanisms for survival. Therefore, it is argued that black families should be evaluated in terms of their own strengths and weaknesses (Billingsley, 1968; Hill, 1972; Hill and Shackleford, 1975; Staples, 1971b).

A variable of major interest when addressing family composition and functioning is marital status. Although increasing numbers of Americans are delaying or eschewing matrimony[1] and divorce rates are rising, marriage still is the expectation for the overwhelming majority of adults. Handicaps

---

Unpublished paper originally presented at the annual meeting of the National Council on Family Relations, Washington, D.C., October 13–16, 1982. Reprinted by permission of the author. The research on which this paper reports was supported partially by NIMH grant RO12740. The author thanks Lynn Robbins, Department of Psychiatry, University of Florida, for her generous research assistance.

for those who are not married can be severe. For example, median income for female-headed black households is only 53 percent of that of black husband-headed households (Bianchi and Farley, 1979).

In spite of objective data such as these indicating certain disadvantages that may be suffered by those who are not married, a contrary viewpoint sometimes is expressed regarding the utility of marriage for at least some low-income black Americans.

Some research has indicated that marital failure almost seems predestined for a substantial proportion of poor black Americans. The inability of many men to obtain steady employment at a living wage causes strains within the marriage and creates expectations of marital failure (Liebow, 1967; Parker and Kleiner, 1969; Rubin, 1978; Schulz, 1969). Other research has shown that some low-income black mothers believe that they are better off without a husband at home (McIntyre, 1966; Rainwater, 1971). Heiss's study (1975) found that fewer than one-third of currently married or unmarried black mothers believed that most men make good husbands, and about one-half agreed that women's best time is when they are married. Slightly over two-thirds indicated that they would marry again. It appears that for some black Americans, at least, marriage is viewed as a losing status.

As pointed out by Billingsley, students of the black family have concentrated on its instrumental functioning (1968). As a result, there is a paucity of empirically backed data regarding the *expressive* functioning of the American black family. The vital subjective dimension all too often has been ignored. In addition, black families that are *not* poor generally have been neglected.

The expressive realm is the focus of this research. The dependent variable for investigation is level of life satisfaction, which is indicative of perceived well-being. The independent variable of greatest interest is marital status. The study is designed to bring data from a representative sample of a black population to bear on the question: What is the impact of marital status on black satisfaction levels? Because of the comparatively high levels of attenuation among American black families, this research focuses on black women.[2]

# Literature Review

Research assessing subjective well-being within the normal population has increasingly been emphasized since the mid-1950s. However, most of this study has been directed toward the white population, with nonwhites either excluded or forming a small subsample of little interest to the researchers.

Most frequently used as indicators of perceived well-being have been responses to items assessing overall happiness or life satisfaction. One of the most consistent findings regarding the general (or white) population is that those currently married and residing with spouse report higher levels of well-being than do those who are not residing with spouse. Intermediate in well-being may be the widowed and the single, with the separated and the divorced lowest in perceived well-being (Bradburn, 1969; Bradburn and Caplovitz, 1965; Campbell et al., 1976; Clemente and Sauer, 1976; Glenn, 1975; Glenn and Weaver, 1979; Gurin et al., 1960; Palmore and Luikart, 1972; Spreitzer and Snyder, 1974).[3]

Much less is available on perceived well-being among black Americans. The comprehensive study of a national sample conducted by Campbell, Converse, and Rodgers (1976) found that among their black subsample both the married and the widowed were equally high in happiness and life satisfaction. Much lower were the single and the separated/divorced (together). A study that included only blacks aged 45 through 74 found marital status and happiness not to be significantly related (Wray, 1974). Gerontological study of only the elderly found little difference in satisfaction levels between married and unmarried blacks (Jackson et al., 1977–1978).

Prior research has shown that a number of variables other than marital status have potential impact on subjective well-being. These variables include income, education, age, social participation, and health.

Research findings on black Americans regarding the effect of income and education are contradictory. Some studies have found positive correlations, others a curvilinear relationship. Contradictory findings also are found in regard to age, although a slight preponderance of evidence indicates that age and well-being are related positively for black Americans. For the general population, self-evaluated health and well-being are positively correlated, and the scant research available indicates that this also holds for blacks. Social participation has been measured in a variety of ways. Generally, it pertains to voluntary contacts outside the home or workplace. Although for the general population social participation tends to be positively correlated with well-being, little and contradictory evidence is available in regard to blacks (Alston et al., 1974; Bradburn, 1969; Campbell et al., 1976; Jackson et al., 1977–1978; Wray, 1974). It is clear that more research is needed on the relations of these variables to subjective well-being among black Americans.

## Method

Data used for this study were collected in four counties of central Florida. Although primarily rural and agricultural, the area includes a number of small towns and two minor standard metropolitan statistical areas (SMSAs). Multistage cluster sampling and the randomization technique developed by Kish (1965) were used to ensure representativeness of respondents. The overall sample consisted of 3,674 persons 18 and over, of whom 626 (17 percent) were black. Of the black respondents, 373 (60 percent) were female. These female black respondents are the subsample for this study. A comprehensive interview schedule was administered in the respondents' homes by trained interviewers. The overall response rate was 86 percent. Comparison of the overall sample to census data on standard socioeconomic variables showed it to be representative (Warheit et al., 1976).

The dependent variable of life satisfaction is measured by responses to the Cantril Self-Anchoring Striving Scale, one component of a series of items designed to help respondents establish their own frames of reference regarding their personal situations. The scale is designed to be "symbolic of the 'ladder of life'" (Cantril, 1965:22). It has ten rungs and allows eleven possible responses, ranging from 0, the lowest possible, to 10, the highest. Those scoring 10 indicate that they have the best possible life for themselves. Other variables investigated are income, education, age, social participation, and health.

An adjusted indicator is used for family/household income. Termed *welfare ratio*, it is determined by dividing a family's total income by its federally determined poverty level. A welfare ratio of 1.0 or lower indicates that the family officially is "in poverty." Poverty levels for the period of data collection were used. Due to the family size and age–sex composition adjustment inherent in the poverty level for any family, this ratio better indicates economic standard of living than does raw income.

Education data are in seven categories (none through college graduate). Age is age at last birthday. Social participation is determined by a composite score on three items. Item one requests frequency of interaction with nearby relatives, including use of the telephone. Item two requests frequency of getting together with nearby friends. Item three asks how often the main worship service of her church is attended. Total possible individual scores range from 0 through 14. Self-evaluated health is indicated by response to an item requesting the individuals' assessment of her current health. Scores range from 1 through 5 (very bad through excellent).

ANOVA is used for bivariate analysis, with multiple correlation and regression with stepwise inclusion of variables used for the multivariate analysis. In order for all calculations to involve the same universe of data, a case with a missing value on any variable has been eliminated completely from the multivariate analysis. Being categorical, marital statuses are coded as dummy variables.

The major hypothesis to be investigated involves testing for differences in life satisfaction levels between black women with different marital statuses. In addition, the impact of other variables previously discussed is studied.

## Research Findings

Table 1 shows life satisfaction scores in bivariate relationship with the independent variables.

## TABLE 1 Life Satisfaction, Bivariate Analysis[1]

| VARIABLE | N | $\bar{X}^2$ | SD | F | P |
|---|---|---|---|---|---|
| Sample | 351 | 6.09 | 2.68 | | |
| (Not available) | (22) | | | | |
| Marital status | 351 | 6.09 | 2.68 | 5.53 | .001 |
| Single | 51 | 4.98 | 2.66 | | |
| Married | 153 | 6.28 | 2.51 | | |
| Widowed | 70 | 6.84 | 2.87 | | |
| Separated | 53 | 5.30 | 2.68 | | |
| Divorced | 24 | 6.75 | 2.25 | | |
| (Not available) | (22) | | | | |
| Welfare ratio | 269 | 6.09 | 2.66 | 2.42 | .05 |
| 0.0–0.5 | 49 | 5.10 | 2.88 | | |
| 0.5–1.0 | 84 | 6.42 | 2.83 | | |
| 1.0–1.5 | 55 | 6.07 | 2.73 | | |
| 1.5–2.0 | 31 | 6.00 | 2.39 | | |
| 2.0 + | 50 | 6.56 | 2.13 | | |
| (Not available) | (104) | | | | |
| Age | 351 | 6.09 | 2.60 | 5.09 | .001 |
| 18–19 | 21 | 5.24 | 2.68 | | |
| 20–29 | 71 | 5.35 | 2.13 | | |
| 30–39 | 64 | 5.38 | 2.68 | | |
| 40–49 | 60 | 6.42 | 2.48 | | |
| 50–59 | 54 | 6.13 | 2.76 | | |
| 60–69 | 52 | 7.08 | 2.83 | | |
| 70 + | 29 | 7.55 | 2.85 | | |
| (Not available) | (22) | | | | |
| Education | 346 | 6.07 | 2.65 | 1.27 | n.s. |
| None | 9 | 6.11 | 3.69 | | |
| 1–4 years | 44 | 6.64 | 3.10 | | |
| 5–8 | 69 | 6.39 | 2.69 | | |
| 9–11 | 122 | 5.80 | 2.74 | | |
| High school graduate | 68 | 6.04 | 2.28 | | |
| 1–3 college | 22 | 5.14 | 1.86 | | |
| College graduate | 12 | 6.67 | 2.02 | | |
| (Not available) | (27) | | | | |
| Social participation | 351 | 6.09 | 2.68 | 6.02 | .001 |
| 0–2 | 5 | 5.20 | 4.44 | | |
| 3–5 | 36 | 4.50 | 2.97 | | |
| 6–8 | 74 | 5.64 | 2.74 | | |
| 9–11 | 123 | 6.24 | 2.32 | | |
| 12–14 | 113 | 6.76 | 2.61 | | |
| (Not available) | (22) | | | | |
| Health | 351 | 6.09 | 2.65 | 3.28 | .01 |
| Very bad | 5 | 2.60 | 1.82 | | |
| Poor | 25 | 5.48 | 3.34 | | |
| Fair | 101 | 5.87 | 2.57 | | |
| Good | 142 | 6.24 | 2.75 | | |
| Excellent | 78 | 6.51 | 2.34 | | |
| (Not available) | (22) | | | | |

[1]Ns vary due to missing data. n.s. = not significant.
[2]Range possible: 0 to 10.

Highest mean level of life satisfaction is found for widows (6.84 of a possible 10.0), followed closely by the divorced (6.75). Slightly lower are the married (6.28), and considerably lower are the separated (5.30). Lowest of all are the single (4.98). The extreme differences are significant at $p < .001$.

Excluding the separated category, life satisfaction levels are higher for the formerly married than for the currently married. However, these differences are slight.

Also statistically significantly related to life satisfaction in bivariate analysis are welfare ratio, age, social participation, and health, as shown in Table 1. Only education lacks significance.

As shown in Table 2, zero-order correlations between control variables are statistically significant in most instances. However, only for age and education and for welfare ratio and education are the $R^2$ values high enough to indicate the potential for distortion of multivariate findings due to multicollinearity.

Table 3 shows the multiple stepwise regression and correlation matrices. Only those in the marital status categories of single and separated show significant variance in satisfaction from the married (the suppressed category). Controlling other variables in the equation, the single and the separated show lower satisfaction levels than do the married ($p < .05$). The widowed and the divorced vary little from the married. Thus, those who never have been married or who are separated, perhaps recently, are lower in life satisfaction than are the currently married, the widowed, or the divorced, independent of levels of the other variables investigated.

Of the other variables in the equation, social participation, age, and perceived health are significantly related to satisfaction. Those who are more involved in interaction outside the home, those who are older, and those who feel that they are in good health tend to be more satisfied.[4] Income and education are not significant, controlling the other variables. Of all variables investigated, social participation has the greatest impact on satisfaction, as shown by its regression coefficient ($B$) and standardized coefficient ($B^*$).

The null hypothesis of no difference in mean satisfaction levels among women in different marital status categories is rejected at $p < .05$. The overall equation is significant at $p < .001$, and the multiple $R^2$ of .209 indicates that about one-fifth of total variance in satisfaction involves linear relationship with these variables.

## Discussion

It appears that marriage is no more conducive to life satisfaction for these black women than is being divorced or widowed. The impact on life satisfaction of having a husband appears to be minimal, except for those who have never had one (the single) or who have recently lost one (often the separated). Those who have had a husband, but who lost him or left him—often some time ago (the divorced or widowed)—are as satisfied as are the currently married.

It might be conjectured that the lower satisfaction scores of the separated than those of the divorced are an artifact of younger age, as the younger tend to be less satisfied. Also, it might be argued that this difference reflects socioeconomic status (SES) differentials, with those with higher SES more likely both to be satisfied and to formalize separation through divorce. However, as age and SES (here income and education) are controlled in the multivariate equation, it appears that recency of marital dissolution is a more plausible explanation for the disparity in satisfaction between the divorced and the separated.

Single women's low satisfaction levels may reflect the desire of many single women to be married. These generally low-income Southern black women, none of whom resides in a large city, may view singlehood as resulting from rejection, rather than from choice.

The comparatively high satisfaction levels of widows may involve several factors, at least two of them unique to this status. As with the divorced, marital dissolution in many cases no doubt occurred some time previous. However, in addition, two other circumstances may be of importance. First, marital dissolution for widows is an "act of God," rather than an event that usually follows an acrimonious relationship. Thus, fault is not an issue, although for the separated or divorced it may lead

TABLE 2   Zero-Order Pearson Product-Moment Correlations ($R$) among Control Variables[1]

| VARIABLE | WELFARE RATIO | AGE | EDUCATION | SOCIAL PARTICIPATION |
|---|---|---|---|---|
| Age | − .15** | | | |
| Education | .40*** | − .58*** | | |
| Social participation | .02 | .06 | .08 | |
| Health | .13** | − .10* | .12* | .13** |

[1]Significance levels, direction unpredicted: * = $p < .05$, ** = $p < .01$, *** = $p < .001$. Ns vary between 373 and 285 because of missing data.

TABLE 3   Life Satisfaction and Marital Status, Multiple Stepwise Regression Model

| VARIABLE | B | B* | SEB | F | P |
|---|---|---|---|---|---|
| Social participation | .219 | .248 | .050 | 19.424 | .001 |
| Age | .038 | .246 | .013 | 9.029 | .01 |
| Health | .368 | .128 | .163 | 5.114 | .05 |
| Welfare ratio | .167 | .068 | .158 | 1.108 | n.s. |
| Single | − 1.163 | − .135 | .534 | 4.750 | .05 |
| Separated | − .899 | − .123 | .448 | 4.031 | .05 |
| Education | .102 | .050 | .148 | 0.479 | n.s. |
| Widowed | − .060 | − .009 | .447 | 0.018 | n.s. |
| Constant: includes married; divorced deleted ($B = .003$, $F = .002$) | .577 | | | | |

| | df | SUM OF SQUARES | MEAN SQUARE | F | P |
|---|---|---|---|---|---|
| Regression | 8 | 389.342 | 48.668 | 8.497 | .001 |
| Residual | 257 | 1472.00 | 5.728 | | |
| Standard error of the estimate: 2.393 | | | | | |

| VARIABLE | R | MULTIPLE R | MULTIPLE $R^2$ | $R^2$ CHANGE | ADJUSTED $R^2$ |
|---|---|---|---|---|---|
| Social participation | .290 | .290 | .084 | .084 | .081 |
| Age | .275 | .384 | .147 | .063 | .141 |
| Health | .140 | .411 | .169 | .022 | .159 |
| Welfare ratio | .118 | .431 | .186 | .017 | .174 |
| Single | − .191 | .442 | .195 | .009 | .180 |
| Separated | − .178 | .456 | .208 | .013 | .189 |
| Education | − .052 | .457 | .209 | .001 | .188 |
| Widowed | .149 | .457 | .209 | .000 | .185 |

to self-denigration and, thereby, dissatisfaction.[5] Second, although age is controlled in the multivariate analysis, because there are comparatively few young widows this control may not function adequately.

That having a husband is not particularly conducive to satisfaction for some women may be tied to exchange theory. One of the basic tenets of this theory is that relationships are discontinued if they appear unprofitable to the actor in comparison with perceived alternatives. In regard to marriage among black Americans, often advanced is the economic perspective that because of racial discrimination, black men have difficulty competing in the labor market. Thus, their economic input into the family sometimes is minimal, or even negative.[6] Perhaps because of this, other inputs, such as those of the expressive realm, may be lessened as well (Liebow, 1967).[7] Thus, after having experienced it, some may not evaluate marriage in retrospect as having been particularly satisfying. After an adjustment period, again being unmarried may seem as satisfying as being married had been.

In the introduction it was stated that some writers believe that black Americans have developed a number of coping mechanisms, including adaptability in family roles. This research indicates that in fact this contention may have validity. Many black women seem as satisfied going it alone as are others who are married and residing with their husbands.[8]

Further study may find variables such as the recency of the separation, divorce, or widowhood and stages of the family life cycle to offer avenues for fruitful research on well-being.[9] Also, although some research has been conducted on satisfaction and happiness levels for specific domains of life in addition to overall well-being, much study remains to be done in the area of domain satisfaction.[10]

Additional opportunities for further research include multivariate investigation of the relationship between marital status and perceived well-being for black men and detailed comparisons between the perceived well-being of black men and women.

---

[1]Currently, a record low proportion of black Americans under age 25 report being married (Bianchi and Farley, 1979).

[2]In 1978, 42.7 percent of all black families were female headed, and 82 percent of these families contained minor children (Bianchi and Farley, 1979; U.S. Bureau of the Census, 1979).

[3]Many of these findings lack comparability not only due to varying methods and analyses, but also because marital status categories are constituted in different ways in separate studies. The separated may be included with the married, placed with all others not currently married, placed with the divorced, or viewed as a unique category.

[4]As might be expected, social participation is important particularly for separated women. Separate analysis shows that it alone accounts for 42 percent of the variance in their satisfaction scores. However, social participation appears much less important for the divorced and the widowed in this context.

[5]It might be hypothesized that life satisfaction leads to marital "success," as evidenced by the higher satisfaction levels of the married and the widowed. This reversal of the cause–effect relationship pursued here is plausible, but is brought into question by the equally high satisfaction levels of the divorced.

[6]Punitive welfare regulations in many states prohibit aid to families in which the husband-father is present, thus exacerbating the situation.

[7]It must be noted that the relationships between marital status and life satisfaction shown in this research hold both in bivariate and multivariate analyses. Thus, regardless of income level, the divorced and the widowed are as satisfied as are the married. For this sample, at least, the economic perspective lacks explanatory power. It appears that discrimination may have taken its toll in additional ways, perhaps involving the fostering of negative self-images.

[8]It should be noted that a consistent research finding is that blacks score lower on happiness and satisfaction scales than do whites, even when variables such as income are controlled. In addition, where investigated, black women have been shown to perceive lower well-being than do black men (Alston et al., 1974; Bradburn, 1969; Campbell et al., 1976; Clemente and Sauer, 1976; Lewinski, 1977; Wray, 1974).

[9]In addition to marital status and age, the life cycle component of having a minor child at home was investigated in this research. Overall, and for each marital status separately, having a child at home did not have statistically significant impact on life satisfaction for these women.

[10]Campbell, Converse, and Rodgers addressed the domain satisfaction of black Americans in their comprehensive study, but primarily relied on bivariate analysis (1976).

# References

Alston, Jon P., G. Lowe, and A. Wrigley
1974    "Socioeconomic Correlates for Four Dimensions of Perceived Satisfaction, 1972." *Human Organization* 33:99–102.

Bianchi, Suzanne M., and R. Farley
1979    "Racial Differences in Family Living Arrangements and Economic Well-Being: An Analysis of Recent Trends." *Journal of Marriage and the Family* 41:537–551.

Billingsley, Andrew
1968    *Black Families in White America.* Englewood Cliffs, N.J.: Prentice-Hall.
1970    "Black Families and White Social Science." *Journal of Social Issues* 26:127–142.

Bradburn, Norman
1969    *The Structure of Psychological Well-Being.* Chicago: Aldine.

Bradburn, Norman, and D. Caplovitz
1965    *Reports on Happiness.* Chicago: Aldine.

Campbell, Angus, P. Converse, and W. Rodgers
1976    *The Quality of American Life.* New York: Russell Sage.

Cantril, Hadley
1965    *The Pattern of Human Concerns.* New Brunswick, N.J.: Rutgers University Press.

Clemente, Frank, and W. Sauer
1976    "Life Satisfaction in the United States." *Social Forces* 54:621–631.

Glenn, Norval
1975    "The Contribution of Marriage to the Psychological Well-Being of Males and Females." *Journal of Marriage and the Family* 37:594–600.

Glenn, Norval, and C. Weaver
1979    "A Note on Family Situation and Global Happiness." *Social Forces* 57:960–967.

Gurin, Gerald, J. Veroff, and S. Feld
1960    *Americans View Their Mental Health.* New York: Basic Books.

Heiss, Jerrold
1975    *The Case of the Black Family: A Sociological Inquiry.* New York: Columbia University Press.

Hill, Robert B.
1972    *The Strengths of Black Families.* New York: Emerson Hall.

Hill, Robert B., and L. Shackleford
1975    "The Black Family Revisited." *Urban League Review* 1:18–24.

Jackson, James S., J. Bacon, and J. Peterson
1977–   "Life Satisfaction among Black Urban Elderly."
1978    *Journal of Aging and Human Development* 8:169–179.

Kish, Leslie
1965    *Survey Sampling.* New York: Wiley.

Lewinski, Robert E.
1977    "A Study of Job Satisfaction and Life Satisfaction in the Mid-Seventies." M.A. thesis, Department of Sociology, University of Florida.

Liebow, Elliot
1967    *Tally's Corner.* Boston: Little, Brown.

McIntyre, Jennie J.
1966    Illegitimacy: A Case of Stretched Values? Ph.D. Dissertation, The Florida State University. Ann Arbor, Mich.: University Microfilms.

Palmore, Erdman, and C. Luikart
1972    "Health and Social Factors Related to Life Satisfaction." *Journal of Health and Social Behavior* 13:68–80.

Parker, Seymour, and R. Kleiner
1969    "Social and Psychological Dimensions of the Family Role Performance of the Negro Male." *Journal of Marriage and the Family* 31:500–506.

Rainwater, Lee
1971    *Crucible of Identity: The Negro Lower-Class Family.* In *Black Matriarchy: Myth or Reality?*, John H. Bracey, Jr., A. Meier, and E. Rudwick, eds., pp. 76–111. Belmont, Calif.: Wadsworth.

Rainwater, Lee, and W. Yancey, editors
1967    *The Moynihan Report and the Politics of Controversy.* Cambridge, Mass.: The M.I.T. Press.

Rubin, Roger H.
1978    "Matriarchal Themes in Black Family Literature: Implications for Family Life Education." *The Family Coordinator* 27:33–41.

Schulz, David
1969    *Coming Up Black.* Englewood Cliffs, N.J.: Prentice-Hall.

Spreitzer, Elmer, and E. Snyder
1974 "Correlates of Life Satisfaction among the Aged." *Journal of Gerontology* 29:454–458.

Staples, Robert
1969 "Research on the Negro Family: A Source for the Family Practitioner." *The Family Coordinator* 18:202–209.

Staples, Robert, editor
1971a *The Black Family: Essays and Studies.* Belmont, Calif.: Wadsworth.

Staples, Robert
1971b "Toward a Sociology of the Black Family: A Theoretical and Methodological Assessment." *Journal of Marriage and the Family* 33:119–138.

U.S. Bureau of the Census
1979 *Statistical Abstract 1979.* Washington, D.C.: U.S. Government Printing Office.

1980 Current Population Reports, series P–60, No. 125. *Money Income and Poverty Status of Families and Persons in the United States, 1979.* Washington, D.C.: U.S. Government Printing Office.

U.S. Department of Labor, Office of Policy Planning and Research
1965 *The Negro Family: The Case for National Action.* Washington, D.C.: Department of Labor.

Warheit, George J., C. Holzer, R. Bell, and S. Arey
1976 "Sex, Marital Status, and Mental Health: A Reappraisal." *Social Forces* 55:459–470.

Wray, Stephen D.
1974 "The Social Factors Associated with the Happiness and Mental Health of People in the Middle Years and Early Old Age." Ph.D. dissertation, Department of Sociology, University of Florida. Ann Arbor, Mich.: University Microfilms.

# PART THREE

# The Family

## Childbearing and Parental Roles

The bearing of children has traditionally been a very important function in the Black community. The sacrifices of Black mothers for their children have been legendary for hundreds of years. While children are still regarded as a strong value to Blacks, attitudes toward having large numbers of them have changed dramatically since 1965. Contributing to this change are the beliefs of many Black women that the responsibility for rearing large numbers of children is destructive to their personal freedom and job mobility, the different problems faced in raising children in urban centers, the decline in biparental households, and the necessity of raising children alone. Around 1983, the lifetime births expected by single Black women aged 18–24 years were the same as that of comparable white women. Women in both groups expected to have fewer than two children in their lifetime (U.S. Bureau of the Census, 1984).

One of the most significant changes in the period 1970–1979 was the change in the Black fertility rate. In 1978, the Black birth rate continued to decline. However, the white birth rate declined even more rapidly (11 percent versus 2 percent), and the total fertility rate in 1979 of 21.5 children per thousand Black women was still higher (14.4 per thousand) than that of white women (U.S. Bureau of the Census, 1984). The Black fertility rate is influenced by a number of factors including regional variations, rural–urban differences, and, most importantly, socioeconomic levels. In 1979, Black women in the South had more children than those who lived in the North, and the birth rate of urban Black women was lower than that of Black women in rural areas. Significantly, college-educated Blacks have the lowest fertility rate of almost every demographic category in the United States, whereas middle-class Catholics and Mormons have the highest. College-educated Black women actually have a lower birth rate than college-educated white women (U.S. Bureau of the Census, 1984).

One of the more significant events since the mid-1970s was the steady increase in the out-of-wedlock births of Black women; at the same time, the birth rate among married Black women showed a steady decline. The illegitimacy rate among whites went from 1.7 to 7.3 per 1,000 unmarried women 15–44 years old between 1950 and 1975, while the rate among Blacks increased from 17.9 to 48.6 during the same time span (Bianchi and Farley, 1979). Some of this racial difference in the illegitimacy rate increase can be attributed to the more frequent and effective use of contraceptives, abortions, and shotgun weddings among white women. The official data show that Black women married before their child was born in only 32 percent of the cases, whereas white women married before their child was born in 63 percent of the cases (U.S. Bureau of the Census, 1984). Another reason has been the substantial decrease in legitimate fertility rates among married Black women over the age of 24. Almost a third of all births to Black women occur to those under the age of 19, the majority of them illegitimate. In 1978, 34 percent of Black mothers only households were maintained by never-married women (U.S. Bureau of the Census, 1984).

Raising a Black child is not, and has never been, an easy task. In light of the obstacles they face, Black parents have done a more than adequate job. Generally, they have more children to rear, with fewer resources, than white parents. They must also socialize their children into the values of mainstream culture in order to adapt successfully to majority group requirements and institutions. At the same time they must teach the children the folkways of their own culture and what it means to be Black in a racist society. Given the poor social conditions under which most Black children are raised, it is not surprising that some fail in life. What is even more surprising is that so many succeed in the face of the adverse circumstances they encounter.

Child-rearing practices do not differ significantly by race. Variations in socialization techniques are more a function of class membership. Middle-class parents, Black and white, are more likely to use verbal than physical punishment to discipline a child. Lower-class Black mothers are often regarded as ineffective parents because of their reliance on physical punishment techniques to control their children. What is not considered in that assessment is the tendency of many Black mothers to combine physical measures with very heavy doses of emotional nurturance. This combination of spankings and affection may be more beneficial for a child's development than the middle class parents' threat of withdrawal of love if the child does not behave correctly. Many observers of the Black family have noticed how children in the lower-class Black community are well treated and seem emotionally and psychologically healthy.

The attitudes and behavior of many Black parents are changing. Fewer children are being born per family and there are indications that those children who are brought into this world are not as well treated. The same trend is also evident in the white community and seems to be part of the tendency of mothers to put their own wishes and goals ahead of everything and everyone else. There are also certain tensions in our society, particularly in urban areas, that affect behavior toward children. Corresponding to an increase in those tensions has

been an elevation of the incidence of child abuse in Black families and a decline in the respect of Black children for their elders. Certain changes in the Black fertility pattern are responsible for some of the inadequate parenting that exists today. While there have been overall declines in the Black birth rate, there has been a significant increase in out-of-wedlock pregnancies, primarily to teenaged women. With the decline in the Black extended family system, immature mothers and one-parent households have fostered the arrogance and negativism emerging among many Black youth.

Although there may be problems stemming from the one-parent household, one study of fatherless Black families found that boys in these homes do not see themselves as less worthwhile than boys who reside in father-present homes (Rubin, 1974). One reason for their high self-esteem is the availability of male role models outside the home and the significance of adult males in the family. Still, one cannot underestimate the importance of the mother and father to the child's development. Those parents provide the necessary aid, values, and encouragement for their children's mobility aspirations. In their survey of female-headed households, Peters and de Ford (1986) note that it is not an easy task to raise children alone but that the households were generally coping well in their circumstances and were a viable form of the family.

# The Extended Family

Kinship bonds have always been important to the Black population. In African societies kinship was and is the basis of the social organization. During the period of slavery many of the bondsmen were organized into an extended family system based on biological and nonbiological standards. Most research studies of Black kinship networks generally indicate that they are more extensive and significant to the Black community than to the white community (Adams, 1970). Whatever the reason, there is little doubt that kinsmen play an important role in the Black family system.

Among the valuable services provided by kin is the sharing of economic resources, child care, advice, and other forms of mutual aid. Those are acknowledged functions of a kinship network, but members of the extended family also serve to liberate children from the confines of the nuclear family unit. Children have someone other than a mother or father to relate to and from whom to receive emotional nurturance. The network also helps socialize children more effectively into values that Blacks held more strongly in rural and southern settings. The function of kinship groups to Blacks is so important that many nonblood relatives are referred to and regarded as kinsmen. Usually, this is a special friendship in which the normal claims, obligations, and loyalties of the kin relationships are operative, such as those of godmothers or play brothers (McAdoo, 1981).

One of the problems the Black family is facing today is a decline in the extended family system. This has occurred, in large part, as a result of Black mobility patterns. Many Blacks have moved from their place of origin to large cities where they have few, if any, kin. Fairly large numbers of Blacks are moving to suburban areas, where they often lack friends or relatives in their immediate neighborhood or community. Changes in the attitudes of Black youth toward their elders have also weakened the role of some older kin. The antiauthority attitudes of many youth have made many of them less responsive to the wisdom and guidance of grandparents and other kin.

## Adolescence and Personality Development

The period of adolescence has been generally regarded as a time of identity acquisition and liberation from parental control. For Black youth the problem of transition from adolescence to adulthood has been compounded by their unique status in the society. Many, for example, do not have a carefree period in which to acquire their identity as do middle-class white youth. Because they come from relatively poor families, large numbers must find jobs to help in the support of their families. Finding employment in today's job market is not an easy task. Without any special skills and with little

education, the majority of Black youth are without regular employment of any kind. In the inner cities of the United States as many as 65 percent of Black teenagers are unemployed (Glasgow, 1979).

Because of that high unemployment rate Black youth are overrepresented in the crime statistics, in the volunteer army, among drug addicts, and in other negative social indexes. There has been a tendency to place the responsibility for the problems of Black youth on their disorganized family system. Although it is true that a slight majority of Black youth are now living in one-parent homes, there is reason to question that those types of families produce uneducable and delinquent children. One-parent households are generally poor families and it is the relationship between poverty and negative youth behavior that bears watching. Taylor (1986) investigated the general sociohistorical context within which the psychosocial development of Black youth occurs. His purpose was to look at role model identifications for these youth and their function in molding their psychosocial identity. What he found was that these youth had at their disposal a rich variety of social and psychological supports as well as a fund of experience on which to rely for the formation of their identity.

## Social and Economic Issues

It is necessary to understand the influence of economics on Black families' lives in order to conceptualize the conditions under which they function—or fail to function—as a viable system. Ever since the release from slavery, economic deprivation has been a fact of life for Black people. Since the forties the rate of unemployment among Blacks has been steadily twice that of whites. The National Urban League's (1974) hidden unemployment index showed the real unemployment rate of Black men to be around 25 percent. Men who can not find work not only have trouble maintaining a stable marital and family life but often can not find a woman willing to marry them in the first place. Only 55 percent of all Black men with incomes of less than $5,000 a year are married, compared to 80 percent of those earning $15–20,000. As incomes rise so does the number of Black men who marry (Glick and Mills, 1974).

Black families have a median income of $13,598 a year compared to $24,603 a year for white families (U.S. Bureau of the Census, 1984). Not only is Black family income 56 percent that of white family income, but that figure indicates a drop in the ratio from 61 percent in 1969. If adjustments for inflation are made, Black families were slightly worse off five years later (National Urban League, 1974). This does not even consider the fact that many more Black families (two-thirds) derive their family income from multiple earners than white households (one-half). The implications of those economic facts are obvious when we observe that the higher the income of Blacks the more likely we will find a biparental family. When we look at Black families headed by women, we see that they had an average income of only $7,510 a year, approximately 38 percent of the earnings of intact Black families in 1981 (U.S. Bureau of the Census, 1984).

## Health Issues

Despite the promise of greater racial equality in American life, most statistics show a widening racial gap in the 1990s. Nowhere is this truer than with regard to health conditions. From 1984 to 1987, the gap in life expectancy between Blacks and whites continued to grow. That trend was almost entirely a function of deaths from preventable causes, such as AIDS, drug overdoses, and other drug-related factors: diseases and disabilities that kill infants in their first year; accidents, mainly those involving motor vehicles; and chronic liver diseases, including cirrhosis caused by alcoholism. During that three-year period, the gap between Blacks and whites increased from 5.6 years to 6.2 years. Actually, this increased gap is largely a result of the high death rate of Black males—especially in their younger years. High unemployment, low self-esteem, and poor social image all contribute to a sense of despair among this group that leads to self-destructive behavior. Homicide, for example, is the leading cause of death among Black men, ages 15–30 years. It is during these years of greatest marriageability that Black men die at a rate triple that of similar Black women. Consequently, the marriage pool is considerably reduced for women who desire marriage to men in the same race. Those who are not victims of homicide die from suicide, AIDS, and drug overdoses. And, almost all of those early deaths occur in the lower socioeconomic classes. Two of the articles in this section focus on the most recent causes of death in the Black American community.

# References

**Adams, B.**
1970  "Isolation, Function and Beyond: American Kinship in the 1960s." *Journal of Marriage and the Family* 32 (November):575–598.

**Bianchi, S., and R. Farley**
1979  "Racial Differences in Family Living Arrangements and Economic Well-Being: An Analysis of Recent Trends." *Journal of Marriage and the Family* 41 (August):537–552.

**Glasgow, D.**
1979  *The Black Underclass.* San Francisco: Jossey-Bass.

**Glick, P., and K. Mills**
1974  *Black Families: Marriage Patterns and Living Arrangements.* Paper presented at the W. E. B. Du Bois conference on American Blacks, Atlanta, Ga.

**Marshall, G.**
1972  "An Exposition of the Valid Premises Underlying Black Families." In *The Black Family: Fact or Fantasy,* Alyce Gullatte, ed., pp. 12–15. Washington, D.C.: National Medical Association.

**McAdoo, H.**
1981  *Black Families.* Beverly Hills, Calif.: Sage.

National Urban League Research Department

1974    *Inflation and the Black Consumer.* Washington, D.C.: Author.

Peters, M., and C. deFord

1986    "The Solo Mother." In R. Staples, ed., *The Black Family: Essays and Studies* (3rd ed.), pp. 164–172. Belmont, Calif.: Wadsworth.

Rubin, R. H.

1974    "Adult Male Absence and the Self-Attitudes of Black Children." *Child Study Journal* 4 (Spring):33–45.

Taylor, R.

1986    "Black Youth and Psychosocial Development." In R. Staples, ed., *The Black Family: Essays and Studies* (3rd ed.), pp. 201–210. Belmont, Calif.: Wadsworth.

United States Bureau of the Census

1984    Series P–20, No. 386. *Fertility of American Women: June 1983.* Washington, D.C.: U.S. Government Printing Office.

# 6 / Childbearing and Parental Roles

## SOCIOCULTURAL INFLUENCES ON ADOLESCENT MOTHERS

### Alva P. Barnett

*This article explores some of the major health consequences and needs of the Black adolescent mother and her child. In the context of sociocultural and structural considerations, the discussion centers on antecedent factors likely to have an adverse affect on the health and well-being particularly of the Black adolescent mother and her child. These factors include inadequate family income and nutrition, lack of accessible quality health care services, and age. The author believes that in order to begin appropriate and effective intervention that is likely to have a positive impact on these young lives, a better understanding of the antecedent factors is needed. Such intervention will increase the functional capacities and optimal abilities of a major segment of our children and youth.*

## Introduction

This paper is intended to contribute to the understanding of the health problems and needs of the Black adolescent mother and the health effects associated with adolescent pregnancy and motherhood. Selected antecedent factors that adversely affect the health and well-being of the Black adolescent mother and her child will be discussed. These antecedent factors are age, inadequate nutrition, family income, changing family structure, and the lack of available and accessible quality health care services. If uncorrected, these factors could have far-reaching implications regarding the functional capacity and optimal ability of these mothers and their infants, who are a major portion of this nation's vital resources.

Quality health care, as a right, should be afforded every individual; it is necessary regardless of race, ethnic identity, social status or economic circumstances of an individual or group of individuals (Zastrow and Bowker, 1984). As Ramsey Clark reminds us, "Youth is the foundation on which quality health is built. If America is to be free and offer fulfillment to its people, it must guarantee every teenager a healthy body, a sound mind and a decent environment" (Clark, 1978).

This American guarantee is a noble gesture

Revised and adapted from an article originally published in *Pediatric Social Work* 3, (4, 1985). © 1985 by Eterna International. Reprinted by permission.

that—no matter how profoundly we hope, desire, and believe it to be—simply flies in the face of reality. That reality is supported by facts that are disturbing and warrant full attention, understanding, commitment, and action by all adults, practitioners, and, most importantly, Black Americans. These facts highlight some of the present conditions that affect the health and well-being of Black families, children, and youth. They include the steady growth of female-headed households; alarming rates of infant mortality; a growing number of poor persons and those below the poverty level as defined by the U.S. government; higher fertility rates, especially among younger adolescents; an increasing percentage of out-of-wedlock births and unemployment; and increasingly low levels of family income. Facts such as these strongly suggest a crisis situation for several reasons.

First, the effects are multiple and will have a negative impact on two subsequent generations of adults, adolescents, and their children. Secondly, adequate and effective intervention and prevention techniques have not been utilized to any measurable degree. The growing body of descriptive literature and statistical reports has not focused significantly on understanding the interactive, multidimensional nature of the situation, which has a particular impact on Black lives. These dimensions include structural barriers to opportunities, cultural values, and individual coping and adaptive patterns in relationship to survival and individual development.

# Present Conditions

In order to understand what the adolescent mother and her infant potentially face, some of the present conditions resulting in multiple effects that adversely impact the well-being mainly of Black families, children, and youth will be discussed in order to understand what potentially faces the adolescent mother and her infant.

The increasing rate of Black female-headed households: In 1982 over 47 percent of Black families with children under the age of 18 years were female-headed households; this represents almost a 40 percent increase of Black female-headed households from the 1950 rate of 8 percent. During this same time frame, white female-headed households increased 12 percent from 3 percent in 1950 to about 15 percent in 1982 (Raspberry, 1984:1; U.S. Bureau of the Census, 1983). These figures show that differences between Black and white family structures are widening, but particularly devastating is that the majority (56 percent) of poor families are female-headed households. It is estimated that 44.9 percent of Black children under 18 years of age live below the poverty line (Mathey and Johnson, 1983).

The gap between Black and white infant mortality rates is not closing but widening at a steady pace. In 1978, the Black infant mortality rate was 86 percent higher than the white infant mortality rate. Four years later, the Black infant mortality rate was 95 percent higher than the white counterparts. According to Dorothy Rice (1984), the federal government's goal to reduce Black infant mortality to no more than 12 infant deaths for each 1,000 live births by 1990 will not be realized if this emerging trend continues. Directly related to infant mortality is the high percentage of underweight babies being born and inadequate nutrition and health care. The most seriously underweight babies have disproportionately been born to Black mothers. For example, in 1981, 6 percent of all white infants were underweight at birth as compared to 31 percent of all Black babies who were underweight at birth (Avery, 1984).

There are many other related facts that have an impact on the level of health and well-being of Black adolescent mothers and their infants, two of which are the higher fertility rates and percentages of the out-of-wedlock births. Also included are higher unemployment levels and lower family income (see Figures 1 and 2 and Tables 1 and 2).

The data presented here disclose the continued lack of parity and, in many instances, the widening gap between minority and majority group circumstances that adversely affects the health and well-being of Black children and youth. The social, health, and structural conditions of which these facts are representative are ultimately surrounded by the issues of wealth and income opportunities.

# Current Knowledge

Since the 1960s, the occurrence of adolescent pregnancy and motherhood has continued to receive an enormous amount of national attention from a variety of disciplines and professional audiences. The steady attention given to adolescent pregnancy and motherhood has resulted in a plethora of descriptive literature and statistics.

Many of the studies have identified such related issues as health risks associated with adolescent pregnancy, childbearing, and the infant; the incidence of adolescent pregnancy and childbearing; and the negative economic social and educational consequences of adolescent motherhood affecting the quality of life (Brown, 1982; Klerman and Jekel, 1973; Ogg, 1976). Descriptive information has been important in learning about the prevalence of problems related to adolescent motherhood; aggregate statistics is also a significant part of this literature. As Resnick (1984) indicates, this type of statistics tends to hide more than it reveals, particularly the patterns and functions of behaviors. Some of the questions arising from these areas that have not been greatly explored are: What are the cultural patterns that must be understood in light of the structural barriers to opportunities afforded Black

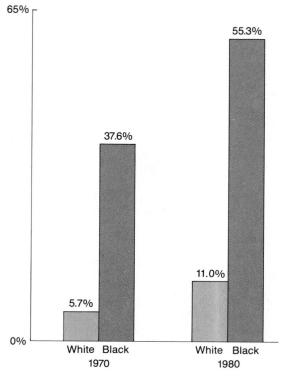

FIGURE 1  Percent of Births Born Out of Wedlock by Race: 1970 and 1980.
Source: National Center for Health Statistics.

TABLE 1    Fertility Rates among Women under Twenty by Age, Race and Marital Status of Woman: 1966, 1970, 1975, and 1978

|  | 1966 | 1970 | 1975 | 1978 |
|---|---|---|---|---|
| All women |  |  |  |  |
| 18–19 | 121.2 | 114.7 | 85.7 | 81.0 |
| 15–17 | 35.8 | 38.8 | 36.6 | 32.9 |
| 10–14 | 0.9 | 1.2 | 1.3 | 1.2 |
| All unmarried women |  |  |  |  |
| 18–19 | 25.8 | 32.9 | 32.8 | 35.7 |
| 15–17 | 13.1 | 17.1 | 19.5 | 19.5 |
| Unmarried white women |  |  |  |  |
| 18–19 | 14.3 | 17.6 | 16.6 | 19.5 |
| 15–17 | 5.4 | 7.5 | 9.7 | 10.5 |
| Unmarried nonwhite women |  |  |  |  |
| 18–19 | 110.5 | 126.5 | 117.4 | 116.3 |
| 15–17 | 61.2 | 73.3 | 72.0 | 64.9 |

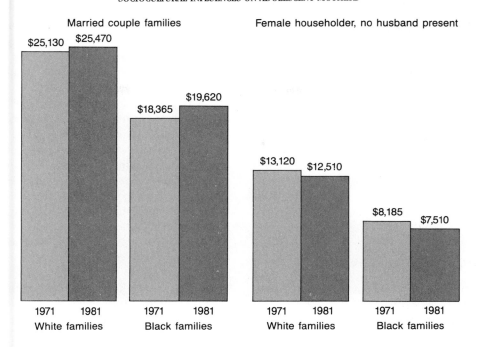

FIGURE 2  Median Family Income by Type of Family and Race of Householder: 1971 and 1981 (1981 dollars)

TABLE 2     Unemployment Rates

|  | 1970 | 1975 | 1980 | 1982 |
|---|---|---|---|---|
| All workers (16 years and over) | 4.9 | 8.5 | 7.1 | 9.7 |
| Black | — | 14.8 | 14.3 | 18.9 |
|   Female | — | 14.8 | 14.0 | 17.6 |
|   Male | — | 14.8 | 14.5 | 20.1 |
| White | 4.5 | 7.8 | 6.3 | 8.6 |
|   Female | 5.4 | 8.6 | 6.5 | 8.3 |
|   Male | 4.0 | 7.2 | 6.1 | 8.8 |
| Female-headed households | 5.4 | 10.0 | 9.2 | 11.7 |
|   Black | 7.5 | 14.0 | 14.9 | 18.7 |
|   White | 4.8 | 8.9 | 7.1 | 8.6 |
| Teens (16–19 years) | 15.3 | 19.9 | 17.8 | 23.2 |
|   Black | — | 39.5 | 38.5 | 48.0 |
|   White | 13.5 | 17.9 | 15.5 | 20.4 |

adolescents? What are the meanings of certain values and beliefs influencing functional behaviors that help to maintain family and community support of U.S. Blacks in light of numerous stresses, such as minimal economic resources? What are the adaptive patterns toward optimal functioning, given the structural nature of various environmental systems or subsystems in which Black adolescents interact? Have these sociocultural and structural issues been adequately addressed from a Black perspective? Have these issues been incorporated in significant numbers of the programs that provide services to Black adolescent mothers and their infants?

## Program Issues

Over 300 programs have been developed to address these issues associated with adolescent pregnancy and motherhood, especially within the age group under fifteen years. Ironically, this growth in program development has occurred since the period of greatest increase of adolescent motherhood, 1960–1974 (Baldwin, 1976).

Many of these programs have been characterized as inadequate in meeting the diverse and multiple needs of the pregnant adolescent and young mother, in part because of the unidimensional aspect of the program (Brown, 1982; McKenry et al., 1979). For example, frequently a biological or physiological approach to intervention is taken without priority being given simultaneously to socioeconomic needs. The inaccessibility of programs and services has been clearly documented, especially in low income areas where inadequate public transportation, lack of child care services, and geographical distance to services represent barriers to the equal access of services (Chilman, 1980; Congressional Budget Office, 1978; Shannon et al., 1969; U.S. Department of Health, Education, and Welfare, 1980). The anticipated outcome goals of these programs are to reduce the incidence of adolescent pregnancy and to minimize the impact of aspects that affect the quality of life associated with adolescent motherhood, which include high morbidity and mortality rates and limited educational gains

and employment skills (Russ-Eft et al., 1979). These expected goals, with the general objective of improving the health and well-being of the adolescent mother and her child, have not been realized in any appreciable measure (Bolton, 1980).

This lack of goal attainment is evidenced by the increasing birthrate since 1960 among adolescents younger than 14 years of age and the steady birthrate among adolescents 14–17 years of age (Bogue, 1977; Guttmacher Institute, 1976). In 1980, almost 600,000 babies were born to adolescents under 20 years of age and over 10,000 of these births were to adolescents 14 years of age and younger (Edelman, 1984:3). Fifty-seven percent of all babies born to adolescents under 15 years of age are Black. For the Black adolescent female, the birthrate remains disproportionately higher than for white adolescents. For example, one out of every four babies is born to Black adolescents, whereas one out of seven babies is born to white adolescents (Meriwether, 1984).

As indicated, there has been an enormous amount of concentrated attention to the growth rates of our young who are having children and choosing to rear them. There has been an increase in the descriptive studies and statistics; also, numerous programs have been developed in hopes of reducing the number of babies that are born to adolescents. Moreover, the overall objective of these intervention strategies over the last few decades has been to improve the health and well-being of these youths and their infants. These efforts have been worthy and for some they have even been effective. However, for Black adolescent mothers, who have consistently had the highest mortality rates, minimal access to services, and disproportionately higher birthrates, these intervention efforts have not significantly altered the impact of adolescent pregnancy and motherhood.

Given this state of affairs, the question arises of why program goals and activities have not significantly improved the health and well-being of the population of adolescents who become pregnant and choose to rear their infants. There may be several reasons for this problem. However, only two major reasons will be discussed with alternative suggestions.

The first major reason that the stated goals are not fully realized might be that adolescent pregnancy and motherhood is viewed as an epidemic rather than a social problem. This perception does not view the problem as structural in nature, limiting targets for intervention. In recent years, this view has been discussed and debated (Klerman, 1980). Many have called into question the extent to which the incidence of adolescent pregnancy is a disease process. Such a view places emphasis on symptomatology and the individual as the problem, rather than broadening its perspective and priority to include the need for understanding antecedent causes that have severe consequences on the adolescent who becomes pregnant and chooses to rear her child, particularly the Black adolescent (Butts, 1981). For example, Lorraine Klerman (1980:777) states:

> *This country is not faced with an epidemic but rather a continuing problem which will fluctuate with the size of the population at risk. . . . No magic bullet will solve the problem; rather its underlying causes must be examined and appropriate interventions designed.*

The second reason for the failure to accomplish the identified program goals is the tendency to view adolescent mothers as a homogeneous group (Falk et al., 1981). For the Black adolescent, this view can mean the difference between prevention and chronic or intractable health and socioeconomic problems. Clearly, the awareness of the cultural and historical context of which the adolescent is a part provides knowledge to the practitioner about her needs, resources, and obstacles to health care. It allows the practitioner to move beyond categorizing or compartmentalizing behaviors and lifestyles. With appreciation and the acceptance of uniqueness that allows the adolescent mother to adapt functionally, the practitioner can intervene and advocate appropriately and in ways that have a positive impact on existing adverse circumstances (Litsitzky, 1956).

Taking into account the need for effective programs to minimize the effects and consequences of adolescent pregnancy and motherhood, the following statement acknowledges issues that must be addressed:

> *We need a new philosophy of health—nothing less. It must be seen in the context of a larger societal whole and the interactions between the person and the environment. Thus, if a better basic income or environment will produce a healthier individual or family, they should be part of the health strategy. (McNerney, 1975:411)*

In further support for minimizing the impact of these areas that affect the quality of life of adolescent mothers and their infants, Karl Fox (1974) has suggested that "the success of a program in promoting well-being must be reflected in the life experiences of its members."

# The Impact of Morbidity and Mortality

## *Maternal Effects*

Research has shown that pregnant adolescents who choose to have their babies are more likely to experience an increased incidence of health problems than their older counterparts. For example, mothers between the ages of 15 and 19 years are twice as likely to die from hemorrhage and miscarriage than mothers over 20 years of age (Bogue, 1977). For this adolescent age group, the maternal death rate from pregnancy and its complications is sixty percent higher than for mothers in their early twenties (Planned Parenthood, 1979).

Similarly, these younger mothers are 23 percent more likely to experience a premature birth with complications such as anemia, prolonged labor, and nutritional deficiency and 92 percent more likely to have anemia than mothers in their twenties (Cooke and Dworkin, 1980; Edelman, 1984; Guttmacher Institute, 1981). Toxemia, hemorrhage, and infections have been identified as major medical determinants of maternal mortality (Minkler, 1979).

For the Black adolescent who chooses motherhood, an even higher incidence of health problems and medical complications is likely to occur when accompanied by adverse antecedent factors. These factors are largely due to the lack of equitable distributed resources and have been identified as inadequate nutrition, financial sources, and income and the lack of an opportunity to secure training, employment, and housing facilities to weather the natural elements, such as winter months; the factor that places Black adolescents in an extremely high risk group for medical complications is inaccessible quality health care (prenatal and postnatal) services (Edelman, 1984; Peoples et al., 1984; Somers and Somers, 1977;411–417). For example, a study by Rothenberg and Varga (1981) found that the health and development of children born to adolescent mothers were not disadvantaged when compared to the children of older mothers, if the socioeconomic backgrounds were similar.

Age, associated with biological immaturity, is being given less attention as an independent risk factor for pregnant adolescents and mothers over 15 years of age (Avery, 1984; Klerman, 1980). Death rates for these mothers are 60 percent higher than female counterparts in their early twenties; one in five adolescents in this age group receives late or no health care, compared to one in ten of pregnant adolescents in all age groups (Children's Defense Fund, 1982).

It is apparent that the risk of maternal morbidity and mortality to Black adolescents is disproportionately higher than that of the majority population. It seems that the adverse antecedent factors significantly contribute to these differences. As Aaron Antonovsky (1974) pointed out, class and race do affect the life chances of an individual. In order to improve the life chances of the Black adolescent mother who is at greatest risk, active attention to change needs to be given to the structural inequities that negatively impinge on the functional capacities of these young people, who are capable of becoming successful, contributing adult citizens.

## Infant Effects

Health, security, and the opportunity to enter a world in which one can develop to maturity in the best possible state of health are considered the right of every child (U.S. Department of Human Resources, 1974). The measures most frequently used in regard to infants include rates of stillbirth, birth weights and birth lengths, and neonatal and infant mortality (Rothenberg and Varga, 1981). This section focuses primarily on infant mortality and the effects of underweight babies.

The infant mortality rate is considered to be the rate that is most sensitive to differences in health care and is inextricably related to social and economic factors. As a result, it is often described as a social indicator or measure determining the level of health. There has been a decrease in the infant mortality rates since the 1960s; however, the gap between Black and white rates has not narrowed. In fact, this widening gap in rates of infant mortality may potentially undermine the slow progress in reducing the nation's infant mortality rate. In the early eighties, almost 20,000 Black infants died during the first year of life who, according to David Anderson (1984:5), would not have died had their chance been equal to that of white infants. Statistics from the U.S. Bureau of the Census (1983) indicate that the cities with the highest infant mortality rates have a majority or near majority Black population.

In 1979, the Black infant mortality rate was 21.8 deaths under the age of one for every 1,000 births and the infant mortality rate for whites was 11.4; in 1982, the rate of Black infant mortality was 95 percent higher than the rate for whites. This is a 9 percent increase within a four year period (Reid, 1982). If this emerging trend continues it is likely to affect adversely the federal government goal of reducing Black infant mortality by 1990.

The most frequently cited adverse outcomes to the infants of young mothers are considered to be prematurity and low birth weight (Rothenberg and Varga, 1981). The high infant mortality is found to be directly related to the high percentage of underweight babies and this is linked to prematurity. In a study done at Johns Hopkins (Battaglia et al.,

1963), it was found that the increase in low birth weights and prematurity were attributed to adolescents under 15 years of age. Two factors that have been frequently associated with premature infants are the inadequate prenatal care and nutrition received by adolescent mothers. Some of the potential outcomes of underweight in babies are epilepsy, cerebral palsy, other disabilities, and death.

Given possible outcomes such as these, it is clear that a combination of intervention strategies is needed. Some of the strategies needed are: (1) health care that is responsive to the needs of these infants and their mothers; (2) an aggressive outreach program that will familiarize mother with services as well as provide educational information and demonstration in such areas as nutrition and infant stimulation skills; (3) accessible and adequate health care service; (4) an adequate number of health care and social service providers whose attitudes about adolescent mothers and their infants are acceptance, high expectations, and encouragement toward self-sufficiency; (5) modification of the philosophy, policies, and practices in social welfare that provide options and resources based on individual needs and acknowledgment of the diversity of life-styles and cultural values; (6) program policy that automatically includes family members and other natural support systems; and (7) sufficient income for basic needs and the opportunity for these young mothers to gain self-sufficiency through job training and available job placements.

Given the information presented in this paper, it seems evident that the problems associated with the incidence of adolescent pregnancy and the prevalence of adolescent motherhood are not so much internal manifestations as results of interactions with a variety of external systems. Therefore, we must understand the individual dynamics within primary systems as well as institutional dynamics that interface with a diversity of people. There also is a need for commitment to prevention intervention along with a commitment to these adolescent mothers becoming self-sufficient and self-determining, and thus contributing, members of this society. The right of every child to health, security, and opportunity can be realized.

# References

Anderson, David
1984    "Study: Black Infant Mortality Rates Not Declining." *National Leader,* January 19.

Antonovsky, Aaron
1974    "Class and the Chance of Life." In Lee Rainwater, ed., *Equality and Justice.* Chicago: Aldine.

Avery, Byllye
1984    "The Status of Black Women's Health." *Congressional Black Caucus Foundation* (Spring).

Baldwin, W.
1976    "Adolescent Pregnancy and Childbearing Growing Concern for Americans." *Population Bulletin* 31:3–21.

Battaglia, F., T. Frazier, and A. Hellegers
1963    "Obstetric and Pediatric Complications of Juvenile Pregnancy." *Pediatrics* 32:902.

Bogue, Donald, editor
1977    *Adolescent Fertility.* Chicago: University of Chicago Community and Family Study Center.

Bolton, Frank
1980    *The Pregnant Adolescent.* Beverly Hills, Calif.: Sage.

Brown, S.
1982    "Early Childbearing and Poverty: Implications for Social Services." *Adolescence* 17 (66, Summer):397–408.

Butts, June Dobbs
1981    "Adolescent Sexuality and Teenage Pregnancy from a Black Perspective." In T. Ooms, ed., *Teenage Pregnancy in A Family Context,* pp. 307–325. Philadelphia, Pa.: Temple University Press.

Children's Defense Fund

1982  *America's Children and Their Families.* Washington, D.C.: Author.

Chilman, C.

1980  *Adolescent Sexuality in a Changing American Society: Social and Psychological Perspectives.* Washington, D.C.: U.S. Government Printing Office.

Clark, Ramsey

1978  *Voices of Concern: Americans Speak Out for Teenage Health Services Pamphlet.* Atlanta, Georgia: Emory University Family Planning Program, Grady Memorial Hospital.

Congressional Budget Office

1978  *Health Differentials between White and Nonwhite Americans.* Washington, D.C.: U.S. Government Printing Office.

Cooke, Cynthia, and Susan Dworkin

1980  *The Ms Guide to a Woman's Health.*

Edelman, Marian W.

1984  "Remembering Our Youngest Mothers," *The Omaha Star,* May 10.

Falk, Ruth, Maria Gispert, and Donald Baucom

1981  "Personality Factors Related to Black Teenage Pregnancy and Abortion." *Psychology of Women Quarterly* 5 (5):737–746.

Fox, Karl

1974  *Social Indicators and Social Theory.* New York: Wiley.

Guttmacher Institute

1976  *Eleven Million Teenagers: What Can Be Done about the Epidemic of Adolescent Pregnancies in the United States.* New York: Planned Parenthood Federation of America.

1981  *Teenage Pregnancy: The Problem That Hasn't Gone Away.* New York: Alan Guttmacher Institute.

Klerman, Lorraine

1980  "Adolescent Pregnancy: A New Look at a Continuing Problem." *American Journal of Public Health* 70 (8):776–778.

Klerman, Lorraine, and James Jekel

1973  *School-Age Mothers: Problem, Programs and Policy.* Conn.: The Shoe String Press.

Litsitzky, Gene

1956  *Four Ways of Being Human.* New York: Viking Press, 1956.

Mathey, William, and Dwight Johnson

1983  "America's Black Population: 1970 to 1982." *The Crises* 90 (10, December).

McKenry, Patrick, Lynda Walters, and Carolyn Johnson

1979  "Adolescent Pregnancy: A Review of the Literature." *The Family Coordinator* (January):17–28.

McNerney, Walter J.

1975  Quoted in A. Somers and H. Somers, eds., *Health and Health Care: Policies in Perspective.* Maryland: Aspen Systems Corporation.

Meriwether, Louise

1984  "Teenage Pregnancy." *Essence* (April):94–96.

Minkler, Donald

1979  "Pregnancy and the Prevention of Undesirable Consequences." In R. Jackson, J. Morton, and M. Sierra-Franco, eds., *Social Factors in Prevention,* pp. 3–15. Calif.: University of California, School of Public Health.

Ogg, E.

1976  *Unmarried Teenagers and Their Children.* Public Affairs Pamphlet, No. 537.

Peoples, M., R. Grimson, G. Daughtry

1984  "Evaluation of the Effects of the North Carolina Improved Pregnancy Outcome Project: Implications for State-Level Decision-Making." *American Journal of Public Health* 74 (6, June): 549–554.

Planned Parenthood

1979  "Teenage Pregnancy: A Major Problem for Minors." In *Zero Population Growth.* Calif.: Planned Parenthood Association of San Diego.

Raspberry, William

1984  "New Interest in an Old Problem." *Chicago Tribune,* February 6.

Reid, John

1982  "Black America in the 1980's." Washington, D.C.: Population Reference Bureau.

Resnick, Michael

1984  "Studying Adolescent Mothers' Decision Making about Adoption and Parenting." *Social Work* (January-February).

Rice, Dorothy

1984  A Report from the National Center for Health Statistics." *National Leader,* January 19.

Rothenberg, Pearlia, and Phyllis Varga

1981  "The Relationship between Age of Mother and Child Health and Development." *American Journal of Public Health* 71 (8, August).

**Russ-Eft, Darlene, Marlene Springer, and Anne Beaver**

1979    "Antecedents of Adolescent Parenthood and Consequences at Age 30." *The Family Coordinator* (April):173–178.

**Shannon, G., et al.**

1969    "The Concept of Distance as a Factor in Accessibility and Utilization of Health Care." *Medical Care Review* 26 (143, February).

**Somers, Anne, and Herman Somers**

1977    *Health and Health Care: Policies in Perspective*. Rockville, Maryland: Aspen Systems Corporation.

**U.S. Bureau of the Census**

1983    *Statistical Abstract of the United States 1984.*

Washington, D.C.: U.S. Department of Commerce.

**U.S. Department of Health, Education, and Welfare**

1980    *Health Status of Minorities and Low Income Groups*. Rockville, Maryland: Office of Health Resources Opportunity.

**U.S. Department of Human Resources**

1974    *Children: The Resource of the Future*. Washington, D.C.: Government of the District of Columbia.

**Zastrow, Charles, and Lee Bowker**

1984    *Social Problems: Issues and Solutions*. Chicago: Nelson-Hall.

# THE MEANING OF MOTHERHOOD IN BLACK CULTURE

## *Patricia Hill Collins*

*This essay explores the relationship between the meaning of motherhood in Black American culture by addressing three primary questions. These questions concern (1) how competing perspectives intersected to form a distinctly Afrocentric ideology of motherhood, (2) what the themes contained in that ideology of motherhood are, and (3) what the effect of this ideology of motherhood is on Black mother-daughter relationships.*

"What did your mother teach you about men?" is a question I often ask students in my courses on African-American women. "Go to school first and get a good education—don't get too serious too young," "Make sure you look around and that you can take care of yourself before you settle down," and "Don't trust them, want more for yourself than just a man," are typical responses from Black women. My students share stories of how their mothers encouraged them to cultivate satisfying relationships with Black men while anticipating disappointments, to desire marriage while planning viable alternatives, to become mothers only when fully prepared to do so. But above all, they stress their mothers' insistence on being self-reliant and resourceful.

These daughters from varying social class backgrounds, ages, family structures and geographic regions had somehow received strikingly similar messages about Black womanhood. Even though

An abridged version adapted from *SAGE: A Scholarly Journal on Black Women*. 4 (Fall 1987):3–10. © 1987 by the SAGE Women's Educational Press, Inc. Reprinted by permission.

their mothers employed diverse teaching strategies, these Black daughters had all been exposed to common themes about the meaning of womanhood in Black culture.[1]

This essay explores the relationship between the meaning of motherhood in African-American culture and Black mother/daughter relationships by addressing three primary questions. First, how have competing perspectives about motherhood intersected to produce a distinctly Afrocentric ideology of motherhood? Second, what are the enduring themes that characterize this Afrocentric ideology of motherhood? Finally, what effect might this Afrocentric ideology of motherhood have on Black mother/daughter relationships?

# Competing Perspectives on Motherhood

## *The Dominant Perspective: Eurocentric Views of White Motherhood*

The cult of true womanhood, with its emphasis on motherhood as woman's highest calling, has long held a special place in the gender symbolism of white Americans. From this perspective, women's activities should be confined to the care of children, the nurturing of a husband, and the maintenance of the household. By managing this separate domestic sphere, women gain social influence through their roles as mothers, transmitters of culture and parents for the next generation.[2]

While substantial numbers of white women have benefitted from the protections of white patriarchy provided by the dominant ideology, white women themselves have recently challenged its tenets. On one pole lies a cluster of women, the traditionalists, who aim to retain the centrality of motherhood in women's lives. For traditionalists, differentiating between the experience of motherhood, which for them has been quite satisfying, and motherhood as an institution central in reproducing gender inequality, has proved difficult. The other pole is occupied by women who advocate disman-

tling motherhood as an institution. They suggest that compulsory motherhood be outlawed and that the experience of motherhood can only be satisfying if women can choose not to be mothers. Arrayed between these dichotomous positions are women who argue for an expanded, but not necessarily different role for women—women can be mothers as long as they are not *just* mothers.[3]

Three themes implicit in white perspectives on motherhood are particularly problematic for Black women and others outside of this debate. First, the assumption that mothering occurs within the confines of a private, nuclear family household where the mother has almost total responsibility for childrearing is less applicable to Black families. While the ideal of the cult of true womanhood has been held up to Black women for emulation, racial oppression has denied Black families sufficient resources to support private, nuclear family households. Second, the assumption of strict sex-role segregation defining male and female spheres of influence within the family has been less applicable to African-American families than to white middle class ones. Finally, the assumption that motherhood and economic dependency on men are linked and that to be a "good" mother, one must stay at home, making motherhood a full-time "occupation," is similarly uncharacteristic of African-American families.[4]

Even though selected groups of white women are challenging the cult of true womanhood and its accompanying definition of motherhood, the dominant ideology remains powerful. As long as these approaches remain prominent in scholarly and popular discourse, Eurocentric views of white motherhood will continue to affect Black women's lives.

## *Eurocentric Views of Black Motherhood*

Eurocentric perspectives on Black motherhood revolve around two interdependent images that together define Black women's roles in white and in African-American families. The first image is that of the Mammy, the faithful, devoted domestic servant. Like one of the family, Mammy conscientiously "mothers" her white children, caring for them and loving them as if they were her own. Mammy is the ideal Black mother for she recognizes her place. She is paid next to nothing and yet cheerfully accepts her inferior status. But when she enters her own home, this same Mammy is transformed into the second image, the too-strong matriarch who raises weak sons and "unnaturally superior" daughters.[5] When she protests, she is labelled aggressive and non-feminine, yet if she remains silent, she is rendered invisible.

The task of debunking Mammy by analyzing Black women's roles as exploited domestic workers and challenging the matriarchy thesis by demonstrating that Black women do not wield disproportionate power in African-American families has long preoccupied African-American scholars.[6] But an equally telling critique concerns uncovering the functions of these images and their role in explaining Black women's subordination in systems of race, class and gender oppression. As Mae King points out, white definitions of Black motherhood foster the dominant group's exploitation of Black women by blaming Black women for their characteristic reactions to their own subordination.[7] For example, while the stay-at-home mother has been held up to all women as the ideal, African-American women have been compelled to work outside the home, typically in a very narrow range of occupations. Even though Black women were forced to become domestic servants and be strong figures in Black households, labelling them Mammys and matriarchs denigrates Black women. Without a countervailing Afrocentric ideology of motherhood, white perspectives on both white and African-American motherhood place Black women in a no-win situation. Adhering to these standards brings the danger of the lowered self-esteem of internalized oppression, one that, if passed on from mother to daughter, provides a powerful mechanism for controlling African-American communities.

## African Perspectives on Motherhood

One concept that has been constant throughout the history of African societies is the centrality of motherhood in religions, philosophies and social institutions. As Barbara Christian points out, "There is no doubt that motherhood is for most African people symbolic of creativity and continuity."[8]

Cross-cultural research on motherhood in African societies appears to support Christian's claim.[9] West African sociologist Christine Oppong suggests that the Western notion of equating household with family be abandoned because it obscures women's family roles in African cultures.[10] While the archetypal white, middle-class nuclear family conceptualizes family life as being divided into two oppositional spheres—the "male" sphere of economic providing and the "female" sphere of affective nurturing—this type of rigid sex role segregation was not part of the West African tradition. Mothering was not a privatized nurturing "occupation" reserved for biological mothers, and the economic support of children was not the exclusive responsibility of men. Instead, for African women, emotional care for children and providing for their physical survival were interwoven as interdependent, complementary dimensions of motherhood.

In spite of variation among societies, a strong case has been made that West African women occupy influential roles in African family networks.[11] First, since they are not dependent on males for economic support and provide for certain key dimensions of their own and their children's economic support, women are structurally central to families.[12] Second, the image of the mother is one that is culturally elaborated and valued across diverse West African societies. Continuing the lineage is essential in West African philosophies, and motherhood is similarly valued.[13] Finally, while the biological mother/child bond is valued, child care was a collective responsibility, a situation fostering cooperative, age stratified, woman-centered "mothering" networks.

Recent research by Africanists suggests that much more of this African heritage was retained among African-Americans than had previously been thought. The retention of West African culture as a culture of resistance offered enslaved Africans and exploited African-Americans alternative ideologies to those advanced by dominant groups. Central to these reinterpretations of African-American institutions and culture is a reconceptualization of Black family life and the role of women in Black family networks.[14] West African perspectives may have been combined with the changing political and economic situations framing African-American communities to produce certain enduring themes characterizing an Afrocentric ideology of motherhood.

# Enduring Themes of an Afrocentric Ideology of Motherhood

An Afrocentric ideology of motherhood must reconcile the competing world views of these three conflicting perspectives of motherhood. An ongoing tension exists between efforts to mold the institution of Black motherhood for the benefit of the dominant group and efforts by Black women to define and value their own experiences with motherhood. This tension leads to a continuum of responses. For those women who either aspire to the cult of true womanhood without having the resources to support such a lifestyle or who believe stereotypical analyses of themselves as dominating matriarchs, motherhood can be an oppressive institution. But the experience of motherhood can provide Black women with a base of self-actualization, status in the Black community, and a reason for social activism. These alleged contradictions can exist side by side in African-American communities, families, and even within individual women.

Embedded in these changing relationships are four enduring themes that I contend characterize an Afrocentric ideology of motherhood. Just as the issues facing enslaved African mothers were quite different from those currently facing poor Black women in inner cities for any given historical moment, the actual institutional forms that these themes take depend on the severity of oppression and Black women's resources for resistance.

## *Bloodmothers, Othermothers, and Women-Centered Networks*

In African-American communities, the boundaries distinguishing biological mothers of children from other women who care for children are often fluid and changing. Biological mothers or bloodmothers

are expected to care for their children. But African and African-American communities have also recognized that vesting one person with full responsibility for mothering a child may not be wise or possible. As a result, "othermothers," women who assist bloodmothers by sharing mothering responsibilities, traditionally have been central to the institution of Black motherhood.[15]

The centrality of women in African-American extended families is well known.[16] Organized, resilient, women-centered networks of bloodmothers and othermothers are key in understanding this centrality. Grandmothers, sisters, aunts, or cousins acted as othermothers by taking on childcare responsibilities for each other's children. When needed, temporary child care arrangements turned into long-term care or informal adoption.[17]

In African-American communities, these women-centered networks of community-based childcare often extend beyond the boundaries of biologically related extended families to support "fictive kin."[18] Civil rights activist Ella Baker describes how informal adoption by othermothers functioned in the Southern, rural community of her childhood:

> *My aunt who had thirteen children of her own raised three more. She had become a midwife, and a child was born who was covered with sores. Nobody was particularly wanting the child, so she took the child and raised him . . . and another mother decided she didn't want to be bothered with two children. So my aunt took one and raised him . . . they were part of the family.*[19]

Even when relationships were not between kin or fictive kin, African-American community norms were such that neighbors cared for each other's children. In the following passage, Sara Brooks, a Southern domestic worker, describes the importance of the community-based childcare that a neighbor offered her daughter. In doing so, she also shows how the African-American cultural value placed on cooperative childcare found institutional support in the adverse conditions under which so many Black women mothered:

*She kept Vivian and she didn't charge me
nothin either. You see, people used to look
after each other, but now it's not that way. I
reckon it's because we all was poor, and I
guess they put theirself in the place of the person that they was helpin.*[20]

Othermothers were key not only in supporting children but also in supporting bloodmothers
who, for whatever reason, were ill-prepared or had
little desire to care for their children. Given the
pressures from the larger political economy, the emphasis placed on community-based childcare and
the respect given to othermothers who assume the
responsibilities of childcare have served a critical
function in African-American communities. Children orphaned by sale or death of their parents
under slavery, children conceived through rape,
children of young mothers, children born into extreme poverty, or children, who for other reasons
have been rejected by their bloodmothers, have all
been supported by othermothers who, like Ella Baker's aunt, took in additional children, even when
they had enough of their own.

## Providing as Part of Mothering

The work done by African-American women in providing the economic resources essential to Black
family well-being affects motherhood in a contradictory fashion. On the one hand, African-American
women have long integrated their activities as economic providers into their mothering relationships.
In contrast to the cult of true womanhood where
work is defined as being in opposition to and in-
compatible with motherhood, work for Black
women has been an important and valued dimension of Afrocentric definitions of Black motherhood.
On the other hand, African-American women's experiences as mothers under oppression were such
that the type and purpose of work Black women
were forced to do greatly impacted on the type of
mothering relationships bloodmothers and othermothers had with Black children.

While slavery both disrupted West African

family patterns and exposed enslaved Africans to the
gender ideologies and practices of slaveowners, it
simultaneously made it impossible, had they wanted
to do so, for enslaved Africans to implement slave-
owner's ideologies. Thus, the separate spheres of
providing as a male domain and affective nurturing
as a female domain did not develop within African-
American families.[21] Providing for Black children's
physical survival and attending to their affective,
emotional needs continued as interdependent dimensions of an Afrocentric ideology of motherhood. However, by changing the conditions under
which Black women worked and the purpose of the
work itself, slavery introduced the problem of how
best to continue traditional Afrocentric values under
oppressive conditions. Institutions of community-
based childcare, informal adoption, greater reliance
on othermothers, all emerge as adaptations to the
exigencies of combining exploitative work with
nurturing children.

In spite of the change in political status
brought on by emancipation, the majority of African-
American women remained exploited agricultural
workers. However, their placement in Southern political economies allowed them to combine childcare with field labor. Sara Brooks describes how
strong the links between providing and caring for
others were for her:

*When I was about nine I was nursin my sis-
ter Sally—I'm about seven or eight years
older than Sally. And when I would put her
to sleep, instead of me goin somewhere and
sit down and play, I'd get my little old hoe
and get out there and work right in the field
around the house.*[22]

Black women's shift from Southern agriculture to domestic work in Southern and Northern
towns and cities represented a change in the type of
work done, but not in the meaning of work to
women and their families. Whether they wanted to
or not, the majority of African-American women had
to work and could not afford the luxury of motherhood as a noneconomically productive, female
"occupation."

## Community Othermothers and Social Activism

Black women's experiences as othermothers have provided a foundation for Black women's social activism. Black women's feelings of responsibility for nurturing the children in their own extended family networks have stimulated a more generalized ethic of care where Black women feel accountable to all the Black community's children.

This notion of Black women as community othermothers for all Black children traditionally allowed Black women to treat biologically unrelated children as if they were members of their own families. For example, sociologist Karen Fields describes how her grandmother, Mamie Garvin Fields, draws on her power as a community othermother when dealing with unfamiliar children.

> She will say to a child on the street who looks up to no good, picking out a name at random, "Aren't you Miz Pinckney's boy?" in that same reproving tone. If the reply is, "No, ma'am, my mother is Miz Gadsden," whatever threat there was dissipates.[23]

The use of family language in referring to members of the Black community also illustrates this dimension of Black motherhood. For example, Mamie Garvin Fields describes how she became active in surveying the poor housing conditions of Black people in Charleston.

> I was one of the volunteers they got to make a survey of the places where we were paying extortious rents for indescribable property. I said "we," although it wasn't Bob and me. We had our own home, and so did many of the Federated Women. Yet we still felt like it really was "we" living in those terrible places, and it was up to us to do something about them.[24]

To take another example, while describing her increasingly successful efforts to teach a boy who had

given other teachers problems, my daughter's kindergarten teacher stated, "You know how it can be—the majority of children in the learning disabled classes are *our children*. I know he didn't belong there, so I volunteered to take him." In these statements, both women invoke the language of family to describe the ties that bind them as Black women to their responsibilities to other members of the Black community as family.

Sociologist Cheryl Gilkes suggests that community othermother relationships are sometimes behind Black women's decisions to become community activists.[25] Gilkes notes that many of the Black women community activists in her study became involved in community organizing in response to the needs of their own children and of those in their communities. The following comment is typical of how many of the Black women in Gilkes' study relate to Black children: "There were a lot of summer programs springing up for kids, but they were exclusive . . . and I found that most of *our kids* (emphasis mine) were excluded."[26] For many women, what began as the daily expression of their obligations as community othermothers, as was the case for the kindergarten teacher, developed into full-fledged roles as community leaders.

## Motherhood as a Symbol of Power

Motherhood, whether bloodmother, othermother, or community othermother, can be invoked by Black women as a symbol of power. A substantial portion of Black women's status in African-American communities stems not only from their roles as mothers in their own families but from their contributions as community othermothers to Black community development as well.

The specific contributions Black women make in nurturing Black community development form the basis of community-based power. Community othermothers work on behalf of the Black community by trying, in the words of late nineteenth century Black feminists, to "uplift the race," so that vulnerable members of the community would be able to attain the self-reliance and independence so desperately needed for Black community development under oppressive conditions. This is the type of power many African-Americans have in mind when they describe the "strong, Black women" they see around them in traditional African-American communities.

When older Black women invoke this community othermother status, its results can be quite striking. Karen Fields recounts an incident described to her by her grandmother illustrating how women can exert power as community othermothers:

> One night . . . as Grandmother sat crocheting alone at about two in the morning, a young man walked into the living room carrying the portable TV from upstairs. She said, "Who are you looking for this time of night?" As Grandmother (described) the incident to me over the phone, I could hear a tone of voice that I know well. It said, "Nice boys don't do that." So I imagine the burglar heard his own mother or grandmother at that moment. He joined in the familial game just created: "Well, he told me that I could borrow it." "Who told you?" "John." "Um um, no John lives here. You got the wrong house."[27]

After this dialogue, the teenager turned around, went back upstairs and returned the television.

In local Black communities, specific Black women are widely recognized as powerful figures, primarily because of their contributions to the community's well-being through their roles as community othermothers. Sociologist Charles Johnson describes the behavior of an elderly Black woman at a church service in rural Alabama of the 1930s. Even though she was not on the program, the woman stood up to speak. The master of ceremonies rang for her to sit down but she refused to do so claiming, "I am the mother of this church, and I will say what I please." The master of ceremonies later explained to the congregation—"Brothers, I know you all honor Sister Moore. Course our time is short but she has acted as a mother to me . . . Any time old folks get up I give way to them."[28]

# Implications for Black Mother/ Daughter Relationships

In her discussion of the sex-role socialization of Black girls, Pamela Reid identifies two complementary approaches in understanding Black mother/ daughter relationships.[29] The first, psychoanalytic theory, examines the role of parents in the establishment of personality and social behavior. This theory argues that the development of feminine behavior results from the girls' identification with adult female role models. This approach emphasizes how an Afrocentric ideology of motherhood is actualized through Black mothers' activities as role models.

The second approach, social learning theory, suggests that the rewards and punishments attached to girls' childhood experiences are central in shaping women's sex-role behavior. The kinds of behaviors that Black mothers reward and punish in their daughters are seen as key in the socialization process. This approach examines specific experiences that Black girls have while growing up that encourage them to absorb an Afrocentric ideology of motherhood.

## *African-American Mothers as Role Models*

Feminist psychoanalytic theorists suggest that the sex-role socialization process is different for boys and girls. While boys learn maleness by rejecting femaleness via separating themselves from their mothers, girls establish feminine identities by embracing the femaleness of their mothers. Girls identify with their mothers, a sense of connection that is incorporated into the female personality. However, this mother-identification is problematic because, under patriarchy, men are more highly valued than women. Thus, while daughters identify with their mothers, they also reject them because, in patriarchal families, identification with adult women as mothers means identifying with persons deemed inferior.[30]

While Black girls learn by identifying with their mothers, the specification of the female role with which Black girls identify may be quite different than that modeled by middle class white mothers. The presence of working mothers, extended family othermothers, and powerful community othermothers offers a range of role models that challenge the tenets of the cult of true womanhood.

Moreover, since Black mothers have a distinctive relationship to white patriarchy, they may be less likely to socialize their daughters into their proscribed role as subordinates. Rather, a key part of Black girls' socialization involves incorporating the critical posture that allows Black women to cope with contradictions. For example, Black girls have long had to learn how to do domestic work while rejecting definitions of themselves as Mammies. At the same time they've had to take on strong roles in Black extended families without internalizing images of themselves as matriarchs.

In raising their daughters, Black mothers face a troubling dilemma. To ensure their daughters' physical survival, they must teach their daughters to fit into systems of oppression. For example, as a young girl in Mississippi, Black activist Ann Moody questioned why she was paid so little for the domestic work she began at age nine, why Black women domestics were sexually harassed by their white male employers, and why whites had so much more than Blacks. But her mother refused to answer her questions and actually became angry whenever Ann Moody stepped out of her "place."[31] Black daughters are raised to expect to work, to strive for an education so that they can support themselves, and to anticipate carrying heavy responsibilities in their families and communities because these skills are essential for their own survival as well as for the survival of those for whom they will eventually be responsible.[32] And yet mothers know that if daughters fit too well into the limited opportunities offered Black women, they become willing participants in their own subordination. Mothers may have ensured their daughters' physical survival at the high cost of their emotional destruction.

On the other hand, Black daughters who offer serious challenges to oppressive situations may not physically survive. When Ann Moody became involved in civil rights activities, her mother first begged her not to participate and then told her not to come home because she feared the whites in Moody's hometown would kill her. In spite of the dangers, many Black mothers routinely encourage their daughters to develop skills to confront oppressive conditions. Thus, learning that they will work, that education is a vehicle for advancement, can also be seen as ways of preparing Black girls to resist oppression through a variety of mothering roles. The issue is to build emotional strength, but not at the cost of physical survival.

This delicate balance between conformity and resistance is described by historian Elsa Barkley Brown as the "need to socialize me one way and at the same time to give me all the tools I needed to be something else."[33] Black daughters must learn how to survive in interlocking structures of race, class and gender oppression while rejecting and transcending those very same structures. To develop these skills in their daughters, mothers demonstrate varying combinations of behaviors devoted to ensuring their daughters' survival—such as providing them with basic necessities and ensuring their protection in dangerous environments—to helping their daughters go farther than mothers themselves were allowed to go.

The presence of othermothers in Black extended families and the modeling symbolized by community othermothers offer powerful support for the task of teaching girls to resist white perceptions of Black womanhood while appearing to conform to them. In contrast to the isolation of middle class white mother/daughter dyads, Black women-centered extended family networks foster an early identification with a much wider range of models of Black womanhood which can lead to a greater sense of empowerment in young Black girls.

[1] The definition of culture used in this essay is taken from Leith Mullings, "Anthropological Perspectives on the Afro-American Family," American Journal of Social Psychiatry 6 (1986), pp. 11–16. According to Mullings, culture is composed of "the symbols and values that create the ideological frame of reference through which people attempt to deal with the circumstances in which they find themselves," p. 13.

[2] For analyses of the relationship of the cult of true womanhood to Black women, see Leith Mullings, "Uneven Development: Class, Race and Gender in the United States Before 1900," in Women's Work, Development and the Division of Labor by Gender, eds. Eleanor Leacock and Helen Safa (South Hadley, MA: Bergin & Garvey, 1986), pp. 41–57; Bonnie Thornton Dill, "Our Mothers' Grief: Racial Ethnic Women and the Maintenance of Families," Research Paper 4, Center for Research on Women (Memphis, TN: Memphis State University, 1986); and Hazel Carby, Reconstructing Womanhood: The Emergence of the Afro-American Woman Novelist (New York: Oxford University, 1987), especially chapter two.

[3] Contrast, for example, the traditionalist analysis of Selma Fraiberg, Every Child's Birthright: In Defense of Mothering (New York: Basic, 1977) to that of Jeffner Allen, "Motherhood: The Annihilation of Women," in Mothering, Essays in Feminist Theory, ed. Joyce Trebilcot (Totawa, NJ: Rowan & Allanheld, 1983). See also Adrienne Rich, Of Woman Born: Motherhood as Experience and Institution (New York: Norton, 1976). For an overview of how traditionalists and feminists have shaped the public policy debate on abortion, see Kristin Luker, Abortion and the Politics of Motherhood (Berkeley, CA: University of California, 1984).

[4] Mullings, 1986, note 2 above; Dill, 1986; and Carby, 1987. Feminist scholarship is also challenging Western notions of the family. See Barrie Thorne and Marilyn Yalom, eds., Rethinking the Family (New York: Longman, 1982).

[5] Since Black women are no longer heavily concentrated in private domestic service, the Mammy image may be fading. In contrast, the matriarch image, popularized in Daniel Patrick Moynihan's, The Negro Family: The Case for National Action (Washington, DC: U.S. Government Printing Office, 1965), is reemerging in public debates about the feminization of poverty and the urban underclass. See Maxine Baca Zinn, "Minority Families in Crisis: The Public Discussion," Research Paper 6, Center for Research on Women (Memphis, TN: Memphis State University, 1987).

[6] For an alternative analysis to the Mammy image, see Judith Rollins, Between Women: Domestics and Their Employers (Philadelphia: Temple University, 1985). Classic responses to the matriarchy thesis include Robert Hill, The Strengths of Black Families (New York: Urban League, 1972); Andrew Billingsley, Black Families in White America (Englewood Cliffs, NJ: Prentice-Hall, 1968); and Joyce Ladner, Tomorrow's Tomorrow (Garden City, NY: Doubleday, 1971). For a recent analysis, see Linda Burnham, "Has Poverty Been Feminized in Black America?" Black Scholar 16 (1985), pp. 15–24.

[7] Mae King, "The Politics of Sexual Stereotypes," Black Scholar 4 (1973), pp. 12–23.

[8] Barbara Christian, "An Angle of Seeing: Motherhood in Buchi Emecheta's Joys of Motherhood and Alice Walker's Meridian," in Black Feminist Criticism, ed. Barbara Christian (New York: Pergamon, 1985), p. 214.

[9] See Christine Oppong, ed., Female and Male in West Africa (London: Allen & Unwin, 1983); Niara Sudarkasa, "Female Employment and Family Organization in West Africa," in The Black Woman Cross-Culturally, ed. Filomina Chiamo Steady (Cambridge, MA: Schenkman, 1981), pp. 49–64; and Nancy Tanner, "Matrifocality in Indonesia and Africa and Among Black Americans," in Woman, Culture, and Society, eds. Michelle Rosaldo and Louise Lamphere (Stanford, CA: Stanford University, 1974), pp. 129–156.

[10] Christine Oppong, "Family Structure and Women's Reproductive and Productive Roles: Some Conceptual and Methodological Issues," in Women's Roles and Population Trends in the Third World, eds. Richard Anker, Myra Buvinic and Nadia Youssef (London: Croom Helm, 1982), pp. 133–150.

[11] The key distinction here is that, unlike the matriarchy thesis, women play central roles in families and this centrality is seen as legitimate. In spite of this centrality, it is important not to idealize African women's family roles. For an analysis by a Black African feminist, see Awa Thiam, Black Sisters, Speak Out: Feminism and Oppression in Black Africa (London: Pluto, 1978).

[12] Sudarkasa, 1981.

[13] John Mbiti, African Religions and Philosophies (New York: Anchor, 1969).

[14] Niara Sudarkasa, "Interpreting the African Heritage in Afro-American Family Organization," in Black Families, ed. Harriette Pipes McAdoo (Beverly Hills, CA: Sage, 1981), pp. 37–53; and Deborah Gray White, Ar'n't I a Woman? Female Slaves in the Plantation South (New York: W.W. Norton, 1984).

[15] The terms used in this section appear in Rosalie Riegle Troester, "Turbulence and Tenderness: Mothers, Daughters, and 'Othermothers' in Paule Marshall's Brown Girl, Brownstones," SAGE: A Scholarly Journal on Black Women 1 (Fall 1984), pp. 13–16.

[16] See Tanner's discussion of matrifocality, 1974; see also Carrie Allen McCray, "The Black Woman and Family Roles," in The Black Woman, ed. LaFrances Rogers-Rose (Beverly Hills, CA: Sage, 1980), pp. 67–78; Elmer Martin and Joanne Mitchell Martin, The Black Extended Family (Chicago: University of Chicago, 1978); Joyce Aschenbrenner, Lifelines, Black Families in Chicago (Prospect Heights, IL: Waveland, 1975); and Carol B. Stack, All Our Kin (New York: Harper & Row, 1974).

[17] Martin and Martin, 1978; Stack, 1974; and Virginia Young, "Family and Childhood in a Southern Negro Community," American Anthropologist 72 (1970), pp. 269–288.

[18] Stack, 1974.

[19] Ellen Cantarow, Moving the Mountain: Women Working for Social Change (Old Westbury, NY: Feminist Press, 1980), p. 59.

[20] Thordis Simonsen, ed., You May Plow Here, The Narrative of Sara Brooks (New York: Touchstone, 1986), p. 181.

[21] White, 1985; Dill, 1986; Mullings, 1986, note 2 above.

[22] Simonsen, 1986, p. 86.

[23] Mamie Garvin Fields and Karen Fields, Lemon Swamp and Other Places, A Carolina Memoir (New York: Free Press, 1983), p. xvii.

[24] Ibid, p. 195.

[25] Cheryl Gilkes, "'Holding Back the Ocean with a Broom,' Black Women and Community Work," in Rogers-Rose, 1980, pp. 217–231; "Going Up for the Oppressed: The Career Mobility of Black Women Community Workers," Journal of Social Issues 39 (1983), pp. 115–139.

[26] Gilkes, 1980, p. 219.

[27] Fields and Fields, 1983, p. xvi.

[28] Charles Johnson, Shadow of the Plantation (Chicago: University of Chicago, 1934, 1979), p. 173.

[29] Pamela Reid, "Socialization of Black Female Children," in Women: A Developmental Perspective, eds. Phyllis Berman and Estelle Ramey (Washington, DC: National Institute of Health, 1983).

[30] For works in the feminist psychoanalytic tradition, see Nancy Chodorow, "Family Structure and Feminine Personality," in Rosaldo and Lamphere, 1974; Nancy Chodorow, The Repro-

duction of Mothering *(Berkeley, CA: University of California, 1978); and Jane Flax, "The Conflict Between Nurturance and Autonomy in Mother-Daughter Relationships and Within Feminism,"* Feminist Studies *4 (1978), pp. 171–189.*

[31] Ann Moody, Coming of Age in Mississippi *(New York: Dell, 1968).*

[32] *Ladner, 1971; Gloria Joseph, "Black Mothers and Daughters: Their Roles and Functions in American Society," in* Common Differences, *ed. Gloria Joseph and Jill Lewis (Garden City, NY:*

Anchor, 1981), pp. 75–126; Lena Wright Myers, *Black Women, Do They Cope Better? (Englewood Cliffs, NJ: Prentice-Hall, 1980).*

[33] *Elsa Barkley Brown, "Hearing Our Mothers' Lives," paper presented at Fifteenth Anniversary of African-American and African Studies at Emory College, Atlanta, 1986. This essay will appear in the upcoming Black Women's Studies issue of SAGE: A Scholarly Journal on Black Women, Vol. VI, No. 1.*

# RACE, ETHNICITY, AND CHILD MALTREATMENT:
## An Analysis of Cases Recognized and Reported by Hospitals

### Robert L. Hampton

*Using the National Study of the Incidence and Severity of Child Abuse and Neglect, the most comprehensive and reliable information available on this problem, it was discovered that Black children were more likely to be reported to child protection agencies as alleged victims of maltreatment than white children. Those data suggested that Black families may be victimized by a process in which their personal characteristics rather than their alleged behavior define them as deviant.*

Violence toward children has existed throughout recorded history. In the view of many historians and social theorists, it is deeply embedded in the social institutions and legal structures of industrialized societies. To combat this phenomenon, the child welfare movement was established in the United States during the middle and late nineteenth century, and societies for the prevention of child abuse have continued to operate in this country since that time.

Hospitals and families share a concern for the well-being of children, but there is little research that specifically addresses the interaction between hospitals and families with respect to child maltreatment. This paper addresses the role of hospitals as gatekeepers in reporting child maltreatment and examines the ethnic differences among reported cases.

## Prevalence

The true prevalence of child abuse is unknown, although nationally reported cases of child abuse have increased 142 percent since 1976. In that year, 416,033 child maltreatment cases were reported to the child protective services (CPS) system. The number of reported cases has increased annually to a total of 1,007,658 in 1983, the latest year for which data are currently available. This increase can be attributed to a number of factors, but we must remember that it is impossible to determine to what

Unpublished paper, 1985. Printed by permission. This research was supported by a grant from the National Center on Child Abuse and Neglect (90CA891), Department of Health and Human Services, Washington, D.C. The author served as a Rockefeller Foundation Postdoctoral Fellow during the period in which this research was conducted.

extent the increase in reporting is directly associated with an increase in the number of maltreated children. Individual states continue to modify reporting legislation to encompass new reportable conditions, such as emotional maltreatment (American Humane Association, 1983). It is likely that the increase in reporting is due to increased public awareness and to improved accountability on the part of state reporting systems.

Official statistics on child abuse (and other forms of family violence) do not show the full extent of child maltreatment in families. For this reason, research has been conducted to obtain better estimates of the prevalence of child abuse. The National Study of the Incidence and Severity of Child Abuse and Neglect (1981) [abbreviated National Incidence Study] was designed from a conceptual model based on the iceberg metaphor: Although substantial numbers of abused and neglected children are recognized as such and are reported to protective services, the reported cases may represent only the tip of the iceberg.

The model assumes that additional children are known to other investigatory agencies such as police and public health departments, courts, and corrections agencies, and to professionals in other major community institutions: schools, hospitals, and social service and mental health agencies. Even a clear-cut case of child maltreatment may go unreported and consequently may never be included in the official record.

. . . . . . . . . . . . . . . . . . . . . . . . . . . . . . . . . . . . . . .

# Factors Associated with Family Violence

Child maltreatment and family violence may be considered most accurately as indicators of families in trouble. Many factors can place a family in jeopardy and lead to family violence, and this multiplicity of causes complicates the task of understanding the origins of family violence. To understand the etiology, one must take into account circumstances that might make a child, parent, or family more suscep-

tible to the particular stresses associated with family violence.

In both empirical studies and reviews of literature, several factors are consistently related to the origins of family violence. Research and clinical findings indicate that parents who use violence against their children were frequently subjected to violence as children (Newberger et al., 1977; Straus et al., 1980). . . . Straus, Gelles, and Steinmetz (1980) not only found support for the hypothesis that "violence begets violence" but also provided data demonstrating that the greater the frequency of violence, the greater the chance that the victim will grow up to be a violent partner or parent. Even so, we must exercise caution in drawing deterministic conclusions from the often-reported association between violence experienced as a child and the subsequent use of violence. Many individuals who experienced violence in their childhoods are not violent adults.

. . . . . . . . . . . . . . . . . . . . . . . . . . . . . . . . . . . . . . .

Discussions of social class differences in family violence alert us to many issues related to the family life experiences associated with social position. Households where the husband was unemployed or underemployed had the highest rates of violence between spouses and violence by parents toward a child (Straus et al., 1980). Unemployed men were twice as likely to use severe violence on their wives as were men employed full time. Among men employed part time, the rate of wife beating was three times the rate for men employed full time. The rate of child abuse among fathers employed part time was nearly twice as high as the rate for fathers employed full time. These findings raise the important issues of family resources acquired through fathers' full-time employment and time at risk. . . .

Another issue is the stress on families associated with lack of employment. A number of researchers have indicated the importance of stress for understanding family violence (Newberger et al., 1977; Straus, 1979). It has been suggested that overzealous physical punishment of children by parents may result as much from the various stresses experienced by the child's parents as from the actual desire or need to control the child's behavior. . . .

## Race and Child Maltreatment

Examinations of the relation between family violence and race have yielded mixed results. In the first large-scale summary of national reports, Gil (1970) concluded that families reported for abuse were drawn disproportionately from the less educated, the poor, and ethnic minorities. Black children were overrepresented as victims of abuse. A more recent compilation of reports gave a similar picture: whites were underrepresented in reported cases of maltreatment, and lower-income families, in general, were overrepresented (Jason et al., 1982).

. . . . . . . . . . . . . . . . . . . . . . . . . . . . . . . . . . . . . . . . .

Newberger and his colleagues (1977) believe that children from poor and minority families are more vulnerable to being labeled as abused than are children from more affluent households; the latter are more likely to be classified as victims of accidents. Support for this proposition, particularly with respect to abuse cases seen in medical settings, comes from several sources. In research conducted among physicians, Gelles (1982) reported that when the physicians made a report of child abuse, they considered not only the child's physical condition but also the caretaker's occupation, education, race, and ethnicity. Five percent of a group of physicians surveyed ($N = 157$) stated that the caretaker's race and ethnicity were so important that they would file a child abuse report on the basis of those characteristics alone (Gelles, 1982).

Using a case vignette model, Turbett and O'Toole (1980) found that recognition of child abuse by physicians was affected by severity of injury and by the parents' socioeconomic status and ethnicity. When children were described as having a major injury, Black children were nearly twice as likely as white children to be recognized as victims of abuse. Physicians were 33 percent more likely to report Black children suffering from a major injury

than children identified as white who were described in identical vignettes. Children described as lower-class whites suffering from major injuries were more likely to be classified as abused than white children with the same injury who were presented as members of an upper-class group (Turbett and O'Toole, 1980).

Data from the national survey of family violence (Straus et al., 1980) indicated little difference between Black and white families in the rates of abusive violence toward children (15 percent in Black families, 14 percent in white families). In a more detailed examination of the national survey data, Cazenave and Straus (1979) concluded that the aid and support, especially child care, provided by Black extended family kin seemed to reduce the risk of abusive violence toward children. These data included only two-parent families; consequently, we advise some caution in interpretation.

In the most complete attitudinal research to date on the topic of ethnicity and violence, Giovannoni and Becerra (1979) explored how the various ethnic and professional groups within the large city define child maltreatment. They presented a series of case vignettes that described specific incidents of child maltreatment, representing a range of behaviors that might be considered maltreatment and that varied in degree of severity. Respondents included professionals and lay people in the metropolitan Los Angeles area.

The respondents were asked to rate each vignette according to the seriousness of its impact on the welfare of the child. The sample population comprised 12 percent Blacks, 17 percent Hispanics, 65 percent white (Anglo), and 6 percent other.

The study sought to test the idea that ethnic minorities and people of lower socioeconomic status are "more tolerant of mistreatment and likely to have a higher threshold for considering actions as mistreatment" (Giovannoni and Becerra, 1979). The results, however, showed just the opposite: In 94 percent of the cases, Blacks and Hispanics were found to give more serious ratings to the vignettes than did the Anglos. Contrary to the authors' expectations, it was found that education and income (the prime indicators of socioeconomic status) were related inversely to ratings of seriousness. That is, the higher the education and income level of the respondent, the lower the seriousness rating. Ethnic differences among respondents were not merely a product of social class differences; ethnic differences persisted even within educational levels. Blacks across all educational levels rated categories of neglect as more serious than did others. The results of analysis by income show similar, though less consistent, trends.

This research suggests that poor and nonwhite families may not share similar attitudes toward maltreatment with white and more affluent families. Nonwhites and people of lower socioeconomic status tended to evaluate the vignettes as more serious (Giovannoni and Becerra, 1979).

# The Framework

Several theoretical frameworks and propositions have been developed from the study of violence and aggression, and these are applicable to the issue of family violence. Gelles and Straus (1979) surveyed fifteen theories ranging from intrapsychic to macrosociological. Many of these approaches are simplistic, unicausal models that fail to articulate the complex, multidimensional process described in some of the earlier works on family violence (Gil, 1970).

To understand violence toward children within a family requires a perspective that takes into account multiple factors interacting within the family system. The ecological model of human development is particularly useful because it not only helps avoid the analytic limitations imposed by unitary theories, but also provides insights into the dynamics of child maltreatment (Garbarino, 1977, 1982a; Bronfenbrenner, 1979).

In its most general form, ecological analysis focuses on the activities of organisms in an environment. This approach locates the child in the setting of the family and explores ways in which the family is connected to other concrete settings and to more general social forces in the social environment (Bowles, 1983). It calls for the separate conceptualization of the environment or context, the characteristics of each actor, and the interaction of actors with each other and with the environment.

Anyone who is concerned with the causes of child maltreatment must be aware of the notion that agents outside the victim–perpetrator dyad have a significant, even controlling effect on the dynamics of maltreatment (Garbarino, 1977; Justice and Justice, 1976). The analysis of child maltreatment involves both the examination of factors within the family microsystem and the identification of other settings in which family members participate individually or collectively. Each setting can be described and analyzed in terms of activities in which people engage, relationships between people, and social roles that organize the activities of different participants and the relationships between participants (Bowles, 1983).

Social institutions such as schools, churches, and medical care facilities are important elements in the family's social environment. To date, little research has examined the connections among these systems with respect to child maltreatment. Gelles (1975) suggested that social agencies are major gatekeepers in the process of labeling and defining a child as abused and a caretaker as abusive. Therefore we must examine the gatekeepers who initially attach the label of abuser to a caretaker, pass this individual through the gate, and reinforce the label (Gelles, 1975).

# Methodology

Data for this analysis were taken from the National Incidence Study mentioned earlier, the most comprehensive and reliable information available on the incidence and severity of child abuse and neglect. This study was conducted in a stratified random sample of twenty-six counties clustered within ten states. Each sample county had a known probability of selection, which provided the basis for computing national estimates. Data were collected on case reports received between May 1, 1979, and April 30, 1980. We reanalyzed data from that study with a specific focus on child maltreatment cases seen in hospitals.

Seventy of the ninety-two eligible hospitals (75 percent) participated in the study (National Incidence Study, 1981: Methodology). From these hospitals 805 cases of child abuse and neglect were brought to the attention of the study. Using an elaborate weighting system to extrapolate from study cases, the study investigators estimated that for the country as a whole, hospital personnel suspected a total of 77,380 cases of abuse and neglect. . . .

For the purpose of this study a child-abuse situation was defined as follows:

> *one where, through purposive acts or marked inattention to a child's basic needs, behavior of a parent/substitute or other adult caretaker caused forseeable and avoidable injury or impairment to a child, or materially contributed to unreasonable prolongation or worsening of an existing injury or impairment. (National Incidence Study, 1981:4)*

. . . Any particular child may have been reported to CPS more than once during the study year and/or may have been described to the study by any number or combination of sources. Enough identifying data were collected, however, to allow us to determine reliably whether or not any two data forms were describing the same child. Duplicate records were purged from the analysis file so that the case was counted only once. Whenever a particular child was identified to the study by a hospital, or whenever another non-CPS source also appeared in the CPS file, the CPS record was retained. In effect, non-CPS sources were given credit only for children who had not also been reported to CPS.

# Results

Previous analyses have shown that in comparison to other agencies in the National Incidence Study, the hospital sample included children who were younger, who had younger mothers, who were more urban (65.8 percent versus 42.1 percent), and who were Black (25 percent versus 16 percent). There were no major differences among hospitals and other agencies with respect to income, mode of medical payment (public or private), proportion of single parents, or sex of child (Hampton and

Newberger, 1985). Table 1 provides a summary of the hospital sample characteristics.

Some important differences existed among samples with respect to the type and severity of recognized maltreatment cases. Hospitals identified many more cases of physical abuse than did other agencies. The proportion of cases in this category alone exceeded the proportion of physical, sexual, and emotional abuse cases recognized by all other agencies; over half the hospital cases belonged to one or another category of abuse. Among hospital cases, the rated severity of injury also tended to be more serious. Twenty-four percent of the hospital cases were rated as serious compared to 13 percent for the rest of the sample (Hampton and Newberger, 1985).

Table 1 reflects maltreatment cases reported to the study either by CPS or directly by hospitals. Because we are concerned with the recognition and reporting process, we must examine carefully this latter set of cases.

As Table 2 shows, Black and Hispanic children were more likely than white children to be reported to child protection agencies as alleged victims of maltreatment. Children from higher-income families were also less likely to be reported.

Younger children were more than three times as likely as adolescents to be reported officially. Single-parent households and families receiving public assistance were also more likely to be reported.

Physical abuse cases were more likely to be reported than unreported but cases of emotional abuse and neglect tended to be underreported. The latter finding is consistent with our expectation that when concrete evidence of injury is absent in cases of emotional maltreatment, professionals tend not to report.

Surprisingly, although hospitals identified more serious cases of child abuse and neglect than other agencies, serious injuries were often unreported.

Multivariate analyses (Table 3) yield a more detailed understanding of the differences between reported and unreported cases. A stepwise discriminant function procedure was used to select variables for inclusion. The variables in Table 3 appear in order of their selection. In our analysis, the fol-

## TABLE 1   Total Sample Characteristics

| CHARACTERISTIC | PERCENT[1] | CHARACTERISTIC | PERCENT[1] |
|---|---|---|---|
| Age of child (in years) | | Receiving AFDC | |
| 0–5 | 54.9 | Yes | 32.2 |
| 6–12 | 28.9 | No | 67.8 |
| 13–17 | 16.2 | Type of maltreatment | |
| Sex of child | | Physical abuse | 35.2 |
| Male | 52.3 | Sexual abuse | 9.3 |
| Female | 47.7 | Emotional injury | 19.4 |
| Mother's education[2] | | Physical neglect | 26.6 |
| 0–8 years | 12.2 | Miscellaneous | 9.5 |
| Some high school | 44.4 | Severity of maltreatment | |
| High school graduate plus | 43.4 | Serious | 33.4 |
| Mother's age (in years) | | Moderate | 36.0 |
| Less than 19 | 10.8 | Probable | 30.6 |
| 20–24 | 21.5 | Number of children | |
| 25–29 | 15.9 | 1 | 35.3 |
| 30–34 | 18.3 | 2 | 22.2 |
| Over 35 | 14.1 | 3 | 15.6 |
| Don't know | 19.4 | 4 | 7.9 |
| Race | | 5 or more | 19.0 |
| White | 66.7 | City size | |
| Black | 25.6 | SMSA over 200,000 | 65.8 |
| Hispanic | 7.6 | Other SMSA | 18.4 |
| Father present | | Non-SMSA | 15.8 |
| Yes | 54.2 | Official report filed | |
| No | 45.8 | Yes | 66.4 |
| Family income[2] | | No | 33.6 |
| Less than $7000 | 49.3 | Weighted $N$ = 77,380 | |
| $7,000–14,999 | 36.6 | Unweighted $N$ = 805 | |
| $15,000–24,999 | 9.3 | | |
| $25,000 or more | 4.9 | | |

[1]All percentages reflect weightings and may not add up to 100 percent because of rounding.

[2]Variable excludes missing data.

lowing factors appeared to affect case reporting most powerfully: income, the role of the mother in maltreatment, race, emotional injury, sex of child, sexual abuse, and mother's education. Disproportionate numbers of unreported cases were victims of emotional abuse in white families of higher income, whose mothers were alleged to be responsible for the injuries.

These data raise a number of important questions regarding the type of cases seen by hospitals and those selected for reporting. It suggests that socially marginal families may be victimized by a process in which their personal characteristics rather than their alleged behavior define them as deviant (Turbett and O'Toole, 1980). This discrimination not only subjects ethnic minority and lower socioeconomic status families to the stigma of being labeled as abusive, but may also subject them to interventions that may be both intrusive and punitive. The same process discriminates in favor of white and high socioeconomic status families. (A latent consequence of this biased reporting may be

TABLE 2    Child Maltreatment Cases Seen in Hospitals by CPS Reporting (Hospital Survey) [1]

| VARIABLE | REPORTED | NOT REPORTED | TOTAL PERCENT |
|---|---|---|---|
| Sex of child | | | |
| Male | 41.7 | 58.3 | 52.3 |
| Female | 44.1 | 55.9 | 47.3 |
| Age of child (in years) | | | |
| 0–5 | 51.9 | 48.1 | 54.8 |
| 6–12 | 45.8 | 54.2 | 26.8 |
| 13–17 | 14.2 | 85.8 | 18.5 |
| Race | | | |
| White | 36.5 | 63.5 | 70.5 |
| Black | 48.3 | 51.7 | 21.7 |
| Hispanic | 85.5 | 14.5 | 7.8 |
| Mother's education | | | |
| 0–8 years | 44.4 | 55.6 | 11.0 |
| Some high school | 57.7 | 42.3 | 37.2 |
| High school graduate | 58.8 | 42.0 | 51.8 |
| Father present | | | |
| Yes | 39.6 | 60.4 | 51.4 |
| No | 46.6 | 53.4 | 48.6 |
| Family income | | | |
| $7,000 or less | 56.1 | 43.9 | 47.9 |
| $7,000–14,999 | 62.9 | 37.1 | 37.9 |
| $15,000–24,999 | 36.8 | 63.3 | 8.2 |
| $25,000 or more | 3.3 | 96.7 | 6.0 |
| Receiving AFDC | | | |
| Yes | 53.5 | 46.5 | 28.4 |
| No | 46.5 | 53.5 | |

[1]Percentages may not add to 100 percent because of rounding. All percentages reflect case weights. Table reflects cases reported to study by sampled hospitals only and excludes cases reported to study by CPS only.

a failure to address the needs of the many middle-class families who, surveys suggest, are at risk for child maltreatment.)

Another central question raised by this analysis concerns differences among the various ethnic groups in the hospital sample. Do they differ in their use of medical facilities? Do they differ in patterns of alleged maltreatment? To what extent might the medical encounter be different for members of different groups?

Table 4 provides an ethnic breakdown of the sample. The groups show several differences in child and family characteristics, as well as in the type of alleged maltreatment. Black and Hispanic chil-dren were younger, had younger mothers, and were more likely to live in urban areas. Whereas 86 percent of the entire sample had incomes below $15,000, 93 percent of the Black and 76 percent of the Hispanic families had incomes below this level. Almost half the Black families were receiving Medicaid and AFDC assistance. Seventy-one percent of the Black households were female-headed.

When we look at differences among the groups with respect to type of maltreatment, we see that almost half the Hispanic children were alleged victims of physical neglect. The other largest category for Hispanics was miscellaneous maltreatment (21 percent), which included involuntary neglect

## TABLE 2    continued

| VARIABLE | REPORTED | NOT REPORTED | TOTAL PERCENT |
|---|---|---|---|
| Type of maltreatment | | | |
| Physical abuse | 52.2 | 47.8 | 30.9 |
| Sexual abuse | 45.8 | 54.2 | 5.7 |
| Emotional injury | 28.3 | 71.7 | 27.3 |
| Physical neglect | 42.7 | 57.3 | 26.8 |
| Miscellaneous | 59.8 | 45.2 | 5.2 |
| Severity of maltreatment | | | |
| Serious | 28.9 | 71.1 | 35.8 |
| Moderate | 33.5 | 66.5 | 39.5 |
| Probable | 45.9 | 54.1 | 29.6 |
| Mother's role in maltreatment | | | |
| Maltreater | 33.0 | 67.0 | 64.9 |
| Not involved | 70.4 | 29.6 | 26.6 |
| Don't know | 39.1 | 65.9 | 8.5 |
| Number of children | | | |
| 1 | 51.7 | 48.3 | 29.5 |
| 2 | 47.3 | 53.7 | 21.9 |
| 3 | 52.3 | 47.7 | 14.1 |
| 4 | 43.1 | 36.9 | 7.1 |
| 5 or more | 25.4 | 74.6 | 27.4 |
| City size | | | |
| SMSA over 200,000 | 46.0 | 54.0 | 66.2 |
| Other SMSA | 41.1 | 58.9 | 16.0 |
| Non-SMSA | 33.4 | 66.6 | 17.8 |
| Total | 93.0 | 57.0 | 100.00 |

Weighted $N = 45,276$
Unweighted $N = 415$

## TABLE 3    Stepwise Discriminant Analysis Results for Hospital Reporting

| VARIABLE | STANDARDIZED COEFFICIENT | VARIABLE | STANDARDIZED COEFFICIENT |
|---|---|---|---|
| Race | .507 | Father in household | .264 |
| Mother's role | .577 | Number of children | .250 |
| Income | .586 | City size | .198 |
| Mother's education | .294 | Canonical *R* | .691 |
| Sex of child | .372 | Wilkes' lambda | .589 |
| Emotional injury | .354 | Percentage of cases | |
| Sexual abuse | .238 | correctly classified | 65% |

TABLE 4  Ethnicity by Selected Household and Family Characteristics: National Incidence Study Hospital Sample[1]

| VARIABLE | WHITE | BLACK | HISPANIC | TOTAL[3] |
|---|---|---|---|---|
| Age of child | | | | |
| 0–5 | 54.3 | 53.6 | 64.4 | 54.9 |
| 6–12 | 25.9 | 36.1 | 30.4 | 28.9 |
| 13–17 | 19.7 | 10.3 | 5.2 | 16.2 |
| Sex of child | | | | |
| Male | 52.6 | 51.6 | 51.0 | 51.6 |
| Female | 47.4 | 48.4 | 49.0 | 48.3 |
| Number of children in household | | | | |
| 1 | 36.0 | 34.7 | 31.2 | 35.3 |
| 2 | 24.3 | 16.7 | 21.6 | 22.2 |
| 3 | 14.3 | 14.8 | 29.9 | 15.6 |
| 4 | 7.8 | 9.7 | 2.7 | 7.9 |
| 5 or more | 17.6 | 24.1 | 14.6 | 19.0 |
| Age of mother | | | | |
| Less than 20 | 10.6 | 9.5 | 16.7 | 10.8 |
| 20–24 | 16.5 | 33.6 | 24.3 | 21.5 |
| 25–29 | 16.3 | 13.7 | 19.1 | 15.9 |
| 30–34 | 19.3 | 13.2 | 26.9 | 18.3 |
| 35 and older | 14.2 | 16.5 | 5.1 | 14.1 |
| Don't know | 23.1 | 13.5 | 7.9 | 15.4 |
| Mother's education[2] | | | | |
| 0–8 years | 10.5 | 9.8 | 29.5 | 12.2 |
| 9–11 years | 39.8 | 58.6 | 35.9 | 44.4 |
| High school graduates | 49.7 | 31.7 | 34.6 | 43.4 |
| Role of mother in maltreatment | | | | |
| Perpetrator | 49.9 | 47.2 | 63.2 | 50.2 |
| Not involved | 42.2 | 42.5 | 27.2 | 42.5 |
| Don't know | 7.9 | 5.3 | 9.5 | 7.3 |
| Family income[2] | | | | |
| Less than $7,000 | 42.9 | 62.8 | 30.8 | 49.3 |
| $7,000–$14,999 | 38.1 | 30.2 | 46.6 | 36.6 |
| $15,000–$24,999 | 12.7 | 3.6 | 2.6 | 9.3 |
| $25,000 or more | 6.3 | 3.3 | 0 | 4.9 |

[1]Percentages may not add to 100 because of rounding.  [3]Missing data excluded.
[2]Cases of unspecified ethnicity are excluded.

due to caretaker hospitalization, financial problems, or other unspecified neglect.

Black maltreatment cases were primarily physical abuse (40.6 percent) and physical neglect (31.4 percent). Emotional injury was alleged only infrequently (10.8 percent).

# Discussion

The ecological perspective suggests that one might approach the issue of child maltreatment and the reporting process by observing factors on different levels of analysis. One could ask which factors

## TABLE 4 continued

| VARIABLE | WHITE | BLACK | HISPANIC | TOTAL[3] |
|---|---|---|---|---|
| AFDC | | | | |
| Yes | 23.1 | 58.5 | 20.5 | 32.2 |
| No | 76.9 | 41.5 | 79.5 | 67.8 |
| Medicaid | | | | |
| Yes | 22.1 | 57.4 | 4.2 | 29.5 |
| No | 77.9 | 41.6 | 95.8 | 70.5 |
| Father in household | | | | |
| Yes | 62.9 | 28.4 | 65.0 | 54.1 |
| No | 37.1 | 71.6 | 35.0 | 45.9 |
| Type of maltreatment | | | | |
| Physical abuse | 35.9 | 40.6 | 10.0 | 35.2 |
| Sexual abuse | 8.6 | 11.1 | 10.0 | 9.4 |
| Emotional injury | 23.8 | 10.8 | 9.7 | 10.4 |
| Physical neglect | 22.1 | 31.4 | 49.2 | 26.6 |
| Miscellaneous | 9.0 | 6.1 | 21.0 | 9.2 |
| Severity of child's injury/impairment | | | | |
| Serious | 30.7 | 40.1 | 37.5 | 33.4 |
| Moderate | 40.8 | 27.7 | 17.6 | 36.0 |
| Probable | 28.5 | 32.2 | 44.9 | 30.6 |
| Urbanicity | | | | |
| SMSA over 2,000,000 | 60.3 | 73.4 | 88.4 | 65.8 |
| Other SMSA | 25.0 | 10.6 | 4.7 | 18.7 |
| Non-SMSA | 16.8 | 16.0 | 6.9 | 15.5 |
| Substantiated (percent of reported) | | | | |
| Yes | 34.7 | 57.6 | 69.7 | 57.1 |
| No | 49.3 | 42.4 | 30.3 | 42.9 |

$N$ = 75,274 (weighted)
$N$ = 777 (unweighted)

among those that directly affect the lives of families increase the risk for maltreatment. Such factors as mundane extreme environmental stress (Peters and Massey, 1983) may be regarded as a macrosystem variable. This factor, combined with the racist or sexist values that demean some minority parents and thus raise the level of stress for their children (Garbarino, 1982a, 1982b), places many children and families at risk. It provides a context of endemic stress (Belle, 1982; Fried, 1982) within which the family members must conduct their daily lives.

Similarly, any analysis of maltreatment in families must acknowledge factors at the institutional level that affect families. Factors that differentially affect the Black family include high unemployment rates, lower incomes, and an overall poverty rate that continues to be about three times as high for Black families as for all families (Glick, 1981; McAdoo, 1982; Pearce and McAdoo, 1981). These factors not only have a direct impact on the quality of family life for Black families, but also appear to have an indirect effect through such factors as marital disruption (Hampton, 1979, 1980), adolescent pregnancies, and mental health problems (Frerichs, Aneshensel, and Clark, 1981). It has been argued that child maltreatment in black families may be a secondary effect of societal violence against Black families (Daniel et al., 1983).

Although macrolevel variables obviously affect child maltreatment in families, the interaction between the family and other agencies is also important. No objective behavior is automatically recognized as child abuse (Gelles, 1975); the agencies that are confronted with suspected cases of maltreatment serve as gates and gatekeepers, which either admit selected cases as abuse or identify them as not being abuse and turn them away. The social process of defining abuse has important political and social implications both for the recipients of the label and for sevice providers.

Medical personnel have a legal mandate to report suspected cases of child maltreatment. All fifty states have enacted legislation that mandates reporting and defines not only the procedure for reporting but also the consequences for failing to report. . . . Nonetheless, reporting is inhibited by a variety of factors, including lack of clarity in defining child maltreatment, the reluctance to intervene in family privacy, and the time and emotional involvement associated with these cases (Newberger et al., 1977; Pfohl, 1977). . . . Our data indicate clearly that even in the presence of these laws, criteria for reporting are applied differentially, often along ethnic and social class lines.

The marginal economic position of many Black families cannot be overstated. Many U.S. Black families do not participate fully in the mainstream health care system and may prefer to use the emergency room as a source of care on an episodic basis. The emergency room is a significant element in the family's social environment not only because it can provide services to relieve acute suffering, but also because emergency services permit nonscheduled visits, often require shorter waiting times than outpatient departments, and are generally accessible by public transportation. These features approximate most closely the conveniences that private care offers to people who can afford it.

The medical encounter represents the interaction between two social systems, whether medical care is provided in the emergency room or in other clinics. This encounter is much more than the interaction between a clinician's expertise and a child's medical condition; most clinicians are majority group members, and the Black family often presents the white physician with socioeconomic differences as well as differences in racial experience (Daniel, 1985; Levy, 1985).

Ethnic families bring to the medical encounter general styles of interaction, attitudes toward authority figures, sex role allocations, and ways of expressing emotion and asking for help that may differ from those of the middle class. These sociocultural factors influence people's interaction in the medical encounter. It has been suggested that culturally based patterns of interaction between Blacks and whites may actually intrude in doctor–patient interactions involving members of those two racial groups (Daniel, 1985; Franklin, 1985; Jackson, 1981; Levy, 1985). Where cultural differences exist, they may affect both the process and the product of the medical encounter.

This encounter typically takes place among strangers who are unequal in ascribed and achieved status. Social distance is inherent in this relationship; the medical provider is always in a superordinate position because the family seeks his or her expertise with respect to the diagnosis and treatment of the child's symptoms. We have learned from labeling theory that the greater the social distance between the typer and the person singled out for typing, the broader the type and the more quickly it may be applied. In particular, the label of child maltreater is less likely to be applied if the diagnostician (gatekeeper) and the possible abuser share similar characteristics, especially socioeconomic status. This is particularly important when the child's injury is not serious or manifestly a consequence of maltreatment.

The assessment of alleged child maltreatment typically involves more than the evaluation of a child's physical symptoms. It implies an evaluation of the family's care-giving potential and behavior that might be related to the child's current symptoms. Although the family and the clinician are allied in a common concern for the child, the alliance is frequently broken by the clinician's responsibility to interrogate the family to determine to what extent their behavior may have caused the child's suffering.

Many of the Black families in our sample are poor, receive public assistance (58 percent), are young (43.1 percent under 25), and are single-parent households (71.6 percent). This combination of factors often leads to the confounding of two sets of variables: those that could make certain people likely to be labeled child abusers and those that previous research has suggested are causal factors in the act(s) of child abuse.

The medical encounter is frequently problematic in its own right and issues of race and ethnicity further complicate these matters. In light of the structured inequality that pervades the lives of Black families, including many factors that contribute to high-risk parenting, being labeled as an abuser holds both symbolic and real implications for child and family. For many families, the label of perpetrator extends beyond the parent–child dyad and can be traced to the larger social structure, which denies many families an opportunity to achieve a reasonable quality of life. Medical professionals frequently contribute to a negative cycle by overintrusion in the guise of help (Newberger, 1985). These practices not only blame the victim for his or her life circumstances but also visit additional cruelty and violence on the Black family and its children.

# References

American Humane Association

1983 *Highlights of Official Child Neglect and Abuse Reporting, Annual Report.* Denver: Author.

Belle, Deborah

1982 *Lives in Stress.* Beverly Hills, Calif.: Sage Publications.

Bowles, R. T.

1983 "Family Well-Being, Family Violence and Rapid Community Growth: An Ecological Perspective." In *Proceedings of the Alaska Symposium on the Social, Economic and Cultural Impacts of Natural Resource Development,* S. Yarie, ed., 146–151. Fairbanks: University of Alaska.

Bronfenbrenner, U.

1979 *The Ecology of Human Development: Experiments by Nature and Design.* Cambridge, Mass.: Harvard University Press.

Cazenave, N., and M. A. Straus

1979 "Race, Class, Network Embeddedness and Family Violence: A Search for Potent Support Systems." *Journal of Comparative Family Studies* 10:281–300.

Daniel, J. H.

1985 "Cultural and Ethnic Issues: The Black Family." In *Unhappy Families*, E. H. Newberger and R. Bourne, eds., pp. 195–254. Littleton, Mass.: PSG Publishers.

Daniel, J., R. L. Hampton, and E. H. Newberger

1983 "Child Abuse and Accidents in Black Families: A Controlled Comparative Study." *American Journal of Orthopsychiatry* 53 (4):649–653.

Franklin, D. L.

1985 "Differential Clinical Assessments: The Influence of Class and Race." *Social Service Review* (March):45–61.

Frerichs, R., C. Aneshensel, and V. Clark

1981 "Prevalence of Depression in Los Angeles County." *American Journal of Epidemiology* 11 (6):691–699.

Fried, M.

1982 "Endemic Stress: The Psychology of Resignation and the Politics of Scarcity." *American Journal of Orthopsychiatry* 52 (January):4–19.

Garbarino, J.

1977    "The Human Ecology of Child Maltreatment: A Conceptual Model for Research." *Journal of Marriage and the Family* 39:721–736.

1982a   *Children and Families in the Social Environment.* New York: Aldine.

1982b   "Healing the Social Wounds of Isolation." In *Child Abuse,* E. H. Newberger, ed. 43–55. Boston: Little, Brown.

Gelles, R. J.

1975    "The Social Construction of Child Abuse." *American Journal of Orthopsychiatry* 45 (April): 363–371.

1980    "Violence in the Family: A Review of Research in the Seventies." *Journal of Marriage and the Family* 42 (4, November):873–885.

1982    "Child Abuse and Family Violence: Implications for Medical Professionals." In *Child Abuse,* Eli H. Newberger, ed. Boston: Little, Brown.

Gelles, R. J., and M. A. Straus

1979    "Determinants of Violence in the Family: Toward a Theoretical Integration." In *Contemporary Theories about the Family,* W. Burr et al., eds. New York: Free Press.

Gil, D.

1970    *Violence against Children: Physical Child Abuse in the United States.* Cambridge, Mass.: Harvard University Press.

Giovannoni, J. M., and R. M. Becerra

1979    *Defining Child Abuse.* New York: Free Press.

Glick, P. A.

1981    "A Demographic Profile of Black Families." In *Black Families,* Harriette McAdoo, ed. Beverly Hills: Sage.

Hampton, R. L.

1979    "Husbands' Characteristics and Marital Disruption in Black Families." *The Sociological Quarterly* 20:255–266.

1980    "Institutional Decimation, Marital Exchange and Disruption in Black Families." *Western Journal of Black Studies* 4 (2):132–139.

Hampton, R. L., and E. H. Newberger

1985    "Child Abuse Incidence and Reporting by Hospitals: The Significance of Severity, Class and Race." *American Journal of Public Health* 75 (1):56–60.

Jackson, J. J.

1981    "Urban Black American." In *Ethnicity and Medical Care,* A. Harwood, ed., 37–129. Cambridge, Mass.: Harvard University Press.

Jason, J., N. Amereuh, J. Marks, and C. Tyler, Jr.

1982    "Child Abuse in Georgia: A Method to Evaluate Risk Factors and Reporting Bias." *American Journal of Public Health* 72 (12):1353–1358.

Justice, B., and R. Justice

1976    *The Abusing Family.* New York: Human Sciences Press.

Levy, D. R.

1985    "White Doctors and Black Patients: Influence of Race on the Doctor–Patient Relationships." *Pediatrics* 75 (4):639–643.

McAdoo, H. P.

1982    "Demographic Trends for People of Color." *Social Work* 27 (1):15–23.

National Study of the Incidence and Severity of Child Abuse and Neglect

1981    Publication No. (OHDS) 81–030326. *Study Findings.*: Author.

Newberger, E. H.

1985    "The Helping Hand Strikes Again: Unintended Consequences of Child Abuse Reporting." In E. H. Newberger and R. Bourne, *Unhappy Families,* pp. 171–178. Littleton, Mass.: PSG Publishers.

Newberger, E. H., R. B. Reed, J. M. Daniel, J. N. Hyde, and M. Kotelchuck

1977    "Pediatric Social Illness: Toward an Etiologic Classification." *Pediatrics* 60:178–185.

Pearce, D. and H. P. McAdoo

1981    "Women in Poverty: Toward a New Understanding of Work and Welfare." In *Thirteenth Final Report.* Washington, D.C.: National Advisory Council on Economic Opportunity.

Peters, M., and G. Massey

1983    "Mundane Extreme Environmental Stress in Family Stress Theories: The Case of Black Families in White America." *Marriage and Family Review* 1 and 2:193–215.

Pfohl, S.

1977    "The Discovery of Child Abuse." *Social Problems* 24 (3):310–323.

Straus, M.

1979    "Stress and Physical Child Abuse." *Child Abuse and Neglect* 4:75–88.

Straus, M. A., R. J. Gelles, and S. Steinmetz

1980    *Behind Closed Doors: Violence in the American Family.* Garden City, New York: Doubleday.

Turbett, J. P., and R. O'Toole

1980    "Physician's Recognition of Child Abuse." Paper presented at the annual meeting of the American Sociological Association, New York.

# 7 / The Extended Family

## GRANDMOTHER FUNCTIONS IN MULTIGENERATIONAL FAMILIES:
### An Exploratory Study of Black Adolescent Mothers and Their Infants

*Sr. Mary Jean Flaherty* · *Lorna Facteau* · *Patricia Garver*

*This qualitative study explores the functions of nineteen Black grandmothers who are engaged in the care of their adolescent daughters' infants. Interviews with grandmothers revealed seven functions related to this role: managing, caretaking, coaching, assessing, nurturing, assigning, and patrolling. Suggestions for future research with Black grandmothers are given.*

Grandparents have been the forgotten subjects in family research. They are emerging as critical figures in the literature which depicts the changing American family at the end of the 20th century. This qualitative study explores the functions of one group of grandparents—Black grandmothers—engaged in primary care activities of infants born to their adolescent daughters. The 19 grandmothers who were selected as subjects of the research were visited in their homes 2 weeks and 3 months after the births of the infants. Open-ended interviews were conducted with the grandmothers. The interview material was subjected to content analysis. Seven grandmother functions emerged from the data: managing, caretaking, coaching, assessing, nurturing, assigning, and patrolling.

## The Central Place of Grandmothers in Poor Black Families

The evidence of teenage pregnancy is so compelling that the concerns of the 1960s (Furstenberg, 1976; Ooms, 1981) have developed into complex health

From *Maternal-Child Nursing Journal* 16 (Spring 1987):61–73. Reprinted by permission. © 1987 by the School of Nursing, University of Pittsburgh. This study was supported in part by a U.S. DHHS Division of Nursing Grant, No. 1PO1 NU01218-01, 1983–1984, and by The Catholic University of America School of Nursing Dean's Research Grant, 1983, 1984, 1985.

and social problems in the 1980s (Baldwin and Cain, 1980; Phipps-Yonas, 1980). Not only does the United States lead most industrialized countries in rates of teenage pregnancy (Jones et al., 1985), the proportion of unwed mothers in the 15–17 year old group has increased from 43% in 1970 to 62% in 1980 (Ventura and Hendershot, 1984). In the present milieu, adolescent mothers bring their babies home and grandparents play critical roles in the rearing of these babies (Furstenberg, 1980; Zuckerman, Winsome, and Alpert, 1979). Kempler (1976) suggests that extended kin, especially grandparents, offer close physical and psychological connections of instrumental and psychological value. The presence of a grandparent can relieve a single parent as the sole source of affection and care.

The involvement of grandmothers in adolescent mothering is particularly significant because the family of the adolescent mother is usually the most consistent provider of care and support (Furstenburg and Crawford, 1978; Zitner and Miller, 1980). Taylor (1975) reports that 15-year-old mothers who experienced supportive relationships with grandmothers, aunts, or counselors, had increased chances of successful mothering.

The availability of alternative caretakers may be critical to adolescents' achievement of dual roles as teenager and mother. However, grandmothers and their adolescent daughters may not agree about their respective positions and responsibilities in families (Sadler and Catrone, 1983). Poole and Hoffman (1981) describe three typical family situations involving urban grandmothers: daughter fails to assume responsibility for infant care and the burden is placed on the grandmother; the grandmother feels disgraced and has responsibility for infant care; and the grandmother is available for emotional and financial support. Smith (1983) developed a similar typology using role concepts of blocking, binding, and sharing. Generally, the literature suggests that support given to adolescent mothers varies with their need for help in mothering roles (Coletta and Lee, 1983).

The central place of Black grandmothers in the rearing of their grandchildren is usually the consequence of family organization as well as historical patterns or role configurations (Burton and Bengt-

son, 1985). LaFargue (1980) argues that Black families survived in the urban north by developing circles of kinfolk who shared responsibilities. Classic descriptions of Black families include studies of relationships which go beyond the mother-father-child tradition (Boszormenyi-Nagy and Spark, 1973; Cohler and Grunebaum, 1981; Stack, 1974). In these families, grandmothers fulfill supportive, child-rearing functions which are integrated into daily family lives (Staples, 1971). Black family households shelter three and four generations where grandmothers mother their own children and frequently take charge of the grandchildren as well (Colon, 1980). While this generational pattern is true for all poor families, Peters (1981) suggests that poor Black families have different child-rearing priorities. They also display attitudes and patterns of behavior which have developed in response to unique cultural, racial, psychologic, and economic pressures (McAdoo, 1981; Stack, 1974). The ordinary pattern of Black families takes on added significance when adolescent family members become mothers.

The ease with which Black grandmothers assume mothering roles for grandchildren may disguise the acceptability of such arrangements. The historical portrayal of Black grandmothers as "guardians of generations" (Frazier, 1939), reflecting wisdom, leadership, and strength (Burton and Bengtson, 1985) is challenged in the 1980s by the competing demands grandmothers fill in multigenerational families.

The question of how young mothers learn to be caregivers and parents is intriguing in any culture. Normal newborns have limited repertoires of behaviors with which to engage their mothers' interests. Yet, the social, intellectual, and emotional development of infants is strongly linked to the quality of early mother-infant interactions. Mercer (1980) identifies four critical periods: the 1st days following birth; at one month; between the 3rd and 4th months; and between the 6th and 9th months of life. Infants born to adolescent mothers may be at higher risk during these periods because their mothers may fail to "cue-in," an elaborate response-reaction-response pattern (Barnard, 1980).

It is not surprising that practical questions arise about what happens when adolescent mothers bring the newborns home to multigenerational families. Do the babies have two primary caregivers? Do the grandmothers allow young mothers to interpret and respond to the baby's cues? What happens to the cue-response model described by Barnard (1980) if infants are cared for by mothers and grandmothers? What part do the grandmothers play in primary prevention of common childhood diseases and in the identification of physical and developmental problems? To what extent do grandmothers participate in decision making about daily care and health care activities?

## Purpose of the Study

The purpose of this study was to explore the functions and extent of involvement of Black grandmothers in primary care activities of infants of young adolescent mothers. Grandmother was defined as the biological mother of the adolescent mother, a girl between 12 and 18 years of age, who delivered a normal first child and lived with her mother. Primary Infant Care Activities were physical care tasks (feeding, bathing, diaper changing, sleeping), comforting tasks (cuddling, holding, talking, singing), developmental tasks (playing, teaching, encouraging motor skills), and health care tasks (immunizations, well baby clinic visits, seeking medical care when illness is present).

## Design of the Study

This descriptive study was initiated in two metropolitan postpartum units and continued in the homes of grandmothers when the infants were 2 weeks and 3 months of age.

There were three data collection periods in the study: (a) during the hospital stay of the adolescent mother or at the first visit of the VNA staff nurse; (b) 2 weeks postpartum; and (c) 3 months postpartum. These times were suggested by Mercer's (1980) identification of critical periods and the investigators' experience with phases of maternal adjustment.

## Method

Tools used in data collection included: Demographic Data Forms and Focused Interview and Observational Field Schedules. The Demographic Data Forms (Hospital and Home Visit Forms) elicited information about grandmothers, mothers, and infants. The Hospital Form described the pregnancy history of the adolescent mother, assessment statistics for the newborn, and information needed to contact the grandmother. The Home Visit Form enabled the investigators to gather information about the daily routines of caring for the newborn, the family structure, the educational and financial status of the mother; the work history and financial status of the grandmother; and a description of the home. These forms were introduced in the hospital and completed at the first home visit.

The interview schedule, developed by the investigators, used primary infant care activities as its organizing framework. During the initial phase of the study a panel of six maternal-child experts reviewed the interview schedule for relevance and design. Their responses influenced the structure, content, and sequencing of the questions. The revised schedule was used at each home visit to elicit specific information about caregiving roles and activities, decision making, and the meaning of being a grandmother.

Interviews were planned so that the grandmothers would be interviewed alone. In practice this proved to be impossible. While privacy is desired interviews, lack of space and family interest in the newborn made the interviews family events. At one visit the grandmother, adolescent mother, new baby, three younger brothers and sisters, the grandmother's sister, and "Uncle Jimmie" were present. Family responses to questions thought to be intrusive (income, food stamps, and involvement of the family in the Women, Infants and Children program—WIC) confirmed literary descriptions of family solidarity. Most family members knew the family business and did not hesitate to give information.

Interviews were recorded, transcribed, and coded to assure anonymity. The tapes were then erased.

## The Subjects

The purposive sample consisted of 19 Black grandmothers who met the study criteria. Adolescent mothers were identified in postpartum units and through VNA offices located in wards of a major city where adolescent pregnancy is common. At the initial meeting, mothers were invited to participate in the study and were asked to sign informed consent forms. Grandmothers were then contacted by telephone and the study was explained. The purpose and conditions of participation were reiterated at the first home visit when the grandmother was asked to sign the same consent form as her adolescent daughter. Attrition occurred at the time of the second home visit despite phone calls and letters to the families. The loss of 10 subjects limited comparative qualitative analysis.

After data collection, the tapescripts were examined for styles of grandmothering and patterns of infant care, notes were made, and preliminary labels were assigned to behavioral and cognitive processes (Patton, 1980). The unit of analysis was difficult to establish because the grandmothers in the study did not speak in sentences or discrete phrases. A thought-behavioral sequence—an identifiable interval which began with a description of thought or behavior and ended when new material appeared on the tapescripts—became the unit of analysis. Seven themes which emerged from the initial sorting of data were used to construct a coding grid. Initial categories were then established around the emergent themes. Two research assistants independently assigned thought-behavioral sequences to derived categories, achieving an interrater reliability of .90. Field notes were employed in this period to verify and clarify information on the tapescripts. The assignment of data was then subjected to evaluation by a social scientist and a nurse scientist in maternal-child health. O'Brien (1982) suggests that categorical assignment of raw data should be validated by experts in the field.

## Demographic Findings

The demographic data supported the descriptions of studies of poor families (Boszormenyi-Nagy and Spark, 1973; Cohler and Grunebaum, 1981; Colon, 1980). Only 3 of the 19 grandmothers in this study lived with their spouses. All grandmothers were rearing their own children (one to 18 years of age) and one or more grandchildren when the new babies were brought home. The grandmothers ranged in age from 29 to 59 years of age with a mean age of 42.

The adolescent daughters were in school (grades 8–12) when they became pregnant. Their mean and median age at the time of delivery was 15.7 years (range 14 to 18 years). Eighteen of the mothers had prenatal care. During the antepartal periods 2 of the study subjects were treated for hypertension and 2 for venereal disease. There were no postpartal complications. One baby was born prematurely; 4 children were cesarean births. The infants weighed from 3 lb. 11 oz. to 9 lb. 9 oz. ($\overline{X}$ = 7 lb. 2 oz.).

The families lived in apartments ($n = 15$) and houses ($n = 4$). Three grandmothers owned their homes; 9 families lived in subsidized housing. Family members shared bedrooms and other living spaces.

Family financial support included monthly salaries, Aid to Families of Dependent Children (AFDC) and food stamps. Eight grandmothers worked outside the home. The 6 families who qualified for AFDC received between \$299–\$750 ($\overline{X}$ = \$457) per month. Ten families received from \$126 to \$431 ($\overline{X}$ = \$217) per month in food stamps. In the 11 families that reported salaries, monthly incomes ranged from \$338 to \$1400 ($\overline{X}$ = \$800). The grandmothers in the study were members of poor families.

In analyzing data obtained by the Home Visit Forms for primary infant care activities (physical care, comforting, encouraging development, and maintaining health), it was found that adolescent mothers emerged as primary caregivers. Two-thirds of the babies slept in cribs in their mothers' rooms; the remaining infants slept in their mothers' beds. Two infants were being breast fed at the first visit. All infants were bottle fed at the second visit. Data obtained at the first home visit revealed that mothers were usually the persons who fed the babies during both the day ($n = 13$) and night ($n = 15$). The patterns of daytime feedings changed when the mothers returned to school. By the time of the second visit all of the mothers who remained in the study were back in school. Data from the second visit revealed that 2 mothers fed the babies during the day and 8 mothers at night. Adolescent mothers made most of the decisions about daily care activities. However, decisions about medical care were made more frequently by grandmothers who also reported that they were advised in these decisions by neighbors, sisters, or their own mothers. All grandmothers gave advice to their daughters about the care of the infants and the need for medical care.

## The Interviews

The mean length of the tapescripts was 16 pages. Four grandmothers accounted for 45% of the thought-behavioral sequences at visit one (VI). Analysis of thought-behavioral sequences resulted in the identification of seven grandmother functions which are defined and described in Table 1. The incidence of these functions is shown in Table 2.

Grandmothers were outspoken in their approaches to daughters and grandbabies. It is clear from the data that grandmothers expected their daughters to care for their infants. These data support the findings of Ladner and Gourdine (1984) who reported that most grandmothers in their study provided child care but did not assume primary responsibility. Grandmothers saw themselves as "back-up persons." However, there was evidence in the interviews of mutual involvement in infant care as grandmothers supplemented maternal care. Grandmothers presented the reality of their families to their daughters and grandbabies: babies must learn to eat the family's food and adjust to family ways. A common theme in the remarks was "No one wants to care for a spoiled baby," and "They have to learn early this is how it is." This realistic approach to family life was softened by the nurturing statements made by the grandmothers, expressive of concern and love for their daughters and the babies.

Managing activities, the category which contained the largest number of items, presented Black grandmothers as strong managers of family life and resources. There is a conceptual link between these data and the survival tactics that LaFargue (1980) reports on the urban Black family. Survival tactics used by the grandmothers in this study included: controlling family members' behaviors; overseeing the recovery of new mothers; fitting work, school, and infant care needs into schedules; providing safety for "their grandbabies"; and applying for government assistance (food stamps, medical care, and public housing). Although caretaking activities encompassed the second largest category, the significance of this function was mediated by the constraints which grandmothers placed on these childcare activities. The study subjects said, "I'll help her for now" or "until she gets back on her feet." It was clear from the transcripts that the grandmothers expected their adolescent daughters to assume most of the infant care. In discussing the mutual responsibility for the care of the infants the grandmothers saw their responsibilities as temporary. Caretaking functions were frequently associated with assigning functions, that is, attributing ownership of the baby. One grandmother said:

> See, this is her responsibility and she gonna have to deal with that. And if you take it from her—if I take it from her—then she's gonna feel that, 'my mother's raising my child, so I ain't gotta worry about it.' And then she goes out and gonna get another one. And when she feels this responsibility herself, and she knows that, 'hey, I don't got time to do nothing else except take care of this kid,' she ain't gonna have time to go out there and get another one. Because, see, if I was to take full charge, then she's not part of her own child. . . . And then who knows what'll happen to a little kid when they feel that way? I know I did. That's how they [her children] got here. 'Cause when my mother took full charge of my son, I said 'no more,' and I went and got [pregnant with] her. Then it was too late. I promised myself I wouldn't make that mistake [with my daughter], because whatever decision she makes about her child, it will be her decision and hers alone. I will not try to change it.

## TABLE 1  Description of Grandmother Functions

| DESCRIPTION | EXAMPLE |
| --- | --- |
| *Managing:* Arrangement of resources and activities so that they synchronize with each to meet family needs. | I didn't have no where to put the crib up . . . and I thought it would look kind of odd setting in the front room. So I told Terri I'd try to get her one of those little playpen cribs which could fit out here in the front room. |
| *Caretaking:* Direct involvement in providing primary infant activities. | . . . in the morning after I get all the other kids out to go to school, I'll go ahead and feed Cecelia, give her a bath, brush her hair and read, and she'll go to sleep, as long as she's full. Or she'll lay in the bed and play . . . and she just really fight . . . and wants me to play with her. . . . |
| *Coaching:* Role modeling or guidance about primary infant care activities or maternal role. | . . . little thing—I always tell her though, if the baby's full, make sure she's burped, or don't lay her down on her back . . . I say 'Now, you have an idea how your baby acts.' |
| *Assessing:* The evaluation of the mother's attitude about or competency in the maternal role. | She's doing better than I really expected that she would do. She really surprised me . . . giving the baby a bath. The baby's very clean. You know, some young girls have babies and they don't really keep 'em . . . the way that she does it. |
| *Nurturing:* Emotional support and love of the mother and grandchild. | . . . the main thing is, that's my daughter, and the second important thing this is my first grandbaby, and I love 'em both, and I wouldn't take nothing for either one of 'em. |
| *Assigning:* Expressions which suggest ownership of the baby. | Because I figure, like if I do it . . . make it too easy on her, she'll go out here again. So, I told her, I said well, this is your body and your life and your baby. |
| *Patrolling:* Overseeing and evaluating the mother's life style and personal life goals. | I took 'em to the doctor, and he told me she was still a virgin. He asked me if I wanted to put her on the pill, so I told him, 'No' . . . so, between the 5th of November and sometime . . . she got this little one. And she is going on the pill though. She's going on something. |

## TABLE 2  Incidence of Grandmother Functions

| FUNCTION | NUMBER | | RANGE PER FAMILY | | PERCENTAGE[a] | |
| --- | --- | --- | --- | --- | --- | --- |
| | V1[b] | V2[c] | V1 | V2 | V1 | V2 |
| Managing | 148 | 37 | 4–18 | 2–8 | 30 | 26 |
| Caretaking | 85 | 34 | 0–16 | 0–7 | 17 | 24 |
| Coaching | 70 | 14 | 1–15 | 1–5 | 14 | 10 |
| Assessing | 68 | 17 | 0–13 | 0–5 | 13 | 12 |
| Nurturing | 47 | 25 | 1–7 | 1–6 | 10 | 18 |
| Assigning | 41 | 10 | 0–10 | 0–4 | 8 | 7 |
| Patrolling | 34 | 5 | 0–10 | 0–2 | 7 | 3 |
| | 495 | 142 | | | 99% | 100% |

[a]Figures are rounded.

[b]V1 = Visit 1 (*n* = 19).

[c]V2 = Visit 2 (*n* = 9).

Grandmothers supported their daughters' returning to school and hoped that their daughters would finish school without becoming pregnant again. The grandmothers, many of whom had themselves been adolescent mothers, expressed worry about their daughters' education and future career opportunities. These concerns echo national studies which report negative correlations between early pregnancy, education, and career advancement (Card and Wise, 1978; Gabriel and McAnarney, 1983; McCarthy and Radish, 1982; Moore, Hoffreth, Wertheimer, Waite, and Caldwell, 1981).

Interview data also revealed the feelings and reflections of the grandmothers on the meaning of the grandmother role and offered insights about caring for the next generation. For example, one grandmother expressed her ambivalence:

> *It's my first time being a grandmother. I haven't even got that feeling of being a grandmother. Feel like it happened too soon. And I don't know . . . it will be different from having my own children . . . I know the baby is in our house. Just like another child come into the family. It still doesn't feel just like my daughter have a child. In a few more months I'll be getting used to it . . . but I be no grandmother right at the moment.*

Another grandmother talked about the need for having babies in the home. "I think I told Connie [the daughter] I am thinking about adopting. Because, you know, children have always been around."

Other grandmothers wanted more knowledge about caring for young babies. In the following vignettes two grandmothers explain:

> *It seems like to me you care for 'em different, you know. Like it's been so long since I cared for a little baby 'cause like Ellie's 16 years old, and you forget a lot of things. 'Cause like I have to call her boy friend's mother and ask her a lot of things.*

> *I was reading the books she [the adolescent mother] brought home, and believe me, I*

> *learned a whole lot. Because when we was having our children, it was all different, not too much different, but it was different. Only thing I know is keep 'em dry, love 'em, feed 'em.*

The grandmothers used a common mechanism to help them express their feelings about their roles. They compared what they had known in raising their own children to how their new grandbabies were being raised. Some decided, "It's a lot to learn if you don't know," and "I just got to get used to it all over again, you know."

## Discussion

This study of Black grandmothers offers insight into the functions of grandmothers in multigenerational families. Seven grandmothers' functions evolved from the data: managing, caretaking, coaching, assessing, nurturing, assigning, and patrolling. These functions emerged as the major activities which grandmothers reported in response to questions about their involvement in the every day care of their grandbabies. The data confirmed the findings of other studies (Coletta, 1981; Mercer, 1980; Smith, 1975; Wilson, 1984) that grandmothers are important persons in the lives of adolescent mothers and in the care of their infants during the early months of life.

The study also highlights the methodological problems associated with home visits with multigenerational families. The visits were difficult to arrange. Alterations in family schedules and changes in phone numbers and addresses made it impossible to locate some of the study grandmothers. Disorganization and mobility are labels often assigned to poor families. This study supported that some poor families live with uncertainty and do not stay in one place. The loss of 10 subjects 3 months after the births of the infants limited comparative qualitative analysis. It could be hypothesized that the grandmothers who were interviewed a second time represent a different population than the original sample. Barnard (1985) argues that initial studies of unexplained phenomena should use cross sectional human behavior techniques. This preliminary work with Black grandmothers suggests that studies of multigenerational families may also be enhanced by cross sectional examination.

# References

Baldwin, W. and Cain, V.

1980   The children of teenage parents. *Family Planning Perspectives, 12,* 34–43.

Barnard, K.

1975   *The nursing child assessment satellite training manual.* Seattle, WA: University of Washington School of Nursing.

Barnard, K.

1985   Studying patterns of behavior. *MCN: The American Journal of Maternal-Child Nursing, 10*(5), 358.

Boszormenyi-Nagy, I., and Spark, G.

1973   *Invisible loyalties: Reciprocity in intergenerational family therapy.* New York: Harper & Row.

Burton, L. M., and Bengtson, V. L.

1985   Black grandmothers: Issues of timing and continuity of roles. In V. L. Bengtson and J. F. Robertson (Eds.), *Grandparenthood* (pp. 61–78). Beverly Hills, CA: Sage Publications.

Card, J. J., and Wise, L. L.

1978   Teenage mothers and fathers: The impact of early childbearing on the parent's personal and professional lives. *Family Planning Perspectives, 10,* 199–205.

Cohler, B., and Grunebaum, H.

1981   *Mothers, grandmothers and daughters.* New York: Wiley & Sons.

Coletta, N. D.

1981   Social support and risk of maternal rejection by adolescent mothers. *Journal of Psychology, 109*(2), 191–197.

Coletta, N., and Lee, D.

1983   The impact of support for black adolescent mothers. *Journal of Family Issues, 4,* 127–143.

Colon, F.

1980   The family life cycle of the multiproblem poor family. In E. A. Carter and M. McGoldrick (Eds.), *The family life cycle: A framework for family therapy* (pp. 343–381). New York: Gardner Press.

Frazier, E. F.

1939   *The Negro family in the United States.* Chicago: University of Chicago Press.

Furstenberg, F. F.

1980   Burdens and benefits: The impact of early childbearing on the family. *Journal of Social Issues, 36,* 64–87.

Furstenberg, F. F., and Crawford, A. G.

1978   Family support: Helping teenage mothers to cope. *Family Planning Perspectives, 10,* 322–333.

Furstenberg, F. F.

1976   *Unplanned parenthood: The social consequences of teenage childbearing.* New York: Free Press.

Gabriel, A., and McAnarney, E. R.

1983   Parenthood in two subcultures: White middle class couples and black, low-income adolescents in Rochester. *Adolescence, 17,* 595–608.

Jones, E. F., Forrest, J. C., Goldman, N., Henshaw, S. K., Lincoln, R., Rosoff, J. I., Westhoff, C. F. and Wulf, D.

1985   Teenage pregnancy in developed countries: Determinants and policy implications. *Family Planning Perspectives, 17*(2) 53–63.

Kempler, H.

1976   Extended kinship ties and some modern alternatives. *The Family Coordinator, 25,* 143–149.

Ladner, J., and Gourdine, R. M.

1984   Intergenerational teenage motherhood: Some preliminary findings. *SAGE: A Scholarly Journal on Black Women, 1*(2), 22–24.

LaFargue, J. P.

1980   A survival strategy: Kinship networks. *American Journal of Nursing, 80,* 1636–1640.

McAdoo, H. P.
1981    *Black families*. Beverly Hills, CA: Sage.

McCarthy, J., and Radish, E. S.
1982    Education and childbearing among teenagers. *Family Planning Perspectives, 14,* 154–155.

Mercer, R. T.
1980    Teenage motherhood: The first year. Part I: The teenage mother's views and responses. Part II: How the infants fared. *JOGN Nursing: Journal of Obstetric, Gynecologic and Neonatal Nursing, 9*(1), 16–27.

Moore, K. A., Hoffreth, S. L., Wertheimer, R. F., Waite, L. J., and Caldwell, S. B.
1981    Teenage childbearing: Consequences for women, families, and government welfare expenditures. In K. G. Scott, T. Field, and E. Robertson (Eds.), *Teenage parents and their offspring* (pp. 35–54). New York: Grune & Stratton.

O'Brien, M. E.
1982    Pragmatic survivalism: Behavior patterns affecting low-level wellness among minority group members. *Advances in Nursing Science, 4,* 13–26.

Ooms, T.
1981    Introduction: Historical perspectives. In T. Ooms (Ed.), *Teenage pregnancy in a family context* (pp. 23–30). Philadelphia: Temple University Press.

Patton, M. Q.
1980    *Qualitative evaluation methods*. Beverly Hills, CA: Sage.

Peters, M. F.
1981    Parenting in Black families with young children: A historical perspective. In H. P. McAdoo (Ed.), *Black families* (pp. 211–224). Beverly Hills, CA: Sage Publications.

Phipps-Yonas, S.
1980    Teenage pregnancy and motherhood: A review of the literature. *American Journal of Orthopsychiatry, 50,* 403–431.

Poole, C., and Hoffman, M.
1981    Mothers of adolescent mothers: How do they cope? *Pediatric Nursing, 1,* 23–31.

Sadler, L., and Catrone, C.
1983    The adolescent parent: A dual developmental crisis. *Journal of Adolescent Health Care, 4,* 100–105.

Smith, E. W.
1975    The role of grandmothers in adolescent pregnancy and parenting. *Journal of School Health, 45,* 278–283.

Smith, L.
1983    A conceptual model of families incorporating an adolescent mother and child into the household. *Advances in Nursing Science, 6,* 45–60.

Stack, C. B.
1974    *All our kin: Strategies for survival in the Black community*. New York: Harper & Row.

Staples, R.
1971    Toward a sociology of the black family: A theoretical and methodological assessment. *Journal of Marriage and the Family, 33,* 119–138.

Taylor, J.
1975    The special needs of school-age parents and their offspring. *Sharing*. Washington, D.C.: Consortium in Early Childbearing and Childrearing.

Ventura, S. J., and Hendershot, G. E.
1984    Infant health consequences of childbearing by teenagers and older mothers. *Public Health Reports, 99*(2), 138–146.

Wilson, M. N.
1984    Mothers' and grandmothers' perceptions of parental behavior in three generational black families. *Child Development, 55,* 1333–1339.

Zitner, R., and Miller, S. H.
1980    *Our youngest parents: A study of the use of support services by adolescent mothers*. New York: Child Welfare League of America.

Zuckerman, B., Winsome, G., and Alpert, J. J.
1979    A study of attitudes and support systems in inner city adolescent mothers. *The Journal of Pediatrics, 95,* 122–125.

# DEEP STRUCTURES OF AFRICAN AMERICAN FAMILY LIFE:
## Female and Male Kin Networks

### *Joseph W. Scott • Albert Black*

*The authors contend that the majority of Black families are best viewed from a kin network perspective rather than from the discrete nuclear family perspective. In order to understand Black family functioning today, researchers need to look at the formation of alliances among heads of single parent households and how they pool resources, do household chores together, and carry out childcare functions in tandem. This article describes Black female-headed kin networks and how they relate, interact, and interlock with one another.*

## Introduction

In 1986, for the U.S. as a whole, married couple families came to about fifty-eight percent of all households, down from seventy-one percent in 1970. Female-headed households increased to twenty percent over this same period. (CPR, P-20, 000, 1986:2).

Black families reached these milestones during the 1970's (Reid, 1982; Pratt et al., 1984). What is more striking is the growing proportion of single-parent headed families *with children under eighteen present*. For all races in the U.S., in 1986, two-parent family groups with such children comprised seventy-four percent of the U.S. total. In contrast, Black two-parent family groups with such children comprised forty-two percent of the Black total. By inference, twenty-six percent of the total U.S. population and fifty-eight percent of the Black family groups were single-parent families (CPR, P-20, 000, 1986).

Looking closely, one finds that ninety-four percent of the single-parent family groups were headed by mothers. Looking even more closely, one finds that a majority of single family heads are parents who *never married* at all. "Approximately forty-nine percent of Black one-parent family groups in 1986 were maintained by a mother who had not married the child's father, and an additional two percent of lone Black parents were fathers who had never married" (CPR, P-20, 000, 1986:11).

Given the corollary that never-married young females and males generally earn poverty wages or near-poverty wages if any wages at all, a majority of these Black women and children are living in need of the basic resources for daily comfort and sustenance (O'Hare, 1987).

In order to adequately understand how African American families such as these *survive* and *function*, male and female *kin* networks must be raised from the subliminal level of perception. In point of fact, the writers believe that the only way to understand how economically deprived Black families, in general, *survive and function*, female and male *kin* networks must be analyzed both as separate entities and together. How kin networks

From the *Western Journal of Black Studies* 13 (Spring 1989):17–24. © 1989 by the Washington State University Press. Reprinted by permission.

function and contribute to Black family survival is the theme of this paper.

Given the nuclear family bias in current analyses of U.S. families, Black male and female *kin* structures are generally ignored in the current discussions of Black *family functioning*. The current analyses routinely omit consideration of female-centered, female-anchored and female-dominated *kin* networks which function in interaction with male-centered, male-anchored and male-dominated *kin* networks. Notwithstanding these omissions, the majority of Black families are best viewed from a *kin network* perspective rather than from the discrete *nuclear family* perspective. This *kin network* perspective considers both blood kin and non-blood kin as a helping network which meets the daily material and social-emotional needs of all concerned.

In the U.S. today, Black males and females are under extraordinary economic and social pressures to form close and obligatory friendships so that their basic physical needs and wants can be satisfied (The Crisis, 1984; Staples, 1985:1005–1015). Under these conditions, friendship becomes defined as "those you can depend on," and includes mostly those individuals one can "count on."

The "unemployment" system and the "welfare" system have combined to push Black men from the center to the periphery of *family kin networks* (Stack, 1974; Staples, 1985). Black men have been made transitory family members, that is to say, they have been made absent fathers, boyfriends, uncles, and stepfathers who live on the margins of the female-centered household networks (Schulz, 1969: 136–144). For the most part, single Black males have become either part-time or floating members of other people's households. Most of these single males do not own or rent their own residences and from time to time must be housed, clothed and fed by female householders (Scott, 1979), especially female-headed households composed of biological sisters, mothers, daughters or some other blood relative on whom they have come to depend.

Even though the public welfare system was initially instituted to allay starvation and destitution (utter want, poverty, indigence and deprivation), it has not provided enough jobs, job training or economic assistance to maintain Black families intact (Piven and Cloward, 1971). The net result has been that the current majority of Black marriage-age adults have been forced into non-nuclear family arrangements (CPR, p-20, 418, 1986); that is, they have been denied sufficient jobs and incomes to support traditional married-couple families: husband-wife families with dependent children, with all family members living in their own separate households, away from their extended family relatives, with the husband-fathers as the principal providers and wife-mothers as childbearers and childkeepers.

During Slavery and after, and even up to the second half of this century, the majority of Black families were husband-wife-children families (Gutman, 1977; Jones, 1985). But, the successive depressions of the 1960s, 1970s and 1980s have forced the majority of Black adults into family arrangements which used to characterize only a minority of Black families even during Slavery, Reconstruction and the Mass Migration and Urbanization periods of the 1920s and 1940s (Staples, 1986:150–157). These new family arrangements are single-parent families and subfamilies largely linked, tenuously, together by scarce economic means and social and emotional ties. A typical arrangement might consist of a couple of nuclear families and subfamilies, single-parent families, and single-person households communally linked together through day to day sharing of economic resources, childkeeping and childrearing. Charles Johnson (1966), a Black social scientist, called it "mutualism," i.e., a "mutual aid" system. Mutual aid practices create and maintain the *family kin networks* (Johnson, 1966:64–65, 85–86).

In census statistics, Black family households appear as though they are separate and discrete family households. In reality, for the most part, these families have had to unite into tight *kin networks* which share food, clothing, furniture, sleeping space, transportation, medicine, and money or its equivalent—like food stamps—in order to survive.

Occasionally, discrete non-family households headed by single males become connected to the *kin* networks which are headed by females. Female-headed and male-headed households become connected with one another at numerous points and in numerous ways depending on the economic, the sociological or the psychological ties the males and females develop among themselves. The memberships of the *kin* networks change as individuals move into and out of the male/female relationships, i.e., social-emotional and economic unions (Drake and Cayton, 1962:570–581).

Male-headed and female-headed family networks may either be multigenerational kin units or unigenerational kin units. That is to say, some kin units may be mother-daughter-children units. Some may be father-sister-children units. Some others may be brother-sister-children units. Still others may be aunt-niece-children units, uncle-nephew-children units, and grandmother-grandchildren units. There are many other combinations (Billingsley, 1968:15–21; Lewis, 1964:82–113).

These units above come into and go out of existence as a result of birth, sickness, death, unemployment, divorce, desertion, eviction and migration. Childcare functions motivate the forming of these family units and kin networks like nothing else does.

In order to survive, heads of single-person households also combine resources and function collectively as though they are a single family group. These single persons may sleep in separate households, but they may pool economic resources and eat together, wash clothes together and carry out occasional childcare functions together. The formation of these alliances among single persons also occurs as a result of food-sharing, clothes-sharing, income-sharing and temporary childkeeping. Socio-economic survival and mutual aid are inseparable. Networking is inescapable.

It should be clear from the foregoing that in order to understand Black family functioning today, family researchers need to look at Black family life as it is played out in *kin* networks. As previously stated, the Bureau of Census has reported that well over half of all Black families *with children* are headed by female single-parents. These families may be linked through blood-kin ties and fictive-kin ties as related sub-families, as unrelated sub-families, as single-person households and husband-wife-children households. An adequate description of Black family life must therefore, of necessity, include network analyses.

Towards this end of better understanding of Black family functioning, the remainder of this paper describes Black female-headed kin networks and Black male-headed kin networks and how they relate, interact and interlock with one another.

# The Formation of Female-Centered Networks

Well over half of *all* Black families *with* children are headed by a single female. These women, for the most part, are either chronically or permanently unemployed (Reid, 1982; Glick and Norton, 1979; O'Hare, 1987). Most of these families are officially recognized as "poor," that is to say, recognized as poverty-level families who suffer from a scarcity of the vital necessities of life (Stack, 1974). For them, food, clothing, shelter, money, heating and cooking utilities and transportation are perpetually in short supply. For them, if there is no gainful employment, they have to engage in other forms of gainful activity to carry out their child-care functions. This means that every day they must seek to alleviate their chronic scarcities of food, other household goods and medical services. They must constantly be looking for and finding people who may be able to contribute money, foodstuffs, childcare services or other resources as their needs require. Their needs include all of the material and nonmaterial resources humans need for the maintenance of life. Thus, an endless network of friends and relatives are needed. For that reason, commensalistic relationships are ever-forming and dissolving among those in need of food, shelter, transportation, money, clothing, heating fuel and child care at one time or other (Stack, 1974).

Borrowing and lending, giving and receiving are the instrumental gainful activities of the poor, in lieu of regular employment. A significant part of every day involves "hunting and gathering." Out of exchanging goods, services and money, social networks emerge. And, this exchange process of acquiring and transferring the vital necessities of life (among members of the near-poverty and poverty class) is what makes survival possible.

While all impoverished people feel pressures to network, unemployed single mothers feel special pressures to form friendships and alliances which can materially benefit them. Single females with children have a continuous and present need for food, shelter, clothes, etc., and thus have a need to look perpetually to form friendship and kinship relationships which will help supply the vital resources necessary to fulfill their chronic needs. If single females with children feel the most pressure to network, they also experience the most pressure to turn male and/or female friendships into kin-type relationships. This tendency is based on the African American belief and tradition that charity begins in the family, and therefore, kin can be *expected* to assist one another willingly and extensively.

Economic and social necessity drive the motivation for kin-type solidarity. Such security can be found in large numbers of friends and kin. While economic reciprocity can gradually transform friendships into kinships, by the same token, the failure to reciprocate can destroy friendships and blood-kin ties. But, since economic resources are always scarce and uncertain, paying back favors is an unreliable, uncertain state of affairs. Hence, network relationships come readily into existence, but also go readily out of existence because of failures in reciprocity involving money, food and other vital services.

As stated above, the norm of reciprocity governs network exchanges. Failure to reciprocate results in shunning, ostracism, and sometimes, violence (Borchert: 38–40). Intentional failure to repay a debt or favor is considered something akin to thievery. Intentional failures are partially disruptive, if not completely destructive, of exchange networks and, hence, non-reciprocity is severely and collectively punished. That is to say, members of networks close ranks in the face of a non-reciprocating person in the system. The members, thereby, maintain reciprocity through collective solidarity and that means by collective condemnation of intentional malfeasance. Network solidarity is "mechanical solidarity."

"Tightening up" social relationships is a constant motivation because obligation-seeking and resource-seeking are basic to the economic survival of the poor and the near-poor. The more people one has indebted to oneself, the more social and economic resources one can call upon in times of need. By expanding one's dependencies, one becomes less vulnerable in case of a loss of a job, an eviction from a residence, a death of a mate or a debilitating injury strike. Blacks survive by family ties (Hill, 1972; Manns, 1981).

## Blood-Kin and Fictive-Kin

The bureau of the Census reports that more Black single females than Black single males become *family householders* (CPR, P-20, 418, 1986). This is probably because Black mothers are usually the childkeepers. Moreover, because of childkeeping responsibilities, Black females have to be concerned about daily sustenance and physical comfort. They have to cultivate friendships they can "count on." For these reasons, Black female heads of households become the anchors of *family kin networks*.

Family roles are somewhat involuntary and somewhat voluntary (Stack, 1974). Even *blood* relatives have a social choice of assuming or not assuming their ascribed roles. A *blood* relative is, therefore, only potentially a *social* relative. Blood relationships may or may not correspond to social role playing such as mother, father, brother or sister (Stack, 1974). Social recognition of certain individuals in certain status-roles depends on the quality of participation; the trades, the swaps, the transfers, and the service performed define the closeness or tightness of relationships (Stack, 1974; Drake and Cayton, 1962:570–581).

Friends who are willing to be obligated as "kin" can "achieve" social recognition as kin— namely, as father, mother, grandmother, grandfather, uncle, aunt, sister, brother or cousin—depending on the role they assume. Anthropologically speaking, these friends are *fictive* kin. In the Black community, they are "play fathers," "play mothers" or other "play" relatives (Stack, 1974; Schulz, 1969:136–144). Those willing to be obligated as siblings are called "sister," or "brother" and are said to "go for" "brothers" or "sisters." Neighbors and blood kin will also publicly recognize them as kin. In sum, those willing to assume the role of kin, such as uncle or aunt, are allowed to assume these designations. Blacks "make" family where they have no blood relatives.

This process of making family relationships causes some conflicts between the expectations of fictive kin and those of blood kin. Occasionally, blood kin want to assert their so-called "natural rights." They maintain that "blood is thicker than water." They say that "blood" is supposed to be synonymous with loyalty, and, therefore, blood relatives are supposed to be more loyal, more faithful and more preferred than fictive kin. But, in reality, blood relatives may not be more giving, loyal, etc., and may even refuse to be obligated. In point of fact, blood kin occasionally follow the norm: "I don't lend and I don't borrow." They want to be left unobligated. Consequently, they become subjects of gossip and derision. If they never need to "fall back" on the family network, they can remain outside of the sea of obligatory reciprocal family relationships. As isolates, they may even achieve respect for their self-sufficiency and independence, but, they are hardly left free from gossip. They usually continue to be pressured into being obligated or continue to be enticed into becoming exchangers.

Despite this potential for conflicts, acquaintanceships grow into friendships and friendships into kinships. The "tightest" relationship in the Black community is kinship, and, as we said, kinship relationships are defined and measured by the nature, the extent and the voluntariness of the exchanges between individuals. For example, friends may exchange clothes, but kin exchange childkeeping rights (Frazier, 1948). Since the nature of the exchanges define the relationships, blood ties do not automatically translate into social kin relationships and vice versa. But, when they do, the kin relationship is doubly "tight."

Sociologically speaking, kinship rights are social rights which can be assumed, granted, transferred or shared (Frazier, 1948; Stack, 1974). Kinship rights grow out of the willingness to assume obligations. With the assumption of socio-economic obligations come kinship rights and vice versa. Normatively, blood relatives are ascribed social ob-

ligations but, factually, the assumption of these obligations becomes a choice for most adults. Thus, the social kinship system among Blacks is a system of rights and obligations among both non-blood and blood kin.

Motherhood, and fatherhood are also socially assumed roles. Even these roles are chosen and allowed, and hard to force on individuals. "Fathers" are those men who *allow* themselves to be obligated, or choose to be obligated, as fathers. That is to say, they choose to become financial providers and social nurturers of children who may or may not be blood-related (Schulz, 1969:136–144). Because they choose to take on a father's obligations, they are offered the role label.

"Mothers" are childkeepers and childrearers. Such role assumption works pretty much the same way as with men. That is to say, birthing a baby does not automatically make a woman the "mother." Motherhood also may be assumed, shared, transferred or loaned temporarily. Motherhood rights are social agreements too (Frazier, 1948:112–113).

# The Formation of Male-Centered Networks

When jobs paying living wages and legitimate business opportunities are absent, male street corner networks form to engage in petty entrepreneurial and semi-criminal activities for economic survival. The "unemployment" system forces Black men into an ever-present quest for money. The unemployed, disemployed and unemployable make up the street corner networks.

The Black ghettoes of our largest cities are areas where there are great concentrations of individuals without subsistence money, basic sustenance, ordinary comfort, physical protection or personal security. The economic scarcity of the ghettoes generates predatory males (and females). It makes human survival desperate. It makes homicides, suicides, and other forms of self-destruction and other-destruction abound. It makes personal security an ever-present need and self-protection a never-ending concern.

The police do not help much in Black ghettoes. Peer networks become the main salvation. Male networks are socially and emotionally vital, for the physical and mental health of the detached, the pushed out, the locked out, and the "down and out." The male networks provide sustenance and comfort when female-based family networks have pushed them out to the margins (Drake and Cayton, 1962: 570–581).

Male *kin* networks come into being too, but usually not as *family* networks. Male *kin* networks usually co-exist with "street-corner societies" (Liebow, 1967; Anderson, 1978; Cohen, 1955; Whyte, 1955). The *kin* network members refer to themselves as "rappies," "drinking buddies" and "stand-up friends."

Typically, male kin networks begin as young adolescent cliques and gangs (Finestone, 1962; Keiser, 1969). The cliques and gangs arise from many personal needs, but foremost are the needs for physical protection, and social and economic support. Accordingly, the clique and gang members provide food, clothes, money, places to sleep and loyal friendship, among other things, to one another. In sum, then, adolescent gangs and adult cliques exist as much for sustenance and comfort as for protection (Dawby, 1973). (Adolescent isolates do not last long in the ghetto environment of organized mayhem and violence. Sometimes the violence is for good reason, sometimes the violence is for thrills. In the ghetto, fear is normal; paranoia is normal; neuroticism is normal.)

As these adolescents become young adults, they begin to function as clubs, lodges, tavern buddies and fraternity brothers. These adult networks also come into existence and are maintained in existence through exchanges of money, food, material resources and in-kind services. The adult networks also satisfy the personal needs for emotional support, physical protection and economic security. Through constant trading and borrowing, lending and sharing, the members bind themselves together in the process.

Males, like females, feel a variety of pressures to convert their friendships to kinship relations in order to maintain access to sustenance, comfort, mutual protection and emergency aid. Those who have been pushed out or locked out of their biological families of origin survive only through networking. Hence, male street corner networks, like the female home-base networks, fall back on kin roles and kin relationships in order to cope with the vicissitudes of everyday ghetto life.

Those willing to engage in unconditional exchanges of money, goods or services among themselves "go for brothers." "Going for brothers" obligates one to unwavering loyalty, trustworthiness and economic support (Liebow, 1967). "Going for brothers," is an assumed role among those who are willing to be obligated in social and economic ways.

Within these kin networks, males compete for status, even in places described as "nowhere to be somebody" (Cohen, 1955; Miller, 1958). They compete for "respect" and "dignity" within the day to day dynamics of the networks. They strive for positive status so that "their credit is always good" (Hannerz, 1970:313–327).

Male street corner societies, over time, differentiate themselves into interest groups (Anderson, 1978; Glasgow, 1981). The law-abiding job-working males gravitate together in special places in cities. They are called "slaves" or "scufflers." The alcoholics gravitate together in other places in the cities. They are called "winos." The underground "businessmen," gravitate together. They are called "hustlers." The drug addicts gravitate together. They are called "dopeheads." The men who maintain a bevy of "working girls" gravitate together (Hare and Hare, 1984:69–91; Staples, 1973:85–88). They are called "pimps." These network differentiations serve various functions within the ghetto context as they overlap at the margins of each of their boundaries.

# The Competition between Male and Female Networks

Male street corner networks compete with female-centered family networks for time, money, and emotional commitments of the males and females who float back and forth among them. On the whole, male street corner networks are antithetical to family networks, even though the male economic "hustles" of one kind or other may bring in some economic support for some families (Aschenbrenner, 1973).

Notwithstanding a few exceptions, most street corner roles and activities, by their nature, exploit females. Pimps, for example, "live off" the labor of women. "Players" provide sex, companionship and protection in exchange for shelter, gifts and money. Pimps "put women to work" prostituting or hustling money in other illegal ways. "Players" corrupt the values of both family men and family women (Glasgow, 1981).

Male tavern networks are cases in point. Tavern networks can be dysfunctional for family life because they drain off time and money that fathers and brothers could be contributing to family networks. "Tavern men do not make good husbands," it is said, because their loyalties, energies and resources are overly divided. Only a few males find a functional balance between the family demands and the tavern demands (Drake and Cayton, 1962: 570–581).

Adult male street corner networks can even threaten the continuance of female-centered networks. By establishing intimate friendships with females entrenched within female-centered family networks, males sometimes draw off valuable members from these female family networks. By establishing romantic alliances with females, males entice females into leaving their family networks and, thereby, use romantic love to undermine long established family support networks among women (Aschenbrenner, 1973). For that reason, romantic alliances may be resisted by some female members of networks as they come to see male street corner networks generally threatening the economic resources of the family networks.

Adolescent male street corner networks can also destabilize family networks by turning law-abiding children into thieves, gang bangers, and drug abusers (Cohen, 1955; Miller, 1958). They can destabilize the family networks by encouraging law-abiding children to engage in sexual promiscuity, shoplifting, drug use, ostentatious displays of money and conspicuous consumption of flashy clothes and jewelry. Adolescent males do not have the choice of

social and economic support without all of the above negatives attached.

# The Role of the Black Churches

Most Black churches are conglomerations of family networks. Family networks which do not "naturally" overlap with one another are brought together by church activities.

Church "welfare" programs facilitate the transfer of goods and resources from one household to another, from one network to another. Church libraries, nurseries, preschools, Saturday schools and Sunday schools also support the family networks. Churches are linchpins which serve as master links among family networks, household networks and isolated individuals. In sum, churches function as a web of life of welfare services for family networks and individuals.

# Male and Female Networks and the Black Church

The Black church exists at the intersection which brings together disparate networks of needy individuals. It preserves the integrity of the existing male and female networks and, at the same time, integrates these networks into a larger whole that functions as a social and economic safety net for all.

The Black church is best viewed as a confederation of networks. The Black church has the same problems as most gender-based networks: It needs a constant flow of new members, and hence, depends on the continued recruitment of single individuals and families.

In order to maintain its charisma, the church has to continue to meet the *instrumental* needs of its members. Inner-city churches, in particular, are composed of people who live under conditions of extreme economic scarcity. As a consequence, the church must provide some subsistence to its neediest members. In this way, the church functions like a family *kin* network system.

The church ritualizes its functions for the "sick and shut-in" by soliciting regular offerings for the "less fortunate" every Sunday. Every Sunday, the church, through its pastor, informs the congregation about sister-so-and-so and brother-so-and-so who are "sick and shut-in." In this manner, the church ritualizes the most basic function of kinship networks, that of economic survival through exchange.

The Black church not only meets the *instrumental* needs of the parishioners but also meets the *expressive* needs of its members. Black church rituals reinforce the values of caring, sharing, and sacrificing. These values are reinforced through songs, prayers and theology. In so doing, the rituals encourage the essential *raison d'etre* of family networks.

The church, in the end, becomes the quintessential "kin" network itself, composed of collectivities of people who commit themselves to material and emotional sharing (Hill, 1972). The church institutionalizes and ritualizes the basic values and norms of these *survival techniques*. The church is an extension of the family. It even uses family terms such as sister, brother, daddy, and mother, and thereby, terminologically reinforces the social and psychological value of familism.

The Black church not only teaches familistic values, it also ritualizes family values. It promotes activities wherein individuals are called upon to actually carry out the requirements of their faith such as visiting the shut-in and giving time and talents to "serving" as deacons, deaconesses, ushers, elders, nurses, and choir members. For example, the church offering is a ritualistic part of each and every religious service; it is also a most symbolic example of turning belief into action. Through the offering, the church addresses the basic needs of the "church family," namely, the need for social support and economic security. Through the offering, the church dramatizes the value of physical survival and ritualizes the process by which that can occur—by communally giving one to the other.

To reiterate, the church functions as the linchpin holding an array of gender-based networks together. It does this ideologically, behaviorally and structurally. The church, however, is not equally attractive to male-centered and female-centered survival networks. Most Black church congregations are disproportionately female. The reasons for this are readily apparent. Church values and norms are those of female-centered kin networks. Church values are familistic values and their norms emphasize the preservation of the home and family. The church ritualizes these familistic values and kinship relationships.

By contrast, the values of most male-centered street corner networks tend to be more associated with the concepts of physical power, easy money and the "survival of the fittest" (Staples, 1973:85–88; Dawley, 1973; Keiser, 1969). Male-centered networks pursue materialistic and physical ends. The church values conflict with these values. If Black males cannot meet family responsibilities in the home setting, they cannot meet the familistic responsibilities of the church. The church services and rituals are constant reminders to males of their shortfalls. Because churches have the same focal concerns as do female-based family networks, street corner male networks clash with the values and practices of the church. Hence, they absent themselves from the church.

## Summary

The Black community should be viewed as a complex of family and kin networks. Blacks establish fictive kin in locales where they have not any blood kin. They form fictive family relationships in new situations and places, even in prisons. Their churches also organize themselves as quasi-families, and the parishioners use kinship labels to refer to one another.

Male and female networks overlap in varying degrees. They cooperate at times and compete at times. They even fight like clans at times. But most of the time, they establish some type of order with the idea of providing material physical security in a racially discriminatory society.

Because the obligations of membership in male-centered street corner networks conflict with membership in female-led, home-centered family networks, males may become part-time or floating members of these female-based networks. Balancing the demands of competing networks at the same time seems to be impossible for a number of Black males; so, they often become men "on the move." For street corner males, life is precarious, and they grow old or lame at a very early age. "They do not make good husbands." The scarcity of marriageable Black males is even more severe than initially perceived.

# References

Anderson, E.
1978    *A Place on the Corner*. Chicago: University of Chicago Press.

Aschenbrenner, J.
1973    *Lifelines: Black Families in Chicago*. Prospect Heights, IL: Waveland Press, Inc.

Billingsley, A.
1968    *Black Families in White America*. Englewood Cliffs, NJ: Prentice-Hall, 15–21.

Borchert, J.
1980    *Alley Life in Washington: Family, Community, Religion, and Folklife in the City, 1850–1970*. Urbana, IL: University of Illinois Press, 85, 38–40.

Cohen, A. K.
1955    *Delinquent Boys*. Glencoe, IL: Free Press.

Current Population Reports
1986    "Marital Status and Living Arrangements," Series P-20, No. 001.

Current Population Reports
1986    "Marital Status and Living Arrangements." Series P-20, No. 418 (March).

Dawley, D.
1973    *A Nation of Lords: The Autobiography of the Vice Lords*. Garden City, NY: Anchor/Doubleday.

Drake, St. Clair and H. R. Cayton
1962    *Black Metropolis*. New York: Harper & Row Publishers: 570–581.

Finestone, H.
1962    "Cats, Kicks, and Color," *Social Problems* 10 (Fall).

Frazier, E. F.
1948    *The Negro Family in the United States*. Chicago: University of Chicago Press: 112–113.

Glasgow, D. G.
1981    *The Black Underclass: Poverty, Unemployment, and Entrapment of Ghetto Youth*. New York: Vintage: 87–104, 181–182.

Glick, P. C. and A. J. Norton
1979    "Marrying, Divorcing, and Living Together in the U.S. Today," *Population Bulletin*, Vol. 32, No. 5 (Population Reference Bureau, Inc., Washington, D.C.).

Gutman, H. G.
1977    *The Black Family in Slavery and Freedom, 1750–1925*. New York: Vintage Books.

Hannerz, U.
1970    "What Ghetto Males are Like: Another Look," in N. E. Whitten, Jr. and J. F. Szwed, *Afro-American Anthropology*, New York: Free Press, 313–327.

Hare, N. and J. Hare
1984    *The Endangered Black Family*. San Francisco: Black Think Tank, 69–91.

Hill, R.
1972    *The Strengths of Black Families*. New York: Emerson Hall Publishers, Inc.

Johnson, C. S.
1966    *Shadow of the Plantation*. Chicago: University of Chicago: University of Chicago Press, 64–65, 85–86.

Jones, J.
1985    *Labor of Love, Labor of Sorrow: Black Women, Work, and the Family from Slavery to the Present*. New York: Basic Books, Inc.

Keiser, R. L.
1969    *The Vice Lords: Warriors of the Street*. New York: Holt, Rinehart and Winston.

O'Hare, W. P.
1987    "America's Welfare Population: Who Gets What?" *Population Trends and Public Policy*, No. 13. Population Reference Bureau, Washington, D.C.

Lewis, H.
1964    *Blackway's of Kent*. New Haven, Conn.: College and University Press, 82–113.

Liebow, E.

1967    *Tally's Corner: A Study of Negro Streetcorner Men*. Boston: Little, Brown and Co.

Manns, W.

1981    "Support Systems of Significant Others in Black Families," in Harriette Pipes Publishers, Inc., McAdoo (ed.), *Black Families*. Beverly Hills: Sage Publishers, Inc., 238–252.

Miller, W. B.

1958    "Lower Class Culture as a Generating Milieu of Gang Delinquency," *Journal of Social Issues* 14(3):5–19.

Piven, F. F. and R. A. Cloward

1971    *Regulating the Poor: The Functions of Public Welfare*. New York: Vintage.

Pratt, W. F., W. D. Mosher, C. A. Bachrach, M. C. Horn

1984    "Understanding U.S. Fertility: Findings from the National Survey of Family Growth, Cycle III," *Population Bulletin,* 39(5):15 (Population Reference Bureau, Inc., Washington, D.C.).

Reed, J.

1982    "Black America in the 1980s," *Population Bulletin*, 37(4) (Population Reference Bureau, Inc., Washington, D.C.)

Scott, J. W. and J. Stewart

1979    "The Notre Dame Report: The Pimp-Whore Complex of Everyday Life," *Black Male/Female Relationships*, 1(2).

Stack, C. B.

1974    *All Our Kin: Strategies for Survival in a Black Community*. New York: Harper & Row Publishers.

Schulz, D. A.

1969    *Coming Up Black: Patterns of Ghetto Socialization*. Englewood Cliffs, N.J.: Prentice-Hall, Inc., 136–144.

Staples, R.

1973    *The Black Woman in America*. Chicago: Nelson-Hall Publishers, 85–88.

1979    "Beyond the Black Family: The Trend Toward Singlehood," *Western Journal of Black Studies*, 3(Fall):150–157.

1985    "Changes in Black Family Structure: The Conflict Between Family Ideology and Structural Conditions," *Journal of Marriage and the Family* 47(Nov.):1005–1015.

———

1984    *The Crisis*. "A Profile of Black America," 91(10) (Dec.).

Whyte, W. F.

1955    *Street Corner Society*, 2 ed., Chicago: University of Chicago Press.

# 8 / Adolescence and Personality Development

## BLACK YOUTH IN CRISIS

### Ronald L. Taylor

*Empirical data from a variety of sources indicate that, compared to the mid-1960s, more black youth today are living in poverty, undereducated and unemployed, involved in crime and drug abuse, and having babies out of wedlock. Despite various federal and community programs to reverse these negative trends, conditions among these youth have continued to deteriorate, with a growing number of these youth joining the ranks of the black underclass—that permanently entrapped population of poor persons largely isolated from the mainstream of American life. This paper examines major social indicators and present data which highlight the negative trends among black youth during the past two decades and discusses programs and policies designed to reverse these negative developments.*

In 1984 there were, according to U.S. Department of Commerce statistics, more than 13.4 million black males and 15.0 million Black females in the population (U.S. Bureau of the Census, 1985). Black youths, 19 years of age and younger, accounted for 10.7 million or 38 percent of the total black population, with more than 2.8 million persons in the 15–29 age group, and nearly three million persons in the age category 20–24. Thus, nearly half (48 percent) of the black population was 24 years of age or younger in 1984, compared to 37 percent of whites in these age categories. Since black youths comprise a much larger proportion of the black population, it is to be anticipated that social and economic problems that affect teenagers in general are likely to have a disproportionate impact on black youth (McGhee, 1982; Wilson, 1984).

In fact, black youths are shown to have fared considerably worse than their white counterparts during the past two decades. Data from a variety of sources indicate that, compared to the mid 1960s, more black youths today are living in poverty, undereducated and unemployed, involved in crime and drug abuse, and having babies out of wedlock.

From *Humboldt Journal of Social Relations*. 14 (Fall/Winter, Spring/Summer 1986–1987):106–133. © 1987 by *Humboldt Journal of Social Relations*. Reprinted by permission.

Despite various federal and community efforts to reverse these negative trends, conditions among black youth have continued to deteriorate, with a growing number of these youths joining the ranks of the black underclass—that permanently entrapped population of poor persons largely isolated from the mainstream of American life. A review of major social indicators highlights the negative trends among black adolescents and young adults during the past two decades and underscore the need for corrective action.

## Living Arrangements of Black Children and Youth

One of the most significant developments of the last two decades has been the rapidly declining proportion of black children under 18 years of age who live in a family structure in which both parents are present. While the proportion of all children living with both parents declined during the past twenty years, this development has influenced the situation of black children and youth much more than their white counterparts. In 1965, nearly 70 percent of black children under 18 lived with both parents; by 1980, the proportion had fallen to 42 percent (U.S. Bureau of the Census, 1983). In 1984, more black children and youth lived with their mother only (48 percent) than lived with both parents (42 percent). In contrast, 81 percent of white children under 18 lived with two parents in 1984, and only 14 percent lived with mother only (U.S. Bureau of the Census, 1985).

Sharp increases in divorce and in births out of wedlock were among the major contributing factors to changes in the living arrangements of black children and youths during the past two decades (Farley, 1984, Bianchi, 1981). The divorce rate of black families with children increased by more than 400 percent during the period 1965–1981, compared to 300 percent for white families. Similarly, the proportion of births to young single black women rose to unprecedented levels during this period. In 1980, 68 percent of births to black women ages 15–24 were outside of marriage, compared to 41 percent in 1955 (National Center for Health Statistics, 1982). While the incidence of out-of-wedlock births to young white women also rose substantially during the past two decades, their rates remain far below the rates for black women. As a result of these trends, a growing number of black children and youth are spending a large proportion of their childhood in households in which one parent, usually the father, is absent.

The dramatic increase in families headed by women has had a substantial impact on poverty among black children and youth because female-headed families suffer much higher rates of poverty than other types of families. The number of poor black children under 18 in female-headed families rose from 1.5 million in 1959, to 3.3 million in 1982, an increase of 122 percent. In 1984, more than half of all black children under 18 lived in poverty, and more than 75 percent of these children lived in female-headed households. In 1983, the median income of black female-headed households was $7,999, compared to $26,389 for two-parent black households in which both spouses worked. Black female-headed households with children are not only more likely to be in poverty but are also more likely than other families to be persistently poor (Duncan, 1983, Hill, 1981). Bane and Ellwood (1983a, 1983b) report that the average child who becomes poor when the family changes from male-headed to female-headed will experience a poverty spell lasting nearly 12 years. But the average black child can expect to experience a poverty spell lasting almost two decades. Thus, a considerable number of black youths can expect to face their first years of adult life in poverty.

These data on changes in black family structure and poverty over the past two decades are perhaps the key to understanding changes in other measures of well being among black children and youths since family structure and poverty are shown to have an adverse effect on educational attainment (Parelius and Parelius, 1978; Rumberger, 1982) and employment opportunities (Freeman, 1978), and to be positively associated with crime and delinquency (Freeman and Holzer, 1985) and teenage pregnancy (Hogan and Kitagawa, 1985).

TABLE 1    Black and White School Enrollment, by Age: 1970 and 1980

(Numbers in percent)

| AGE | BLACK | | WHITE | |
|---|---|---|---|---|
| | 1970 | 1980 | 1970 | 1980 |
| 3–4 | 14.4 | 38.2 | 12.1 | 36.3 |
| 5–6 | 67.8 | 95.4 | 73.1 | 95.8 |
| 7–13 | 95.8 | 99.4 | 97.5 | 99.2 |
| 14–15 | 93.7 | 97.9 | 96.3 | 98.3 |
| 16–17 | 84.3 | 90.6 | 90.1 | 88.6 |
| 18–19 | 47.7 | 45.7 | 57.7 | 46.3 |
| 20–21 | 18.2 | 23.4 | 32.2 | 31.9 |
| 22–24 | 8.8 | 13.6 | 15.2 | 16.4 |
| 25–34 | 4.9 | 7.8 | 6.2 | 7.8 |
| Total 3–34 | 54.4 | 53.9 | 54.2 | 48.9 |

Sources: Bureau of the Census, 1970 Census, 1970 Census of Population, General Social and Economic Characteristics, United States Summary, PC(1)-C1, 1972, Tables 88 and 131; and "School Enrollment—Social and Economic Characteristics of Students: October 1980," Current Population Reports, Series P-20, No. 362, May 1981, Table 6.

# Education

Trends in school enrollment rates for black children and youths show marked improvement over the past two decades (see Table 1). For example, in 1960 over 83 percent of whites, ages 16–17 were attending school, compared to 77 percent of black youths. By 1970, the proportion of 16 and 17 year olds in school exceeded 90 percent for whites and 84 percent for blacks. In 1979, black 16 and 17 year olds were slightly more likely to be enrolled in school than their white counterparts.

Despite the racial convergence in school attendance, there remain significant differences between black and white youths in rate of delayed education (i.e., being behind in school) and in non attendance. Black youths are much more likely to be enrolled below the modal grade for their age group than are white youths, and this differential increases in higher grades. In 1979, more than half (54 percent) of black males age 17 who attended school were behind their modal class, compared to 26 percent of their white counterparts (U.S. Bureau of the

Census, 1981a). Indeed, at all ages and for both sexes, black youths are more likely than whites to be enrolled at grade levels below their age group. For black males in particular, the delay rate has consistently been twice the rate for white males since 1960 (U.S. Commission of Civil Rights, 1978). As a consequence, there remains a significant racial difference in the completion of high school: 21 percent of all black 18 and 19 year olds, and 25 percent of these 20 and 21 years old, had neither completed nor were enrolled in high school in 1980, compared to 14.9 percent and 14.5 percent respectively of white youths in these age groups. In 1983 nearly a quarter of black youths in the 19–21 age group failed to complete their high school education, leaving them ill-equipped to enter the job market, military service or post secondary education.

Recent studies have shown that delayed education and dropping out of school are related to a number of factors, including family income, experience in school, and non school related experiences (Rumberger, 1982; Mare, 1980; Bickel and Fuller, 1983). Analyses of data from the *National*

**TABLE 2  Employment and Unemployment Rates, 1954–1984**

| | BLACK AND OTHER | | | | | WHITE | | | | |
|---|---|---|---|---|---|---|---|---|---|---|
| | 1954 | 1964 | 1969 | 1977 | 1983 | 1954 | 1964 | 1969 | 1977 | 1983 |
| **Percentage of labor force unemployed** | | | | | | | | | | |
| Age: 16–17 | 13.4 | 25.9 | 24.7 | 38.7 | 47.3 | 14.0 | 16.1 | 12.5 | 17.6 | 22.6 |
| 18–19 | 14.7 | 23.1 | 19.0 | 36.1 | 43.8 | 13.0 | 13.4 | 7.9 | 13.0 | 18.7 |
| 20–24 | 16.9 | 12.6 | 8.4 | 21.7 | 27.2 | 9.8 | 7.4 | 4.6 | 9.3 | 13.8 |
| **Percentage of population employed** | | | | | | | | | | |
| Age: 16–17 | 40.4 | 27.6 | 28.4 | 18.9 | 13.7 | 40.6 | 36.5 | 42.7 | 44.3 | 36.2 |
| 18–19 | 66.5 | 51.8 | 51.1 | 36.9 | 31.3 | 61.3 | 57.7 | 61.8 | 65.2 | 58.0 |
| 20–24 | 75.9 | 78.1 | 77.3 | 61.2 | 57.2 | 77.9 | 79.3 | 78.8 | 80.5 | 74.2 |

Source: U.S. Department of Labor, Employment and Training Report of the President, 1982, and Employment and Earnings, January, 1984.

*Longitudinal Survey of Youth Labor Market Experiences* (Center for Human Resources Research, 1980), found that students from families living below the poverty level were almost four times as likely as non-poor students to fall behind in school and that low socioeconomic status significantly increased the risk of dropping out of school, particularly for black youths. Indeed, a recent study by the National Urban League reports that many black males leave school for family economic problems, academic difficulties or disciplinary problems. However, for a growing number of black females, failure to complete high school is due largely to pregnancy (McGhee, 1982). Whatever the reasons, failure to obtain a high school diploma imposes serious long term limitations on the social and economic mobility of black youths, and virtually assures membership in the black underclass.

# Youth Unemployment

While black youths have traditionally fared less well in the labor market than white youths, the past twenty years have seen a dramatic deterioration in their labor market positions (see Table 2). For example, in 1954 black and white unemployment rates for 16 to 24 year olds were 15.8 and 9.9 percent respectively, a difference of 5.9 percentage points. The difference widened to 8.7 percentage points by the early 1960s and to 12.9 percentage points during the 1970s. In 1983, 45 percent of black youths ages 16–24 were unemployed compared to 19.5 percent of white youths. Similarly, the percentage of 16–24 year olds who were employed declined for black youths from 47.2 percent in 1954 to 39.0 percent in 1983, but increased for white youths from 49.7 percent in 1954 to 64.0 percent in 1983 (U.S. Department of Labor, 1982, Employment and Earnings, 1984).

However, official statistics on youth unemployment understate the actual level of joblessness among black youths since they fail to include "discouraged workers" (i.e., those who have given up an active search for work), a disproportionate number of whom are black (Flaim, 1973). A recent study by the Urban League (1981) found that when such workers are included in the unemployment figures, the jobless rate among black teenagers increased by at least 50 percent. Its index of *Hidden Unemployment* placed the actual jobless rate for black teenagers at 50 percent in 1980, and the actual number of unemployed black youths at more than double the official level. It was estimated that in some inner city areas, the actual jobless rates for black youths approached 80–90 percent.

Many proposed explanations for the disastrous increase in black youth unemployment focus on social and economic factors which are presumed to affect black youths disproportionately: minimum wage legislation and equal employment activities; inadequate demand for labor due to slow economic growth; changes in job mix and physical location of industry; increased job competition among youths, women and immigrants; employer discrimination; and a lack of skills and/or aspirations on the part of black youths (e.g., Thomas and Scott, 1978; Freeman, 1980; Osterman, 1980; Hill, 1981; Marc and Winship, 1984). Although much remains to be learned regarding the quantitative impact of these factors on the black youth unemployment problem, recent data reported by Freeman and Holzer (1985), based on a survey of more than 2,000 black males, ages 16–24, in the inner city areas of Boston, Chicago and Philadelphia provide some important insights.

The principal results of their analysis can be summarized in seven basic propositions:

1. While sluggish economic growth contributed to the increase in black youth joblessness over the period from 1959 to 1979, it was not a major cause; for in spite of slow economic growth, the economy produced more than 22 million new jobs from 1970 to 1983, few of which were secured by black youths.
2. With respect to the effects of minimum wage legislation and equal employment activities, neither appears to have had a significant impact on black youth participation in the labor market.
3. While evidence suggests that increases in the rate of white female participation in the labor force, particularly in the service sector, have adversely affected the job opportunities for young blacks, there is no evidence that the rise in the Hispanic population (the most significant immigrant group) has had a similar effect.
4. The movement of jobs from the city to the suburbs is not a major factor in the rise of joblessness among inner city youths, particularly in places like Chicago, since the unemployment experiences of black youths in areas where jobs are nearby differ little from the unemployment experiences of black youths who reside in areas of the city where jobs are scarce. Even jobs located at the borderline between predominantly black and white areas of the city are secured by white youths. Thus the problem is not intra-city changes in job location, but an increase in the aggregate level of demand for jobs in a city as a whole.
5. Employer discrimination is less of a factor in black youth unemployment than is the lack of references (e.g., teachers, previous employers, etc.) or connections to the job market through job holders in the family or community. However, perceived employer discrimination does have an effect on the work performance of black youths.
6. Black youths' attitudes toward work and employment aspirations are important contributors to the joblessness problem among these youths. Black youths with positive attitudes toward work, and strong long-term career aspirations are more likely to find work than are youths without such attitudes or desires.
7. While black youths are highly responsive to economic and social incentives which increase their prospects of employment, increasing joblessness among these youths reflect, in large measure, their increasing responsiveness to negative incentives (i.e., poor employment opportunities or attractive criminal opportunities) and social-family developments (i.e., growing family instability and dependency) of the 1970s.

Whatever the mix and contribution of these factors to the black youth joblessness problem, the cost of high unemployment among black youths is more than economic. Conditions which prevent or make it difficult for youths to find work discourage them from trying to attain economic independence. Moreover, high unemployment is likely to promote growing disaffection or alienation from society, and may contribute to a range of social pathologies, including crime, substance abuse and other life styles destructive to social and economic mobility (Gibbs, 1984; Ullah, 1985).

TABLE 3    Total Arrests, Percent Distribution by Age and Race, United States, 1983

| | ARRESTS UNDER 18, PERCENT DISTRIBUTION | | |
| OFFENSE CHARGE | White | Black | Other |
| --- | --- | --- | --- |
| Total | 72.7 | 25.7 | 1.6 |
| Murder and nonnegligent manslaughter | 49.6 | 48.8 | 1.6 |
| Forcible rape | 41.5 | 57.4 | 1.1 |
| Robbery | 29.4 | 69.3 | 1.2 |
| Aggravated assault | 59.4 | 39.4 | 1.3 |
| Burglary | 72.1 | 26.5 | 1.4 |
| Larceny-Theft | 68.1 | 29.9 | 2.1 |
| Motor vehicle theft | 70.9 | 26.9 | 2.1 |
| Arson | 82.8 | 15.9 | 1.2 |
| Violent crime | 44.0 | 54.7 | 1.2 |
| Property crime | 69.5 | 28.6 | 1.9 |
| Crime Index total | 66.6 | 31.6 | 1.8 |

Sources: U.S. Department of Justice, Federal Bureau of Investigation, Uniform Crime Reports for the United States, 1983.

# Crime, Delinquency and Substance Abuse

Relative to their numbers in the youth population, black youths are disproportionately represented in arrest statistics on crime and delinquency. Black youths constituted approximately 14 percent of all youths aged 15–19 in 1983, but, as reported in Table 3, they were involved in 69.3 percent of the robbery arrests, 57.4 percent of the rape arrests, and 39.4 percent of the aggravated assaults attributable to persons under 18 years of age. Indeed, more than half of all arrests for violent crimes, and a quarter of all property crimes reported in 1984 involved black youths. Thus, the rate of crime and delinquency among black youths increased from 19.3 percent of all juvenile arrests in 1965, to 23.1 percent in 1984. The growing involvement of black youths in crime and delinquency is reflected in their increasing numbers among inmates in local jails and other public and private residential facilities for juvenile offenders. In 1982, 32 percent of all youths in public or private juvenile facilities were black, with an average age of 14.9 years (U.S. Bureau of the Census, 1986).

Black youths are not only more likely to be arrested for violent crimes, but are also more likely to be the victims of such crimes. According to a recent report from the Department of Health and Human Services (1986), homicide is the leading cause of death for black males and females between the ages of 15–24 (see Table 4). In 1983 alone, more than 2,000 black youths 15–24 years of age were slain, the majority of whom by other black youths (Federal Bureau of Investigation, 1984). The black homicide rate is highest in major urban areas where black youths constitute a greater percentage of the population. In 1980, 60 percent of the black population, and 56 percent of all blacks under 25 lived in central cities. A study of black homicide rates in 14 major cities with the largest black populations in 1980 revealed that black homicide rates in all but one of these cities exceeded the national black rate, which stood at 38 per 100,000 persons in that year. In the cities of St. Louis, Los Angeles, and Cleveland, the black homicide rate was more than double the national black rate (U.S. Department of Health and

TABLE 4    Black Males and Females: Death Rates for Five Leading Causes of Death, 1981, Selected Age Groups

| AGE GROUP | HOMICIDE | DISEASES OF THE HEART | CANCER | MOTOR VEHICLES | CEREBROVASCULAR DISEASE |
|---|---|---|---|---|---|
| **Black males** | | | | | |
| 15–24 | 73.2 | 6.7 | 7.0 | 30.8 | 1.5 |
| 25–34 | 136.9 | 29.3 | 14.1 | 42.2 | 7.2 |
| 35–44 | 106.1 | 129.3 | 75.8 | 40.0 | 29.2 |
| **Black females** | | | | | |
| 15–24 | 16.9 | 4.2 | 4.6 | 7.7 | 1.6 |
| 25–34 | 23.2 | 13.7 | 17.4 | 8.2 | 6.6 |
| 35–44 | 16.3 | 56.0 | 73.7 | 7.7 | 21.0 |

Source: Health United States, 1984.

Human Services, 1986). Despite recent declines in the rate of black homicide, black youth, especially black males, continue to be over represented as homicide victims relative to their proportion of the national population.

The disproportionate involvement of black youths in crime and delinquency has been attributed to a variety of factors, including bias on the part of law enforcement agencies in the treatment and/ or disposition of cases involving black youths, excessive rates of poverty, joblessness and welfare dependency among these youths and their families in inner city neighborhoods, and a "subculture of violence" created by these conditions which foster high levels of interpersonal violence of homicide among blacks (Curtis, 1975). Acknowledging the contributions of these conditions to the growth of black crime and delinquency does not diminish the depth and social significance of these problems. As Gibbs (1964) observes, the disproportionate involvement of black youths in the Juvenile Justice system result in "severe limitation on their educational and occupational opportunities . . . creating a vicious cycle of delinquency, incarceration, recidivism, and chronic criminal careers, or unemployment and marginal social adaptation in adulthood" (p. 9).

In accounting for the rise in crime and delinquency among black youths, some researchers point to the increase in drug abuse among these youths in recent decades as a major contributing

factor (Leukefeld and Clayton, 1979; Gandossy et al., 1980; Brunswick, 1980). Indeed, evidence indicates that some forms of drug abuse are strongly associated with increases in property and/or violent crimes among youths and adults (Weissman, et al., 1976; Ray, 1983). It has been estimated that as many as two-thirds of all drug addicts engage in crime against persons (e.g., muggings and armed robberies) and as many as one-third of all addicts commit such crimes as their primary means of support (Chambers, 1977). Moreover, a study by the National Institute on Alcohol Abuse and Alcoholism (1975) reported that three-fifths of all murders involved alcohol, as did 40 percent of all reported assaults and one-third of forcible rape cases. National data on drug related criminal offenses for black youths are unavailable, but a national survey of youths involved in drug abuse treatment programs indicated that a disproportionate number of black youths in these programs have been arrested and convicted of criminal offenses involving property, the use and sale of drugs, violent and non-violent crimes, and weapons offenses (Leukefeld and Clayton, 1979).

Whatever its contribution to crime and delinquency, substance abuse is a major problem among black children and youths. For example, the percentage of black youths reporting current marijuana use rose from 12 percent in 1971 to 23 percent in 1982 among those 12–17 years of age, and from 48 percent to 61 percent among black youths, ages

16–25 (National Survey on Drug Abuse, 1983). In the 1979 National Survey on Drug Abuse, nonwhite youths, ages 18–25 were nearly equal to or exceeded the drug abuse rates of their white counterparts in every major drug category except inhalants and hallucinogens. In fact, on all major indicators of drug use, black youths, particularly low income youths in northern inner cities, are found to lead their white counterparts in: 1) age at initial drug use; 2) the "hardness" of the drugs they use; and 3) the number of drugs they use (National Institute on Drug Abuse, 1979a; O'Donnell and Clayton, 1979; Brunswick and Boyle, 1979). While such drug use patterns among black teens are undoubtedly a function of demographic and socioeconomic characteristics of urban areas where these youths are concentrated in substantial number, such patterns may also reflect a growing sense of despair and alienation among black youths ensnared in a complex web of poverty, joblessness and community disorganization. To the degree that social circumstances become more uniform for black and white youths, we may expect a convergence in black and white prevalence rates.

## Teenage Pregnancy

While birth rates for black teenages declined from a high of 173 per 1,000 in 1957 (data for years prior to 1969 refer to nonwhites) to 89 per 1,000 in 1982, the rate of out-of-wedlock childbearing among black teens continued to rise during the past two decades, becoming one of the major contributors to the increase in black female-headed households during this period (U.S. Commission on Civil Rights, 1983; Farley, 1983). Data from the 1964–66 National Natility Survey indicated that 72,400 black children were born to unwed teenage mothers in 1965. In 1982, the number had grown to 128,000 (National Center for Health Statistics, 1982). Thus, since 1965, the incidence of childbearing among unmarried black females ages 15–19 rose from 57 percent to 83 percent in 1981, and approached unity in 1985, when 90 percent of births to black teenagers were born out-of-wedlock. The incidence of out-of-wedlock births

to white teenagers also rose to unprecedented levels during this period, but their rates remain far below those for black teens (U.S. Bureau of the Census, 1975; National Center for Health Statistics, 1982).

An increase in the proportion of sexually active teenagers and deferral of marriage are two reasons cited for the precipitous rise in the rate of unwed pregnancies among black youths in recent decades. A recent study by the Alan Guttenmacher Institute (1981) indicated that the number of sexually active teenagers increased by two-thirds during the 1970's and accounted for 18 percent of women "capable of becoming pregnant," 46 percent of all out-of-wedlock births, and 31 percent of the abortions during the decade. While much of the increase was attributed to white teenagers, on an age by age basis, black teens were shown to have a higher prevalence of premarital intercourse and a lower mean age at first intercourse than their white counterparts. According to one survey, the proportion of black teenage women who reported having premarital intercourse increased from 52 percent in 1971, to 66 percent in 1979 (Zelnik, Kantner & Ford, 1981). These changes were accompanied by a decrease in the mean age of first intercourse from 15.9 years to 15.4 years during this period (Zelnick and Kantner, 1980). Although the use of contraceptives became more prevalent among black youths over the past decade, such increases failed to offset increases in the proportion of sexually active black youths, resulting in a net increase in premarital pregnancies and births (Zelnik and Kantner, 1980; Hogan, Astone and Kitagawa, 1985). Moreover, the growing tendency among black youths to defer marriage (either before or after pregnancy) has contributed to the problem of illegitimate births by increasing the proportion of black females at risk of becoming pregnant outside of wedlock (O'Connell and Moore, 1980; Cherlin, 1981). Since 1960, the proportion of never married black females increased from 65 percent to 82 percent in 1983 for those ages 14 to 24. As Wilson and Neckerman (1984) have pointed out, the tendency to defer marriage on the part of young black women is directly related to the dearth of marriageable young males whose numbers are diminished by high rates of unemployment, incarceration, and homicide.

In addition to these demographic factors, some point to the welfare system, in particular broadened eligibility for income transfer programs, as an incentive for young women to have babies. According to one study, 71 percent of females under 30 who received AFDC (Aid to Families with Dependent Children) had their first child as a teenager (Moore and Burt, 1982). While it is true that teenage mothers are disproportionately represented among welfare recipients, evidence suggests that welfare dependency is the result rather than the cause of teenage childbearing (Presser and Salsberg, 1975; Moore, 1978; Moore and Burt, 1982). However, the availability of welfare may influence the teenager's decision to rear the child rather than marry the father, resort to adoption or submit to abortion.

Whatever the cause, unwed teenage childbearing is a problem of epidemic proportion in the black community, with enormous consequences for the teenage mother and her child. It has been repeatedly documented that, compared to youths who postpone childbearing, teenage mothers have lower educational attainment, less income, higher unemployment (Card and Wise, 1979), are more dependent on welfare (Moore and Burt, 1982), are more likely to experience psychological problems associated with pregnancy (McLaughlin and Micklin, 1983), have higher levels of completed fertility (Mott, 1986), are more likely to abuse or neglect their children (Furstenberg et al., 1981), experience higher rates of marital dissolution (Glick and Norton, 1979), and are more likely to have daughters who also became unwed teenage mothers (Chilman, 1983). In addition, pregnant teenagers are at a higher risk of medical complications, and are more than twice as likely as older women to die in child birth (Alan Guttmacher Institute, 1981). Moreover, babies of teenage mothers are more likely to be premature, to have low birth weight and to die within the first months or year (National Center for Health Statistics, 1980). Should they survive, these children are more likely to experience long term medical problems such as mental retardation, cerebral palsy, and other birth injuries or neurological defects which require lifelong care (Alan Guttmacher Institute, 1981).

While the impact of premature fatherhood on adolescent males is less well documented, most teenage fathers are generally unprepared psychologically to assume the role of parent and provider for a family (Rothstein, 1978; Card and Wise, 1978). It is often alleged that adolescent fathers impregnate young women as a means of proving their masculinity or resolving other psychic needs, but some research indicates that many young fathers experience depression and emotional conflict over the impending change in their status and responsibility (Robinson and Barret, 1985). Few adolescent fathers are in a position to contribute to the financial support of their children, although some may leave school and find employment in order to assume partial responsibility. In doing so, these youths diminish whatever limited opportunities they may have had for educational and economic mobility.

Beyond the personal tragedy that premarital pregnancy and childbearing often creates for Black youths are the larger implications of these unfortunate developments for the black family and community. On the basis of current trends in black teen pregnancies and out-of-wedlock births, it has been estimated that "the turn of the century could well see three-quarters of all black families headed by single women" (Center for the Study of Social Policy, 1984). These families are likely to be overwhelmingly poor and welfare dependent, resulting in severe limitations on the social and economic life chances of a significant segment of black children and youths. Accordingly, the problem of black teenage pregnancy should be regarded as a "natural catastrophe ... a threat to the future of black people without equal" (Norton, 1984).

# Some Implications for Programs and Policies

From the foregoing analysis it is clear that the situation of a large number of black youths has deteriorated significantly during the past two decades, reaching a level of crisis proportions on some indicators of social and economic wellbeing. Such ominous developments are undoubtedly related to the dramatic rise in the number of black youths which occurred during this period and to their increasing concentration in the inner cities of major urban areas (Wilson, 1985). For example, black youths ages 16 to 19 increased by 72 percent in urban areas between 1960 and 1970, while the age category 20 to 24 increased by 66 percent during that decade. By 1980, 56 percent of blacks under 25 years of age lived in central cities, or more than twice the percentage for whites (U.S. Bureau of the Census, 1980). Thus, it was to be anticipated that the abrupt increase in the number of black youths would likely have an "exponential effect on the rate of certain social problems" (Wilson, 1977, p. 20). Wilson speculates that there may be a "critical mass" of young persons such that when that number is reached or increased suddenly and substantially, "a self sustaining chain reaction is set off that creates an explosive increase in the amount of crime, addiction, and welfare dependency" (1977, p. 20). Under such conditions, community institutions and local labor markets prove inadequate to meet the needs and cope with the consequences of a substantially enlarged teenage population.

However, changes in the age structure of the black population cannot alone account for the deteriorating condition of black youths during the past two decades. To such demographic changes must be added real declines in the supply and value of legitimate opportunities for these youths through education, training and employment in the nation's central cities. Thus, problems of crime and delinquency, drug abuse, and out-of-wedlock births among black teens may owe their existence and increase in recent years as much to the crippling effects of poverty, inadequate education and joblessness as to the demographic changes which occurred during this period.

What measures should be taken to interdict, constrain and reverse the negative trends in unemployment, crime, drug abuse, and out-of-wedlock births among black youths? The usual prescription calls for improvements in family, community, school, employment and human services environments of black children and youths, together with an assortment of individualized treatment approaches designed to induce attitudinal and behavioral changes in youths while imparting skills and education. But the development of successful strategies for ameliorating the problems of black youths has proved elusive, and a good deal more needs to be learned regarding the effectiveness of competing models of social intervention. It is clear, however, that public and private efforts to aid black youths cannot be limited to a single policy or social program, but must be multi-dimensional, and must include not only the efforts of government, but a broad range of public and private institutions— from the welfare systems, employers and schools to the criminal justice system, and families.

Since so many of the problems afflicting black youths are bound up with the lack of job opportunities and training, the first imperative for action is the establishment of a national youth affirmative action program, along the lines suggested by Thomas and Scott (1979). The object of such a program would be the establishment by law of the right of all youths to the educational and job training experiences that would enable them to assume productive adult work roles in society. A major activity of the program would include the development and implementation of a centralized strategy to deal with the unemployment problems of all youths, but with an aggressive emphasis on meeting the training and employment needs of minority youths from economically disadvantaged backgrounds. An essential part of the strategy to deal with minority youth unemployment would involve the development of formal and informal networks of individuals and groups (e.g., in schools, the community and labor market) to "sponsor" unemployed minority youths, from the point of job entry to the point at which they acquire marketable job skills and realistic employment options. Without these features, as Thomas and Scott point out, "any new policy effort to attack current minority youth unemployment is likely to resemble past employment programs for minorities" (p. 178).

While the federal government would coordinate activities under this program and engage in long-term planning and program evaluations, the actual administration of the program would occur at the state and local levels, and would involve a wide range of experimental projects and services designed to break the cycle of poverty, crime and other forms of antisocial behavior. Evidence suggests that a well developed jobs program can be very effective, especially when linked to schools. A network of part-time jobs, school attendance payments, and offers of guaranteed minimum wage jobs during the summer to minority youths who continue their schooling would provide work experience in addition to prolonging their education (Freeman and Holzer, 1985). Whatever the precise mix of programs, the major objective of a national youth affirmative action program would be to expand job opportunities for black teens, and to make employment a realistic alternative to crime and delinquency.

To the degree that job programs are effective in developing and expanding employment opportunities for black youths, they may be expected to have a positive impact on the level of drug abuse among these youths, since unemployment is a major contributing factor to drug use behavior in the black community (Brunswisk, 1980). But the remedy for substance abuse is not as simple as providing job training and employment, however essential these may be. Indeed, no one factor is sufficient to explain why black children and youths become involved with drugs. For some, drug use may be a response to or an escape from boredom, psychic distress, or the problems created by family disorganization. For others, drugs may serve an occupational or business function, satisfying a work role as well as an economic need (Preble and Casey, 1969). Moreover, in many inner city communities, exposure to drugs and pressure to experiment can hardly be avoided and come to be accepted as a fact of community life. Thus, just as it took a complex of conditions to produce the problem, it will require a range of remedies to dissolve it.

Drug education programs have been one approach to early prevention, but the effects of such programs on the behavior and attitudes of youths has been minimal, due in part to the narrow scope of these programs, a lack of clearly defined goals, and the lack of a clear understanding of the individual's motivation to use drugs (Ray, 1983). Many different intervention and early prevention approaches need to be tested and systematically analyzed. Educational programs whose main focus is not on drugs and drug counseling but on the youth's entire life style, as it intersects larger social and economic structures, are likely to be more effective than didactic or information-giving approaches to the problem. An early intervention program with this orientation would aim to reinforce the strengths and aspirations of black youths and seek to provide them with alternative models for understanding their social environment, and appropriate techniques for managing their personal and social problems.

With regards to treatment and rehabilitative services for youthful drug abusers, most current programs are ill-suited to deliver effective services to adolescents since they are designed for older, hard core drug users. Moreover, these programs which are structured to accommodate adolescents are typically small components of larger social service systems and usually lack high visibility and resources for effective treatment. While evaluations of the effectiveness of particular treatment modalities or programs show mixed results, some program designs seem more effective than others. Treatment programs which provide comprehensive and integrated services to youth, ranging from drug and psychiatric counseling, sex, educational and vocational counseling, to medical and recreational services, are shown to produce more positive results than programs offering a more narrow range of services (Smith, Levy and Striar, 1979). One program which has gained national recognition for its multimodality approach and comprehensive services to youth is The Door, established in 1972 in the city of New York. This program places equal emphasis on prevention, treatment and rehabilitation on the assumption that only a holistic approach to the problem is likely to be effective. Accordingly, it provides a broad range of free services to drug abusers, ages 10–21 and draws on a wide range of human and financial resources in the community in responding to the multiple problems of these youths. This program has been very effective in reducing or eliminating drug abuse among its clients and should be replicated in other communities across the country.

As in the case of drug abuse, teenage pregnancy is a complex phenomenon, with numerous determinants, and will require a multiplicity of preventive and corrective strategies to reduce its incidence among black youths. Since most teenager pregnancies are unintended, and are often the result of misinformation, ignorance or "excessive risk taking" on the part of youths, major emphasis has been given to sex education and family planning as primary prevention measures for early pregnancy, unwed childbearing and marriage. But evidence shows that sex education programs have had little if any impact on preventing these behaviors among youths (Kirby, Alter and Scales, 1979). Most sex education programs generally fail to take a broad analytic view of the causes of teenage pregnancy, i.e., the varied factors that determine sexual and fertility behavior among youths, and have been slow to include information and materials of direct utility to teenagers—contraceptive techniques and the interpersonal dynamics of their use (Moore and Burt, 1982). However, some studies show that sex education, combined with contraceptive services and an integrated approach to the physical, social and psychological needs of teenagers are very effective in reducing the incidence of teen pregnancy (Edwards et al., 1979).

There are limits, however, to what sex and contraceptive education can accomplish. Sexual activity and contraceptive use are shown to be strongly linked to such factors as level of self esteem, a sense of personal and interpersonal competence, personal and familial values and expectations, quality of family relations, the availability of contraceptives, and attitudes toward their use (Cvetkovich and Grote, 1980; Moore and Burt, 1982). The role of these factors in influencing sexual and fertility behavior among teenagers is unlikely to be much affected by sex information and referral services. Rather, to be effective, sex education must be reconceptualized to include strategies for building youths problem-solving skills, self confidence, perceptions of alternatives and consequences, and motivation to postpone sexual activity or practice effective contraception should they become sexually active.

For those teenagers who do become pregnant, there are a variety of public and private programs available. The majority of these programs are geared toward helping teenage mothers receive adequate medical care and counseling, and to complete their education. While there have been some successes, the long term results are disappointing (Lancaster and Hamburg, 1985). Such programs as school-based clinics, nurse home visitors, community women, social and work skills training, and several types of counseling and mentor models have all, on occasion, shown positive results, but in other settings, the same program has failed to reduce first pregnancies, or the effects do not persist once the program ends (Moore and Burt, 1982). Perhaps a major reason for the relative failure of such efforts is that they constitute a form of intervention that offers too little too late. As Chilman (1983) points out, many of the young women for whom these programs have been designed are the victims of a network of deprivations: "deprivations stemming from poverty, racism, poor health and educational services, community disorganization, and family conflicts. These deprivations have adversely affected their physical, social, and psychological development. Moreover, many of these adolescent girls see little hope for their future lives in terms of further education and adequate employment. Attempts to finish school, preventing the birth of another child, trying to find a well paying job strike many as fruitless endeavors" (1983, p. 304).

One sorely neglected source of amelioration of the problem of teen pregnancy is the adolescent father, who is as uninformed about sex and sexuality as most teenagers. Most teenage fathers never practice contraception, nor discuss the possibility of pregnancy, and believe that it will never happen to them (Alan Guttmacher, 1982). Such behavior and attitudes are especially prevalent among low income black adolescents and undoubtedly contribute to the problem of repeated and unwanted pregnancies among these youths. Thus, the failure of most programs to actively involve adolescent fathers in their remedial programs for unwed mothers neglect an important opportunity to promote sexual responsibility among these youths and discourage their long term active involvement in the care and support of their offspring. The value of programs designed to include adolescent fathers has only recently been recognized and preliminary results from such innovative programs as the Teen Father Collaboration, coordinated by the New York City Bank Street College of Education and the Teenage Pregnancy and Parenting Project in San Francisco, suggest that such programs may prove effective in helping to reverse the cycle of children having children.

# Conclusion

The future grows out of a present that has been shaped by the past. Thus the fate of many black youths will be determined to a substantial degree by the negative trends outlined above, and by developments yet to unfold. In addition, their future will be shaped by concerted efforts made in the present to remove the network of disadvantages which diminish their life chances in society. As the preceding analysis has sought to make clear, the problems of black youths are multidimensional and action in any single direction is likely to prove inadequate. Im-

proving the quality of urban education and job training for these youths, while essential, will not by themselves improve the employment prospects for these youths unless an adequate supply of jobs is available. Similarly, efforts to combat crime, delinquency, drug abuse and out-of-wedlock births among black teens will not yield substantial results without attention to the more central problems of poverty, discrimination and the material conditions of the inner cities. Yet such efforts may turn out to be no more than a series of Sisyphean exercises if there is validity in Rainwater's (1969) observation that "the central fact about the American underclass is that it is created by the operation of what in other ways is the most successful economic system known to man. It is not, in short, so much that the good system has not included the underclass, as that in the manner of its operation it produces and reproduces it" (p. 9). However, the perception is growing that the costs associated with the production and reproduction of the black underclass are socially, politically and morally unacceptable.

# References

**Alan Guttenmacher Institute**

1981 *Teenage Pregnancy: The Problem That Hasn't* (1982) *Gone Away.* NY: Alan Guttmacher Institute.

**Bane, M. J. and Ellwood, D. T.**

1983a Slipping Into and Out of Poverty: The Dynamics of Spells. National Bureau of Economic Research Working Paper No. 1199.

1983b The Dynamics of Dependence: The Routes to Self-Sufficiency. Supported by U.S. Dept. of Health and Human Services grant. Contract No. HHS-100-82-0038.

**Bianchi, Suzanne**

1981 *Household Compositions and Racial Inequality.* New Brunswick, NJ: Rutgers University Press.

**Brunswick, Ann**

1980 Social Meanings and Developmental Needs: Perspectives on Black Youth's Drug Abuse. *Youth and Society*, pp. 449–473.

**Brunswick, Ann and Boyle, John**

1979 Patterns of Drug Involvement. *Youth and Society*, 11, pp. 139–161.

**Card, J. J. and Wise, L. L.**

1978 Teenage Mothers and Teenage Fathers: The Impact of Early Childbearing on the Parent's Personal and Professional Lives. *Family Planning Perspectives*, 10, pp. 199–205.

**Center for Human Resource Research**

1984 *The National Longitudinal Surveys Handbook:*

*1981*. Columbus: College of Administrative Science. 1981. The Ohio State University Center for the Study of Social Policy. The 'Flip-Side' of Black Families Headed by Women: The Economic Status of Black Men. Working Paper.

Chambers, C. D.

1977   A Review of Recent Sociological and Epidemiological Studies in Substance Abuse. Paper presented at the Neurobiology Seminar, Vanderbilt University, Nashville, Tenn.

Cherlin, N. A.

1981   *Marriage, Divorce, and Re-Marriage*. Cambridge, MA: Harvard University.

Chilman, C.

1983   *Adolescent Sexuality in a Changing American Society*. NY: John Wiley.

Curtis L. A.

1975   Violence, Race, and Culture. Lexington: Lexington Books.

Cvetkovich, G. and Grote, B.

1980   Psychosocial Development and the Social Problem of Teenage Illegitimacy. In C. Chilman, (ed.), *Adolescent Pregnancy and Childbearing*. U.S. Government Printing Office, pp. 15–41.

Duncan, G. J.

1984   *Years of Poverty, Years of Plenty*. Ann Arbor, MI: Institute for Social Research, University of Michigan.

Edwards, L. E., Steinman, M. E., Arnold, K. and Hakanson, A.

1980   Adolescent Pregnancy Prevention Services in High School Clinics. *Family Planning Perspectives*. 12, pp. 6–14.

Farley, Reynolds

1984   *Blacks and Whites: Narrowing the Gap*. Cambridge, MA: Harvard University.

Federal Bureau of Investigation

1983   Crime in the United States, 1983. Washington, D.C. Government Printing Office.

Freeman, R.

1978   Black Economic Progress Since 1964. *The Public Interest*. 52 (Summer), pp. 52–68.

1980   Why Is There A Youth Labor Market Problem? In Anderson, B. and Sawhill, I. (eds.), *Youth Employment and Public Policy*. Englewood Cliffs, NJ: Prentice-Hall, Inc.

Freeman, R. and Holzer, N.

1985   Young Blacks and Jobs—What We Now Know. *The Public Interest*. 78, pp. 18–31.

Furstenberg, F., Linclon, R. and Menken, J.

1981   *Teenage Sexuality, Pregnancy and Childbearing*. Philadelphia: Univ. of Pennsylvania Press.

Gandossy, R., Williams, J. and Harwood, H.

1980   *Drugs and Crime: A Survey and Analysis of the Literature*. Washington, D.C.: U.S. Dept. of Justice.

Gibbs, J. T.

1984   Black Adolescents and Youths: An Endangered Species. *American Journal of Orthopsychiatry*. 54, pp. 6–19.

Glasgow, D.

1981   *The Black Underclass*. NY: Vintage Books.

Glick, P. and Norton, A.

1979   Marrying, Divorcing and Living Together in the U.S. Today. *Population Bulletin*. 32, Washington, D.C.: Population Reference Bureau.

Hill, M. S.

1981   Some Dynamic Aspects of Poverty. In M. S. Hill, D. H. Hill, and J. N. Morgan, (eds.), *Five Thousand American Families: Patterns of Economic Progress*. Vol. IX. Ann Arbor: Institute for Social Research, Univ. of Michigan Press.

Hofferth, S. and Moore, K.

1979   Early Childbearing and Later Economic Well Being. *American Sociological Review*. 44, pp. 784–815.

Hogan, D. P. and Kitagawa, E. M.

1985a  The Impact of Social Status, Family Structure, and Neighborhood on the Fertility of Black Adolescents. *American Journal of Sociology*. 90, pp. 825–55.

Hogan, D. P., A. Stone, N. M. and Kitagawa, E. M.

1985b  Social and Environmental Factors Influencing Contraceptive Use Among Black Adolescents. *Family Planning Perspectives*. 17, pp. 165–169.

Kirby, D., Alter, J., and Scales, P.

1979   An Analysis of U.S. Sex Education Programs and Evaluation Methods. Washington, D.C.: U.S. Dept. of Health, Education and Welfare.

Lancaster, J. B. and Hamburg, B. A.

1985   *School-Age Pregnancy and Parenthood: Biosocial Dimensions*. NY: Aldine Publishing Co.

Leukefeld, C. and Clayton, R.

1979   Drug Abuse and Delinquency: A Study of Youths in Treatment. In Beschner, G. and Friedman, A., (eds.), *Youth Drug Abuse*. Lexington, MA: Lexington Books, pp. 213–227.

Mare, R. D. and Winship, C.

1980   Changes in the Relative Labor Force Status of Black and White Youths: A Review of the Literature. Special Report prepared for the National Commission for Employment Policy. Institute for Research on Poverty, Univ. of Wisconsin, Madison.

1984   The Paradox of Lessening Racial Inequality and Joblessness Among Black Youth. *American Sociological Review.* 49, pp. 39–55.

McGhee, James

1982   The Black Teenager: An Endangered Species. In James Williams, (ed.), *The State of Black America.* NY: National Urban League.

McLaughlin, S. D. and Micklin, M.

1983   The Timing of the Birth and Changes in Personal Efficacy. *Journal of Marriage and the Family.* 45, p. 47.

Moore, K.

1978   The Consequences of Age at First Childbirth: Family Size. Working Paper 1146-02. Washington, D.C.: The Urban Institute.

Mott, F.

1986   The Pace of Repeated Childbearing Among Young American Mothers. *Family Planning Perspectives.* 18, pp. 5–12.

National Center for Health Statistics

1980   Final Natality, 1978. *Monthly Vital Statistics Report.* U.S. Department of Health and Human Services.

1982   Advance Report of Final Natality Statistics, 1980. *Monthly Vital Statistics Report.* U.S. Department of Health and Human Services.

National Institute on Alcohol Abuse and Alcoholism

1975   Alcohol and Health: New Knowledge. U.S. Department of Health, Education and Welfare. Washington, D.C. Publication No. (ADM), pp. 75–212.

National Institute on Drug Abuse

1979   National Survey on Drug Abuse. U.S. Dept. of Health and Human Services.

1983   *National Survey on Drug Abuse.* 1979. U.S. Dept. of Health and Human Services.

1983   *National Survey on Drug Abuse: Main Findings.* 1982. U.S. Department of Health and Human Services.

Norton, E. H.

1985   Restoring the Traditional Black Family. *New York Times Magazine.* June 2, p. 79.

O'Connell, M. and Moore, M.

1980   The Legitimacy Status of First Births to U.S. Women Aged 15–24, 1939–1978. *Family Planning Perspective.* 12, pp. 16–25.

Papagiannis, G., Bickel, R. and Fuller, R.

1983   The Social Creation of School Dropouts: Accomplishing the Reproduction of an Underclass. *Youth and Society.* 14, pp. 363–392.

Parelius, A. and Parelius, J.

1978   *The Sociology of Education.* Englewood Cliffs, NJ: Prentice-Hall.

Preble, E., Casey, J.

1969   Taking Care of Business—The Heroin User's Life on the Street. *International Journal of Addictions.* 4, pp. 1–24.

Presser, H. and Salsberg, L.

1975   Public Assistance and Early Family Formation: Is There a Pronatalist Effect? *Social Problems.* 23, pp. 226–241.

Rainwater, L.

1969   Looking Back and Looking Up. *Transaction.* 6 (Feb.), p. 9.

Ray, O.

1983   *Drugs, Society and Human Behavior.* St. Louis: C. V. Mosby.

Robinson, B. E. and Barret, R. L.

1985   *Fatherhood.* NY: Guilford Press.

Rothstein, A. A.

1978   Adolescent Males, Fatherhood, and Abortion. *Journal of Youth and Adolescence.* 7, pp. 203–214.

Rumberger, R.

1982   Recent High School and College Experiences of Youth: Variations by Race, Sex, and Social Class. *Youth and Society.* 13, pp. 449–470.

Smith, D., Levy, S., Striar, D.

1979   Treatment Services for Youthful Drug Users. In Beschner, G. and Friedman, A., (eds.), *Youth Drug Abuse.* Lexington, MA: Lexington Books, pp. 537–569.

Thomas, G., and Scott, W.

1979   Black Youth and the Labor Market: The Unemployment Dilemma. *Youth and Society.* 11, pp. 163–189.

Ullah, Philip.

1985   Disaffected Black and White Youth: The Role of Unemployment Duration and Perceived Job Discrimination. *Ethnic and Racial Studies*. 8, pp. 181–193.

U.S. Bureau of the Census

1975    *Historical Statistics of the United States*. Vol. 1. Washington, D.C.: GPO.

1982    1980. *Characteristics of American Children and Youth*.

1981    *Current Population Reports*. Series P-20, No. 360.

1982    *Statistical Abstract of the United States*. Vol. 1. Washington, D.C.: GPO.

1982    1980. *Characteristics of American Children and Youth*.

1981    *Current Population Reports*. Series P-20, No. 360.

1982–    1982. *Statistical Abstract of the United States*.
83        Washington, D.C.: GPO.

1985    *Statistical Abstract of the United States*. Washington, D.C.: GPO.

1986    *Statistical Abstract of the United States*. Washington, D.C.: GPO.

U.S. Bureau of Labor Statistics

1984    *Employment and Earnings*. January 1984. U.S. Department of Labor.

U.S. Commission on Civil Rights

1978    *Social Indicators of Equality for Minorities and Women*. Washington, D.C.: GPO.

U.S. Commission on Civil Rights

1983    *A Growing Crisis: Disadvantaged Women and Their Children*. Washington, D.C.: GPO.

U.S. Department of Health and Human Services

1986    *Black and Minority Health*. Vol. V: Homicide, Suicide & Unintended Injuries. Washington, D.C.: GPO.

U.S. Department of Justice

1983    Federal Bureau of Investigation. *Uniform Crime Reports for the United States*.

U.S. Department of Labor

1982    *Employment and Training Report of the President*. Washington, D.C.: GPO.

Weissman, J., Marr, S., Katsampes, P.

1976    Addiction and Criminal Behavior: A Continuing Examination of Criminal Addicts. *Journal of Drug Issues*. 6, pp. 153–165.

Williams, J. (ed.)

1981    *The State of Black America*. 1981. New York: The National Urban League.

Wilson, J. Q.

1977    *Thinking About Crime*. N.Y.: Vintage Books.

Wilson, W.

1984a   The Urban Underclass. In L. W. Dunbar, (ed.), *Minority Report*. New York: Pantheon, pp. 75–117.

1984b   The Black Underclass. *Wilson Quarterly*. 8, pp. 88–99.

Wilson, W. and Neckerman, K.

1985    Poverty and Family Structure: The Widening Gap Between Evidence and Public Policy Issues. Paper presented at the Conference on Poverty and Policy: Retrospect and Prospects. Williamsburg, VA, 1984.

Zelnik, M. and Kantner, J.

1980    Sexual Activity, Contraceptive Use and Pregnancy Among Metropolitan-Area Teenagers, 1971–1979. *Family Planning Perspectives*. 12, pp. 230–237.

Zelnik, M. and Ford, K.

1981    *Sex and Pregnancy in Adolescence*. Beverly Hills, CA: Sage.

# EARLY PARENTHOOD AMONG LOW-INCOME ADOLESCENT GIRLS

*Lorraine P. Mayfield*

*It has been believed that many women become trapped in poverty because of out-of-wedlock children born during their adolescence. Data are presented which show this to be more true for whites than for Blacks. Black adolescents who become mothers are less likely than whites to marry and move away from home and are more likely to be living with their parents and receiving assistance with child care. For the Black adolescent, motherhood is less likely to terminate education and preparation for the future.*

## Introduction

By 1980, two-thirds of female-headed families received child welfare and two-thirds of the long-term poor were women (U.S. Commission on Civil Rights, 1983). This rapid rise of female-headed families is due partly to the rising failure rate of marriage and the low income of women who were separated and divorced and partly to a massive rise in the number of babies born to unwed teenage mothers. The contemporary trend toward out-of-wedlock teenage motherhood is particularly striking in both Black and white low-income communities. Between 1975 and 1979, out-of-wedlock births to teenagers 15–19 years old increased from 223 to 253 per 1,000 live births (U.S. Department of Health and Human Services, 1981).

Many researchers have examined the implications of teenage childbearing for education, employment, and other factors related to poverty. Research shows that early motherhood has serious negative consequences for young women (Chilman, 1983; Furstenberg, 1976; Presser, 1975; Waite and Moore, 1978). Teenage mothers in these studies were much more likely to drop out of school because of pregnancy, be without employment experience, bear other children early, and be on public assistance after the birth, in comparison to youth who began childbearing in their early twenties.

Usually uneducated, unskilled, and unsupported, teenage mothers are in need of financial and emotional support. This paper examines the role of family support and family formation for low-income adolescent women who are coping with motherhood. I focus on poor teenagers because they are more likely to become pregnant and less likely to terminate an unwanted pregnancy than youth from affluent backgrounds (Chilman, 1983). In addition, youth from poor families are more likely to be vulnerable to the intergenerational transmission of poverty. In particular, this paper explores the family support available and attempts to explain young mothers' marital status. I hypothesize that family support and marital status vary by racial background. The following propositions are discussed in this study:

1. Low-income adolescent Black mothers have more role models of single-headed households

Paper prepared for presentation at the American Sociological Association Annual Meeting, San Antonio, Texas, August 28, 1984. Printed by permission.

than whites, which reduces the urgency of an early marriage.

2. Low-income adolescent Black mothers receive greater family support than whites because of strong kinship ties in the Black community.

3. Low-income young Black mothers marry later because they aspire to higher upward mobility aspiration than low-income young white mothers.

The implications of these hypotheses may provide important insights to process of whether or not poverty is transmitted across generations and assist with social policy geared to reduction of poverty in women's lives and their disadvantaged children.

# Theoretical Overview and Review of Literature

## Status Transition

The status transition perspective is used to assess whether young mothers view themselves as moving from one status to another, leaving adolescence to enter adulthood. The early entry into the role of parent is often synchronized with other role transitions that interfere with the normative central activity of adolescent years—that is, schooling. The single most evident consequence of early role transition is the depressing effect on schooling (Furstenberg, 1976; Hofferth and More, 1979; Presser, 1975; Waite and Moore, 1978). Whether or not young mothers aspire to remain in school and seek its completion provides evidence of how they view their status in the life course.

Some researchers (Ladner, 1972; Stack, 1974) report that low-income teenage Black mothers gain maturity, autonomy, and respect as mothers in the community after the birth of their first child. Ladner (1972), in her anthropological study of Black adolescent females in a St. Louis ghetto, advances the idea that a girl becomes a woman through having a baby; she performs motherhood functions and joins the community of experienced mothers. According to

Ladner, adolescence is not seen as a life stage and as a period of preparation for maturity; rather, children move directly into adulthood when they become parents, even though premarital birth of a first child is characteristically viewed as a mistake (Ladner, 1972:216). Stack (1974), in her anthropological study of a midwestern city of low-income Black families and youth, found that young Black mothers often stated that having a baby made them feel more mature and responsible. She found that within their homes, young Black mothers are granted freer social lifes. Although early and out-of-wedlock childbirths are not held to be desirable in the low-income Black community, it is usually accepted as an unfortunate but often inevitable event.

However, other researchers view early motherhood as an event that has serious negative consequences but does not necessarily propel youth into the adult role. Furstenberg (1976), in his longitudinal survey study of 400 predominantly Black and economically disadvantaged adolescent mothers in Baltimore, found that early motherhood may present no serious obstacles to continued high school education. Furstenberg's sample showed that young Black mothers were most apt to return to school if they held high educational goals and had help with child care. In his study, remaining single was highly correlated with more help from the teenagers' family in many ways, including child care. Presser (1975), in her study of 408 women in several age brackets from New York City, found that 60 percent of the first births were unplanned and that teenage mothers, although unprepared for motherhood, did not consider themselves adults.

The literature on young white mothers, especially from low-income family backgrounds, is scant. Rubin's (1976) in-depth study of white working-class families shows that marriage is viewed as an absolute requirement by both men and women if a girl becomes pregnant; thus, the white teenage mother is likely to enter the role of wife.

## Value of Early Marriage

In conventional thinking, when a young woman marries she assumes the role of adult. Overall, the dominant U.S. cultural norms prescribe entry into the marital role during the youth's twenties. The costs of teenage marriage are great to individuals and society because early marriages are associated with higher fertility, economic difficulties, and greater risk of divorce.

In the blue-collar California families that Rubin (1976:41) describes in her study,

> *for most working-class girls getting married was, and probably still is, the singularly acceptable way out of an oppressive family situation and into a respected social status and the only way to move from girl to woman.*

For this group, premarital pregnancy automatically means marriage for both men and women (Rubin, 1976:67). Elder and Rockwell (1976) carried out an analysis of the causes and consequences of timing of marriage among white women born between 1925 and 1929. Using data from the National Fertility Studies of 1965 and 1970, they found that early-marrying women were more likely to come from low socioeconomic origins, especially if they failed to finish high school. Howell and Frese (1982:46) confirm this finding in their study of 945 southern teenagers in 1975, in which they found that white females tended to marry earlier and drop out of school at higher rates than Blacks. Kenkel (1981) reports in his study of 311 low-income southern high school girls that white girls were less willing to postpone marriage and were more likely to have goals of being wives and mothers only.

Within low-income Black communities, marriage to legitimize a child has often been seen as not practical (Ladner, 1972; Stack, 1974). Although fertility is highly valued in the Black community, early marriage to legitimize children is not the dominant practice (Furstenberg, 1976; Ladner, 1972). In addition, early marriages are perceived as having negative consequences on youths' educational achievement. All too often, the father of the baby is an unemployed or underemployed youth with little chance for financial improvement. The community usually holds that marriages should be entered into because they have a good chance of succeeding and because the couple wants to (and can) live together and establish its own home. Otherwise, the young mother and her child can live with relatives. With the concept of status transition, we examine some of the social consequences, particularly as it relates to marriage and family support.

# Data and Methodology

## Data

The data for this study came from the Youth Incentive Entitlement Pilot Project (YIEPP), funded by the U.S. Department of Labor and managed by Manpower Demonstration Research Corporation. In response to high unemployment among young people, especially Blacks, Congress in 1977 enacted the Youth Employment and Demonstration Projects Act. YIEPP was one of the four experimental programs established under the act. The research design for this study of the program impact of YIEPP incorporated interviews with a sample of 7,553 youths at four locations and four matched comparison sites. The urban sites were Baltimore, Maryland; Cincinnati, Ohio; and Denver, Colorado. In Baltimore, only a third of the city was included in the area of study, whereas the entire cities of Cincinnati and Denver were included. The fourth study site consisted of eight rural counties in Mississippi (Adams, Claiborne, Covington, Franklin, Jefferson, Jones, Wayne, and Wilkinson). The four comparison sites chosen were Cleveland, Ohio; Louisville, Kentucky; Phoenix, Arizona; and a group of counties in western and eastern Mississippi (Clarke, Humphreys, Lauderdale, Shirley, Smith, and Washington).

The following criteria were used to choose eligible youth for the sample: (1) The youth must live in the geographic areas of the Entitlement project for 30 days prior to the survey, (2) the youth is aged 15–19, (3) the youth has not received a high school diploma or certificate of high school equivalency, and (4) the youth is economically disadvantaged, either by constituting a family of one or by being a member of one, and the family income is at or below the poverty level as determined by the Office of Management and Budget.

During 1978, household screening interviews were administered to a stratified random sample of about 130,000 households to determine the presence of youths. Interviewers subsequently returned to each eligible household and conducted baseline interviews with eligible youths and their parents.

The purpose of the baseline survey was to collect data on demographic characteristics, family background, and self-esteem of the youths as well as on the behavior of these youths with regard to their schooling, training, and work experience. The baseline survey was not officially identified with YIEPP demonstration program. The findings of the baseline survey are reported in *Schooling and Work among Youth from Low-Income Households* (Barclay et al., 1979).

## The Full Sample

The entire sample consisted of 7,553 youths interviewed in their households in the areas listed previously. Minority representation was very high because of the southern locations and the greater minority populations in the inner city. The sample consisted of white, Black, and Hispanic youths ranging from 15-year-olds to 19-year-olds. Fourteen percent were age 15, 30 percent were 16, 27 percent were 17, 18 percent were 18, and 11 percent were 19.

The sample was 48 percent male and 52 percent female. The mean level of family income for the total sample was $6,395 in 1975. Over 50 percent of family income is derived from earned income in most sites, except Baltimore, Cleveland, and Cincinnati. In these study sites, the Aid to Families with Dependent Children (AFDC) component is high. Slightly more than 55 percent of all youths and their families were receiving some type of welfare assistance.

This YIEPP baseline survey sample was in no way identified with the demonstrations and included all youths eligible for the program. One strength of this data set is that it sheds light on an infrequently surveyed population—older teenagers from poverty families living either in inner cities or rural areas and who are making slow progress in school. In contrast to the National Longitudinal Study of High School Seniors of the Class of 1972,

this data set provides insights into the behavior of the U.S. poor in their formative years. Another advantage is that the large sample size makes it possible to categorize respondents by motherhood status and race. The effects of motherhood are inferred by comparing the outcome variables for the nonparenting groups.

For this paper, I focus the analysis on a sample of 3,832 Black and white female teenagers. This sample consists of 56 percent Black nonmothers, 21 percent white nonmothers, 17 percent Black mothers, and 6 percent white mothers. Much of the analysis focuses on the young mothers.

## Methodology

Cross-tabular analysis of the outcome variables of family support and marital status were presented by racial and parenting status for comparison. Measures of family support included questions on residential, financial, and child care assistance. Respondents were asked "Do you live with parent/guardian now?" Unfortunately, if the teenager did not live with parent/guardians, no other question was asked about whom else she may be living with. Financial dependence on parents or guardians was determined from responses to the question "Do you receive any allowance or money from your parents or guardians on a regular basis?" Child care assistance was ascertained by the question "Is your child regularly cared for by someone else during the day?"

Measures for upward mobility aspirations related to educational status and were gleaned from the following questions: "Are you currently enrolled in a junior high school, or any kind of high school, or in a G.E.D. program?" "What was the highest grade you completed in school?" "How much education would you really like to get, if everything worked out just right?"

The girls' parents' current household status was taken from the parents' response to this question: "Are you currently married and living with your (husband/wife), widowed, divorced, separated, or have you never been married?"

# Portrait of Teenage Mothers and Nonmothers

Table 1 shows how teenagers who are mothers differ in many respects from those who do not have children. Background factors (e.g., age, marital status, present living arrangements) are compared across race and parenting status. Table 1A shows the age range of the sample is 15 to 19 years old. Young mothers are slightly older than nonmothers and, regardless of race, youths tend to be mothers as their age increases.

From Table 1B, we learn that the overwhelm-ing majority of Black mothers have never married, but the marital status of white mothers is quite different—40 percent of them were once married. Table 1C shows that older youths are more likely to marry than younger ones. This is especially the case for white mothers; 51 percent of the 19-year-old white mothers were previously married. Only 11 percent of the 19-year-old Black mothers were ever married.

Table 1D shows the present living arrangements of the teenagers, if the youth was living with parents/guardians at age 14. Black youth and white nonmothers are overwhelmingly likely to continue living with their parents and guardians. About 1 out

**TABLE 1**   Portrait of Teenage Mothers and Nonmothers by Age, Marital Status, Living Arrangements, and Child Care Support and by Race and Parenting Status

|  |  | BLACK MOTHERS | WHITE MOTHERS | BLACK NONMOTHERS | WHITE NONMOTHERS |
|---|---|---|---|---|---|
| A. | Age (in years) |  |  |  |  |
|  | 15 | 8% | 2% | 21% | 20% |
|  | 16 | 16 | 15 | 32 | 30 |
|  | 17 | 27 | 25 | 26 | 26 |
|  | 18 | 26 | 34 | 15 | 15 |
|  | 19 | 24 | 24 | 6 | 9 |
|  |  | 100% | 100% | 100% | 100% |
|  |  | (667) | (219) | (2,128) | (818) |
| B. | Never married | 95% | 60% | 99% | 86% |
|  |  | (667) | (219) | (2,128) | (818) |
| C. | Never married by age (in years) |  |  |  |  |
|  | 15 | 97% | —[1] | 100% | 100% |
|  |  | (32) | (5) | (455) | (165) |
|  | 16 | 99% | 70% | 100% | 98% |
|  |  | (110) | (33) | (675) | (244) |
|  | 17 | 98% | 57% | 99% | 95% |
|  |  | (187) | (54) | (550) | (214) |
|  | 18 | 94% | 65% | 99% | 91% |
|  |  | (177) | (74) | (326) | (125) |
|  | 19 | 89% | 49% | 97% | 87% |
|  |  | (160) | (53) | (122) | (70) |
| D. | Living with parents *now* | 83% | 49% | 98% | 86% |
|  |  | (391) | (159) | (1,197) | (450) |

[1]Number of cases is too small for percentage.

of 2 white mothers live with parents/guardians. Unfortunately, the survey does not provide data on where youths live if they do not live with parents.

Table 2 presents some characteristics of the teenagers' family of origin. In particular, Table 2B shows that Black youths, both mothers and nonmothers, are more likely to live with parents who are without spouses than are white youths. Not only are Black youths more likely than whites to live in single-parent households, the young Black mothers also are more likely than any other category to live in a household in which their mothers have never married. Hence, the family structures of these low-income groups differ by race.

There are other variations in the households. The amount of deprivation varies within these low-income families. Table 2C shows that the young mothers' families, both Black and white, are more likely to receive public assistance than nonmothers' families.

Table 2D presents the distribution of the youths' parents' education. The mean grade completed for all the youths' parents is the ninth grade. Black parents are slightly more likely than white parents to have received more education, although few if any of the parents continued their education beyond high school. Table 2E shows that Black parents were not able to turn their slight education advantage into increased labor force participation. Approximately half of Black parents were out of the labor force in the past three years. In summary, young mothers' parents are little able to provide financial assistance and working role models as they struggle with poverty.

# Results

Analyses of the Black/white differences in family formation for low-income adolescent girls are present in relationship to each of the three hypotheses.

1. Low-income adolescent Black mothers have more role models of single-headed households than whites, which reduces the urgency of an early marriage.

2. Low-income adolescent Black mothers receive greater family support than white mothers because of strong kinship ties in the Black community.
3. Low-income young Black mothers marry later because they aspire to higher upward mobility aspirations than low-income young white mothers.

The first proposition suggests that the family background and structure influence the type of future structure that young mothers may adopt. The profile of young mothers shows that a greater percentage of young Black mothers live in single-headed households than whites. This experience confirms previous research showing that young women brought up by female heads of household are less favorably disposed to traditional patterns of family structure (Crowley and Shapiro, 1982:414). Black youth, regardless of parenting status, are still living at home and may learn and value the viability of a single-parent home. Black adolescent mothers learn that the high rates of unemployment for Black men, particularly adolescent males, makes viable two-parent families difficult to achieve and maintain.

The second hypothesis concerning family support addresses the families' resources and strengths that low-income families can provide to their daughters. This section provides an analysis of the young women's continued dependence on their parents and society. Four types of dependence are examined: residential, financial, child care assistance provided by family, and welfare dependence on society (in particular, direct AFDC support to young mothers).

Table 3 shows the percentages of respondents who live at home with parents or guardians. The overwhelming majority of youths, regardless of parenting status, are more likely to live with their families.

Table 4 shows residential arrangement by marital status. As expected, never-married young women are more likely to live with their families. Of those youths who were previously married, 68 percent of Black mothers live at home and only 28 percent of white mothers live with their parents.

## TABLE 2    Family Background Data by Race and Parenting Status

| | BLACK MOTHERS | WHITE MOTHERS | BLACK NONMOTHERS | WHITE NONMOTHERS |
|---|---|---|---|---|
| A. Relationship between parent and teenager, if teenager lives with parent | | | | |
| Mother | 85% | 83% | 85% | 82% |
| Father | 5 | 12 | 5 | 11 |
| Other relative | 10 | 5 | 10% | 7 |
| | 100% | 100% | 100% | 100% |
| | (544) | (108) | (1,986) | (721) |
| B. Parents' marital status | | | | |
| Married, living with spouse | 26% | 41% | 31% | 53% |
| Widowed, divorced, separated | 63 | 56 | 61 | 45 |
| Never married | 11 | 3 | 8 | 2 |
| | 100% | 100% | 100% | 100% |
| | (551) | (109) | (2,005) | (725) |
| C. Percent of family receiving AFDC | 63% | 61% | 47% | 43% |
| | (550) | (109) | (2,002) | (725) |
| D. Parents' education | | | | |
| 8th grade or less | 34% | 53% | 35% | 47% |
| 9th grade | 12 | 19 | 12 | 13 |
| 10th grade | 19 | 8 | 17 | 12 |
| 11th grade | 16 | 7 | 16 | 11 |
| 12th grade | 18 | 12 | 18 | 14 |
| Beyond high school | 1 | 1 | 2 | 3 |
| | 100% | 100% | 100% | 100% |
| | (538) | (108) | (1,950) | (707) |
| E. Parents' time in labor force for past 3 years | | | | |
| All of the time | 22% | 24% | 19% | 16% |
| Most of the time | 8 | 9 | 9 | 9 |
| Some of the time | 20 | 25 | 19 | 26 |
| None of the time | 50 | 42 | 53 | 49 |
| | 100% | 100% | 100% | 100% |
| | (551) | (109) | (2,004) | (725) |

The percentages of single respondents who stay home is high, and marriage for white young mothers seems to be an impetus for moving away from home. On the other hand, motherhood for Blacks does not appear to be a compelling reason to leave home. In general, Black families continue to provide residential assistance to their daughters.

Another form of family support is financial assistance. Table 5A shows the percentage of respondents who receive regular financial support. Overall, nonmothers are more than twice as likely than young mothers to receive financial help. When young mothers do receive help, Blacks receive slightly greater financial assistance than their white counterparts, even when we take residential arrangements into account. Table 5B reveals that the

**TABLE 3    Present Living Arrangements of Teenagers (If Teenagers Lived with Parents in the Past)**

|  | BLACK MOTHERS | WHITE MOTHERS | BLACK NONMOTHERS | WHITE NONMOTHERS |
|---|---|---|---|---|
| Not living with parents | 17% | 51% | 2% | 14% |
| Living with parents | 83 | 49 | 98 | 86 |
|  | 100% | 100% | 100% | 100% |
|  | (391) | (159) | (1,197) | (450) |

**TABLE 4    Living with Parents/Guardian by Marital Status and by Race and Parenting Status**

|  | BLACK MOTHERS | WHITE MOTHERS | BLACK NONMOTHERS | WHITE NONMOTHERS |
|---|---|---|---|---|
| Ever married | 68% | 28% | —[1] | 1% |
|  | (19) | (64) | (7) | (25) |
| Never married | 85% | 63% | 99% | 90% |
|  | (371) | (95) | (1,190) | (425) |

[1]Number of cases is too small for percentage.

youths' age influences whether or not they receive financial assistance. For all the categories of teenagers, as their age increases financial support decreases, especially for young mothers. The financial support for younger teenagers better enables them to continue their schooling; families may expect older adolescents to work or seek other means of support.

The availability of child care assistance is assessed by a number of indicators. Although these respondents were not directly asked who provides child care assistance, it is possible to speculate on possible candidates by examining their responses to the following questions:

1. "(Is/Are any of) your child(ren) regularly cared for by someone else during the day?"
2. "About how much does this care usually cost you per week?"

3. "About how many hours each day are they usually cared for?"
4. "How many miles, if any, do you have to travel to deliver your child(ren) to this care?"

Table 6A reports the percentage of young mothers who receive regular child care. Approximately half of Black mothers reported they can depend on someone else for child care assistance, whereas only a quarter of white mothers can do so. Black teenage mothers are more likely than white mothers to receive child care aid. Table 6B reveals that over three-fourths of Black mothers have child care assistance for five days of the week. Table 6C displays the percentages of the cost of child care to the young mothers. Black young mothers are more likely to receive free assistance than their white counterparts, and a larger percentage of white mothers pay a higher cost for child care than Blacks.

|  | TABLE 5 | Financial Help | | |
|---|---|---|---|---|
|  | BLACK MOTHERS | WHITE MOTHERS | BLACK NONMOTHERS | WHITE NONMOTHERS |
| A. Financial support from family by race and parenting status | | | | |
| Yes | 14% | 7% | 33% | 22% |
| No | 86 | 93 | 67 | 78 |
|  | 100% | 100% | 100% | 100% |
|  | (663) | (216) | (2,121) | (813) |
| B. Percentage of teenagers receiving financial aid from family by race, parenting status, and age | | | | |
| Age (in years) | | | | |
| 15 | 39% | —[1] | 42% | 33% |
|  | (31) |  | (455) | (164) |
| 16 | 16% | 19% | 36% | 26% |
|  | (110) | (32) | (672) | (243) |
| 17 | 23% | 13% | 31% | 19% |
|  | (185) | (53) | (547) | (212) |
| 18 | 10% | 1% | 23% | 12% |
|  | (175) | (73) | (323) | (124) |
| 19 | 4% | 2% | 18% | 8% |
|  | (162) | (53) | (124) | (70) |

[1]Number of cases is too small for percentage.

Table 6D shows that all young mothers use child care assistance for the large portion of the day and that white mothers receive more hours per week.

Table 6E shows the miles traveled for child care help. Young mothers (both Black and white) often do not travel at all for child care assistance. Fewer than 5 percent of the mothers traveled beyond four miles for this help.

It is suggested by the extensive free child care, long hours provided, and lack of travel that parents or other relatives are providing help to these mothers. Black adolescent mothers who for the most part live at home receive more child care assistance than whites.

Although only 5 percent of all 3,832 youths—mothers and nonmothers—received any public assistance directly, Table 7 shows that Black young mothers were more likely than the other groups to receive this assistance. Because Black mothers come from homes that are more likely to be welfare-dependent, they may be more familiar with public assistance's eligibility criteria and procedures.

In summary, Black mothers are found to be more dependent on their families than their white counterparts. By living at home, Black adolescent mothers receive not only room and board but also regular financial help and child care assistance. For the very small percentage of youths who receive welfare support directly, Black mothers appear to be more dependent on societal resources than their white counterparts.

We next examine the hypothesis that low-income young Black mothers marry later than whites because they have high upward mobility aspirations. In particular, we explore educational attachment and aspirations as indicators of mobility aspirations.

---

**TABLE 6    Child Care Assistance**

---

|     |                                      | BLACK MOTHERS | WHITE MOTHERS |
| --- | ------------------------------------ | ------------- | ------------- |
| A.  | Child care by someone else           |               |               |
|     | Yes                                  | 48%           | 23%           |
|     | No                                   | 52            | 77            |
|     |                                      | 100%          | 100%          |
|     |                                      | (658)         | (214)         |
| B.  | Number of days child care used       |               |               |
|     | 1                                    | 1%            | 3%            |
|     | 2                                    | 3             | 2             |
|     | 3                                    | 2             | 5             |
|     | 4                                    | 1             | 5             |
|     | 5                                    | 78            | 59            |
|     | 6                                    | 2             | 7             |
|     | 7                                    | 13            | 19            |
|     |                                      | 100%          | 100%          |
|     |                                      | (313)         | (49)          |
| C.  | Cost of child care                   |               |               |
|     | $0                                   | 69%           | 51%           |
|     | $1–14                                | 10            | 10            |
|     | $15 and over                         | 21            | 39            |
|     |                                      | 100%          | 100%          |
|     |                                      | (309)         | (49)          |
| D.  | Child care hours used                |               |               |
|     | 1–7                                  | 23%           | 9%            |
|     | 8                                    | 13            | 8             |
|     | 9–24                                 | 64            | 83            |
|     |                                      | 100%          | 100%          |
|     |                                      | (313)         | (49)          |
| E.  | Miles traveled for child care        |               |               |
|     | 0                                    | 86%           | 80%           |
|     | 1–3                                  | 10            | 15            |
|     | 4 and over                           | 4             | 5             |
|     |                                      | 100%          | 100%          |
|     |                                      | (286)         | (49)          |

---

Table 8A shows that the overwhelming proportion of Black nonmothers are currently enrolled in school; over half of white nonmothers and over two-fifths of Black mothers are attending school. White mothers are most likely to drop out—93 percent are not currently enrolled.

The highest grade completed provides a measure of school progress. Table 8B shows that white mothers made the least amount of educational progress; only 34 percent of them completed the ninth grade. Although white mothers are older than the other groups, they are less likely to be in the

**TABLE 7   AFDC Income by Race and Parenting Status (from January 1977 to August 1984)**

|  | BLACK MOTHERS | WHITE MOTHERS | BLACK NONMOTHERS | WHITE NONMOTHERS |
|---|---|---|---|---|
| Yes | 69% | 48% | 26% | 7% |
| No | 31 | 52 | 74 | 93 |
|  | 100% | 100% | 100% | 100% |
|  | (149) | (111) | (53) | (72) |

**TABLE 8   Educational Experiences and Aspirations**

|  |  | BLACK MOTHERS | WHITE MOTHERS | BLACK NONMOTHERS | WHITE NONMOTHERS |
|---|---|---|---|---|---|
| A. | Currently enrolled | 41% | 7% | 82% | 52% |
|  |  | (667) | (219) | (2,128) | (818) |
| B. | Highest grade completed |  |  |  |  |
|  | 8th or less | 15% | 30% | 6% | 14% |
|  | 9th | 17 | 34 | 17 | 23 |
|  | 10th | 27 | 22 | 32 | 31 |
|  | 11th | 26 | 11 | 25 | 20 |
|  | 12th | 15 | 3 | 20 | 12 |
|  |  | 100% | 100% | 100% | 100% |
|  |  | (636) | (204) | (2,089) | (795) |
| C. | Plans to return to school | 73% | 39% | 90% | 71% |
|  |  | (645) | (207) | (2,090) | (785) |
| D. | Education desired |  |  |  |  |
|  | Less than high school | 5% | 9% | 2% | 8% |
|  | Finish high school | 47 | 57 | 33 | 48 |
|  | Some college | 15 | 12 | 17 | 14 |
|  | Finish college | 27 | 16 | 39 | 23 |
|  | Graduate school | 6 | 6 | 9 | 7 |
|  |  | 100% | 100% | 100% | 100% |
|  |  | (656) | (212) | (2,107) | (803) |

upper high school grades. Black nonmothers are more likely to be in school and to have completed higher grades than the other groups. From this sample, we conclude that Black mothers are not as educationally handicapped by their parenting status as are whites. Table 8C shows the percentage of youths who are looking forward to returning to school in September. Clearly nonmothers are planning to return to school and 73 percent of the Black mothers are anticipating school in the upcoming fall. However, the majority of white mothers do not plan to return to school.

Virtually all the teenagers plan to finish high school (Crowley and Shapiro, 1982). An important part of the American dream is to complete college. College education assists upward mobility. Forty percent of all the female youths aspire to complete college. Among our typology of youths by race and parenting status, Table 8D indicates that Black non-mothers are most ambitious—approximately half of them desire a college or graduate education. Thirty-three percent of Black mothers desire at least a college education. Only 30 percent of white non-mothers ideally plan to finish college and graduate school and white mothers are least likely to consider college in their life plans. Overall, Black teenagers, regardless of parental status, are more likely to aspire to the middle-class aspiration of college education and advanced training.

In summary, we find that low-income Black youth and Black mothers have a greater school attachment than low-income white youth. A larger percentage of Black mothers are attending school and completing more grades. In addition, we find the educational goals of impoverished Black adolescent girls, regardless of parenting status, are higher than white youth. As other researchers (Crowley and Shapiro, 1982; Dawkins, 1981) report, minority youth realize that they are more dependent on educational institutions to achieve upward mobility. Our research confirms that motherhood is correlated with less ambitious educational goals and school participation, but more so for white girls than for Blacks.

## Conclusion

American cultural stereotypes focus on how Blacks more than whites are caught in the devastating "culture of poverty" or "underclass" because of higher incidences of out-of-wedlock children born during their adolescent years. Our data suggest that these generalizations apply more to young white women than to Blacks. For the most part, young Black mothers are not demoralized about their future; in fact, they are more likely to have high educational expectations, greater school attachment, and access to child care (because of the proximity to their supportive families). We find that young white mothers tend to marry earlier and to drop out of school at higher rates than Blacks. White females are most likely to experience accelerated adult role entry by becoming not only mothers but wives. Young Black mothers are willing to postpone marriage and accept the low-income Black community norm that the role of mother is more important than wife, particularly when an unstable marriage is foreseen. The role of adolescence, when time is used to prepare for the future by completing school, does not appear to be terminated for a substantial number of Black mothers. The aspirations of young Black mothers concerning delayed marriage entry and higher education are more compatible with the trends in the larger society than are those of whites.

Although a longitudinal study would better assess whether poor households transfer poverty to successive generations, this research suggests that young white women suffer more immediate educational handicaps from counternormative role transitions than young Black women. In addition, the general problem facing low-income Black and white mothers is the lack of institutional support. To avoid economic disadvantages associated with early childbearing, teenage mothers must be afforded the opportunity to complete their education. In order to do this, many young mothers need low-cost child care services; and family financial assistance is needed for youth who remain at home. Vocational training programs and public service jobs are necessary to assist them to achieve economic independence and adult status, and to minimize the perpetuation of the feminization of poverty.

# References

Barclay, Suzanne, et al.
1979    "Schooling and Work among Youth from Low-Income Households: A Baseline Report from the Entitlement Demonstration." New York: Manpower Demonstration Research Corporation.

Chilman, Catherine
1983    *Adolescent Sexuality in a Changing American Society, Second Edition.* New York: Wiley.

Crowley, Joan E., and David Shapiro
1982    "Aspirations and Expectations of Youth in the United States. Part I. Education and Fertility." *Youth and Society* 13 (4):391–422.

Dawkins, Marvin P.
1981    "Mobility Aspirations of Black Adolescents: A Comparison of Males and Females." *Adolescence* 16 (Fall):701–710.

Elder, Glen, and R. Rockwell
1976    "Marital Timing in Women's Life Patterns." *Journal of Family History* 1 (Autumn):34–53.

Furstenberg, Frank
1976    *Unplanned Parenthood: The Social Consequences of Teenage Childbearing.* New York: Free Press.

Hofferth, Sandra, and Kristen Moore
1979    "Early Childbearing and Later Economic Well-Being." *American Sociological Review* 44: 787–815.

Howell, Frank M., and Wolfgang Frese
1982    "Adult Role Transitions, Parental Influence, and Status Aspirations Early in the Life Course."

*Journal of Marriage and the Family* 44 (1): 35–49.

Kenkel, William F.
1981    "Black-White Differences in Age at Marriage Expectations of Low Income High School Girls." *The Journal of Negro Education* (Fall):425–438.

Ladner, Joyce A.
1972    *Tomorrow's Tomorrow: The Black Woman.* Garden City, N.Y.: Doubleday.

Presser, Harriet
1975    "Some Consequences of Adolescent Pregnancies." Paper presented at the National Institute of Child Health and Human Development Conference, Bethesda, Md.

Rubin, Lillian
1976    *Worlds of Pain.* New York: Basic Books.

Stack, Carol B.
1974    *All Our Kin: Strategies for Survival in a Black Community.* New York: Harper & Row.

U.S. Commission on Civil Rights
1983    Clearinghouse Publication 78. *Disadvantaged Women and Their Children.* Washington, D.C.: U.S. Government Printing Office.

U.S. Department of Health and Human Services
1981    *Vital Statistics of the United States Annual.* Washington, D.C.: U.S. Government Printing Office.

Waite, L. J., and K. A. Moore
1978    "The Impact of an Early First Birth on Young Women's Educational Attainment." *Social Forces* 56 (March):845–865.

# 9 / Social and Economic Issues

## POVERTY: NOT FOR WOMEN ONLY—
## A Critique of the "Feminization of Poverty"

### Alliance Against Women's Oppression

*This paper criticizes the feminization of poverty perspective, which—ignoring differences in race and class—suggests that all women are in danger of becoming poor. Rather, the "poor" are members of the lower working class—an unemployed or underemployed reserve of surplus workers segregated more by racism than sexism. The economic status of Black men has actually deteriorated since the sixties, with 50 percent now unemployed.*

- *"2 out of 3 American adults living in poverty are women."*
- *"Families headed by women live on 40% of the income of those headed by men."*
- *"The causes of women's poverty are different from men's."*
- *"A man becomes single and a woman becomes a single parent."*
- *Women are only a husband away from poverty."*

These are but a few of the most popular catch-phrases of an analysis termed the "feminization of poverty." This perspective has captured the imagination of a diverse array of political forces ranging from the Democratic Party to the Democratic Socialists of America (DSA), from liberal feminists of the National Organization for Women (NOW) to the radical sector of the women's movement, from *Off Our Backs* and the feminist press to the *Guardian* newspaper.

The heart of the "feminization of poverty" perspective is the proposition that women are bearing the brunt of economic hardship in the Reagan era and now make up the "new American underclass." Specifically, it argues that all or almost all of today's poor are women and that all or almost all women are in imminent danger of becoming poor.

Two trends are used to back up this assertion: first, the disintegration of two-parent families which leaves women to bear the responsibility and expense for child-rearing alone; and second, the low-wage status of women and their reliance on ever scarcer social services in order to survive.

From *AAWO Discussion Paper No. 3* (September, 1983). Reprinted by permission. Footnotes have been renumbered and some art and tables have been deleted.

"Feminization of poverty" is not only an analysis of women's declining status. Its promoters also see it as the basis for an organizing strategy with the potential to mobilize millions of women and revive the women's movement in the 1980s. This vision is shared by liberals, radicals and socialists alike. According to the May 1983 issue of the DSA's Bay Area newsletter, "A focus on the feminization of poverty is important for the women's movement. . . . It offers a new bond which cuts across class, age, race and sexual preference because women are in fact just a husband away from poverty." Vulnerability to impoverishment is seen as the common condition of all women and, thus, the issue to organize them into united political action.

Although it is riddled with distortions about who indeed has borne the brunt of poverty in this country, the "feminization of poverty" analysis has rapidly gained widespread popularity as an accurate depiction of women's current condition. That the liberal feminists have advanced such an analysis is no particular surprise. They have never gotten high marks for remembering the widely divergent class realities faced by different strata of women. But the fact that the left, too, has swallowed this analysis hook, line and sinker is highly problematic. It indicates the superficial understanding of the relationship between women's oppression, class exploitation and racism that prevails among left forces, including those within the women's movement. The "feminization of poverty" analysis deserves to be carefully critiqued rather than embraced without question. This discussion paper is written in order to initiate that process.

# Class and Racial Blinders

The "feminization of poverty" view does, in fact, point to certain economic realities affecting many women in the U.S. There is also no question that Reaganism includes a ruthless sexist attack on women's rights and living standards. However, the fatal flaw of the "feminization of poverty" analysis is that it treats all women as members of an oppressed class. On the one hand, it minimizes the differences in condition and consciousness among women. On the other hand, it minimizes the commonality in condition and consciousness between women and men of the same class or racial group.

Liberal advocates of the "feminization of poverty" perspective are quite direct about the fact that any class or racial differences that might exist among women are distinctly secondary or even irrelevant to their analysis. Diana Pearce, Director of Research for the Center of National Policy Review at Catholic University in Washington, D.C., and the one who coined the phrase "feminization of poverty," writes that her analysis is concerned with "those women who are poor because they are women. . . . For a woman, race is a relatively unimportant consideration in determining economic status."

The socialist feminist proponents of the "feminization of poverty" have incorporated the same essential vantage point into their analyses. They submerge the class and race differences that exist among women and then focus on the fate of one particular sector. In an article for *Ms.* magazine entitled "The Nouveau Poor," Barbara Ehrenreich and Karin Stallard tell the story of "Avis . . . , one of the 'nouveau poor': middle class by birth and marriage, she is now raising her three youngest children on a tenuous combination of welfare, child support, and her native Yankee ingenuity. . . . With her handsome New England features and hearty outgoing manner. . . . Not the kind of person you would expect to catch paying for her groceries with food stamps, she is in some ways typical of the new female poor."

The focus on the "human interest" dimension of this story has a political objective: to bridge the gap between two different sets of women. First and foremost, white middle class women, the actual or potential "new poor," are supposed to identify with Avis' "native Yankee ingenuity" and "New England features." Second, the "old poor," women for whom poverty is a chronic condition, are supposed to empathize with Avis' plight as a newcomer to the welfare rolls.

This attempt to bring women together by minimizing the class and race differences between them leads to distortions on three fronts. First, it paints a false picture of women. Second, it redefines poverty, its causes as well as its historic and current victims. Third, it gives rise to a political strategy that speaks to the problems faced by a certain sector of white middle class women—but which is incapable of representing the interests of those poor women who suffer not only from sex discrimination but also from class and race oppression.

# Not All Women Are Poor

- *"Virtually all women are vulnerable— a divorce or widowhood is all it takes to throw many middle class women into poverty."*[1]

This "feminization of poverty" line is wrong—empirically and theoretically—in its starting assumption that all women are in relatively equal and imminent danger of becoming poor. Women are far from a homogeneous group. Some women are indeed poor and getting poorer, but many others are rich and getting richer.

It is popular among radical sectors of the feminist movement to cast the ruling class as a bunch of greedy white men who oppress every other social group. But this description conveniently drops out the fact that women of the ruling elite enjoy the prerogatives of the rest of their class and stand in an exploitative relation to men and women of the working class. These women own and control much of the wealth of the ruling class and are not about to slip into poverty, regardless of their marital status. The only thing they have in common with working class women is their biology.

While women of the petit bourgeoisie have a long way to go to overcome sex discrimination within their class, most are not "just a husband away from poverty." It is true that, in the case of divorce, they may experience a fairly dramatic drop in income and standard of living. However, many of these women have the independent property, financial resources, education and skills to live comfortably with or without men. Furthermore, the majority of these women remarry. And, when they do, it is generally to men of their class.

In addition, the greatest impact of the affirmative action and special admissions programs won through the civil rights struggles of the 1960s has been to increase the access of women of the petit bourgeoisie and some of the upper strata of the working class to middle management, to a number of the professions and to institutions of higher edu-

cation. For example, in 1981, women made up 14% of the nation's lawyers and judges, up from 4% in 1971, while Black men had gained only 1.9% and Black women only 0.8% of these positions. In 1981, women were 22%, or one in five, of all doctors, up from 9% in 1971. By contrast, 2.7% of all doctors were Black men, and 0.7% were Black women. From 1972 to 1980, women increased their share of Master's degrees from 40% to 50% and doubled their share of doctoral degrees from one-sixth to one-third.

These women are overwhelmingly white; they are not particularly vulnerable to Reagan's social austerity program; and they do not become welfare mothers upon divorce.

# Poverty Is a Class Condition

Before [we rush] to "feminize" poverty, a note on the causes of poverty and its principal victims is in order. Poverty is overwhelmingly the problem of the "old poor." The adage "the poor get poorer" identifies the deepening emiseration of the entire lower strata of the working class.

Many hopes and illusions are fostered about the possibility of ending poverty in the U.S. But poverty is a class condition and is structural to U.S. capitalism. It is the constant companion to members of the least stable strata of the working class and afflicts men, women and children. A more or less permanent reserve of unemployed or underemployed workers is the by-product of a profit oriented economy. This is the sector of the population most devastated by dislocations in the economy and by political attacks on the class.

There are, to be sure, millions of women whose lives are shaped by sex-segregated, low-paying, low-status jobs; unemployment; and cutbacks in vital social services. But these are not women in general—they are women of the working class. The class exploitation suffered by these women guarantees that they experience women's oppression in a way qualitatively different from women of the owning classes.

Yet, even within the working class there are major differences among women. These differences occur between the sector of the class that has enjoyed stable economic conditions and a relatively high standard of living and the sector that has been kept on the lowest rungs of the economic ladder. In the U.S., it has been *racism*, not sexism, that has been the main factor determining who falls on which side of this divide. This division within the working class makes all the difference in a woman's standard of living, income, vulnerability to recessions, unemployment and poverty, the condition of her neighborhood, the schools her children attend, and her access to decent health care.

Women in the lower strata, especially minority women, have long been forced to seek wage work. In the past, minority women's participation in the labor force has been much higher than that of white women. The lower incomes of minority men required that every able-bodied adult in the family, female and male, look for work, since family survival depended on multiple wage earners. It is the lower strata of the working class, with its high concentration of minority workers, that makes up the "working poor."

However, over the years the odds have gone up that the men of this strata may either be permanently unemployed or incarcerated. Many leave their families because they can no longer fulfill the role of male breadwinner. In any case, poverty is the principal source of the enormous social pressure that leads to the disproportionately high rate of divorce among Black families.

In addition, many men and women of this strata continue to be denied the education, training and opportunity to enter the labor market at all. Thus, they are dependent on the "largesse" of the U.S. government to meet their survival needs. Given that the attitude toward the poor ranges from "benign neglect" to outright hostility, this is a precarious existence indeed.

## Sexism and Working Class Women

Of course women are affected in a particular way by poverty because of the role they play in childrearing. Since sexism has assigned them principal or sole responsibility for raising children, the meager wages that poor women receive, or the inadequate welfare checks, must stretch to sustain the kids as well. These are the factors that have locked portions of the working class into a cycle of poverty that will not be broken short of a major social transformation. But it is not these women (or men) that the "feminization of poverty" advocates are primarily concerned about. Their main focus is on the "Avises" of the world—the so-called "nouveau poor," the women who had become accustomed to economic stability and for whom not having quite enough to make ends meet comes as a rude shock.

Poverty has, in fact, claimed some new victims. Many women who were part of the more stable and comfortable sector of the working class have been caught in the squeeze between two trends. First, over the past 40 years, white women's participation in the labor force has risen dramatically to 50%, almost catching up with the 53% of minority women who work. Since World War II the deepening exploitation of the working class has made the two-wage family the norm and the only way to maintain a comfortable standard of living. Entry into the paid labor force has been a double-edged sword. On one hand, it affords women an important measure of economic independence from men. On the other hand, since women's incorporation into the workforce takes place on a discriminatory basis, their substandard wages mean that they face economic hardship if they become the sole support of their families.

Secondly, the increasing instability of the "nuclear family" has meant that more and more women from the stable strata of the working class find themselves in exactly this position. When the men in two-parent families leave, the standard of living of these families drops, both because of the women's low-wage status and because of the vacuum of social supports available for raising children. In the current period of social austerity, the lower strata is growing in size and changing in composition. New social groups are being forced to face the bottom-line realities of U.S. capitalism, creating the "new poor." Among them are the women caught in the nexus of these two social trends—the women for whom poverty has been "feminized."

But, before taking pity of the plight of the "nouveau poor," it might be useful to recall that

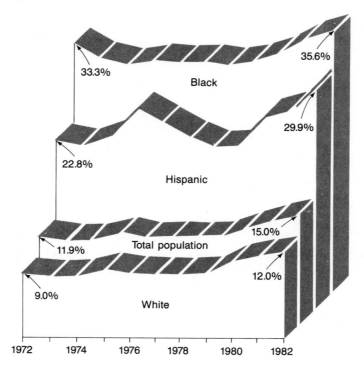

**FIGURE 1** Poverty Rates in the United States, 1972–1982

For each category, percentage of the population living below the poverty level.
Hispanic people may be of either race. Source: U.S. Bureau of the Census.

women who thought that the color line and a working husband would protect them from the worst that capitalism has to offer have shown no particular concern for the permanently impoverished sectors of the U.S. population. The oppressive conditions faced by the poor were acceptable and easily overlooked, as long as they mainly affected those people whose poverty was viewed as almost a genetic deformity—the "coloreds" and "foreigners." Poverty has been rediscovered now that increasing numbers of working class whites are in danger of defaulting on their mortgage to the "American Dream."

Whether this sector will establish political unity with the "old poor" or whether they will struggle to regain their material privileges remains to be seen. But there is nothing yet to indicate that the branch of American womanhood represented by Avis will become the most reliable combatants in

the struggle to defend the poor against political and economic attack and to strike at the class roots of poverty in the U.S. The potential for these women to identify with and fight against the conditions suffered by the "old poor" depends entirely upon the extent to which sharp and consistent struggle is taken up against racism and class oppression.

# Not All Poor People Are Women

- *"By the year 2000, all of the nation's poor will be women and their dependent children."*[2]

This prediction is a favorite in "feminization of poverty" literature. It seems to assume that by the year 2000 all of those men who are presently poor will be either rich or dead. Furthermore, it indicates that the "feminization of poverty" perspective not only provides a distorted view of women but also leaves men, minority men in particular, entirely out of the analysis.

While poverty is intensified by sexism, women's oppression is not its sole or even fundamental determinant. The profile of the poor is incomplete without putting men back into the picture. Here again the conditions faced by minority men most starkly reveal the life conditions of the lower strata of the class. . . .

While 20 years ago 75% of Black men were employed, today an astounding 45% of all Black men do not have jobs. . . . Men who immigrate from Mexico, Central America and the Caribbean in search of work hardly fare better. The educational and employment opportunities available to Puerto Rican, Native American and Mexican-American men are severely restricted.

Thus, for many minority men, the military (poverty draft), the streets or prison have become the only remaining "career" options open. Those who do find work are generally at the lower end of the wage scale in the service and agricultural sectors of the economy.

While poor women were forced into dependence on Aid to Families with Dependent Children (AFDC) to raise the kids, it should not be forgotten that general assistance, which provided some support for adult men, was virtually eliminated some time ago. Other programs designed to improve the employment opportunities of minority men have also gotten the axe. It should not need saying, but the men who depended on such programs and services have neither disappeared nor become wealthy. In minority communities, poverty has not been "feminized." Though women face distinct kinds of difficulties and hardships, poverty is the common condition of a large portion of these communities which include men, women and children. The "feminization of poverty" analysis is unlikely to find many adherents among the women who inhabit the inner cities, ghettos, barrios and reservations of America. For these women, reality includes the fact that their male children will have only a fifty-fifty chance of ever finding a job. It includes the fact that many of the adult men of their community have

been driven close to desperation by the bitter dynamics of capitalism and racism.

## "Feminization of Poverty" or Poverty of Socialist Feminism?

- *"2 out of 3 people in poverty are women. What if we all went to the polls?"*[3]

This slogan now being popularized by feminist organizers aptly sums up the strategic implications of the "feminization of poverty" perspective. Although not everyone attracted to the "feminization of poverty" line has linked it to a definite strategy to rebuild the women's movement, the women who lead liberal feminist organizations such as NOW and the National Women's Political Caucus certainly have. For them, the "feminization of poverty" analysis provides a lever to widen the "gender gap" (the significantly greater percentage of women than of men supporting Democrats over Republicans). The issue of female poverty is seized upon as an electoral tool to cohere the Democratic Party's base of support among women voters. Of course, it is no small matter that the U.S. government is currently headed up by reactionary, anti-woman Republicans, the likes of Ronald Reagan. Supporting politicians committed to a more liberal social program is certainly in the common interest of the vast majority of women. However, there are serious problems in promoting the illusion that getting more Democrats into office can qualitatively alter, much less reverse, the trends in women's oppression, racism and poverty.

But the liberals of the feminist movement and of the Democratic Party cannot be expected to sort out the complexities of class, race and sex nor to create a program that focuses on the issues that most affect working class women. What is extremely disturbing, however, is that some of the most avid and prolific adherents of the "feminization of poverty" view are those feminists who identify as socialists. In particular, the trend of social democracy, represented primarily by the DSA, has become a highly active advocate of this analysis and strategy.

One might expect that socialist feminists and social democrats would be more wary about adopting a perspective that, in its origins, explicitly drops class and race out of consideration. Quite to the contrary, these particular socialists have built a political career wishing that the knotty problems of race and class that divide women would simply do a disappearing act. "Feminization of poverty" as a strategy provides a new magic wand—attractive because of its seeming concern for the poor and oppressed.

The incidence of women's oppression and poverty is a critical question which does shape the survival of peoples of color and significant sectors of the rest of the U.S. working class. However, promoting the "feminization of poverty" as the issue that can "unite women across class, race, age and sexual preference" is a highly dubious enterprise. Feminist strategies that seek to unite women across the class spectrum while remaining oblivious both to the particularities of the conditions faced by minority and poor women and to the oppression suffered by minority and other working class men have always doomed the women's movement to remaining under the hegemony of white women of the middle classes. The "feminization of poverty" analysis and strategy promises to be a repeat performance.

The "feminization of poverty" will certainly be projected, with greater frequency as the 1984 elections approach, as the guide to women's fightback in the 1980s and as the antidote to Reaganism. But, this analysis should be treated with great suspicion by the left. It draws the class line incorrectly, ejecting minority and other working class men from the fight against poverty while including women who are not threatened by poverty at all. It envisions no independent voice for working class forces in the women's movement. It must be rejected as an analysis of women's condition and a strategy for women's liberation.[4]

---

[1]*From* Poverty in the American Dream/Women and Children First, *by Karin Stallard, Barbara Ehrenreich and Holly Sklar.*

[2]*From the 1980* National Advisory Council on Economic Opportunity *report to then-President Carter and cited in* Ms. *magazine, July/August 1982, and the* Guardian, *June 29, 1983.*

[3]*Slogan of the East Bay Women's Coalition.*

[4]*In preparing this discussion paper we have primarily used the following sources:* A Dream Deferred: The Economic Status of Black Americans, *The Center for the Study of Social Policy, Washington, D.C., July 1983.* Unemployment and Underemployment among Blacks, Hispanics, & Women, *U.S. Commission on Civil Rights, Nov. 1982.* A Growing Crisis—Disadvantaged Women and Their Children, *U.S. Commission on Civil Rights, May 1983.* Equal Employment Opportunity for Women: U.S. Policies, *U.S. Dept. of Labor, Office of the Secretary, Women's Bureau, 1982.*

---

# CAN THIS LINE BE SAVED?

The "feminization of poverty" analysis has recently been given a dramatic face-lift. In particular, the pamphlet entitled *Poverty in the American Dream—Women and Children First*, by Karin Stallard, Barbara Ehrenreich and Holly Sklar is a significant improvement on the article entitled the "Nouveau Poor" written by the same authors for *Ms.* magazine in August 1982.

The pamphlet more consistently incorporates the conditions faced by minority women and includes many individual stories of women of color struggling to survive the rigors of the welfare system or low-wage jobs. In addition, in recounting the story of Avis (whose fine New England features were a focal point of the *Ms.* article), the most blatant appeal to WASP interests is dropped. The character trait that enables Avis to make ends meet is transformed from "native Yankee ingenuity" to a colorless "thriftiness." Presumably, these kinds of changes come as the result of some criticism directed at the social democratic advocates of the "feminization of poverty." To the extent that these writers have been forced to take some note of the considerable material differences among women, this is a positive development.

However, the pamphlet does not correct any of the basic flaws in the "feminization of poverty" analysis. Once again, all women are depicted as confronting essentially the same economic prospects. And, once again, minority and poor men are entirely absent from the picture. The pamphlet contains such tell-tale bloopers as the following:

- *"While individual women moved up the career ladder, women as a class slid backwards, with those who were doubly discriminated against—women of color—taking the heaviest losses."*

Women of color have, indeed, taken the heaviest losses. But it is simply not true that "women as a class slid backwards." Women of a *particular* class did the sliding. But women of the petit bourgeoisie and ruling class (who represent more than just "individual women") have done just fine.

- *". . . there is a fundamental difference between male and female poverty: for men, poverty is often the consequence of unemployment and a job is generally an effective remedy. While female poverty often exists even when a woman works full-time."*

What this has conveniently obscured is that the effective remedy of employment is absolutely unavailable to large numbers of men. True, sexism imposes an additional burden on poor, women-headed households since, in the majority of instances, the children stay with the mother. But this does not negate the *fundamental similarities* between the causes of male and female poverty. Both are caused by unemployment and underemployment in an economic system that regenerates an impoverished layer of the working class made up of women, men and children.

- *"The short-lived 'war on poverty' has become a war on the poor in which women and children are the main casualties. . . . Women are the first fired, last hired and lowest paid in the best of times."*

In attempting to capitalize on the consciousness developed to target the oppression of minority peoples, the authors have converted "last hired, first fired" into a feminist slogan. Thus, the historic racialization of poverty in the U.S. is effectively downplayed as is the fact that it is minority women whose economic condition is the *main* factor behind the escalation in female poverty.

The "feminization of poverty" analysis distorts reality and cannot be salvaged by the addition of references to women of color. This is because the "feminization of poverty" framework, even the new and improved version, highlights the commonality of all women as a group (*"virtually all women are vulnerable"*), thereby *glossing* over the class and racial privilege enjoyed by white women of the middle and upper classes. At the same time, this analysis argues for the fundamental difference between male and female poverty, thereby driving a wedge between poor and minority women on the one hand and their class brothers on the other. In conclusion, the "feminization of poverty" analysis misleads both the overall struggle against poverty and the struggle to improve the condition of poor women.

# THE POLITICAL ECONOMY OF BLACK FAMILY LIFE

## Robert Staples

*This article reviews the changes in Black life
and its relationship to larger sociological
factors that are responsible for current Afro-
American family patterns. The author points
out the larger economic changes occurring
in the United States and their implications
for the future trajectory of Black family
trends. The author concludes with a best-case
scenario and some recommendations for
strengthening Black families.*

Any discussion of the changes that have occurred in the black family over the last 35 years commonly assumes that black family problems are a function of the decline of familial values and the triumph of hedonism over the discipline and perseverance necessary for marital stability. In some quarters the old canard is that slavery and its concomitants destroyed the value of family life for many Afro-Americans. But any objective analysis of marital and family patterns in the United States would reveal a weakening of the patriarchal, monogamous and nuclear family for all racial groups during the past third of a century.

One remarkable and understated fact is that the statistics used as an indicator of black family determination 20 years ago are almost the same for white families in the decade of the 1980s. The direction of change, although not necessarily the cause, has been the same for all racial groups in American society. However, the definition and interpretation of those phenomena tend to be negative when applied to black Americans. As Marie Peters once noted:

When blacks are studied, so-called problem populations are often the focus of research— single parents, parents of emotionally disturbed, mentally retarded, or academically nonachieving or delinquent children and youths, or low income families.[1]

## Decline of Nuclear Family

There are a combination of etiological forces in the decline of the nuclear family, among them the weakening of the patriarchy by the increasing economic and psychological independence of women, the sexual revolution, greater mobility and urbanization patterns and the liberalization of divorce laws. While many of those same causes impact on black family instability, a more central source appears to be the declining participation of black males in the labor force.

I will address the reasons behind the growing unemployment and underemployment of black males and how these problems contribute to the shortage of black mates, the increase in single parent households, marital dissolutions and out-of-wedlock births.

Historically, black men have endured higher rates of unemployment than white males. In 1950 that difference was only twice the rate of white males, but in 1986 it is three times greater.[2] This increasing racial differential in unemployment rates occurred during the 1970s and 1980s, a period when affirmative action regulations and anti-discrimina-

From *The Black Scholar* 17 (September/October 1986):2–
11. Copyright 1986 by Robert Staples. Reprinted by
permission.

tion laws should have reduced the racial unemployment gap. Other forces were at work, nonracial forces, that produced racially based outcomes.

Foremost among those forces were the Vietnam War and the Watergate scandals, events which created a crisis of confidence in many American institutions and leaders. The result was a cultural narcissism among whites that took the form of reduced support for measures designed to foster racial equality and a desire to keep a higher share of personal income by cutting government expenditures on the poor.

The Reagan Administration and opponents of racial equality have taken the ideological initiative and redefined affirmative action as reverse racism. Programs designed to assist the poor were interpreted as creating black dependency on government handouts and as disrupting family life. Those social programs were cut, and tax cuts favoring the wealthy were used to redistribute wealth—sort of a Robin Hood in reverse.

Moreover, employment in government service, an important source of jobs for blacks, declined when government agencies used tax monies to subcontract services to private businesses. Subcontracting was particularly true in defense work that was generally given to private firms whose work force was largely white and male.

That these changes occurred under the Reagan Administration was no coincidence. In Reagan's re-election campaign of 1984, only 10 percent of the black population voted for him compared to 65 percent of the white male population.

## Job Flight to Suburbs

While the Reagan Administration set the tone and direction of the black unemployment trends, other forces were at work. One of them was the shift of jobs from the racially diverse inner cities to the largely white suburbs. Almost two-thirds of all new office construction now takes place in the suburbs.[3] Consequently, many jobs are moving away from the poorly skilled and displaced racial minorities. As Kutscher has noted, "There are two reasons for that. Those who need jobs do not have the abilities re-

quired, and jobs are leaving aging cities and manufacturing areas for the suburbs."[4]

Along with the shift of jobs from cities to suburbs has been the fact that the greatest increase in jobs has occurred in small businesses, another factor that works against blacks. Small businesses often recruit workers through informal means and look for a "personality fit" in workers. This type of recruitment often means that currently entrenched white workers bring in their friends and relatives to work for the same firm, a process that largely excludes blacks.

The advantage for blacks of huge, bureaucratically organized, strongly led organizations is that it is easier to change their racial employment patterns than in small ones. Small businesses hire friends and relatives or people of the same ethnic background, and the personal prejudices of the employer can be decisive.

A critical factor in black unemployment trends has been the decline of industrial manufacturing jobs and the proliferation of jobs in the service and information processing spheres. In 1986, only 25.2 million Americans are employed in goods-producing industries, a net loss of 700,000 since the peak in 1979, compared to 74.5 million now earning their living in services, an all-time high and net increase of 10.1 million since 1979.[5]

## Non-Union Jobs

These services jobs often require no specific skills beyond literacy and tend to be non-unionized, meaning they lend themselves to subjective, and hence arbitrary, recruitment and employment practices. Industrial manufacturing jobs had the distinction of being highly unionized, with retention being determined by seniority, not employer discretion. These jobs rarely required standardized tests for entry level jobs and the demonstration of job proficiency was fairly precise.

It is alleged that large numbers of black males lack the minimal literacy skills necessary for employment in the service and information processing industries. A shocking 44 percent of black males are estimated to be functional illiterates, a considerably higher number than 30 years ago.[6] Certainly, the responsibility for these high rates lie with the public school system which promotes these males without their having obtained reading and writing skills. The federal government has decreased its funding of public education over the past seven years.

In the South, the causes of black male illiteracy might be attributed to the fact that the increasingly black public schools are now controlled by whites. For example, in Georgia where 52 percent of the state's 187 school districts have a majority black student population, only four school superintendents are black, and only one school outside Atlanta is black-controlled.[7]

## Black Underground Economy

A constellation of interlocking factors has pushed black males out of the labor force and into the shadow economy of drug sales, stolen goods and petty thefts, increasing their percentage of the American jail population to 49 percent.[8] The malfunctioning of America's capitalist economy has created a million millionaires and forced several millions into a new kind of poverty. America's constant emphasis on competition and the loss of millions of jobs to foreign nations using cheap labor to provide inexpensive imports has propelled most literate high school graduates to seek college degrees as an entry into the white collar sphere of the private sector.

Black males face a double dilemma in this evolving economy: They are not competitive with white and black women whose literacy and interpersonal skills are better, and the menial jobs that once were their monopoly must now be fought over with newly arriving third world immigrants. All three groups, women, black men, and third world immigrants, are exploited by this situation. Of the white collar jobs added since 1980, mostly occupied by women, a third of them were in retail where the average annual salary in 1980 was $9,063, below the government's poverty level of $10,000 for a family of four.[9]

## White Indifference

Meanwhile, the white male electorate and their wives, who must depend on their husbands' higher income, have twice elected to political office an administration widely perceived as representing the interests of the wealthy. The small benefits that have trickled down have gone largely to middle class white males. Between 1980–86, government expenditures on the military increased by 100 percent, and the major beneficiaries have been white males.[10] The trillion dollars this country has spent on its military buildup has diverted capital away from the improvement of basic industries in such vital areas as steel, automobiles and machine tools, the very sector where more black men were located.

A false sense of gender and racial self-interest has led members of the white population to ignore such things as a jobless rate of 40 percent among young black Americans. As Richard Reeves has observed: "One of the secrets of the acceptance of the doubled crisis in unemployment is the fact that unemployment among adult white males is still in the old range, below six percent."[11] Certainly, the captains of industry would not want full employment, which would create a situation where employers would have to bid for workers rather than the reverse.

## The Contemporary Black Family

As a basic element in black social organization, the family is an institution which is of considerable importance to the history, present status, and future of the black community. Although the charge was incorrect, Moynihan's thesis, that "at the heart of the deterioration of Negro society is the deterioration of the Negro family," gives recognition to the importance of black family life in shaping the personality of black children, carrying out survival functions and adapting its form to the requisites of a society that is admittedly hostile to people of color.[12]

Because the black family has been an adaptive unit, its form and dynamics have varied according to the conditions black people have faced. When times have been harsh, the family has been a strong and resiliant institution. In periods of relative "prosperity" or group disunity, the family has weakened under the stresses and strains common to a fragile arrangement of diverse personalities into a solidarity unit.

It can reasonably be stated that the federal government's efforts to promote black family solidarity have been misguided and ineffective. The purpose of this article is to review the changing status of black families and its implications for future efforts to strengthen black family life. In describing the contemporary condition of black families, I have already attempted to deal with the larger sociological factors responsible for current black family patterns. My intent is to point out the changes that are taking place and the trajectory of future trends among black families.

# Economic Deprivation

It is necessary to understand the interplay of economics on black families' lives in order to conceptualize the conditions under which they function— or fail to function—as a viable system. Ever since black people were released from slavery, economic deprivation has been a fact of life. Over the past 40 years the rate of unemployment among blacks has been steadily twice that of whites. The National Urban League's hidden unemployment index shows the real unemployment rate of black men to be around 25 percent.[13] Men who cannot find work not only have trouble maintaining a stable marital and family life but often cannot find a woman willing to marry them in the first place. Only 55 percent of all black men with incomes of less than $5,000 a year are married in comparison to 80 percent of those earning between $15,000 and $20,000. As incomes rise so do the number of black men who marry.[14]

Intact black families have a median income of $13,598 a year compared to $24,603 a year for white families. Not only is black family income 56 percent as much as white family income, but that figure indicates a drop in the ratio of 61 percent in 1969. If

adjustments for inflation are made, black families were slightly worse off five years later. This does not even consider the fact that many more black families (two-thirds) derive their family income from multiple earners than white households (one-half).

The implications of those economic facts are obvious when we observe that the higher the income of blacks, the more likely we will find a biparental family. When we look at black families headed by women, we see that in 1981 they had an average income of only $7,510 a year, approximately 38 percent of the earnings of intact black families in 1981.[15]

# Black Sex Ratio

According to the Census Bureau, there are many more black women than black men in the U.S. over the age of 14. This is the official sex ratio. That number of marriageable black men does not exist if we look at other forces that tend to make black men ineligible for marriage, such as the number in prison, the number in the military and the number who died at an early age. Mortality rates among black men are three times higher than among white men between the ages of 15 and 30.

For example, according to mortality data in the state of Michigan, black men are losing almost an average of one year a decade from their life expectancy. In addition, many are drug and alcohol abusers, some in mental institutions, a fairly large number are marrying interracially, and a significant number have joined the Gay Liberation Movement.[16]

As a result of the shortage of marriageable men, there are large numbers of female-headed households among blacks. These houses are regarded as pathological because we live in a society in which a man is expected to be at the helm of the family ship, and that society is not structured to accommodate families in which women are the heads. Approximately 48 percent of all black families are headed by women, and it is estimated that at the end of the decade the majority of black families will be headed by women.[17]

# Female-Headed Households

For a number of reasons, the proportion of female-headed households is increasing among all racial groups, including whites. But a major difference is that there are not many opportunities for black women to form monogamous relationships. This does not mean that these female-headed households cannot meet their functional obligations to carry out what we call the functional prerequisite of the family.

One of the major reasons we find pathological social indexes associated with the female-headed households is that they are confounded with problems of poverty. If you look at female-headed households among both blacks and whites, you will find that the majority of them have an income less than $10,000 a year, defined by the Labor Bureau as the minimum poverty level. The majority of female-headed households are poor, because society still consigns women to the lowest paying jobs.[18]

# Role of Black Men

The basis of a stable family rests on the willingness, and ability, of men and women to marry, bear and rear children and fulfill socially prescribed familial roles. In the case of women those roles have traditionally been defined as the carrying out of domestic functions such as cooking and cleaning, giving birth to children and socializing them, and providing sexual gratification, companionship and emotional support to their husbands. There is abundant evidence that black women are willing and able to fulfill these roles.

Conversely the roles of men in the family are more narrowly confined to economic provider and family leader. There are indications that a majority of black American males cannot implement those roles. When it comes to a choice between remaining single or getting married, individuals often do a cost-benefit analysis. Marriage is frequently a *quid pro quo* arrangement. The desire to enter and maintain a conjugal relationship is contingent on women's and men's perceptions of the benefits that can be acquired and, conversely, with the anticipated costs.

When selecting a mate, black women must consider the nature of the pool from which they will draw. In 98 percent of marriages with a black female bride, the groom will be a black male. Hence, the female's pool consists of the unmarried black males with a variety of attributes. The most distinguishing characteristics of that pool is the excess number of women over men during the marriageable years.

According to the U.S. Census Bureau there are almost 1.5 million more black women than men over the age of 14. By the Census Bureau's own account, the undercount of black males means that about 925,000 black males exist that were not added to the black population total. It should be noted that the uncounted black male is likely to be transient and unemployed.[19] Since there is an excess number of black males at birth, the subsequent shortage of black males over the age of 14 must be attributed to their higher infant mortality rate and the considerably greater mortality rate of young black males through such means as homicide, accidents, suicide, drug overdoses and war casualties.

# Unemployment and Underemployment

The biggest problem for black women, however, is not the quantity in the available supply of potential mates, but the quality. Whereas black women may select a mate on the basis of a number of attributes, a minimum prerequisite is that he be gainfully and regularly employed.

According to a study by Joe and Yu, almost a majority of working age black males fail to meet those minimum prerequisites. After an analysis of the economic and census data, Joe and Yu concluded that 46 percent of the 8.8 million black men of working age were not in the labor force. Based on 1982 statistics, they found 1.2 million black men were unemployed, 1.8 million had dropped out of the labor force, 186,000 were in prison and 925,000 were classified as "missing" because the Census Bureau says it could not locate them.[20]

This study, moreover, overstates the number of "desirable" and available black males in the marriage pool. Even with the census undercount, there are still a half million more black women over the age of 14 than black men. We must also subtract from the marriage pool black men with certain characteristics that substantially outnumber black women. Among those characteristics would be blacks serving in the Armed Forces. Approximately 90 percent of them will be male. The Census Bureau reports that there were 415,000 blacks under arms in 1982, representing 20 percent of all U.S. military personnel.

It can be reliably stated that a large number of those black males had poor prospects for employment in the civilian labor force. While the salary and other benefits of military personnel have improved in recent years and a number of black soldiers are currently married, the military does take a number of marriage-age black males out of circulation by stationing them in foreign posts and isolated military stations. Furthermore, once their period of enlistment ends, black veterans experience a higher rate of unemployment, even in relation to black civilian males with no military service.[21] Hence, military service only postpones the entry of black males into the ranks of the unemployed, one reason black males have a higher rate of re-enlistment than their white counterparts.

## Marriage Pool

Included in the factors that reduce the number of desirable black males in the marriage pool is the high rate of underemployed black males. The U.S. Civil Rights Commission reported that black men are overeducated for their jobs and have greater difficulty translating education into suitable occupations. Even college educated black males have an unemployment rate four times greater than their white peers.

Among black males employed in the labor force, one out of three will suffer from unemployment in a given year.[22] These facts serve to explain why black marriages dissolve, not why they never take place. In Hampton's study, the respondents who reported the highest number of employment problems had a marital disruption rate three times higher than the overall rate for the sample.[23]

Another group of black males regarded as undesirable or unavailable are those confined to mental institutions or otherwise mentally unstable. While their exact numbers are unknown, black males are more likely to be committed to mental institutions than black women. Furthermore, the constraints of racism are such that blacks are more likely to suffer from mental distress. In 1970, 240 non-whites per 100,000 population were confined to mental institutions compared to 162 whites per 100,000 population. Blacks also used community health centers at a rate almost twice their proportion in the general population.

The rate of drug and alcohol abuse is much greater among the black population, especially males, based on their overrepresentation among patients receiving treatment services. It is estimated that as many as one-third of the young black males in the inner city have a serious drug problem.[24] Many of the mentally unstable, drug and alcohol abusers will have been included in the figures on black males who have dropped out of the labor force or are incarcerated in prison. The magnitude of the problem simply reinforces the fact that black women are severely disadvantaged in choosing from the eligible and desirable males in the marriage pool.

A large category of black males who fit into the desirable group are not available. By all reliable estimates the black male homosexual population is considerably larger than that of similar women, based on the often quoted Kinsey estimate that 10 percent of the adult male population is homosexual. That would mean about 800,000 black men are not available to heterosexual black women.[25]

Of course, many of these gay men do marry, for a variety of reasons, and serve well in the roles of husband and father. Due to the increasing public acceptance of overt male homosexuality, it is reasonable to expect that fewer gay males will choose to enter into heterosexual marriages in the future. Finally, it should be noted that black men marry outside their race at a rate twice as great as that of black women.[26]

## College Educated Blacks

Although the shortage and desirability of black males in the marriage pool affects the non-college educated black woman's marriage chances, the college educated black female is not spared the problem if she desires to marry within her race and socioeconomic level. In 1980, there were 133,000 more black women enrolled in college than black men, about 57 percent of all black college students. However, black male students have a much higher attrition rate than their female peers.

In the University of California system, for instance, only 12 of every 100 black male students graduate within four years. Thus, in 1981, 36,200 of 60,700 bachelor's degrees awarded to blacks went to women, or 62 percent. Between 1976 and 1981, black women receiving bachelor's degrees increased by nine percent; comparable black males declined by nine percent. These same trends existed for graduate degrees during the years 1976–1981. At the master's level, black women declined by 12 percent and black men by 21 percent. At the doctoral level, black men declined by 10 percent and black women increased at a rate of 29 percent.[27]

College educated black women do have the option of marrying men of lesser education and making a viable choice. In the past, as many as 50 percent of college educated black women married men of a lower socioeconomic level. Increasingly, however, there is resistance among these women to marrying down. Almost one-third of college educated black women remain unmarried past the age of 30.

These women face a similar shortage in the marriage pool of male high school graduates and must compete with lesser educated black women for these same men. Also, such middle level men tend to marry early and have the most stable marriages in the black community. The marriage patterns of college educated black males tend to put college educated black women at a disadvantage. Many of these men marry women of a lower educa-

tional level, and the interracial marriage rate is highest in this group of black men.[28]

## Future of the Black Family

The future of the black family is inextricably tied up with the current and future status of the black male. Current figures indicate that 46 percent of black males between the ages of 16 and 26 are not active participants in the American labor force, a figure closely associated with the 48 percent of black families headed by women and the 52 percent of black children born out of wedlock. If the employment rate of black men does not improve, demographic projections are that 59 percent of black families will be headed by women by the year 1990, and that only eight percent of black children born in the year 1980 will spend all their childhood lives with two parents.[29]

Unless unforeseen social forces reverse current trends, the future is likely to bring one of the first cases in history where women have achieved superiority over men in the vital areas of education, occupation and income. Already black women are more educated than black men at every level except the doctorate and should exceed them in the number of doctorates received by the year 1990. The 1980 census reveals that 15.8 percent of black women are managers and professionals compared to 10.8 percent of black men. College educated black women currently earn 95 percent of the income of college educated black men.[30]

As black women gradually move ahead of black men, it is possible that a role reversal may take place. Since black women will not need to marry a man in order to attain a decent standard of living, many of them may begin to select dating partners and husbands on the basis of sex appeal rather than the traditional criterion of socioeconomic status. Conversely, black men may become the gender that barter their sexuality for a "good marriage" with a successful woman.

## Shortage of Black Men

The shortage of black men who are desirable and available for marriage will continue into the 21st century. Black women may adapt to their situation by a variety of means. Lesbianism may increasingly be viewed as a viable option by women who want their emotional and companionship needs met. Among the women who experience the greatest shortage of men, those over the age of 60, a kind of gray lesbianism may emerge in response to the unavailability of men.

In the college educated segment of the black female population, marriages to men of different races may become one of the adaptive responses to the male shortage. Some of them may seriously consider a more formalized participation in polygamous relationships or liaisons with married men instead of remaining celibate and childless their entire lives.

For the vast majority of black women, there will continue to be some involvement with black men. Chances are that many will continue to be sexually active at an early age, bear children out of wedlock and rear them with the assistance of a female based kin network. Black women will likely have varying periods of cohabitation with men, but legal marriage rates will continue to decline except for college educated black males, the one subgroup in the black community not plagued by low income, high rates of unemployment and a shortage of compatible mates.

## Demographic Changes

As for black men, their employment chances will rise or fall with changes in the economy and other demographic changes in American society. If the economy continues its transformation from a goods production to a service dominated economy, black men's participation rate in the labor force may decline since the latter type of economy favors female workers. Such a transformation will mean black men's continued dependence on the underground economy, cohabitation with a woman of some means or living at home with their parents.

One countervailing force could be the shortage of young workers predicted by the year 2000, when large numbers of the baby boom generation reach retirement age. Demographic projections show that by the year 2000, 40 percent of the school population graduating into the work force will be black.[31] Given a substantial improvement in black employment, the likely result will be an increase in marriage rates and a decline in out-of-wedlock birth rates.

These demographic changes, however, are already being manifested in many parts of the United States, with no discernible improvement in the employment prospects for young black males. While employers in low wage industries, such as fast food outlets, are complaining of an inability to fill job vacancies in the affluent suburbs, there are still more young workers than jobs in the central cities. Young white workers are often obtaining part-time and summer work at wages of $9 to $10 an hour while black teenagers find it difficult to secure minimum wage jobs at $3.35 an hour. Many black teenagers rightfully perceive fast food and other minimum wage jobs, even when available, as dead-end positions that have no long-term payoff.

Other barriers to employment remain. A director of a youth employment program states that "minorities have a 30 percent chance of being hired when dispatched to an interview. But when we send someone who is not a minority, they get hired."[32] Sadly, these teenagers often find themselves competing with their older neighbors for such jobs. This sharp distinction between summer job prospects in central cities and the suburbs belies the rosy projections for young workers in the 1990s.

## Full Employment

A best case scenario for black families would be the election of an enlightened government that would provide the conditions for the strengthening of black family life. First, and foremost, would be the implementation of a full employment policy. This policy would require a substantial redistribution of income from the relatively affluent to the poor accomplished by a rigidly enforced system of progressive income taxation and the reduction of military expenditures to the bare minimum necessary to defend the country from an attack by foreign nations.

A huge federal bureaucracy would not be created since it would only need to fund already existing projects and agencies such as highway construction, housing, education, the postal service, water conservation, public parks, child care and other services. There would be no reason to make the system racially based since blacks would automatically share in the benefits of a full employment economy. Some government-financed training programs in community based institutions would be necessary to develop and improve skills of some undereducated workers.

Another governmental act would be the formulation of a family allowance plan, already in effect in most Western nations. This family allowance should be set at the level most economists agree is a "good" standard of living, not the poverty level which only permits families to exist at the lowest standard of misery. The family allowance would be provided to all American families, reducing the stigma of current welfare programs, and the rigid system of progressive income tax rates would retrieve it from more affluent families.[33]

A family allowance plan would permit all families to have a decent income and to work out other difficulties in their relationship as best they can. While it will work to the advantage of most American families, a family allowance should benefit black families most by lifting their ability to create and maintain a family from under the scourge of economic pressure.

[1] Marie Peters, "Racial Socialization of Young Black Children," in Black Children: Social, Educational and Parental Environments, eds. H. McAdoo and J. McAdoo (Beverly Hills, California: Sage, 1986).

[2] Lynn C. Burbridge. "Black Unemployment: Current Trends," Focus, April 1986: 6–7.

[3] "Back to the Suburbs," Newsweek, April 21, 1986: 60.

[4] Ronald Kutscher quoted: "Jobs Up, But Are They Helping the Poor?" The San Francisco Sunday Examiner and Chronicle, June 8, 1986, p. A-12.

[5] Paul Shinoff, "The Elusive Idea of Full Employment," San Francisco Examiner, April 24, 1986, p. C-7.

[6] Jonathon Kozol, "Illiteracy in America" (New York: Morrow, 1985).

[7] Dudley Clendinen, "Keeping Control: Southern Whites Keep Their Grip on the Black Schools," The New York Times, June 23, 1986, p. 11.

[8] Robert Staples, "American Racialism and High Crime Rates," The Western Journal of Black Studies 8 (Summer 1984): 62–72.

[9] "Jobs Up, But Are They Helping the Poor?" loc. cit.

[10] Lester Brown, et al., State of the World 1986 (Washington, D.C.: Worldwatch Institute, 1986).

[11] Richard Reeves, "A Look at Unemployment," San Francisco Chronicle, June 13, 1986, p. 85.

[12] Daniel P. Moynihan, The Negro Family: the Case for National Action (Washington, D.C.: U.S. Government Printing Office, 1965).

[13] National Urban League Research Department, Quarterly Economic Report on the Black Worker 2 (Spring 1975): 1–8.

[14] P. Glick and K. Mills, Black Families: Marriage Partners and Living Arrangements (Atlanta University Press, 1975).

[15] United States Bureau of the Census, America's Black Population, 1970 to 1982: A Statistical View, July 1983 (Washington, D.C.: U.S. Government Printing Office, 1983).

[16] Robert Staples, Black Masculinity: The Black Male's Role in American Society (San Francisco: The Black Scholar Press, 1982).

[17] T. Joe and P. Yu, The "Flip-Side" of Black Families Headed by Woman: The Economic Status of Black Men (Washington, D.C.: The Institute for the Study of Social Policy, 1984).

[18] U.S. Bureau of the Census, loc. cit.

[19] Joe and Yu, loc. cit.

[20] Ibid.

[21] James Stewart and Joseph Scott, "The Institutional Decimation of Black Males," Western Journal of Black Studies 2 (Summer 1978): 82–92.

[22] Staples, 1982, loc. cit.

[23] Robert Hampton, "Institutional Decimation, Marital Exchange and Disruption in Black Families," Western Journal of Black Studies (Summer 1980): 132–139.

[24] United States Department of Health, Education and Welfare, Health Status of Minorities and Low-Income Groups (Washington, D.C.: U.S. Government Printing Office, 1979).

[25] Alan Bell and Martin Weinberg, Homosexualities (New York: Simon and Schuster, 1978).

[26] Staples, 1982, loc. cit.

[27] National Center for Education Statistics, Participation of Black Students in Higher Education: A Statistical Profile from 1970–71 to 1980–81 (Washington, D.C.: U.S. Department of Education, 1983).

[28] Robert Staples, The World of Black Singles: Changing Patterns of Male-Female Relations (Westport, Connecticut: Greenwood Press, 1981).

[29] Thomas Espenshade and Rachel Braun, "Life Course Analysis and Multistate Demography: An Application to Marriage, Divorce and Remarriage," Journal of Marriage and the Family 44 (November 1982): 1025–1036.

[30] U.S. Bureau of the Census, 1983, loc. cit.

[31] U.S. Bureau of the Census, Estimates of the Populations of the United States, by Age, Sex and Race: 1980 to 1985 (Washington, D.C.: U.S. Government Printing Office, 1986).

[32] George Suncin quoted in "Summer Vocation Travails," San Francisco Examiner, June 8, 1986, p. D-1.

[33] Alfred J. Kahn and Sheila B. Kamerman, "Social Assistance: An Eight-County Overview," White Plains, New York. The Institute for Socioeconomic Studies 8 (Winter 1983–84): 93–112.

# 10 / Health Issues

## SUBSTANCE ABUSE AND THE BLACK FAMILY CRISIS:
## An Overview

### Robert Staples

*The author reviews the statistical data and popular literature on substance abuse among Black Americans and its impact on Black family stability. He also looks at the effect on Black family life of the increasing arrest rate of Black males and the foster home placement and drug exposure of Black children, as a result of drug sales and consumption. The adaptation of the extended Black family to this situation and the role of racism are delineated.*

In the 1980s the focus of social concerns changed from sexism, racism, poverty, and war to drugs, animal abuse, and the destruction of the environment. While the latter problems have a legitimate claim on the society's attention and resources, it is clear that they represent little threat to the prevailing social order as presently defined. Moreover, only one of those issues, drugs, directly affects Afro-American communities as a salient concern. And, the issue of drugs is viewed by the public as mostly a "Black problem." Almost all of the media coverage is of Blacks dealing drugs in a public area. As the government's efforts to control the distribution and consumption of illicit drugs, such as cocaine, have escalated, the percentage of Blacks arrested and jailed for drug-related offenses increased from 30 percent in 1984 to 38 percent in 1988.[1] These statistics have led many public officials to declare that the war on drugs has, in effect, become a war on Black people.[2]

The war on drugs may be doomed to failure, because drugs are legally defined as the problem only because their purchase and consumption are illegal. Alcohol, prescription drugs, and cigarettes combined may be more destructive of individuals and the social order than the illegal drugs. For instance, the health effects of alcohol consumption are alarmingly devastating to Black people. In Black males the death rate for cirrhosis of the liver was 70 percent higher than in comparable white males in

Previously unpublished paper, 1990.

1987. The Black female death rate from the same cause was almost double that of white females.[3] In general, alcoholism is highly implicated in job absenteeism, motor vehicle fatalities, suicides, violent crimes, and homicides.[4]

While alcohol is legal, drugs such as cocaine and heroin are not. Hence, the government's efforts to control substance abuse is limited to the illicit drugs. Certainly, members and leaders of the Afro-American community agree that drugs are the greatest scourge of the Black community. According to social psychologist Wade Nobles, the prevalence of drugs in the Black community, with its concomitant violence, has served to reduce the quantity and quality of Black life. "Substance abuse," he says, "in many ways is becoming an American condition. However, in relation to the African-American community, substance abuse can be judged as an instrument of genocide."[5] At the Second Annual Conference on the Black Family and Crack Cocaine, a former drug dealer confessed, "I didn't know that I was selling death to my people when I was peddling crack. We need you to teach us to love the Black culture because the drug culture has its arms wide open for young brothers."[6]

Certainly, the health implications, especially for young Black men, from drug use are ominous. Between 1984 to 1987, the gap in life expectancy between Blacks and whites has increased from 5.6 years to 6.2 years. According to health statisticians, a white child born in 1987 could expect to live about 75.6 years while a Black child could expect to live about 69.4 years.[7] Students of this subject claim that this trend is almost entirely the result of deaths from AIDS, drug abuse, alcoholism, and car accidents. The one thing these causes have in common is that they are all preventable.[8] The causes of death that increased much more for Blacks than whites, and were the chief factors in the widening life expectancy gap, were mostly drug related. Even AIDS, a mainly sexual disease among Afro-Americans, has been largely caused by the incidence of drug use. The sharing of needles, common among heroin users, represents the primary mode of transmission of the virus in the Black population. The number of Blacks diagnosed with AIDS increased from 25 percent in 1984 to 29 percent of all AIDS cases in 1988.

In September 1988, Blacks composed about 55 percent of all AIDS cases among children under age 13.[9]

Amazingly, the devastating impact of drugs and alcohol consumption on Black mortality rates is not reflected in the various surveys comparing whites and Blacks on consumption patterns. While the surveys are sparse in number, and inconsistent in their findings, they reveal Blacks to have lower rates of mind-altering substance levels. In a report by the U.S. Department of Health and Human Services, it was found that Black youths tend to drink at slightly lower rates compared to white youths and suggest that the young Black population has a lower rate of heavy drinkers and a larger proportion of abstainers.[10] Byram and Fly also discovered that in contrast to white families, there are fewer adult members who drink, fewer friends who drink, and a greater level of family closeness in disrupted Black families than in intact families.[11] Separate studies by the FBI and the National Institute for Drug Abuse concluded that Blacks comprise only 12 percent of the United States' drug users.[12] Studies of those who consume drugs reveal slightly lower percentages for Blacks and Latinos than for whites. The consensus of national research analyzing cocaine addiction by income and race is that cocaine use in all forms, snorted, injected, or smoked, is greatest among white single men in metropolitan areas of the Northeast and West.[13] Drug therapy clinics consistently report that most of their patients are middle-class addicts with good jobs.

This disparity between the results of surveys and the conventional wisdom that drug abuse is a "Black problem" begs the question as to why the jails are full of Blacks arrested and convicted of drug-related crimes. Using the typical Black explanation that it is a racist conspiracy to commit genocide against the Black population is not sufficient. After all, the mayors and police chiefs of America's largest cities are themselves Black, and not likely to prey unfairly on their own people. Most likely, it is a function, in part, of the poverty and violence associated with drugs in the Black community. In a political climate that requires some action on the part of the government, Blacks are the easiest to arrest. Because white addicts have more to lose in terms of income, property, and reputation, they are very secretive about their addiction. They take their drugs in tight little cliques and their purchases are made in office buildings, or at somebody's home. In the Black communities, sellers standing on the corner and shootouts over drug turfs bring addicts to the attention of the police.[14]

Moreover, Black residents are often the ones demanding greater police presence in their communities, because of the murders, robberies, and other crimes associated with drugs. While the drug problem may be largely a symptom of other problems in the Afro-American community, it threatens to tear Black families asunder. Because crack cocaine (a cocaine derivative) is so accessible and cheap, it has affected Black families in a way heretofore unknown. Although drug and alcohol consumption have always been problematical for Black people, the peculiar nature of crack cocaine addiction has exacerbated the already existing problems of crime, poverty, unemployment, and racism. And it has invaded the Black family in some of the following ways:

1. Children are taking over as heads of their families largely because of their incomes from selling crack.
2. Young, pregnant mothers are risking their lives to secure the drug and, in some cases, exchanging sexual relations for it or the money to buy it.
3. Some adolescent girls are deserting their families and forming violent gangs to sell and buy crack.
4. In some communities, female addicts exceed male users for the first time in the race's history. Because many of them are in their childbearing years, there are increasing reports of drug use or drug addiction among pregnant Black women. The result is the increasing numbers of infants prenatally exposed to drugs and at risk for later developmental problems.
5. Although the extended family network in Black communities has traditionally absorbed needy children, the drug culture has created holes in its safety net. Unlike the individuals ravaged by poverty and racism, the drug-addicted individual is markedly different in behavior, temperament, and willingness to cooperate.

# Young Black Men as an Endangered Species

Recent studies indicate an increase in hard drug use and a decline in alcohol consumption among American youth. Although alcohol is legally sold, it is hardly a benign beverage when used to excess. Indeed, considering the alcohol-related deaths from drunken driving, cirrhosis of the liver, homicides, some suicides and family violence, alcohol is probably a more destructive drug than heroin and cocaine combined. Its impact on Black communities is particularly negative. The combination of economic, social, and psychological problems faced by Black youth render them vulnerable to the enticement of alcohol so readily available in their communities. Because those problems so easily interface with the patterns of alcohol consumption, alcohol abuse must be seen as more than a legal or medical problem: It is also a political problem.

Throughout America, Black youth must struggle merely to survive. Their forms of coping with Euro-American rule are often nothing more than a slow death for many of them. One of these coping mechanisms is simply to become so narcotized that their subjugation under Euro-American rule is tolerable. While alcohol consumption has become pervasive throughout the United States, young Black abusers still come from the least educated and poorest segment of the Black community. Alcohol abuse is pure and simple a way of coping with a society in which young Blacks see themselves as powerless and without any kind of future.

Institutional racism and economic marginality have forced Black males to disproportionately experience the ravages of inner city life. Unlike poor women with children they are not eligible for public welfare. Bereft of any income from legitimate sources, only a limited number of options are available to them. Many are living with their parents. Some of them may find temporary shelter with a woman who is eligible for public assistance (if no adult male is living with her). After those two options, all that is left is homelessness and public begging or participation in the underground economy. Increasingly, the sale of drugs to alienated and powerless young Black men has produced an alternative economy that can provide high wages and self-esteem to young men denied both in mainstream America. With the lack of equally successful role models in the inner city, drug dealers often become heroes to ghetto youth.

A combination of the above named forces threaten to institutionally decimate much of the Black male population. The public schools fail to provide them with marketable skills in today's economy, and increasing competition among a variety of cultural groups for the scarce jobs available place them among the most vulnerable groups to unemployment status. For those with no jobs, hence no income, commission of street crimes leads to a life-long career in prison. Those who survive by other means are still left with nothing meaningful to do in a society where money and work define masculinity. Instead, they will define their masculinity by siring children that they cannot support, and defend their masculinity by a violent response to any slight or provocation. Their time will be occupied by the use of alcohol and drugs to allow them to blot out the awareness of their superfluous existence in a country that devalues and fears them. The predictable consequences are fatherless families, homicides that occur at a rate six times higher than among white men, an early death from drug and alcohol-related causes, including acquired immune deficiency syndrome (AIDS), and a life expectancy that is the shortest of all sex-race groups.[15]

This morbid situation is not unknown or unprecedented in the history of white settler societies. The fate of the American Indian is a prototype of a similar form of genocide in this country. Similar parallels can be found among the Maoris of New Zealand and the Aboriginals of Australia. All these groups had in common a forced coexistence in a white-dominated culture that had appropriated their land or their labor. Because their conformity to Anglo Saxon demands could not be elicited, they were perceived as a continuing threat to the existence of white rule. Because the economy was able to function without them, they became excess baggage and a competitive threat to the privileges of white males. Hence, idleness and powerlessness created the opportunity for self-destruction through the use of alcohol and drugs, fratricidal violence, and suicide.[16]

Alcoholism, on the legal level, is formally known as the crime of public intoxication. This type of behavior should be considered a medical problem, not a crime. Because of the oppressive conditions under which they live, Black youth consume alcoholic beverages to cope with the stress in their lives and escape from reality. No law ever stopped a man from drinking and the medical problem of alcoholism is not going to be solved by putting people in jail.

Enforcement of this law fits well into the typical pattern of class and racial discrimination. The society creates conditions that lead Black youth into heavy drinking. It controls the disposition of licenses to engage in liquor sales. Since this is a profitable enterprise, leading to significant economic gains, few Blacks are allowed to participate in the alcoholic beverage industry. Hence, whites create the conditions that motivate Black indulgence in alcohol consumption, from which they financially benefit. Upper-class whites can do their drinking in bars, clubs, and restaurants, because of their greater wealth, where they are less exposed to arrest for intoxication. Poor Black youth, who live in substandard homes, are more likely to remain in the streets, and the constant surveillance of the ghetto by police forces makes them more vulnerable to detection and arrest.

Drug abuse is another medical problem that is defined as a crime. Although Blacks make up only about 12 percent of those who regularly used illicit drugs in 1988, they accounted for some 38 percent of all drug arrests in 1988.[17] A number of studies have found a strong relationship between heroin addiction and minority group status. In some parts of the inner city, addicts represent as much as 30 percent of the total population. The use of heroin by poor Blacks can only be seen as an effort to cope with the stresses related to survival.[18]

A population with a large number of drug addicts provides the police with a rationale to patrol the Black community to "protect" its inhabitants from their criminal behavior. At the same time the police are managing to control and intimidate its residents by their presence. It is well known that Blacks are not in control of the manufacturing, importation, and sale of drugs. The point of origin of heroin is often Turkey, from where it is sent to France to be processed; then it is smuggled into this country from Latin America and Canadian ports. But the public clamor for new controls to get the addict off the street leads to repressive laws that increase the penalties for pushers. The effect of these laws is to punish the poor ghetto addict (who must sell to support his habit) while dealing leniently with the manufacturer who is not directly involved in drug sales or the middle-class drug user who can afford to purchase his drugs.

As Professor Norval Morris has declared, "The whole law and order movement that we've heard so much about is, in operation, anti-Black and anti-underclass, not in design, not in intent, but in operation."[19]

In effect, the war against drugs may only exacerbate the problems of Black families. Clearly the disproportionate numbers of Blacks arrested for drug-related offenses is a function of the nexus between race and drug dealing. In New York City a judge threw out crucial evidence in the drug arrest of a young Black woman in the Port Authority Bus Terminal on the ground that the profiles of people to be searched were almost exclusively aimed at Black and Latino travelers. Statistics showed that all but 2 of the 210 people arrested in 1989 in a drug interdiction program at the bus terminal were either Black or Hispanic.[20] The Legal Aid Society's defense of such racially biased results was "that most people who committed crimes were poor, and Black and Latino people were the poorest groups in New York City."[21] While the poor are most vulnerable to such unjustified arrests and seizures, the characteristic that most of those detained share is their race. As a Houston defense lawyer notes, "The darker your skin, the better your chances."[22] A Nigerian pharmacist was stopped at the Houston airport after a flight from his native Nigeria, questioned, x-rayed, handcuffed, and detained for eight hours. He had the misfortune to fit the profile of a drug courier, because heroin frequently is smuggled into the United States from Nigeria.[23] Wealthy Blacks are often stopped by the police and searched because their luxury cars draw the suspicion of police officers.

The tactics of the federal government's drug effort are largely aimed at law enforcement, not treatment, education, and job training. Its goals are the jailing of street drug sellers and an 85 percent increase in the number of federal prison cells. Already, Blacks comprise nearly half the jail population in the United States. The incarceration of the Black, mostly male, population is occurring at an alarming rate. One in four Black men in their 20s is either in jail, in prison, on parole, or on probation.[24] Lower-income Black families are being broken up as adults, already hampered by a lack of education and job skills are incarcerated, only to be released later with felony records that render them even less employable. Between the years of 18 and 24, the main years in which Black women are looking for a mate, Black women outnumber the marriageable Black men by sizable ratios. This has an impact on the out-of-wedlock birth rate among young Black women. A study of low-income neighborhoods in Chicago discovered that a man who has a job is twice as likely to marry the mother of his children as a man who is unemployed.[25]

The young Black male's involvement in drug activity affects Black family life in other ways. As Noble and Goddard have observed, "The drug culture is, in fact, creating a 'psychopathic' environment wherein 'effective family functioning' is not determined by the rules or moral values of one's social cultural group but by the dictates of a system of deviancy and chaos."[26] They also note that for individuals and families involved in the drug culture, the drug-related behaviors and the pursuit of the means necessary to sustain the drug-taking life-style become the central life interests and the primary determinants of all social relations. One of the reversals of normal family functioning is the breakdown of the normal lines of parental authority. Some teenagers sell crack to their own parents, giving them an enormous power over the older generation. There are cases where teenagers use the profits from their drug sales to help support the family.

Mainstream society is not blameless for the proliferation of substance abuse in Black communities. Because society holds out the goals of materialistic consumption for everyone in America but differentially distributes the means for achieving them, Black youth in poor, economically deprived communities are often surrounded by affluent suburban residents that create in them a sense of envy and they feel devalued as people. When they see affluent white neighborhoods, they ask themselves, "Why should I be poor?" Advertisers target Black youth for ads on sneakers that cost as much as $200. Where will they get the money for such items other than drug sales? Some scholars have suggested that middle-class Blacks must share some of the responsibility for drug activity among Black youth. The withdrawal of respectable role models, they say, to the suburbs has left only the known drug dealer as a role model for impressionable youth to emulate.[27]

Although drugs and alcohol are considered separate, the typical substance abuser uses both (the abuse of both drugs and alcohol is known as *polydrug use*). Young people who start off using the less toxic beer move on to hard liquor and eventually the more addictive drugs. Many Black neighborhoods do not have grocery stores but they always contain liquor stores. Because alcohol and tobacco consumption has been declining faster among whites, Blacks are increasingly the target of those products' advertising. Surveys across the United States show that Black communities have much more tobacco and alcohol advertising than white communities.[28] This marketing strategy is coming under fire. A cigarette company was forced to withdraw a cigarette aimed mostly at Blacks. As alcohol sales have begun to decline, the liquor industry has been left with a disproportionate number of poor and uneducated people as their primary clients. And, they know that Blacks are overrepresented among the poor and uneducated.

## Young Black Women and Drug-Addicted Infants

Substance abuse among the female population in any large numbers is historically unprecedented.

Yet, the National Institute on Drug Abuse found that there were almost 17.5 million female illicit drug users in the United States in 1985, 84 percent of whom were women of childbearing age. About 5 million were cocaine users. Black women constitute about 10 percent of these self-reported drug users.[29] More than 44 percent of the women admitted to federally funded alcohol and drug treatment programs are in poverty and 19 percent of them belong to racial minority groups.[30] While any statistics on the use of alcohol and drugs have to be regarded with caution, it seems safe to assume that the rise in female substance abusers is a function of the greater freedom women have gained in recent years. Just as they are approximating males in education and the workplace, they suffer, in addition to the stresses caused by multiple role demands and sexism, the same consequences of alienation, poverty, and unemployment.

The involvement of Black women in drug activity, however, has more serious implications for Black family stability. And, in some parts of the United States, such as, New York, Washington, D.C., Kansas City, and Portland, crack cocaine related arrests of women are higher than that of men.[31] In the past, women appeared to have lower rates of substance abuse than men, in part, because it made them more vulnerable and susceptible to male sexual advances. The sexual revolution of the 1960s may have made that concern a moot point. Anyway, Black women addicted to drugs are known to exchange sex for the mind-altering substance. In crack houses, which are generally dilapidated rooms in abandoned buildings, teenage girls may perform oral sex in exchange for a smoke. The adults at the crack houses are often parental figures and called 'Ma' and 'Pappy.'[32]

Women's involvement in the drug activity is more disruptive of family relationships. At early ages, they may leave school and home, hang out on the streets, and begin selling drugs. Observers report more women and girls are selling drugs, and they are more organized. Some of the drug lords prefer women as sellers because they are less likely than men to be searched by undercover policemen, since only policewomen may search females. While the crack sellers are mostly men, a changing scene in inner cities is the formation of female gangs to sell or buy it. This is a change because women were rarely allowed access to Black street culture. The drug trade has reduced the male's power to keep them off the streets. Relationships between daughters and parents are often fractured. Because of the behavioral changes precipitated by drug usage, parents feel powerless to control their daughters. The use of crack cocaine can make a woman erratic and aggressive. Some have to steal in order to finance the purchases. The parents are often the objects of their thefts. One mother said she locked everything of value in a back bedroom to prevent her daughter or her associates from stealing them.[33]

Almost all female drug users are sexually active; many of them engaged in prostitution to finance their drug habit. In the eastern part of the United States, heroin is a popular drug because it brings users down from the high of crack. Heroin acts biochemically as a sedative, crack as a stimulant. Consequently, female drug users may share needles with a male sexual partner, increasing the risk of contracting the AIDS virus. And the sexual activity frequently leads to pregnancy in the largely young female population, the most tragic consequence being the transmission of the AIDS virus to the newborn infant. Nationally, a majority of the babies born with the AIDS virus have Black mothers.[34] Their numbers are small, however, compared to the consequences of birth to a drug-addicted mother. Throughout the United States, it is estimated that 10 percent of all babies born in this country have some illicit drug in their veins. Approximately 375,000 children in 1988 were born to mothers who used drugs during pregnancy.[35] Those babies exposed to cocaine prenatally are at greater risk of being born prematurely, dying before birth and acquiring a number of deformities. Again the ugly specter of racism is raised in a study of Black and white women reported to authorities for drug use in a Florida county. Although Black and white women who are pregnant use drugs and alcohol in equal numbers, the Black women were ten times more likely to be reported to state authorities for drug use than white women.[36]

# What about the Children?

Prior to 1960 very little information was published about addicted mothers and congenitally addicted newborns. It was not until the late 1960s that research related to drug-complicated pregnancies and questions about its effects on the developing fetus received much attention. For instance, it was 1973 before fetal alcohol syndrome was even identified.[37] Several reasons may account for the lack of scientific interest in the drug-dependent mother/infant population. One possibility is, before 1970, it was believed that women addicts were infertile. A study by Gaulden on heroin-addicted women claimed that long-term ingestion of heroin led to menstrual irregularity and decreased libido.[38] Several studies have subsequently demonstrated that female addicts are no less fertile than the general population.[39] Other reasons for the lack of interest in studying the population of addicted mothers and congenitally addicted newborns concern the multitude of difficulties an examiner encounters in collecting accurate data and finding a homogeneous group. The lifestyles of drug addicts, in general, are not stable and reports on patient history are unreliable. The majority of the pregnant women received inadequate or no prenatal care.[40] The kind of drug(s) used, the amount of drug(s) used, and the duration of drug(s) used vary among the population of drug abusers across city, state, and country. Much of the variation depends on the availability of the drug(s); commonly more than one kind of drug is used. Medical screening for multiple drug use is not effective and is expensive. The ingredients in street drugs vary daily and from supplier to supplier. Additives in the drugs are not always known; consequently, their effects are also unknown.

Issues related to the drug-dependent mother and her drug-addicted child have been identified as problematic. The existence of prenatal drug exposure has been recognized, and the steadily increasing incidence of newborns born with congenital addiction has been acknowledged. Despite the limited support of past empirical data, researchers are beginning to delineate and study the consequences of prenatal drug exposure.

Infants exposed to drugs before birth are at greater risk of being stillborn or prematurely born. As many as 18 percent to 50 percent of the drug-exposed infants are born preterm.[41] The actual cause for the premature births is unknown. Some drugs, such as cocaine, can cause hypertension and in turn cause the placenta to separate. Anatomical examination of the spontaneously aborted fetuses has presented a clearer picture of the effects of drugs on the developing fetus. Studies have shown that an abusing mother's crack binge can cause physiological responses in the infant. Crack binges trigger spasms in the baby's blood vessels, which in turn can severely restrict the flow of oxygen and nutrients for long periods. Fetal growth, including the head and brain size may be impaired. In addition, there is a possibility that strokes and seizures may occur and that malformation of the kidneys, genitals, intestines, and spinal cord may develop.[42] A given pattern of symptoms and signs of drug exposure is determined by the type, amount, and number of drugs used, the length of time between delivery and last drug exposure, and the fetus' ability to metabolize the drugs.[43]

It is generally acknowledged that premature infants are at greater risk for many problems, including learning disabilities. Among school age children, who were born prematurely and entered the regular school system, 40 to 50 percent had difficulties such as learning and behavioral problems. A low socioeconomic status heightened the potential risk, but could not explain the cause of the resulting high percentage of children showing later school difficulties.[44]

It is not known what the relationship is between the behavior problems and intrauterine drug exposure. The caregiving environment and, if applicable, premature birth of the child are influences that complicate the analysis, but must be considered when examining the child's behavior. However, indications are that drug-exposed infants who demonstrate organizational and processing difficulties, that is, disturbed behavior and motivation and attention problems, also later demonstrate poorer school performance than anticipated by the tested IQ.[45]

Supporters of fetal rights argue that women who knowingly and willfully place their unborn child at risk are criminals (child abusers) and should be treated as such. This punitive reaction to substance-abusing women, who are believed to be harming their fetus, is rebutted with arguments saying that criminalizing pregnant substance-abusing women is counterproductive. Supporters of mothers' rights argue that substance-abusing mothers should not be criminally victimized but rather should be encouraged to seek medical treatment.[46] Their opinion is that the addicted mother's fear of prosecution or having her child taken away could possibly worsen an already bad situation. One feared consequence is that less prenatal care, overall, will be sought by the expectant mothers and more children will be born at home or elsewhere without medical attention. Putting the mother in jail could destroy the bond between mother and child, which could be fostered if the pair receives adequate treatment.

## The Death of Black Motherhood

The surge in drug addiction among young Black women has accomplished what colonialism, slavery, racism, and economic deprivation could not—subordinate the maternal instinct to the pursuit of an addiction. All available historical evidence shows Black women to have an unbreakable bond with their children. The universal testimony of observers of the Black family was that the Black mother's love for her children was unsurpassed in any part of the world.[47] Yet, the crack epidemic is blamed for many of the 2.2 million cases of child neglect and abuse reported to child protective services in the USA each year.[48] Some of the deaths of children reported to have died from neglect and abuse by a parent are also associated with crack. According to Dr. Elizabeth Rahdert, a research psychologist, "We know that it (crack) chemically impairs people's functioning so they can't make decisions, can't take responsibility for paying the rent or seeing that there is food on the table for the children."[49]

Among the negative consequences of Black parental neglect is the forcible removal of Black children from their mothers and placement in foster care facilities, many of them run by whites. In the state of California, up to 60 percent of drug-exposed infants are placed in foster care. The number of children in out-of-home care increased from 47,700 in 1985 to 78,900 in 1989 in that state.[50] A majority of those children are Black because the number of drug-exposed children has outstripped the capacity of the Black community to absorb them. A similar problem exists with a glut of Black children awaiting adoption. Nationally, Black children constitute 40 percent of children waiting to be adopted in 1990.[51] Statistics show that Black families adopted children from public welfare agencies at four and a half times the rate of whites and Latinos.[52] The need is so great that some Black children are being placed with white families as foster or adoptive parents, a practice that has generated a great deal of controversy in the past.[53]

One reason for the rising number of Black children placed in foster or adoptive homes is the number of their mothers serving time in jails and prisons. The number of women in state and federal prisons increased from 13,420 to 30,834 during an eight-year period.[54] In states with sizable Black populations, Black women represent the majority of such prisoners. That has been true for a number of years. The difference nowadays rests in the nature of charges brought against them—felony drug charges compared to misdemeanors. Crack has created a window for petty dealers to sell the drug in contrast to higher-priced drugs, which tend to be tightly controlled by male drug lords. In a similar vein as Black male street drug dealers, a Black woman is more subject to arrest and detention than white women, because of the heavy police presence in the Black neighborhoods and the public nature of the Black woman's drug transactions.

Probably most children of Black female addicts do remain within their extended families. In a few cases, the biological father and his family may assume care of the children. Most observers of the drug scene say that does not happen too often in the case of the female addicts who go to jail. When men are taken off to prison, their girlfriends and wives take care of the children and often come for visits. Women with substance abuse problems are more likely to lose their partners. According to one prison official, "You see that with the visits. You rarely

see the boyfriends coming out here. With men, the women take care of them. But the men don't take care of the women. They abandon them. It's pitiful."[55]

Generally, the family members who replace the mother are grandmothers, aunts, and sisters. Social agencies estimate that as many as 70 percent of the children in neighborhoods ruled and ruined by crack are being reared by older relatives.[56] Most likely, it is the grandmother who will assume care of the children abandoned by their drug-abusing mothers. Often they do not have formal custody of the children, which prevents them from being eligible for traditional sources of public support. Because they are related to the child, the grandparents may get only a third of the amount allotted to children who are in licensed group homes.[57] In addition to the financial burden, the grandparents' entire routine is changed because the sudden responsibility for small children has been imposed on them. As a 67-year-old grandmother complained, "Here I am an old lady and I have inherited four kids. I find myself changing diapers again. It's a lot of work and there's nobody to help me with them."[58]

While the extended family may adapt its routine to help raise the children abandoned by crack-using mothers, it is at great sacrifice. As they approach what should be their leisure years, the grandmothers are forced into a second wave of parenting and find themselves involved in transporting toddlers to day care centers, reading bedtime stories, and rushing to PTA meetings and little league games. Although the grandmothers take the children out of a sense of duty, they can find themselves under siege from the violence and erratic behavior of the child's mother. One woman's daughter left her son with her, stole her car, and threatened to kill her when confronted.[59] Such behavior can render the extended family network ineffective when the drug culture tears at its fabric. Parents have to get restraining orders to prevent their adult children from visiting them or their children.

Hence, drugs and alcohol abuse are particularly destructive of Black family stability, because they disrupt the integrity of the nuclear and extended family. The risk to children caused federal anti-drug chief William Bennett to call for removal of children from drug infested neighborhoods and placement of them in orphanages. According to Bennett, "We may just have to find some way to get children out of the environment which they're in, to go to orphanages, to go to Boys Town, to expand institutions like that, where they will be raised and nurtured."[60] Such a draconian solution belies the federal government's understanding of substance abuse in the inner cities. Bennett would wage a war on drugs by institutionalizing all the victims, the parents in prisons and the children in orphanages. While substance abuse has become a part of the American condition, spread throughout a cross-section of the population, the efforts to eliminate it seem to target the most economically vulnerable segments of society. Black women have the lowest income of all race/sex groups in the United States, a fact reflected in the poverty rate of 45 percent of all Black children in this country in 1987.[61] In essence, lower-income Blacks are being penalized for their poverty, not for the unfortunate consequences of being addicted to legal and illegal substances that millions of affluent Americans have in common with them.

## Summary

In assessing the causes and nature of substance abuse in the American population, it is clear that rapid social changes can bring about psychological dislocation. Among those changes are declining faith in American institutions and the growth of values such as materialism, consumerism, and narcissism. The latter value may be directly tied to substance abuse because it promotes behavior that is associated with individual fulfillment. Drugs and alcohol are "feel good" mechanisms that self-centered individuals use to achieve a pleasure release. Moreover, as the political and economic elite have demonstrated a rapaciousness in their management of the body politic and economy, ordinary citizens have become alienated from the values of thrift, hard work, and sobriety that characterized an earlier America. For Blacks of the underclass, alcohol and drugs have traditionally been opiates used to ease the pain of their oppressed status. Since poorer Blacks feel the sting of racism and poverty more directly, they are more likely to seek the palliative effect of drugs and alcohol than the more affluent Blacks. Because of their poverty and powerlessness, they are the most public of drug users and sellers, thus the easiest people to arrest.

While the war on drugs continues to fill up the expanding prison facilities with people of color, the use of illicit drugs and equally destructive—but legal—use of alcohol will continue unabated as long as the social conditions that cause their use are extant. Without resorting to conspiracy and genocide theories, it is instructive to note that drug abuse is identified as America's number one problem while inequality of wealth, homelessness, poverty, massive unemployment, and a host of problems directly traceable to class and racial oppression are removed from the public discourse. Substance abuse has the advantage of being viewed as a personal trouble whereas, in reality, it is a public issue. It is a public issue because the causes of substance abuse are embedded in the social structure. Only by eliminating the machinations of a chaotic and exploitative economy can we expect to reduce its concomitant of substance abuse among America's Black population.

[1] Sam Meddis, Drug Arrest Rate Higher for Blacks. USA Today. December 20, 1989, p. A-1.

[2] Ron Harris, "Experts Say the War on Drugs Has Turned into a War on Blacks." San Francisco Chronicle. April 24, 1990, p. A-12.

[3] Department of Health and Human Services, Health, United States, 1989. Washington, D.C., 1990.

[4] Wade W. Nobles and Lawford Goddard, "Drugs in the African-American Community: A Clear and Present Danger," in The State of Black America 1989. New York: The National Urban League, 1989, p. 165.

[5] Quoted in Joanne Ball, "Life Span for Blacks Is Getting Shorter." San Francisco Examiner, June 11, 1989, p. A-9.

[6] Quoted in Evelyn C. White, "Black Family Conference Assails Crack." San Francisco Chronicle, April 27, 1990, p. A-18.

[7] National Center for Health Statistics, Health, United States, 1987, DHAS Pub. No. (PHS) 88-1232, Public Health Service. Washington, D.C.: U.S. Government Printing Service, 1987.

[8] Ibid.

[9] "White Americans Are Getting Healthier." San Francisco Examiner, March 23, 1990, p. A-17.

[10]*Department of Health and Human Services,* Report of the Secretary's Task Force on Black and Minority Health. *Washington, D.C.: U.S. Government Printing Office, 1985.*

[11]*Wayne Byram and Jerry W. Fly, "Family Structure, Race and Adolescents Alcohol Use: A Research Note."* American Journal of Drug and Alcohol Abuse *10:467–478, 1984.*

[12]*Meddis,* loc. cit.

[13]*Andrew H. Malcolm, "Crack, Bane of Inner City, Is Now Gripping Suburbs."* The New York Times, *October 1, 1989, p. A-1.*

[14]*Harris,* loc. cit.

[15]*Ramon G. McLeod, "Young Black Men Endangered—Steep Rise in Violent Death."* San Francisco Chronicle, *February 23, 1989, p. A-6.*

[16]*C. F. Robert Staples,* The Urban Plantation, Racism and Colonialism in the Post Civil Rights Era. *Oakland: The Black Scholar Press, 1987, pp. 51–75.*

[17]*Meddis,* loc. cit.

[18]*Nobles and Goddard,* op. cit.

[19]*Quoted in Harris,* loc. cit.

[20]*Ronald Sullivan, "Law Authorities Say Drug Program Profiles Do Not Discriminate."* The New York Times, *April 26, 1990, p. A-20.*

[21]*"Lisa Belkin, Tools AGAINST Drugs Attacked as Racist."* San Francisco Chronicle, *March 20, 1990, p. A-9.*

[22]Ibid.

[23]Ibid.

[24]*John Flesher, "Report: 235 of All Young Black Men Afoul of Law."* San Francisco Examiner, *February 27, 1990, p. A-1.*

[25]*William E. Schmidt, "Study Links Male Unemployment and Single Mothers in Chicago."* The New York Times, *January 15, 1989, p. A-12.*

[26]*Nobles and Goddard,* op. cit., *p. 172.*

[27]*William J. Wilson,* The Truly Disadvantaged. *Chicago: The University of Chicago Press, 1987, pp. 55–57.*

[28]*"An Uproar Over Billboards in Poor Areas."* The New York Times, *May 1, 1989, p. C-8.*

[29]*National Institute on Drug Abuse,* National Household Survey on Drug Abuse 1985 Population Estimates. *Rockville, MD: National Institute on Drug Abuse, 1985, pp. 19–21.*

[30]*National Council on Alcoholism,* A Federal Response to a Hidden Epidemic: Alcohol and Other Drug Problems Among Women *18:32–40, 1987.*

[31]*Gina Kolata, "In Cities, Poor Families Are Dying of Crack."* The New York Times, *August 11, 1989, p. A-10.*

[32]Ibid.

[33]Ibid.

[34]*"White Americans Are Getting Healthier."* The San Francisco Examiner, *March 23, 1990, p. A-17.*

[35]*"Drug Abuse's Most Innocent Victims: Babies,"* Children's Defense Fund Reports, *May 1989.*

[36]*"Study Probes Use of Drugs, Alcohol by Pregnant Women."* San Francisco Examiner, *April 26, 1990, p. A-14.*

[37]*Vivian Weinstein and Kathleen West, "Drug Babies—Their Lives, Their Future."* Children's Advocate *1–4, January/February 1986.*

[38]*E. C. Gaulden, "Menstrual Abnormalities Associated With Heroin Addiction."* American Journal of Obstetrics and Gynecology *90:155, 1964.*

[39]*Gael Wagner and Lois Keith, "Drug Addiction,"* Maternal-Fetal Medicine, Principles and Practice, *Vol. 3 (Robert Creasy and Robert Resnik, Eds.). Philadelphia: W. B. Saunders, 1989, pp. 1–10.*

[40]*H. Sardemann, R. Madsen, and B. Friis-Hansen, "Follow-up of Children of Drug-Addicted Mothers."* Archives of Disease in Children *51:131–134, 1976.*

[41]*Wagner and Keith,* loc. cit.

[42]*G. Aylward, "Methadone Outcome Studies. Is It More Than Methadone?"* Journal of Pediatrics *101:214–215, 1982.*

[43]*Wagner and Keith,* loc. cit.

[44]*Heidelise Als, "Patterns of Infant Behavior: An Analogue of Later Organizational Difficulties,"* in Dyslexia: A Neuro-Scientific Approach to Clinical Evaluation *(F. Duffy and N. Geschwind, Eds.). Boston: Little, Brown and Company, 1985, pp. 67–91.*

[45]*Weinstein and West,* loc. cit.

[46]*K. R. Kaufman, M. E. Weekes and E. R. Kaufman, "Right to Healthy Birth: Medico-Legal Issues in Phencyclidine Ingestion."* Child Abuse and Neglect *10, 1986.*

[47]*Patricia Hill Collins, "The Meaning of Motherhood in Black Culture and Black Mother-Daughter Relationships."* Sage: A Scholarly Journal on Black Woman *2:3–10, Fall 1987.*

[48]*Michael deCourcy Hinds, "Addiction to Crack Can Kill Parental Instinct."* The New York Times, *March 17, 1990, p. A-1.*

[49]Ibid.

[50]*Rick DelVecchio, "State Fails Foster Kids Group Says."* San Francisco Chronicle, *April 27, 1990, p. A-4.*

[51]*Charisse Jones, "Drugs Add to a Glut of Adoptable Black Children."* Los Angeles Times, *May 21, 1989, p. A-1.*

[52]Ibid.

[53]*Joyce A. Ladner,* Mixed Families: Adopting across Racial Boundaries. *New York: Doubleday, 1977.*

[54]*Celestine Bohlen, "Number of Women in Jail Surges with Drug Sales."* The New York Times, *1989, p. A-1.*

[55]Ibid.

[56]*June Gross, "Grandmothers Bear a Burden Sired by Drugs."* The New York Times, *April 9, 1989, p. A-1.*

[57]*Evelyn C. White, "Crack Crisis Turns Grandmothers into Moms."* San Francisco Chronicle, *May 22, 1989, p. A-2.*

[58]Ibid.

[59]Ibid.

[60]*William Bennett, U.S. Drug Chief, cited in Gregory Lewis, "Bennett Idea on Children Draws Jeers."* San Francisco Examiner, *April 28, 1990, p. A-1.*

[61]*"Child Poverty Tragedy for U.S."* San Francisco Chronicle, *April 27, 1990, p. A-22.*

# A PERSPECTIVE ON AIDS:

## A Catastrophic Disease But a Symptom of Deeper Problems in the Black Community

*Andrew D. McBride, M.D., M.P.H.*

*This article, written by a medical doctor, describes the gamut of issues affecting AIDS in the Black community, including the heterosexual spread of AIDS, the reporting of the disease in the Black community, its peculiar clinical manifestation in Blacks, AIDS among Haitians and Africans, and the federal government's response to funding research for AIDS prevention. The author notes that AIDS is interrelated with some old problems in the Black community and Blacks must work to remove the root causes that contribute to the spread of AIDS.*

Acquired Immune Deficiency Syndrome (AIDS) is undisputedly the most significant public health problem facing the Black community today.

AIDS is an infectious disease known to be caused by a virus, Human Immunodeficiency Virus (HIV). This virus mainly attacks the body's immune (T4 + Helper/inducer lymphocytes) and neurological systems. The most outstanding feature of the disease is that it renders the body defenseless against otherwise non-fatal infectious agents and certain cancers (Ho, Pomerantz, Kaplan, 1987). First identified in 1981, AIDS is a disease that once it has manifested itself is almost uniformly fatal. AIDS has no known cure or vaccine. To date over 50,000 United States cases have been documented by the Centers for Disease Control (CDC).

From the outset, it was apparent that AIDS disproportionately affected Blacks. In 1981, CDC noted that 21.5 percent of the first 107 cases of previously healthy persons displaying AIDS-related symptoms were Blacks and Hispanics, most of whom were homosexual/bisexual males (Houston-Hamilton, 1986).

AIDS in the United States occurs chiefly in two populations: male homosexuals/bisexuals, and intravenous drug users. These two groups represent 90 percent of reported U.S. cases of AIDS.

## Heterosexual Spread of AIDS

If the heterosexual spread of AIDS is of major concern to public leaders and the public at large, it should be of dominant concern to Black people. Whereas heterosexual transmission represents only 4 percent of the total AIDS cases, heterosexual transmission represents 11 percent of the cases of AIDS in Blacks. Blacks represent 70 percent of the cases of heterosexual transmission of AIDS (Centers for Disease Control, 1987).

In the Black community, the HIV infection rate via IV drug use has grown. In Newark, N.J., 61 percent of the new cases of AIDS are reported to be intravenous drug users (Institute of Medicine, National Academy of Sciences, 1986). Blacks (51%) and Hispanics (29%) are overwhelmingly represented

From *Urban Research Review* 11 (1988):1–4. Copyright 1988 by the Institute for Urban Affairs and Research, Howard University. Reprinted by permission.

**TABLE 1    United States Cases Reported to CDC as of September 21, 1987**

| TRANSMISSION CATEGORIES[1] | BLACK NOT HISPANIC | | TOTAL | |
|---|---|---|---|---|
| | Cumulative Number | (%) | Cumulative Number | (%) |
| **Adults/Adolescents** | | | | |
| Homosexual/Bisexual Male | 4046 | (40) | 27483 | ( 66) |
| Intravenous (IV) Drug Abuser | 3473 | (35) | 6853 | ( 16) |
| Homosexual Male and IV Drug Abuser | 696 | ( 7) | 3129 | ( 8) |
| Hemophilia/Coagulation Disorder | 20 | ( 0) | 379 | ( 1) |
| Heterosexual Cases[2] | 1151 | (11) | 1644 | ( 4) |
| Transfusion, Blood/Components | 128 | ( 1) | 882 | ( 2) |
| Undetermined[3] | 508 | ( 5) | 1232 | ( 3) |
| SUBTOTAL [% of all cases] | 10022 | [24] | 41602 | [100] |
| **Children[4]** | | | | |
| Hemophilia/Coagulation Disorder | 5 | ( 2) | 31 | ( 5) |
| Parent with/at risk of AIDS[5] | 282 | (89) | 456 | ( 79) |
| Transfusion, Blood/Components | 19 | ( 6) | 70 | ( 12) |
| Undetermined[6] | 10 | ( 3) | 23 | ( 4) |
| SUBTOTAL [% of all cases] | 316 | [54] | 580 | [100] |
| TOTAL [% of all cases] | 10338 | [25] | 42182 | [100] |

[1]Cases with more than one risk factor other than the combinations listed in the tables or footnotes are tabulated only in the category listed first.

[2]Includes 902 persons (196 men, 706 women) who have had heterosexual contact with a person with AIDS or at risk for AIDS and 742 persons (582 men, 160 women) without other identified risks who were born in countries in which heterosexual transmission is believed to play a major role although precise means of transmission has not yet been fully defined.

[3]Includes patients on whom risk information is incomplete (due to death, refusal to be interviewed or loss to follow-up), patients still under investigation, men reported only to have had heterosexual contact with a prostitute, and interviewed patients for whom no specific risk was identified.

[4]Includes all patients under 13 years of age at time of diagnosis.

[5]Epidemiologic data suggest transmission from an infected mother to her fetus or infant during the perinatal period.

in the IV drug population (See Table 1). Therefore, heterosexual Black and Hispanic people who are sexual partners of HIV-infected heterosexual drug users become one of the obvious "bridges" of transmitting HIV infection to the remainder of the heterosexual community.

# Reporting of AIDS in the Black Community

AIDS is only one, although the most malignant, manifestation of HIV infection. For every person with AIDS, there are an estimated 100 persons infected with HIV without any sign of disease or lesser manifestations of disease. Physicians and other health providers are generally required to report only AIDS and not HIV infection. Because male homosexuality/bisexuality and intravenous drug use are the predominant risk factors in the U.S., it is obvious that in addition to having a devastating disease there is the added social stigma attached to being infected with HIV.

Because of racial factors and the relatively low socio-economic status of most Blacks, one can reasonably expect that the dominant medical establishment will have a strong proclivity to report more stringently AIDS cases in Blacks, Hispanics and lower socioeconomic groups as compared to middle and upper class whites. Medicine has a long history of this type of bias towards reporting diseases. For example, in the 1800's, physicians readily identified tuberculosis as such in the poorer classes and called the same illness a "melancholia" when it occurred in upper classes (Swan, 1985).

In addition, there is the perennial undercounting of Blacks in the population census. This would make AIDS incidence, mortality, morbidity and other population-based rates falsely high. Even taking these factors into account, it appears that AIDS is more likely to be under-reported in whites than over-reported in Blacks.

## Peculiar Clinical Manifestations of AIDS in Blacks

Recent reports indicate that Black AIDS victims are dying at faster rates than other persons with AIDS (Mason, 1987). Blacks with AIDS have been found to have a higher incidence of manifestation from opportunistic infections when compared to whites, and a lower incidence of Kaposi's Sarcoma. Any number of possibilities exist as an explanation for these occurrences, ranging from the lack of access to quality medical services to pre-existing poor health of Blacks. However, to date, neither CDC nor other national public health authorities have reported any detailed explanations for these findings.

## Stigmatizing of Haitians in the United States

AIDS was first reported in Haitians in 1982 (Hockstader, 1987); based on only a few initial cases, incidents of HIV infection in the Haitians were initially over-estimated. Since that time, CDC estimates of the incidence of HIV infection in Haitians has been revised down from 4.5 percent before 1984 to 1.5 percent in 1986 (Institute of Medicine, National Academy of Sciences, 1986). The actual incidence among the many Haitians who have been in this country for years is not fully known but it is reasonable to expect that these Haitians have even a lower incidence of infection. In 1985, CDC officially dropped Haitians in the United States as a "high risk" AIDS group. Nonetheless, Haitians in this country remain stigmatized by this official CDC mislabeling.

In fact, the case for labeling all men from San Francisco as high risk has just as much public health justification. It is estimated that homosexual/bisexual males represent at least 25 percent of the male population in San Francisco (Institute of Medicine, National Academy of Sciences, 1986). Current estimates state that 37 percent to 75 percent of homosexual/bisexual males are infected (Jones et al., 1987). Thus, it can be conservatively estimated that 9.25 percent of the men from San Francisco are infected when compared to 1.5 percent of the Haitian population (Jones et al., 1987).

While CDC was quick to prematurely label all Haitians as a high risk group, the public health response has been slow and relatively weak in alerting the Black community to the threat posed by AIDS. Only recently have federal public health authorities forcefully advocated for programs in the Black and Hispanic community (Mason, 1987). Even today, when it is fashionable for Blacks and Whites alike to advocate "education and counseling" in the high-risk community, a relatively small portion of public monies is allocated for Black communities. The mere $7 million nationally for AIDS education in the Black community is roughly equivalent to the cost of a single issue of a daily newspaper for each Black person in the United States.

## The Hemophiliac Response

Contrast the belated and anemic federal support for AIDS prevention in the Black community with the federal response to hemophiliacs. In 1986, federal funds were appropriated for AIDS counseling and education. A total of $2.5 million was earmarked for hemophiliacs (a group 83% white and a high risk AIDS group) (National Hemophilia Foundation, 1987). Hemophiliacs who received contaminated blood products in the past are an extremely high risk group. Between 32 percent to 92 percent of the hemophiliacs who received blood products before 1984 have HIV infection. Since that time, procedures for sterilizing the blood products used by hemophiliacs (MMWR, 1987) and methodologies for screening the blood supply for HIV have been applied. Therefore, from a public health perspective, hemophiliacs as a group will become a progressively smaller at-risk group.

Interestingly enough, the federal government never instituted a similar program for hematologic patients, people with sickle cell disease. While persons with sickle cell disease, as a rule, did not receive the same concentrated blood products (clotting factors) as the hemophiliacs, many persons with sickle cell disease received multiple transfusions with HIV-infected blood. There is little doubt that persons with sickle cell disease who received multiple transfusions were at high risk of HIV infection. While large scale studies on the incidence of HIV infection in persons with sickle cell disease have not been performed, there are many case reports by sickle cell clinicians of HIV infection in sicklers. Given the large number of persons with sickle cell disease, 50,000 Black Americans annually (Howard University Center for Sickle Cell Disease) as compared to 20,000 hemophiliacs, (National Hemophilia Foundation), there is apparently little public health policy justification for instituting a program for hemophiliacs and not one for sicklers.

# The Gay Movement Response to AIDS

It has been known for years that homosexual/bisexual males have been at high risk for sexually transmitted disease. In retrospect, it is not surprising that a new sexually transmitted disease when planted in the male homosexual/bisexual community would flourish.

Blacks, as a group, are at higher risk than whites of having a sexually transmitted disease but in addition, Blacks are at greater risk of being intravenous drug users. These two conditions put Blacks at double risk.

In contrast to the Black community, the response of the white Gay movement to AIDS has been swift and effective. White homosexual/bisexuals have exerted their influence on AIDS policy and programs from the outset of the discovery of AIDS. In every community in which AIDS is prevalent, they are potent political forces. Moreover, not only have monied white homosexual/bisexuals donated funds to the cause, they have put in much time in voluntary humanitarian services to educate and aid their fellow homosexual/bisexuals. Although their work in many cases was too late, the work of the Gay movement to combat AIDS is beginning to pay off.

White homosexual/bisexuals appear to be reducing their high-risk AIDS status; for example, as devastatingly ill Black and Hispanic AIDS babies (mostly the products of drug-abusing mothers or fathers) were accumulating in Northeastern hospitals, such as Harlem Hospital in New York City, white homosexual/bisexuals in New Mexico, New York and San Francisco had fewer cases of sexually transmitted diseases (STDs) (gonorrhea, syphilis) than in previous years (Jones et al., 1987). In spite of the high prevalence of the HIV virus in the homosexual/bisexual population, public health officials concede that this drop in STD in male homosexuals demonstrates reduced risk in contracting HIV infection. In addition, it is believed that STD may be an important co-factor in converting an asymptomatic HIV infected person into a full blown AIDS patient. Thus, it is possible that the decrease in STD in male homosexuals will prevent or delay AIDS in those already HIV infected (Institute of Medicine, National Academy of Sciences, 1986).

# AIDS in Africa

Inevitably, AIDS will kill thousands of people in the U.S. and many millions in Africa. The U.S. press and public health establishment have been intensely interested in Africa and the Caribbean, because AIDS appears to be spreading there heterosexually (Institute of Medicine, National Academy of Sciences,

1986). For example, reports of the 3rd International Conference on AIDS cite that the masses of people in Central Africa in the rural areas are largely not HIV infected. The distribution of the HIV virus in East and Central African countries (e.g., Zaire, Zambia, Burundi, Rwanda, Uganda, Tanzania) appears to be more restricted to the "urban" areas. In South Africa the distribution of HIV is along the truck routes taken by the migrant Black male mine workers, displaced from their families, imported from surrounding Black nations. These routes are the strongholds of the HIV-infected female prostitutes (3rd International Conference on AIDS).

HIV infection in Africa is not yet at pandemic levels, but HIV infection is firmly seated in Africa. It does not strain the imagination as to the impact that AIDS will have on Africa and the poorer Caribbean countries such as Haiti when one considers the case of measles. Today 50,000 African children die of measles, a disease with an available vaccine. Measles is the single leading cause of childhood death in Africa. In many instances 1/3 of the children die before the age of six years (UNICEF, 1986). This illustrates the extremely limited capacity of African countries to respond to a disease, unlike AIDS, that is practically 100% preventable.

# A Reasonable Response to the AIDS Epidemic in the Black Community

Blacks already infected with HIV will need both financial and human services. Clearly, federal, state and local governments should provide resources for these services. The Black community groups should be strong advocates of and provide additional financial and human services to the Blacks already HIV-infected. There is an obvious role that the Black churches and other community groups should play in this area.

Blacks are over-represented among those infected with HIV; but 99% of Blacks are not infected. HIV infection is not a "Black" or "Hispanic" disease. The Black community should resist the label.

"Where you see hoof prints do not look for zebras." HIV virus has been found to be in most body fluids; to survive outside of the body for 36 hours (MMWR, 1987) and is found in mosquitoes. It has been contended that the virus was introduced into the Black community as part of a White conspiracy (personal communication at a church conference on AIDS). These reports vary from being technically true to being outlandish. The Black community should be aware of all new information about HIV infection; but *the best epidemiological evidence suggests that the Black community concentrate on three primary means of transmittal of the virus: (1) Sexual contact; (2) dirty drug needles and (3) being born of a mother infected with HIV.*

**Sexual contact**　The Black community should promote programs, policies and practices that decrease sexual promiscuity and promote discretion in selecting sexual partners. A major step would be the promotion of monogamous sexual relationships, especially Black marriages. Marriage is an institution that is being wholeheartedly abandoned by young Black people. According to the D.C. Department of Human Services, in 1986, 92.8 percent of births to Black women under age 20 were to single mothers.

Non-monogamous sexually active persons should properly use condoms and spermicide and avoid anal intercourse. Condoms are not failsafe but are reported to be about 83 percent effective in preventing the spread of HIV infection (Goedert, 1987).

The voluntary testing for the HIV antibody and counseling should be encouraged in the Black community. However, Blacks should stand with the Gay movement in watch-dogging the issues of confidentiality of reporting in regard to the HIV antibody test.

Black homosexuals/bisexuals have special problems of social rejection not completely shared with their white counterparts (National Coalition of Black Lesbians and Gays, 1986). These differences should be acknowledged and preventive health programs directed to minimize HIV transmission in Black homosexual/bisexual males.

**Dirty drug needles**　Obviously, programs that treat and prevent drug abuse should be promoted in the Black community. Sterile needles should be made available to the addicted population. In addition, the addicts should be taught to sterilize their needles by simply using a diluted solution of household bleach.

**Children born to an HIV-infected mother** About 80 percent of children with AIDS are Black or Hispanic. All pregnant women should be offered the HIV test and be given appropriate counseling. An HIV-infected pregnant woman should be given the most current available information to protect her health and that of her unborn child. According to recent data, the risk of transmittal of HIV to the unborn is 30 percent to 60 percent. The reports of the International Conference point to strong evidence that the chances of an infected woman passing the virus to her unborn child are nearly 50 percent.

## AIDS Education in School

The federal government is undertaking a relatively anemic effort to educate the minority community about AIDS (See Table 2). The Surgeon General has recommended that AIDS education be taught at the elementary school level. It is difficult not to look at these educational proposals without a jaundiced eye. How can the public leadership be preaching AIDS education, when by almost every measure the education system is failing Blacks.

### TABLE 2  Summary of PHS Funding For AIDS

| | |
|---|---|
| 1982 | $   5.5 million |
| 1983 | $ 28.7 million |
| 1984 | $ 61.5 million |
| 1985 | $108.6 million |
| 1986 | $233.8 million |
| 1987 | $494.1 million ($30 million, on a one-time only basis, to cover the cost of AZT. $130 million for AIDS information, health education, and risk reduction. $129 million for effective treatment in FY 1987). |

In the 1987 supplemental appropriation, $7 million were made available to initiate a special emphasis on preventing AIDS among minorities at risk.

Fewer Black are going into higher education than in previous years. The urban Black grade and high schools continue to languish far below an acceptable level of academic achievement. Blacks, particularly males, are dropping out of school in record numbers. In the health professions (medicine, professional nursing, and dentistry), Blacks are severely under-represented. Enrollment in these areas continues to decline. Clearly, one cannot be sanguine about the efficiency of AIDS education in the schools.

## General Recommendations

In addition to AIDS, most major communicable diseases (tuberculosis, syphilis, viral hepatitis, pelvic inflammatory disease, diphtheria, pertussis) inordinately affect Blacks (Report of the Secretary's Task Force On Black And Minority Health, 1985). Research does not show that Blacks are in fact genetically more susceptible; however, economic, educational, nutritional and environmental influences, as well as the inadequacies of the health care systems are the major contributors (Williams, 1975).

AIDS is an infectious disease that is growing in the Black community. The Black community must not only deal with the exigency of this particular disease but work to remove the root causes that contribute to its spread. A careful examination of contributing factors to AIDS in the Black community will reveal some very old interrelated problems: social disruption with the dismantling of the Black family; weakened Black education and training systems; weakened Black economy; growing social and economic influences of the criminal justice system fueled by drugs and alcohol; unhealthy environmental conditions; negative treatment by the media; and the diminution of the values of Black culture and history.

*Oddly enough, what the Black community does to defeat these old enemies will contribute to the fight against a new one, AIDS.*

# References

1986 Acquired immunodeficiency syndrome (AIDS) among Blacks & Hispanics—United States. *Morbidity and Mortality Weekly Report*, 35(42), 655–666.

Centers for Disease Control

1987 *Weekly Surveillance Report*, September 21.

1987 *Epidemiology—AIDS in Developing Countries*, Session of 3rd International Conference on AIDS, June, Washington, D.C.

Goedert, J.

1987 What is safe sex? Suggested standards linked to testing for human immunodeficiency virus. *New England Journal of Medicine*, 316(21), 1339–1342.

Ho, D., Pomerantz, R., Kaplan, J.

1987 Pathogenesis of infection with human immunodeficiency virus. *New England Journal of Medicine*, 317(5), 278–286.

Hockstader, L.

1987 "AIDS in Haiti." *Washington Post Health*, 12–17.

Houston-Hamilton, D.

1986 A constant increase: AIDS in ethnic communities. *Focus*, 1(11), 1–2.

Institute of Medicine, National Academy of Sciences

1986 *Confronting AIDS: Directions for public health, health care and research*, Washington, D.C.: National Academy Press.

Jones, C., Waskin, H., Gerety, B., Skipper, B., Hull, H. and Merty, G.

1987 Persistence of high-risk sexual activity among homosexual men in an area of low incidence of the acquired immunodeficiency syndrome. *Journal of the American Venereal Disease Association*, 14(2), 79–82.

Mason, J.

1987 Statement made at the Congressional Black Caucus Health Braintrust, September, Washington, D.C.

National Coalition of Black Lesbians and Gays

1986 Position Paper.

National Hemophilia Foundation

1987

1987 Recommendations for prevention of HIV transmission in health-care settings. *Morbidity and Mortality Weekly Report*, 36(25), 35–185.

1985 *Report of Secretary's Task Force on Black and Minority Health*, DHHS, October.

1987 Survey of Non-U.S. hemophilia treatment centers for HIV seroconversions following therapy with heat treated factor concentrates. *Morbidity and Mortality Weekly Report*, 36(9), 121–124.

Swan, P.

1985 History of TB. *Nursing Times*, 81, 47–49.

UNICEF

1986 *State of the world's children 1986*.

Williams, R. A.

1975 *Textbook of Black-related diseases*. New York: McGraw Hill.

# PART FOUR

# Black Families and the Future

## Alternative Life-Styles

Making predictions about the future nature of any group's family life is a risky endeavor. Few, for instance, could have projected what has happened to the American family as a whole since 1970. Certainly there were trends leading us in certain directions, but it was the acceleration of those trends that caught many of us by surprise. In the case of the Black family, the research literature is still so sparse and biased that we have practically no attempts to analyze Black families of the future or alternative family life-styles. Certain barometers of the future can be seen in light of the existing social conditions for Blacks and the trends in sexual behavior, fertility patterns, sex role changes, and marital adjustments.

Some adaptations to alternative life-styles will occur because large numbers of Blacks, especially in the middle class, are taking on the values of the majority culture. Family relations in the majority culture are changing and many Blacks will follow their trends. However, Blacks as a group will continue to face certain problems that may not be unique to them except to the extent of their prevalence. The continuing high unemployment rate among Black men and women will still have serious ramifications for the kind of family life they will have. That will primarily be a problem of the lower-class group, but all classes will have to adapt to the increasing critical problem of a male shortage and the consequences thereof.

Up to this time the problem of the male shortage has been handled by a type of serial polygyny whereby Black men have more than one wife in a lifetime but not at the same time. Some men remain married but are free-floating in their relations with other women. This kind of male-sharing may be necessary for a group with such an imbalanced sex ratio. It, however, gives rise to many conflicts between men and women who are strongly socialized into monogamous values. The instability of many Black marriages can be accounted for by this factor as well as by the general range of forces that cause marital disruption. In the future alternative family life-styles should be well thought out and implemented in ways conducive to individual and group harmony.

## Public Policy and Black Families

According to Bell and Vogel (1968), the family contributes its loyalty to the government in exchange for leadership, which will provide direct and indirect benefits for the nuclear family. Although there is little doubt that Black families have been loyal to the political state in the United States, it appears that they have derived few reciprocal benefits in return. Although the political system has the power to affect many of the conditions influencing Black family life, it has failed to intervene in the service of the Black population and, in fact, has been more of a negative force in shaping the conditions under which Black families must live. As Billingsley (1968:177) has stated, "no subsystem has been more oppressive of the Negro people or holds greater promise for their development."

Historically, we find that state, local, and federal governmental bodies have been willing collaborators in the victimization of Black families. Under slavery, marriages between slaves were not legal because the slave could make no contract. The government did nothing to ensure stable marriages among the slave population or to prevent the arbitrary separation of slave couples by their owners. Moreover, the national government was committed to the institution of slavery, a practice that was most inimical to Black family life (Frazier, 1939).

One function of government has been to protect the sexual integrity of the female population. Until recently, the government has not provided legal or physical protection for the Black woman against sexual advances of white males. Many Black women were forced to engage in intercourse with white males because there was no law that prevented their involuntary seduction. Some state governments passed laws that held that no white man could be convicted for fornication with a Black woman. Other states required a white person as witness to any act of rape against a Black woman (Berry, 1971).

However, the government did pass, and strongly enforce, laws against interracial marriage, which were mainly designed to prevent the mating of Black men and white women. These laws ostensibly were passed to prevent racial amalgamation; but, as Heer (1974) noted, antimiscegenation laws served other functions. The requirement of racially homogamous marriages prevented Blacks from inheriting wealth from any white person through marriage into a family of means. The ban on interracial marriages denied Blacks a chance to become familiar with the white world and to obtain jobs requiring such familiarity. Their class mobility was also restricted by the lack of informal social contacts with whites that can facilitate their entrance into certain jobs, which are acquired through pull and connections.

In more recent years, state governments have tried to impose middle-class values on lower-income families, many of whom are Black. Various state legislatures have passed laws designed to reduce or eliminate welfare benefits to women who have given birth to a child out-of-wedlock. A few states have even attempted to pass laws sterilizing women on welfare who have had more than one "illegitimate" child.

For reasons that may be related to the sacrosanct nature of the family in the United States, this country has rarely had any clearly defined plans or policy concerning the family. The closest thing to it has been the welfare system, which actually worked to disrupt more families than it did to keep them together. In light of the continuing decline of the extended family, which once provided valuable backup services to the nuclear family, some sort of family support system seems necessary. Although the Black family has an extended family character, there is some decline in its viability as a support force. At the same time the central problems facing Black families require to a much greater extent some kind of remedy by a well-formulated public policy and action program addressed to their needs.

Scott (1978) delineated what those needs are in relation to Black women in our society. She described them, most accurately, as a lower-income group with high rates of unemployment and densely concentrated in low-level service-related jobs. Even if employment were offered to Black women who are unemployed, they would have problems because quality day care centers are not often available to them. Some critics of day care program expansion argue that taking care of children is a function of the family, not of the government. Such arguments ignore the realities of today's families, which necessitate either low-cost, government-supervised care of children or the relegation of women to a permanent category of second class citizens.

Those same critics are advocates of involuntary birth control and sterilization programs to prevent women from having "too many" children. This is especially imposed on low-income Black women, who are stereotyped as irresponsible breeders of children. Scott (1978) noted that birth control and sterilization programs often have a higher priority than prenatal health services and sex education programs for Black adolescents. She suggested a number of programs that would assist Black women to maintain healthy families. Elevating their pay and status in the work force is a key one, along with the development of quality day care facilities and promotion of research activities on the mental and physical health problems of Black women, the needs of the Black aged woman, the role of women in the media, and other areas.

In an early article on "Public Policy and the Changing Status of Black Families," Staples (1973) reviewed the past relationship of government to the structure of Black family life. In general, the government's efforts, few as they have been, were sporadic, misguided, and ineffective. Because future trends are in the direction of increasing numbers of female-headed households, which are characterized by a below-average income and above-average number of children, Staples suggested the specific contents of a public policy relevant to Black families. It includes a universal family allowance, elimination of sex discrimination in employment, community controlled day care centers, a child development program, and expanded government employment. Only through a combination of these measures will Blacks have a choice of family arrangements.

# References

**Bell, N. and E. Vogel**

1968  *A Modern Introduction to the Family.* New York: The Free Press.

**Berry, M.**

1971  *Black Resistance—White Law: A History of Constitutional Racism in America.* New York: Appleton-Century-Crofts.

**Billingsley, A.**

1968  *Black Families in White America.* Englewood Cliffs, N.J.: Prentice-Hall.

**Frazier, E. F.**

1939  *The Negro Family in the United States.* Chicago: University of Chicago Press.

**Heer, D.**

1974  "The Prevalence of Black–White Marriage in the United States, 1960 and 1970." *Journal of Marriage and the Family* 36 (May):246–258.

**Scott, P. B.**

1978  "Black Female Liberation and Family Action Programs: Some Considerations." In *The Black Family: Essays and Studies* (2nd ed.), R. Staples, ed., pp. 260–263. Belmont, Calif.: Wadsworth.

**Staples, R.**

1973  "Public Policy and the Changing Status of Black Families." *The Family Coordinator* 22:345–353.

# 11 / Alternative Life-Styles

## FROM TEENAGE PARENTHOOD TO POLYGAMY:
### Case Studies in Black Polygamous Family Formation

*Joseph W. Scott*

*In this article the author describes a type of polygamous family formation in the Black community that develops when a single female parent becomes sexually involved with a married man and reaches a stage of sharing him with his wife on a regular and continuing basis. The author defines polygamy as a situation in which legally married men and never married women become permanently invested in children and other aspects of family life.*

## Introduction

Polygamy in the United States has been virtually forgotten as a subject of serious study by American behavioral scientists. The writer surveyed the various journals in sociology, anthropology, and marriage and the family, and was not able to find any systematic research other than his own (Scott, 1976; Scott, 1977) on the practices in the United States of polygamy outside the early studies of Mormons (Muncy, 1974) and later studies of Puerto Ricans in Puerto Rico (Stewart, 1956).

If one accepts the subjective understanding of the people one observes and if one accepts the efficacy of the consensual agreements they make, polygamy is indeed a growing family form in the U.S., and, in addition, the practice is not new.

What has happened is that generally social scientists who study family relations in the United States have come across polygamous families among their cases, but they systematically treat them as "extramarital" affairs or "illicit" relations. As a result the polygamous families in the U.S. have been ignored with the consequence that the researched picture of American family life—especially that outside the law—has been quite incompletely reported (Schulz, 1969; Hertz and Little, 1944; Staples, 1973; Liebow, 1967; Pope, 1967).

From the *Western Journal of Black Studies* 10 (Winter 1986):172–179. Copyright 1986 by the Washington State University Press. Reprinted by permission.

This study is a first step in an attempt to give a more complete picture of American family life without imposing value judgements of policy implications about the phenomenon in question.

## Review of Literature

The Black American family has been the subject of many articles in recent years—especially since the Moynihan Report (Moynihan, 1965). Nearly all of these discussions, however, ignore the fact that the Black family has been changing in the same ways as white families have been changing—although at a faster rate (Farley, 1971). More recent research indicates that matrifocal Black families are the result of more and more destabilizing forces pressing upon the Black nuclear family, rather than the result of Black males and females of marriage age giving up on the *value of* marriage (Young, 1970; Aschenbrenner, 1973; Stack, 1972; Belcher, 1967). Demographic and economic forces within the larger political economy have been pressing upon the Blacks contributing to their growing number of single-parent female-headed households in contrast to the typical husband-wife headed family.

To speak of the single-parent family as a growing family form is also to beg questions of *Black family formation processes*, in general. In Black America there are many types of families: for example, couple-headed families, single-parent headed families and polygamous families. Common beliefs to the contrary, most Black families are still husband-wife families (56 percent) even though decreasing. Farley (1971:279) found that since 1930 the percentage of adult Black men married with a spouse has been decreasing. In 1930, for example, 65 percent of the Black men of marriage age headed such families; in 1982, only 42 percent of these Black men headed such families (Farley, 1984). During this same time that husband-wife families were decreasing in number, mother-headed families were increasing in number too (31 percent). From 1930 to 1969 the *proportion* of husband-wife families declined from 80 to 69 percent (Farley and Hermalin, 1971). Today that proportion is 56 percent (Reid, 1982).

Although increases in female-headed households have been caused by divorce, separation and widowhood, female-headed households increased in great number largely because *single women of marriage-age have been setting up their own independent households in greater number*, largely because single never-married women have been becoming mothers with the benefits of husbands. Farley's (1971:284) research supports this contention. For example, he found that from 1930 to 1969 a very rapid increase in female-headed households resulting from single women leaving their parental homes and setting up their own independent households. Furstenberg (1978:324) found, in fact, that out-of-wedlock births to single Black females did contribute to young mothers leaving their parental homes to set up their own households earlier than other young women their age in their socio-economic circumstances. In addition to biological events such as out-of-wedlock births, this author also thinks that socio-economic stresses in many poor families have operated as "pushes" causing many young women to leave their parental homes around age 18 in order to set up independent households to relieve the burdens on their parents by living on public assistance. Black women, aged 20–24, who once largely were married by this age are remaining single. The percentage single is 72 percent (Farley, 1984). While they are remaining single, they are not remaining childless.

As suggested above, female-headed households have also increased due to increasing marital breakups. Compared to whites, proportionately fewer Black adults who ever marry, remain married and continue to live with their spouses. Compared to whites, significantly more Blacks are widowed, divorced and separated. Blacks spend much more of their adult lives as singles. In 1979, the distribution of Black females 25 to 44 was 23 percent never-married, 16 percent separated, 3 percent widowed, and 13 percent divorced (Cherlin, 1981). Is there any wonder that more than 41 percent of the Black family and non-family households today are female-headed, and that this percentage is more than three times the proportion for Whites (Glick and Norton, 1979:3)? Is there wonder that *one-half* of all Black families *with* children are headed by single females?

## Family Formation Processes

Clearly then, one of the most common ways that female-headed households are formed today is by way of the out-of-wedlock births to single females. Furstenberg (1978:324) found that "from pregnancy to the five-year postpartum interview, a growing proportion of the young mothers predictably made their way out of the household of their parents." By the time the women Furstenberg studied had reached their early 20s, the proportion of these women living with parents had dropped to 46 percent, and that there was a "a sizeable increase in the proportion of women living alone, and only a slight increase in the proportion currently living with their spouses." (Furstenberg, 1978:325) Furstenberg concluded that teenage parenthood seemed to result in an earlier home-leaving than would otherwise be the case. Therefore, it is reasonable to say that out-of-wedlock teenage parenthood is a very relevant factor in single-parent family formation today.

## Teenage Parenthood

It is commonly reported than 1 in 10 teenage girls in the U.S. becomes pregnant every year (Intercom, 1977:12) and that teenage pregnancy is nearly three times as common among Blacks as among whites (Zelnik and Kanter, 1974, 1978a, 1978b). However, an increasing number of women of all races have been bearing children outside of marriage: 5 percent of all births in 1960 were out-of-wedlock compared to 14 percent in 1975. For Blacks alone in 1975, the percent of births out-of-wedlock was 49 (Glick and Norton, 1977:6). Even more revealing is that among Black and white teenagers together in 1975, 39 percent of their births were out-of-wedlock; the percentage for whites was 23 percent, compared to the Blacks' 78 percent (Intercom, 1977:11).

From these data above, one of the most common processes generating family formation among Blacks is out-of-wedlock births. In point of fact, 55 percent of all Black births annually are out-of-wedlock. Given the finding that out-of-wedlock births do cause young women having babies outside of marriage to set up independent households *be-*

*fore* they might otherwise do so, increasing single-parent households are inevitable, if premarital births continue to rise. Widowhoods have also been contributing to the growing number of Black female-headed households. A second point of fact is that for women 15–44 the non-marital birth rate is 83 per 1000 for Blacks compared to 18 per 1000 for whites (Matney and Johnson, 1983).

Where are the marriage-age Black men? Jacquelyne Jacksons (1971) reported that there were only about 85 black adult men for every 100 black women in the marriage ages in the largest urban areas. Today, there are about 1.8 million more Black females than males in the U.S. The sex ratio at 15 to 19 is 100, but by 40 to 44 it is 82. Why? Staples (1973), Scott and Stewart (1978) have turned up data that indicate that Black males have been disproportionately eliminated through various wars, so-called justifiable homicides, death sentences, industrial accidents, poor medical care and Black-on-Black crime. Excess mortality of Black males is caused by heart disease, homicide and cancer (U.S. Dept. of HHS, 1986). Blacks have 2.5 to 5.3 times more widows than whites in the age groups from 25–44. Mansharing, therefore, may be a demographic imperative in some urban places, especially, where the sex ratio is even lower than 85, for marriage-age Blacks. Substantial single parenthood results from the biological shortage of Black males.

## Black Polygamous Family Formation

The foregoing discussion now enables one to begin to understand polygamous family formation in the U.S. This research indicates that such families grow out of the increasing single female parents in the Black community. Polygamous families may be formed in a number of ways: One style of polygamous family is a female-headed family combined with a second female-headed family, with the two females sharing the never-married father of their children between them. Another style is for a legally married man and an unmarried female to begin an extramarital courtship which eventually grows into a full-fledged familial relationship with children and subsequent regular visitation and financial support patterns. In this latter type of polygamous family formation, the consensual "wife" is often a never-married mother living independently who began as a teenage parent and for various social, sexual and economic reasons became sexually involved with a married man and came to the point of sharing him with his legal wife on a regular and continuing basis.

This article describes the latter type of polygamous family formation: the families involving legally married men and never-married women who became "permanently" invested in children and other aspects of family life.

## The Sample

The first sample is an availability-snowball one of Black women between the ages of 18 and 32. Interviewed were a total of 22 young Black women, one-half of whom were married and one-half of whom were single. No interviews were completed with any *two* women who were knowingly sharing the *same* man between them. The sample of 22 women consented to open-ended interviews recorded on tape. All of the women were either still in a polygamous relationship or had recently been in that situation for some considerable period of time prior to the interview. These relationships had lasted from about 2 years to over 12 years.

In a separate paper, published elsewhere, the views and life experiences of the *consensual* "wives" are compared to those of the *legal* wives (see Scott, 1980). This paper deals exclusively with the consensual "wives" and the process by which they became attached to married men on a routine basis.

All eleven consensual "wives" in this subsample were of lower socio-economic status, although some had started college. Most were regularly unemployed, although a few were employed. Generally, they had childhoods typical for their socio-economic status in the sense of having been more-or-less close to both of their parents up to the age of 10 and thereafter from 10–15 they became less close to their parents, most particularly less close to their fathers due to parental separations and divorces. However, they usually remained close or very close

to their mothers, but these parent-child relationships were not without their problems too.

On the whole, these single females started "seeing" young males at an early age—usually 14 or 15; that is, they were "receiving company" about this age, sometimes with and sometimes without parental permission. About seventy percent of them became sexually active between 16 or 17 and hence, as one would expect, became pregnant usually at 17 or no later than about 18. As a result of these early sexual involvements and pregnancies, they had their first babies out-of-wedlock. For the majority, these babies were unwanted, unplanned and untimed. In addition, socially and educationally, these young teenagers were not ready for motherhood.

Given the secretive nature and the antagonistic nature of these triadic relationships, the writer has not interviewed (as yet) any of the men involved with these particular women. The immense cooperation of openness required to interview all corners of these triadic relationships are being cultivated. Hence, the demographics on the male role players are still unattainable.

The woman legally married to the man who is being shared is called the legal wife; the woman not legally married to the married man being shared is called the consensual "wife." The word "wife" is preferred because of the familial nature of these relationships and because some respondents used the term to refer to themselves. This is an ethnographic study, using life histories.

## From Teenage Parenthood to Polygamy

The typical women in this sample came from the lowest socio-economic levels in the community, and their families or orientation were typically headed by a single mother who was either separated, divorced or never married. Family background was described in these words:

*My mother and father separated when I was twelve years old. He would come to visit us every once in a while, but my mother mostly*

*raised us from then on. She was understand-*
*ing, and she was lovable; and she tried to*
*give us the things that we needed, moreso*
*than the things that we wanted. With several*
*kids, you can't give them too much. She*
*wasn't working. We were on welfare.*

For the most part, they had trouble with their mothers and felt it necessary to leave home in late adolescence. They were usually fifteen through eighteen years of age, still in school and still relatively unsocialized as to adult statuses when they left.

Leaving home was described this way:

*I left home because I felt that I should have*
*more freedom than my mother wanted to*
*give me and I realized that I had to give her*
*respect. . . .*
     *. . . my biggest problem was getting away*
*from her. You know, 'cause I was a teenager*
*going to school. I didn't have nice things like*
*other girls so I had to come home and cook*
*and iron; she didn't even give me lunch*
*money. So the most thing I dreamed was get-*
*ting away from home.*

More often than not, upon leaving, they got pregnant and had to leave school too. (Schools for the most part did not have provisions for school-age mothers.)

During this period they had their first sexual experiences. To be more precise, they had their first continuous sexual relations which as one would expect soon led to their first pregnancies. Almost all of them became pregnant by their first lovers or their first regular sexual companions largely because they were ignorant of and inexperienced in this most critical aspect of adult socialization—sexual intercourse. Leaving home (and not sex) was uppermost in their minds:

*All I ever thought about was getting away*
*from home. You know what, I never did*
*think about babies or anything. I figured that*
*one day I would get pregnant, but I wasn't*
*thinking about babies then. I was thinking*
*about getting away from Mama.*
   *My first (sex intercourse) was at his*
*house . . . I was just doing something cause*
*he asked me to. I didn't even know what feel-*
*ing I was supposed to get; that is a shame. I*
*didn't know no better and I didn't care, I*
*guess. . . . I just didn't feel anything, about it.*
*I didn't know if I should like it or not. He was*
*telling me this is the normal thing to do and*
*this is the only way we are going to go to-*
*gether and all this kind of stuff; he said that I*
*had to understand and the fact that he was a*
*man and he can't just be kissing and patting*
*and stuff like that, you know. . . . When it*
*happened I could have died; when it was*
*over and it was very painful, very painful. . . .*
*He was about 17 'cause I was 15.*

Not having had much formal or informal instruction in the art of sexual intercourse and in the technology of birth control they were destined to get pregnant, barring any congenital maladies.

When asked if they were trying to get pregnant most said they did not want to get pregnant or become school-age mothers, even though they wanted to become mothers at some point in the future.

The first out-of-wedlock pregnancy was usually immediate:

*Well, I had my first child when I was fifteen.*
*And I didn't go back to school because I had*
*the baby. And by my mother having all my*
*other brothers and sisters, I couldn't very well*
*have her take care of my baby. And I wasn't*
*going to have her adopted. I wasn't married.*

Once they became pregnant their personal values, scripted from their mothers, prevented them from getting abortions or even considering giving up their children for adoption. The traumas of out-of-wedlock pregnancies were not enough to change their minds or their behaviors.

After confirming their pregnancies, a few considered marriage, but most did not. Even though most of their male friends offered to marry them, the girls refused them pretty much to the man. The women responded with a wholesale rejection of the institution of marriage. As they saw it, marriage was not necessarily an adequate coping mechanism for teenage pregnancies. Neither were motherhood and marriage necessarily to be combined. They had grown up under an existential pattern concerning motherhood and marriage that males and females could live happily compartmentalizing these two activities. The disjunction between motherhood and marriage had long been forced upon their friends and relatives by societally imposed socio-economic circumstances.

Early in their childhoods as girls, they, like others in this society had held the American family dream: individually, they had expected to have a marriage, a husband, about three children, a home and a stable income. However, they were soon to learn that these simple goals held out to everyone were not materially or institutionally possible for everyone.

They had held these ideas up to the time of their pregnancies, and now their pregnancies and attendant problems caused these ideals to slowly slip out of their grasps. When asked for their hands in marriage the women had said "no" because they knew that neither they nor their male friends could even remotely come close to supporting a house and a family. They must have sensed that their physical, emotional, and social immaturity were prohibitive too.

That immaturity comes through in these statements:

> *Well you know—another reason I didn't want to get married was because I felt sexually I wanted to branch out, have me some more fellows. That is a sad way to think about it, but I wanted to look and see if this was really what I wanted to be stuck with the rest of my life. I wanted to find out if this was the right one. So, this is why I didn't want to just jump up and marry, you know.*

Even though the women refused to marry them—usually for a good reason—the fathers nevertheless continued regular visitations and ties.

Contrary to the mythologies surrounding Black males, they did not desert these women at the outset of pregnancy or at the births of the babies. At birth most started to make financial contributions within the limits of their meager incomes. For those out of school with sporadic employment, they made contributions up to the level of financial responsibility they could assume. But one must remember that the young teenage Black males have been the main "rejects" of this money economy.

Most of the fathers reportedly wanted to make contributions in order to be able to have paternity rights and visitation rights without marriage and its attendant contractual rights. But, even though they were *willing* to contribute more than they did, they were not able to do so because of either their lack of employment or their low income from the employment they could find. They understood the rejection by the women very well. The American family ideal was more remote than it seemed at first glance, through the eyes of all these young adolescents.

The out-of-wedlock pregnancies and births caused their American family dreams to fade fast, and caused the realities of their situations to dominate: Matters of coping with stigma, with economic self support and child support, with socially and emotionally stunted men became the most pressing realities.

The unavailability of "good men" highlighted their problems:

> *I feel that the good men are getting scarce. The good ones out here now are the hustlers and the so-called pimps. Even what you call the professional ones, they are doing the same thing; they are hustling but they are doing it a little more discreetly. They are getting that money from those girls and having different kinds of girls, and if they don't do certain things or if they don't give them money they don't want to be bothered with them, you know. Fellows are staying with the ones that are giving them the money.*

What of marriage? Marriage to immature, financially insolvent men was hardly a solution. Marriage to "legitimize" the births in the eyes of whites was hardly a solution: that type of "legitimacy" did not matter to most members of the Black community. Marriage to convey upon them an adult status was hardly a solution; in point of fact, motherhood without marriage not only conveyed an adult status, but it also conveyed adult rights and privileges, and qualified them for public child support at a time when private child support was not at all certain. Most commonly, therefore, the women opted for motherhood without marriage.

Motherhood without marriage was a sort of decision they drifted to:

> *I dreamed, you know, I wanted to be married have a nice husband and children, although I didn't get married to the one I wanted to. I wanted to get married someday but I'm glad I didn't get married. I was too young in the first place. Getting married at fifteen, even though you have a baby, that was too young.*
>
> *Now, marriage is not the right thing to do—it is just a piece of paper that both of you have an agreement. You can also get that by means of an understanding. You can also get that understanding without that piece of paper. That piece of paper cost you very little to get it but costs you a hell of a lot of money to get rid of it. You don't have to have that piece of paper to have that understanding. I never thought of living my life without a husband. But if that is what is in store for me, that is what I accept.*

The prior socialization for adulthood now loomed larger than ever. Ignorance of birth control and its uses clearly become a most serious omission in the socialization of school-age mothers because their out-of-wedlock pregnancies and births subsequently forced most of these women into several self-defeating decisions. Early motherhood had the effect of rearranging the shapes of their lives. For example, pregnancies and births made them dependent upon those same mothers and relatives from whom they wanted to be independent. These same pregnancies and births made them dependent upon

public agencies which put them through continuous degradation rituals. Finally, these pregnancies and births made them dependent upon male companions who pressured them to do things they may not have wanted to do.

How men shaped their lives is illustrated as follows:

> *A lot of men don't want to get married, especially if you have a child. Well, men don't want to be bothered with another man's child. It's hard to find a man who would take a woman on with children. The children's fathers are always somewhere in the background . . . coming, knocking, and going through all these changes. Some men just don't feel like being bothered with all that. If I were a man and I married a woman, I wouldn't want her ex-husband or ex-man to come knocking on the door, saying, "Can I see my kids?" But that's the problem. You have to face it.*

What all of this suggests is that these out-of-wedlock pregnancies and births reduced their options very considerably and made them more dependent upon those on whom they did not want to be dependent.

As if these reduced options were not enough, the women found that they had fewer options in the marriage marketplace too. They found an abundance of companionship from men who were the least likely to be employed and emotionally stable. They found that while they were not sexually "loose," they were considered sexually "experienced" and many males believed them to be sexually "available."

The confusion that out-of-wedlock babies caused was revealed in these words:

> *After you have a baby, then you have all kinds of suitors knocking at your door. They feel that if a woman has had a baby, she's easy for everybody else. That's not true for a lot of women or a lot of girls. I mean, if you make a mistake and have a baby, it's not saying that everything is open for everybody else.*

*It's not like that. But I have had a lot of offers. But I'm the kind like this: I don't believe in a whole bunch of men even though I'm single.*

Their pregnancies and births were indicative of a brief sexual experience but many males assumed more and acted on it. By contrast the school-age females who had not had any out-of-wedlock births did not give the appearance of being sexually active or available, and hence males who were looking for sexually active and available women looked for those of demonstrated experience . . . the school-age mothers.

For most of these mothers, their first out-of-wedlock pregnancies often led to second out-of-wedlock pregnancies and with these their options became still further reduced. Their semi-permanent dependency on parents, public agents or male friends was now complete. More often than not the men who now came around were either single men looking for sex and money without familial attachments or married men looking for sex as a permanent consensual arrangement.

The difficulty of finding a "good" man was described this way:

*Nowadays, you can forget about having a man all to yourself. If he is going with you, you can take for granted that he has at least one more somewhere else. If it ain't nothing but where he works at, he got somebody. Nowadays he is going for everything that he can get: He is going for sex; he is going for money; if you got a car, he'll take that. The first thing that they ask you is "Do you have a job?" "You working?" If you ain't working, they ain't got the time.*

The stable employed men who were marriageable were not looking for women who have had one or more children out-of-wedlock. Thus, one time, these women were forced to drift towards married men—into polygamous relationships. The drift was more by circumstance than by plan, but it was definitely in the direction of married men.

The women usually became consensual mates while their men were still married and living with their wives. Sometimes they became consensual mates of men who were married but separated from their wives. Rarely did these women ever find their men free and clear of other conjugal relationships. The men who were "free and clear" were usually either habitual drug users, or criminals, or homosexuals, and none of these types, the women maintained, were desirable as mates, especially, as father figures. In point of fact they could be neither stable husbands, father figures nor lovers. The men most available and most desired were married men:

*Most of the available single men have either been killed in the war, or they have been put in prison, or they are queers or funnies. You're damn right there is a shortage because when you run across a good one that wants to give you something and has got something, nine out of ten times he is married. He is married; you better believe it.*

*I rather go with a single man. But is is hard to find a good single man. But most of those married men are good, better than those single men. You find women today that won't go with nothing but a married man because they can't stand no static.*

Considering the choices, married men turned out to be the more sought after. Because the married men were more accepting of maternal situations, they were also more desirable. Being kinder in demeanor, more stable in life-style, more frugal in spending habits and more reliable in visitation habits also made married men more desirable. Married men revealed themselves to be more knowledgeable than single men about the psycho-sexual satisfaction of women and about all other aspects of their lives. That consideration was compared in these words:

*As far as a single man and a married man is concerned, if you find a nice single man that really has himself together, it is nice; but if you don't find that kind, you are just about as well off with a married man. If it like this, some married men will do all they can possibly do for you. . . .*

*A single man don't have the patience, nor understanding. If things don't go like they want them to, then they are mad. They are ready to fight. Like if they make a date. They say: "Well, I'll be at your house tonight at eight o'clock." If you got kids, and your child gets sick and you can't make it he's going to say: "Well so-and-so and so-and-so." And he's going to get mad and Bam: He's gone. But now a married man, if he's got a family and your child gets sick, he says: "Well, I understand. Let me know how everything works out." Even when it comes down to sex, a married man respects a woman more than a single man, because he wouldn't want nobody to curse his wife out or curse in front of her. Whereas a single man, he might be used to cursing a woman out.*

When these women found married men whom they like sexually and personally, they did not break off the relationships with the men because they turned out to be married. They took no great steps to avoid sexual and personal involvement with them perhaps because they thought they could eventually "tighten up" the relationships and make them exclusive. Hope springs eternal and hope caused these women to stay in these relationships and get deeper and deeper into them. They neither wanted to nor did they plan to share these men with anyone else permanently. Sharing married men turned out to be one of the pitfalls of the rating and dating game for unwed mothers. As the contradiction became apparent they felt further trapped, but still hopeful. When questioned about the contradiction, the women believed that they had no other real choice given their circumstances. They had to stay in these relationships to have any at all.

In the final analysis, *drifting into polygamy* has been for these women and to outside observers who know the socio-economic facts of this society, a forced choice. School-age pregnancies and births without provisions for the adequate economic support reduced their subsequent choices to largely forced ones. Educationally, familially, occupationally and financially they generally came out of compel-

ling circumstances and continued to get mired in even more compelling circumstances. Having babies out-of-wedlock clearly restricted their subsequent choices with regard to marriage and the family, and resulted in their social, emotional and economic dependency on married men.

Their dependency on married men finally produces a polygamous arrangement:

*I have to share him, which I am doing. . . . I thought about this. I really cried when he went back. It broke me up; but like my girlfriends said, "Well, let him make up his own mind and go on like you've been doing and just don't drop out of the picture right now because he definitely wouldn't have a choice." So I think my choice would be to go on and stay with him until he leaves her and treat him like I have been treating him. He is not really married, so he can't stay with her forever. . . .*

*As far as leaving him, I feel like—there is not enough men to go around . . . I mean somebody that really wants to do thing for me. It would give me hard time to try to find somebody else; although, I know I could, it would be hard. As far as leaving . . . I don't think I would.*

*You can say you'll let him go before you share him, but then you let him go today and meet one tomorrow, well, that is the same problem. So, I don't know what choices we would really have . . . other than not to share him.*

Married men turned out to be the ones with whom these women could not put together some semblance of family lives even if only consensual rather than contractual family lives. So, even though their married men had family and paternity commitments elsewhere, these women allowed themselves to become involved. Man-sharing was not the choice the women most wanted. Though polygamy was less than a desired choice, it became a tolerable choice within the social, economic and personal choices they had.

## Towards a Theory of Polygamous Family Formation

Developmental Task Theory seems applicable. Magrabi and Marshall (1965:454-459) postulate that a failure to perform satisfactorily the developmental tasks at one particular stage will result in difficulty with the performance of later developmental family tasks. For example, the lack of successful use of contraception in premarital sexual intercourse is likely to lead to difficulty in planning the family size in the future stages. Even though one cannot say with certainty what behaviors or activities contribute most to later future accomplishments, the evidence of the eyes suggests that there is a relationship between behavior at one stage and success at tasks at later stages.

If one were to follow these women through the transition from virginity to sexual activity, from that to contraception use, from that to pregnancy from that to childbirth or abortion or without marriage and so on, one could see that the behaviors and activities at one stage precondition the accomplishments at the next stage.

Throughout this study the author has used the terms "forced choice" to refer to the limited skills, knowledges and performances available to these teenage subjects. The author has also intimated that these limitations preconditioned their subsequent choices and influenced the future stages they could arrive at (without extraordinary assistance). The author therefore reasoned that these women mostly "drifted" into polygamy.

It seems abundantly clear that over "time" certain "tasks" such as child-rearing and income maintenance grow out of certain "situations" such as teenage parenthood, calling for the successful performance of tasks before advancement to a next stage can occur. If one were to identify the stages and activities required for passage to a new level and compare these to those options actually available at each stage, one would conclude that polygamous relationships could be possible and discernible outcomes of a teenage parenthood.

Developmental Task Theory suggests that there are tasks arising at a certain stage in the life of a family which, if successfully performed, leads to satisfaction as well as success with later tasks. On the other hand the inability or incapacity to accomplish these developmental tasks leads to either failure, or difficulty with later tasks if not to disapproval by the society at large. The drift into polygamous relations is explained very well by Developmental Task Theory.

# References

Aschenbrenner, J.
1973 "Extended Families Among Black Americans," *Journal of Comparative Family Studies* 4:256–269.

Belcher, J.
1967 "The One Person Household: A Consequence of the Isolated Nuclear Family," *Journal of Marriage and the Family* 29: (Aug)584–590.

Farley, R.
1971 "Family Types and Family Headship: A Comparison of Trends Among Blacks and Whites." *The Journal of Human Resources* VI: (Summer)275–296.

Farley, R. and A. Hermalin
1971 "Family Stability: A Comparison of Trends Between Blacks and Whites." *American Sociological Review* 36:1–17.

Farley, R.
1984 *Blacks and Whites: Narrowing the Gap?*, Cambridge, Mass.: Harvard U. Press.

Furstenberg, F. and A. Crawford
1978 "Family Support: Helping Teenage Mothers to

Cope." *Family Planning Perspective* 10: (Nov/Dec)322–333.

Glick, P. and A. J. Norton

1977    "Marrying, Divorcing, and Living Together in the U.S. Today." *Population Bulletin* 32: (Population Reference Bureau) Washington, D.C. 1–39.

1979    "Marrying, Divorcing, and Living Together in the U.S. Today," *Population Bulletin*, Vol. 32, No. 5 (Population Reference Bureau, Inc., Washington, D.C.).

Hertz, H. and S. Little

1944    "Unmarried Negro Mothers in a Southern Urban Community," *Social Forces* 23: (Oct)73–79.

Intercom

1977a   Vol. 5 (Feb):11.

1977b   Vol. 5 (Sept):5.

Jackson, J.

1971    "But Where are the Men?" *Black Scholar*: (Dec)30–41.

Liebow, E.

1967    *Tally's Corner*. New York: Little Brown & Co.

Magrabi, F. and W. Marshall

1965    "Family Developmental Tasks: A Research Model." *Journal of Marriage and the Family* 27 (Nov):454–459.

Matney, W. C., Jr. and D. L. Johnson

1983    "America's Black Population: 1970 to 1982, A Statistical View," *The Crisis*, Vol. 90, No. 10, 10–18.

Moynihan, D.

1965    *The Negro Family: The Case for National Action*. Washington, D.C.: U.S. Depart. of Labor.

Muncy, R.

1974    *Sex and Marriage in Utopian Communities*. Baltimore: Penguin Books, Inc.

Pope, H.

1967    "Unwed Mothers and Their Sex Partners." *Journal of Marriage and the Family* 29: (Aug)555–567.

Reid, J.

1982    "Black America in the 1980s," *Population Bulletin*, Vol. 37, No. 4 (Population Reference Bureau, Inc., Washington, D.C.).

Schulz, D.

1969    "Variations in the Father Role in Complete Families of the Negro Lower Class." *Social Science Quarterly* 49: (Dec)73–79.

Stack, C.

1972    "Black Kindreds: Parenthood and Personal Kindred Among Urban Blacks." *Journal of Comparative Family Studies* 3:194–206.

Staples, R.

1973    *The Black Woman in America*. Chicago: Nelson-Hall.

Stewart, J. B. and J. W. Scott

1978    "The Institutional Decrimation of Black American Males." *The Western Journal of Black Studies* 2: (Summer)82–92.

Stewart, J. and Associates

1956    *The People of Puerto Rico*. Urbana, IL.: University of Illinois Press.

U.S. Department of Health and Human Services

1986    "Report of the Secretary's Task Force on Black and Minority Health," Vol. 35, No. 8, Feb. 28.

Young, V.

1970    "Family and Childhood in a Southern Negro Community." *American Anthropologist* 72:269–288.

Zelnik, M. and J. Kanter

1974    "The Resolution of Teenage First Pregnancies." *Family Planning Perspectives* 6: (Spring)74–80.

1978a   "First Pregnancies to Women Aged 15-19: 1976 and 1971." *Family Planning Perspectives* 10: (Jan/Feb)11–20.

1978b   "Contraceptive Patterns and Premarital Pregnancy Among Women Aged 15-19 in 1976." *Family Planning Perspectives* 10: (May/June)135–142.

# Sociocultural Facets of the Black Gay Male Experience

## Susan D. Cochran · Vickie M. Mays

*This article reviews the literature on Black gay and bisexual men. It reports on the development of a Black gay identity, the integration of Black gay men into the Black heterosexual world, some of their sexual practices, behavior that places them at risk for AIDS and alcoholism, and their social networks. The authors caution that the experiences of Black gay men cannot be interpreted in terms of a white gay male standard.*

Prior to the appearance of AIDS in this country, studies on the sexual preferences and behaviors of gay men generally ignored the specific experiences of Black men (Bell, Weinberg, and Hammersmith, 1981). With the press of the AIDS epidemic to develop baseline information on men's intimate behaviors, this tendency rarely to study Black gay men, or do so in the same manner as White gay men, persists. While many researchers may recognize the importance of possible cultural differences, their approach has been to assume that Black gay men would be more like White gay men than Black heterosexuals. Questionnaires, sampling procedures, and topics of focus have been more consistent with White gay men's experiences (see Becker and Jo-

seph, 1988, for a comprehensive review of behavior change studies). This proclivity has resulted in an emergence of comparisons between Black and White men using White gay standards of behavior that may be obscuring our understanding of important psychosocial determinants of sexual behaviors in Black gay men. Given the differences that have been observed in family structure and sexual patterns between Black and White heterosexuals, there is no empirical basis upon which to assume that Black gay men's experience of homosexuality would perfectly mimic that of Whites (Bell, Weinberg, and Hammersmith, 1981). Indeed, very little is known empirically about the lives of Black gay men (Mays and Cochran, 1987), though there are some indications, discussed below, that they are more likely to engage in activities that place them at greater risk for HIV infection.

In the absence of any data we need to proceed cautiously with assumptions that imply anything other than [that] same-sex *activities* of Black gay men resemble those of White gay men. This caution is particularly true for AIDS studies that purport to study psychosocial behavior. Studies of this type report not only on behavior but also attempt to describe motivations and circumstances that led to the behavior. In the absence of a set of questions or

An abridged version of the article "Epidemiologic and Sociocultural Factors in the Transmission of HIV Infection in Black Gay and Bisexual Men" printed in *A Sourcebook of Gay/Lesbian Health Care* (M. Shernoff and W. A. Scott, eds.) Washington, D.C.: National Gay and Lesbian Health Foundation, 2nd ed. Copyright 1988 by the National Gay and Lesbian Health Foundation. Reprinted by permission. Support for this chapter was provided by a grant from the National Institute of Mental Health to both authors—a California State University, Northridge Foundation grant to the first author, and a USPHS Biomed grant from the University of California, Los Angeles, to the second author. Work on this chapter was completed while the second author was a National Center for Health Services research fellow at the Rand Corporation, Santa Monica, California.

framework incorporating important cultural, ethnic, and economic realities of Black gay men, interpretations emanating from a White gay male standard may be misleading.

# Development of a Black Gay Identity

In recent years, researchers (Spanier and Glick, 1980; Staples, 1981; Guttentag and Secord, 1983) have noted differences between Whites and Blacks in their intimate heterosexual relationships. Differential sociocultural factors presumably influence the development and specific structure of sexual behavior within Black heterosexual relationships. These factors include the unavailability of same ethnic group partners, fewer social and financial resources, residential immobility, and lack of employment opportunities. Many of these same conditions may surround the formation, maintenance and functioning of Black gay male relationships.

Popular writings in past years by Black gay men describe the difficulty in finding other Black gay men for potential partners, the lack of a visible Black gay community, an absence of role models, and the dearth of Black gay male social or professional organizations (Soares, 1979; Beame, 1983). While gay bars, gay baths and public places existed where White gay men gathered, some of these were off limits to Black gay men either due to actual or perceived racism within the White gay community or the danger of passing through White neighborhoods in order to participate in gay community activities. Thus, expectations that the experiences of Black gay men are identical to those of White gay men seem unwarranted.

In examining differences between Blacks and Whites in the emergence of a homosexual orientation, Bell, Weinberg, and Hammersmith (1981) found that, for the White males, pre-adult sexual feelings appeared to be very important. In contrast, among Black males, childhood and adolescent sexual activities, rather than feelings, were stronger predictors of the development of adult homosexual sexual orientation. Thus Blacks started to act at an earlier age on their sexual inclinations than Whites

did (Bell, Weinberg, and Hammersmith, 1981). This would be consistent with Black-White differences in the onset of heterosexual sexual activity if socioeconomic status is not statistically controlled for (Wyatt, personal communication).

The typical conceptualization of sexual orientation is that individuals are located in terms of their sexual feelings and behaviors on a bipolar dimension where one extreme is heterosexuality, the other is homosexuality, and lying somewhere in between is bisexuality (Bell and Weinberg, 1978). This definition does not include ethnicity or culture as an interactive factor influencing the expression of sexual behavior or sexual orientation. For example, Smith (1986) makes a distinction between Black gays and gay Blacks complicating the demarcation between homosexuality and bisexuality:

> Gay Blacks are people who identify first as being gay and who usually live outside the closet in predominantly white gay communities. I would estimate that they amount to roughly ten percent of all Black homosexuals. Black gays, on the other hand, view our racial heritage as primary and frequently live "bisexual front lives" within Black neighborhoods. (p. 226)

These two groups are probably quite different in both social activities and sexual behaviors. The Black gay man, strongly identified with Afro-American culture, will often look and behave much like the Black heterosexual man except in his sexual behavior. The extent to which his same-sex partners are integrated into his family and social environment may be a function of his class status (Soares, 1979). It has long been noted by Blacks that there are differences, both in values and behaviors, between middle-class and working-class Blacks. There is no reason to assume that within the Black gay community such diversity would not persist. While Smith (1986) has described the Black gay community in only two dimensions we would be remiss if we stopped here. There is a growing population of Black gays who have forged an identity acknowledging both statuses:

*At times I cried just remembering how it is to be both Black and gay during these truly difficult times. But here we are, still proud and living, with a culture all our own. (Sylvester, p. 11, 1986)*

We know less about the behavior of Black men who identify as bisexual and least about those black men who engage in same-sex sexual behavior but identify as exclusively heterosexual. When the factor of social class is added the distinction between homosexuality and heterosexuality may become even more blurred. Among lower socioeconomic Black men, those engaged in same-sex sexual activities, regardless of their sexual object choices, may appear on the surface no different from Black heterosexuals. If the support systems of Black gay men are like those of Black lesbians (Cochran and Mays, 1986), fewer economic resources results in a greater reliance on a Black social network (both gay and heterosexual) for tangible and emotional support, a strong tendency to live in predominantly ethnic neighborhoods, and the maintenance of emotionally and economically close family ties.

This extensive integration into the Black heterosexual world may not only be a function of fewer economic resources, but also of ethnic identification. The culture of gay life, generally perceived to be White, may not be synonymous with the norms of Black culture. Choices of how to dress, what language to use, where to live, and whom to have as friends are all affected by culture. The White gay community, while diverse, has developed norms concerning language, social behavior, and other demarcations (Warren, 1974) that may not mesh well with certain subgroups of Black gays. For example, in the past there has been a heavy emphasis in the gay White community (except among the middle-aged, middle-class closeted gay men) on socializing in public places—bars, beaches, and resorts (Warren, 1974). In contrast, the Black gay community places greater emphasis on home entertainment that is private and not public, perhaps as a holdover from the days when discrimination in many public places was common. This pattern of socializing would facilitate the development of a distinct Black gay culture (Soares, 1979).

It is perhaps this difference in socializing that has frustrated health educators attempting to do AIDS education through the social network in gay bars. Generally, they have found that they do not reach a significant number of Black men using this technique. An understanding of the Black gay community makes salient that risk reduction strategies should focus on "risk behaviors" and *not* "risk groups." Emphasizing risk reduction strategies that rely on group membership require a social and personal identification by Black men that for many may not be relevant.

# Sexual Behavior

Bell and Weinberg, in a 1978 study comparing sexual activities of White and Black gay men, found that Blacks were more likely to report having engaged in anal sex, both passively and actively, than White gay men. In terms of our current knowledge of AIDS, this appears to be one of the highest risk factors for contracting the HIV virus (Friedland and Klein, 1987).

A second aspect of Black gay men's sexuality is that they may be more bisexual in their behaviors than White gay men. Evidence for this comes again from Bell and Weinberg (1978) who reported that Black gay men were significantly more likely to have engaged in heterosexual coitus (22 percent) in the previous twelve months than White gay men (14 percent). This seems to be borne out nationally by the AIDS statistics. Among male homosexual/bisexual AIDS patients, Black men are more likely than White men to be classified as bisexual (30 percent versus 13 percent) rather than homosexual (70 percent versus 87 percent). Due to the intense homophobia in the Black community and the factors we discussed above, men may be more likely to remain secretive regarding their homosexual activities (Mays and Cochran, 1987). This may provide a mode of transmission of the AIDS virus outside of an already identified high risk group.

There are several other differences between Black and White gay men noted in the Kinsey Institute data that have implications for contracting the HIV virus. Looking at sexual behavior both pre- and post-Stonewall, Black gay men, in comparison to White gay men, were more likely to be sexually active across ethnic boundaries and less likely to report that their sexual partners were strangers (Gebhard and Johnson, 1979; Bell and Weinberg, 1978). Sexual practices post-Stonewall underwent profound change in the gay community. Black gay men were a part of that change (Gebhard and Johnson, 1979; Bell and Weinberg, 1978). However, these differences in meeting partners or choice of partners remain. They are apparently less malleable to change than specific risk-related sexual behaviors.

While the 1978 Bell and Weinberg study was conducted on a small sample in the San Francisco area, it is suggestive of the need for further research to assess the prevalence of risk behaviors and strategies most effective for decreasing risk. Indeed, a recent report of ethnically based differences in syphilis incidence rates (Landrum, Beck-Sague, and Kraus, 1988) suggests Black gay men are less likely than White gay men to be practicing "safer sex." Sexual behavior has multiple determinants and it is important that variables such as culture, ethnic identification, and class be incorporated into health education programs designed to promote sexual behavior change by Black men.

# Intravenous Drug Use

IV drug use is more common in the Black community (Gary and Berry, 1985), which may explain the higher than expected prevalence of Blacks in the co-categories of IV drug user and homosexual/bisexual male. HIV infection is endemic among IV drug users in the urbanized Northeast who themselves are most likely to be Black (Ginzburg, MacDonald, and Glass, 1987). Ethnic differences exist between the percentage of homosexual/bisexual men with AIDS who are also IV drug users; for White gay and bisexual men with AIDS, 9 percent have histories of IV drug use, while for Blacks the figure

is 16 percent. Black gay and bisexual men who do not use IV drugs may also be at increased risk because they are more likely than Whites to be sexual partners of Black men who are IV drug users. In the Bell and Weinberg study (1978), 22 percent of White men had never had sex with a Black man, whereas for Black respondents, only 2 percent had never had sex with a White man.

# Alcohol as a Cofactor

Recently, alcohol use has been implicated as a cofactor facilitating the occurrence of high risk sexual behavior among gay men (Stall et al., 1986). In predicting alcohol use among Black gay and bisexual men, one might expect that normative use patterns will be influenced by what is common behavior in both the Black community and gay community.

Norms for alcohol use in the Black community reflect a polarization of attitudes, shaped on the one hand by traditional religious fundamentalism and rural southern heritage and on the other by a focus on socializing in environments where drinking is common, such as bars, nightclubs, and home parties (Herd, 1986). This latter norm is more prevalent in urban Black communities. Blacks and Whites vary in small ways in their drinking patterns, although Blacks are more likely to suffer negative consequences, including alcohol-related mortality and morbidity, from their drinking than are Whites. Current rates of mortality due to liver cirrhosis indicates that rates are 10 times higher in Black men aged 25–34 as compared to White males. While drinking is found across all socioeconomic groups of Blacks, health and social problems associated with drinking has been found more often in low income urban Blacks (Lex, 1987). Similarly, for this group it was found that Black males 30–59 were most likely to use alcohol to face the stress of everyday life situations. This is the group most affected by HIV infection.

Within the gay male community, alcohol abuse is a serious problem (Icard and Traunstein, 1987). This may result from both the sociocultural stress of discrimination and the tendency for gay-oriented establishments to be drinking establishments as well. Thus, gay men frequently socialize in environments where alcohol consumption is normative.

Black gay and bisexual men, depending upon their relative identification with the Black or gay community, would be expected to demonstrate behavior consistent with these norms. For some, this might mean a high level of abstinence apart from social drinking consistent with other Black Americans; for others, alcohol consumption might more closely resemble that of White gay men with concomitantly higher rates of alcohol dependency.

## Crossing Traditional Risk Groups' Boundaries

Early AIDS epidemiologic tracking programs conceptualized the disease as a result of the gay lifestyle (Mays, 1988). Indeed, now discarded names for different manifestations of the illness included Gay-related Immunodeficiency Disease and Gay cancer. This focus on discrete risk factors continues to the present, although the additional populations of IV drug abusers, hemophiliacs, persons born in Haiti and Central Africa, and recipients of blood transfusions after 1978 have been added to the list. For Whites, this approach is highly successfully, describing the presumed HIV transmission vector in 94 percent of cases; for native-born Blacks, the percentage of cases accurately labeled by a single risk factor (including the combination of IV drug use and male homosexual sexual contact) drops to 88 percent (Cochran, 1987). This underscores the reality that sociocultural factors varying across ethnic groups strongly influence individuals' behavior, and by this their risk of contracting HIV.

For Black gay and bisexual men, the reliance on highly specified risk groups (or factors) ignores the fundamental nature of their behavioral location in society. The multiplicity of their identities may indirectly increase their risk for HIV infection by exposing them to more diverse populations (Grob, 1983).

First, as Blacks, they are behaviorally closer to two epicenters of the AIDS epidemic: IV drug use and foreign-born Blacks (primarily those from Haiti and Central Africa where HIV infection is more common). Social and behavioral segregation by ethnic status is still a reality of the American experience and Black gay and bisexual men suffer, like other Blacks, from pervasive racism. As we noted above, if their social support systems are similar to what we know of Black lesbians (Cochran and Mays, 1986), extensive integration into the Black heterosexual community is common. Behaviorally, this may include both IV drug use and heterosexual activity with HIV infected individuals. Thus Black gay and bisexual men are at increased risk for HIV infection simply by virtue of being Black.

Second, as men who have sex with other men, Black gay and bisexual men are often members of the broader gay community in which ethnicity probably reflects the general U.S. population (84 percent White). Black gay and bisexual men may have relatively open sexual access to White men, although racism in the community may preclude other forms of socializing (Icard, 1985). Data from the Bell and Weinberg study (1978) suggests several interesting differences, as well as similarities, between White and Black gay men. Blacks reported equivalent numbers of sexual partners, both lifetime (median = 100–249 partners) and in the previous 12 months (median = 20–50), as Whites. Although they were significantly less likely than White gay men to engage in anonymous sexual contacts (51 percent versus 79 percent of partners), more than two-thirds reported that more than half their sexual partners were White men. In contrast, none of the White respondents reported that more than half their partners were Black. It should be kept in mind, however, that a greater percentage of the White sample (14 percent) was recruited at bath houses than the Black sample (2 percent). Nevertheless, at least sexually, Black gay men appear to be well integrated into the gay community. Therefore, Black gay and bisexual men are also at higher risk for HIV infection because they are behaviorally close to another epicenter of the AIDS epidemic: the gay male community.

Third, as a social grouping unto itself, the Black gay and bisexual male community may be more diverse than the White gay community (Icard, 1985). Some men identify more closely with the Black community than the gay community (Black gay men); others find their primary emotional affinity with the gay community and not the Black community (gay Black men). To the extent that this diversity of identity is reflected in behavioral diversity as well, HIV transmission may be greatly facilitated (Denning, 1987).

Thus Black gay and bisexual men are individuals often located behaviorally at the crossroads of HIV transmission. Their multiple social identities make it more likely that the practicing of high risk behavior, whether sexual or needle-sharing, will occur in the presence of HIV.

## Perceptions of Risk

There may be a reluctance among Black gay and bisexual men to engage in risk reduction behaviors because of the perception by some members of the Black community that AIDS is a "gay White disease," or a disease of intravenous drug users (Mays and Cochran, 1987). In addition, many risk reduction programs are located within outreach programs of primarily White gay organizations. These organizations often fail to attract extensive participation by Black gay men.

Research findings suggest that the personal perception of being at risk is most often influenced by accurate knowledge of one's actual risk and personal experiences with the AIDS epidemic (McKusick, Horstman, and Coates, 1985). There may be a variety of reasons why Black gay and bisexual men do not see themselves as at risk. These include the notion of relative risk and a lack of ethnically credible sources for encouraging risk perceptions (Mays and Cochran, 1988). Relative risk refers to the importance of AIDS in context with other social realities. For example, poverty, with its own attendant survival risks, may outweigh the fear of AIDS in a teenager's decision to engage in male prostitution. Economic privilege, more common in the White gay community, assists in permitting White gay men to focus their energies and concerns on the AIDS epidemic. For Black gay men of lesser economic privilege other pressing realities of life may, to some extent, diffuse such concerns. Credible sources relate to the issues that we have presented here of ethnic identification. Black gay men who are emotionally and behavioral distant from the White community may tend to discount media messages from White sources.

# References

1988    Acquired Immunodeficiency Syndrome (AIDS) Weekly Surveillance Report, United States AIDS Activity, Center for Infectious Diseases, Centers for Disease Control, April 4, 1988.

Bakeman, R., J. Lumb, R. E. Jackson, and P. N. Whitley
1987    "The Incidence of AIDS among Blacks and Hispanics." *Journal of the National Medical Association* 79:921–928.

Beame, T.
1983    "Racism from a Black Perspective." In *Black Men/White Men: A Gay Anthology.* M. J. Smith ed. San Francisco: Gay Sunshine Press.

Becker, M. H. and J. G. Joseph
1988    "AIDS and Behavioral Change to Reduce Risk: A Review." *American Journal of Public Health* 78:394–410.

Bell, A. P. and M. S. Weinberg
1978    *Homosexualities: A Study of Diversity among Men and Women.* New York: Simon & Schuster.

Bell, A. P., M. S. Weinberg, and S. K. Hammersmith

1981 *Sexual Preference: Its Development in Men and Women*. Bloomington: Indiana University Press.

Bureau of the Census

1983 "General Population Characteristics, 1980." U.S. Department of Commerce: U.S. Government Printing Office.

Centers for Disease Control

1987 "Human Immunodeficiency Virus Infection in the United States: A Review of Current Knowledge." *Morbidity and Mortality Weekly* 36 (Suppl. no. S-6):1–48.

Cochran, S. D.

1987 "Numbers That Obscure the Truth: Bias in Data Presentation." Paper presented at the meetings of the American Psychological Association, New York, August.

Cochran, S. D. and V. M. Mays

1986 "Sources of Support among Black Lesbians." Paper presented at the meetings of the American Psychological Association, Washington, D.C., August.

Cochran, S. D., V. M. Mays, and V. Roberts

1988 "Ethnic Minorities and AIDS." In *Nursing Care of Patients with AIDS/ARC*, A. Lewis ed., pp. 17–24. Maryland: Aspen Publishers.

Denning, P. J.

1987 "Computer Models of AIDS Epidemiology." *American Scientist* 75:347–351.

Friedland, G. H. and R. S. Klein

1987 "Transmission of the Human Immunodeficiency Virus." *New England Journal of Medicine* 317: 1125–1135.

Friedman, S. R., J. L. Sotheran, A. Abdul-Quader, B. J. Primm, D. C. Des Jarlais, P. Kleinman, C. Mauge, D. S. Goldsmith, W. El-Sadr, and R. Maslansky

1987 "The AIDS Epidemic among Blacks and Hispanics." *The Milbank Quarterly* 65, Suppl. 2.

Gary, L. E. and G. L. Berry

1985 "Predicting Attitudes toward Substance Use in a Black Community: Implications for Prevention." *Community Mental Health Journal* 21:112–118.

Gebhard, P. H. and A. B. Johnson

1979 *The Kinsey Data: Marginal Tabulations of the 1938–1963 Interviews Conducted by the Institute for Sex Research*. Philadelphia: W. B. Saunders Co.

Ginzburg, H. M., M. G. MacDonald, and J. W. Glass

1987 "AIDS, HTLV-III Diseases, Minorities and Intravenous Drug Abuse." *Advances in Alcohol and Substance Abuse* 6:7–21.

Gottlieb, M. S., H. M. Schanker, P. Fan, A. Saxon, J. D. Weisman, and I. Posalki

1981 "Pneumocystic Pneumonia—Los Angeles." *Morbidity and Mortality Weekly Report* 30:250–252.

Grob, G. N.

1983 "Diseases and Environment in American History." In *Handbook of Health, Health Care, and the Health Professions*, D. Mechanic, ed., pp. 3–23. New York: Free Press.

Guttentag, M. and P. F. Secord

1983 *Too Many Women: The Sex Ratio Question*. Beverly Hills, Calif.: Sage Publications.

Herd, D.

1986 "A Review of Drinking Patterns and Alcohol Problems among U.S. Blacks." In *Report of the Secretary's Task Force on Black and Minority Health:* Volume 7, M. Heckler ed. USDHHS.

Icard, L.

1985 "Black Gay Men and Conflicting Social Identities: Sexual Orientation versus Racial Identity." *Journal of Social Work and Human Sexuality* 4:83–93.

Icard, L. and D. M. Traunstein

1987 "Black, Gay, Alcoholic Men: Their Character and Treatment." *Social Casework* 68:267–272.

Landrum, S., C. Beck-Sague, and S. Kraus

1988 "Racial Trends in Syphilis among Men with Same-Sex Partners in Atlanta, Georgia." *American Journal of Public Health* 78:66–67.

Lex, B. W.

1987 "Review of Alcohol Problems in Ethnic Minority Groups." *Journal of Consulting and Clinical Psychology* 55 (3):293–300.

Macdonald, D. I.

1986 "Coolfont Report: A PHS Plan for the Prevention and Control of AIDS and the AIDS Virus." *Public Health Reports* 101:341–348.

Mays, V. M.

1988 "The Epidemiology of AIDS in U.S. Blacks: Some Problems and Projections." Unpublished manuscript.

Mays, V. M. and S. D. Cochran

1987 "Acquired Immunodeficiency Syndrome and

Black Americans: Special Psychosocial Issues." *Public Health Reports* 102:224–231.

—— 1988 "Issues in the Perception of AIDS Risk and Risk Reduction Activities by Black and Hispanic Women." *American Psychologist* 43:11.

McKusick, L., W. Horstman, and T. J. Coates
1985 "AIDS and Sexual Behavior Reported by Gay Men in San Francisco." *American Journal of Public Health* 75:493–496.

Morgan, W. M. and J. W. Curran
1986 "Acquired Immunodeficiency Syndrome: Current and Future Trends." *Public Health Reports* 101:459–465.

Samuel, M. and W. Winkelstein
1987 "Prevalence of Human Immunodeficiency Virus in Ethnic Minority Homosexual/Bisexual Men." *Journal of the American Medical Association* 257:1901 (letter).

Smith, M. C.
1986 "By the Year 2000." In *In the Life: A Black Gay Anthology*, J. Beam ed. Boston: Alyson Publications.

Soares, J. V.
1979 "Black and Gay." In *Gay Men: The Sociology of Male Homosexuality*, M. P. Levine, ed. New York: Harper & Row Publishers.

Spanier, G. B. and P. C. Glick
1980 "Mate Selection Differentials between Whites and Blacks in the United States." *Social Forces* 58:707–725.

Stall, R. S., L. McKusick, J. Wiley, T. J. Coates, and D. G. Ostrow
1986 "Alcohol and Drug Use during Sexual Activity and Compliance with Safe Sex Guidelines for AIDS: The AIDS Behavioral Research Project." *Health Education Quarterly* 13:359–371.

Staples, R.
1981 *The Changing World of Black Singles*. Connecticut: Greenwood Press.

Sylvester
1986 Foreword. In *In the Life: A Black Gay Anthology*, J. Beam ed. Boston: Alyson Publications.

Warren, C. A. B.
1974 *Identity and Community Formation in the Gay World*. New York: John Wiley & Sons.

# 12 / Public Policy and Black Families

## DISADVANTAGED WOMEN AND THEIR CHILDREN

### United States Commission on Civil Rights

*A summary and analysis of the employment problems of women, especially Black women, as they are caused by gender-linked occupations and employer discrimination. Practical solutions to the low wages paid women are explored, such as comparable worth methods and enforcement of equal opportunity laws. Federal welfare programs and their ability to reduce female poverty are examined.*

Poor women do participate in the labor force. Their work orientation and life goals are quite similar to those of other Americans.[1] The problem is they are often unable to find work, must work part time, or the jobs do not pay a wage adequate to support a family. The Commission has found that 61 percent of black, 51 percent of Hispanic, and 45 percent of white women in the labor force in 1980 were either unemployed or underemployed, compared to 35 percent of white men.[2] Not all of these women were poor, but in 1979, 3.1 million women sought public assistance because they were unable to support their families.[3] Inadequate earnings, dependence, and poverty over time are associated with loss of confidence, making efforts to improve their status more difficult.[4]

This chapter discusses the relationship of employment status and poverty, the concentration of women in low-wage jobs, inequalities in wages paid to women, and work disincentives in Federal programs. Labor market data presented are for fully employed[5] women unless otherwise noted because they provide the most realistic means of comparison to men.

## Employment and Poverty

Recent studies have shown that millions of working Americans endure economic hardship, and the most disadvantaged of these are women. Bureau of Labor Statistics studies of poverty by employment and marital status in 1979 and 1980 are most revealing.[6] Although no poverty rates are given by both race and sex, the rates are reported for women maintaining families alone and express the severity of their problems.[7]

Many fully employed women heading households are poor in spite of their work efforts. In 1980,

From *Disadvantaged Women and Their Children*, U.S. Commission on Civil Rights (Washington, D.C.: U.S. Government Printing Office, 1983), pp. 13–35. Tables and some footnotes have been renumbered.

23 million women were fully employed, of whom 3.2 million were heads of household. The poverty rate for the women heading their own families was 5.4 percent, almost 2.5 times that for nuclear families, and twice the rate for men maintaining families with no spouse present (see Table 1). Since all cash income is included when calculating poverty rates,[8] the data show that, in spite of full-time work, these women are poor, and after welfare payments (if they are eligible), they are still poor.

Of all persons who have less than full-time employment, women heading families are most likely to be poor. The poverty rates for those who could only find part-time work in 1980 exceeded 56 percent for women maintaining families and 26 percent for husbands (in nuclear families).[9] Almost 56 percent of women maintaining families who were unemployed at any time during 1980 were poor. The corresponding rate for husbands experiencing unemployment was 14 percent. The poverty rates for women who looked for, but could not find work at all during 1980 were extremely high, reaching 85 percent for women maintaining families alone. The rate for husbands was 53 percent.

In general, the poverty figures in Table 1 for women maintaining their own families indicate their lack of personal financial resources to carry them through periods of unemployment or reduced employment. In some cases a dependent child or other relative living in the home may help out, but they are frequently unable to make up the income lost by the primary breadwinner.[10]

The minimum wage provides a benchmark for determining the adequacy of employment. In 1980 full-time work[11] at the minimum wage ($3.10) provided an income of $6,448, just under the $6,570 poverty level for a family of three that year. (The average size of a family headed by a woman receiving aid to families with dependent children is three.)[12]

The 1980 earnings distribution for full-time workers shows disparities at the high as well as the low end of the scale. Over 2.8 million women (13 percent) who were fully employed had earnings of $7,000 or less, compared to 4.4 percent of fully employed men (see Table 2). Eighty-eight percent of the men earned over $10,000, compared to 63 percent of white, 57 percent of black, and 48 percent of

Hispanic women. These figures do not tell the whole story, however. Most of the women were clustered in the $7,000 to $15,000 range, with a total of 9.6 percent earning over $20,000, while most of the men earned over $15,000, with 46.5 percent earning over $20,000. Among the women, 10 percent of whites, 6.4 percent of blacks, and 5.1 percent of Hispanics earned over $20,000.

The poverty level is a severe measure of hardship and does not give a complete indication of how many families are really under stress trying to make ends meet. Table 3 presents another view of fully employed women and how they and their families are concentrated at the low end of the income and earnings distribution. By increasing the hardship standard to 1.25 times the official poverty threshold, the proportion of female-headed families in distress almost doubles. The proportion for men who maintain families alone increases at almost the same rate; however, only half as many men meet this definition of hardship.

Acquiring full-time employment will not necessarily solve the poverty problem for the many women who are unemployed or employed less than full time. This is apparent from the poverty figures for fully employed women given above. Guaranteed employment at the minimum wage may not be enough either. The fact is that a job often is not enough to enable women to leave poverty. The next section discusses aspects of occupations and wages, illuminating further the dilemma of women in the labor market.

# Occupations and Wages

A woman's occupation has a major effect on her earnings. However, most women are concentrated in a few occupations that are typically low wage with little room for advancement. This concentration of women in certain occupations may be due to discrimination, which is a process that can be transposed from individual attitudes and actions into social structures and business organizations.[13] Once institutionalized, discriminatory procedures cause: "unequal results along the lines of race, sex, and national origin, which in turn reinforce existing practices and breed damaging stereotypes which

TABLE 1    Women and Men Maintaining Families below the Poverty Level,[1] 1980

| | WOMEN WHO MAINTAIN FAMILIES[2] | HUSBANDS IN NUCLEAR FAMILIES | MEN WHO MAINTAIN FAMILIES[2] | TOTAL ALL MEN AND WOMEN |
|---|---|---|---|---|
| Fully employed[3] | 5.4% | 2.6% | 2.8% | 2.5% |
| Partially employed[4] | 39.9 | 11.0 | 20.2 | 11.8 |
| Involuntary part-time[5] | | | | |
| Could only find part-time work | 56.6 | 26.2 | ([6]) | 22.2 |
| Slack work, material shortage | 28.3 | 11.8 | 22.0 | 11.9 |
| Unemployed at some time* | 55.6 | 14.3 | 24.0 | 17.5 |
| Did not work | 53.5 | 13.7 | 21.3 | 20.9 |
| Ill, disabled | 49.3 | 20.8 | 24.9 | 33.3 |
| Taking care of home | 59.4 | ([6]) | ([6]) | 18.1 |
| Going to school | 81.9 | 37.7 | ([6]) | 20.5 |
| Unable to find work | 85.1 | 53.4 | ([6]) | 44.7 |
| Retired | 11.1 | 7.9 | 11.3 | 13.5 |

*This item may be read as follows: Of all persons who were unemployed at some time during 1980, 17.5 percent were in poor families. Of women who maintained families alone and experienced unemployment, 53.5 percent were poor, compared to 21.3 percent of men who maintained families alone.

Notes: The employment categories may overlap. Data are not available by race.

[1]After inclusion of cash transfers and excluding in-kind transfers such as food stamps and housing.

[2]Men and women maintaining families have no spouse present.

[3]Persons who worked 50–52 weeks of the year usually at a full-time job. Also referred to as full-time, year-round workers.

[4]Persons who worked less than 50 weeks of the year in either full-time or part-time jobs, and persons who worked part time 50–52 weeks.

[5]Persons who worked less than 35 hours for at least 1 week during the year (a) because they could only find part-time work or (b) because of the slack work or material shortages.

[6]Data not shown where base is less than 75,000.

Source: U.S., Department of Labor, Bureau of Labor Statistics, *Linking Employment Problems to Economic Status: Data for 1980* (1982), tables 4, 10, 13, 17 and 26.

TABLE 2    Earnings of Fully Employed Workers, 1980

| | ALL MEN | ALL WOMEN | WOMEN White | Black | Hispanic |
|---|---|---|---|---|---|
| Total | 100.0% | 100.0% | 100.0% | 100.0% | 100.0% |
| Under $4,000 | 1.1 | 2.2 | 2.1 | 3.1 | 2.6 |
| $4,000–6,999 | 3.3 | 10.8 | 10.1 | 15.6 | 21.4 |
| $7,000–9,999* | 7.7 | 24.6 | 24.6 | 24.3 | 28.1 |
| $10,000–14,999 | 20.1 | 36.4 | 36.8 | 34.3 | 30.7 |
| $15,000–19,999 | 21.4 | 16.5 | 16.4 | 16.3 | 12.0 |
| $20,000–24,999 | 19.1 | 6.2 | 6.5 | 4.1 | 3.2 |
| $25,000 & over | 27.4 | 3.4 | 3.5 | 2.3 | 1.9 |
| Median earnings | $18,910 | $11,287 | $11,413 | $10,609 | $9,769 |

*This item may be read as follows: In 1980, 28.1 percent of fully employed Hispanic women earned between $7,000 and $9,999.

Source: U.S., Department of Labor, Bureau of Labor Statistics, unpublished tabulations, 1980.

then promote the existing inequalities that set the process in motion in the first place."[14]

Large disparities in income, occupational, and wage statistics lend credence to the theory of discrimination. The Supreme Court has noted that statistics showing racial or ethnic imbalance are important in legal proceedings:

*[B]ecause such imbalance is often a telltale sign of purposeful discrimination; absent explanation, it is ordinarily to be expected that nondiscriminatory hiring practices will in time result in a work force more or less representative of the racial and ethnic composition of the population in the community from which employees are hired.[15]*

Since the passage of Title VII of the Civil Rights Act of 1964 and other equal employment legislation, employers have been required to give women equal consideration in employment, training, promotions, and salaries.[16]

## Occupations

Before legislation requiring equal opportunity, and even now, most women worked in occupations traditionally dominated by females. . . . Although the jobs are not always low skill, they do tend to be low wage and to have little promotion potential. The Commission has found that more than 26 percent of black, 23 percent of Hispanic, and 20 percent of white women are overeducated for their jobs.[17] This means they may have a college education, but work in jobs only requiring a high school diploma, or have a high school diploma, but work in jobs requiring an elementary school education. Even in "female" professions such as nursing, teaching, social work, and academic librarianship, men are disproportionately represented in positions that involve supervision, direction, and planning, and they consistently earn higher wages.[18]

Two major explanations for occupational segregation have been investigated by Andrea Beller. The first is that women choose traditionally female occupations, and the second is that employer discrimination leaves them no choice. Research by Beller supports the latter theory.[19] The first theory

is a human capital approach,[20] developed by Solomon Polachek.[21] The theory is based on sex role differentiation and contends that women "find occupations attractive in which skills deteriorate the least with absences from the labor force, and they enter them disproportionately."[22] The second explanation is a discrimination theory of employer choice developed by Barbara Bergmann.[23] It holds that:

*because women face barriers to entry into certain occupations, they tend to become crowded into a small number of occupations without barriers. Increasing the supply of labor reduces earnings in these . . . occupations, and limiting the supply of labor raises earnings in the occupations that become male.[24]*

In research concerning these theories, Beller states:

*if women freely choose to enter only a third of all occupations and those occupations pay less, then women's lower earnings may not be a fundamental social problem. The major issue is whether the dramatic differences in the occupational distributions of the sexes result from different choices made by each, given equal opportunities, or from unequal opportunities to make similar choices.[25]*

Occupational discrimination diminished somewhat during the 1970s, and enforcement of Title VII of the Civil Rights Act of 1964 and the Federal contract compliance program were found to be associated with an increase in the probability of a woman's being employed in a male-dominated occupation compared to a man's probability, thus supporting Bergmann's theory of employer discrimination.[26]

## Women in Traditional Occupations

Women accounted for a disproportionate share (65 percent) of the increase in employment during the period 1972–82, and the occupations experiencing the greatest growth in employment tended to be

TABLE 3    Poverty Status of Families of Fully Employed Workers, 1980

| | TOTAL (1,000) | BELOW POVERTY[1] | BELOW 1.25 POVERTY LEVEL | BELOW 1.50 POVERTY LEVEL | BELOW 2.00 POVERTY LEVEL | MEDIAN FAMILY INCOME |
|---|---|---|---|---|---|---|
| Women who maintain families* | 3,240 | 5.4% | 10.4% | 17.4% | 34.1% | $15,843 |
| Median personal earnings | | $5,192 | $6,130 | $6,900 | $ 8,347 | |
| Husbands | 31,063 | 2.6% | 4.5% | 6.9% | 13.8% | $27,677 |
| Median personal earnings | | $4,489 | $6,515 | $8,220 | $10,446 | |
| Men who maintain families* | 1,038 | 2.8% | 5.6% | 9.3% | 18.3% | $22,788 |
| Median personal earnings | | ([2]) | ([2]) | ([2]) | ([2]) | |

*These items may be read as follows: Although median family income for men who maintained families alone in 1980 was $22,788, median income for women maintaining families was $15,834. Of women maintaining families, 17.4 percent had incomes below 1.5 times the poverty level (median earnings were $6,900), and 9.3 percent of men maintaining families had earnings below 1.5 times poverty (median earnings not available).

[1]The 1980 poverty level for a family of three was $6,570. The data presented here take into account the poverty thresholds for families of different sizes.

[2]Data not shown where base is less than 75,000.

Source: U.S., Department of Labor, Bureau of Labor Statistics, *Linking Employment Problems to Economic Status: Data for 1980,* (1982), table B–1.

those already dominated by women, such as secretaries, cashiers, registered nurses, and bookkeepers.[27] Women accounted for at least half of the increase in each occupational category experiencing growth, with the exception of craft and kindred jobs, where they accounted for 20 percent of the increase.[28]

The concentration of women in a few traditionally female occupations is closely related to low wages. (A discussion of women's low wages follows this section.) A large number of women can be found in jobs characterized as marginal. They "tend to have low wages and fringe benefits, poor working conditions, high labor turnover, little chance of advancement, and often arbitrary and capricious supervision."[29] In a recent report, the Commission found that 21.6 percent of black, 18.5 percent of Hispanic, and 13.9 percent of white women were employed in relatively low-paying jobs requiring less than 3 months of training.[30] Of all majority males, just 5.3 percent were in such occupations.[31] Table 4 gives the occupational distribution and the ratio of female to male salaries of all fully employed men and women in 1980.

Women of all races are concentrated in the clerical and kindred category that, although it provides approximately 18 percent of all full-time jobs, employs 40 percent of white, almost 35 percent of black, and 36 percent of Hispanic women. These jobs include bank tellers, billing clerks, bookkeepers, and cashiers.[32] Median annual earnings for women clerical and kindred workers were $10,909; for men, $18,474.[33]

Another occupational category in which women are overrepresented is service work. Although 8.7 percent of all full-time workers are in this field, more than 24 percent of black, 13 percent of Hispanic, and 10 percent of white women work in such service jobs as cooks, dishwashers, food counter and fountain workers, cleaning service workers, waiters, nurse's aides, child care workers, and dental assistants.[34] Less than 7 percent of men are service workers. Median annual earnings for service workers were $8,043 for women and $13,140 for men.[35]

Hispanic women are particularly underrepresented among professional, technical, and kindred workers (11 percent compared to 18 percent for both sexes and 19.5 percent for white women). The professions they have penetrated are probably those typically associated with women, such as librarians, teachers, nurses, and health technologists.

In 1980 women in professional and technical occupations earned $11,140, compared to $18,750 for men.[36]

Hispanic women are especially overrepresented among operatives. Although 10 percent of all fully employed workers are operatives, 22 percent of Hispanic women are in these jobs. This rate compares with 9.7 percent of white and 11.3 percent of black women. The operative jobs in which women are predominantly employed include laundry and dry cleaning operatives, packers and wrappers, sewers and stitchers, shoemaking machine operatives, and textile operatives, such as spinners, twisters, and winders.[37] Median annual earnings of operatives were $9,476 for women and $15,743 for men.[38]

Most of the women earning low wages are in typically female occupations. Among the 2 million fully employed women who earned less than $6,000 in 1980 (less than the minimum wage), 31 percent were service workers, 23 percent were clerical and kindred workers, and 11 percent were operatives.[39] These low earners constituted 8.8 percent of all fully employed women. The proportion of men earning low wages was 4.8 percent.[40]

## Women in Nontraditional Occupations

Women in nontraditional employment tend to have children, have usually tried other jobs, and have realized that they could never earn an adequate living at them.[41] In fact, the probability that a working woman is employed in a nontraditional occupation increases as the number of her children increases.[42] However, just 2 percent of all female workers are craft and kindred workers (traditionally male occupations). Nevertheless, recent Bureau of Labor Statistics data show that, as a proportion of all craft workers, they increased from 3.6 percent in 1972 to 6 percent in 1980.[43] This translates into an increase of 365,000 during the period.[44]

Table 5 reflects some of the gains women have made in these occupations. In spite of large percentage gains, the absolute numbers are small (generally less than 0.05 percent in each occupation) relative to total women in the work force, and

women have much to achieve to gain access to apprenticeships and vocational training in these better paying, nontraditional occupations.

Assuming no barriers to women's entering traditionally male occupations, 60 percent of currently employed women would have to change occupations for women to have the same occupational profile as men, and this figure has changed little since 1900.[45] However, it takes a strenuous, conscious effort for change to take place.

A recent study of sex segregation concluded that, "Neither demographic trends, technological change, nor bureaucratic imperatives are 'natural' forces that lead to balanced sex ratios within jobs or firms," and that, "policy intervention is unlikely to make matters worse—most establishments are about as segregated as they can possibly be."[46]

Severe external pressure and, where possible, a large percentage of women already employed in an organization facilitate desegregation of the work force.[47] Desegregation occurs most easily in large firms that have government contracts and are subject to Federal regulations.[48] However, the outlook is not bright for women employed in smaller and less visible firms that may do nothing or make only token changes, since they are less likely to be subject to enforcement activities.[49]

Changing jobs is not a practical solution to the low-wage problems of many currently employed women. Women already in traditionally female occupations would lose seniority and vested benefits in their current jobs, would have to pay for retraining, and would have no guarantee that they would be hired by employers in their new field. It is important, however, that young women receive adequate counseling on the benefits or possible drawbacks of nontraditional employment. It is also important that equal employment opportunity laws be strictly enforced so that investment in nontraditional training will pay off. The following section reviews other explanations for women's low wages relative to men's.

## Wages

Women earn less than men: 59 percent as much in 1981, a decrease from 64 percent in 1955.[50] Table 6

## TABLE 4   Occupations of Fully Employed Workers, 1980

|  | ALL MEN | BOTH SEXES | WHITE WOMEN | BLACK WOMEN | HISPANIC WOMEN | RATIO OF MEDIAN EARNINGS OF WOMEN AND MEN |
|---|---|---|---|---|---|---|
| Total | 100% | 100% | 100% | 100% | 100% | 59.4% |
| Professional, technical, and kindred | 17.6 | 18.2 | 19.5 | 17.6 | 10.9 | 65.6 |
| Managers and administrators, except farm | 18.2 | 15.3 | 11.0 | 4.3 | 7.1 | 55.3 |
| Sales workers | 6.1 | 5.5 | 4.7 | 2.6 | 4.0 | 48.9 |
| Clerical and kindred workers* | 6.2 | 17.9 | 40.2 | 34.8 | 36.2 | 59.1 |
| Craftworkers, foremen, and kindred | 21.5 | 14.6 | 2.2 | 1.4 | 3.2 | 61.5 |
| Operatives, except transport | 10.1 | 10.1 | 9.7 | 11.3 | 22.0 | 60.4 |
| Transport equipment operatives | 5.2 | 3.5 | 0.4 | 0.3 | 0.1 | 61.5 |
| Laborers, except farm and mine | 4.5 | 3.3 | 1.0 | 1.4 | 1.4 | 59.0 |
| Private household workers | (¹) | 0.3 | 0.6 | 2.0 | 2.3 | 75.1 |
| Service workers | 6.9 | 8.7 | 10.1 | 24.4 | 13.0 | (¹) |
| Farmers and farm managers | 2.5 | 1.7 | 0.3 | (¹) | (¹) | 61.2 |
| Farm laborers and foremen | 1.1 | 0.9 | 0.4 | (¹) | 0.1 | (¹) |

*This item may be read as follows: In 1980, 17.9 percent of all fully employed workers were in clerical and kindred jobs; however, 6.2 percent of all men, compared to 40.2 percent of white women, were in these occupations. The median earnings of all women in these jobs were 59.1 percent of the earnings of men in these jobs.

¹Data not shown where base is less than 75,000.
Source: U.S., Department of Labor, Bureau of Labor Statistics, calculated from unpublished data, 1980.

## TABLE 5   Female Craft and Kindred Workers

|  | 1972 | 1980 | PERCENT GAIN |
|---|---|---|---|
| Carpenters | 5,000 | 18,000 | 260 |
| Other construction craftworkers | 11,000 | 50,000 | 354 |
| Machinists | 2,000 | 18,000 | 800 |
| Heavy equipment mechanics* | 5,000 | 15,000 | 200 |
| Telephone installers and repairers | 6,000 | 27,000 | 350 |

*This item may be read as follows: Between 1972 and 1980, the number of women employed as heavy equipment mechanics increased from 5,000 to 15,000, a 200 percent increase.

Source: Carol Boyd Leon, "Occupational Winners and Losers: Who They Were during 1972–80," *Monthly Labor Review*, June 1982, p. 28.

shows how earnings are distributed by sex, race, and ethnicity for fully employed workers.

All women are at an earnings disadvantage when compared to men, but black and Hispanic women are the most disadvantaged. Hispanic women earn one-half the median income of white men, while black and white women earn 54 and 58 percent, respectively.

Some of the explanations that have been offered on women's occupational distribution and wages include both direct and indirect discrimination. Following are possible reasons for the unex-

TABLE 6   Median Earnings of Fully Employed Persons, 1980

| | WOMEN | MEN | RATIO OF FEMALE TO MALE EARNINGS | RATIO OF FEMALE TO WHITE MALE EARNINGS |
|---|---|---|---|---|
| White | $11,413 | $19,570 | 58.3% | 58.3% |
| Black* | 10,609 | 13,737 | 77.2 | 54.2 |
| Hispanic | 9,769 | 13,717 | 71.2 | 49.9 |

*This item may be read as follows: In 1980 fully employed black women earned 77.2 percent as much as fully employed black men and 54.2 percent as much as fully employed white men.

Source: U.S., Department of Labor, Bureau of Labor Statistics, unpublished tabulations.

plained disparities in wages between men and women.[51] Not all researchers agree on the importance of different factors, and although no single one will suggest a solution to all of the economic problems of women, an investigation of each highlights issues that concern both female employees and their employers.

**Personal Choice or Sex Role Stereotyping** Many women continue in jobs in spite of their low rates of pay. A study done for the Equal Employment Opportunity Council concluded that, "It is difficult to assess the relative importance of the choices women make in the labor market and of the factors affecting their choices."[52]

The first factor is the effect of socialization, in which some women come to believe that only certain jobs are appropriate for women, and they may never even consider other types of jobs.[53] Second, women may have chosen or have been directed into courses of study or training that did not provide qualifications for other jobs.[54] The third explanation says that women lack information about other jobs, their salaries, working conditions, and how to obtain access to them.[55]

A fourth explanation is that women know they have other options, but choose to limit their training and labor force participation because of actual or expected family obligations. If they do work, they take jobs requiring limited overtime and travel or jobs they would not mind leaving if their husbands' career advancement requires transfer.[56]

Fifth, discrimination may cause women to believe that they cannot gain access to certain jobs or

that the jobs themselves would be made unpleasant. This belief guides their education and training decisions.[57]

Once employed in a low-wage, low-skill job, a woman may find her employer reluctant to invest in on-the-job training for her because he may not believe she is interested in advancement, or because he thinks that she may soon leave her job.[58] All women suffer as a result of these experiences and decisions, for it is likely that they will spend more years in the labor force than expected at the time they made choices regarding education and training.[59]

**Discrimination** Discrimination against women in the form of low pay is well documented. While men tend to obtain good jobs with rapid advancement, women receive unequal pay for equal work and are assigned to low-level jobs without promotion potential.[60]

Minority women have had to deal with the effects of both racial and sex discrimination. In 1920 black women were largely restricted to agricultural labor, domestic service, and laundry work, which accounted for 75 percent of jobs held by black women in the labor force.[61] During this period black women were able to replace immigrant women in unskilled jobs in candy factories and to replace men in some heavy jobs,[62] but:

> To do so, they had to accept less pay than a white person doing an equivalent job would have received. One observer commented that as soon as Washington, D.C., laundries real-

*ized they might have to pay a minimum wage, they "began to ask the employment bureaus about the possibility of obtaining white girls" to replace the Negro women. Married women could be hired to do the heavy unskilled work of men for up to one-third less than employers had to pay the latter. Yet these jobs were attractive to women who had few options.[63]*

In 1940 more than half of the 2 million women who earned wages working in someone else's home were black and Hispanic.[64] They were among the poorest paid and hardest working, but were not protected by the Fair Labor Standards Act or other protective legislation.[65] In Lynchburg, Virginia, $6.00 for a 72-hour week was a typical wage for a domestic.[66]

The facts that the median earnings of black women are now 94 percent of those of white women and that the occupational distribution of young black women has improved dramatically in the last 20 years have created concern that policymakers will conclude that black women are no longer disadvantaged (on the basis of race) in the labor market.[67] To compare black and white women is to compare one disadvantaged group to another. And because black men continue to be discriminated against, one author concludes: "Although the elimination of sex discrimination would, by definition, produce economic equality between white men and women, black women would fare no better than black men and continue to earn less than white men (and white women)."[68]

**Research on Wage Disparities** Factors such as education, age, and work experience generally explain less than half of the difference in wages between men and women.[69] Statistical studies have tested whether enforcement of equal opportunity provisions has had an effect on reducing discrimination and, thus, wage disparities between men and women. One study found that variables related to work experience, such as years of training and on-the-job training, accounted for 29 percent of the gap. However, formal education (usually defined as years of school) explained just 2 percent of the difference between white men and white women.[70]

Education explained 11 percent of the difference between white men and black women.[71] Although poverty rates for both men and women decline as educational levels increase, proportionally more women are poor because they earn less than men at all educational levels. . . .

The effectiveness of equal employment laws varies depending on the following factors:

*(1) the completeness of the law in specifying every manifestation of discrimination as illegal behavior; (2) the percentage of employment covered by the law; (3) the enforcement of the law; and (4) the extent of the penalties imposed. If the law makes certain forms of discrimination illegal but leaves others unmentioned, then employers are free to adjust their behavior so that discrimination persists and is reflected in new and unanticipated forms of disadvantage. But even illegal forms of discrimination will persist if the benefits of continued discrimination are seen to exceed the costs, in terms of the chances of being caught and the penalty if and when that occurs.[72]*

Andrea Beller has found that enforcement of equal employment opportunity laws increased female earnings by 4.7 percent between 1967 and 1974.[73] Enforcement for race discrimination had a net effect on the earnings of black women of 1.2 percent during the same period.[74] Executive Order 11246, issued in 1965, which requires Federal contractors to establish goals and timetables for achieving reasonable representation of minorities and women in their labor force, and Title VII of the Civil Rights Act of 1964, which established sex as one of several bases for protection against discrimination in employment, were studied. Using Current Population Survey and Equal Employment Opportunity Commission data for the 1968 to 1974 period, Beller reached the following conclusions:

1. Enforcement of Title VII increases female earnings within industries and occupations, while the Federal contract compliance program increases earnings by lessening entry restrictions across industries and occupations.[75]

2. When enforcement activities are visible, they provide a deterrent effect that extends beyond the scope of the original charge.[76]

3. Although black women have benefited from Title VII enforcement against racial discrimination, they seem to have benefited more from enforcement against sex discrimination.[77]

4. The most powerful tool for increasing the earnings of women is probably enforcement against sex discrimination.[78]

5. Worsening economic conditions, as measured by unemployment rates, curtailed, but did not eliminate, the effectiveness of Title VII, for the sex differential in earnings might have increased.[79]

Although an overall effect on wages at the national level may be difficult to measure, there is no doubt that many women are better off as a direct result of litigation on their behalf, and countless others benefit from the deterrent effects of visible enforcement. Had equal employment opportunity legislation not been passed, the gap between men and women in wages earned could have increased more than it did during the last decade.[80]

**Comparable Worth**   An explanation for wage disparities that has gained considerable momentum in recent years is referred to as "comparable worth." This theory is based on the concept that, "within a given organization, jobs that are equal in their value to the organization ought to be equally compensated, whether or not the work content of these jobs is similar."[81] The literature located for this report on comparable worth was based on sex differentials, not both race and sex. However, a major study conducted for the Equal Employment Opportunity Commission states:

*despite the apparently greater immediate relevance of the comparable worth issue to women than to minorities, our analysis is applicable whenever substantial job segregation between different groups exists and whenever particular jobs are dominated by particular groups.*[82]

Proponents of this theory believe that many jobs in which women predominate are compensated at a lower rate because they are held by women, constituting discrimination.[83] Furthermore, employers may separate similar jobs, providing lower wages and less upward mobility for those held by women.

The Congress clearly indicated that it rejected the comparable worth theory and favored a strict equal work requirement when it passed the Equal Pay Act of 1963.[84] To claim equal wages, the burden of proof falls on the plaintiffs suing under the Equal Pay Act of 1963, which is restricted to equal pay for equal work. Equal work is that "which requires equal skill, effort, and responsibility . . . performed under similar working conditions. . . ."[85]

Title VII of the Civil Rights Act of 1964 has thus become central to the comparable worth issue because it affects the full range of employment practices and specifically forbids discrimination in compensation.[86] Title VII affords protection against employment practices that, although fair in form and administration, have disparate impact.[87] When neutral policies and practices affect a protected group more harshly than others, there may be a basis for a Title VII complaint.

Although some employers have established job evaluation systems to provide objective standards of job worth to be used in setting wages,[88] studies indicate that they have violated their own standards, "either to implement an explicit decision to pay women or minority workers less than men or whites or to conform to an external standard for establishing pay rates."[89] Many employers survey the local labor market and use the "prevailing rate" as a basis for establishing their own wage schedule. In doing so they may assume they are being nondiscriminatory, but in fact they may be continuing disparities and discriminatory personnel practices of the other firms or those that were established because of discrimination in the past.[90]

Wage disparities for jobs of comparable worth have been found in several cities and States that have performed job evaluations to determine if they underpay predominantly female jobs. For example, in Minnesota, the predominantly female position of typing pool supervisor was rated higher than the predominantly male position of painter, yet the women were paid $334 a month less than the men (see Table 7). In Washington State, licensed practi-

TABLE 7  Comparable Jobs Inequitably Paid

| | JOB TITLE | MONTHLY SALARY | NUMBER OF POINTS |
|---|---|---|---|
| Minnesota | Registered nurse (F)* | $1,723 | 275 |
| | Vocational ed. teacher (M) | 2,260 | 275 |
| | Typing pool supervisor (F) | 1,373 | 199 |
| | Painter (M) | 1,707 | 185 |
| San Jose, California | Senior legal secretary (F) | 665 | 226 |
| | Senior carpenter (M) | 1,040 | 226 |
| | Senior librarian (F) | 898 | 493 |
| | Senior chemist (M) | 1,119 | 493 |
| Washington State | Licensed practical nurse (F) | 1,030 | 173 |
| | Correctional officer (M) | 1,436 | 173 |
| | Secretary (F) | 1,122 | 197 |
| | Maintenance carpenter (M) | 1,707 | 197 |

*This item may be read as follows: In Minnesota, the traditionally female job of registered nurse was rated equal to the traditionally male job of vocational education teacher according to standards of training and responsibility established by the State; even so, the nurses were paid $537 a month less.

Source: Nancy D. Perlman, chair, National Committee on Pay Equity, testimony before the U.S. House of Representatives, Subcommittees on Civil Service, Human Resources, and Compensation and Employee Benefits, Sept. 16, 1982.

cal nurses received more than $400 a month less than correctional officers even though their jobs were rated as being equal according to standards established by the State.

The Equal Employment Opportunity Commission asked the National Research Council of the National Academy of Sciences to make a judgment as to whether low-paying jobs are low paying because of the sex, race, or ethnicity of the people who tend to hold them or because the jobs themselves are not worth higher pay. The study concluded:

> several types of evidence support our judgment that . . . in many instances jobs held mainly by women and minorities pay less at least in part because they are held mainly by women and minorities. First, the differentials in average pay for jobs held mainly by women and those held mainly by men persist when the characteristics of jobs thought to affect their value and the characteristics of workers thought to affect their productivity are held constant. Second, prior to the legis-

> lation of the last two decades, differentials in pay for men and women and for minorities and nonminorities were often acceptable and were, in fact, prevalent. The tradition embodied in such practices was built into wage structures, and its effects continue to influence these structures. Finally, at the level of the specific firm, several studies show that women's jobs are paid less on the average than men's jobs with the same scores derived from job evaluation plans. The evidence is not complete or conclusive, but the consistency of the results in many different job categories and in several different types of studies, the size of the pay differentials (even after worker and job characteristics have been taken into account), and the lack of evidence for alternative explanations strongly suggest that wage discrimination is widespread.[91]

Many women are not made aware of the effect of the undervaluation of traditionally female jobs or of the economics of self-support when they are young enough to make crucial training and employment decisions. The result has meant poverty for a large number.

One alternative to economic independence is public assistance. The next section reviews Federal programs assisting the poor to see how they affect the efforts of poor women trying to become self-sufficient.

# Federal Welfare Programs and Work

As a result of the factors discussed above, it is not surprising that many women who rely on earnings to support themselves and their children are poor. Women do have other resources; however, the biggest factor in reducing their poverty rate is welfare programs. One study found that 51 percent of unmarried household heads with children[92] were poor in terms of their earnings in 1975. Private pension plans and annuities reduced the rate to 50.8 percent. Social security payments, unemployment benefits, and worker's compensation payments reduced the rate to 45.2 percent. The women still in poverty were dependent upon outside (and sometimes unreliable) sources of income such as alimony, child support, money from friends and relatives, and welfare payments. These sources reduced the rate by 9.3 percent. After all of these payments, 28.7 percent were still poor.[93]

The effect of welfare payments on reducing poverty for the working poor was very low; it reduced by 0.4 percent the 4.6 percent who were in poverty.[94] . . .

## *Aid to Families with Dependent Children*

The aid to families with dependent children program is administered by State and local governments under Federal guidelines. . . . 80 percent of AFDC recipient families in 1979 were headed by women. Forty-three percent of AFDC families were black, 40 percent white, and 14 percent Hispanic.[95] In 1979, 3.4 million families, with 7.2 million children, received AFDC.[96] Forty-nine percent of the children were white and 46 percent were black. Five percent were of other races or ethnicities.[97] Fifty-five percent of AFDC families had a child under 6 years of age, a factor affecting the employability of the mother. Mothers of children under 6 were not required to register for work or training in 1979; however, they could volunteer and be given preference in the provision of services. (The Omnibus Budget Reconciliation Act of 1981 requires mothers of children 3 years of age or older to register for community work experience programs (CWEP) in States that have them.)[98] Based on data for 1979, 64 percent of AFDC families would be required to meet job search or work requirements under CWEP unless exempt because of age, disability, or remoteness of residence.[99]

Many recipients of aid to families with dependent children have a commitment to work in spite of personal handicaps such as lack of schooling and the presence of young children. Of 3.1 million mothers receiving AFDC in 1979, the latest year for which data are available, almost 9 percent were employed full time, over 5 percent were employed part time, and 10.5 percent were seeking work or awaiting recall. Among those not employed, 6.6 percent were incapacitated, 2.8 percent were in school, and 39.8 percent were homemakers.[100]

As noted at the beginning of this chapter, 5.4 percent of fully employed women maintaining their own families had incomes below the Federal poverty threshold in 1980, even after including cash welfare payments. The poverty rates for those women who worked part time involuntarily or who were unemployed exceeded 55 percent. Recent changes in AFDC eligibility may have the effect of making their work efforts seem even more futile. The Federal Government establishes general eligibility criteria for AFDC, but individual States determine their own "standards of need" (poverty thresholds) for eligibility purposes and the amount of their welfare payments. States are not required to provide welfare benefits equal to their own standard of need or the Federal poverty threshold.

Federal AFDC eligibility criteria and benefit levels changed considerably with the passage of the Omnibus Budget Reconciliation Act in 1981. Previously, AFDC recipients who worked knew they could increase their disposable income. AFDC regulations permitted administrators to disregard the first $30 of monthly earnings plus one-third of the remaining earnings when recalculating eligibility for AFDC. Reasonable work-related expenses were also disregarded.[101]

A major study by Tom Joe of the Center for the Study of Social Policy reported the effects on the working poor of the changes that became effective in fiscal year 1982 and also projected the effects of the proposed changes for 1983.[102] One of the primary measures used by Joe was the reduction in allowance for work-related expenses, which has the effect of reducing net income available to the working recipient. . . . Joe's study was not designed to prove whether working welfare recipients would actually decrease their work efforts. His primary concern was to show that welfare benefits were being decreased extensively and that the working poor were especially hard hit—to the point where it might seem rational to give up trying to hold a job.[103] . . .

## Summary

Employment is generally considered the key to economic independence in our society, but it does not unlock the door for many women. A combination of socialization and apparent discrimination has created a situation in which women do not obtain labor market benefits comparable to those earned by men with similar education and training. Although equal employment laws have affected the occupational distribution and wages of some women, a large gap remains between men and women in these two areas that will require major efforts to overcome if women are to achieve economic security comparable to that enjoyed by most men.

As a proportion of white males' income, fully employed white, black, and Hispanic women earned 58.3, 54.2, and 49.9 percent, respectively. Such large disparities are a reflection of both past and present discrimination by race and sex. Studies indicate that women are concentrated in occupations already dominated by women and that these jobs are undervalued relative to men's jobs.

Although many women are poor in spite of their work efforts, other poor women are not able to obtain work because they lack training, experience, or important supportive services, such as child care and transportation. It is not clear whether workfare programs for welfare recipients will provide the type of experience or training necessary for these women to obtain private sector jobs and become economically independent. In addition, changes in eligibility requirements for aid to families with dependent children have created incentives in some States for welfare recipients to quit work because benefits are higher for nonworkers.

Executive orders and laws requiring equal employment opportunity have been most effective in businesses that already employ large numbers of women and are subject to government regulations. Considerable effort is required to reach smaller firms, which have little incentive to provide equal opportunity to women.

Federal support for employment and training programs has decreased dramatically, and therefore, special efforts will be needed to provide alternative sources of skill training for poor women unable to gain access to currently available resources. If not, they may find themselves trapped in poverty in spite of their best efforts to avoid or overcome their dependency.

[1]U.S., Department of Labor, Employment and Training Administration, The Work Incentive (WIN) Program and Related Experiences, by Leonard Goodwin, R&D monograph 49 (1977), pp. 10–11.

[2]U.S., Commission on Civil Rights, Unemployment and Underemployment among Blacks, Hispanics, and Women (1982), p. 5 (hereafter cited as Unemployment and Underemployment).

[3]Henrietta J. Duvall, Karen W. Goudreau, and Robert E. Marsh, "Aid to Families with Dependent Children: Characteristics of Recipients in 1979," Social Security Bulletin, vol. 45, no. 4 (April 1982), p. 6 (hereafter cited as "AFDC: Characteristics").

[4]U.S., Department of Labor, The Work Incentive (WIN) Program and Related Experiences, p. 11.

[5]*A fully employed woman is defined as one who has worked at least 35 hours a week, at least 50 weeks during the year.*

[6]*U.S., Department of Labor, Bureau of Labor Statistics,* Linking Employment Problems to Economic Status, *Bulletin 2123 (January 1982), and* Linking Employment Problems to Economic Status: Data for 1980 *(1982).*

[7]*To produce most of its general labor force studies, the Bureau of Labor Statistics uses data from the Current Population Survey, conducted monthly by the Bureau of the Census. Because of the sample size, the data are not considered reliable for minority groups such as Asian and Pacific Island Americans, American Indians, and Alaskan Natives. Reliable data for these groups are obtained only during the decennial census, and special reports from the 1980 census are not yet available. Although tabulations for blacks and Hispanics would have been reliable, they were not produced for these reports. (The report using 1981 data is expected to provide data for these two groups.)*

[8]*Poverty data used by the Bureau of Labor Statistics are provided by the Bureau of the Census and include all cash transfer payments (such as social security, AFDC, pensions, interest income) as income before determining whether the family is in poverty. In-kind benefits such as food stamps and housing are not counted.*

[9]*The "husband" rate includes all married men whether or not their wives are in the labor force. All poverty rates are based on total family income.*

[10]*U.S., Department of Labor, Bureau of Labor Statistics, calculated from unpublished data for 1981.*

[11]*Full-time work in this example is defined as working 40 hours a week, 52 weeks a year.*

[12]*Duvall and others, "AFDC: Characteristics," table 3, p. 7.*

[13]*U.S., Commission on Civil Rights,* Affirmative Action in the 1980s: Dismantling the Process of Discrimination *(1981), p. 5.*

[14]*Ibid.*

[15]*International Brotherhood of Teamsters v. United States, 431 U.S. 324, 339 n. 20 (1977).*

[16]*The Civil Rights Act of 1964, 42 U.S.C. §2000e–2(a) (1976 & Supp. IV 1980), makes unlawful the following employer practices:*

*(1) to fail or refuse to hire or to discharge any individual, or otherwise to discriminate against any individual with respect to his compensation, terms, conditions, or privileges of employment, because of such individual's race, color, religion, sex, or national origin; or*

*(2) to limit, segregate, or classify his employees or applicants for employment in any way which would deprive or tend to deprive any individual of employment opportunities or otherwise adversely affect his status as an employee, because of such individual's race, color, religion, sex, or national origin.*

*The Equal Pay Act of 1963, 29 U.S.C. §206(d)(1) (1976 & Supp. IV 1980), states that an employer may not discriminate between:*

*[E]mployees on the basis of sex by paying wages to employees in such establishment at a rate less than the rate at which he pays wages to employees of the opposite sex in such establishment for equal work on jobs the performance of which requires equal skill, effort, and responsibility, and which are performed under similar working conditions, except where such payment is made pursuant to (i) a seniority system; (ii) a merit system; (iii) a system which measures earnings by quantity or quality of production; or (iv) a differential based on any other factor other than sex[.]*

*Title IX of the Education Amendments of 1972, 20 U.S.C. §1681(a) (1976), provides:*

*No person in the United States shall, on the basis of sex, be excluded from participation in, be denied the benefits of, or be subjected to discrimination under any education program or activity receiving Federal financial assistance.*

*Executive Order No. 11246, 3 C.F.R. 339 (1965), amended by Executive Order No. 11375, 3 C.F.R. 493 (1967), reprinted in 42 U.S.C. §2000e app. at 1233 (1976), requires that employers holding Federal contracts and federally assisted contracts:*

*[W]ill not discriminate against any employee or applicant for employment because of race, color, religion, sex, or national origin. The contractor will take affirmative action to ensure that applicants are employed, and that employees are treated during employment, without regard to their race, color, religion, sex, or national origin. Such action shall include, but not be limited to the following: employment, upgrading, demotion, or transfer; recruitment or recruitment advertising; layoff or termination; rates of pay or other forms of compensation; and selection for training, including apprenticeship.*

[17]Unemployment and Underemployment, *pp. 9–10.*

[18]*Wendy Wolf and Neil Fligstein, "Sex and Authority in the Workplace: Causes of Sexual Inequality,"* American Sociological Review, *vol. 44, no. 2 (April 1979), p. 236; and James W. Grim and Robert N. Stern, "Sex Roles and Internal Labor Market Structures: The 'Female' Semi-Professions,"* Social Problems, *vol. 21 (1974), pp. 690–705.*

[19]*Andrea H. Beller, "Occupational Segregation by Sex: Determinants and Changes,"* The Journal of Human Resources, *vol. 17, no. 3 (Summer 1982).*

[20]*Human capital theory uses characteristics of individuals, such as education, training, ability, experience, and personal choice, to explain differences between men and women in occupational distribution, occupational status, and wages.*

[21]*Solomon W. Polachek, "Occupational Segregation Among Women: Theory, Evidence, and a Prognosis," in* Women in the Labor Market, *ed. Cynthia B. Lloyd (New York: Columbia University Press, 1979).*

[22]*Beller, "Occupational Segregation by Sex," p. 372. See Polachek, "Occupational Segregation Among Women."*

[23]*Barbara Bergmann, "Occupational Segregation, Wages and Profits When Employers Discriminate by Race or Sex,"* Eastern Economic Journal, *vol. 1 (April 1974), pp. 103–10.*

[24]*Beller, "Occupational Segregation by Sex," p. 372. See Polachek, "Occupational Segregation Among Women," and Bergmann, "Occupational Segregation, Wages and Profits," pp. 103–10.*

[25]*Beller, "Occupational Segregation by Sex," p. 372.*

[26]Ibid., *p. 391.*

[27]*Carol Boyd Leon, "Occupational Winners and Losers: Who They Were During 1972–80,"* Monthly Labor Review, *June 1982, pp. 18–19.*

[28]*Ibid.*

[29]*Peter Doeringer and Michael Piore,* Internal Labor Markets and Manpower Analysis *(Lexington, Mass.: Heath Lexington Books, 1971), p. 165, cited in* Unemployment and Underemployment, *pp. 7–8.*

[30]Unemployment and Underemployment, *pp. 7–8.*

[31]Ibid., *p. 8.*

[32]*Nancy F. Rytina, "Earnings of Men and Women: A Look at Specific Occupations," in U.S., Department of Labor, Bureau of Labor Statistics,* Analyzing 1981 Earnings Data from the Current Population Survey, *Bulletin 2149 (September 1982), p. 27.*

[33]*U.S., Department of Labor, Bureau of Labor Statistics,* Linking Employment Problems to Economic Status: Data for 1980, *table 2.*

[34]*Rytina, "Earnings of Men and Women," p. 29.*

[35]*U.S., Department of Labor, Bureau of Labor Statistics,* Linking Employment Problems to Economic Status: Data for 1980, *table 2.*

[36]*Ibid.*

[37]*Rytina, "Earnings of Men and Women," p. 29.*

[38]*U.S., Department of Labor, Bureau of Labor Statistics,* Linking Employment Problems to Economic Status: Data for 1980, *table 2.*

[39]*Ibid.*

[40]Ibid.

[41]*U.S., Department of Labor, Employment and Training Administration,* Enhanced Work Projects—The Interim Findings from the Ventures in Community Improvement Demonstration, *Youth Knowledge Development Report 7.5, by the Corporation for Public/Private Ventures (May 1980), p. 11.*

[42]*Beller, "Occupational Segregation by Sex," p. 383.*

[43]*Leon, "Occupational Winners and Losers," p. 24.*

[44]Ibid.

[45]*William T. Bielby and James N. Baron, "A Woman's Place is with Other Women: Sex Segregation in the Workplace" (paper prepared for the National Research Council's Workshop on Job Segregation by Sex, May 24–25, 1982, Washington, D.C.), p. 2.*

[46]*Ibid., pp. 39–40.*

[47]*Ibid., pp. 40–41.*

[48]*Ibid., p. 40.*

[49]Ibid.

[50]*See Cynthia B. Lloyd and Beth T. Niemi,* The Economics of Sex Differentials *(New York: Columbia University Press, 1979), p. 152.*

[51]*Donald J. Trieman and Heidi I. Hartmann, eds.,* Women, Work, and Wages: Equal Pay for Jobs of Equal Value *(Washington, D.C.: National Academy Press, 1981), pp. 52–66.*

[52]Ibid.

[53]*Ibid., p. 53.*

[54]Ibid.

[55]Ibid.

[56]Ibid. *See Polachek, "Occupational Segregation among Women."*

[57]Ibid.

[58]*Steven H. Sandell and David Shapiro, "Work Expectations, Human Capital Accumulation, and the Wages of Young Women,"* The Journal of Human Resources, *vol. 15, no. 3 (Summer 1980), p. 337.*

[59]Ibid.

[60]*Winn Newman, "Pay Equity Emerges as a Top Labor Issue in the 1980's,"* Monthly Labor Review, *April 1982, pp. 49–50.*

[61]*Alice Kessler-Harris,* Out to Work: A History of Wage Earning Women in the United States *(New York: Oxford University Press, 1982), p. 237.*

[62]*Ibid., p. 238.*

[63]Ibid.

[64]Ibid.

[65]*Ibid., p. 270.*

[66]*Ibid., p. 271.*

[67]*Allan G. King, "Labor Market Racial Discrimination against Black Women,"* The Review of Black Political Economy, *vol. 8, no. 4 (Summer 1978).*

[68]*Ibid., p. 334.*

[69]*See Lloyd and Niemi,* The Economics of Sex Differentials, *pp. 232–39 for a list of over 20 such studies.*

[70]*Mary Corcoran and Greg J. Duncan, "Do Women Deserve to Earn Less than Men?" Institute for Social Research, Univ. of Michigan (undated), p. 8.*

[71]Ibid.

[72]*Lloyd and Niemi,* The Economics of Sex Differentials, *pp. 301–02.*

[73]*Andrea H. Beller, "EEO Laws and the Earnings of Women" (paper presented at a joint session of the Industrial Relations Research Association and the American Economics Association, Sept. 16–18, 1976), p. 8.*

[74]*Ibid., p. 9.*

[75]*Ibid., p. 11.*

[76]Ibid.

[77]Ibid.

[78]Ibid.

[79]*Andrea Beller, "The Effect of Economic Conditions on the Success of Equal Employment Opportunity Laws,"* The Review of Economics and Statistics, *vol. 62 (August 1980), p. 387.*

[80]*Lloyd and Niemi,* The Economics of Sex Differentials, *p. 306.*

[81]*Trieman and Hartmann,* Women, Work, and Wages, *p. i.*

[82]*Ibid., p. 16.*

[83]*Ibid., p. 9.*

[84]*See the Supreme Court's discussion of the legislative history of comparable worth in Corning Glass Works v. Brennan, 417 U.S. 188, 198–205 (1974).*

[85]*29 U.S.C. §206(d)(1) (1976).*

[86]*42 U.S.C. §§2000e–2000e (17).*

[87]*Griggs v. Duke Power Co., 4011 U.S. 424 (1971) cited in John R. Schnebly, "Comparable Worth: A Legal Overview," Personnel Administrator, April 1982, p. 44.*

[88]*In general, standards of job worth are based on job evaluation plans that try to rate numerically the basic features of jobs, such as skills, effort, responsibility, and working conditions. These features may have different weights, depending on the nature of the job. The ratings are totaled to provide an overall measure of job worth. The process can be quite complicated; it can be biased, but it has been done successfully. For a further discussion, see Trieman and Hartmann,* Women, Work, and Wages, *pp. 71–80, and 115–30. Also see table 7 in this chapter.*

[89]*Trieman and Hartmann,* Women, Work, and Wages, *pp. 56–57.*

[90]*Ibid., p. 61.*

[91]*Ibid., p. 93.*

[92]*Richard D. Coe, "Dependency and Poverty in the Short and Long Run," in* Five Thousand American Families, *ed. Greg J. Duncan and James N. Morgan (Ann Arbor: The Institute for Social Research, Univ. of Michigan, 1978), vol. VI, p. 277. The data do not distinguish between male and female unmarried household heads with children; the great majority, however, are female.*

[93]Ibid.

[94]Ibid.

[95]*U.S., Department of Health and Human Services, Social Security Administration,* 1979 Recipient Characteristics Study *(1982), part 1, p. 1.*

[96]*Ibid., p. 37.*

[97]Ibid.

[98]*42 U.S.C.A. §609(b)(2) (West Supp. 1975–1981).*

[99]*U.S., Department of Health and Human Services,* 1979 Recipient Characteristics Study, *part 1, p. 17.*

[100]*Duvall and others, "AFDC: Characteristics," p. 3.*

[101]*U.S., Department of Labor,* WIN Handbook *(3rd ed.), p. XIV–3.*

[102]*Tom Joe,* Profiles of Families in Poverty: Effects of the FY 1983 Budget Proposals on the Poor *(Washington, D.C.: Center for the Study of Social Policy, February 1982).*

[103]*Tom Joe, director, Center for the Study of Social Policy, Washington, D.C., interview by telephone, Nov. 17, 1982.*

# SOCIAL POLICIES, BLACK MALES, AND BLACK FAMILIES

## *Bogart R. Leashore*

*This chapter illustrates how social policies operate to maintain racial inequality, especially with respect to Black males. It is shown how domestic policies related to taxes and budget cuts have differentially affected Black families and how racism and ideologies have influenced the development of social policies in the United States. Health care, employment and income support, and crime and justice are three areas delineated for alternative social policies.*

The convergence of some socioeconomic indicators between Blacks and whites over the last few decades has prompted some social scientists and others to conclude that the significance of race has declined in the United States.[1] Statistically significant differences between Blacks and whites on several socioeconomic measures have declined.[2] However, it is erroneous to conclude therefore that racial inequality no longer exists in the United States. For example, in April 1985 the net seasonally adjusted unemployment rate for Blacks age 16 to 19 years was 37 percent, compared to 14.4 percent for whites in the same age group.[3] Similarly, significant differences exist between Blacks and whites on family income, infant mortality, life expectancy, incarceration, the number of children living in poverty, and in other areas.[4] As was recently observed by a white U.S. journalist:

> *It was only yesterday that racial discrimination was legal in vast parts of the country. . . .*

> *Racism remains a fact of life in this country—it may be abating, it may be weakening, but it is certainly not ready to be mounted for the Smithsonian.*[5]

In short, race remains a critical factor in the quality of life in the United States.

This chapter draws attention to the roles played by social policies in maintaining racial inequality, particularly with respect to Black males; why and how this has occurred; and how social policies might be altered to enhance the well-being of Black males, Black families, and other Americans as well. Black males are of special interest because of the high risk status they face compared to white males, and the significant roles they continue to assume in Black family life despite the "feminization of poverty."[6] . . .

## Tax Increases and Budget Cuts

A comprehensive analysis of U.S. domestic policies observed that between 1980 and 1984 Black families, regardless of the presence or absence of a male head, were helped less than or hurt more than were white families.[7] Analysis of the current U.S. tax system indicated that the federal government is taxing the poor at levels "without equal in history."[8] A disproportionate number of blacks—males and females—are low wage workers, or working poor and near poor. This group has experienced the sharpest increases in taxes over the past few years,

Unpublished paper, 1985. Printed by permission. Footnotes have been renumbered.

TABLE 1    Budget Cuts in Programs with High Black Participation

| PROGRAM | DEGREE OF BLACK PARTICIPATION | BUDGET CUT |
|---|---|---|
| Public Service Employment (CETA) | 30% | − 100% |
| Employment and Training | 37 | − 39 |
| Work Incentive Program | 34 | − 35 |
| Child Nutrition | 17 | − 28 |
| Legal Services | 24 | − 28 |
| Compensatory Education (Title I) | 32 | − 28 |
| Pell Grants and other Financial Aid for Needy Students | 34 | − 16 |
| Food Stamps | 37 | − 14 |
| Aid to Families with Dependent Children | 46 | − 11 |
| Subsidized Housing | 45 | − 11 |

Source: Center on Budget and Policy Priorities, *Falling Behind: A Report on How Blacks Have Fared under the Reagan Policies* (Washington, D.C.: Author, October 1984), p. 12.

as well as the sharpest cutbacks in social programs. Further, prior to the 1981 tax act, most families in poverty were exempt from federal income tax. In 1978, a family of four at the poverty line paid only $269 in federal taxes, which increased to $460 in 1980. By 1984, a family of four at the poverty line paid $1,076 in taxes.[9]

Since 1980, budget cuts in social programs designed for those with low and moderate incomes have been greater than cuts in programs not designed for this group. Programs designed for low and moderate income persons represented less than one-tenth of the federal budget, yet these programs accounted for close to one-third of the total number of cuts in all federal programs. Black Americans comprise 30 percent to 40 percent of the beneficiaries of most of the low income programs that received the greatest cuts. It has been shown that the 1981 budget cuts cost the average Black family three times as much in lost income and benefits as they cost the average white family. This has been attributed to cuts in programs with high participation by Blacks. For example, as shown in Table 1, employment and job training programs received the greatest cuts in 1985—and more than 30 percent of the participants in these programs were Black.[10]

# Racism, Social Darwinism, and Laissez-Faire Ideology

The social welfare policies of the United States lag significantly behind those of many countries of the world.[11] For some, the existence of this lag is deliberate and is not coincidental. Claiming that race impacts on the development as well as the implementation of social welfare policies can be a highly controversial position. Nevertheless, it seems clear that Blacks disproportionately have to turn to social programs for assistance in providing for their daily needs. Drawing on the premises of social Darwinism and laissez-faire ideology, some social and behavioral scientists, policymakers, and others attribute this disproportionate reliance to the failure of individuals and tend to absolve government from sharing any responsibility.[12] The paradox of these circumstances becomes more apparent when recognition is given to the role the U.S. government has historically played in promoting and maintaining racial inequality. For example, little more than a decade ago, federal, state, and local governments knowingly participated in and supported a racist medical experiment on uninformed Black males.

The experiment was conducted from 1932 to 1972 and is documented in the work *Bad Blood: The Tuskegee Syphilis Experiment*.[13] More recently, national efforts have turned to child support enforcement in response to the increasing numbers of families headed by women.[14] Rooted in coercive and punitive social policy, Black males are more likely to be the victims of child support enforcement programs because they experience a higher rate of unemployment, receive lower wages, and are therefore less likely able to pay than white males....

With specific reference to Blacks, conservatives and some liberals raise their voices against affirmative action and other federal interventions to promote racial equality. There is an insistence that adequate opportunities are available for those who are motivated toward individual achievement. Pathological views of Blacks and the poor suggest that the problems of poverty are rooted in individual deficits, such as indolence. Futile and endless rhetoric continues about the deserving and nondeserving poor. It is assumed that people are poor because they don't try, that governmental assistance is more of a hindrance than help, and that little can be done to improve "the lot of the less fortunate." Little regard is given to the demographics of poverty, which include the following facts: close to one-half of the adult non-aged poor work part time or full time but do not earn enough to escape poverty; others, for health or child care reasons, cannot enter the labor force; and most poor families do not remain in poverty for prolonged periods nor do they perpetuate a "culture of poverty" from one generation to the next. It has been stated that conservative attacks on government-sponsored social programs are "replete with erroneous conclusions flowing from doubtful assumptions" and that these conservatives "offer no alternative means of bolstering opportunity and advancement for the nation's disadvantaged and working poor."[15]

# Mobilizing for Alternative Social Policies

Although the United States is hailed as the land of opportunity, and indeed is so for some, too many Black Americans continue to face structural barriers that block their entry into the socioeconomic mainstream of the society. Joblessness, low wages, poverty, inadequate medical care, substandard housing, poor education, and incarceration are conditions of life that need to be addressed if the defeminization of poverty is to occur. Too often, these conditions of living have reduced the family availability of many Black males....

The probability of being able to function as family provider is related to opportunities for working and receiving adequate financial compensation. Given these highly probable relations, it seems that serious attention should be given to the life circumstances of Black males. In the context of social policies, efforts should be directed toward the elimination of social welfare assaults on Black males and others. Special emphasis should be given to the following areas: health care, employment, wages and income support, and crime and justice.

## *Health Care Policy*

The overall health status of U.S. Blacks continues to lag behind that of whites on several measures. These include higher rates of infant and maternal mortality and shorter life expectancy. Research has shown that Black women are more likely than white women to die because of childbirth complications; that low birth weight is more prevalent among Black than white infants; that Blacks in general and Black males in particular live shorter lives than whites; and that whites receive considerably more preventive and routine medical care than Blacks.[16] These results ring clear the need for an effective program of national health insurance.

Historically, health care policy has focused on three issues: access to care, quality of care, and cost of care. However, preoccupation with cost has resulted in less interest in access and quality of care. For example, profit-oriented hospitals have been shown to be more expensive than nonprofit or public institutions. Those most likely to be without health insurance including Medicaid are women, people of color, and older people. If they cannot pay, health services are not accessible. If they have little to pay with, the quality of care is likely to be what has been characterized as "junk medicine"—

for example, unnecessary tests and procedural duplications.[17]

Politicians, labor, religious, service, and charitable organizations, and consumer groups should reassert the need for a program of national health insurance with wide coverage and a larger federal financial role. These forces must seize control of the health care industry from the hands of physicians, private hospitals, and private health insurance companies.[18] A universal program of quality health care that is attractive to the nonpoor, as well as the poor, is needed. Broad benefits, public financing, and administration by the federal government should be key features of social policy for national health insurance.[19] Various industrialized nations of the world have implemented a range of programs that guarantee equal access to medical care as a citizen right.[20] That the United States remains without such a health care policy not only defies reason, but also continues to be a source of international embarrassment.

## *Employment and Income Support Policies*

Poverty statistics, economic, and employment differences between Blacks and whites have been established. What seems needed are social policies that will reduce and eliminate economic inequality, which is deeply embedded in the structure of U.S. society. Programs increasing the taxes of those with low and moderate incomes while reducing the tax burden of the affluent and big business have done little to improve the U.S. economy. The failure to ensure equal job opportunities for Blacks have placed them at the bottom of the U.S. socioeconomic structure. Weakened commitments of government to civil rights and affirmative action have only worsened the situation. Federal policies to create jobs can reduce unemployment and ensure minimal adequate incomes. Moreover, tax credits and wage subsidies designed for low income and low skill workers can be as economically efficient as public employment policies.[21]

Classical economic theory accuses trade unions of pushing wages up, which prices workers out of jobs and thereby keeps unemployment high.

On the contrary, other evidence indicates that productivity can be improved by giving workers a formal voice in the workplace. If unions coalesced, broadened their interests, and shifted pressure for wage increases, they could become a greater positive force for full employment. In lieu of short-run wage increases, an organized and cohesive labor movement could bargain for full employment, egalitarian wage distributions, opportunities for retraining, workplace enrichment, and welfare objectives.[22]

Aid to Families with Dependent Children (AFDC) has long been stigmatized as a program for those who do not want to work. As a means-tested program, it separates "them" from "us" and has a history of contributing to father absence and family breakup. Family allowance and cash housing allowances based on family size and family income exist in much of Europe. They are available to all moderate income families as well as to the poor. The combined allowances have been considered an income support system that guarantees a higher standard of living, especially for those families with special needs (e.g., female-headed families).[23]

As an expression of important U.S. values, the development of AFDC policy has been consistently directed toward punishing poor parents, especially single mothers, while moving away from promoting the well-being of dependent children. Specifically, values related to capitalism, liberalism, and positivism have been influential in the development of AFDC. The work ethic, individualism, personal freedom, the free market, and the worthiness of individuals have greatly influenced AFDC policy. Racial discrimination against Black families in the early days of AFDC further contributed to the humiliating welfare system of today.[24]

A recent historical study of the Social Security system in the United States vividly depicts the process of institutionalizing antipoor biases in the system. Among other things, it is shown why and how the phrase *social security* has come to mean social insurance even though the legislation of 1935 included public assistance. It is concluded that policy developments relative to public assistance were so constrained that many of the needy went without adequate support.[25] Critical assessments of the Social Security Act of 1935 have posited several relations between the state and the economy, or how political power gets translated into economic power. A recent assessment concludes that

> *in a hierarchical state structure, capitalist groups with varying economic interests exerted their influence at different levels in the hierarchy. . . . Economic power then gets translated into political power through the direct intervention of corporate liberals and through the hierarchical structure of the state, which allows competing factions to petition state managers for direct agendas in social policy.*[26]

Actions for Social Security reform should include a comprehensive analysis of the age requirement for receipt of benefits. Particular attention should be given to any disparities between males of color and white males relative to life expectancy and the age at which benefits can be received. Should Black and other males of color be eligible for Social Security benefits at an earlier age than white males because the latter have a longer life expectancy?[27] Relative to AFDC all states should be prohibited from using the absence of father in families as an eligibility requirement. In the case of child welfare, federal and state legislation and policies should be modified to include subsidized and legal guardianship as another plan of care for abused and neglected children, in addition to foster care and adoption. Far too many Black children, as well as others, linger in foster care.[28] More importantly, efforts need to be directed toward eliminating circumstances that necessitate taking children from their biological families, especially inadequate income and housing. Entitlement programs of the federal government for children, specifically AFDC, continue to lag behind those for other groups (e.g., veterans, the aged, the disabled, and those who are retired). Equal treatment for children through some form of federalized payments is not beyond the capacity of our government.[29]

Cutbacks in federal funds for child day care and nutrition should not only be restored, but increased. Similarly, federal aid for low and moderate income college students and food stamps should be restored and/or increased.

## Crime and Justice

One of the most glaring differences between Blacks and whites in the United States is the disturbingly higher involvement of Blacks as compared with whites in the criminal justice system. . . .

Conditions of prison overcrowding, environmental conditions, idleness, violence, limited staffing, and inadequate medical care characterize many state prisons. Resulting court actions have included orders to reduce prison populations, to provide meaningful work, to provide meaningful opportunities for educational and vocational training, to expand prerelease transition programs, to provide medical care and staffing that meet certain standards, and to prevent violence.[30] With specific reference to Black homicide, the highest rates have been found among unemployed and underemployed Black youth and young adults. Thus, it can be argued that, like reduction of poverty and other social problems, homicide reduction can be achieved through major political and social changes.[31]

Given the high incarceration rate for Black males, new policy initiatives need to be established. These should include sentencing reform, plea bargaining, and employment opportunities for ex-offenders. Regarding the latter, any significant reduction in crime will require better employment opportunities for ex-offenders as well as for delinquents. New policy initiatives for the employment of ex-offenders can be specifically designed for ex-offenders, or created in conjunction with new programs for the employment of disadvantaged workers in general.[32] Suggested areas for prevention and intervention concerning homicide include gun control, community organization and education, and more effective responses to prehomicide behavior.[33]

## Summary and Conclusions

This chapter has focused on social policies and how they have had an impact on Black males in particular and Black families in general. It is shown how domestic policies related to taxes and budget cuts have differentially affected Black families and how racism and ideologies have influenced the development and implementation of social policies in the United States. Attention is called to three areas in which there is a need for alternative social policies: (1) health care, (2) employment and income support, and (3) crime and justice. National and local efforts are needed to provide an effective program of national health insurance, full employment, family allowances, and actions to reduce incarceration.

The achievement of the social policy initiatives presented in this chapter will require deliberate efforts on the part of many parties, including Blacks and other people of color and supportive whites. In so doing, system-challenging political strategies should be used both within and outside of social institutions. Mass actions and collective efforts by multiethnic liberal challenging coalitions can result in social change for female-headed families and others who do not have basic power resources. Strategies that can be used include demonstrations, congressional lobbying, and voting. Black leaders and organizations can function in a national leadership capacity to achieve desired social change.[34] In the meantime, fraternal, business, and religious organizations should implement broad-based supportive and educational programs targeted for Black males including those who are institutionalized (e.g., those in prison).

Several conscious strategies should be developed within the Black community. These should include an internal Black agenda with a recommitment to Black community development or institution building. Further, Blacks can generate an internal economy with a capacity to absorb the marginally unemployed. Resources can be pooled into economic development institutions that go beyond providing technical assistance to small businesses but can also provide capital for large-scale enterprises that contribute to meaningful employment. An economic development institution could plan the organization and distribution of financial resources in order to promote economic stability and security within Black communities. Political activities should include mobilizing the voting power of the Black community so that officials are elected who are sensitive to and understand their needs. Black institutions such as churches can establish

*priorities* of social needs and can commit resources toward designated ends—as has been the case with a national network of Black churches that was organized to provide financial assistance to needy Black college students. This requires the involvement of organizations cutting across special interests, social classes, and resources so that a sense of community is restored. Special uses of mass media can be applied in order to bring leadership together to plan and promote goals and strategies. Local needs should be clearly linked to national issues; similarly, national activities should involve local programming.[35]

The mobilization of people of color and others for meaningful social change requires removal of blocks or barriers to power including internal and external political and economic forces that serve to maintain powerlessness among oppressed groups. Through the process of empowerment, Blacks and others can exert influence and overcome obstacles to meeting their needs. Basic to the process of empowerment, Blacks and others must understand the consequences of powerlessness. Moreover, there should be an understanding of and an appreciation for the capacity to bring about change.[36] With particular reference to Black males, it has been suggested that myths have been perpetuated in response to "an unmitigated fear of black male power."[37] Intertwined with racism and other factors, this fear has resulted in a range of social and economic assaults, which have been operationalized through punitive and coercive social policies and social services.

Black social and behavioral scientists, as well as others, should draw attention to research that supports the need for new social policy initiatives. Black scholars and researchers can ill afford the luxury of academic isolation, lest their contributions be minimized. Fresh perspectives and progressive thinking are needed for examining social issues related to the well-being of Black people and that of all Americans. This should include a more balanced view of racism that analyzes not only the consequences for the victim, but also the motivations of the perpetrator. Knowledge and understanding is needed regarding why and how racism is nurtured and sustained in the United States, and what mechanisms can be used to eliminate it. In addition, white Americans should be educated about the social benefits which they stand to gain through the enactment of constructive social policies.

---

[1]*William Julius Wilson*, The Declining Significance of Race: Blacks and Changing American Institutions *(Chicago: The University of Chicago Press, 1980); Michael Hout, "Occupational Mobility of Black Men: 1962 to 1973,"* American Sociological Review, *49 (June 1984), pp. 308–322.*

[2]*Reynolds Farley*, Catching Up: Recent Changes in the Social and Economic Status of Blacks *(Cambridge: Harvard University Press, 1983); Richard B. Freeman*, The Black Elite *(New York: McGraw-Hill, 1976).*

[3]*U.S. Department of Labor, Bureau of Labor Statistics, USDL85-184, Washington, D.C. (May 1985), Table A-3.*

[4]*Theodore Cross*, The Black Power Imperative: Racial Inequality and the Politics of Nonviolence *(New York: Faulkner Books, 1984); Children's Defense Fund,* Portrait of Inequality: Black and White Children in America *(Washington, D.C.: Children's Defense Fund, 1980); National Urban League, Inc.,* The State of Black America, 1984 *(New York: National Urban League, 1984).*

[5]*Richard Cohen, "Racism Recollected,"* Washington Post, *August 10, 1985, p. A19.*

[6]*Lawrence E. Gary and Bogart R. Leashore, "High-Risk Status of Black Men,"* Social Work, *27 (January 1982), pp. 54–58; Gary and Leashore, "Black Men in White America: Critical Issues," in* Color in a White Society, *Barbara White (ed.) (Silver Spring, Md.: National Association of Social Workers, 1984), pp. 115–125.*

[7]*John L. Palmer and Isabel V. Sawhill*, The Reagan Record: An Assessment of America's Changing Domestic Priorities *(Cambridge, Mass.: Ballinger, 1984).*

[8]*Daniel Patrick Moynihan, "Family and Nation," Cambridge, Mass.: Harvard University, the Godkin Lectures, 1985).*

[9]*Center on Budget and Policy Priorities,* Falling Behind: A Report on How Blacks Have Fared under the Reagan Policies *(Washington, D.C.: Author, October 1984).*

[10]*Ibid.*

[11]*Robert Kuttner,* The Economic Illusion *(Boston: Houghton Mifflin, 1984).*

[12]*Ibid.; Sar A. Levitan and Clifford M. Johnson,* Beyond the Safety Net: Reviving the Promise of Opportunity in America *(Cambridge, Mass.: Ballinger, 1985), pp. 6–18.*

[13]*James Jones,* Bad Blood: The Tuskegee Syphilis Experiment *(New York: Free Press, 1981).*

[14]*Joyce E. Everett, "An Examination of Child Support Enforcement Issues," in Harriette McAdoo and T. M. Jim Parham (eds.),* Services to Young Families Program Review and Policy Recommendations *(Washington, D.C.: American Public Welfare Association, 1985), pp. 75–112.*

[15]*Levitan and Johnson,* Beyond the Safety Net, *pp. 6–18.*

[16]*A Dream Deferred: The Economic Status of Black Americans, a* working paper *(Washington, D.C.: The Center for the Study of Social Policy, 1983).*

[17]*Michael Clark, "What Hath Reagan Wrought,"* Health PAC Bulletin, *15 (July–August 1984), pp. 3–4.*

[18]*Kuttner,* The Economic Illusion, *pp. 249–250.*

[19]*Theodore R. Marmor, Judith Feder, and John Holahan,* National Health Insurance: Conflicting Goals and Policy Choices *(Washington, D.C.: The Urban Institute, 1980).*

[20]*Kuttner,* The Economic Illusion.

[21]*Irwin Garfinkel and John L. Palmer, "Issues, Evidence, and Implications," in* Creating Jobs: Public Employment Programs and Wage Subsidies *(Washington, D.C.: The Brookings Institution, 1978).*

[22]*Kuttner,* The Economic Illusion, *pp. 136–186.*

[23]*Kuttner,* The Economic Illusion, *pp. 243–247.*

[24]*Jan Mason, John S. Wodarski, and T. M. Jim Parham, "Work and Welfare. A Reevaluation of AFDC,"* Social Work, *30 (May–June 1985), pp. 197–203.*

[25]*Jerry R. Cates,* Insuring Inequality: Administrative Leadership in Social Security, 1935–54 *(Ann Arbor: The University of Michigan Press, 1983).*

[26]*Jill S. Quadagno, "Welfare Capitalism and the Social Security Act of 1935,"* American Sociological Review, *49 (October 1984), p. 645.*

[27]*Gary and Leashore,* Social Work, *27 (January 1982), p. 57.*

[28]*Bogart R. Leashore, "Demystifying Legal Guardianship: An Unexplored Option for Dependent Children,"* Journal of Family Law, *23 (1984), pp. 391–400.*

[29]*Moynihan, "Family and Nation," pp. 43–44.*

[30]*Alvin J. Bronstein, "Prisoners and Their Endangered Rights,"* The Prison Journal, *LXV (Spring–Summer 1985), pp. 4–5.*

[31]*Darnell F. Hawkins, "Black Homicide: The Adequacy of Existing Research for Devising Prevention Strategies,"* Crime and Delinquency, *31 (January 1985), p. 94–97.*

[32]*James B. Jacobs, Richard McGahey, and Robert Minion, "Ex-Offender Employment, Recidivism, and Manpower Policy: CETA, TJIC, and Future Initiatives,"* Crime and Delinquency, *30 (October 1984), pp. 486–503.*

[33]*Hawkins, "Black Homicide," p. 96.*

[34]*Ronald Walters, "Imperatives of Black Leadership: Policy Mobilization and Community Development,"* The Urban League Review, *9 (Summer 1985), pp. 20–41.*

[35]*Ibid.*

[36]*Barbara Bryant Solomon,* Black Empowerment: Social Work in Oppressed Communities *(New York: Columbia University Press, 1976).*

[37]*Robert Staples, "The Myth of the Impotent Black Male," in* The Black Family: Essays and Studies *(2nd ed.) (Belmont, Calif.: Wadsworth, 1978), p. 99.*

# USE OF SOCIAL WELFARE PROGRAMS AND THE DISINTEGRATION OF THE BLACK NUCLEAR FAMILY

## K. Sue Jewell

*Written for policy makers as well as for scholars of Black studies, sociology, psychology, social work, and public policy, this article argues that social policies and their absence have negatively affected the status of Black family structures. In particular, the author advances the thesis that these social policies not only failed to bring about significant Black progress expected out of the civil rights era but also destroyed the mutual aid and support networks of Black American families.*

## Introduction

Over the last decade American men and women have experienced an alarming rate of divorce. For Black couples living in the United States divorce statistics are even more staggering. According to census data, in 1982 the combined divorce ratio for Black men and women (220 per 1,000) was approximately double that for white men and women (107 per 1,000). Simultaneously, the divorce ratio for Black women was 265 per 1,000. This represents a significant rise from 1970, when the divorce ratio for Black women was only 104 per every 1,000 married couples. Comparatively, the divorce ratio among white women rose from 56 to 128 per 1,000 during this same period. This increase in the ratio of divorces among Black couples indicates that the tra-

ditional nuclear familial structure is undergoing significant change. According to Weitzman (1981), the relatively young and poor are overrepresented in the population at large among those couples obtaining divorces. In relation to Black Americans, Staples (1981) asserts that the higher the level of educational attainment for females the greater the likelihood that marriages will culminate in divorce, and for lower income Blacks separation continues to be the desired method of ending marriages. Moreover, Staples maintains that among Black singles the largest number are separated while the divorced represent the second largest grouping. With 2 out of 3 marriages ending in divorce the tendency for Black couples to terminate marriages has become endemic to Black American culture. Further, studies reveal that the inordinate number of Black women and children living in poverty is directly related to the increase in divorces among Black American couples (Pearce, 1979; Cummings, 1982; Jewell, 1982). Studies which have attempted to establish a relationship between the effects of welfare on marital stability among Blacks have been inconclusive.

For example, Honig (1974), Ross and Sawhill (1975), and Moles (1976) found that the relative size of welfare benefits was correlated with the proportion of families headed by females. Conversely, Bane (1975) discovered that the average amount of welfare payment was unrelated to divorce. In another study, Bahr's (1979) findings revealed that the re-

From the *Western Journal of Black Studies* 8 (Fall 1984): 192–198. Copyright 1984 by the Washington State University Press. Reprinted by permission. Presented at the 1983 Association for the Study of Afro-American Life and History (ASALH) Conference, Detroit.

ceipt of welfare was not associated with higher levels of marital dissolution among low-income Blacks.

These and other studies which have attempted to establish a relationship between the effects of welfare on marital stability among Blacks have yielded inconsistent findings. One reason for the apparent uncertainty is the failure of these studies to examine the interrelationships between values, belief systems and monetary incentives on marital dissolution among Black men and women. It is not sufficient to attempt to establish a linear relationship between welfare payments and marital break-up between Black couples without examining these salient variables.

As such, this paper seeks to examine the method by which the use of social welfare programs contribute to Black women's decisions to terminate their marriages by modifying existing beliefs and values. Moreover, incorporated in this conceptual model is the important role of monetary incentives in influencing this decision-making process.

Recognizing the serious consequences of conflict in Black male–Black female relationships, academicians as well as non-academicians have begun to focus on the analysis of conflict in these relationships. Prior to 1970 there was a dearth of literature on Black male–Black female relationships. Increasingly, emphasis is being placed on Black male–Black female conflict (Wallace, 1979; Frankin, 1980; and Poussaint, 1982). Numerous theories have been posited in an attempt to provide a causal explication of dissension among Black couples. While scholars and policy makers recognize the prevalence of dissolution of the Black nuclear family, there appears to be little consensus regarding the basis for this erosion. Although researchers acknowledge that economic conditions, high rates of unemployment, contribute to divorce among Black couples, there is a paucity of studies that examine the relationship between the use of social welfare programs and the decline of Black families. Because the former conditions increase the necessity for reliance on systems external to the nuclear family it is surprising that this area has been largely neglected by scholars.

In a related study the University of Michigan's Institute for Social Research, examining culture of poverty theories, found that among Blacks long-term welfare dependency as a child does not lead to long-term welfare dependency as an adult. Furthermore, the findings revealed that children from poor households are more likely to be poor as young adults.

Yet, the study did not explore the relationship between welfare dependency and family instability. In an earlier study Daniel Moynihan (1965), relying largely on census data, posited that problems which confront the Black community are a result of the deterioration of Black families. Citing matriarchal families, delinquency, out of wedlock births, economic dependency, etc., Moynihan advanced that Black families, not society were responsible for their own problems. Generalized indictments of Black families in the absence of sound theoretical formulation and rigorous scientific investigation into the relationship between social welfare policy and the formation of attitudes, beliefs and behaviors of its beneficiaries does little to ameliorate the social and economic plight of Black families or the Black community.

In addition to exploring the relationship between welfare utilization and intergenerational poverty, researchers must begin to investigate factors which promote the use of and dependency on social welfare programs by Black women.

## Historical Overview

The Black family's ability to make positive contributions to society and to successfully socialize its offspring, while confronted with social barriers, has necessitated its dependency on sources external to the two-parent family unit. McCray (1980) refers to the Black family's reliance on the mutual aid network. Historically, there has been an interdependent relationship between the Black family, relatives, neighbors and church members who comprise the mutual aid network.

In the absence of social institutions designed to address the needs of Black family members, informal mutual aid networks were established. These networks provided basic goods and services such as food, shelter, clothing, and the like. In addition to providing goods and services for physical survival they also rendered guidance and counseling regarding personal and family matters. Mutual aid networks enabled Black men and women to identify strategies for ensuring the survival of the two parent family unit.

Billingsley (1972) states that during the period after slavery, when the Freedmen's Bureau was disbanded, social services were not provided by the larger society, and the Black community, through "informal neighbor to neighbor" systems had to provide resources for the care of children. According to McCray (1980), "the sense of caring and social responsibility in the Black community, plus strong kinship bonds and other reinforcements kept families together and strengthened their functioning."

Stack (1974) in her studies of Black urban poor families revealed considerable sharing of goods and services, and the care of children. She considers this mutual aid as an adaptive strategy to cope with poverty and racism.

The Black church occupied a significant role in the mutual aid network. In addition to functioning as one of the chief providers of social services, it prescribed sharing and giving as tenets which were to be followed by members of the Black community. Historically, the Black church has been active in the area of social service (Lincoln, 1974; Wilmore, 1975).

The mutual aid network's commitment to maintaining intact Black families was reinforced by the Black church. It was the Black church that served as an agency of social orientation, providing encouragement, guidelines and reinforcement for the traditional values of marriage, family, morality and spirituality in the face of the devastating effects of slavery (Blassingame, 1979).

As a result of the Black family's dependence on the mutual aid network to provide goods and services, the network exercised considerable control on Black family members. The mutual aid network, with its high degree of integration in the Black church, established values and role expectations governing interaction between husbands, wives and children. Thus, Black family members received positive or negative sanctions depending on their willingness to exhibit prescribed behaviors. Ostensibly, deviation from established norms resulted in the withdrawal of goods and services or other social sanctions. Understandably, reinforcement in conjunction with the threat of the loss of services resulted in adherence to prescribed norms. Consequently, Black men and women confronted with family problems sought and utilized strategies for problem resolution which seldom included separation or divorce.

## Decline of Mutual Aid Networks

Increasing involvement of the government in the delivery of social services has caused social scientists to raise questions about the continued ability of mutual aid networks to affect the maintenance of the traditional Black family unit. McCray (1980) voiced this concern, "For Black families and Black people there is but one danger; if these informal adaptive coping mechanisms are pulled into the bureaucratic structure, the informal nature of the network and the network itself could be destroyed."

Seemingly, government-sponsored social service programs have served to diffuse the mutual aid network's influence on Black family stability. Basically, there are three fundamental problems associated with government provision of social services to Black family members. First, when the government initially became involved in the delivery of social services, policies were established which necessitated that the husband be absent from the home, in order for a woman and her children to receive financial assistance. Secondly, the bureaucratic structure of the government resulted in decentralization of service delivery; whereby, certain goods and services were provided at one location while others were made available at another facility. Finally, the nature of the exchange relationship was altered from the perspective of the recipient.

When the government began providing fundamental goods and services eligibility determination was frequently based on the woman's inability to care for herself and her children due to the absence of the husband. Frequently, men were forced to abandon their families in order for their wives to receive public assistance. For Black men, confronted with unemployment and underemployment, it often meant leaving their families to ensure the survival of their wives and children. In effect, government policies were antithetical to the maintenance of the two parent family. In essence, the government's position in the provision of social services was opposite that of the mutual aid network. For the mutual aid network, the condition for rendering services was maintenance of the traditional two parent family.

Government bureaucracy resulted in families acquiring basic goods and services from diverse agencies. In the past, Black families obtained goods and services along with family counseling from the same source. Crises were handled with a greater degree of immediacy. In obtaining counseling services from formal social agencies individuals are generally referred from one agency to another. This often results in the scheduling of appointments and a prolonged waiting period. Despite the exigency of the situation, individuals seeking family counseling must follow established policies and procedures. Of equal importance is the lack of confidence which Black clients have in white counselors who provide individual and family counseling. The trust which exists in mutual aid networks is due largely to the familiarity and frequency of social interaction of family members of the mutual aid network. Race and class differences of the counselor and the Black client may represent impediments to effective counseling relative to family matters. The lack of empathetic understanding on the part of the counselor, for the client, is commonly a result of these differences.

In the mutual aid network individuals changed roles frequently. Black men and women moved freely between the role of provider and recipient. They were able to discharge their indebtedness as a recipient by becoming a provider. Generally, no norm of reciprocity operates when individuals receive services from social welfare agencies. The recipient seldom returns goods or services. Therefore, the recipient remains in the dependent status. Although some social welfare programs have established programs requiring re-

cipients to work (workfare), they have been temporary menial work relief programs of relatively short duration. A consequence of government's expanded role in social service delivery is a decline in the mutual aid network.

## Availability of Alternatives: Rewards Minus Costs = Outcome

Social exchange theory sheds considerable light on the Black family's interdependence on mutual aid networks and the decision of Black males and females to abandon this relationship for one with government social service agencies.

Thibaut and Kelley, two social psychologists, using a pay-off matrix to explain social exchange principles, investigated numerous issues related to group processes. Although they placed emphasis on the mutual interdependency of persons in dyadic relationships, their work has applicability to small group interaction as well. Thibaut and Kelley maintained that a person will not remain in a relationship where the services provided seem relatively meager compared to what the person knows about other relationships. Accordingly, outcome of a relationship is derived using the formula rewards minus costs equals outcome. Of equal importance is Thibaut and Kelley's interjection of the cognitive variable "actor expectations." They suggest that outcome value in a social relationship must always be measured in terms of actor expectations.

Black males' and Black females' willingness and perhaps eagerness to acquire social services from social welfare agencies can be attributed to two conditions (1) limited or meager rewards provided by mutual aid networks and (2) costs incurred by individuals receiving the rewards (goods and services).

Although members of the mutual aid network are committed to providing services to Black family members, the resources of the network's members are equally as limited as are those of the Black family. To give to others often means reducing one's own resources. Furthermore, obtaining resources from the mutual aid network is a highly capricious endeavor. It may mean soliciting assistance from several members of the network before obtaining needed goods and services.

Conversely, receiving goods and services from social welfare agencies increases the reliability and dependability of service acquisition. This is not to suggest that individuals receiving goods and services from government-sponsored social service agencies obtain them in quantities sufficient to meet their needs. Rather, individuals are better able to determine the amount of goods and services which they will be allotted. As such, recipients can establish realistic expectations regarding household expenditures and other financial obligations.

Costs incurred in the relationship between Black family members and members of the mutual aid network also serve to dissuade individuals from using the mutual aid network as the primary source of social service delivery. The obvious costs are monetary and material.

In addition to these costs, Black men and women incur latent costs. These costs Emerson (1962) labels "motivational investment." Emerson in his principles of social exchange invokes the concepts "motivational investment" and "availability of alternatives." These concepts were introduced to explain power-dependence relationships. Though not stated explicitly the concepts of "reward" and "cost" are underlying assumptions. A major postulate of Emerson is that "the power of one actor in a dyadic relationship is equal to the dependence of the latter actor on the former actor." The dependent person's willingness to remain in the relationship is determined by the actor's valuation of rewards received and by the availability of alternative sources of rewards. Thus, one's desire to maintain a relationship is reflected in his or her motivational interest. When Black men and women become aware of alternative sources of goal mediation, as is the case with social welfare programs, they may choose to discontinue the relationship with the mutual aid network. When this occurs the relationship with social welfare agencies is perceived to be more rewarding and less costly than the relationship with the mutual aid network.

Emerson's concept of "power" is quite useful in explaining the willingness of Black men and women to maintain a relationship with the government through social service agencies. The dimension of power and dependence appears clear in one's relationship with neighbors and members of the community. However, in a relationship where services are provided by the government, it is difficult for individuals to envision themselves occupying a dependent status. The concepts of "behavior control" and "fate control" which are set forth by Thibaut and Kelley to explain control which the provider of services maintains over the recipient may be beyond the grasp of the recipient due to his/her enigmatic conception of the government.

Nevertheless, the relationship which the Black male and female maintain with government social service agencies is dependent rather than interdependent. As stated earlier, there are relatively few instances in which recipients are expected to discharge their indebtedness by performing a service in exchange for the goods and services received. In some instances Black male and female recipients may reverse roles in the exchange relationship. In so doing, they may perceive themselves to be providers. Thus the government becomes the recipient. Justification for this perception can be found in the attribution of social inequities to the government and the belief that the tax liability incurred by Black Americans requires the government to discharge its indebtedness.

Applying the fundamental concept of social exchange to marital dissolution, Levinger (1965, 1976) maintains marriages are held intact by the perceived rewards and costs of the relationship, of marital dissolution and costs and rewards of alternative relationships. Although social exchange theory adequately explains the relationship between Black family members and social welfare agencies, a synthesis of social exchange and equity theory (a specific formulation within exchange theory) is necessary for analyzing and understanding dissension in, and the dissolution of, Black male–Black female relationships. Specifically, equity theory provides an elucidation of how the use of social welfare programs influence Black women's decisions to terminate their marriages by separation or divorce.

Equity theory (Walster, Berscheid and Walster, 1973) with its emphasis on contributions of individuals in dyadic relationships sets forth the following major postulates: (1) Individuals will try to maximize their outcomes, (2) when individuals perceive a relationship to be inequitable they become distressed and (3) the more distressed individuals become the more they will try to restore equity in the relationship.

The Black female's perception of her relationship with the Black male as inequitable is related to the dual functions which she performs. As breadwinner and the primary socializing agent she perceives her contribution to the relationship to be greater than that of her spouse. Moreover, the media's success in perpetuating an idealized image of the American family in which males assume exclusive responsibility for breadwinning and females are assigned to expressive functions is instrumental in the Black female's devaluation of her spouse and the marital relationship.

## Expectations vs. Realization

Clearly, structural factors have necessitated that Black families systematically rely on external sources for the acquisition of goods and services. The increased availability of social welfare programs has served to supplant rather than supplement existing social support systems, giving rise to a perception of government social welfare programs as a more viable alternative to marital relationships. A consequence of this favorable valuation of social welfare programs is that irrespective of their abundance, resources made available to divorced Black women through this means is not sufficient to enable them to maintain or increase their preseparation or predivorce standard of living. Weitzman's (1981) study revealed that the standard of living, for women divorced after one year, decreased by 73 percent. During the same period divorced males experienced a 43 percent increase in their postdivorce standard of living. Although these figures apply generically to divorced men and women, high rates of unemployment of Black females, the proportion of Black women in service occupations, more than one-fourth in 1980, and the failure of men to comply with child support payments would suggest that the postdivorce Black woman's standard of living declines as well. This is substantiated by census data which reveal that 50 percent of Black families maintained by females account for 70 percent of all Black poor families in America.

## Implications

The foregoing theoretical formulation has several implications for social policy and scientific investigation. The degree to which Black women's decisions to terminate their marriages is based on the use or projected use of social welfare programs raises several issues regarding the organization and administration of social service delivery, establishment of policies designed for the inclusion of two parent family members in educational and job training programs, incorporation of goal oriented family counseling in social service delivery, coordination of self help networks with government agencies and the identification and proliferation of alternative methods of conflict resolution for Black American couples.

Finally, the disintegration of the Black nuclear family has serious social implications for Black American culture and the larger society. Attendant problems such as family violence, crime, out of wedlock births, mental illness, etc., are inextricably related to the absence of a cohesive family structure. Certainly, scientific investigation into this phenomenon is warranted.

# References

1983   *America's Black Population: 1970 to 1982*. U.S. Department of Commerce, July.

Bane, M. J.
1975   *Economic Influence on Divorce and Remarriage*. Cambridge, Massachusetts. Center for the Study of Public Policy.

Bahr, Stephen
1979   "The Effects of Welfare on Marital Stability and Remarriage." *Journal of Marriage and the Family*, 41 (August), pp. 553–650.

Billingsley, Andrew
1972   *Children of the Storm: Black Children and American Child Welfare*. New York: Harcourt Brace Jovanovich.

Blassingame, John W.
1979   *The Slave Community*. New York: Oxford University Press.

Blood, Robert O. and Donald M. Wolfe
1960   *Husband and Wives: The Dynamics of Married Living*. New York: The Free Press.

Chadwick-Jones, John K.
1976   *Social Exchange Theory: Its Structure and Influence in Social Psychology*. New York: Academic Press.

Cummings, Judith
1983   "Disintegration of Black Families Threatens Gains of Decades." *The New York Times*, November 20, p. 36.

Emerson, Richard M.
1962   "Power-Dependence Relations," *American Sociological Review*, 27: pp. 31–41.

Franklin, Clyde W. II.
1980   "White Racism as the Cause of Black Male–Black Female Conflict: A Critique," *Western Journal of Black Studies*, 4: pp. 42–49.

1982   *Theoretical Perspectives in Social Psychology*. Boston: Little, Brown and Company.

Glasgow, Douglas
1981   *The Black Underclass*. New York: Vintage Books.

Hill, Robert
1974   *The Strengths of Black Families*. New York: Schocken Books, Inc.

Honig, Marjorie
1974   "AFDC Income, Recipient Rates, and Family Dissolution." *Journal of Human Resources* 9: (Summer), pp. 302–322.

Jewell, Sue
1983   "Reviving the Self-Help Network," *The Detroit News*, November 20, p. 17-A.

Levinger, George
1965   "Marital Cohesiveness and Dissolution: An Integration Review." *Journal of Marriage and Family* 27: (February), pp. 19–28.

1976   "A Social Psychological Perspective on Marital Dissolution," *Journal of Social Issues* 32: (Winter), pp. 21–47.

McCray, Carrie Allen
1980   "The Black Woman and Family Roles," in LaFrances Rodgers-Rose, ed., *The Black Woman*. Beverly Hills, Calif.: Sage Publications, Inc.

Moles, Oliver C.
1976   "Marital Dissolution and Public Assistance Payments: Variation Among American States." *Journal of Social Issues* 32: (Winter), pp. 87–101.

Moynihan, Daniel P.
1965   *The Negro Family: The Case for National Action*. Office of Policy Planning and Research, United States Department of Labor (U.S. Government Printing Office, March), pp. 29–44.

Pearce, Diana
1979   "Women, Work and Welfare: The Feminization of Poverty," in Karen Wolk Feinstein, ed., *Working Women and Families*, Beverly Hills, Calif.: Sage Publication, Inc., pp. 103–124.

Poussaint, Alvin F.
1982   "What Every Black Woman Should Know About Black Men," *Ebony* (August), pp. 36–40.

Ross, Heather L. and Isabel V. Sawhill
1975   *Time of Transition: The Growth of Families Headed by Women*. Washington, D.C. The Urban Institute.

Schrag, Clarence
1974   "Elements of Theoretical Analysis in Sociology" in Llewellyn Gross, ed., *Sociological Theory: In-*

*quiries and Paradigms*. New York: Harper and Row.

Stack, Carol
1974 *All Our Kin: Strategies for Survival in a Black Community*. New York: Harper & Row.

Staples, Robert, ed.
1971 *The Black Family*. Belmont, Calif.: Wadsworth.
1981 *The World of Black Singles*. Westport, Conn.: Greenwood Press.

Statistical Abstract of the United States 1981 102nd ed.
1981 *National Data Book and Guide to Sources. U.S. Department of Commerce*. Bureau of Census.

Steinmetz, Suzanne K. and Murray R. Straus
1974 *Violence in the Family*. New York: Harper & Row.

Thibaut, John W. and Harold H. Kelley
1959 *The Social Psychology of Groups*. New York: John Wiley.

Wallace, Michele
1979 *The Black Macho and Myth of the Superwoman*. New York: Dial Press.

Walster, Elaine; E. Berscheid, and G. W. Walster
1973 "New Directions in Equity Research," *Journal of Personality and Social Psychology*, 25: pp. 151–176.

Weitzman, Lenore J.
1981 "Economics of Divorce: Social and Economic Consequences of Property, Alimony and Child Support Awards," *UCLA Law Review*, Vol. 28:1181.

Wilmore, Gayraud S.
1973 *Black Religion and Black Radicalism*. Garden City, New York: Anchor Books.

# Little Giant

# Little Giant

## BY CARL ALBERT
### With Danney Goble

University of Oklahoma Press
Norman and London

Permission is acknowledged for the use of photographs on the following pages: Carl Albert Collection in the Carl Albert Congressional Research and Studies Center, University of Oklahoma, pages 6, 14, 72, 88, 152, 154, 168, 169, 187, 197, 204, 249, 250, 261, 282, 303, 314, 322, 328, 363, 369, 377; Western History Collections, University of Oklahoma Library, pages 10, 12, 15, 42; Dev O'Neill, pages 228 and 364; National Park Service, photograph by Abbie Rowe, page 209; and KNOE-TV, Monroe, Louisiana, page 259.

*E*
*840.8*
*A36*
*A3*
*1990*

Library of Congress Cataloging-in-Publication Data

Albert, Carl Bert, 1908–
    Little giant : the life and times of Speaker Carl Albert / by Carl Albert ; with Danney Goble.
        p.   cm.
    ISBN 0-8061-2250-1 (alk. paper)
    1. Albert, Carl Bert, 1908–    .   2. Legislators—United States—Biography.    3. United States. Congress. House—Biography.
    4. United States. Congress. House—Speaker—Biography.
    I. Goble, Danney, 1946–    .    II. Title.
    E840.8.A36A3    1990
    328.73′092—dc20
    [B]                                                            89-29013
                                                                    CIP

    The paper in this book meets the guidelines for permanence and durability of the Committee on Production Guidelines for Book Longevity of the Council on Library Resources. ∞

Research and writing for this book were made possible through the generous support of
W. Lee Brown and the National Bank of McAlester
Jack T. Conn
Mrs. Tom Garrard
Elmer Hale
Walter Neustadt, Jr.

# Contents

# Illustrations

# Little Giant

# Albert Is My Name

$O$n May 22, 1927, a single headline streamed across the entire front page of Oklahoma's largest newspaper. "WEARY AIRMAN CONQUERS PARIS," it announced triumphantly. The lead story's first sentence captured the magnitude of Charles A. Lindbergh's achievement and gave him the heroic nickname he would never lose: "A lone eagle, flying without radio or signalling devices of any kind, winged his way from the American continent Saturday on the long hop to Paris."

No fewer than ten other stories plastered the front page of that day's *Daily Oklahoman*. Collectively, they gave a hungry audience such details of the flight as Lindbergh's fuel cost ($175), mileage (ten miles to the gallon), and diet (five sandwiches and two canteens of water). Only one other story ran on the front page. Only one name other than Lindbergh's appeared in a headline. It said: "CARL ALBERT GOES EAST."

I was leaving Oklahoma and going to Washington. There I would speak on the Constitution of the United States. It was twelve days past my eighteenth birthday.

What put a high school from McAlester, Oklahoma, up there with the company of the Lone Eagle was a contest sponsored by the *Daily Oklahoman* and forty-nine other metropolitan newspapers. In 1924, the papers had launched the National Oratorical Contest on the American Constitution. Open to any high school

3

student in the country, the contest divided the nation into seven regions. In each, preliminary and state competition would identify every state's best orator on the Constitution of the United States or the work of an individual associated with it. The seven regional contests then pitted champions of neighboring states against one another. The prize for seven regional winners was a trip to Washington for the national finals, to be judged by justices of the United States Supreme Court. Each of the seven also received an award that it had been my ambition to win for years: an expense-paid, three-month summer tour of Europe.

That prize was almost beyond the comprehension of a boy who had seen little more than the farm fields and coal mines of Pittsburg County, Oklahoma, but the contest's requirements were perfectly fitted to me. Each contestant—three million entered the initial eliminations that year—would write and deliver a ten-minute oration. Other than that, the rules were brief: "The only requirement is that he do his best."

By 1927, I had done my best three times. As a sophomore, I entered the district contest at Ardmore. I placed third. There were three in the contest. As a junior, my best was better. I won both the district and the state eliminations and fell just short of capturing the regional championship at Kansas City. Finally, in 1927, untold hours of work and dreams paid off. I won the contest at Kansas City, and Carl Albert went east.

I took with me my first real suit, a gift from some proud hometown merchants. On my wrist was a brand new Bulova President, a fifty-dollar gold watch donated by Newton's Jewelry Store. Suitably outfitted, I left McAlester with my high school principal, R. L. McPheron, aboard the Texas Special on May 23. We rode all night to Saint Louis, where we took the Baltimore and Ohio's best train, the American.

When that train pulled into the Washington station, two men met us. One was my official sponsor, the *Daily Oklahoman*'s Washington correspondent; the other was Senator Elmer Thomas. I had seen Mr. Thomas the year before during his campaign when he spoke at the McAlester courthouse. This was my first time, though, to meet him. New to the Senate—he was then beginning his third month in office—he looked just as I thought a United States senator should. Six feet, four inches tall, weighing a sturdy 240 pounds, Thomas had steel-gray hair combed sleek, and his attire was immaculate. Little wonder, then, that Oklahomans elected to the Senate for four six-year terms, a record of service still unequaled. When I met him on my very first day in the capital, I began a friendship that would stretch over that entire time and beyond.

The next morning, I put on my new suit and watch, left the Raleigh Hotel, and went with the other contestants to the White House to meet the president. Calvin Coolidge sat relaxed and comfortable at his desk in the Oval Office. Because there were no color photographs, I had an unsuspected surprise: the president had red hair, like my own. I was not surprised by his greeting. As each of us was introduced to him, all we got back was a mild handshake and a quick and quiet "Pleased to meet you." Afterward, President Coolidge said not a single word, not even as he joined our group to record the occasion with an official photograph behind the White House. Silent Cal certainly lived up to his nickname that day.

Mrs. Coolidge proved to be much different. As she took us through the White House, she charmed us all with a graciousness and warmth that made me wonder how such a deadpan president could have earned such a charming first lady. In time, I came to know every first lady after her. All have been lovely, but few so impressed me as did the dour president's wife who so fully earned her name, too: Grace Coolidge.

That evening, we were all the guests at the mansion of John Hayes Hammond, a multimillionaire and old hunting buddy of Teddy Roosevelt. His home, destined to become an embassy, looked even bigger and better than the White House. For such an occasion, I put on my first tuxedo and took a cab right to the front door. Determined to make a suitable impression, I walked right up to the gentleman in tails who stood at the open door. I confidently extended my right hand, softened my Oklahoma accent, and solemnly announced, "Albert is my name." He took no pains

*President Coolidge said not a single word.* Carl Albert, second from the left, on the White House lawn with President Coolidge in 1927, with the other finalists in the National Oratorical Contest sponsored by forty-nine newspapers.

at all with his perfect English accent. Bowing almost to the floor, he rose to declare, "I am the butler."

As I recovered my pride, I made my way past the stairway into a large living room that featured a magnificent grand piano. At its bench sat Mr. Hammond's daughter. She sized me up perfectly but gently. As I stood there, barely five feet, two inches tall, she smiled at me and said, "You are so tiny and cute, you simply look like a doll in that dinner jacket." She did not look like a doll in her gown, but she looked very good to me just then. It turned out to be a wonderful evening for a McAlester boy in the Hammond mansion. For one thing, they gave me the best meal I ever ate.

Sixty years since that night, I remember that meal. I remember even more clearly my return to the hotel. To my surprise, Senator Thomas was there, ready to show his young constituent the sights of Washington. He drove me in his car up Independence Avenue. Ahead of us was the United States Capitol, awash in lights. It was my first glimpse of that magnificent building. As the senator parked his car, I stood on the sidewalk to the right side, the House side, of the West Front. I had never seen such a view. I stood there, my eyes drawn to one window. In time I learned that the window belonged to the office of the majority leader of the United States House of Representatives. Standing there that warm evening, I already knew that of all the places on earth I could ever be, this would always be the most special.

We had the contest the next evening. We spoke before a full audience at Constitution Hall in the stately building owned by the Daughters of the American Revolution. Seven high school students—seven out of the three million who had entered the eliminations—came to the stage, each a little nervous, all mighty proud. I spoke first, opening with the words that I had rehearsed thousands of times: "Our Constitution, in the course of its existence, has weathered many storms arising within and without our country."

I was just a boy, and I was a long way from home. Home was and always would be Oklahoma, but I would return to Washington many times. Always I would have something of the feeling that I had experienced on a spring night in 1927, when I knew that of all the things I could ever want to do, this was it. I would meet more presidents, know more first ladies, visit more mansions. In my last months there, I would greet the queen of England. For thirty years, I would make the House side of the Capitol my workshop. For nine of those, I would look through the majority leader's window from the other side. For another six, I would occupy the Speaker's chair. I would be there as our Constitution weathered its most severe storms since the Civil War.

This is the story of how I came to be there.

# CHAPTER ONE

# We Had Everything but Money

$W$hen I was a boy, I often heard my grandfathers speak of territorial fever. It was a condition that had stirred my family for generations. My earliest Albert ancestors came from Germany's Rhine Valley to Pennsylvania in the early 1700s. My mother's people were of Scottish, English, French, and German descent. Whatever their origin, they were of common pioneer stock. Most of them reached America before the Revolutionary War; all were here by 1800. They fought in each of America's wars from the Revolution onward. All went west at early dates, and all continued west, part of the human waves that settled the continent.

The particular fever that my immediate kin experienced occurred as the last of those waves swept across the nation's final frontier. As the nineteenth century ended, virtually all of the North American continent had been settled, its soil plowed, its resources applied. Everywhere this was true, except for a large hole that most maps still labeled "The Indian Nations." Now Oklahoma, those lands lay as a patchwork of Indian domains, each assigned to a different tribe, each closed to all but a trickle of white pioneers, all ready for the next outburst of territorial fever.

For the Choctaw Nation, which occupied eight million acres in the southeast corner, the fever rose just after the Civil War with the discovery of coal. After 1872, when the Missouri, Kansas and

*Oklahoma's first industrial city.* McAlester in 1904.

Texas (MK&T or Katy) tracks reached the coalfields, the fever became an epidemic. Within a generation, nearly fifty mining companies opened more than one hundred mines in the area. Rich veins of what was called the "best steam coal west of Pennsylvania" ran two to eight feet thick and produced three million tons of coal annually. The town of McAlester lay at the center of the bustling activity. Named for J. J. McAlester, a storekeeper and Indian trader who had opened the first commercial mine, the sleepy village of 646 people in 1900 was Oklahoma's first industrial city ten years later with 12,000 residents.

My own family was part of that increase and typical of it. My grandfather, Granville Albert, had been a farmer most of his life. He had farmed in Kansas for a while but was living in Barry County, Missouri, when he heard about the Choctaw country. In the late 1880s, he took his entire family there. My mother's people crossed the Red River about the same time, coming north from Gainesville, Texas. The men on both sides did work related to mining. My mother's father, Robert Carlton Scott, and his brother, Charles, were carpenters who built houses and mining tipples for the coal companies. Grandfather Albert briefly fired the boiler at the Number Nine mine in Krebs before he opened a hotel down the MKT line at Savanna. Mostly, though, they did what they always had done. They farmed, hoping to get better land, better crops, and better markets.

My father, Ernest Homer Albert, was my family's first to work underground. He began mining coal at sixteen and became a well-paid, highly skilled miner. An old Scotsman taught him to be a gasman, a job that fully earned him his pay and demanded his skills, for it was one of the most dangerous in the industry. Before the mine opened each morning, he would go alone into each dark entry and room. Armed only with a tiny lamp to register lethal gases, he would probe each cavity, checking for fire, air circulation, and accumulated gas. A good gasman could turn a potential tragedy into a routine day. On the other hand, a gasman's error could bring grief and disaster to an entire community.

That happened not once but many times. There were ten major mine disasters in the McAlester area before statehood. On average, the blood of thirteen men stained every million tons of coal mined. One of those men was Lewis Durman, one of my uncles, who was the victim of a rock fall in the Number One Samples mine. After my uncle's death, Mr. Samples gave Aunt Minnie some leftover lumber, and some of her kin used it to build an extra story on the house she owned. With the added space, she could take in boarders to eke out a living for herself and her three small children. The only other thing Mr. Samples gave her was the right to dig around the slate dump for any scrap coal that might have fallen into the

*I was named for my mother's father.*

pile. He offered to pay three dollars per ton for what the widow and orphans could scrape together. That was her compensation for a husband killed working in the world's deadliest mines.

My father was boarding with Aunt Minnie when he married my mother, Leona Ann Scott, on March 2, 1907. After their wedding, my parents moved into the Bolen-Darnell mining camp. They lived in a cheap, unpainted, four-room house. It was a company house, and it sat across the street from the company store. Beside it ran the Katy spur that carried coal from the Big Bolen mine, which lay two blocks west.

It was in that company house in that mining camp that I was born on the tenth day of May in 1908. Those who recall the occasion better than I remember that it was about eight o'clock on a bright and beautiful spring morning when my father rushed to the company store to summon Dr. Virgil Barton. Three miners' wives helped the doctor, my mother—and me. I was named for my mother's father (Carl being a shortened form of Carlton) and my father's brother, Bert.

My earliest memories go back to the Bolen camp. Most are trivial, such as being sent across the street to buy a loaf of bread and returning from the company store with a sack of candy. Another was a horrifying event: the fatal shooting of a man near our front yard. Frank Miller had black, curly hair and was a great favorite of mine. He boarded with our next-door neighbors. One morning the man of the house unexpectedly returned home early to find Miller in bed with his wife. The neighbor grabbed his gun as Miller dashed out the back door and headed for our house. The first shot missed as Miller passed through our yard. The second killed him instantly. My mother was looking through the window and saw the fatal shot. She was a witness at the trial. The jurors acquitted the neighbor.

More substantial events left less-permanent impressions. I do not at all recall the birth of my brother, Noal, in February of 1910. I do know that I and everyone else have always called him Budge. Only later did I learn that the nickname came from my own babyish efforts to say "brother." Budge it is.

The "Little Bolen" mine, opened by Carl Albert's father about 1910.

With two babies, my mother became very fearful of the dangers of my father's mining. Those fears were nearly realized while my father was working in a mine in Baker, a tiny community three miles west of McAlester. Working underground one day, my father was hit by a large, falling rock. Had not another miner been there to roll it off him, he likely would have died. My mother had had all she could take, so she laid down the law: my father had to get out of the mining business. That is how I came to live in Bug Tussle.

Bug Tussle is not a city. It is not even a town. It is (or was until 1968) a rural school district. It lies along Gaines Creek ten miles

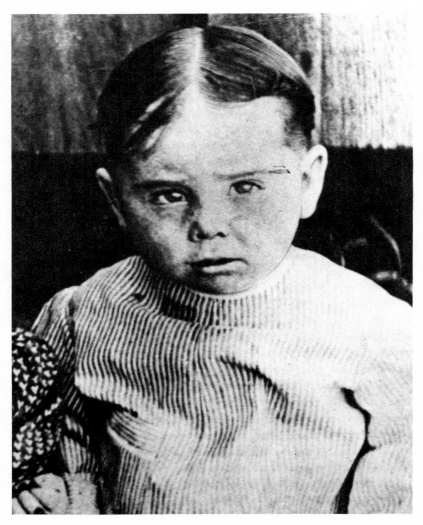

*My earliest memories go back to the Bolen camp.* Carl Albert, aged two.

northeast of McAlester and runs about four miles east and west, five miles north and south. When we moved there, my Grandfather Scott already lived in the community with about fifty or sixty other families. Like other rural communities, its center and most important feature was the schoolhouse. Before statehood, there were no public schools in the Indian lands. Subscription schools, usually charging each pupil a dollar per month, were about all there were. There were at least two subscription schools in private homes before 1900, when parents volunteered to put up a schoolhouse. It, too, was a subscription school until statehood gave it public, tax-supported status. About 1912, it was replaced by a new two-room school built one mile to the south.

Both buildings were not only schools but community centers, sites of preaching, singing, and holiday festivities. The story is told that it was at one of these that the school and community acquired their memorable name. Thousands of insects would swarm around the kerosene lamps that lit the building for night use in the early 1900s. Particularly during the summers, the insects were fearsome. One resident, a rowdy young man whose own name was Ran Woods, took to referring to the place as a real bug tussle. Bug Tussle it is.

Since all my father had ever done was mine coal and farm, if he had to leave the mines he had to find a farm. That was hard because the allotment of the Choctaw lands just before statehood left land difficult for a farmer to buy. Most were tenant farmers renting from landlords who had acquired the Indian allotments. For instance, Grandpa Scott's family was renting land owned by the country doctor who served the community. We initially rented a farm owned by Kyle Tennant, the doctor's daughter. After a year there, my father rented a large piece of bottomland a quarter-mile east. Because it was too large to work by himself, he went in with his father and his brother. The three of them rented and farmed the land for four years.

The Bug Tussle community had few people of wealth. J.J. McAlester had a country home, large ranch, and several thousand acres of land, but that lay four miles north of us in the community known as Reams Prairie. In Bug Tussle itself the resident gentry were families like Robert Sawyer's. Mr. Sawyer had a large ranch, cattle, a fine white frame house on Fish Creek, and the distinction of owning the community's first automobile. Otherwise, most of the families there were like ours: poor dirt farmers. John Virden, who grew up there with me, later described the place as "poor as gully dirt, the land *and* the people. Not just *kinda* poor, but real poor, the kind of poverty you can not only see, you can *feel it,* and *taste it,* and *smell it.*" How we all made it I will never know. But because my father was the hardest-working man I have ever known, we always had enough to eat. While our clothes were few and sometimes patched, my mother saw to it that they were always clean. As Budge says, we did not think we were poor. We had everything but money.

One of the things we had was family in abundance. All of my living grandparents lived nearby. Grandpa and Grandma Albert lived on our place, and my father's only brother lived two hundred yards away with his own two children. Grandpa Scott and my mother's stepmother lived a quarter-mile up the road. My mother's only full sister, Myrtle, lived in a town called Alderson, just a few miles away. Dozens of other relatives lived nearby. Our family ties were strong and deep.

The nearness of my grandparents was especially important to me because they provided a living link to my own roots. Grandpa Scott would tell me about his own parents, grandparents, and even great-grandparents. Grandma Albert—her name was Mary Jane, but everyone called her Mollie—was always pleased to have me ask about my ancestors. She loved to talk about her own childhood in Kentucky. One day she was washing dishes and I wiped for her. She told me about her own father, a really bright man, small in stature like herself. Her mother's name had been Ash, and she told me that she had an uncle named Green Ash. Then she laughed.

Grandpa Albert hardly ever talked about his ancestors. His own grandparents had died before he was old enough to know them.

Also, Grandpa Albert did not talk about much of anything. He was a very quiet person who always attended to his own business and never bothered anyone else. My brother and I would sometimes work with him in the field. He would never raise his voice, not even to his horses. Neither I nor anybody I have ever asked once heard him raise his voice to anything or anybody. He was a devoted Baptist, but he kept his religion and his politics to himself.

Grandpa Scott shared his own opinions, particularly on religion, with everybody. He was well read, very witty, and always talkative. He got religion late, for in his younger days he was very high tempered. Not long after he had come into the Choctaw lands, he and his brother Charles killed a man in Krebs. In June 1896, a man named Frank Newburn shot and killed their oldest brother. Granddad ran out with a shotgun, and Newburn started shooting at him. He tried to shoot back, but the shotgun was empty, so he hit him in the head and knocked him down. As Newburn started to get up, Uncle Charlie took the pistol out of his hand and shot him between the eyes. He lay there next to their brother, two dead men lying two feet apart.

My grandfather and great-uncle buried their brother in the McAlester cemetery. A federal marshal arrested them at the graveyard right after the funeral. He also arrested their father, who was just an innocent old man. The marshal took my grandfather and uncle over to the federal court in Fort Smith for trial. Because my grandfather had two little girls, the authorities let him post bond. Uncle Charlie had no children, so he stayed in jail until the trial. It was ten months before they were acquitted for acting in self-defense. After the trial, my grandfather met up with the marshal who had arrested them all. He pulled him out of a store and offered to fight a duel with guns. He put a chip on his shoulder and dared the lawman to knock it off so he could kill him. He meant it, and the marshal knew it. My grandfather had to satisfy himself with beating the man senseless.

It was later that Grandpa Scott got religion, and when he found it, he truly was born again. He turned completely around. He never met a person he did not try to convert. He preached in nearly every church and school building as well as in many homes in the area. He was an unrelenting missionary for the Lord.

His wife shared his zeal. My mother's own mother had died when she and her sister were children. My grandfather remarried and had three more children. His second wife was a small, dark-complected Texan whose maiden name was Mary Elizabeth Clark. Owing to her looks, everyone always called her Pedro. She had gone to college and was the only one in the family or the community with much formal education, but she was a literalist on the Bible, particularly in its prophetic and apocalyptic visions.

My grandfather's religious prejudices ran deep, but his own convictions were sure. I know that I was satisfied that everything he talked about was correct until I was about thirteen. For instance, because he believed so strongly in divine healing, I believed it was almost a sin to take medicine. Once when I suffered from fever and chills, the only cure I wanted was Grandpa Scott's prayer.

Grandma Albert believed in Sloan's Chill Tonic. She most certainly did not believe in Grandpa Scott's prayers. Her own religious convictions were just as strong as my grandfather's, and her prejudices ran just as deep. She was a Baptist, and she rejected every doctrine and every belief that did not square with Baptist teachings. This included faith healing.

She tried to push her beliefs on to her own children. When they were young, she would haul my father and his brother to Baptist services twice on Sunday as well as Wednesday nights. My father went no further in school than the fourth grade. He probably would have gone longer, but the family moved to Krebs. The only school there was operated by the Catholics. When he came home one day carrying a catechism, his mother jerked him out of school and never let him go back.

Aside from her religious prejudices, Grandma Albert was one of the most remarkable persons I ever knew. She and Grandpa Albert lived in a two-room log shack, but after they had lived there a few months one would have thought it had been touched by a fairy's wand. Tiny, quick, and industrious, she could do more for a run-down cabin and weed-ridden yard than anyone I ever saw; and she could do it with practically nothing. There were flowers all over her yard. There was never a stick or a tin can out of place. She had little money for niceties, so she made them. Her hands turned old rug strips into bright crocheted coverings. Her fingers knitted and sewed and made beautiful lace curtains to adorn the old windows. She dusted her furniture daily, and she scrubbed her wooden floors at least twice a week.

My father inherited his mother's zeal for work though not for religion. It seems that my grandmother's passions had burned any significant beliefs out of him. Like most of my people, he was small in stature. His own father stood five feet two, his mother five feet. He himself was a very stocky five feet, five inches. With muscles like pine knots, my father was known through the community for his wrestling talent. Even more was he known as a worker. With no education to speak of, he never doubted his ability to get his family through good times and bad. He never gave us cause to doubt it either.

I respected my father; I loved my mother. Where he gave strength, she gave love. She was small, too—about five feet two, and one hundred and ten pounds. That hardly measured the love she gave her children. They were her life, her devotion. She would clean us up for school, comfort our petty hurts, and worry over our mischief. Like my father, she had no more than a fourth-grade subscription-school education, but she read books, particularly the Bible, to her children. She read Scripture with the same fundamentalist convictions as Grandpa Scott, her father. Her concern for our welfare prohibited drinking, dancing, and gambling. If my father smoked, he would have go to off somewhere to do it. She would not allow anyone, including our father, to smoke in front of her children, and he respected her beliefs. We were nearly grown before any of us saw him use tobacco.

While we were on the farm that my father and his kin rented, we lived in a house typical of the Bug Tussle community. It was a double log cabin: two log rooms separated by a dog trot (an open breezeway) running north and south. Attached to the eastern room was a small lean-to that we used as a kitchen. A frame smokehouse sat to the rear on the north side. Drinking water came from an old well near the house.

In the backyard stood the universal and indispensable instrument of life in rural Oklahoma: a huge, black iron boiling pot, its three short legs resting on rocks. In the summer, it heated water for shoeless children to wash their feet nightly. In the fall, it converted ashes and hog fat into lye soap. Year round, it boiled our clothes, which my mother then washed with the lye soap on a scrub board set in a No. 3 washtub.

The barn was about thirty yards to the west. Surrounding it were cattle and horse lots, pigpens, and chicken coops. My father usually kept ten to twelve hogs. Cows provided milk and a few calves to butcher. We always had horses for farm work and riding. Mine was that shade of gray that gave him the name Blue. Adjoining the barn lots was a large garden that produced our vegetables. Fruit came from the orchard of trees and berry vines east of the house. My father kept the corncrib filled with corn, the shed with hay, and the smokehouse with hams and bacon.

Inside the house, there was no sign of luxury. A wood cookstove and family dining table occupied the lean-to. The children slept in the west log room. My parents slept in the east room, which was also our living room, where we gathered around the potbellied stove that was our sole source of winter heat. Other than the Bible, there were never many books. Newspapers covered the walls. They were all we could afford for wallpaper.

All in all, that layout was about average in Bug Tussle. Few Bug Tussle people had more worldly goods than we. Several had much less.

We were living there when my sister was born exactly two weeks before my fifth birthday. As I left my bed and entered the breezeway, I saw a strange horse and buggy in the front yard. They belonged to the community's doctor. He carried his black pill bag out of my parents' room. When I came in, I saw my mother lying in bed. Grandma Albert was washing the pink baby in a galvanized dishpan. My parents named her Kathryn, and she grew to be a beautiful girl with my mother's black eyes and black hair. She was to be the one girl in the family.

My extended family continued its nomadic ways. Grandpa Scott moved out of Bug Tussle to a farm near Adamson. In 1916, Grandpa Albert moved into the house where Grandpa Scott had been living. Uncle Bert followed his wife's people out west that same year to grow cotton in Beckham County. For a year, we were all that were left on the big farm that we once had all worked together.

In January 1917, we moved, too. It was about a mile west. My father rented 120 acres from Guy McCulloch. Mr. McCulloch put up a barn on the place and hired a well driller to drill us a well. Grandpa Albert selected the site, as he did for most of the wells in the community. He always used a peach-tree water witch; good water came in at eighty feet.

Our new house was one of the Bolen camp houses that Mr. McCulloch moved onto the place. It was similar to the one in which Budge and I had been born. Two more Albert boys would be born there. Homer arrived a month after the United States entered World War I. My youngest brother, Earl, was born on December 7, 1921. Thus, all four of us were born in unpainted coal mining camp houses. Only the last was born in one that we owned. My father had bought the place from Mr. McCulloch in 1918.

Earl would always be the family's baby and precious for it. His birth was a blessing to all of us. Homer was a determined and fearless boy. He would often frighten our youngest brother by taking him through the little country cemetery. Even as a small child the blackest darkness held no terror for him. His life was cut short by wounds suffered in Normandy on June 9, 1944. When I heard of his fate, I remembered my mother's unusual sorrow after his birth. One day she had called me to her side. She said that she just could not stop crying. She had brought a boy into the world at war. She was consumed with dread at the sadness and horror that might await him. Her own early death spared her the knowledge of

Homer's fate in another world war, the one that began on Earl's twentieth birthday.

All four of us kids called our parents Mama and Papa. Their generation used Ma and Pa, the terms they themselves used to address our grandparents. Words like Daddy were unused until my own children's generation. To us, that term sounded babyish, and Mother and Father were too formal for ordinary speech. My parents were Mama and Papa to me as long as they lived.

While we all lived together in Bug Tussle, we shared the family's labor. Mama and Papa worked tirelessly. The home was my mother's domain. She kept her scant furnishings orderly and clean. She did the same for her children, too. From time to time, my father would add to the family's income by working in the coal mines. This occasionally meant that he would toil underground in distant mines through the week before riding the train home for weekends with the family. The farm, though, remained his major work. At times, Papa would hire an extra hand; always, he made full use of ours.

Each of us worked before and after school. Daily we would collect and haul the wood and water that my mother would use for heating, cooking, and washing. Budge and I usually fed and watered the animals. Budge and I usually fed and watered the animals. Milking was another of our daily chores, done morning and evening. Cows, unlike boys, did not mind cold weather. It seems that my hands were never colder than when on a cow's udder on a typical January morning.

Our seasonal work moved with the natural rhythms of the crops. Spring and summer meant chopping (weeding) cotton, an activity calculated to tire every muscle and blister every finger. Summer's hottest days seemed reserved for baling hay and threshing oats. In the one-hundred-degree heat, it was all one needed to know of hell. But fall was worst of all; then hell became real. It was cotton-picking time.

The long rows of fleecy cotton plants stretching across a wide field were an awesome sight. The thousands of stalks must have been designed by Satan himself to foretell of the bottomless pit. The short plants would not allow a boy to pick from his knees. In a few hours they numbed, rendering him unfit to walk. Stooping merely transferred the agony to the lower back, quickly making it impossible to stand. The cursed burrs pricked my fingers until the blood ran. This surely was the temporal form of the eternal damnation of Grandpa Scott's sermons.

For all of the pain it inflicted upon us, the Bug Tussle farm made us a good living. A succession of good crops and decent prices had provided us the money to own at last a place of our own, and when they continued, my father would actually have money in the bank. At a minimum, the farm sustained us.

All our basic food was homegrown. Gardens gave us the vegetables that Mama served fresh in season and canned for year-round use. In a wood-burning oven she baked biscuits every morning, corn bread every two or three days. Wheat bread—what we called light bread—was a once-a week luxury. The pigpens gave us our basic meat: pork, ham, bacon, and sausage, all of which we prepared ourselves. Without refrigeration, beef was less common. About once every three or four weeks, we or a neighbor would butcher a calf and divide it with the community.

In other ways, we had to meet our own needs. The swarming insects that gave our community its quaint name had no charm at all in the summer, when clouds of mosquitoes brought malaria. Most kids caught it every summer. It is a wonder more did not die. The only way we had to fight it was with tin cans of burning oily rags to keep the mosquitoes at bay. They were about as useless as old Doc Tennant's little bag of pills.

More routine childhood diseases also required home remedies. Doc Tennant's treatment of mumps, for instance, was mare's milk. When I had the disease, we happened to have a mare nursing a new colt. I took one drink of the milk and declared that I would rather have the mumps.

There was no cure at all for the seven-year itch that afflicted the state during World War I. That common label was only slight exaggeration, since the malady persisted for months. Like others', my body was covered with sores that I scratched until they bled. Even Doc Tennant could not treat it. All we ever found that would ease the suffering was sulphur. For a while, everyone smelled like a sulphur well.

The international outbreak of swine flu after the war stretched its deadly hand into our little community. For that, we had no defense at all. Several of our neighbors died, one of them the brother of my good friend John Virden.

Johnny Virden's family was poor, even by Bug Tussle standards. He had lost his mother at an early age, and his father was an old man to have such a young child. Several of his older relatives were already living in Bug Tussle when Johnny moved into our old log house on the Kyle Tennant place. Years later, he would describe his first recollection of me. As he remembered it, I was walking down a country lane that ran due north of the Bug Tussle school. By then I was in school, so I was reading a book. According to John, I was oblivious to the world as I walked along, intently reading, my bare feet kicking up a great cloud of red dust. He recalls that I was dressed in the best Bug Tussle fashion:

> blue and white striped overalls with mismatching blue denim patches on the knees. [I] wore a hickory shirt and a broad-brimmed straw hat that had "shot up to seed" from being rained on too many times. And that was all. . . . We said "howdy" and told each other our names, and shook hands with the one-pump handshake peculiar to country kids and fullblood Indians.

Johnny and I became fast friends, perhaps because we shared a capacity for innocent mischief. One such incident occurred at the local swimming hole on Bucklucksy Creek. In the summer's drought, my father had rolled his farm wagon into the creek's shallow side, where the creek's water would soak the wooden wheels and keep their iron tires snug. Johnny and I decided that it would be great fun to pull the wagon over to the other, deeper side. We did. We had a good laugh as it disappeared beneath ten feet of muddy water.

A week or so later, we smiled—to ourselves—when my father stopped by Mr. Virden's place to ask if Mr. Virden had seen his wagon. It seemed he could not find it, and he thought Johnny's father might have borrowed it. He had not. But he did have an idea. With us boys in tow, Mr. Virden took Papa down to the creek. The men stripped and waded in. It was Johnny's father who found the wagon—when he stepped on its tongue. It took the two men and the two boys to pull it out. Only the boys saw the humor in it. John Virden can finish the story:

> Once the wagon was hub-deep and snugged to a tree with a rope, each father cut a limb that looked as big as a hoe handle. For the next three minutes any passerby would have thought somebody was killing a yearling in that thicket, the hollering and bellowing was that loud.

In time, Johnny's father wandered away from Bug Tussle, taking him to the little community of Ulan. I lost track of him after that, only to meet him again when we were both students at the University of Oklahoma. He was studying journalism, but what he really wanted was an appointment to West Point. He could never find a sponsor, so he went into the Army Reserve and built a career as a newspaperman. Eventually, he landed on Dwight D. Eisenhower's staff. He served as Ike's public relations officer when the general headed America's North Atlantic Treaty Organization forces. Since his Bug Tussle days, when ability counted, John Virden had it. He won several army citations for a superior performance.

John Virden was largely self-educated. As soon as he got near a library, he started reading. He taught himself more about the Civil War than any man I ever knew. He knew strategy, tactics, and details by the thousand, particularly about the Battle of Gettysburg. His grandfather had been an unsung Confederate soldier there, and John became so expert on it that he laid the wreath honoring the Southern dead at the battle's centennial ceremony. It was U.S. Grant's grandson who laid the Northern wreath. In time, John Virden would be invited to lecture at the school he could never attend: West Point.

I always think of Johnny Virden whenever anyone wonders

how a notable person could come from a place as obscure as Bug Tussle, Oklahoma. That tiny, rural community with the curious name had within it people who were just like Carl Albert and John Virden. They are people I have known and respected all my life. There was certainly nothing special about the two of us then or there.

Even our innocent escapades were typical. They helped lighten the heavy routine of farm work. Fishing and hunting helped, too. It seemed that every boy had a .22 rifle and single-barrel shotgun. Abundant quail and rabbit were our game. If there was a hunting season, we did not know it; we certainly paid no attention to it.

Staying overnight with a friend was always a great treat, particularly if that friend was Bill Anderson. Our friendship stretches beyond my memory; I cannot recall not knowing him. His mother was Mama's dearest Bug Tussle friend, and his family was almost as close to me as my own. When he was a boy, Bill Anderson was loaded down with more names than any person I ever knew. For some reason, his teachers always called him Charlie. All of his friends called him Mook. His father called him Smook. When he finally got to high school in another community, he ended the confusion—or maybe added to it—by declaring that his name was Bill. His birth certificate gave his name as William Kitchell Anderson. If he was ever called William or Kitchell, I never heard of it.

I loved staying over with him (under whatever name) and his older brothers, Roy and Ray. We were known to swipe watermelons in season and hunt out of season. Later, I enjoyed playing with his little sister Ruth and brother Howard, who was called Happy and now goes by the name James.

More organized entertainment came in such special events as the annual Pittsburg County Fair. The fair was partly good-natured competition between folks for the best livestock and finest produce. To a country kid, it was also a special world of mechanical rides, thrilling side shows, and exotic foods. It was also the one time of the year that I could count on getting a dollar bill. Folding money just naturally made one feel rich, especially when earned by chopping a farmer's cotton for a day. I always hated to break a dollar bill, so I would survey the entire fair's offerings before doing it.

Bug Tussle afforded more frequently social events, but most were off-limits to Mama's children. Her moral disapproval of smoking, drinking, and gambling extended to dancing. Thus, we were spared the excitement of the occasional dances held at some of the farmhouses. Sometimes those dances were exciting. Young rowdies, their blood heated by moonshine whiskey and local Choctaw beer, often disrupted the dances with fights. Gunfire was not an unheard sound amid the country band's tunes.

Religious meetings may have brought some of this type to repentance. To us, they were social events as well as spiritual gatherings. When I was a boy, I hardly knew that formal denominations even existed. Occasionally, someone would teach a Sunday-school class, open to all, at the schoolhouse, and almost weekly we would attend gospel singing conventions at the Bug Tussle school or in one of the nearby country districts. Without a preacher, Sunday-night singings were our regular services. They were well attended and attracted the best singers from the entire area, even extending into Arkansas. The local residents joined in enthusiastically through the aid of shape-note hymnals. By reducing every possible note of any song into one of eight different shapes, these hymnals made it possible to create instant four-part harmonies.

Summers brought revivals. Some were held in brush arbors along Bucklucksy Creek, right below our house. More often, we would drive up to Reams Prairie, just north of us. Country preachers, including Grandpa Scott, exhorted far into the night. Their congregation included no idle pew-warmers. The people's own testifying, singing, shouting, and praying for the sick were very much a part of the service. The preachers expounded a holiness version of Christianity. Many believed in and practiced glossolalia. Speaking in tongues was the highest form of religious expression, for it gave tangible evidence of the baptism of the Holy Ghost that followed salvation and sanctification.

The sinner's conversion marked only the start of that process. It was made manifest and celebrated by baptism. A good preacher could get ten to fifteen baptisms at a time. The number would include repeaters, for many would redo the process from time to time. It seems that there were a lot of backsliders among us. The sacred site was a big hole in a creek under a culvert near the highway.

Coal Creek was the scene of one quite memorable baptism. Brother Alexander was a Freewill Baptist preacher up at Reams. One of his converts was a little old lady who was raising a mentally retarded daughter. Beulah, the child, was a large girl of sixteen. She would walk faster than a horse, swinging her arms, looking neither left nor right. For church, she had her own seat in the Reams schoolhouse. If anybody got there first, she would just knock him or her right out of it.

As the crop of converts came down to the creek, Beulah rose on both legs, staring wildly. Every time Brother Alexander dipped one under, she would shout, "Oh!" Then came her mother's turn. The preacher blessed the old lady in the name of the Father, the Son, and the Holy Ghost. As he put her under the water, Beulah yelled, "Damn you!" The girl pulled her mother out, threw her over her knee, and proceeded to beat the Devil out of her. Brother Alexander stepped in to save the poor woman. Beulah beat him, too.

I remember an even more notable conversion that occurred in a nearby community. It involved a woman who was fairly notorious for her activities, not only with her husband but with other men of the town. Her husband was arrested for luring a small girl down in a cellar and taking indecent liberties with her. He was thrown in jail, due to be charged with statutory rape.

During this time, the town was holding a camp meeting. The wife was so upset that she sought solace in the Almighty. She went to the meeting, made her way down to the mourners' bench, and met the Lord. She said she was saved. She said that the Savior wanted her to confess all her sins, and she was ready to tell it all. She confessed that she had done many evil things with many men in the community. She promised that she would recount them all at the next night's meeting. Before the next night came, some of those community men, including some who were county officials, released her husband and dismissed the case. The sinful couple quietly slipped away.

Aside from such events, our family's relief from toil largely consisted of visiting its kin scattered across rural Oklahoma. Grandparents stayed close enough for regular visits. Other relatives wandered farther away—far enough away to make a trip an adventure, given the primitive transportation. Henryetta can be reached in an hour by automobile now, but in 1913 it required a farm wagon, two railroads, a rented hack, and an entire day. That was what it took to reach the home of my mother's only full sister and her husband, a man whose 1876 birth date was commemorated in his name: Liberty Centennial Williams. That was an adventure.

It was adventure enough to whet my appetite for travel. Even in Bug Tussle we had heard of the *Titanic*'s sinking. I was fascinated by the gigantic ship and those like it. I thought of them as floating cities, moving across dark seas to strange lands. For hours I would sit holding to my ear some sea shells that Grandpa Scott had picked up in Galveston. I heard the ocean's roar, and I wanted to be on it. I wanted to be on one of those ships. I wanted to reach through a porthole into salt water. I wanted to meet different people. I wanted to see a world larger than I knew.

For the time being, though, I had to content myself with what came to us. A good crop and war-induced prices in 1916 gave us enough money to see some of the world at home. We went to the Ringling Brothers Circus. It was a marvelous sight for a country kid; African lions, Asian tigers, Arabian horses, Indian elephants, Japanese acrobats, Chinese rope walkers—it seemed that the world had come to me.

Ringling Brothers came once. Gypsies came through every month or so. From as far back as I can remember until the time that I was grown, they plied their trades from Mexico City to Chicago along the old dirt trail that used to be the Texas Road. Later it was the Jefferson Highway. Today it is U.S. 69. It runs through McAlester, where the Gypsies used to camp on a stream just outside town. They were remarkable people. They had strange accents, strange clothing, and they had cultivated thievery into an art.

I watched once as they worked over a store about a mile and a half from our house. The owner had stacked five cases of soda pop outside the store. Every bottle disappeared in fifteen minutes. Yet not one native had seen any Gypsy take a single bottle. While the band outside performed its magic, the Gypsies inside were ravaging the store. I slipped in to watch. They alternated between predicting the owner's coming good fortune and prophesying his imminent doom. One old woman picked up a jar of pickles and asked the owner if she could have it. He answered bewilderedly that he could not just give things away. She warned that if he did not, his barn would burn that very night. He told her to take the pickles. I do not know whether what the owner respected was the Gypsies' habit of arson or their claim to prophecy, but they certainly had a gift for larceny. The barn did not burn, but the store was stripped.

They really were remarkable. I would have liked to visit their camp, but I was afraid. It was said that Gypsies stole children, too.

The area's resident population was surprisingly cosmopolitan. The coal mining boom that had summoned my grandparents to Indian Territory had been heard literally around the world. Especially after 1890, immigrants came to make up a large share of the mining population. Italians were the largest single group, but Russian, Mexican, Syrian, and Bulgarian accents were also common sounds to my boyhood.

A caste system, informal but real, had developed around the mines. Americans and some Englishmen generally managed the mines and held the highest-paying jobs. The dirty and dangerous job of digging the coal usually fell to the "foreigners." This caste system also carried over to the social life of the miners and their families. I remember that some of the people in my community would not even vote for a well-qualified Scotsman for mine inspector because of his "funny" accent. I also remember visiting my relatives in Krebs, Alderson, Bache, and Dewar, where kids would make fun of other children whose parents could hardly speak English.

These habits, reinforced by the identification of different towns with different aspects of the mining industry, resulted in the concentration of definite ethnic groups in certain communities. At statehood, McAlester's population was one-quarter immigrant stock, but in the surrounding towns, where the actual mining occurred, immigrant families made up a much larger share. In both Krebs and Hartshorne, for instance, they comprised a majority of the population.

These ethnic identities have proved to be quite durable. To this day, Hartshorne has a richly diverse population. Late in my congressional career, I addressed its high school commencement; the senior class included several full-blooded Indians, as well as graduates of Russian, Italian, Polish, and Mexican descent. A black girl was valedictorian. Hartshorne also is one of the few places west of the Mississippi to maintain a Russian Orthodox church.

Thinking about these towns later in my life, I recall the time I got a call from Manlio Givonni Brosio, the Italian ambassador to the United States. He said he had been looking through a congressional directory and it appeared that Krebs, Oklahoma, was in my district. I told him that it was, and he asked if I would accompany him to Krebs. "Nearly all the mail I get from that state," he explained, "comes from Italians there who want to bring their kinfolk from Italy to Krebs, Oklahoma." I agreed and contacted King Cappo, who lived across the street from me in McAlester. He was a prominent figure in the Italian community. He and his Italian friends planned to give the ambassador a regular Oklahoma wingding.

I introduced Ambassador Brosio at a large reception. He began speaking in English; after a few minutes he shifted entirely to Italian. I was walking through the crowd to gauge its reaction. A small Italian man about seventy-five years old, with a visored cap on, came up to me. He asked in a strong accent, "Are you Carl Albert?" I said, "Yes." He said, "I knew your papa. I worked with him in the coal mine a long time ago."

"That big shot up there," the old man continued. "him your friend?" I said that he was. He said, "You know what, Carl Albert? Him a-talka Italian better than me, I think."

Back in Bug Tussle when I was a boy, there were only a few Italian families living on farms. There were also some Choctaw families in the community, but the largest ethnic minority was the blacks. Several families lived there, and there were more living across Gaines Creek. Quite a few lived to the north of us. One of them, Joe Thomas, was a frequent childhood playmate. Fletch Tilford and his family ran a garage and country store—the store ravaged by the Gypsies—just down the road from our house. I used to play with his kids and with the Scott boys, whose father farmed in the community. Often I would start walking to school with the Tilford and Scott kids. When we would get to Kyle Tennant's meadow, I would angle off left to the Bug Tussle school. The black kids turned right.

Like every other school district in Oklahoma, ours had rigidly segregated schools. It was required by the state constitution. The Scotts and the Tilfords and about fifteen to twenty other black kids went to a school about a mile west of ours. Like the law's demand, it surely was separate; unlike the law's claim, it hardly was equal.

Theirs was a little old one-room schoolhouse on the creek bank. Its sessions were no more than six months, with school let out to send the black kids into the fields to pick cotton. They had one teacher, a young girl whose only education was through the eighth grade in a similar school up in Reams. They could not do better. The constitution required that the black schools be financed by a different—and lesser—tax base from ours. They could pay only sixty dollars for each of the six months. I was just a boy who was himself part of the world, but I knew even then that those black kids never had a chance. I felt that it was unfair, un-human, and un-Christian. I promised myself that if I were ever in a position to do something about it, I would.

Our own school was blessed, not only in comparison with the separate black school but with most rural schools in Oklahoma. The Missouri, Kansas and Texas Railroad was the largest taxpayer in Pittsburg County. About five miles of its track ran right through the Bug Tussle district, and we got a good share of its property tax. Ours was a two-room schoolhouse, quite enough for our needs, sturdily enough built that it is still used as a community center. We had a full nine-month term. We paid the lower-room teacher (the one with the first four grades) $75 to $100 a month; the upper room (grades five through eight) had its own teacher, usually the principal. The job paid $150 per month, a sizable sum at the time and equal to that paid in the largest city systems. In addition, a teacherage, a separate, well-built dwelling, adjoined the school and afforded the principal year-round, rent-free hous-ing. Thus, while the black kids (and many rural white kids) had a poorly prepared teacher with at best a state third-grade certificate, Bug Tussle could demand teachers with a first-grade or lifetime certificate. The result was that all of our teachers were unusu-ally well prepared. Most had normal-school or four-year-college training.

My own parents had very little education. Their subscription-school education had lasted only a few months a year, and none at all after four years. They hoped that their children could do better, but I doubt that they ever had any idea that any of us would ever go beyond high school, if that far. My parents never once required me to open a book. No one ever checked my schoolwork. But they sent me to school. And I wanted to go.

I started school in the first week of September 1914. For the first day, Papa drove me to the schoolhouse in a buggy, but he showed me how I could walk through the woods to and from school. I carried a brand-new aluminum lunch bucket that Mama had carefully packed. I also had a satchel. I had insisted on taking it, although the only thing in it was one little red book that my father had bought the week before. It was the primer that we would use. I had been looking forward to this day for some time. Six years old, I expected it to be the greatest day of my life.

It turned out to be a disappointment. Mrs. Lottie Ross taught the first four grades; her husband, Charles C. Ross, had the upper room. Mrs. Ross helped me pick out a desk near the center of the room. She told us what we would be doing and what she would expect of us over the year. Then she dismissed us. I did not know what to do until Ray and Roy Anderson told me I could go home. Bill Anderson went back with his older brothers. I started back through the woods alone. I made it home, and I remember that my mother met me, saying, "Are you home already?" I started crying and said, "I went to school but they didn't give me time to eat my dinner." I was not very impressed with my first day of school.

The second day *was* one of my life's greatest days.

I opened my primer to find a story about a little boy and a goat. I looked at the pictures a few minutes, then I went to Mrs. Ross's desk and asked her to read it to me. I stood by her, watching the words as she read them. She read the story slowly, carefully, and with great feeling. Every once in a while, I would look up at her and we would smile at each other. I went back to my seat a very happy boy.

When the morning recess came, the other kids ran out to play. I went to Mrs. Ross's desk and asked her to read the same story again. She did, pausing to let me talk about the boy and imagine what he was like. At my desk, I went over the story again and again, maybe fifty times in all. By the noon lunchtime, when I asked Mrs. Ross to read it for me again, she said, "I believe you can read the story to me now. Try and see if you can." I did, getting every word perfectly.

I took the book home and showed my mother and my father that I could read. Then I started going through the book's other stories. I found that I could recognize every word that had been in the goat story. With Mama's help on the new words, I could read those stories, too. At bedtime, I told my mother that I did not want to go to bed. "I want to sit up and read."

I have never had quite the feeling that I had when I finished that little red primer. I know I cannot describe it. I had learned to read. I was so thrilled that I literally sat up and clapped my hands. I had discovered a new world. It was a world that stretched beyond Bug Tussle, beyond Pittsburg County, beyond Oklahoma. It was a world without boundaries and without end, and I had the key to open it. Born that day was a joy and love of learning that would take me to four degrees in two universities. But I would never learn more than I had at Lottie Ross's side on the second day of first grade at Bug Tussle School.

I was blessed with a succession of good teachers all through my Bug Tussle years. Mrs. Ross not only taught all of the first-grade subjects, she did the same for the second, third, and fourth grades, all of us together. The school day ran from nine in the morning to four in the afternoon. Fifteen-minute recesses, one before and one after noon, helped break up the day. An hour gave us time to eat our home-packed lunches and run off some surplus energy.

Mrs. Ross was obviously an organized teacher, as well as an important one to me. However, she never did get used to the school's most ungenteel name. One fine spring day in 1915, she announced that Bug Tussle was an ugly name. Buttercups and daisies blanketed the little mound upon which the school sat. With meadowlarks and other songbirds accompanying her words, she declared that henceforth the school would be known as Flowery Mound. In time, that became its official name. Those who grew up there, however, still cling to the more rugged title that Ran Woods had first given it.

Lottie Ross taught the next year at Mountain View School, a suitably delicate name, though it was only the country district immediately south. Bessie Kelley replaced her. Hers was a remarkable ability to tell stories, long, involved fairy tales that kept our attention for weeks until another would begin. Mrs. Ross returned for my third year. A fine Syrian girl, Salima Moussa, from Krebs started me on my fourth-grade year. Halfway through it, I was advanced into the fifth grade. The teachers and my parents believed that the lower grade had little challenge for me. Though I was now in the upper room, I found it not much more challenging.

Fanny Ross, stepmother to Charles Ross, taught that grade. She also served as the school's principal and was one of the first women to hold public office in Oklahoma. In 1918, while serving as my teacher, she won election as Pittsburg County superintendent of schools.

The sixth and eighth grades each had challenge enough. In those years, I had two of the finest teachers I would ever see. I would have distinguished professors who knew more than they, but I probably never would have better *teachers,* not even at Oxford, than Walter Gragg and Robert Craighead.

Walter Gragg was my sixth grade and first male teacher. He was proficient in all subjects. He was absolutely inspiring with language; I doubt that a better grammar teacher ever lived. He would have us parsing sentences and conjugating verbs for hours—and loving it. Later I would learn Latin, Spanish, and Japanese. I never had to study their rules of grammar or the structure of their language. Walter Gragg had taught me all I would ever need to know of those.

Robert Craighead was a born teacher. He loved to teach children, especially those hungry for learning. He would stay after school; he would even invite a student to the teacherage at night to pursue a worthy idea. He came to us after several years of teaching country schools in Missouri and Oklahoma. He brought a wide range of experiences with him. He had been a rail splitter in Texas, he had fought in the Spanish-American War, he had lived three years in Puerto Rico, and he had attended a fine little college in Missouri.

Of course, he had long since mastered the subjects that he taught. He was in full command of all of the fundamentals of elementary education. He also knew and loved great literature. He was a fine speaker who often read poetry to us in his melodious voice. With his own money, he brought literary masterpieces into the school. He introduced me to the wealth of the English language and taught me about those who spoke and wrote it best.

It was just a little country school, and despite Lottie Ross's efforts, we persisted in calling it Bug Tussle. However, it provided a basic education exactly as excellent as any child might make it. Its subjects were the universal ones. I enjoyed and did well at them all. I was especially fond of geography, for it opened the world about me. American history enthralled me, and my best teachers always seemed to love it and teach it well. They taught it as a grand story, a pageant of heroes marching past for our inspiration and as our models.

I still remember the very first history lesson in our little American-history text. It was about Columbus persuading Queen Isabella to finance his trip to India by sailing west. When he was confronted by doubters of his belief that the world was spherical, my history book said that he took out an egg and dared them to make it stand on its end. They could not do it and asked him how. Columbus cracked the egg on its point and set it on the table with that end down. One of the ministers snorted that he could have done that if he had thought of it. Columbus answered, "Yes, but I thought of it."

History for me was full of such heroes—men who had thought of it and had acted upon that thought. I became a great admirer of men like Washington, Jefferson, Jackson, and Lincoln. After I had read every biography of them at the little school, my parents gave me more for Christmas. I read and reread them, moved each time by their subjects' bravery and achievement. Lincoln's story was especially inspiring. The boy who had read by a log cabin's firelight to prepare himself for the presidency meant a lot to a kid living in a log cabin, even if he was reading by kerosene lamps.

The Bug Tussle school not only served to educate the community's children, it also was the center for community festivities. Particularly at Christmas, it was the site of a grand community party. The children received small gifts and treated their parents with skits and recitations. My talent for memorization landed me such prize assignments as "The Night Before Christmas," the one sure favorite in those days. Under Mr. Gragg's and Mr. Craighead's influence, I also recited such memorable orations as Theodore Roosevelt's "The Strenuous Life" and Woodrow Wilson's speech recommending war. More forgettable was the occasion in which the schoolchildren dressed as fruits and vegetables. I sang out, "I am a little onion, O!" It was not all serious.

We made our own playground games with minimal equipment. Baseball, basketball, and blackman were favorites. Track—races of every distance and variation—was common. I inherited some of my family's wrestling ability. I was also a pretty good runner, but only a fair baseball player. Lyman Pope, a full-blooded Indian boy, had us all beat. He was our local Jim Thorpe. He could out-run and outhit any other boy in the school.

Bug Tussle's one prosperous family provided my first boyhood crush. Ruth Sawyer's father was a cattleman with extensive land holdings. His daughter was a sparkling child with black eyes and black hair. I was convinced that she just had to be the prettiest girl in the world. It took no small act of courage for me to bid on her pie at a community pie auction. I kept enough courage to stay in the bidding until I won the pie and the right to share it with her. That was my bravery's limit. We ate the pie silently, neither daring to glance at the other.

My schoolwork came easily for me. Sometimes it came too easily. In a few minutes I could grasp any assignment well enough to get by. Only when I had an excellent teacher—and I had some—did I reach for excellence myself. I suppose that it was precisely their ability to make me better that made them the best.

I also came to appreciate the teachers' likes and dislikes. On through high school and college, I seldom saw a teacher without a personal slant, prejudice, or theory. I would instinctively give them and the class their own views when I answered questions. In other words, I told them what they wanted to hear.

This was a trait that was to serve me well all my life. As a young congressman, it helped me win the attention of men like Sam Rayburn. Later, it helped me gather the support and goodwill of powerful legislators. I have not always been sure that it was the most intellectually honest approach; on the other hand, I have seldom seen reason in the ordinary course of affairs for a person always to bow his neck and insist on his own point of view. After all, I have never known a mule to get very far in life.

For whatever reason, my teachers always seemed to be especially fond of me. Lottie Ross once confided to my mother, "He's going to make a great man someday." She remembered that Mama laughed and replied, "He'll have to. He's too lazy to work." I was not lazy and Mama knew it, but I did learn early on something of the tangible value of an education.

Perhaps the only thing that ranked below my affection for farm work was my ability at it. In particular, I was one of the sorriest cotton pickers that ever lived. Papa had a rule, though: "Don't come in until you pick a hundred pounds." Budge could almost do it by noon; I was lucky to get there by sundown.

My father usually hired pickers to help. During World War I, these were two little black boys, Joe Scott and Nathaniel James, who lived just down the hill from us. They could pick even faster than Budge. So every morning we would line up, each assigned a row. They raced ahead while I straggled farther and farther behind.

Then I started to tell them stories about the war. I would start one as soon as we got going. I might tell them that I had read that the government was going to draft little boys. We were going to have .22 rifles, but instead of lead bullets, we would shoot cotton seeds. That way we would not kill the little German boys, but we would keep them back. Another tale was that the government was going to build a big lake and put little ships on it. Boys would serve in the navy, wear blue uniforms, and sail the ships.

Every time we lined up to start our rows, I would start my story. They got ahead of me, but they kept listening. Then I would talk in a lower and lower voice. When they stopped picking to hear, I would stop talking. I told them that I could not talk loud enough for them to hear me, that I would have to quit until I caught up with them. But they wanted to hear the story, so all three of them—Budge, Joe Scott, and Nathaniel James—would turn and pick back to me in my row.

The only trouble was they were putting the cotton in their own sacks. I explained that that would not do. Papa would wonder why my rows made so much less cotton than theirs. They would have to put it into my sack. Their fingers a blur, they would pick and put it in my sack so I could keep up. As long as I told my story, they would keep me up with them. I stretched that story out the whole season. That is how I picked my hundred pounds.

That may have been my most immediately valuable use of education. The most enduring came in 1914, my first year in Bug Tussle School. The Honorable Charles D. Carter, member of Congress from the Third Congressional District of Oklahoma, came out to Bug Tussle in a buggy. He was a mixed-blood Chickasaw Indian and our district's original congressman; he was also one of the most handsome men I had ever seen, the most articulate I had ever heard. I had seen and heard some of our county's politicians, but never anything like him.

He spoke to the student body at Bug Tussle school. He told us about meeting with President Wilson. He talked about Congress and how it worked. Then he said the words that burned into my soul, leaving a life's fire: "You know, I'm an Indian boy, and it's wonderful in this country that a man who's a member of a minority can be elected to Congress. A boy in this class might someday be the congressman from this district." I was sitting in the same seat where I had just learned to read. And I knew. I had no doubt. Mr. Carter was talking to me. I was that boy.

That was in the fall of 1914, the same school year in which the same student body assembled again for its group portrait. I stood exactly in the center of the front row with the other first-graders. My hair tousled, my head cocked to the side, I knew that day what I would know every day of my life thereafter. This little boy is going to Congress.

I told nobody. They would probably laugh and shrug me off. But that is why I studied history so intensely, finding inspiration

*Exactly in the center of the front row, . . . this little boy is going to Congress.*

in the lives of great public men. That is why I loved and worked so hard at language, grammar, and oratory. Those were the tools of public men. That is also why Robert Craighead was so important to me.

Mr. Craighead was from Callaway County in Missouri's Ninth Congressional District. He was a constituent, admirer, and friend of Champ Clark, the district's congressman and the current Speaker of the House of Representatives. He told us of Champ Clark's life, the life of a poor boy, born—like Lincoln and many of us—in an unpainted log cabin. He told us of his devotion to the House, how he had turned down an appointment to the Senate after the incumbent's death. Mr. Craighead told us how close Clark had come to winning his party's presidential nomination and certain election, only to have them snatched away by Wilson in the 1912 Baltimore convention.

Perhaps because of his devotion to Champ Clark's career, Mr. Craighead knew a lot about the office of the Speaker. He explained how Clark and the great Republican rebel George Norris had led the fight to smash the rule of Speaker Joseph G. Cannon, the czar whose power nearly reduced the democratic body to one-man rule. As Speaker, Champ Clark modernized the House of Representatives. He used his power, but he did not abuse it. He was a Speaker who respected the rights of the minority and of individual members. He made legislative policy in the Democratic caucus, not in the Speaker's Rooms. He had done more to make the House of Representatives the people's branch than had any man since the Constitutional Convention.

Robert Craighead convinced me that Champ Clark was a great man. He convinced me, too, that being Speaker of the United States House of Representatives would be a great goal. That ambition, however, was tempered by Champ Clark's own counsel: "The Speakership is the hardest office in the world to fill, and the hardest to get." I later learned just how right he was. Even at the time, I sensed it. Politics had already cost me one of the finest teachers I had ever seen.

John Perteet headed one of the biggest families in the community. His father had lived there since the original land allotments, and the old man's many children had families there, too. John Perteet's eight children attended the Bug Tussle school, which was about two hundred yards from their home. One was Henry, a boy a little older than I, who was the school's champion speller. He also was crippled, and sometimes Henry Perteet would have to crawl to school.

For some reason, John Perteet came to dislike Mr. Gragg. He maneuvered to get himself elected to the school board. He was determined to fire my sixth-grade teacher; in fact, he came by our house and talked to my parents about it. He even asked me if I would not want to have Mr. Charles Ross back at the school for my seventh grade. I did not answer. I loved Mr. Gragg. We all did. But it counted for nothing. The school board dismissed Walter Gragg at the end of the year. Mr. Ross, stepson of Fanny Ross, county school superintendent, took his job.

By that time, I had also learned something of politics on a larger scale. We had greeted the news of Europe's World War with initial indifference. The immigrant miners must have felt loyalty to their homelands, as well as concern for their relatives there. Most people in our community, however, had no direct stake and little personal interest in the fighting. Our inconveniences were slight. For instance, we could not get German-made blue dye. But aside from the steady bleaching of our overalls and chambray shirts, Europe's war was not Bug Tussle's.

Germany's sinking of the *Lusitania* in 1916 did stir up considerable indignation. It was a principled resentment: a German submarine cowardly had attacked an unarmed British passenger ship. Our concern, however, was still neither immediate nor personal. Though Americans had died, none were our neighbors or relatives. Nonetheless, many greeted America's declaration of war in April 1917 with relief; at last the indecision of our country's role was resolved. Now, American forces would quickly settle the score and permanently resolve the issue. They would make the world safe for democracy.

We boys were certainly ready. Our newspapers told us that the Germans were a cruel and evil people. Their soldiers bayoneted Belgian babies and machine-gunned French civilians. Their wicked Kaiser plotted to rule the world. General Pershing's doughboys must return the help of Lafayette's brave men who had won us our own freedom. We sang with the departing troops, "Goodbye Broadway, hello France, we are going to pay our debt to you."

We only regretted that we could not go, too. We all wanted to be soldiers. In fact, we youngest boys formed ourselves into a military company. We marched through the woods, the fields, and the schoolyard, our chins high, our backs straight, sticks firmly held to our shoulders. Because one of Papa's hired hands had taught me the commands of his National Guard drills, I was their captain, and I put them smartly through their paces. For Christmas 1918, I received the grandest present I ever had: a tiny toy cannon that shot a rubber shell. Budge got a set of soldiers. We played that winter with my cannon blasting away at his charging infantry.

Otherwise, the war's immediate effect on my family and most of the community was economic. War demand ran cotton prices up to forty cents a pound, three and four times their customary level. We all wore better clothes. My father's bank account climbed, for the first time, to four figures. Papa bought a new horse-drawn hack, a poor man's surrey, and it was a great improvement over the secondhand buggy and Springfield wagon. Mama finally decorated the house with store-bought wallpaper.

Then the bodies started coming home. The first was Claude Tedrick's. He had been one of those young men—Claude was about twenty—who had come by the farm, looking for work. My father had hired him, giving him meals and a roof until the crop work began and his pay started. Claude was like a lot of people there; he could neither read nor write. He told me once how much he admired Doc Tennant. Claude said that he did not "know 'A' from a pig track," but the doctor "could make all them little crooks" without even looking at the paper.

He wanted something better and bigger than farm work, so he joined the army and served on the Mexican border. He went to Europe with Pershing's troops, one of Bug Tussle's first men to enter the war. Claude Tedrick died in a French ditch. By the time another of Papa's hands went to war, we did not hear as much about our debt to Lafayette. Carrying their draft orders, boys were leaving every week. There was crying, not singing, when we drove our new hack into McAlester and put Dave Williams on the train for Camp Robinson.

We boys, too young to fight or to understand, kept our war fever high. I was one of them. But it was obvious that war weariness was rising. People resented wartime regulations. Abstract principles gave way to personal fear for our sons and our friends and the future. My mother was not the only one to feel it. A rebellion of antiwar sharecroppers and tenant farmers erupted not far north, in the Canadian River valley.

The self-styled patriots were alarmed. Maybe they had cause to be. Oklahoma's governor, Robert L. Williams, created a state council for defense, and county councils appeared in most of the state. These were nearly hysterical where the foreign-born population was large, where poverty had eroded community bonds, and where patriotism had lost its lust.

Pittsburg County was just that kind of place. Our county council sought out the rebellious, and we had some. It vigilantly searched for slackers, and we probably had a few of those, too. The trouble was that the council could not tell the difference and it did not know how to handle either.

Grandpa Scott, as independent and as opinionated as any man who ever lived, was no slacker, but the local patriots thought any man so contrary just had to be one. They called on him, demanding that he nail a flag to his house to prove his loyalty. He showed them that he already had one flying from his mailbox. He also showed them the medal that his own father had won as a Civil War soldier fighting for that same flag. Grandpa invited them to nail up all the flags they wanted. They left.

They came back. This time, they wanted him to sign a card swearing loyalty to the president and everything it took to go into a war. They asked this of a man who had stood trial for murder, a man who had beaten the officer who arrested him, and a man who had found apocalyptic religion. He would sign no card. He would give his country his loyalty. But he would not swear to any man. In fact, he would not swear at all. In his view, swearing violated the Commandments, and that card was the mark of the beast, Revelation's symbol of fealty to the Antichrist.

So they arrested him and threw him into the Pittsburg County Jail. There a gang of patriots, joined by common drunks and thieves, bound him, and whipped him, two hundred lashes in all.

*Grandpa Scott, as independent and as opinionated as any man who ever lived.*

Grandpa Scott asked the Lord to forgive him and signed the card. He did it with his soul's reservation that he would recant if the Lord asked it of him. The Lord must have understood.

Through such experiences, I came to know and understand something about my community. Nature had blessed it abundantly. Beneath its soils ran the rich coal veins that had called our people forth. The hills and valleys received the gentle rain that nourished the daisies, buttercups, wild roses, and lilies of our fields. Spring sparkled with their brilliant color. Red oaks, hickories, sweet gums, maples, and evergreens renewed nature's palette in the fall. Yet for all of nature's wealth, most of our people were poor. Only a few owned their own farms or had any hope of ever owning them. For many miners, life was dirty, brutal, and short. Few country kids had decent clothes. Most went barefoot until winter. Some of the adults did, too.

McAlester, only a few miles away, was the area's metropolis, and many of its founders still lived there. Most of the coal companies had their headquarters there. Local promoters had built a school system that was envied across the state. They also had won for it the state institution that gave the place a reputation and the community a large and steady payroll: the Oklahoma State Penitentiary.

Most of our people believed in the old-time religion. They also believed in the old-time politics. In what was already called Little Dixie, that meant the Democratic party. Two hundred Democrats were registered to vote in our precinct; there were six Republicans, though no one knew why.

Outside our immediate area, a good number of people were turning to Socialism. Socialists governed Krebs, and a Socialist represented the working-class section of McAlester on the city council. Pittsburg County gave Eugene V. Debs, the Socialist party nominee, exactly one-fourth of its presidential vote in 1912. From the year of my birth through 1914, Socialists controlled the United Mine Workers.

Though my father was a union man, he was never a Socialist. He continued to believe in a man's hard work, not the overthrow of society. Considering what he had achieved with so few advantages, it was a reasonable belief, one that I could share.

That was, perhaps, the greatest lesson I learned in Bug Tussle. We lived no differently from most of the people there. I never thought myself any better than anyone there, yet I knew that there had to be something better than growing cotton or mining coal for a living. My family and my life had given me the means to see that. A visiting congressman traveling in a buggy had defined what it was. My teachers had shown me the path to it.

That was why I took so hard the news of 1922. In the spring, my father grew a good crop of cotton and our little class passed the county examinations with ease. We had a fine and moving graduation ceremony at the schoolhouse, for the Bug Tussle school went no higher than the eighth grade. If a student went to high school, he or she would have to go away. McAlester, only a few miles away, had a splendid high school. But cotton prices collapsed during the summer and Papa could find no way to get me there. He could not afford a car, and it was too far for me to ride Blue. There was no money to board me. So when other kids were ready to go to high school, I went to the cotton patch. I could not yet leave Bug Tussle.

In a sense, I never would.

# CHAPTER TWO

# *A Little Giant*

$\mathrm{N}$o one could have convinced me of it at the time, but the dropout year that followed my graduation from Bug Tussle School was one of the most important I ever had. The year gave me plenty of time to think about what I wanted to do with my life.

One thing I wanted had not changed. My disappointment only steeled my resolve that I *would* go to Congress one day. In that dropout year I decided to do everything possible to get me there. I would go to high school. I would go to college. I would take a law degree. I would excel in all my studies. Along the way, I would also master debate and oratory to prepare myself for public life. For the same reason, I would study government, and I would travel to study the world.

What kept me out of school breathed purpose into those ambitions. The collapse of farm prices—a collapse that began two decades of agricultural depression—briefly hurt me, but it nearly ruined my father. It did ruin thousands. In southern and eastern Oklahoma, the rout of prices occurred on a battlefield. For years most of our farmers had struggled in a hostile marketplace, their greatest foe the sharecropping system, their only weapon cotton stalks. Now, men less energetic or merely less fortunate than my father slid into bankruptcy or deeper into tenancy.

I watched as the colors faded from their clothes and the hope from their eyes. I saw their kids (not one of my classmates could go to high school that year either) take up hoes and plows to start lives that would lead to—I did not know where. But I did know that if our people were ever to go anywhere, government would have to help them. My classmates and their parents deserved better, and there was nothing else that could get it for them. The recent world war enlarged my awareness. I had seen the bodies come home. I had heard my mother's fears. I had touched my grandfather's scars. I believed that if war ever were to be prevented, it would have to be government that did it.

Binding these convictions together were bands of my own experiences. There were teachers who taught our history as a tale of individual struggle and achievement. There was Representative Charlie Carter, who told us kids that Congress could make a difference. Robert Craighead had explained how that institution worked and how important personal integrity was to it. I had, too, the examples of my father's persistence, my mother's devotion, and my grandfather's resolution. All of this summed to a boy's determination that his life would have a moral impact upon his world, his country, his state, and his community. This is what I learned that year. It is what I wanted to do and why I wanted to do it.

In the meantime, there were cows to be milked and crops to be tended. I did that, but I also tried to keep up with my education. Mr. Craighead, my eighth-grade teacher, knew how sharp my hurt was and one way to treat it. He gave me some books and lessons on English composition and ancient history. With his encouragement, I began to teach myself elementary algebra.

I also found work to do on my own. I had loved grammar. In fact, I had found it exciting for its order, its precision, and its ability to lift one beyond circumstances. I honestly did not understand why so many other kids found it difficult, boring, and irrelevant. So, I wrote an English grammar for twelve-year-old children.

I had two grammar books, one from the sixth grade, the other from the eighth. I compared them subject by subject. I then set out to express the grammatical rules in the simplest language, language that any kid could understand.

I wrote that our language could be reduced to a few simple rules. For instance, in all of English there were just eight different kinds of words. These were called parts of speech. Every word anyone would ever use belonged to one of these eight groups. I gave many examples for most parts. Of course, I mentioned that there was but one common expletive, the word *there,* as in "There was a boy who had a goat." From words, I moved to phrases, from phrases to clauses, from clauses to sentences. I used two whole Big Chief tablets fixing up that grammar.

My zeal was not shared by my family. When Budge and I were in school together, I usually sat in the front row, where I could listen to everything. He sat in the back, where he could have a little fun. No one in my family—and, aside from the teachers, no one in my community—had any education to speak of. Still, my mother's love stretched to embrace any ambitions her children cherished. My father, however, thought that eight years of schooling were plenty. Sometimes he would fuss when I studied so much. For all his fussing, though, he was the one who helped me to do it. My mother had persuaded him to leave the mines for her children. For us children, he now knew he must go back.

A revival of mining had opened new jobs in the mines. Mine owners sought out my father, knowing that he could do anything around a mine from digging coal to supervising a crew. The owners also knew of his skill in the two most dangerous jobs underground: gasman and shot firer.

Papa returned to the mines in August 1923, working as both a gasman and shot firer. He also finished the year's harvest, and he would keep and supervise our farm thereafter, though others would work it. As a very skilled miner, he sometimes made more than four hundred dollars a month, an unusually high wage at the time. He earned every penny of it. There would be one stretch of seven years in which he would work on the night shift seven nights a week, every night save one for seven years. The one time

*Papa returned to the mines.* Carl, Homer, Leona, Earl, Kathryn, Ernest, and Noal Albert.

that he had to take off sick, the mine exploded, killing eighteen men. It was another one of the Samples mines. My father always believed that had he been at work it would not have happened.

As soon as we could, we would have to move closer to the mines and give the farm's renters our house. Until then I was able to start school, thanks to Mr. Craighead. He bought a brand new Model T. He had a son, Edwin, about my age. Edwin drove into McAlester for high school, and I rode with him. In September, we bounced over the country roads into McAlester to enroll for high school.

The school that I was starting was more than just a high school. In the first place, high school itself meant far more then than it does today. Only a minority of the American population at the time had earned high school diplomas. In rural southeastern Oklahoma, it was a rather small minority. Then, high school was a *high* school, roughly equivalent to a community college today.

McAlester High School was at least the equal of a very good community college. The city was home to some of Oklahoma's outstanding lawyers, engineers, accountants, and businessmen— educated professional people with pride in their city and expectations for their children. The school system they built and supported was one of the state's finest; McAlester High School was its crowning jewel.

The building itself was nearly new. Sitting high atop a hill overlooking the business district, its architecture of red brick and white limestone was flanked with columns and turrets to follow the day's collegiate style. Almost all of its teachers were university graduates, and several had done considerable work beyond the baccalaureate. What other school would have a teacher like Arthur Coole, who coached the football team? In his spare time, he studied Mandarin Chinese to prepare himself for a subsequent career as a missionary to China.

He was also a pretty good coach. The school took its athletics seriously. In fact, one of its students, Tom Poor, had gone to Europe recently as a high jumper with the United States Olympic team. It was the competition, the triumph of excellence, that gave the school's athletics significance. It gave athletes a certain status, but one no higher than that of debaters, orators, or scholars. McAlester High School was known for entering just about every competitive speech and academic contest in the state. Its teams did not often lose. Its graduates were stars of the best universities in the region. Shirley Buell, who came up through the school system and was salutatorian of my class, remembers it just right: "At that time, in that town, in that school system, of that state, there were giants."

Everyone in the school—everyone in the town—knew just who

the giants were. Academic achievement was greatly respected, and the record that she had compiled even before entering high school already made Shirley Buell one of them. It gave her and a dozen other students a popular stature equal to Tom Poor's. I knew who they were even before I started school. Like everyone else, I respected them. In fact, I was in awe of them. I was a country kid, barely five feet tall. It would be hard for me to be a giant, too.

My enrollment underscored that. English and algebra were required ninth-grade subjects. Edwin and I had agreed upon ancient history and Latin as our electives. When we handed in our enrollment cards, the principal, Mr. McPheron, told us we could not take Latin. He would not allow freshmen from the country schools to take it because they were not prepared well enough for it. We masked our feelings and signed up for the first alternative, public speaking. The teacher happened to be in the office with us, and she redeemed something of our day. "I want these two boys," Miss Perrill Munch laughed. "I may not teach them to speak Latin, but I will bet you they speak good English when I get through with them."

For a while, I was not even sure that I could speak decent English. I began school feeling out of place, full of doubt, intimidated by the city giants of superior preparation and academic reputation. I know I looked out of place. Befitting the school's prominence, the girls' standard dress included heels and silk stockings. The boys wore suits, white shirts, and ties. One who was there recalls that I came to the first algebra class dressed in Bug Tussle fashion: overalls, a work shirt, and brogans. I honestly did not mind that. What I dreaded was my inability to compete intellectually with what I feared were superior people, city people from city schools, their homes filled with books.

My first effort in class multiplied those fears. Our English teacher, Maureen Watson, called on me to explain a very simple paragraph in our composition text. I arose and started—started stammering, stuttering, and searching for a way to give up unnoticed. The classroom erupted with laughter as I shrank into my seat in the middle of my muttering.

It was two weeks before I said another word in any class. It was in the same English class. We were reviewing grammar. The teacher was calling upon students to identify parts of speech. Students clamored for her recognition to answer questions. Then Miss Watson wrote on the blackboard a simple sentence, something like "There was a beautiful house on the hill."

"What," she asked, "is the word *there?*"

Many tried. Several guessed. No one knew.

"Does anyone have any idea?" she asked.

There was silence until I bashfully raised my hand. I said quietly but confidently, "It is an expletive." Not one of the city kids even knew the term.

That happened more than sixty years ago, now, but I still remember that day. I remember it because I knew then that I had arrived. In a place that treasured competition, I could compete with anybody, and I would. I vowed that I would not make a single grade under ninety on a single assignment, and I knew that I could do it. I knew, too, what stature that could bring me. After our first report cards came out—I was in the nineties in every subject—my algebra teacher told the class that the faculty had singled out Carl Albert for setting an extraordinary standard for work. In that same class, one of the students congratulated me for having solved a problem that no one else had. She did not know that I considered it a triumph just to speak with her. Her name was Shirley Buell.

Just after we got our first report cards, Papa rented a house in town and we moved. It was to the northwest part of town, near the state penitentiary. We did not improve our situation much. We were in an old frame house. Our utilities were a two-hole chick sale (outdoor toilet) and a single hydrant, in the yard, too. It was our first painted house. Our new home was walking distance (just two miles) from the high school.

Our part of town was called formally Talawanda Heights. It was otherwise known as Guard Town. My father mined coal on the state prison grounds, and we boys fooled around the penitentiary. On Sundays, we would buy cigarettes for the women prisoners— our fee was a nickel—and then watch the women's warden take the smokes away. Next door to us lived a more successful entrepreneur: he was a bootlegger. Our neighbor to the north was old man Ritchie, who for some time had been the prison's bloodhound man. He was known for an occasion on which three convicts attempted to escape by taking a prison secretary hostage. Mr. Ritchie shot and killed all three without harm to himself or the terrified secretary.

Next to him lived that prison's most renowned employee, Richard Owens. Mr. Owens had built the state's electric chair back in 1915. For thirty-three years, he was its sole operator. He also got quite a bit of work in surrounding states. Wardens agreed that he was the perfect executioner. He got neither pleasure nor pain out of pulling the switch. It was just a job. I used to run into him as he walked casually home in the morning, his cowboy boots moving briskly as he came down the street after having used his trade one, two, even three times the night before.

Mr. Owens was a large, tall man who had been a local boxing champion in his youth. The story is that he killed his first man when he was fifteen when somebody stole his father's horse. He found the horse and a man on it. When he challenged the man about the horse, the fellow jumped on him. Rich Owens got his knife out and cut the guy's head off before he could get loose. He had been killing men ever since.

He had started with the prison as a regular guard. Not long after, two convicts grabbed him. One put a knife at his throat; the other led him through the prison yard as their hostage. Rich told them, "Now, you all better make this good. If you don't, I'll make good on you." Then he shouted at the tower guard, "Shoot 'em! Kill 'em both!" The guard did shoot and kill the one leading him. The other dropped his knife in terror and ran into a coal house. Richard Owens followed him in, took up a long-handled shovel, and knocked him down. "Please don't, Mr. Owens," the convict cried, "don't kill me." Richard Owens cut him off. "I told you you'd better make it good, 'cause it was either you or me." Then, with his big cowboy boots, Richard Owens literally stomped the inmate's brains out. The story was all over the front page of the *Daily Oklahoman,* and Owens's picture was in every newspaper. It was the heyday of his life.

For all his notoriety, there was something about Mr. Owens that sometimes made him seem apprehensive. When I would talk with him, he could not look me in the eye for ten seconds. His own eyes darted about, never resting anywhere. That was the way they were moving when I ran into him one time later on, after I had been away from home for some time. I asked about his health. He said it was fine. Then he asked about mine. His eyes flicked aside as he added quietly, "I have been praying for you."

At school, I threw myself headlong into every subject. I threw head, feet, body, and soul into the one I had not intended to take: public speaking. When Perrill Munch got through with me, I could speak very good English indeed.

Miss Munch was a young graduate of the University of Oklahoma. She also had studied speech and drama at a private school in Martha's Vineyard, Massachusetts, where she earned more than the equivalent of a master's degree. Her dark hair lay in the tight waves that were fashionable at the time. Her dress was always professional and always immaculate.

She was everything a teacher should be. She knew her material, and she had it organized to the most minute detail. She delivered it with a clarity and a force that made her the finest classroom lecturer I would ever hear. To this day I keep a little black loose-leaf notebook in which I set down my lessons as Perrill Munch dictated them to our fourth-hour class in 1923. I still find use of it.

Miss Munch lived her work and put her whole life into it. She taught five or six classes during school hours, and at night she coached debate and directed plays. In between and afterwards, she made time for any student who needed her. That is why her first-floor classroom attracted practically every outstanding student in the school. Had I taken Latin, I would have learned Caesar's *Veni, vidi, vici* (I came, I saw, I conquered); in public speaking, I came to see what conquering was all about.

Before the common use of microphones, amplifiers, and other mechanical aides, public speaking was a form of oratory lost to a modern age of gadgetry and conversational address. Merely to be heard required training in breathing, diction, and inflection. Miss Munch worked us tirelessly on those now-lost skills.

She emphasized that one method of learning good oratory was to read and recite good oratory. I memorized that first year in high school orations that I can still recite, classics like Demosthenes's "Oration on the Crown," Patrick Henry's liberty-or-death speech, and Abraham Lincoln's immortal trinity, the "Gettysburg Address" and first and second inaugurals. She urged us to recite poetry, for it encouraged one to speak with feeling and passion. I memorized some great poems (and some not-so-great ones), and I recited them on every possible occasion. Frank Sittle, one of my class-mates, still remembers crying at my version of Lord Tennyson's "Crossing the Bar." Even Budge was moved to tears with my ren-dition of Senator Graham Vest's "Eulogy on the Dog."

It was my newfound interest in public speaking that first intro-duced me to the world of politics. Slick advertisements and thirty-second television spots were innovations not yet inflicted upon the electorate. Politicians still earned votes the hard way: on the stump. Candidates for governor, senator, and congressman spoke every election year at the county courthouse. Aspirants for local office flowered each biennial fall at every country school and crossroads store. For the office seekers, stump speaking was the only way to reach a large audience. For the voters, it was a rare opportunity for entertainment and excitement. For me, it was a chance to see and to hear oratory at its most practical level.

In rural Oklahoma, stump speaking was an art form. I still re-call my parents' taking me into McAlester in 1922 to hear Jack Walton campaign at the courthouse. Walton was Oklahoma City's mayor. He was also the gubernatorial candidate of Socialists, debt-ridden farmers, and hard-up union men, all allied into the Farmer-Labor Reconstruction League. Finally, Walton was a born stump speaker, a man capable of moving crowds to laughter, to rage, to praise, to bitterness—and to the polls. He won the Democratic nomination and election to the governorship that year by record margins. Walton served only eight months before the legislature impeached and removed him. His fatal mistake was crossing the Ku Klux Klan. Oklahoma counted many Klansmen in the early 1920s, including a majority of the state's legislators.

The object of my oratory was different from Walton's. It was in the year that I entered McAlester High School that newspaper publishers began the nationwide competition that offered the winners a trip to Washington, an ocean crossing, and a summer in Europe. It was the only contest in America that afforded such opportunities. It surely was the only way that a country kid from Bug Tussle could hope to go. Our entry, Cecil Peters (Cecil placed second in the state contest), was my idol that year. By my sophomore year, the contest was my obsession.

I began that year a serious study of the Constitution of the United States. Knowing that a speaker could not express a thought he did not have, I read everything I could find on it in the McAlester library. I wrote and rewrote my speech a dozen times, always finding it difficult to purge its most ringing lines. I eventually shaped it to my satisfaction and won the McAlester High School contest.

Finally, the day came to catch that worst of trains, the one that took all day to run across 130 miles of rough track to Ardmore, site of the Third Congressional District contest. I thought enough of my speech that I offered to show it to a fellow passenger and competitor, Earl Hirschmidt from Wilburton, but he was so proud of his own that he would not let me see it. Some of his pride was deserved, for he won second place at Ardmore; a local boy took first. I rode the train back carrying my speech and wearing the bronze medal for third place. I wore the medal until my fellow students learned that there had been only three entries.

I knew it, though; and I was pretty blue when I got back home. I went to see Miss Munch. She told me not to be discouraged; she would not give up on me if I would not give up on myself. I could win that contest, but the only way to do it was to outwork every single student in the district, state, and region. She believed I could do that because she believed in me.

Years later—after I had won it and after I had gone to the House of Representatives—some of Perrill Munch's friends and former students gave her a testimonial dinner. I spoke there, saying that "this is the first time I have ever traveled halfway across a continent to attend a banquet. I would have gone halfway around the world if it had been necessary." Then I told about that trip to Ardmore so long ago. I told about my failure, about my talk with Miss Munch, about what she had said. I told them the truth: "It was that little talk that put me in Congress twenty years later. That expression of faith was one of the highlights of my life, not simply because it encouraged me to go on, but mainly because of the confidence it gave me in the dignity and the power and the importance of honest labor."

For the next eleven months, I gave that contest nearly every spare minute I had. I read everything I could find on the Constitution. I wrote my speech. I rewrote it. I threw it away. And I wrote it again. When I was finally satisfied, I started working on the delivery. I worked on the first sentence for more than a month. I said it over and over on my way to school, in my back yard, wherever I could. I worked on making it as direct and natural as possible. I saw my audience before me, and I worked on projecting my voice to that person standing at the back wall. I took parts in school plays to help me deliver the oration in an unaffected manner. One of the best speech teachers in the country kept her promise and stayed right with me.

When the time arrived for the district contest, I was ready. A young journalist named Tom Steed reported the event for a local newspaper. We later served together in Congress for twenty-eight years. Tom Steed always remembered when I was a little freckle-faced, redheaded kid in a borrowed, ill-fitting suit. Then I started talking, and I "damn near blasted the paint off the walls." What did it was the sentence that I had worked on for an entire month:

> In the year 1787 a group of earnest men, representatives of the American states, met in the city of Philadelphia to formulate a Constitution which would provide for a more perfect union of these states and guarantee the individual rights of men to themselves and their posterity.

This time, the train ride home was a triumph. I carried twenty-five dollars, and I wore the gold medal.

In April, I took the oration to two contests on the same day. At Norman in the morning, I entered it in the state interscholastic contest. An OU speech professor named Josh Lee was the judge. When he heard me speak, he wrote "100 percent" by my name and waited to see if any of the twenty-four other contestants would cause him to change it. None did. He gave me first place. My real interest, though, was that evening's finals of the state contest on the Constitution. After we finished, the results were read, starting with the lowest-ranking entry. All the names except mine had been read before the announcement, "Carl Albert of McAlester won first!" My response was odd for someone who had worked eleven months on one speech: I could not say a word.

I went to Kansas City for the regional finals with Mr. McPheron, the principal whose concern for my inferior preparation had put me in public speaking. The finest orators of five states were there. I was the last speaker. Only the one who spoke immediately before impressed me. He was Joseph Mullarky from a well-known private academy in Augusta, Georgia. When he finished, Mr. McPheron turned to me and said, "You have a real opponent there."

I surely did. The first four judges split their votes evenly. Two ranked me first with Mullarky second; the other two reversed the order. The fifth judge decided the contest by ranking another contestant first with Mullarky second and me third. The Georgian won first place and the coveted prizes by a single point. After all that work, I had finished one point short. But I had another year, and the confidence in hard work, to make it up.

I returned to McAlester and news that devastated my happiness. My mother was going to leave us. During my sophomore year, she had contracted tuberculosis, one of the most fearful and deadly diseases of the day. Her spells of suffering had worsened steadily during the previous two years. She had spent more and more time in bed, growing weak and worn. Papa had taken her to almost every doctor in the area, but none could help her. They finally told him that her best chance to survive was to go out west; it was the last, desperate hope for remedy. Just after I returned from Kansas City, she and some of the other kin took the younger children in an old Buick out to Albuquerque, New Mexico, to be under the care of a respected TB specialist. Papa and I took the train out to join them later that summer. The warm, dry climate and the physician's care seemed to be doing Mama a lot of good. Our arrival helped, too, for the family was together for the summer.

We lived in a tourist court, the forerunner of a modern motel. Mama talked with me, laughed with Papa, and played with the kids. She showed us off to her neighbors, a Mr. and Mrs. Bellknap. Mr. Bellknap was especially kind. He helped Mama look after things and got Budge and me jobs with a building contractor that he worked for.

When the summer ended, we had to get back to Oklahoma for school. My brother and I asked the contractor for our summer's wages. He put us off and kept putting us off. I told Mr. Bellknap, who promised to bring either our wages or the contractor back in a sack. He brought the money, and we left Mama in fine spirits under her doctor's and good neighbor's care.

Imagine my surprise when I received a letter from Mama about two weeks later. She wrote that the Bellknaps had left their tourist cabin late one night. They were in an Amarillo jail. They were not married, and their name was not Bellknap. She had heard that they were wanted somewhere for bank robbery. I soon found out where.

The next spring, the prison warden needed some free entertainment for the inmates. Miss Munch took a group of us speech students out to the penitentiary, where we put on a show for the convicts. I recited an Edgar Guest poem, "It Can Be Done." My performance was put quite deeply in the shade by our girl debaters, particularly those who upheld the affirmative on the proposition "Resolved: that capital punishment should be abolished." The girls made the most of their entirely captive audience.

While I sat on the platform enjoying the girls' success, I happened to look down to the very front row. I noticed a big, tall, bug-eyed prisoner. He gave me a smile and a wink that covered the entire side of his face. I suddenly realized who the inmate was: Mr. Bellknap from Albuquerque.

As we were breaking up, I yelled at him, "Are you Bellknap?

"Yeah," he answered. "Remember that old heifer I was keeping out there?"

I said that I did.

"She pulled the rug out from under me, and here I am." He walked off with the other convicts and I never saw him again.

Bellknap was a prisoner, a thief, and an adulterer, but he had been my friend. He got me a job. He got my wages and brought them to me. He looked after my sick mother and her helpless little children. I have seen church deacons who were not his equal.

Everyone's senior year was a time of recognition and achievement. Boys who had sat on the bench put on the black and gold uniforms of McAlester High and became local celebrities. Girls blossomed in musical performances. Students like Shirley Buell continued to compile impressive academic records. It was a year for us all to stand as giants.

I had changed a lot by then. I had not grown much taller—I stood five feet, two inches when I graduated—but I was not the same timid, insecure boy who had arrived from Bug Tussle three years earlier. I had come just short of winning a European tour, I was keeping my vow of academic achievement, and I had made lasting friends of nearly every student in the school. At the start of classes, they elected me president of the student body. I also was president of my homeroom and two school organizations, the Poetry Club and the Golden M Club. The latter was particularly rewarding.

The Golden M Club was Miss Munch's creation of the previous year. Because it required outstanding speech or dramatic performance for membership, it was a small but prestigious organization. Eleven of us were charter members. It was a remarkable group. With me, its original members went on to include a federal judge, a New York attorney, a successful surgeon, a law-school professor, an executive of the American Bankers Association, and three corporation executives. All of us later would point to our high school speech training as indispensable to our lives. The lesson that we each had learned there involved the highly competitive character of things worthwhile.

Our Class of 1927 was outstanding. We swept the interscholastic academic contest held at the teachers college in Durant, taking ten first-place medals in contests on fifteen subjects. I won three of the firsts: in government, physics, and declamation. Our debate teams crisscrossed the state and won the state championship on the topic "Resolved: that the United States should enter into an agreement for the cancellation of the interallied war debts." Taking the negative, my partner and I were undefeated. I wrote a new oration on the Constitution—one probably not as good as the previous year's—and won the district, state, and regional rounds of competition. A week before graduation, I went east, saw the U.S. Capitol, met President Coolidge, and spoke before justices of the Supreme Court. I did not win there, but being there was victory enough.

My grades in class improved. At the year's end, I was named class valedictorian. My four-year average was the highest of any student yet to graduate from the school. It was just a few hundredths of a point above Shirley Buell's.

Just before graduation, we all received our copies of the *Dancing Rabbit,* the McAlester High School yearbook. Beside my senior picture was a list of my activities and awards. There was no men-

# Seniors

Carl Albert

Valedictorian; Student Body Pres. '27; Home Room President '27; Golden M Club President '27; Poetry Club President '27; Debate '26, '27; Constitutional Oration Contest '25, '26, '27; Original Oration Contest '26; Dramatic Reading Contest '26, '27; Declamation Contest '27; Golden M Club '26, '27; Poetry Club '26, '27; Romani Novi '25, '26; Dramatic Club '25, '26, '27; Honor Society.
*A little giant.*

*I only wish my mother could have seen it.* Carl Albert's page in the McAlester High School yearbook, 1927.

tion of my initial insecurities, but at the bottom was an epigram of which I was mighty proud: "A little giant." I only wish that my mother could have seen it.

Just before Christmas, we learned that Mama was worsening. We immediately caught the train to Albuquerque, where others of her relatives met us. Our presence seemed to give her new hope and new life, and we had a joyous Christmas. Her gift to us was her assurance that she was going to get well and live to raise her children. She faded almost immediately afterwards. The TB specialist gave us no hope. On the last day of 1926, her family gathered around Mama's bed. Little Earl, just barely five years old, could hardly see over the edge. Homer stood beside him, crying. Mama took my hand and said, "Son, take care of my little boys." She breathed deeply, shuddered, and she left us.

Papa went to the local undertaker and arranged to send her body back to Oklahoma for the funeral. He and Homer and Earl rode the train back with her. The rest of us set out in the old Buick for home across hundreds of miles of desolate, snow-covered plains. We traveled silently, lost in our sorrow, across the frozen roads until the car slid off into a ditch. We could not move it. As we sat there, the long train carrying my mother passed us, and we saw my father and brothers through the windows. Finally, another motorist arrived and tried to push us out. He could not. He said he had to leave and wished us luck. I explained the situation, that my mother had just died, that her train had passed us, that we had to get home for her funeral, and that the old car had no heater. I offered him twenty dollars, all we had, to get us out somehow. After several hours, he did. In all that time, not one other car had come by.

We left the snow behind in the Texas Panhandle and drove through mud across western Oklahoma. The next morning, we came through Seminole, then the center of Oklahoma's legendary oil boom. The streets of Seminole were part of that legend. Tons of oilfield equipment had turned the narrow pathways into either ruts or mud. On that day, they were mud, mud to our axles, as we inched our way toward McAlester and Mama's funeral.

When we finally pulled in, Papa had made the final arrangements. My mother had a country funeral, the only kind Papa had ever seen or would allow. Her friends and relatives stayed up all night with her body, which was kept in our house. The services were the next day, in the yard. Brother Alexander (he had baptized Mama in Coal Creek) preached the service. Her father, Grandpa Scott, was there and could have done a better job, had he been able to do it at all. Mama's many other relatives were there, too, along with her neighbors from Bug Tussle and most of my schoolmates at McAlester. We buried her in the first of our family plots in the local cemetery. She was forty years old.

The next summer took me away from my grief. Miss Munch may have been right. I must have outworked every other student around. I was going to Europe as a champion orator.

Even the train ride to New York was an adventure. Some of my fellow passengers were from Oklahoma and recognized me from the pictures in the *Daily Oklahoman*. One man recalled reading that my father was a coal miner and cotton farmer. He was determined to take me out of my dismal background. The one way to do that, he was sure, was to get me an appointment to West Point. He wanted to call his senator (Senator Thomas) about it right away. He was absolutely sure that a boy of my record and ability could rise to be a general. As such, he predicted, I would meet "presidents, senators, cabinet officers, and big-city bankers." I thanked him for his concern but explained that I had my own plans.

Another passenger who recognized me was Lorraine Gensman, wife of a former Oklahoma congressman, L. M. Gensman. Old enough to be my grandmother, she decided to take me under her wing. She knew New York City as well as she did Lawton, Oklahoma, her hometown. After we reached New York, she took me down to Coney Island. I must have ridden every ride there, and there were a lot more than there were at the Pittsburg County Fair. Coney Island was also where, for the first time, I heard the ocean's roar.

The next day, I was on that ocean. I boarded the largest pas-

*The reward for my faith, the realization of things hoped for, the substance of things finally seen.* Carl Albert, in the back row on the left, in Cannes, France, in 1927, touring Europe as a champion orator.

senger ship of the time, the *Leviathan.* I had never seen anything so spectacular or so beautiful. It had been built by the Germans before World War I and seized by the United States during the war. It was one of the most luxurious vessels crossing the Atlantic during the Roaring Twenties. Only Lindbergh had made the trip by air yet, but each summer the *Leviathan* carried thousands of Americans to European vacations. Surely, none had one more spectacular than mine.

I do not know how many times the adults with us claimed that I was going to run out of superlatives before I reached our next stop. They all remarked on the joy that I never thought to conceal.

I suspected that I was amusing some of them, but the boy seeing these things had never before seen two hundred dollars in one place in his life. My father crawled miles under the earth to dig us a living from black rock, or he chopped it out of a cotton patch. But I had found a way to do what I had wanted to do. I had found the reward for my faith, the realization of things hoped for, the substance of things finally seen.

In England, I marveled at Big Ben, the sturdy watchman over the world's oldest deliberative body, the British Parliament. I visited the House of Commons, where I heard David Lloyd George, Winston Churchill, and Ramsay MacDonald. I saw *Hamlet* performed in Stratford-on-Avon, William Shakespeare's birthplace. I visited the Poets' Corner of Westminster Abbey and saw the tombs of some of the greatest figures in the history of the English-speaking people. I saw the spires at Oxford. I remembered that one of my teachers back at McAlester had told us about Cecil Rhodes, that he had left money to send some of America's best college men (women were not then eligible) to study at Oxford as something called Rhodes scholars. I decided then and there that that would be my next goal. I guess I was not the only one. Three of the six male finalists in the 1927 high school contest—Max Lancaster, Jim Tunnel, and myself—did become Rhodes scholars.

In France, I saw the world's most beautiful city: Paris. I stood beneath the Arc de Triomphe, where General Pershing supposedly had saluted and declared, "*Lafayette, nous sommes ici.*" I saw, too, living reminders of the horror of war. At the edge of a French battlefield, there was a young man selling cheap mementos. Along the whole right side of his face and across both eyes, nothing showed but silver. His face literally had been shot off at Verdun. I saw, too, Versailles, where Woodrow Wilson's dreams of a world of order backed by American might had crumbled.

Across the Pyrenees into the Spanish Basque country, down the Mediterranean coast along the Riviera, through Florence and Venice into Rome, I saw the art and architecture of our civilization. In Rome, our group met privately with the Pope. Alone, I walked all over the Colosseum, sat in its seats, hugged its stones, lay on its floor. I walked alone over the Appian Way, a boy from Bug Tussle feeling the same ground beneath his feet that Caesar's legions had felt.

From Rome, we went to Geneva before returning to Paris. We sailed from Cherbourg on the SS *United States*. I had to get to Norman, Oklahoma, to start college.

When I went to the University of Oklahoma in the fall of 1927, the school was rather new, somewhat small, and hardly prestigious. Norman promoters had wanted the capitol but had accepted the university from the 1890 legislature. Four to five thousand students attended its classes, mostly in a few buildings clustered around an oval north of the library. The university had few nationally recognized scholars. That year's football team placed sixth in the conference but did hold Central State Normal School to a 14-14 tie.

For me, however, it was the perfect place. My mother's sister lived in Norman, and I could hold down my living expenses by staying with Aunt Myrtle. The tuition was reasonable. There was no government aid available to college students, no matter how deserving or how needy, but Mr. McPheron believed that he could help me get a student job with the school. He did. With his introduction, I landed a job in the registrar's office. It paid the going wage for college students: thirty cents an hour. It was not much, but it would have been a whole lot had I not gotten it.

My father had little enough that he could give me. The day after I had returned home from Europe, I packed my things and got ready to leave. Papa came into the room. He handed me a twenty-dollar bill. I knew how much he needed it, but I knew that he needed even more to give it to me. It was the last money I ever got from home in my life. I hitchhiked from McAlester to Oklahoma City, where I spent my first fifty cents on college. That was the fare for riding the interurban down to Norman and the University of Oklahoma.

I walked on campus knowing what I wanted to take from there; I would work for the highest possible grades. There was a

*I walked on the campus knowing what I wanted to take from there. Carl Albert enrolling at the University of Oklahoma, 1927.*

collegiate-level contest for oratory on the U.S. Constitution, and I would compete in it. I wanted the grand prize: the Rhodes scholarship. I knew I had the desire, I had the drive, I had the self-discipline, and I had the will to work. And I knew by then that such goals, the deliberate work toward them, and their realization—all of these were what made me Carl Albert.

I also decided that Carl Albert would enjoy life in the process.

My most important class in my first semester was a step toward each of those purposes. Josh Lee was the head of the speech department, author of an excellent text, and a speaker of considerable renown himself, good enough to talk his way into a House seat in 1934 and into the Senate two years later. He was also the judge who had received my high school oration so favorably. He insisted that I take his advanced class in oratory, and he promised that he would work with me for the intercollegiate contest on the Constitution.

Throughout the school year, I polished my oratory by entering two campus contests. I won both and picked up some two hundred dollars in prize money. The money gave me some breathing room. I was living on a close budget of thirty dollars a month. Every male student had to enroll in Reserve Officers' Training Corps during his first two years, so I cut costs by wearing my ROTC uniform to class when my one suit was at the cleaners.

At my freshman year's end, I became one of seven finalists in the intercollegiate oratorical contest. We met in Los Angeles because of the sponsorship by the Better America Federation of California, a group that included publisher Harry Chandler. Chandler's *Los Angeles Times* gave the contest and the finalists steady publicity. As I looked over the *Times*'s issue for the day of the finals, it seemed that the writers sensed the intensity of the competition that I faced. Amid outstanding scholars from America's greatest schools, I was listed last, the only student from a state college and the only freshman to reach the finals. Because I lacked the others' achievements, they identified me as "the son of a coal miner and proud of it."

I was a freshman from an unhonored college, but I beat the best there was. The next day's *Los Angeles Times* could not resist the drama of my victory, nor could it resist the impulse to exaggerate it into even more of a Horatio Alger tale. According to the news account, I had begun my forensic career "while attending classes, more or less iregularly, in a ramshackle two-room schoolhouse." One of the things that the story got exactly right was my reward: a check for fifteen hundred dollars. It was enough to finance my remaining college education.

That turned out to be only the start of the publicity. Harry Chandler's *Los Angeles Times* kept stories running daily, reporting my appearances before area civic groups. Nearly thirty years later I came to appreciate just how extensive that publicity had been; it was in 1947 on my first day as a new congressman from Oklahoma. Another freshman member came up to me and asked if I was the same Carl Albert who had won the college oratorical contest back in 1928. He remembered reading about it in the papers. He added that he later had entered the same contest, too, but he had been eliminated early. His name was Richard Nixon.

With the appearances came additional money and rewards. I spoke before several clubs and groups for a few weeks, usually picking up a hundred dollars or so as an honorarium. Harry Chandler himself presented me to the sponsoring Better America Foundation. After hearing my speech, he and some other Los Angeles businessmen offered to get me into Stanford and pay all of my expenses through college and law school. I thanked them but told them that I wanted to go back to Oklahoma. My home was there. I wanted to go to Congress, and I figured that Oklahoma was the place I could best represent. Besides, I was and always wanted to be an Oklahoman.

My appearance before the Elks Club did pay a big dividend. A group of Elks was sailing to Honolulu for a few weeks' vacation and invited me to join them. I jumped at the chance. We sailed, the jet-setters of that day and I, out of Los Angeles on *The City of Honolulu.* When I reached Hawaii's capital, I came to appreciate just how important the Elks were there. The Elks Club of Honolulu owned one of only two large buildings that sat at the water's

*I never felt myself such a big shot before or since.* In Hawaii, 1928.

edge on Waikiki Beach; the other was the newly opened Royal Hawaiian Hotel. The Elks put me there in an elegant ground-floor suite. The mayor made me an official guest and furnished me with a Cadillac limousine and full-time chauffeur. I never felt myself such a big shot before or since.

With a cute native girl that I had met on the ship, I saw every sight Hawaii had to offer. My Elks friends also arranged for me to give my oration before several civic groups. One audience included the president of the Dole Pineapple Company, Hawaii's corporate colossus. My speech so impressed him that he offered me two thousand dollars if I would give it four more times over the next few weeks. I took the offer and the money and stayed over. Upon my return to the mainland by way of San Francisco, one of the Los Angeles Elks called me. He had three more speeches and three more honoraria awaiting me. I took the train, made my speeches, drew down my bank deposits, and bought a railroad ticket back home.

The oratory contest and everything that came from it lasted almost the entire summer. The money I earned, well over four thousand dollars, lasted for the rest of my college years. The memories of that time will last forever.

At OU, my speech activities gave me my first introduction to campus life. Because of press reports, I may have entered the university as the best-known freshman on campus. It certainly did not take long before I was asked to join just about every club there.

In my first semester, some older students from McAlester invited me over for dinner with their fraternity, Kappa Alpha. Only a year old, the house at the corner of College and Cruce was impressive with its Georgian-Southern architecture. In fact, I found everything about the chapter impressive. I pledged Kappa Alpha, thereby making friends who would stand with me for decades.

My grades were good. Most of my early classes were introductory required subjects, and except for Spanish, which I began my first semester, few were intrinsically exciting. Nonetheless, I kept up the study habits that I had developed back at Bug Tussle with the same reward. I finished my first semester as one of only two freshmen to earn all A's.

That record qualified me for membership in the freshman academic honorary society, Phi Eta Sigma. William B. Bizzell was OU's president at the time, and Phi Eta Sigma was one of his principal interests. After I spoke at the society's initiation ceremonies, Dr. Bizzell became a close friend. In time, he had me accompany him on speaking and fund-raising tours, where he introduced me to some of Oklahoma's most prominent and powerful citizens. One was Lloyd Noble, a millionaire oilman from Ardmore. Another was Lew Wentz, a similarly situated Ponca Citian and for decades the state's No. 1 Republican. Despite Mr. Wentz's party beliefs, both became my lifelong friends and supporters, politics included.

My speaking also introduced me to less-prominent men, one of whom was Daredevil Dick Mormon. Daredevil Dick had thought up a great promotion for selling cars. He would chain himself to a steering wheel and drive continuously, without stop and without rest, for a week. He talked some Chevrolet dealers in Oklahoma City into sponsoring him. Still, he needed a speaker to drum up a crowd as he passed by the Chevy agencies. That was my part.

For that week, I spoke at Chevrolet dealerships. Daredevil Dick would come by, chained to the wheel but beaming as I embellished his steadily lengthening exploits. I was speaking when he finished the ordeal. As he pulled into a Chevrolet agency, he collapsed. His chains were removed, and Daredevil Dick was carried, asleep, to a bed in the dealer's show window. He lay sleeping in public view for twenty hours.

Easily the most interesting figure that I met through my speech activities was Thomas Pryor Gore. A Populist during his youth in Texas, Gore had moved to Oklahoma during territorial days. At statehood he was elected, along with Robert L. Owen, as one of Oklahoma's original United States senators. By this time a Democrat, Senator Gore kept something of his Populist past alive. Washington knew him as a fierce foe of trusts, of bankers, and of warlords. It was the last quality that seemed to have ended his career. Gore had resisted stoutly Woodrow Wilson's preparedness measures before our 1917 declaration of war. Once it came, he remained a steadfast critic. What many voters saw as his lack of patriotism cost him his Senate seat in 1920.

Ten years later, the old senator was poised for a comeback. By many his opposition to the war was forgotten; by others it now was applauded. The onset of the Great Depression, nowhere more disastrous than in Oklahoma, transformed this champion of the common people into a prophet. But this one cried in no wilderness; rather, crowds gathered whenever and wherever he campaigned to reclaim a Senate seat.

I had heard him speak before, and I had been awed. In fact, I still consider Thomas Gore the finest American political speaker that I have ever heard. In 1930, he had lost none of his eloquence. However, he did need someone to introduce him at his campaign talks. Since I was just a college student, I bore no political scars, and my appearance would antagonize no local faction. He asked me to speak briefly, introducing him at his rallies. Besides, he needed someone to drive for him. Since childhood, Senator Gore had been blind.

Through the long, hot summer of 1930, I drove the old senator over the roads of Oklahoma to crowds of dispossessed farmers, frightened merchants, and unemployed oil-field workers. My remarks were brief; the old senator's were masterpieces of political oratory. One thing that made them masterpieces was Gore's never-failing wit. He was an expert humorist, one capable of moving the most desperate crowds to laughter, but he used his humor well. He never felt compelled to start a speech with a wisecrack. Rather, he wove his wit into the warp and weft of his addresses.

He also was capable of the perfect spontaneous quip. I remember his campaign back home in McAlester that summer. Gore was to speak from a platform set up on one end of Choctaw Avenue. As the crowd was gathering, the assistant county attorney started speaking from the street's other end. His name was Bob Bell, and he was managing the campaign of Gore's Democratic primary opponent. Bob Bell was a feisty little man, an able speaker himself, though when excited he spoke in a high-pitched voice. On this occasion, his voice got higher and higher as he proceeded to give the old senator quite a bit of Pittsburg County hell.

When Gore got ready to speak, several of us offered to get Bob Bell to stop. But Gore waited for him to finish. Bell finally ran down, and Senator Gore stepped on the platform. He always looked upward, his eyes almost pure white, as he spoke. He did this time as he slowly said: "I seldom refer to my affliction. I cannot see. But it seems that somewhere in the far, far distance I hear the tingling and the jingling of a tiny little Bell." Bob Bell told that story on himself for years. Even he got a laugh out of it. "Boy, he set me down," he would say.

Thomas Gore had a way of setting just about anybody down. The story was already told—and is still told in the Senate—of Senator Gore's dressing down another senator. One of his target's friends rose to say that the senator from Oklahoma was taking advantage of his colleague. If the senator from Oklahoma could see, the other senator would not take it. Gore roared back, "Well, blindfold the senator and send him this way."

The old senator's wit was always devastating and always on the mark. But he was no mere crowd pleaser. His eloquence approached the poetic on issues about which he cared deeply. One involved my old high school debate topic: Should America cancel the war debt owed us by Britain and France? Gore had not changed. He was against canceling the debt. He believed that we had given enough to the British and the French when we gave them our boys. His sightless eyes looked toward heaven as he spontaneously uttered the words that I recall more than a half-century later:

> I see the soldier
> Over there
> Who will never again,
> Even in death,
> Feel the warm soil of Oklahoma.
>
> There he lies,
> With no sentinel

Save the distant star,
With no mourner
But the winds of night.

And I sometimes wonder
If the moaning winds
That play among the tuft above his grave
Do not disturb the slumber of those
For whom he died to save.

He was the best. He was also the winner, in both the primary and the general elections.

In my years at the University of Oklahoma, I developed friendships that have lasted throughout my life. The university remained relatively small and thoroughly friendly. *Howdy* was the byword on campus. One heard it dozens of times while going to classes, attending student meetings, or just hanging out.

Many of the students that I met there would be active in politics in my early career. Aubrey and Bill Kerr, whom I first encountered as leaders of a rival student political party, I would see again as allies in Oklahoma's "real" political party. They became and long remained major figures in the Democratic party, their voices magnified by that of their older brother, a young graduate of the teachers college at Ada. He was Robert S. Kerr, Oklahoma's wartime governor and subsequently the fabled uncrowned king of the United States Senate. Just a year or so ahead of me were several men whom I met as a student and would often see again. One was Luther Bohanon, a leader of the bar and Senator Kerr's choice for the federal judgeship in Oklahoma City. Mike Monroney was another. Mike served four years with me in the House before moving to the Senate for three terms. Such friendships have been among the things that have caused me never to regret turning down Harry Chandler's offer of a free Stanford education.

For all of Stanford's exalted reputation, I doubt that I would have encountered better students—or stiffer academic competition—than I met at OU. I know that I never, anywhere, saw any student the equal of Dean Woolridge. Dean was an OU legend, and properly so. He had entered the university at age fifteen, and he became the first of its graduates to finish with a perfect four-point grade average.

I remember that Dean and I shared nine and eleven o'clock classes. During the hour's break, we always headed for the student union, where we played pool. We would put our French texts on the window ledge and study our lessons during the games. At eleven, we would head for French class. I averaged about 97 percent for the course; Dean Woolridge averaged a perfect 100. At semester's end, the teacher said she did not know which made her angrier: was it Dean for never making a single error in vocabulary, grammar, spelling, or punctuation, or herself for being unable to think of anything that he did not know in French? We chose not to increase her frustration with the knowledge that he had learned his French in a pool hall between shots.

Maybe not as efficiently as Dean, I also managed to find time for play among my studies. I took up the college man's game, bridge, and became a pretty good player in nightly games over at the Varsity Shop, our local hangout. I never could beat Paul Hodge, who took his before-dinner games with deadly passion. Paul's eventual reward was twice to represent the United States in world championship matches. I became a decent chess player and one of OU's very best checker players. I took my reward while campaigning over cracker barrels in the country stores of rural southeastern Oklahoma.

We also had our student celebrities. One, George Milburn, had a national reputation, even as a student. George wrote books, people bought them, and he made money out of them. George Milburn was one of OU's most talented students—and one of its nastiest.

I discovered both qualities when he gave me a copy of one of his books. It was a collection of stories, some poignant, many hilarious, loosely based upon George's experiences in a little town near Tulsa. One of the best was about the town's big shot, a merchant who installed its first indoor toilet. The local folks thought it terribly unsanitary to have human waste right in his house, but he went ahead and put it in and covered his old outdoor pit with boards. Thinking he heard a prowler, the fellow went outside one night and crashed through the boards, into the pit. He began screaming, "Fire! Fire! Fire!" Rescuers finally came and pulled him out. When they found no fire, they asked him why he had shouted "Fire!" He answered, "Because you sons of bitches wouldn't have come if I yelled 'Shit! Shit! Shit!'"

I read the book the day he gave it to me. The next day, George called up and accused me of stealing his book. He yelled that I was a kleptomaniac, that a thief was the lowest creature that crawled the earth, and that a book thief was the lowest form of that species. He threatened me with violence and a lawyer. I yelled back, but I agreed to return the book. When he received it, he called me again. He said I could have the book back if I wanted it. Then he started raving at me again! I hung up just after I screamed back: "Fire! Fire! Fire!"

For organized fun, there was the university's principal pep club, the Ruf Neks. Members shared the privilege of running onto the football field armed with white paddles to complement their bright red shirts. My brief membership was more organized than fun. The Ruf Neks' hazing reputation was unbelievable; the reality was far worse than the reputation.

On initiation night, we pledges were ordered to take a truck-load of barrel staves down to a spot on the Canadian River. We knew what that meant: paddles were not merely members' trademarks but gruesome reminders of initiation. To prepare ourselves, several of us sewed big stakes into our shorts. They were little help. During the hazing, I thought once or twice that I was being beaten to death.

I awoke the next morning, crawled out of bed, and limped to class. I expected at least to share our rewards with my fellow sufferers. I reached campus only to discover that we were members of a nonexistent group; sometime after midnight, the university's disciplinary authorities had abolished the club. The cause was our initiation. So I did not run out onto the football field and carry a white paddle to match my red shirt, not until the club was reorganized and invited the old members back. By then, I was a member of Congress.

Far better disciplined was a student group that I came to enjoy: the Reserve Officers' Training Corps. After the required two years' military training, I signed up for the advanced program in my junior year. I had gone to Fort Sill with my brother for a National Guard camp the previous summer and genuinely enjoyed it. Besides, advanced ROTC paid a little money: about thirty cents a day plus six weeks' summer-camp pay. Plus, I got to keep my uniform to wear to class.

Our summer training was also at Fort Sill. We trained with other college units, but we were the most fortunate tenants. Most of the others were infantry units, but the OU corps was in field artillery, and the Lawton military post was one of the world's foremost artillery training grounds. Our equipment was the army's best, though it was of World War I vintage. We used French 75 artillery pieces and wooden caissons, all horse drawn.

Daily, we harnessed our horses, hitched them to the caissons, and drove our big guns out to the firing ranges. We took our training seriously and competed fiercely to bracket our salvos before zeroing in on the exact targets. It was good that we did so, for our officers from the university accompanied us. There to greet us were the old-time Regular Army sergeants. They took everything military seriously. By summer's end, we could have performed creditably on the battlefield. Thus, my decision to take advanced ROTC was a good one.

An even better one arose literally from luck. Paul Hodge came by on one semester's last day. This time he had found a better game than bridge: a big poker game drawing upon the players' last college money. Except for my savings, my last was fifty dollars. I decided that I could lose that and still hitchhike home. By 2:00 A.M., I was down to my last ten. I borrowed twenty-five from a friend and stayed in the game. In the next hand, I drew four queens, paid the money back, and kept going. When the game broke up at four o'clock, I counted my pile: $255. With my bag already packed, I went over to the intersection of U.S. 77 and Main Street, the favored spot for college hitchhikers. I decided to take the first ride I got to anywhere it went.

It went to San Antonio, Texas, and I decided to keep on heading south. I hitched a ride to Laredo, got a permit, and crossed the Rio Grande. For eight dollars, I bought a third-class railroad ticket to Mexico City.

I had been interested in Mexico since my high school trip to Europe. Accompanying us was Arturo García Formentí. He had won a similar contest on Mexico's government and would compete in Europe against other national champions. Arturo became my closest companion in Europe, though neither of us knew more than a few words in the other's tongue. At OU, I had taken two years of Spanish, no doubt because of Arturo's influence. Now I would try it out on the natives.

I was lucky to catch Arturo just before he left the capital for a month's speaking tour on behalf of the president. He found me a rooming house for the *muy pobre* (very poor). It was economical, though not poor. For ten dollars a week, I got a small but attractive room and two meals a day. I probably never had a better bargain in my life. The regular paying guests were all intelligent, and several were well educated. One was a distinguished Castilian Spaniard from Madrid, a true member of the gentry. Another was a Russian émigré who longed for the czar's return. The natives included an educated and cultured civil servant with a keen interest in Mexican history and the guitar, which he played as he sang lovely Mexican ballads. Another made a prosperous business of cutting old automobile tires into strips, punching holes and running straps through them, and selling the product as shoes. Many wore them in the Mexico City of 1929. Most native of all was a very dark, full-blooded Aztec. Tall, straight, and proud, he could have descended from Montezuma.

Our times in the rooming house were a continuous classroom for me. We lingered for hours over the dinner table, discussing politics, art, literature—everything Mexican. My fellow boarders seemed to be pleased, maybe even surprised, at my interest in and love for things Mexican. Gringos were hardly known for their appreciation for the country, but sometimes it would be the natives who had to curb my obvious enthusiasm.

I remember one evening in which I was declaring my affection for their country when the civil servant stopped me. "But, Señor Albert," he said, "we don't complete many things. We start them, but we do not finish them." He told me of taking a visiting Spaniard to the opera house. The Spaniard noted that the building was not finished. They heard an opera. The visitor's judgment was that it was fine, but it was not finished. Later, they went to a speech by Mexico's dynamic one-armed president, Alvaro Obregon. My friend enthused, "Wasn't he great?" The Spaniard answered, "Yes, but he is not finished."

During most days and many nights, I tried to follow the counsel of my OU Spanish professor: "Learn your Spanish from a walking dictionary with a dress on. That is the best kind."

I visited Mexico City's theaters, operas, and cabarets with several dictionaries. With others, I visited the shrine to the heroic Mexican cadets who had stood and died at Chapultepec against Winfield Scott's army. With an attractive student from the University of Mexico, I explored one of the world's most beautiful campuses and one of its largest cathedrals. Alone, I crawled all over the enchanting ruins of San Juan Teotihuacan, just as I had those of Rome. This time, however, my enthrallment cost me: our rickety tourist bus left during my private explorations. Stranded, I spent the night in a hut of some local *peóns*. My fellow boarders in the adjoining room were a loud and smelly group of pigs.

My summer in Mexico may have lacked the glamour and the prestige of my European summer two years earlier, but altogether it was just as thrilling and just as important. My skill in and appreciation for the Spanish language grew immensely and has remained a lifelong affection. As a student, as a congressman, and as a citizen, I have always believed that there are no better people on God's earth than our own neighbors. If the people of this country only could see them as equals and treat them as our friends, both countries—but especially the United States—would be better off.

I believe that it was a wiser person that left Mexico City with a third-class ticket to Laredo. I know that it was a happy and tired one that hitchhiked back to Oklahoma to finish college.

At the university, my academic interests depended somewhat on the professors' abilities. I suppose that is always so; I know that it had been the case with me since my days in the schoolhouse at Bug Tussle. At OU, I had several outstanding professors, among the best I would ever know.

Quite by accident I first met the professor who would serve as my teacher, my mentor, and my friend. In my sophomore year, some of us were preparing for a debate on democratic institutions. I went by to talk with OU's principal authority on political theory, Cortez A. M. Ewing. I had that day a long session with the greatest teacher I yet had met, a man at once knowledgeable, articulate, and warm. I decided then to make his office my intellectual headquarters as long as I was at OU. I followed his counsel in working out my remaining academic curriculum: a government major with a strong history minor.

I started in Dr. Ewing's own classes almost immediately. They were always filled with the university's very best students, for each one seemed to be a model class. My first, ancient political theory, opened up the ancient world to me. Professor Ewing traced the origins of politics, permanently impressing me with the centrality of ethics in politics and government. The same theme reappeared in his subsequent courses on comparative political theory, modern European political theory, and American political theory. More than a half-century later, I still can think of no better preparation for a career in public service.

With other students, I would often visit Dr. Ewing's home in the evenings. He and Mrs. Ewing were delightful hosts. Most of the entertainment was the spontaneous exchange of reasoned and informed opinion on issues of the day, and it was a day of weighty issues. Russians were still talking of global revolution, Italians bowed beneath Mussolini's fascist dagger, Germans were discussing an odd book titled *Mein Kampf*. In America, the spasms of depression were shaking loose Republican control of government and awakening a somnolent nation. Those were heady days, made more momentous by Professor Ewing's incisive observations. He and his wife seemed genuinely to enjoy my frequent visits. Mrs. Ewing probably explained their pleasure much later when she commented upon the tenacity of my student days. "You had to be tenacious," she added, "when you had nothing but a dream to go on."

Professor Ewing helped that dream along immeasurably. With his encouragement, I applied for the coveted Rhodes scholarship during my junior year. The odds against me were long; had I won, I would have gone to Oxford without an undergraduate degree. Nonetheless, I was runner-up in the state finals to select Oklahoma's recipient. Just as I had after placing second in the high school speech contest, I vowed to redouble my efforts and go all the way the next year.

My senior year was rich with honors. It began with my selection as president of the men's council. Later, there followed election as most popular student, a Phi Beta Kappa key, and the Dads' Day Cup as outstanding male student. The year ended with the competition for a Rhodes scholarship. Five hundred thirty-nine of the very best American students competed for the world's most prestigious academic prize. Mine was one of thirty-three awarded.

Winning a Rhodes scholarship was a big part of what Mrs. Ewing had sensed as the dream that I went on. It was a dream born in a cotton patch, nurtured in a country schoolhouse and a special high school, fed by some exceptional men and women. The prize was mine, but the goals that I had set and the achievement of them—for these I was indebted to very many.

The scholarship could not have come at a better time. The Great Depression was fully upon us in 1931. Cotton prices had collapsed. Mines had closed. My fellow graduates often had little hope for a job. Hungry men were rioting in Oklahoma City. Tens of thousands of my fellow citizens were fleeing to California. John Steinbeck and others would call them Okies. I called some of them my friends and neighbors. Cecil Rhodes's trust granted me a different fate: three years of Oxford University schooling and an

. . . *The Dads' Day cup as outstanding male student.* Velma Jones and Carl Albert, the outstanding female student and the outstanding male student in 1931 at the University of Oklahoma.

annual stipend of four hundred pounds, or roughly two thousand dollars.

My first money would come only when I arrived in Oxford. Knowing that I did not have the money to get there, Lew Wentz, Oklahoma's richest man and chief Republican, lent me five hundred dollars. I got my steamship ticket from an Italian agent in McAlester. I hitchhiked to Saint Louis, where I took a bus to New York City and boarded an Atlantic liner sailing for Southampton. This Okie was going to Oxford.

# CHAPTER THREE

# Up to Oxford, Down to Oklahoma

I came from a community founded on Indian lands. I carried a degree from a university younger than my parents. I represented a state not even a year older than myself. I was bound for Oxford, England.

Life there was different. The city of Oxford had eighty thousand residents, making it the largest place in which I yet had lived. Lying at the confluence of the Cherwell and the Isis rivers, it surely was the oldest. The Romans knew the place as Oxonia. The earliest bridges across the rivers were built by its first Norman ruler. It was nothing to walk along streets and see buildings that were thriving with commerce when Christopher Columbus pointed his ships westward across the Atlantic. Some of the merchants in those buildings were investors in John Smith's enterprise, the Virginia Company of London.

Oxford's university, chartered in 1571, was the oldest and most prestigious in the English-speaking world. Its origins dissolve into medieval mists, but three of its colleges (University, Balliol, and Merton) date to the thirteenth century. Its earliest scholars included men like Roger Bacon, John Duns Scotus, John Wycliffe, Erasmus, and Sir Thomas More. Richard Hakluyt, whose writings sparked England's earliest interest in colonizing America, had been a geographer there. One of his students, Sir Walter Raleigh, led the first body of English settlers to the New World. Centuries

90

later, another Oxford man, Cecil Rhodes, took Britain's flag across another continent. At his death, the six million pounds that he took out of Africa provided the scholarships that brought talented colonials back to Oxford. What they found there was a system of higher education unequaled in the world and unlike any in the United States. It did not take long to see just how different it was.

Even the language was different. To begin, the English sharply distinguish between a college and a university. A college is a place of residence and of higher learning. Though largely self-governing, their colleges have no authority to hold examinations or award degrees; only universities have those rights. Thus, one could be a student at any of Oxford's twenty-seven colleges of the time, but his examinations and degree came not from his college but from the university. These exclusive privileges of the universities were guarded jealously. In fact, for more than 250 years, Oxford and Cambridge (chartered in 1573) had granted the only degrees in all of England.

Even after that monopoly was broken, the two retained their towering influence and prestige. Theirs were ancient traditions, sizable endowments, honored presses, and massive stocks of books, for by law their libraries received copies of every book printed in England. They also maintained their status as the aris-tocracy's preferred path into political, ecclesiastical, or academic power. The relative democracy of American higher education was still somewhat foreign to Oxford. The international competition for the Rhodes scholarships likely was its most democratic single feature. It certainly was the only way that a boy from Bug Tussle, Oklahoma, could have gotten there with England's elite.

The language differences carried over into one's studies. I learned that one does not enter Oxford; rather, one comes up to Oxford and thereby becomes an Oxonian. Upon graduation, one does not leave; the Oxonian goes down. In between, one does not study a subject, one reads. Thus, I came up in 1931, read law for three years, and went down in 1934.

Though I was a graduate of the University of Oklahoma, I was called an undergraduate at Oxford. For most Oxonians, the first degree is the bachelor of arts. In law, the B.A. in jurisprudence was awarded after two years. After my third year, I earned Oxford's graduate degree in law, the bachelor of civil law.

One thing that I learned quickly was that each of Oxford's colleges holds over its students a disciplinary authority unknown to American schools. Parliament had made them courts unto themselves, having jurisdiction that the civil courts could not overrule. My college, St. Peter's, was Oxford's newest. Founded only two years before my arrival, its disciplinary code was fashionably light. Other colleges, though, had rules so hoary and so strict that their walls reminded me of the McAlester penitentiary's.

Disciplinary authority beyond the college's walls was the university's. Included in that was the demand that undergraduates wear half-gowns extending to the waist. So clad and identifiable, they could not drink in the city's pubs, sits in the front sections of its cinemas, or date girls from the town.

Enforcing these rules were the university's proctors. Attired in full cap and gown, they roamed the streets, eager to pounce upon the errant undergraduate. Finding one, they would approach him, tip their caps, and say, "Sir, are you a member of the university?" The offender was in a situation similar to that of an automobile driver caught speeding in a small Amish community of Pennsylvania. His misdeed suddenly loomed disproportionately large before him. I was told that it was not a pleasant experience, but I cannot offer personal testimony. My own minor infractions always eluded the proctors.

We lived in housing provided by the separate colleges. Mine was quite modern and impressive. At OU's Kappa Alpha house, two of us had shared a single room. At St. Peter's, each student's quarters consisted of two rooms: a living or study room and a bedroom. Both were well furnished.

Twelve of us students had rooms on a single stairway. Each stairway had its own maid and its own scout. The latter was a high-class servant, a combination valet and army sergeant whose mission was to look after the new recruits. Our scout was a distinguished gentleman whom we knew only as Hamilton. He began my every day from the first with a loud knock at the door. With the broadest *a* in the English language, he would shout, "Five and twenty past eight, sir." At its sound, I always jumped from bed, threw on my trousers, shirt, jacket, and half-gown and hurried over to the chapel. In my college, morning services were the required opening of our every day.

After our classes, we usually gathered in one of our quarters for an afternoon tea. This was an English tradition that I learned to love. The drink itself was secondary. What was important was the pleasant conversation, sometimes fun, sometimes serious, always with some of the brightest young men in the Western world.

I still remember my very first Oxford tea. I had taken the railroad from London through fifty-seven miles of English countryside to Oxford. A taxi brought me to St. Peter's gate, where I met my first fellow Oxford student, an Englishman named George Done. He introduced me to some of his friends, including another American Rhodes scholar, Gordon Siefkin. Some British students met us for tea in Siefkin's quarters. One of them asked where I was from.

"Oklahoma," I answered.

"Oklahoma? Oklahoma?" he puzzled in a perfect Oxford accent. "Is that near Hollywood, or would it be up Chicago way?"

I realized how far I was from Oklahoma, and that it was very different, indeed.

Compared with that offered in most American law schools, an Oxford legal education was a true education, not a form of vocational training. Oxford stressed the institutional basis of the law's growth, not the practical skills of a lawyer's daily work. Of course, a student grappled with knotty problems of contracts and torts, but even more important were the principles of jurisprudence that he followed back to their Roman and oldest English origins.

The instructional method was no less different from the American style. Each Oxford scholar is assigned a single tutor, a don, who guides the student to his degree. When I went there, St. Peter's was still too new and small to have its own law don. For that reason, the college assigned me to work with C. H. S. Fifoot of Hertford College.

When I got Fifoot, I got the finest law tutor in the entire university. He had graduated with distinction from Oxford, where he had read law under G. C. Cheshire, one of Britain's great legal scholars. It was Fifoot's generation that fought the World War, and he had been badly wounded in France. Afterwards, he remained self-conscious of the scars along his neck and lower face. But he was a witty conversationalist, a warm and gentle man, a first-rate scholar. His lectures were among the university's most popular, his scholarly treatises among its most esteemed. Of all the great teachers that I ever had, none topped C. H. S. Fifoot for a depth of knowledge matched with an ability to teach it.

Normally, we had one tutorial session a week. Each usually lasted an hour. To prepare for the tutorial, Mr. Fifoot would give me a reading assignment from standard texts and leading court decisions. He also gave me a specific question to research.

The first course that I read with my tutor was torts. On the day I first met him, he assigned me the text for the course, showed me the law library, and introduced me to the most pertinent cases. He then gave me the topic for our first tutorial session: "How far is a master liable for the torts of his servant?"

A week later, I returned with a ten-page, handwritten essay on the topic. Alone with my tutor, I read it aloud. Over tea, we then discussed my essay, the topic, and the issues involved. Everything was fair game. If I had misread or overlooked a case, I heard about it. If I wanted to pursue a line of reasoning, I did. And so it continued, through torts, contracts, trusts, equity, Roman law, constitutional law, personal property, real property—most of the curriculum.

The tutorial system was at once Oxford's most distinctive quality and its greatest strength. To an American always comfortably harnessed to structured classwork, it might look like chaos, no system at all, but I swiftly learned that its freedom could be either a license to fail or a license to learn. I was there to learn, and the intense sessions, each directed to my needs rather than a general average, made it easier. Neither Mr. Fifoot nor I was interested in wasting my time.

Lectures often supplemented the tutorials, but they only supplemented them. Formal lectures were being held all around Oxford every weekday morning, and they were given by the very top men in the various subjects. Unlike American lectures, however, these were totally unrestricted. Students attended any lecture they wanted to, but only if they wanted to. Moreover, the general understanding was that attendance was not to be indiscriminate. Overdone, it could even be disreputable. No one took roll, neither did anyone dare interrupt the lecturer with a question. A lecturer might be speaking before a handful or a hundred. Some did not seem to care. Others did not seem to notice.

The lectures did allow students to hear some of the world's most respected scholars. One that I heard was Sir William Searle Holdsworth. His specialties were constitutional law and equities, but all of English law was his domain. He was a tireless worker who published nine volumes of his *History of English Law* while holding the demanding rank of tutor. Upon that basis, he was elected, in 1922, Vinerian Professor of English Law. His magisterial *History* continued to grow, eventually stretching to fifteen volumes, each covering the totality of the law's growth and work.

Professor Holdsworth was a large man, large in achievement, large in appetite (before writing each evening, he drank three glasses of port), and large in appearance. He looked like nothing but an Oxford professor, and when he lectured on England's legal history, I felt as though I were hearing the Gospel from the lips of Luke. So complete was his knowledge and so thorough was his presentation that I hardly noticed how poor was his delivery. Determined to impart his knowledge fully, Holdsworth would repeat each sentence three times in three different ways.

The uniform intellectual brilliance of the lecturers covered a diverse range of their personalities, a range running from the staid to the strange. Of course, Oxford insisted that its professors were free to run their lectures as they pleased. In one case, that of a notorious history professor, the consequence was quite memorable. The man simply and utterly hated women, and at each term's beginning, students would flock to his initial lecture to see what would happen. Among the all-male colleges, Oxford had four women's colleges at the time. Their mischievous tutors often suggested that new students attend the old fellow's lectures. The repeated result was an Oxford legend.

One term, I accompanied a friend who was reading history to see if the legend were true. It was. Entering the lecture hall was an old buzzard who looked as disheveled as any tramp. His eyes maliciously searched the audience until he spotted the ladies. "Get those women out of my lecture," he roared.

Stunned, the unsuspecting women sat frozen.

This only made the professor angrier.

"Go! Go!" he screamed.

The women filed out, the professor breathed deeply, and muttered, "When are those bloody tutors going to quit sending those idiots to me?"

Apparently, his rhetorical question calmed him. The old fellow smiled, reached his hands into his pockets, and offered his final judgment. "It's getting around this bloody university to where a man won't be able to use his own bloody vulgarity to emphasize the points of his own bloody lectures." He had no need to say that three times—if any at all.

Considerably tamer were seminars. Although they were common to legal education in America, Oxford began offering seminars only after 1903, making them a contemporary innovation by its standards. As in an American classroom, a teacher and his students gathered around a table to dissect legal doctrines as if in a science laboratory, the seminar's original inspiration. Not surprisingly, some of the best were directed by visiting Americans. One of the finest that I had was under Felix Frankfurter, then a Harvard law professor and later a Supreme Court justice.

A final component of Oxford's legal education was the student's own reading, deep and heavy reading from lists prescribed by his tutor. It was usually done during the long intervals between terms.

In some measure, each student's final education consisted of an individualized mix. Some subjects would be covered almost exclusively in tutorials. Others would involve more lectures. For some, seminars were essential. Some, such as international law, I did largely by reading. One way or another, all the elements of a broad and sound legal education were there. I was blessed to be there, too.

That system's greatest source of strength was its incredible range of opportunity. Its greatest source of potential anxiety was that the student never knew exactly where he stood. There were occasional simulated tests, but grades were never taken. In fact, the student received no grades at all until the very end. Then Oxford University exercised the power that none of its colleges held. Oxford gave the examinations, and Oxford awarded the degrees. A scholar's whole record rested entirely upon two examinations. The more important was a long and gruesome written test that stretched over several days. Morning and afternoon sessions covered each of the subjects in the curriculum. That was when all the tutorials, all the lectures, all the seminars, all the reading—everything—came together. And everything depended on the outcome of those precious few hours.

After the university's three examiners graded the written examinations, they called each student before them for a second ordeal, his oral examination, called the viva. They could, and sometimes did, quiz the student on any aspect of any subject. Their purpose, however, was not to uncover specific lapses of fact or of memory. Rather, it was to judge the candidate's general ability.

Only at that point did the student receive any grades, an alpha, beta, gamma, or delta (corresponding to our A, B, C, or D) for each subject. Upon that basis, he received his degree, known as an honors degree and divided into four classes: first, second, third, fourth.

Altogether, that was the Oxford system. I had never encountered anything like it before. Most Americans never would. But as I think of it now, most of my schooling had prepared me for just that. What kept one moving through the system was a love of learning. My Bug Tussle teachers had given me that; those at

*The lovely times we spent together.* With Max Lancaster in Spain, 1932, during the Rhode scholarship years.

McAlester had nourished it; the OU faculty had cultivated it. Amid the spires of Oxford, it bloomed.

It bloomed for all of us. And for all of us, our lives would be altered by our experiences as Rhodes scholars. Fifty years after that experience, one of us, Morris Shaffer, spoke for all of us when he judged that the most enduring legacies of our experience were "the lovely times we spent together" and what we learned from one another "regarding alternate ways of looking at life." I know that I treasure those memories of times spent together. I know, too, that I learned much from the brilliant young men who became my friends.

One was already my friend, and knowing him rightly prepared me for the intellectual company that I was entering. Max Lancaster had been a finalist with me in the 1927 high school oratory contest, and we had traveled through Europe together that summer. Now we were meeting again. I knew enough about Max Lancaster to know that he had the kind of mind that Cecil Rhodes had wanted to find and train.

Max read modern languages at Balliol. It was said of the Oxford colleges that it was Brasenose for brawn, Christ Church for blood, and Balliol for brains. Max only added to his college's reputation. He had been teaching French at Indiana University when he won his Rhodes. He also knew German well. He read Latin better than any English Etonian I ever met. Ahead of him was an outstanding academic career teaching Italian at Vanderbilt. While there, he would win Chile's order of merit, the Bernardo O'Higgins Award, for his stirring English translation from Spanish of the national epic *Arauciad*.

For all of Max's abilities, he was in no way unusual as a Rhodes scholar. It was a class—my class, designated by the year that we all went up as the Class of '31—that met Cecil Rhodes's expectations of scholarship. If there was anything special about that class, it was the record of achievement that lay ahead of us and was so indebted to our Oxford years. Many stayed in academics to build distinguished and varied careers. James Pettegrove became an internationally recognized scholar of German drama as well as the collaborator of the celebrated philosopher Ernst Cassirer. Byron Trippet would hold the presidencies of distinguished colleges in both the United States and Mexico. Austin Faricy became both an outstanding professor of the humanities and an honored harpsichordist. Ferdinand Stone taught law in America and in France, Italy, and England, where the monarch named him to the Honorary Order of the British Empire. Others, like John Pirie, later the general counsel of America's leading airline, built businesses and careers upon their brains.

One unique quality of my class was the number of us, almost a third, who went on to justify Cecil Rhodes's faith with careers in public service. In time, Oxford's Rhodes scholars of 1931 provided America with a naval scientist (Francis Coleman), a leader in public education (Robert Jackson), two senior diplomats (William Koren and Alexander Daspit), a special assistant to the president (John Martin), the first head of the Agency for International Development (Fowler Hamilton), a chairman of the Federal Reserve Bank of New York (Alfred Hayes), a judge of the United States Circuit Court of Appeals (Benjamin Duniway), and a four-star general (Charles Bonesteel). Two of us, Secretary of State Dean Rusk and I, rose to the two highest positions of government service ever occupied by beneficiaries of Cecil Rhodes's trust. At the time, though, none of us knew that was in our futures. But we did know that in the future we would hold dear those lovely times that we were spending together.

It was the warden of Rhodes House who, after consulting with the various colleges, assigned me to St. Peter's. Oxford's newest college may have been its least prestigious, but it did have one big benefit: the Rhodes stipend completely covered its smaller costs and left me the money to travel. Oxford's schedule gave me the time. The university ran three terms, each about two months long. Thus, nearly half my time was free to see as much of Europe as I wanted. I wanted to see it all, and seeing it with some of my classmates gave me the loveliest times of all.

Our favored spot was along Spain's Mediterranean shore. The area is now known as the Costa del Sol. Fully developed, it rivals the French Riviera for expensive tourism. In the early 1930s, the coast was quite primitive and hardly a lure for the jet set. What brought us there was the favorable exchange rate, the best in Europe for impecunious college students. Because the Spanish peseta was so cheap, I was able to sleep and have two meals a day for as little as ninety cents.

Spring was our favorite time to visit. The coastal climate is always spectacular but never more so than in the spring. Oxford's climate is never worse than in the winter. The contrast made us appreciate Spain all the more. So spring usually called my very

*Spring usually called my very closest friends and me.* With Spanish students and two gypsies at Granada.

closest friends and me to the Spanish coast. From there, we would travel forth to places like Cadiz, Seville, Cordova, and Grenada.

Travel was cheap, the weather was perfect, and the country was free. There was talk of a leftist uprising against the republic, but we saw nothing of one. We certainly saw no sign of the fascist revolt to come. We traveled freely through the country, mixing with peasants and workers and students and Gypsies. Sometimes, though, the times were not so lovely.

Our first Oxford term ended in early December, and Max Lancaster and I decided to spend Christmas in Paris. The family of one of Max's Balliol friends, Vala Zetlin, lived there. They agreed to put us up near their apartment at 11, rue Nicolo, just off the Champs-Elysées. We had been to Paris four years earlier. The city was still as lovely, but we could sense a difference. Maybe it was the depression. Maybe it was the unease over a fitful Germany. Whatever it was, the city seemed to be nervous, caught between a world of gentility destroyed and another of horror unborn.

Crime seemed to be rampant. It was nothing to read in the paper of a public guillotining drawing hundreds of curiosity seekers. One took place during the few days we were there. It involved a rapist. His victims were twenty teenage girls. We did not join the crowd, for we were not among the curious. We did join the Zetlin family for a holiday dinner.

The Zetlins were a family of victims, victims of those dangerous times. They were all well educated and highly cultured. Each spoke French, Russian, German, and English and spoke them well. The Zetlins were Russian Jews. Mrs. Zetlin's first husband had been prominent in the provisional government that replaced the czar. When the Bolsheviks overthrew that regime, the Zetlins fled, bribing their way to Paris. Now they were giving us our holiday dinner. Joining us on Christmas Day 1931 was their neighbor and fellow exile Alexander Kerensky.

Here was the man who had headed the ill-fated provisional government. His regime was no match for the Bolsheviks, and his graciousness was no match for Lenin's ruthlessness. His government had collapsed in the October Revolution, which gave birth to the world's first Communist state. Kerensky had barely managed to escape Red firing squads. Over dinner, he told us of fleeing the Soviet state, crossing its frozen border on a motorcycle. We listened enthralled, two American students sitting with a man who had made history and was now, like our hosts, its victim.

The next Christmas I saw another man who would make history—and millions of victims. I wanted to visit Central Europe that year and I made sure to go to Munich. There, I ran into one of St. Peter's dons, an excellent German historian and linguist. We talked briefly before he happened to ask, "I say, Albert, did you know Hitler is going to speak here on Thursday?" After that, there was nothing that could have pulled me out of Munich before Thursday. When Thursday came, we went—with fifty thousand Germans—to hear the man they called "*der Führer.*" It was a spectacle. A huge band blasted out martial tunes in front of a platform alive with waving Nazi flags and banners. The songs became ever more martial, the brass section louder, the beat stronger and faster, as the time for Hitler's speech approached.

He was not there, but we had no doubt of his whereabouts. Every few minutes, one of his Brown Shirts stepped to the microphone. His clothes pressed to a saber's edge, his posture as rigid as a rifle, he would notify the crowd of Hitler's movements.

"Heil Hitler! *Der Führer* is on his train approaching Munich."

Hands clapped, voices shouted, "Heil Hitler!"

After a few minutes, "*Der Führer* has reached the station."

More applause, more voices, "Heil Hitler!"

Another, interchangeable Brown Shirt: "*Der Führer* is traveling in his motorcar."

Much applause, many shouting "Heil Hitler!"

Now, the first Brown Shirt: "*Der Führer* is in sight!"

Caps sailed through the air. Nazi salutes shot up in unison. Spontaneous applause bunched into a rhythmic, pulsating beat of flesh upon flesh.

Just as the noise was passing its crescendo, a Brown Shirt shot to the microphone. "*Der Führer,*" he screamed, "has arrived."

The place came alive with a quickening, throbbing sound. It

continued, driving toward a final spasm as *Der Führer* came across the stage.

He looked like anything but the object of such hysteria. To me, he just looked tired, maybe sleepy, mostly bored. Facing fifty thousand erect, straining arms, he reached his right hand into his pocket and returned their salute with a casual, limp left arm.

As my friend translated for me, Hitler began to speak. His words dragged forth slowly at first. His sentences stopped in mid-thought, then began again somewhere else. Until he lit upon an emotional point. Suddenly and steadily, his voice grew stronger. Then he started to move. His rambling gave way to pacing and that to marching as he stomped back and forth across the plat-form. The words came faster and faster, louder and louder. Each time he paused for breath, that breath was heated by screams from thousands of throats.

Then, just as suddenly, Hitler's voice softened. For a few moments, the crowd sat silent, ears cocked to hear slow, soft, rhyth-mic streams of Hitler's words. Until one word became a shout, fol-lowed by another and another, each louder than the one before. At the top of his voice, he continued through his peroration. He ended with the crowd afire, a mad pentecost of hysteria.

It was the most remarkable performance I had ever seen. I left the place and I left Munich with the belief that this pathetic little creature had but one talent: he could incite an entire nation to madness. On that particular evening, it was his personal mad-ness. Within a few weeks, the feeble hands of Baron Paul von Hindenburg handed Hitler the chancellorship of Germany, and *der Führer's* personal madness became national policy.

Back in Oxford, Hitler's madness was no more than an odd curi-osity. The concerns of an American seemingly were unshared by Britain's elite. Unlike us, the British had fought four years of bloody war against one German army and were in no mood to face another. Maybe they were in no mood to think about it.

Much more pleasant was the safe world of Oxford in its spring.

Then and there the weather is always perfect, the flowers always beautiful, the countryside always enchanting. When not studying, I joined the other students in the gentlemanly ritual of punting on the Cherwell. We rented boats and with long poles pushed them up and down the river, pausing for box lunches on its graceful banks.

Sports were another diversion. I had not been there long before I realized that competitive athletics were at least as important to Oxford as to any American university. The games were different— the major sports were cricket, rugby, hockey, and rowing—but the intensity of competition was just as fierce. Equal, too, was the athlete's status: a member of the rowing team that faced Cambridge was as honored as an All-American football player for OU.

The Oxford Union was another diversion, though a more substantial one. It sat a few paces from St. Peter's, and I joined it early and attended its debates. They were full-dress affairs held every Tuesday night and featured outstanding student debaters, as well as political leaders. Among the latter, David Lloyd George and Winston Churchill were spectacular. I could have listened to either for hours.

Lloyd George spoke in a beautiful, lilting Welsh manner. Like Churchill, his grammatical constructions were perfect. Perfect, too, was their sense of metaphor and timing. Churchill in particular had an absolutely devastating wit. But it was passion, not wit, that he invoked to warn the union repeatedly and vainly of Hitler's menace.

Academically, my second year was nearly consumed by Roman law. It was Oxford's way to make the law of ancient Rome nearly central to the curriculum. It also was Oxford's way to ground its study in the original *Institutes* of Gaius. Written in the second century A.D., the *Institutes* recorded the earliest development of legal interpretation and did it entirely in Latin. Most English scholars, schooled since childhood for an Oxford degree, read Latin as a second language. I had exactly two years at McAlester High School and knew only the simplest words. For that reason, I spent most of a term in battle with the *Institutes,* the text open before me, a Latin dictionary beside it. I could call in Max Lancaster to help with some of the more obscure constructions, but most of the struggle was word-to-word combat. I slugged my way through it so slowly that I could not help but learn it thoroughly.

At the second year's end came our examinations. I spent a good part of the last term systematically reviewing all of my earlier work. The real push came, though, when the ordeal began. I slept well the night before the first day's exam. I did not sleep again for three nights. As soon as one day's test finished, I began studying for the next. The resulting written examinations thereby tested one's endurance as much as his intelligence.

Compared to that, the vivas (oral examinations) were no challenge at all. In fact, a group of us got ready for them by relaxing on a trip through Scotland. In an old car we drove through the countryside and slept every night in pup tents pitched in farmers' fields.

We spent our first night in the borderlands of Scotland, sleeping in the territory made famous as Sir Walter Scott's setting for his "Lady of the Lake." Our tents sat right where

> The stag at eve had drunk his fill,
> Where danced the moon on Monan's rill,
> And deep his midnight lair had made
> In lone Glenartney's hazel shade.

We left Glenartney's shade for Edinburgh. We had our lunch on the second floor of a Princess Street restaurant overlooking the great gorge that separated us from the beautiful castle of Edinburgh. We then made it a point to go much farther north by Loch Ness. The famous monster, Nessie, had been getting a lot of press coverage and we wondered how she was doing. We did not find her, so we dropped down south, toward Oxford. Before getting there, we made sure to camp "by the bonnie, bonnie banks of Loch Lomond."

When we reached Oxford, we were all fresher and better for our vivas. Mine went very well. I satisfied Oxford's examiners and received Oxford's initial degree. To celebrate, I planned a summer in

*We slept every night in pup tents pitched in farmers' fields . . . in the territory made famous as Sir Walter Scott's setting.* In Scotland, 1933; above, with Gordon Siefkin and George Done.

Europe. My destination was Germany. I wanted to see how a different monster was doing.

I went to Germany expecting to spend much of the summer there. As was often true on these trips, I had no elaborate itinerary. All I knew for sure was that I would sail to Hamburg and travel the country until I could see if Hitler was making much difference. Otherwise, I did not even know where I would stay in Hamburg. A fellow passenger helped me out there. He was a student, too, attending the University of London. A German native, he was quite familiar with Hamburg. He also was Jewish.

We reached Hamburg and registered at a small hotel. After dinner, we decided to take a walk through the city. It was lovely, if a bit quiet for a couple of vacationing students, so we resolved to visit some of the beer gardens. In our third one, we met two local girls. Both had taken English in school, and they seemed delighted to have an American to use it on. We four had a great time over steins of good German beer.

I remember well one of the girl's pride because she had traveled quite a bit. She reached into her purse and pulled out a heavily stamped passport and visas that recorded her travels. As I was looking them over, some of Hitler's Brown Shirts stepped up to our table.

My German was far too poor to make out what they were saying, but I could not mistake their attitude. Gruff, boisterous, and arrogant, they were badgering the other fellow. His initial politeness in the face of it gave way to anger, then to fear, as the brown-shirted hooligans grabbed him and pulled him away. I was too stunned to move, but I did not have to. The gang seized me and threw me into the street, where my fellow student was. Shaking with rage and alarm, he explained our transgression: we had been talking with two Aryan women, he a Jew, and I a foreigner. That answered the question that had brought me to Germany.

I left the next day. At Lübeck, I bought a ticket for a Swedish boat bound for Copenhagen. Policemen crowded the boarding area, carefully inspecting every person getting out of Germany. I expected no trouble and I had none—until I handed over my passport. It was not mine. It was the one the girl had been showing me in the beer garden.

Instantly, German officers surrounded me. They threw questions at me. The Swedish captain quickly stepped in to act as my interpreter. The German officials scrutinized my own passport before they finally accepted my story and let me board the vessel. They took the young girl's passport with them. I never learned what happened to it or to the little German girl who was so proud of her English and her freedom to travel.

My third and final year at Oxford was a bittersweet one. There were undeniable advantages to that year. Because I now held an Oxford degree, I shed my half-gown and the restrictions that went along with it. I could visit pubs, and I did. I could occupy a front seat in a cinema, and I did. I could date local girls, and I did that, too. Of course, I now wore the long gown that denoted an Oxford graduate, and I was proud to be one.

No longer an undergraduate, I had to find my own housing (digs was the Oxford term), and I was extraordinarily lucky. One of the dons at Oriel College was taking a year's leave. With George Carlson, a Rhodes scholar from Colorado, and Wilmore Kendall, a Rhodes scholar from my home county, I rented his apartment. It was in a perfect location: No. 4, Oriel Street, just opposite the college.

We easily had the most lavish digs of any of the Rhodes students. The apartment required three floors for its four bedrooms, four bathrooms, kitchen, den, and living room. All were handsomely furnished; the last held a grand piano.

The place swiftly became something of a social center for the Rhodes scholars and many of our English friends. People came and went, sometimes staying so long that I had to lock myself in the uppermost floor's bedroom; it was the only place quiet enough to afford a little study time. Still, the apartment and the enlarged privileges accounted for much of the year's sweetness.

The bitterness came from the realization that I would not have such opportunities much longer. My legal studies continued, steadily becoming less academic and more practical. They were preparing me less as a scholar, more as a lawyer. That, too, was a reminder that my years in Oxford were ending. They had been years of great challenge and of great opportunity.

They also had been years removed from much of the real world. I could listen to Hitler, but I need not be governed by him. I knew that America, Britain, and the entire world struggled in a deep, global depression, but I did not feel it. Beneath the fairy castle spires of Oxford, we held quiet tutorials. We cheered our rowing crew, we debated at the union, we punted the Cherwell. All along we knew there would be life after Oxford, and we knew that it would be something very different.

At the end of the spring term, I got ready to join that life. I passed Oxford's examinations and took Oxford's advanced law degree, the bachelor of civil laws. I celebrated and reminisced with my English friends and the Americans who expectantly had crossed the Atlantic as I had three years earlier. Then we left, sailing from Southampton, not knowing this time what to expect. We went our separate ways; mine was back to McAlester, Pittsburgh County, Oklahoma. Life there was different.

I returned to an America still held tight in the Great Depression's jaws. The bite was especially severe in rural Oklahoma. In no time, I felt it myself. I got home only to learn that there was not a single job opening in the county that was not some form of government work relief. Every lawyer in McAlester agreed that the local legal business was all but nonexistent. Some confessed that the only reason they had any at all was because they took chickens and eggs for fees.

I could not even get that until I passed the state bar exam. Through the fall of 1934, I stayed at the university's law library, studying for the test. I also scouted out future employment, only to learn that things were not much better anywhere else in the state. I took and passed the bar exam with no job prospects at all; by then it was winter. I was far from Oxford and close to desperate.

A break finally came with an article in the *Daily Oklahoman*.

President Franklin D. Roosevelt's New Deal had created a Federal Housing Administration in 1933. According to the paper, the FHA soon would be opening an Oklahoma City office. The office would need a few administrators, a handful of secretaries, and one other employee: a legal assistant.

I ran to the nearest telephone and called Washington. Senator Elmer Thomas remembered his high school visitor; Senator Thomas Gore remembered his college driver. They gave me their recommendations and put me in touch with the local administrator. He hired me on the spot to my first real job. The pay was $150 a month, exactly $16.67 less than I had been paid for going to school at Oxford. I was mighty glad to get it.

Working with the FHA gave me an education as well as a check. I had not worked there long before I understood that I was right at the center of some major national problems.

The housing industry had been unhealthy long before the 1929 stock-market crash. Indeed, its deterioration had been one source of the economic erosion that led to the overall collapse. With the Depression, the housing industry and the general economy began a mad dance leading to total exhaustion. Swelling unemployment rolls left fewer and fewer Americans able to build, buy, or repair homes. Home construction, sale, and repair slowed, swelling those unemployment totals. The resulting spiral could never reverse itself.

Moreover, the housing industry was tied directly to the banking industry. Unemployed men could not meet their mortgage obligations. Lenders could not collect on their loans. The only available recourse, mortgage foreclosures, benefited no one. Homeowners lost their homes. Creditors accumulated buyerless properties. Families took to the streets. Banks closed their doors.

Here, too, was a deadly spiral that threatened nothing less than total financial collapse. Already it had doomed much of the country to be that one-third of the nation that FDR knew was ill fed, ill clothed, and ill housed. Unless somebody did something, too many would stay there too long. Buyers needed mortgage money they could use with with monthly payments they could handle.

Lenders needed assurance that they could recover larger loans requiring smaller down payments and stretched over longer periods. Everyone needed protection against shoddy and hazardous construction methods.

To any but a mossback reactionary, the crisis called for decisive government action to relieve the present misery, to reform the underlying problem, and to recover a large piece of the American Dream. It was the mission of Franklin Roosevelt and his Democratic party to take that action. It was their genius to do it not by reversing American capitalism, but by rescuing it. They helped capitalists save capitalism from itself.

The housing act enlisted the existing private elements—the bankers, the buyers, and the builders—in a systematic attack on national needs. It encouraged financiers to require smaller down payments (twenty percent became standard) and to lengthen repayment schedules, usually to twenty years. For these reasons, monthly payment schedules fell markedly and borrowers had some assurance that they could keep their homes, even if hard times returned again.

In exchange for these liberalizations, the federal government maintained a fund to guarantee the lenders' loans against default. A fee of one-half of 1 percent added to each borrower's monthly payment financed the fund. The guarantee, while virtually painless to the homeowner, assured lenders' participation and cooperation in the entirely voluntary program.

Finally, reasonable but detailed rules prescribed loan standards. Some sought to ensure that borrowers would be capable of repayment; others governed the properties to be financed. These protected the buyer, the lender, and the government from unscrupulous building practices that already had defrauded Americans of billions of dollars.

Altogether, the national housing act was a model of modern statesmanship. I am proud of the president who proposed it, proud of the party that sponsored it, proud of the Congress that adopted it. I am proud, too, to have worked in its administration.

Up in a second-floor office across from the old post office, we worked in Oklahoma City to bring the FHA to Oklahoma. Some called us bureaucrats, but all we were was a very hardworking group of people, about a half-dozen, trying to help other people. Our chief responsibilities were central and western Oklahoma, where we maintained offices in the principal towns. Local people employed by the Works Progress Administration (WPA) regularly staffed these. Local chambers of commerce usually donated the office space.

Much of my work was in those scattered offices. I bought my first car, a Model A costing $475, and drove across much of the state. As the legal assistant, I helped interpret and explain Washington's rules and prepare the paperwork. Most of my work, however, was more personal than legal. In one community after another, I met with loan applicants and helped them fill out their applications. I visited the local bankers and the savings-and-loan directors, explaining the program and urging their cooperation. It was a pretty good use for an Oxford education.

It was also an education in itself. Driving across Oklahoma, I saw things that I can never forget. One was on the MK&T Railroad running north into McAlester. I was driving home one weekend when I passed a long freight train. It had a string of at least fifty coal cars, all empty of coal, each filled with desperate men and boys. They were economic refugees trying to find some kind of work somewhere else.

I got home still shaken. For some reason, I went out to Bug Tussle. I visited one of my old schoolmates. He, his wife, and their nine children were living there in a three-room shack. No one in the family had had a pair of shoes in more than two years. His only income was fifty dollars a month, earned with the WPA.

"How do you get by?" I asked.

He answered, "Oh, I fish in the spring and summer, trap and skin wild animals in the winter."

My friend's lips smiled but his eyes did not when he added, "I have to steal chickens on the side."

You never can forget things like that. All you can do is try to understand them.

My fieldwork with the FHA contributed to my understanding. It gave me my first real experience with western Oklahoma. Up until statehood, there were two distinct and entirely separate territories, Indian Territory and Oklahoma Territory. The first became roughly the eastern half of the state, and it was where my people had settled. Its lands were rolling, forested hills, later cleared for small cotton farms, usually worked by tenants. Its people were migrating southerners, Baptists and Methodists mainly, Democrats almost always.

Oklahoma Territory was considerably different—different enough to have justified a separate statehood. It was flatter, drier, almost treeless. Migrating midwesterners settled there. They plowed up wheat farms, built Church of Christ and Presbyterian churches, and voted Republican.

Despite those historic differences, every corner of the state suffered mightily in the 1930s. Oklahoma's people were proud people and strong people, but they, no less than some of the Europeans I had seen, were victims of a history larger than they. In the old Indian Territory, the tenant system collapsed under the weight of ten-cent cotton. In the old Oklahoma Territory, the hardworking men who had plowed the prairie to grow wheat in the twenties tasted dust in their mouths in the drought-stricken thirties. All over the state, the oil boom that followed Oklahoma's birth ended when crude oil prices hit a dime a barrel.

Cotton, wheat, and oil—everything—had collapsed. The resulting emergency overwhelmed state and local governments. Human needs swelled as public revenues shrank. They did their best, but their best could not even slow the tide of ruin. Neither could it slow the human tide. Abandoned farm cabins and oil-field shacks lined the roads that I drove. After all, Oklahoma lost a fifth of its population in the 1930s.

The photographs of Dorothea Lange and others recorded the faces of many of those migrants, the ones called Okies. There were haunting photographs, too, of the ones who stayed. Some captured the awesome, fearsome majesty of the howling winds and billowing clouds of dust that roared across the western plains, hollowing out the Dust Bowl. Some caught old people without hope, young people without work, small children without promise. To see those pictures is to know something of what it was to go down from Oxford to Oklahoma in the 1930s.

The reality was worse than the photographs. Driving across the state in my model A, carrying federal loan applications, I saw things that remain more vivid than any mere picture. I remember driving right through the heart of the Dust Bowl in the summer of 1936, when the temperature was 120 degrees. A little west of Guymon, I pulled into a tiny filling station that sat upon a sterile plain. A little boy—he could have been no more than thirteen—came out to the car and filled my tank.

"Mister," he said, "this is the first sale I have made today."

I knew then that this little boy was in charge of the station. Then he told me why.

"Sir," he said, "it looks like this country is going to burn up. We can't make it here. My parents have gone to California to look for work, and they left me here to take care of things. 'Doesn't look like there's much left to take care of."

There was not much left. Just a little boy with the oldest eyes I had ever seen.

I climbed back into the car and kept going. Blowing dust howled about me. Before long, I had to pull off the road and wait for the duster to pass. I finally made it to Boise City, the county seat of Cimarron County and epicenter of the Dust Bowl.

If God had not forsaken the place, He was one of the few that had not. Stores, banks, nearly everything seemed abandoned. I did find a resident leaning on a light post. We talked a bit, and I asked him how long the place had been without rain.

"Fella," he answered, "I got a boy three years old that has never seen a drop of rain."

But drought was not really the problem. It was raining elsewhere in Oklahoma, but the people were no better off. Right in the state's capital, where the North Canadian River literally had flowed with oil, a camp had sprung up on the riverbanks. I went through it once with a McAlester doctor, there to attend a dying child. I saw five hundred people living in shacks, most made of cardboard, their only toilet and running water the river itself.

This was man's depression, not God's. It would not help much to wait for rain, any more than it would help to wait for the sinking economy to raise itself. This was government's task. Here was its purpose.

That is what I learned when I went down from Oxford and back to Oklahoma. It added to my resolve to go to Congress. I wanted to be part of a government that accepted that task and met that purpose. In time that happened. What Franklin Roosevelt began, others would extend. I was able to be one of them. I was able to do my part to see that the government of all of us would act in remembrance of these, the least of us.

In the years ahead, I would never once see that happen without seeing, too, a little boy left behind to take care of things.

## CHAPTER FOUR

# *I Think I'll Go Back Home and Run for Congress*

$B$y the spring of 1937, I had spent nearly two years with the Federal Housing Administration. It had been a valuable experience in many ways, but money was not one of them. I was still earning Depression wages with no raise in sight. I knew that I was ready to move on for the right opportunity. It came in May.

The Sayre Oil Company was a family-owned business that took its name from the town of Sayre, home of its founder and president, E. L. Martin. Buddy Martin was his son and the company vice president; he also was my Kappa Alpha fraternity brother. It was Buddy who asked me if I would be interested in working as the in-house attorney at the company's Oklahoma City headquarters.

I jumped at the chance. Sayre Oil had wide and diverse holdings that belied its localized name, and I could count on some interesting work. Oil was second only to agriculture in its economic significance to Oklahoma. I knew that I could never really know or serve the state without understanding the industry. Finally, the job paid $250 a month and that was nearly double my FHA salary.

Mr. Martin had built his company on some very profitable leases and wells in the fabulous East Texas field. To them he later added wells and leases in the Permian Basin of West Texas. The

Texas crude that he sold refiners was bringing in better than $3 million a year at the time. The company also had oil properties in Oklahoma and Kansas, and Mr. Martin owned extensive tracts of land in western Oklahoma and the Texas Panhandle. All in all, there was plenty of work for the company's legal department: me.

Much of the work—easily the most interesting work—was out in the field. Oil had just been discovered in southern Illinois, and Mr. Martin and some wildcatters were busy buying up leases and drilling wells in America's latest pool. It made for a lot of legal business. It also gave me my first close-up view of some of the world's biggest gamblers and smoothest operators. Few of the oil men were well educated; some had no education at all. Mr. Martin certainly had no Oxford degree, but I came to believe very quickly that none of my Oxford dons could have outsmarted him on a business deal.

There was a banker up in southern Illinois who learned the same thing, and his education cost him more than mine. Mr. Martin was buying leases and entrusting them to a small-town banker in the new oil patch. In no time the lease prices shot upward. I went over to the county courthouse, looked in the land records, and found out why. Our banker friend had taken advantage of our trust to start buying royalties in his own name. That was what was running the prices up on us. He should not have done that.

When I told him what was going on, Mr. Martin sent me out to buy up leases in two different parts of the county. The leases in one, the one where our geologists told us we could expect oil, I kept with me. The other, in a place of no promise at all, I recorded with the clerk at the courthouse. Sure enough, the banker started frantic buying in the new area. He was taking everything he had made off our trust and pouring it into the new leases, jacking the prices up, and buying still more at the inflated prices. Meanwhile, we kept buying quietly and cheaply in the other area without recording the leases.

After a few weeks, Mr. Martin had me spring the trap. I recorded every one of the leases that covered nearly an entire field— Sayre Oil had it all. Our competitor ended up with a trunk full of worthless paper. Too late, he learned that he had paid a fortune for leases to a field as dry as a banker's eye.

One of the best things about my new boss was his politics. Mr. Martin was a Democrat, a down-the-line, Franklin Roosevelt, New Deal Democrat. Of course, I was, too. I had seen too many of Oklahoma's neediest people to be anything else. In a place like Oklahoma, at a time like the Great Depression, I did not know how one *could* be anything else.

It appeared that not many Oklahomans were anything else. Although Republican nominees carried the state in two of the three presidential races of the 1920s, the popular identification of the Depression with the GOP decimated the party. In 1932, Franklin Roosevelt became the first presidential candidate to carry every one of Oklahoma's seventy-seven counties. In 1936, he got two out of every three Sooner votes. One of his record total was my first presidential ballot.

Oklahoma's voters had every reason to support the president so faithfully. The relief and recovery projects of the New Deal were chipping away at some of their towering economic troubles. The Federal Housing Administration saved homes that would have been lost. The Federal Deposit Insurance Corporation saved banks that would have failed. The Works Progress Administration created jobs for people who would have stayed idle. The National Youth Administration kept youngsters in school who would have withdrawn. The Agricultural Adjustment Administration got government checks to farmers who faced doom without them. The National Recovery Administration kept small-town merchants in business. A dozen relief projects kept families eating.

One thing that Roosevelt and the New Deal could not do was give shape to the state Democratic party. Oklahoma Democrats have always been a fractious crowd. In the 1930s, they were something of a mob, and the party tended toward catch-as-catch-can chaos. One symptom of that attracted considerable national attention, attention that was either bemused or hostile. It was my state's penchant for famous-nameism.

It began in 1932 when an obscure schoolteacher filed for election as a representative at large. His name was William C. Rogers, and his few friends had always known him as Bill. But when he filed for office, this Mr. Rogers instructed the election board to enter him on the ballot as Will Rogers. So identified, he ran all over twenty opponents to capture the Democratic nomination. He went on to lead the entire ticket in the general election. He drew even more votes than Franklin Roosevelt.

Two years later, this Will Rogers sought a second term. I returned from Oxford to discover his name among those of the 241 candidates who sought 31 offices on a Democratic ballot that measured 531 square inches. He won that year, too. In fact, Will Rogers won five consecutive terms. He served until the office was abolished after the state lost a House seat following the 1940 census.

It is said that this particular Will Rogers contributed little humor to national affairs—little humor apart, that is, from his own elections. Over the years, he kept returning to Washington after beating back challenges from men named William Cullen Bryant, Brigham Young, Sam Houston, Robert E. Lee, and Wilbur Wright.

Congressman Rogers's success encouraged others to try their hands and famous names at winning steady employment through the Democratic primary. In 1938 alone, thousands of Oklahoma's Democrats marked their ballots for Oliver Cromwell, Daniel Boone, Huey Long, and Patrick Henry. Sixty-seven thousand Democrats voted that year for an Oklahoma City housewife named Mae West. All lost—all except Will Rogers—but all contributed mightily to my state's reputation for political buffoonery.

Far more serious was the inability of the state party to work with the national administration. Few politicians dared criticize the president or his policies openly; FDR and the New Deal were far too popular with far too many for that. But at the same time, some of the congressional delegation feuded openly with the White House and their party's leadership in Congress. In Oklahoma City, William H. Murray, known as Alfalfa Bill, who was the state's governor from 1931 to 1935, stubbornly refused to cooperate with New Deal agencies. After Murray's term, much of the legislative leadership stayed in open and permanent rebellion against its party's policies in Washington.

None of this was unique to Oklahoma. America's federal structure never has promoted the party loyalty and party discipline sustained by Britain's unitary system. During the 1930s, this became steadily graver. A growing number of conservative Democrats, especially southern conservative Democrats, were deserting the New Deal. In Congress, they were moving toward an informal alliance with the bitterly anti-Roosevelt Republican minority, an alliance that threatened to bury FDR's program on Capitol Hill.

Of course, many southerners in Congress were steadfastly loyal to the administration. It was my early friend Elmer Thomas who pieced together much of FDR's farm program in the Senate Agriculture Committee. Josh Lee, my speech professor at the University of Oklahoma, joined Thomas in the Senate in 1936. He proved to be an even firmer friend of the New Deal, a dependable vote for FDR and an eloquent champion of his policies.

It was while I was working for Sayre Oil in 1938 that Senator Thomas faced a tough reelection fight. E. W. Marland, the legendary oilman who had built and lost an empire, was closing out a frustrating term as governor and seeking solace in the Senate seat. Gomer Smith, who had served very briefly in the House of Representatives, had run awfully well against Senator Thomas six years earlier. Smith subsequently had risen to the vice-presidency of the Townsend Clubs, the group agitating for generous pensions for the elderly. Fortified by the old folks' votes, he was running again.

Both of these were formidable contenders, and neither was as dependably for FDR as Senator Thomas. I wanted to help the old senator, and I asked Mr. Martin one day if I could take a month's unpaid leave to campaign for him. Mr. Martin would hear nothing of it; he insisted that I take as long as I wanted at full pay. That would be his contribution to the Thomas campaign and to the New Deal.

I spent most of the summer campaigning for Senator Thomas. I must have given a hundred speeches or more, speaking at every crossroads in southern Oklahoma, all the way from the Arkansas line to the Texas Panhandle. In July, I got some mighty powerful help: President Roosevelt came to Oklahoma.

That summer, the president took a decided and singular gamble. His program was stalled in Congress, so, in order to move it, he resolved to throw himself into the Democratic congressional primaries. In a few carefully selected races, he would campaign personally and directly for the renomination of his most loyal supporters who were facing strong challenges. More important, he would actively enter other races to call for the defeat of powerful Democratic apostates. Never before had a president so directly intervened in his party's congressional nomination process.

That is what brought FDR to Oklahoma. Three days before the July primary, his train roared into the state, stopping at towns along the Santa Fe line before pulling into Oklahoma City for a climactic address at the state fairgrounds. Estimates are that a fifth of Oklahoma's electorate came to one or another of the stops to hear the nation's most popular public man. Seventy-five thousand of us heard his address at the fairgrounds. It was the finest stump speech I ever heard. The president really laid the lash to the Republicans. Then he moved on to what he called the "yes, but . . ." Democrats. Yes, they wanted prosperity, but not to underwrite it. Yes, they wanted reform, but not this one. Yes, they called themselves Democrats, but they voted like Republicans. The crowd went right along, shouting its agreement. There was an explosion when the president urged them to give him in Washington the strong right arm of "my old friend, Senator Thomas."

Our old friend did return to Washington, where he continued to support the president in peace and in war. Others of FDR's friends—Hattie Carraway in Arkansas and Alben Barkley in Kentucky—fended off strong conservative challengers with Roosevelt's assistance that year. In these cases, the president could persuade voters to return his friends. He almost never could convince them to defeat his foes. Not even FDR's earnest and public pleadings could defeat senators like Ellison D. ("Cotton Ed") Smith in South Carolina, Millard Tydings in Maryland, or Walter George in

Georgia. Each of them returned to Washington, too. They returned to positions of power and authority. Unchastened and unafraid, their influence actually grew, for they had withstood the assault of a politician heretofore believed to be invincible. Their survival and success only emboldened other conservative Democrats to break with the White House and the national party.

FDR's gamble had failed. Worse, it had backfired. After 1938, a conservative coalition of most Republicans and many conservative Democrats emerged as a political phenomenon that would survive for most of my own public life. Not even Franklin Roosevelt could overcome it; no subsequent president could ignore it. I later learned just how much the congressional leadership had to understand it, too.

My legal work in the Illinois field became more and more interesting. I enjoyed the work and my colleagues, too. I was not the only attorney working for the only oil company in the area. In fact, I was not the only one from McAlester, Oklahoma. Tom Ed Grace had been a friend since high school. Like me, he had been valedictorian at McAlester High and had gone on to OU, where we had been bridge partners. I ran into Tom while he was working for Carter Oil, one of the Standard Oil companies. Tom had the original idea, but I thought it a grand one: we both left our salaried jobs to open a new firm, Grace and Albert of Mattoon, Illniois.

Grace and Albert hung its shingle in an excellent location. We occupied the second floor of a building on Main Street in Mattoon. The first floor belonged to a Greek restaurant, the most popular eatery in the whole area. Across the street sat Carter Oil Company, my partner's former employer. It was the chief source of our bread-and-butter business, title examinations that the legal department farmed out to Grace and Albert.

Title examinations remained our specialty. From time to time, we did have litigation. For instance, Tom took on a divorce and child-custody case and won a splendid victory. I also went into court to argue a complicated case regarding land transfer. Most days were spent poring over land records. I must have studied thousands of abstracts, plowing steadily through uncountable records of deeds, conveyances, and covenants. Our clients demanded secure leases. Their landmen got the leases; we saw that they were secure. It was not glamorous work, but it was work, and in the late thirties that still meant a lot more than glamour.

At their start, the 1940s seemed not to offer much more glamour. In the spring of 1940, I accepted a good job with The Ohio Oil Company. The Ohio—*The* was part of its formal name and always capitalized—went back in the oil business to the days of the original Standard Oil and old John D. Rockefeller. Although it never reached the size of Standard or the Texas Company, it was a fine, well-run, fully integrated firm. It refined its own crude oil from its own wells in Illinois, Texas, and other fields. A subsidiary, Illinois Pipeline Company, was a major midwestern shipper. Another subsidiary, Marathon, had filling stations all across Ohio, Indiana, and Illinois. For all its reach, The Ohio proudly bore the image of the founder and his family. James Donnell, a pal of old John D. himself, established the company and passed it down to his son, then President Otto Donnell. Otto's son, James, was steadily moving upward at the time.

The Donnell influence pervaded the company. As a Democrat and a Methodist, I had to notice how many of the other employees were Republican and Presbyterian, as were the Donnells. My own boss later told me that he had been a Methodist when he started with The Ohio, but he had changed. According to him, that was true of nearly every man who wore The Ohio's white collar.

My office was with the company's district headquarters in Marshall, a little town near the Indiana border. In effect, I was in charge of all the company's legal business in Illinois. I chose the work I wanted for myself and farmed out the rest to independent firms. In the first year, I took three cases into the courts, and I sent a lot of abstracts out of the office. It was an excellent job. It paid well—three hundred dollars a month was awfully good money at the time—the work was challenging, and the people were great. I still clung to the dream of one day representing Oklahoma in Congress, and I took every opportunity to keep up with the folks in my home state. Lest I be tempted to quit The Ohio, though, I only had to recall how tough it had been to find any legal work at home. Things there had hardly improved by 1940. In some ways, they had worsened, as the largest waves of Okie migrants were only then leaving. The lingering uncertainty of the Great Depression was no occasion for me to make a sudden career move.

There was one other uncertainty at the time, but its resolution came with frightful dispatch. While I was searching land abstracts in the American midwest, Hitler had been seizing national estates in central Europe. Events showed Britain and France the ugly truth of which Churchill had warned and toward which they had been so stubbornly blind. Adolf Hitler was not just another politician; this mad genius would stop at nothing to build his thousand-year Reich and stretch its influence across the Continent. He would rule in Europe or he would serve it hell. Too late, the democracies had drawn the line at the border of Poland. When Hitler's panzers crashed across the Polish frontier and his Stukas rained death upon Poland's cities, war was again upon the world.

Unlike Americans just a little older than I, I could not say with President Roosevelt, "I have seen war," but I had seen its results (the young man's silvered face at Verdun appeared before me often) and I could say with FDR, "I hate war." Like millions of others, I supported his pursuit of an unprecedented third presidential term, hoping that that personal abhorrence and his great political skills could make a difference. They could not. The neutrality laws hastily and idealistically assembled early in the 1930s crumbled before awesome reality. Just as quickly, America accepted the role of democracy's arsenal, furiously began lending and leasing war matériel to the Allies, and looked toward its own anemic forces. In 1940, after ferocious debate, Congress gave the nation its first peacetime conscription law, the Selective Service Act.

Watching these events rush past, I thought to look into my own military liability. After four years of college ROTC, I had graduated from OU with a commission in the Army Reserve. I hardly had thought about it since. Now I did, and I realized that my commission had expired. I had missed the required annual training while I was at Oxford. I checked with the adjutant general and learned that the army's policy was not to reinstate any expired commission.

Still, the country was not at war and might not be. I was in my thirties, and I saw no reason to volunteer. When the new Selective Service Act set up a lottery to determine the order of induction, I knew enough to know that the odds were that it would be a long time before my number was drawn. Secretary of War Henry Stimson did the drawing, pulling slips of assigned numbers from a revolving drum. Mine was the second number he drew. Early on the morning of June 16, 1941, I boarded a train, as ordered, bound for Camp Grant, Illinois. By noon, I was a private in the army of the United States.

I was not at Camp Grant long. Within two days, all of us new recruits were traveling through the southern darkness, headed for Camp Polk, Louisiana. I suspect that several of the boys wanted to leave even earlier. At least, some said they were thinking about taking off and heading for home—until the officers lined us up and read us the Articles of War. That part about punishment by "shooting to death with musketry" really got our attention.

Our arrival at Camp Polk hardly increased our delight in our new experience. We rode a train for a day and a half and reached the Louisiana post late at night, carrying all of our gear through mud for a mile to our barracks. We had just dropped, exhausted, onto our cots when a tall, skinny, blond corporal busted through the door. In a voice I had thought reserved for the announcement of Armageddon, he welcomed us with the memorable words: "Get off them damn bunks! Who in the hell do you think you are? You had better learn right now that you are not going to lie on your fat asses around here."

After that, we were not inclined to. Neither were we apt to forget the corporal's gratuitous judgment that "I don't like college boys. I want you to know that there ain't gonna be no book reading around here." A tough-looking draftee from Chicago looked around and said, "He's a nice son of a bitch, ain't he?" Some of us smiled. All of us knew we were in the army now.

Actually, basic training was not bad. I was assigned to Battery C of the Fifty-fourth Armored Field Artillery Battalion. Much of our training was exactly what I had already done at Fort Sill with my college ROTC unit. We even used the same weapons: old French 75s. I just polished up the skills that I had acquired in summer camp and really impressed the officers. Before long, our field artillery officer, Colonel Vincent Meyer, had me transferred to his office.

That was a good break, less because it took me out of the field than because it put me in an important place at an important time. I had a desk in the same room as Colonel Meyer. That summer, our entire Third Army was taking part in a massive training exercise, the largest military movement since the Armistice. The 240,000-man Third Army was "invading" Louisiana, which was defended by the 180,000 men of the Second Army. Colonel Meyer's office thereupon became a major headquarters.

I was working there one day when some senior officers came through. At their center was a hawk-nosed general outfitted in riding boots and a brace of ivory-handled pistols. George S. Patton, Jr., needed no introduction; he was already a legendary figure. Nonetheless, he systematically shook the hand of every officer and enlisted man in Colonel Meyer's office. General Patton inspected our operations—he seemed to like what he saw—and stayed to lecture us on his favorite subject: the tank in modern warfare. When Colonel Meyer asked him if he thought our artillery would be more effective at some distance behind advancing tanks, Patton answered him with "Hell, no. I think they should go right up with the tanks."

Colonel Meyer tactfully retreated by telling Patton, "Well, you know more about tank warfare than anyone."

"That is right," the general affirmed instantly.

I was so intrigued with Patton's performance that I barely noticed the men who accompanied him. Later, one of Colonel Meyer's aides told me that another of our visitors had a pretty good reputation among professional soldiers, too. He told me his name: Colonel Dwight Eisenhower. It was the first time that I heard that name.

I enjoyed my work with Colonel Meyer enough that I decided to apply for Officer Candidate School. The colonel told me to forget it; I could apply directly for a commission. With Colonel Meyer's recommendation and encouragement, I started the application through the channels to the adjutant general. The papers were moving somewhere a few days later when Congress passed a bill amending the Selective Service Act. The original statute conscripted men for one year only. The brass who had trained those men did not want to lose them, not when the world picture was worsening. Not in August of 1941. After a bitter struggle, Congress agreed. By a vote of 203 to 202, it extended the draftees' service another eighteen months. At least it did so for those under twenty-eight; those older, it released immediately.

So it seemed that my military service was to be a grand anticlimax. I went back to my job with The Ohio and took up right where I left off. Again, I picked my own cases, often to allow me the chance to travel. I remember one of those, a suit filed by a Marathon distributor, because it took me into Waynesville, Missouri. What made the town so memorable is that I was there on the morning of Sunday, December 7, 1941.

Within days of the Pearl Harbor attack, I went to Washington. Certain to be called into the army again, I had to see how my commission request was proceeding. I knew enough about the military and the government to know how slowly paper could move through it even in the best of times. I had little idea how to hurry the process, for these truly were the worst of times. I was walking up Connecticut Avenue, wondering what to do, when I heard someone say, "Hello, Carl."

The tone was as natural as could be. I looked around to see someone in a major's uniform. That someone was Frank Rogers; I had known him at McAlester High School. I had seen him just once since then: when I learned that Frank was in the army and making it his career. What I had not known is that he had risen so fast, that he was with the very top of the Army Air Corps, that he worked with commanders responsible for commissions and promotions, and that I would walk into him on Connecticut Avenue. Until then, I did not even know how lucky I was.

Once I told him the situation, Frank offered to help. In no time he had the matter worked out with the Air Corps command. I left my civilian work and reported back to the army. In mid-March, I received my commission as a second lieutenant. On March 20, 1942, I reported as ordered to the judge advocate general's office, United States Army Air Corps, Washington, D.C.

I reported to my commander, a Colonel Snodgrass, with the air judge advocate's office. Young attorneys were daily coming into the army, and the colonel was glad to get one who had some military training. For that reason, he appointed me his assistant executive officer.

Our headquarters was in the old Munitions Building. While construction proceeded on the Pentagon, that building housed much of the War Department. General George C. Marshall, the army's chief of staff, had his office there; Eisenhower had moved in to help him on December 14. Just beyond my work station sat a desk in a hallway. I noticed that no one ever sat there, though it was assigned to a Major Doolittle. Apparently, he was on a training mission somewhere else. I learned why Jimmy Doolittle was away when his bombers visited Tokyo.

The office next to mine belonged to a Colonel James Fechet. I soon learned that the colonel had been a great World War I pilot. With his close friend Billy Mitchell, he had helped build the Army Air Corps. For four years, he was its commander. He had worn a general's stars until the great military contraction of the post–World War I years, when his rank was reduced to colonel. At that grade he had retired, but he had volunteered to serve his country in the new emergency. He returned to Washington and the Air Corps, but he returned as a colonel, outranked by dozens of men of considerably fewer years and considerably lesser achievements.

I had an instant liking for old Fechet, and I instinctively

thought his present situation unfair. In my spare time, I started looking into the statutes and military precedents, wondering whether he could be restored to his original rank. Sure enough, after some digging I discovered that such things occasionally had been done in war. I took my information and precedents to my senior officers, and they jumped right on it. In less than a week, Fechet proudly wore again his two stars.

General Fechet's new responsibilities included approval of all Air Corps staff promotions, and one of his first approvals was to raise my rank to first lieutenant. In fact, it came at his own initiative, the general explaining that a man could not live in Washington on a second lieutenant's salary. I was awfully appreciative of the improvement, as I am sure the general had been of his own. I was appreciative again in August 1942 when he approved my rise to captain. Each promotion improved my pay and status. I was glad for the prestige, and I needed the money because I had met someone else in the air judge advocate's office. Her name was Mary Harmon.

Mary was a South Carolina girl, raised in Columbia. After high school, she had attended a business college and worked for the telephone company. She had taken a federal civil service exam for a secretarial job and scored well enough to be called to Washington during the military buildup before Pearl Harbor. She had been a civilian secretary with the Air Corps for about a year when I arrived. Later, we learned that our co-workers had played quiet matchmakers for us. She had been home sick with the measles during my first week in the job, but the other secretaries made sure that I learned her name and one thing else about her: just under five feet, Mary Harmon was my size. They gave her the same information about me.

The next Monday, I was working away when I heard the assured rhythm of heels clicking briskly across our marble floor. I looked up into sparkling blue eyes. I mumbled some pleasantry, and Mary Harmon introduced herself in a gentle Carolina accent that softly sheathed an inordinate poise and confidence. She could

*August 20, 1942, we exchanged vows in a little Lutheran church.* Carl and Mary Albert.

have been anything from three feet to seven; it made no difference. I knew then and there that Mary Harmon was just the right size for me.

We began to date. I remember that our first was to see the Ringling Brothers Circus. Mary was sharing a room over by the national zoo, and we practically made the zoo a second home for each of us. With some other young couples, we enjoyed the capital's other most scenic and least expensive sites. In early August we even celebrated my new captaincy by taking in New York with some friends.

Pretty soon, the only thing preventing our marriage was Mary's insistence upon her sister's approval. We invited Frances, her sister, up, and she and I hit it off instantly. As I recall, Frances bestowed her blessings on our plans as we were heading for the zoo.

The army gave us four days' leave for a marriage and honeymoon. Most of the first was consumed by a tiring ride on a long and packed train to Columbia. On the second, August 20, 1942, we exchanged vows in a little Lutheran church. On the third, we had our honeymoon, a whole day of it, in Charleston. On the fourth, we rode the train back to Washington, back to work, back to the war.

There is no job that does not allow a person to do something for someone else. Done well, the payment is a satisfaction that transcends any mere salary. To some, work as an army attorney during wartime might seem a battle with boredom, its skirmishes the shuffling of paper across a Washington desk. I quickly learned that the work's object was not paper but people. It was not a safe sinecure, it was an opportunity for service.

One of my first assignments was certainly that. One morning, an officer walked into my office. With him was a staff sergeant. The officer laid out the enlisted man's story. He had joined the army in the late thirties and was assigned to Clark Field in the Philippines; that is where he was when the Japanese attacked the base with a ferociously surprising air raid on the war's second day. Oblivious to his personal safety, the young man had set up a machine gun and had taken on the warplanes singlehandedly. He shot down two and stayed with his machine gun until the attack ended. His commander was so impressed with his courage and resourcefulness that he recommended him for the Distinguished Service Cross, the award that is second only to the Congressional Medal of Honor. He rightly won it.

In the process, however, the army had learned something about the young hero: he was not a citizen. He was not even a legal alien. He had been born in Hungary and had gone to Canada. With no visa, no passport, no identification of any kind, he had tried to enter the United States, but American officials had turned him back at the border. The fellow subsequently had hidden in a freight car and had come into the country illegally.

No one paid attention to that when he enlisted in the peacetime army. No one bothered to look into his papers when he served in the sweltering Philippines. Certainly no one thought his citizenship too important when he grabbed that machine gun at Clark Field. Now, though, it was important. In fact, the young man wanted and needed America's citizenship more than he did its military honors.

I knew that Congress had passed a law providing for accelerated citizenship to servicemen during the war. The problem was that the statute explicitly applied only to legal immigrants. In fact, his application already had been rejected on just that basis. His cause seemed unquestionably hopeless until I dug up an obscure statute from World War I. It empowered the courts to grant citizenship to any serviceman who rendered extraordinary national service in time of war.

I drew up the necessary papers and prepared the petition for a court hearing by our staff attorney, who was most experienced in Washington's federal courts. By this time, however, the young soldier had built up such confidence in my work that he insisted that I argue his case in court. Although I was not a member of the local bar, I got special permission to appear. Of course, the judge had no problem in ordering the boy's award of citizenship. The young soldier was the hero, but his infectious gratitude left me feeling awfully good.

A lot of the rest of my Washington work left me less impressed with mankind's virtues. In the winter of 1942–43, I attended the law courses run by the army's judge advocate general (JAG) at the University of Michigan. My record was such at the JAG school that I returned to Washington as a department head: chief of the military justice division. My section's major responsibilities were in criminal matters.

There was no little of that. Much of it involved the black markets that sprang up as our troops advanced on every front. The black market in currencies was probably the most lucrative for the criminals and the most troublesome for us. Troops were forbidden to change currency in any but official exchanges. Nonetheless, wholesale operations appeared around the globe, their only business the trade in black-market money. We tried to crack down hard, but the job was almost impossible.

In the case of one airman who had made a tidy profit dealing in black-market dollars, our attempt at prosecution failed because most of the witnesses had been dispersed by troop movements. That was a common occurrence, and it thwarted more than this one prosecution. In this case, however, we were able to see some measure of justice. We had an order issued transferring the culprit to the United States. Patiently, we waited until the fellow filed his income taxes, and then we pounced. We had no trouble proving that he had failed to report income that we knew he had—never mind how he got it. He went to prison for a while and paid a fine that wiped out his ill-gotten gains.

Another problem was the scope of operations. Millions of dollars were involved in exchanges weaving through several countries. One notable case, for instance, began with a Frenchman in North Africa. Before the trail ended, it involved immense sums of dollars fed through Turkey into Nazi Germany. The radio reminded us in those days that Lucky Strike green had gone to war.

Working where I was, trying to follow that trail of money, it seemed that the Mafia had gone to war, too.

I knew that my brothers had.

"Son, take care of my little boys" had been Mama's last words, and I had done it as best I could. Only Homer had wanted to go to college, and I had paid all his expenses to Oklahoma A & M (now Oklahoma State University) while he was there. I also had helped my other two brothers and my sister Kathryn from time to time.

When the war began, my two youngest brothers went into the army. Homer was first. He trained at Camp Barclay, Texas, before his assignment to the Ninetieth Division. Earl went into the 457th Parachute Field Artillery and was stationed at Camp McCall, North Carolina. That was close enough to Washington that Mary and I took the train down to see him. We stayed at a dinky, dirty, old hotel. Earl was allowed off the post to stay with us there until we had to go back.

Meanwhile, Homer's unit went out to California for desert training. We expected that that would put him in the 1942 invasion of North Africa, but instead his division got no closer than Indiantown Gap, Pennsylvania, where it sat some time for overseas readiness. During the layover, he took the train down to visit us once in Washington; otherwise, we stayed in touch through the mails. In time, though, both brothers' letters stopped coming. When the mails resumed, Earl's letters came from New Guinea, Homer's from England. Earl's unit was preparing for MacArthur's return to the Philippines. Homer's was ready for the Normandy crossing.

At just about the same time, I got my own overseas orders. Mary moved back to Columbia, and I boarded a Liberty ship in California to sail into the Pacific. None of us knew where we were going until the ship docked. The first solid ground was Oro Bay, New Guinea. I was not there long—just a few days—but I was there long enough to run into one of the last people I expected to see in that place: my youngest brother, Earl. His paratrooper division was already there when our Liberty ship arrived. Running into each other a half-world away from our McAlester home was quite a shock for us both. Earl had another one for me. He was the one who informed me that Homer had been badly wounded at Normandy. I instantly recalled that it was Homer's birth during the First World War that had caused our mother such forebodings.

I only wished that I could have taken better care of him.

My assignment was with General MacArthur's Far East Air Service Command in Brisbane, Australia. I was there as part of the huge army buildup in preparation for the invasion and conquest of the Philippines, Okinawa, and Japan itself. In a C-47, several other officers and I flew from New Guinea to Brisbane.

It was hard to tell there was a war going on. Australia had been MacArthur's refuge since his flight from the Philippines three years earlier. Most of the men with him had never had it so good. They were about as far from Washington and its supervision as one could get and stay on this planet. Japanese forces were only a fading line on a map; they were no military threat to Brisbane. The Australians genuinely welcomed the Americans. Many soldiers took Australian wives; more took Australian girlfriends. Many lieutenant colonels and everyone of higher rank maintained private quarters, usually in fine homes. They made their own rules and had pampered enlisted men for their errands. It was small wonder that officers and men stationed in Australia relished their assignment. They stubbornly resisted transfers, including rotation back to the States.

They resisted, too, the influx of new troops into their pleasant operation. It was a sign that their war party was about to end. And it was. General MacArthur was determined to restore military discipline. For that reason, he wanted a strong JAG branch, one particularly fitted to criminal prosecution. That was the assignment that brought me to Brisbane.

I had not been there long before I realized just how important that task was. Black markets operated openly. Theft—organized, massive theft—was gaining momentum. Both officers and men had grown accustomed to treating government property as their personal possession. The intelligence units that MacArthur had ordered beefed up had no trouble at all locating offenders and gathering evidence. The judge advocate staff had the more difficult mission: winning convictions in an environment that had come to expect such misdeeds as routine, even the soldier's fair reward.

In that regard, one case was particularly critical. A certain lieutenant colonel from Kansas City was charged with numerous criminal offenses, most involving the large-scale misappropriation of government property. As I looked over the documents compiled by the investigating authorities, I was amazed. The scale and the audacity of the man's operations were almost unbelievable.

What I found even more unbelievable was the prevailing belief that we could never win a conviction against him. It was that thinking that made the case so critical. A defeat would doom any hope to restore discipline, and we would lose control of our obligations. A victory for the prosecution would be a victory for military authority. Our duty was to fight for that victory.

The preparation and trial of the case fell to me. Part of my task was to serve the formal charges on the accused. I made sure that he knew when I would be there. I could tell he was ready for me. I met him at his quarters, an excellent, neat private home. The fellow graciously introduced himself and invited me to join him for refreshments in the dining room. He directed me to a seat. As I sat down, I noticed an open letter, laid out ever so casually, before my hand. It was on the stationery of the United States Senate, and the signature at the bottom belonged to a pretty important Missouri politician: Senator Harry Truman. I later learned that my man had known the senator when both were with the Pendergast machine. I was thoroughly underwhelmed by the old boy's connections, if that was his point. I was not sure, since I did not try to read the letter. I just served him my papers. I was pretty sure that he would read them.

The trial was long and complex. Through it, the accused and

his attorneys all but sneered as we assembled and placed our evidence before the court. Slowly but deliberately it grew, until it became a large, heaving volcano of proof. My final speech before the trial officers must have ignited it. We won our conviction.

The lieutenant colonel got five years in a federal prison. Military prosecutors got the feeling that future convictions would be much easier, free-living soldiers got the word that discipline was real, and I got something, too: a Bronze Star for meritorious service.

From Brisbane, Australia, I next moved to Hollandia in northern New Guinea. MacArthur, in fact, moved the entire operation there as the American army began to rush northward through the Pacific toward Japan. The Australian cities had looked like American cities, except that their civilian quiet and calm made them look like a city from earlier in the 1900s. Hollandia looked like nothing that belonged to America or to this century. It was spectacular country with stunning hills, a splendid harbor, and a beautiful lake. Its permanent residents were semicivilized natives who spoke an Indonesian dialect. The army gave us booklets to help us converse with them, and I studied mine carefully. With some practice, I became fairly adept at it, enough so that I could visit with them in their grass houses built on stilts in the lake.

Not too far away was Mount Hagen, which the army used as a rest area. Its native population still lived in the Stone Age. They really did use stone tools, and their only dress was grass skirts. Until the world war and the United States Army reached them, their entire contact with white men or the outside world consisted of two Catholic priests from Pennsylvania. With their senior priest's help, I set out to learn their language, too. I worked up to a functioning vocabulary of around five hundred words. This so impressed the native chief, a man of many wives and forty children, that he got up a dance in my honor. The entire tribe and many of their neighbors gathered for quite a memorable festival.

The army kept up a steady flow of legal work. As MacArthur's forces grew to outnumber a good-sized city, the JAG prosecutors confronted as many criminal cases as an urban district attorney's office. Many were just about the same kind. We tried assault cases, theft cases, murder cases, and rape cases. On one occasion we hanged five men for raping a nurse.

I suppose the only difference between our work and that of civilian district attorneys was that we confronted situations and crimes that rose largely from our military circumstances. One such case involved an army doctor determined to make enough in the service to buy and equip a medical clinic when he returned home. His method was to sell alcohol to the enlisted men. In no time he came to run a complete bootlegging network that involved supply officers and other agents. What he sold was government-issue alcohol, requisitioned in massive quantities for claimed medicinal uses and peddled through his dispensary. When we caught up with him, he already had socked away forty thousand dollars from the racket. We got it all back in fines—and another five years of his life in prison.

When General MacArthur kept his promise to return to the Philippines, we went, too. We built our camp just outside Manila. This time, there was no doubt that there was a war going on. There were still pockets of Japanese resistance within a few miles of our office. We saw its victims—Americans, Japanese, and Filipinos—almost daily. I remember interviewing one of them. She was an old American lady whom the Japanese had imprisoned when they overran Luzon. She had spent nearly three and a half years in the prisoner-of-war camp that the Japanese had made of the honored religious site Santa Tomas. She described her confinement as the most forlorn experience a human could have. Rotten food, lousy clothing, inadequate medicine—all of these were a part of a day's physical tribulations. Worse, though, was the psychological strain. In particular, she never had any news of the outside world except for what the Japanese told her. That was always bad and rarely true. One day it might be that the emperor's forces had besieged San Francisco. The next might be that they had overrun California. So many times had she heard of the eminent surrender of the United States that she quit believing anything. She resigned herself to dying a prisoner of the Japanese.

And then one morning she was awakened by a lot of noise in the prison yard. Before she could get to her window, she heard an American-accented shout: "Get them damn trucks out of here!" She described it as the sweetest music she had ever heard. In the person of a salty-tongued U.S. Army sergeant, her liberator had arrived. The American army had taken the prison during the night and had killed all of the Japanese guards.

Our command outpost was almost as much of a rumor factory as the POW camp had been. Of course, most of the rumors had to do with the long-awaited and much-dreaded invasion of the Japanese homeland. The favored topic was what American unit would spearhead the assault. It was an honor that few combat veterans wanted, for whichever it was, it was sure to suffer horrendous causalities. The odds-on favorite was the Eleventh Airborne Division, the one in which my brother Earl served. After what had happened to Homer at Normandy, I did not want to see Earl part of an even bloodier invasion of Japan.

That is why the radio news one morning was such music to us. A military announcer told us that a single powerful new weapon had leveled an entire city, Hiroshima. A few days later, we heard that a second such bomb had destroyed a second city, Nagasaki. The next news—by then it was no surprise—was that Japan had given General MacArthur its complete and unconditional surrender. Unlike Hiroshima, we had expected the end to come a full year later, and we thought it would come on a tide of American blood, the blood of a million paratroopers, soldiers, marines, and sailors. Instead, it came in a dignified ceremony on the calm waters of Tokyo Bay.

I am told that President Harry Truman never once regretted his decision to spare all those lives by dropping those two bombs. I know that Earl never regretted it. Neither did I.

My brother and I both got to Japan after all, but it was as part of an occupation army, not an invasion. My unit moved into Haneda Airstrip, about halfway between Tokyo and Yokohama. It was quite a place. There was not one flyable Japanese plane in the vicinity. The whole area was a blackened desert, its landscape of bomb craters littered with twisted cactuslike steel beams, yet the airstrip itself was untouched. It looked for all the world like a civilian runway in Kansas. The contrast was a testimonial to our flyers' skills. They had destroyed the field's military value to the enemy while preserving the airstrip for their own use after the certain conquest.

Haneda was an appropriate introduction to the whole country. Everywhere it was a land of contrasts. There was the contrast between Japan's beauty and its devastation. Even amid the greatest destruction in the history of warfare, carefully nurtured trees and shrubs still bloomed. Every morning, Japan's industrious people scurried about like a huge team of ants steadily clearing away the rubble. And yet they always found unlimited time to be gracious to their conquerors, particularly those like me who bothered to learn some of their language. It seemed strange to think that such beauty-loving, hard-working, and gentle-living people had only recently made war upon my own country. Until a few weeks earlier, they were my mortal enemy. But that was true, and I saw the consequence of that truth. As soon as possible, I visited Hiroshima. It was an awesome sight, one forever seared into my memory. Looking at it, I saw what man could do and what man must avoid.

Otherwise, my chief interest in Japan was that of nearly every other serviceman there: to get out, to get back home, and to get on with my life. The American army was demobilizing fast, but barely fast enough for me. My turn finally came in February 1946. With twelve thousand other homesick boys, I boarded the USS *West Point*. In ten days, we crossed the Pacific, passed through the Panama Canal, and docked at New York City.

My feet had barely touched American soil when I ran into a McAlester boy who was returning from the European theater. It was Frank Rogers, the same Frank Rogers whom I had encountered on Connecticut Avenue in Washington four years earlier. We talked briefly about our war assignments. Frank had been in

Vienna and said he intended to go back with the service. He asked me what I was going to do.

"Why, Frank," I answered, "I think I'll go back home and run for Congress."

When I told Frank that I might run for Congress, it was not the first time that I had thought about it. That had happened in a country schoolhouse more than thirty years earlier. But 1946 was a rare opportunity. I feared as much as I hoped that it might be a once-in-a-lifetime opportunity.

I had been watching the politics of Oklahoma's Third Congressional District since I was a boy. If there was one dependable fact about its Democratic politics, it was the tremendous power of incumbency. The district had had only three congressmen since statehood. Once elected, each tended to stay in Washington about as long as he wanted. Twice incumbents had lost reelection campaigns, but both of those had been very close contests involving very prominent challengers in very unusual circumstances. Only the last of those elements seemed to involve me in 1946. This would be the first election after the greatest war in American history. Anybody could reckon that a returning veteran would have a rare opportunity against a sitting politician.

The problem was just that; anybody could calculate it. And one already had. His name was Bill Steger, and he came from a prominent Bryan County family. His father was a director of the First National Bank of Durant, the county seat. Bill had gone to Harvard and held a law degree from OU. He had begun his political career before the war when he was elected Bryan county attorney. After Pearl Harbor, he had resigned his office and enlisted in the navy. He had been discharged in October 1945 and had started running for Congress the day he got back to Oklahoma. By the time I got there, you could not drive down a highway in the Third District without seeing one of Steger's signs on some farmer's fence post, and his cards and pamphlets were in every café and crossroads store. His friends were talking up his candidacy all

*I think I'll go back home and run for Congress.* Back row, Earl, Ernest, Kathryn, and Noal Albert; front row, Homer and Carl Albert.

over the place. Part of the talk was that he was prepared to spend an unheard-of sum—fifty to sixty thousand dollars—on the race.

The incumbent was Paul Stewart, the Old Man from the Mountain. He may have been a sitting politician, but he was no sitting duck, not for Bill Steger or anyone else. Stewart published a newspaper over in the county-seat town of Antlers. For years he had been a major figure in the state senate, and in 1942 he had pulled off the feat of himself beating an incumbent congressman, Wilburn

Cartwright. Two years later, he beat him again in a campaign that left bitter enmity between the two. Paul Stewart was not going to be easy to beat. Beating him and Bill Steger both looked pretty formidable.

There were a few ready to try, however. State Senator Bayless Irby was already running, and state senators had quite a few friends in that day's courthouses. The word was that one or two others were ready to try their hands, too. Any other entries would not make much difference, though. The Democratic primary would decide the winner (not for nothing was the Third District called Little Dixie), and the primary was almost sure to be a two-stage affair. No one was likely to get a majority of the votes in a large field; thus, a runoff election would be necessary for the top two contenders. Paul Stewart and Bill Steger seemed to have those slots in their sights, maybe in their grasp.

Through the spring months, however, I went over the district. In a rickety old public bus, I rode around to the various county seats. Anybody who knew politics—anybody who knew me—could tell what I was doing. I was testing the waters. I found them muddy.

Everywhere I went I found encouraging signs. I had friends and potential supporters all over the district. The contest was still a race, yet I knew that the other horses were out of the gate ahead of me and moving on down the track. Realistically, I had no money beyond the wartime savings that Mary had hoarded carefully. Not only had I never held a public office, I had never even campaigned on my own behalf. Because of OU, Oxford, law practice, and the war, I had been away from home and the district pretty steadily since leaving high school in 1927, nearly twenty years earlier.

I talked it over with men I trusted. I counseled with my McAlester friends. I even discussed it with Congressman Stewart, whom I found to be open, honest, and respectful. Then I made my decision just two weeks before the filing period opened. I would not run for Congress. It turned out to be the best decision I ever made.

At 7:00 A.M. on Monday, April 22, the state election board in

Oklahoma City began accepting filings for public office. Bill Steger was there early on Monday. Paul Stewart filed on Tuesday, Bayless Irby on Wednesday. Two more Democrats and a lone Republican filed on Wednesday. Friday ended the week and, at five o'clock, the filing period. That afternoon, I was pretty depressed. A chance had come to realize the boyhood dream that literally had carried me around the globe. In missing this one, I might well be missing the only one I would ever have. Bill Steger was five years younger than I, and if he took that seat from Paul Stewart, he might keep it for an awfully long time. Even if he did not do it in 1946, he would be set to move upon any opportune vacancy.

That is why I was pretty miserable on that Friday afternoon in 1946. I walked up and down the McAlester streets most of the day. Only occasionally did I stop by the apartment or my law office. At one of those stops, the phone rang. It was Truman Bennet, our county superintendent of schools and one of my best friends. I had never heard him so excited. Paul Stewart had been trying to get hold of me, Truman said. Unable to find me, the congressman finally had called him. He wanted me to know that he had come down with some worsening heart pains—no one even knew he had a problem—and had decided to withdraw from the race. He was so appreciative that I had chosen not to run against him that he wanted me to know.

The next sound I remember was Truman Bennet's car horn on the street outside. I ran through the door, jumped in the car, and we took off for Oklahoma City. If there was a bump, we did not notice it. If there was a speed limit, we did not heed it. At twenty-five minutes past four o'clock, we ran into the office of the state election board and I filled out some papers. I handed them to a weary clerk, one too tired to notice my face. Surely no one had ever worn a bigger smile at the exact moment that he officially became a candidate for the United States House of Representatives. I would not have traded that filing form for any oil well, ranch, farm, or bank in the whole state of Oklahoma.

I was in the race but I was still far behind, and it was only two months until the primary election. Instinctively, I decided to spend the first of those organizing. In the second, I would take the stump.

Folks have always taken their politics seriously in Oklahoma's Third District. The saying was, even then, that everything was political in the district, everything except politics. That was personal.

My organization was certainly personal. Like every other Oklahoma candidate, I had no regular party mechanism to turn to. What I did have was a network of friends, most dating to my high school or college days. Once I announced my candidacy, it seemed that they came out of every valley and from behind every hill in the district. This one thought he could help over in Latimer County. That one had a lot of kin down in Pushmataha County. Here was one who had some influence back in LeFlore County.

Money? That was personal, too. Mary cashed in our $9,000 worth of War Bonds and thereby became my major contributor. Some of my Bug Tussle playmates threw in. Bill Anderson, my best friend since before I had shoes, came up with $500. J. G. Puterbaugh, one of the coal industry's prestatehood pioneers, pitched in $1,500. Julian Rothbaum, whose father had been a merchant among the miners at Hartshorne, put in $1,000—the first of many generous contributions during my career. Norman Futor, a friend from OU and still a soldier in the army, added another $500. That was about it. Any other support we hoped to get by passing a hat at my speakings.

By June, I was doing those speakings at the rate of five to ten a day. Wherever two or three were gathered, there I tried to be also. At first, I did it alone. Driving over the district, I made every political rally my organizers could get up. In between, my eyes searched for groups to address. I remember one morning, about seven o'clock, driving through the little hamlet of Clayton on my way to a county rally. Nine old men were hunkered down on the sidewalk, whittling and spitting. I pulled up, hopped out, and handed them my cards with my solemn picture and slogan: "From a Cabin in the Cotton to Congress." I stayed to make a little talk.

For ten minutes, I laid some fiery championship oratory before that audience on a sidewalk in a village.

Pretty soon, I got some campaign help in the form of a three-piece string band and a seventeen-year-old redheaded girl singer. In the hot, early days of summer, we would pull into some village like Howe or Fox or Tom and set up under a shade tree. The little girl blasted out something like "Sioux City Sue" or "Tumbling Tumbleweeds." After her singing attracted a crowd, I would make my speech, work the crowd with handshakes and cards, and move on to the next stop.

If we passed a farmer out in his fields, I always tried to stop. I would talk a bit about his crops and a lot about his price supports and rural electricity. I promised to help him keep the first and get the second. I would always mention, too, that I was from a cabin in the cotton. Usually, I left a friend ready to help send me to Congress.

When we hit a good-sized town, I would walk up and down every street, go in and out of every store, and shake every hand I found. Back in the car, back on the road, all over the district, I met the voters where I found them.

I recall driving over those back roads down by the Red River, not quite sure where I was. Finally, I came across a little store and saw three or four men standing around outside. I rolled up, handed them my cards, and asked for their support. One of them looked at the card, looked at me, and asked, "Congress? Is that for the state?"

"No, sir," I said. "It's for the United States House of Representatives. In Washington," I thought to add.

He put my card down, looked me over again, then said to his friends, "I don't think he can beat Sam Rayburn, do you?"

Sure enough, I had wandered across the river into Texas—just one of the places where no one could beat the great Mr. Sam.

But Sam Rayburn I did not have to beat. My friends and I figured all along that we could not overtake Bill Steger. Our hope was to place second, force a runoff, and use the extra time to catch him. To do that, my greatest asset was my energy, a passionate, driving energy fueled by a life's ambition. My greatest weapon was my speaking.

All the skills that I had worked to acquire and sharpen from McAlester High School to the Oxford Union went into stump speeches delivered all over southeastern Oklahoma. In most of them, I was careful to tie myself to the New Deal's record, a record of changing "soup lines into production lines and relief rolls into payrolls." Usually, too, I would talk about the world war, about what I had seen in the Pacific graveyards and at Hiroshima, about America's new and awesome responsibilities.

A supporter later told me about one of those speakings. He had brought along a full-blooded Choctaw, a poorly educated but quite respected fellow, one whose judgment influenced a lot of votes in the Indian community. The story was that when I stood up to speak, the Indian noted my slight stature and mumbled, "Don't know. Congress takes a *big* man." But he listened to my speech and smiled broadly when I finished. "What do you think now?" my man asked him. "I think the little owl has a big hoot."

I may have never gotten a better evaluation in my life; certainly I got no more important one. By July 2, Election Day, I had given enough speeches, met enough voters, passed out enough cards, and shaken enough hands to pass every Democratic contender save one. Bill Steger, as predicted, led the pack. Carl Albert, as I had dared to hope, was second, twenty-seven hundred votes back, headed for a runoff, and coming up fast.

Three terribly hot weeks separated the first and second primaries. Looking over the results of the first, it seemed to me that one county, Carter, was the key to the election. It was the district's most populous county, and Steger had run up a big total there. If I could cut into that significantly while making lesser gains elsewhere, I could catch and pass him. So I concentrated everything I had left on Carter County and its seat, Ardmore. I found there an unexpected but important ally: Lloyd Noble, the Republican millionaire whom I had met when I was at the university. Mr. Noble offered to pay the cost of all of my newspaper and radio advertising in the county. The total was only seven hundred dollars, but it was seven hundred dollars that I did not have and could not afford to miss.

The runoff results were close enough that the difference could be credited to that seven hundred dollars, or, for that matter, almost anything. The earliest counts gave me a 95-vote lead. The official tabulation put the margin at 259. Steger, of course demanded a recount, but that only drove the margin up to the final official figure: 27,574 to 27,244—a 330-vote majority. I was as happy as if it had been by a million.

The general election was but a formality. John Fuller had been the lone Republican to want the hopeless honor of carrying the GOP banner through Little Dixie. John was a longtime friend of mine. In fact, his wife was my distant cousin. When I won the Democratic nomination, John gave me a one-hundred-dollar campaign contribution and withdrew from the race. The Republican Central Committee found a willing substitute, Eleanor Watson. She and they knew how hopeless was the cause. Like most Democratic nominees, I carried the district by a lopsided margin of six to one. Winning every single precinct, though, was pretty special. To tell the truth, I would have been as happy if it had been by one.

Just after the general election, Mary and I got ready to move to Washington. We bought a new car (the one new car available in town) and put nearly everything we had in the trunk and back seat of the two-door Pontiac. Then we pointed the car east and started driving.

In 1946 there was not one mile of four-lane highway between Oklahoma and Washington. So we drove on narrow, two-lane pavement except in parts of Tennessee and West Virginia, where the route was a gravel pathway through the mountains. In 1946 there was not a single bypass along the way, so we drove through every city, town, and village. In 1946 it took me three hard days' driving to get to Washington and the Congress.

Or thirty-eight years, depending on how you look at it.

# CHAPTER FIVE

# *The House Habit*

$A$fter such a long time driving, I was in a hurry to get to Congress. I was in so much of a hurry, in fact, that when Mary and I drove that road-weary Pontiac into the capital we did not as yet even have a place to live. Luckily, a Washington friend from our World War II days arranged for us to sublet a suite at the Jefferson Hotel. With some awfully cheap furniture that we got from a manufacturer in Guthrie, Oklahoma— he asked no down payment and gave us unlimited time to pay— we set up housekeeping.

The new Congress had not even convened, but I could not wait to get to the Capitol. As quickly as we could, Mary and I inspected the office that I would occupy as the United States representative from the Third Congressional District of Oklahoma. It was a letdown.

The Republican victory of November, the first since the start of the Depression, made me a freshman congressman of the minority party. As such, I was about at the bottom of the list for office assignments. So I started in Room 452 of the Old House Office Building in a space vacated when Albert Cole, a Kansas Republican, moved to better quarters. It would not have taken much to have been better than what he left for me. Every chair needed new upholstery. The carpet was threadbare. The blinds did not work. There was no desk adequate for a congressman, even a freshman minority congressman. In fact, there was no usable desk or file cabinets for his secretary. For a time, I would have to operate the office out of cardboard boxes and manila envelopes. Still, I was a congressman and I did have a place to hang my hat. Besides, as Mary said, I might someday be able to do better.

That day looked to be pretty far off, though. I might have been a freshman, but I knew that a congressman's entire career was launched down the path of his committee assignments. It was in the committee rooms that a congressman's work was done and measured. It was his assignment to the right committee that led most directly to a member's influence within the House and tangible rewards for his grateful district. Knowing that, I had aimed high. The ink was barely dry on my election certificate when I wrote the Democrats' committee on committees with my preferences. Each newcomer was allowed to list three choices. My three, in order, were rules, appropriations, and ways and means. These were the big three, the most powerful, the most prestigious committees in the House of Representatives. They were also the most difficult to land. Seasoned congressmen of several terms' outstanding service always sought assignment to each. Even they were not often successful.

I did not have a chance. Even when I lowered my sights appreciably (by offering to serve on the Public Works Committee), my case was hopeless. Years of accumulated grievances against the New Deal and the Democratic party had festered through the world war. President Roosevelt's death had removed the most articulate champion we had. Harry Truman, as yet unappreciated, had assumed FDR's office but neither his popularity nor his leadership. His first rocky months in office were bedeviled by labor strikes, consumer frustration, and business hostility. All of this the Republican party had played upon with its 1946 slogan of artful simplicity. "Had enough?" the GOP had asked. And the voters had answered, sending fifty-five veteran Democratic congressmen (and twelve senators) packing and giving the Republicans control of both houses of Congress.

The unaccustomed Republican majority took over every committee, leaving few slots for even veteran Democrats. A newcomer had some pretty poor pickings left, and mine were about the poorest of all. Despite the GOP's national landslide, Oklahoma sent three other freshmen Democrats (Glen Johnson, Toby Morris, and Preston Peden) with me to Washington. Each represented a district less securely Democratic than mine. For that reason, our party's leadership was more interested in bolstering their reelection chances with attractive assignments. By the time they got to

The Oklahoma congressional delegation of 1947–49: Toby Morris, Glen Johnson, Mike Monroney, Bill Stigler, Preston Peden, George Schwabe, Ross Rizley, and Carl Albert.

me, all the leaders could offer was the unrequested House Committee on the Post Office and Civil Service. In all the later years when I would have a voice in committee assignments for hundreds of freshmen members, not once did I know of one who sought post office and civil service.

Still, I accepted my assignment: maybe someday I might do better there, too. In fact, I was grateful enough that I was ready to thank our party's House spokesman, the great Sam Rayburn. Speaker after 1940, Mr. Rayburn would have to serve as minority leader in the Republican-controlled House. I visited his office, only to encounter his secretary since 1919, the formidable Alla Clary. Miss Clary glanced over my youthful appearance and slight stature. Coolly she informed me that Mr. Rayburn did not have time to talk with pages.

However inauspicious those first few days may have been, I was thrilled beyond words on January 3, 1947. It was my first official day as a congressman. There was another first on that day, too. Through the new medium of television, millions of Americans were watching the House convene. With befitting solemnity, the clerk of the House began calling the alphabetical roll of members. The first called, Thomas Abernathy of Mississippi, did not respond. The second was Carl Albert of Oklahoma. "Here," I answered. It was the sweetest word in the English language.

Behind that response was my entire life's experience. Sitting on the House floor, looking up at the massive Speaker's dais, I remembered one that went all the way back to Bug Tussle, back to the eighth grade and Mr. Craighead's little talks about a man who had once stood right there. Speaker Champ Clark, my teacher had told us, loved the House of Representatives. It was from that very spot that Champ Clark had rejected the Missouri governor's offer of an appointment to fill the unexpired term of a dead United States senator. That was where Champ Clark had read his telegraphed answer. "There is a House habit and a Senate habit," he had said, "and I have got the House habit so bad that I can never get out of it."

I wanted to have the House habit, and another of Mr. Craig-

Carl Albert at a freshman congressman.

head's little talks told me how to get it. He had told us of Champ Clark's observation that a man has to learn to be a congressman, just as he must learn to be a farmer or a carpenter or a lawyer or anything else. If his constituents were "to select a man of good sense, good habits, and perfect integrity, young enough to learn," and keep returning him to the House, he and they would both profit. For as he learns his job, as a congressman acquires the House habit, "such a man grows into power and high position as surely as the sparks fly upward." For myself, I was ready to keep my end of that bargain. The spark glowed within me to learn the House habit. Maybe someday, that spark would carry me upward, too.

For many days, though, it carried me only between Capitol Hill and the little apartment at the Jefferson Hotel. After just a few of them, I wrote myself a letter dated February 2, 1947, the last day of my first month in Congress.

Looking over that letter now, I see it as the testament of another dream. Just as I had earlier dreamed of winning oratorical contests, traveling to Europe, capturing a Rhodes scholarship, or going to Congress, I dreamed again, this time of what I hoped to accomplish there. It had to be a long letter, for, as always, I dreamed big, but then I had never known a little dream to carry anyone anywhere.

Only months before I wrote, my country and the world had been at war. I had stood in the black deserts that that war had made of Japan's cities. And so I prayed earnestly that "God give me the power and the resolution to work daily as long as I am in Congress for world peace." For me, that path was illumined by the blunders that I saw following the First World War. I believed that the path to peace lay in an active international organization, the new United Nations, which must not be allowed to go the way of Woodrow Wilson's old League of Nations. America could not afford to ignore its responsibilities once more, nor must it ever again lack "military preparedness equal to that of any potential hostile power on earth." The old idea of a Fortress America had died at Pearl Harbor; its tombstone was a mushroom cloud. In a dangerous world of armed might, "we must unite with other free nations to insure the continuation of both their freedom and ours."

The freedom that we were defending also had to be enlarged. Already I believed that "no baby should be born into this land to drag a chain only because of the race or color which God gave it." At the time, I could only hope that "my career in Congress is long and that I will have the ability and political and personal courage to make a contribution to the civil rights of all people."

One right that I wanted all people to share was the right to a quality education. My own life bore witness to its power, and it left me persuaded that "this tommy rot about the education of our children being the sole responsibility of local communities, however poor, is disgraceful. There is nothing so sinister about educating our children that would tarnish our national government by getting into it."

Because my state was poor and my district poorer, federal aid was no demon; it was a deliverer. Directed to their schools, Washington's dollars could deliver my people from ignorance. Federal dams could save their farms from floods, reclaim their soils from erosion, and ease their toil with electricity. Sensible farm programs could bring prosperity to the poor children of pioneer parents, the rural folk who were both my neighbors and my constituents. Those townsfolk who made their living from oil and gas production needed a watchdog for their interests. Those with special needs—Indians with unsettled claims, veterans with ruined lives, employees of my hometown's naval ammunition depot, and all the rest—deserved an attentive champion in Washington.

There was pride in that letter of February 1947. "After all," I wrote, I was living "the fulfillment of a life-long dream." But there was humility, too. I closed it with these earnest words: "As much as I like my job I would not want it unless I could help my people. I hope, when I am through, it will be said that I represented them well and that I served my country as a congressman in my day and generation to a best of my ability."

In 1947, I was just a freshman congressman of the minority

party, the lowest-ranking member of the most obscure committee in the entire Congress. Never again would I find the time or the compulsion to write out my dreams. I was too busy making them come true.

It is unfortunate that Americans who know next to nothing about any other congressional session can recognize readily the Congress that I entered in 1947. It was the famous Do-Nothing Eigh-

*Truman had a special place for me.* President Truman and Democratic congressional leaders: Senator Mike Mansfield, Congressman Carl Albert, Speaker Sam Rayburn, Senator Carl Hayden, and House Majority Leader John W. McCormack.

*I do remember first knowing the two future presidents.* John Kennedy is in the third row from the back on the right side, five seats in from the center aisle; Carl Albert, two seats to his left; Richard Nixon, second row from the back in the fifth seat in from the center, on the opposite side of the aisle. The photograph, taken in 1947, is of military veterans serving in Congress.

tieth Congress. Harry Truman appended the nickname when he made the Republican-controlled legislature his election foil in 1948, and the name stuck. The tactic certainly served Truman well: his presidential campaign in '48 remains the miracle election. The memorable adjective, however, obscures the fact that this was a Congress of remarkable figures and remarkable achievements.

First elected with me to the House side of the Do-Nothing Congress was a group of ninety-two men and women who remained my friends for years. They included two future presidents, John F. Kennedy and Richard M. Nixon. The latter would also serve as vice-president under Dwight Eisenhower. In addition, nine would serve in the United States Senate, and five went on to become state governors. Outside elective politics, another five became judges, seven became high officials in the executive branch, and two became American ambassadors. In 1971, when I was first elected Speaker, eight of the original members of the Class of the Eightieth Congress still served with me in the House. No longer green freshmen, five then were chairmen of House committees or major subcommittees.

I cannot claim to have been able to foretell their futures at the time, but I do remember first knowing the two future presidents. I met them both on my very first day in the House. I was standing on the floor when Richard Nixon came up, introduced himself as Dick Nixon, and asked me about that college oratorical contest on the Constitution of nearly twenty years earlier. He grinned when he told me of his own quick elimination in a later contest. While we both served in the House until Nixon went to the Senate in 1950, we got along quite well, often finding ourselves in agreement on bipartisan matters of foreign policy.

Later that same day, John Kennedy (he called himself Jack) introduced himself to me. He asked if I was the new Oklahoma congressman who had been a Rhodes scholar in the 1930s. He seemed pleased to know me, and he mentioned that he had often visited Oxford while his father was our ambassador to Great Britain. Before Kennedy, too, moved on to the Senate on his way to the

White House, we often conferred as House members, particularly about the knotty issue of labor-law reform.

On that same day, I met another future president, though not a freshman congressman. Lyndon Johnson had come to the House in the mid-1930s as a supporter of Franklin Roosevelt and had become a protégé of Sam Rayburn. Mike Monroney, Oklahoma City's veteran congressman, introduced us in the Democratic cloakroom. I soon learned that it was Johnson's favorite habitat. I never spoke with him there without being impressed by his burning political ambitions. Never did I sense that he had, or wanted to have, a House habit. I already sensed that the Senate's much different habit was more fitted to Lyndon Johnson's ways.

Because the Republicans were the majority, they provided the formal House leadership of the Eightieth Congress. Joe Martin, a Massachusetts representative since 1924 and the Republican floor leader since 1939, won pro forma election as Speaker over our Sam Rayburn, who thereupon became the minority leader. Quite conservative by temperament—Martin had opposed most of Roosevelt's New Deal and would marshal his Republican forces to bury much of Truman's Fair Deal—the new Speaker proved to be both affable and effective. In the Speaker's role, he put aside most of his partisanship to work well with the Democratic leaders. His oft-repeated observation that "you've got to follow in order to lead" testified to his awareness that there were many political facts that transcended partisan maneuverings.

Never was that clearer, or more important, than in the critical field of foreign policy. Hitler's defeat had removed the basis of our alliance with Soviet Russia. Stalin's brutal installation of puppet regimes in Central and Eastern Europe had removed hope for a postwar partnership. Even as we freshmen congressmen were learning our way around Washington, events were transpiring overseas that would permanently alter America's way in the world. In February 1947, the nearly bankrupt British told our government that they could no longer afford to support the Greek government's civil war against Red insurgents. The British were leaving Greece, Turkey—the entire eastern Mediterranean—a vacuum, a vacuum that seemed doomed to be filled by the Soviets. In that same grim winter, the second after World War II, 125 million Europeans remained malnourished. National Communist parties in France and elsewhere were ready to feast on their misery. All that blocked their way was Harry Truman, the leaders of Congress, and the members who had learned too well the costs of isolation and appeasement.

In a breathtakingly short period, Harry Truman and the Eightieth Congress checked the threat of Stalinist advance and laid the foundation for a generation of American diplomacy. First was the Greek-Turk loan, $350 million that preserved the independence of Greece and Turkey and kept the Mediterranean from becoming a Russian lake. Next was the European Recovery Program (the Marshall Plan), $13.5 billion that honored Secretary of State George C. Marshall and drowned the Communist threat in a flood of new prosperity. In between was the epoch-making Truman Doctrine. Its declaration that it would be "the policy of the United States to support free peoples who are resisting attempted subjugation by armed minorities or outside pressure" reversed sixteen decades of American isolation and defined our mission as protector of the Free World.

Thus, in the spring of 1947, in my first months of Congress, America shouldered the burdens of global leadership that it had shunned after the First World War. President Truman pointed the way. Speaker Martin and Sam Rayburn led the Congress. Jack Kennedy, Lyndon Johnson, Dick Nixon, two-thirds of both houses, and I marched along. I did because the Second World War had taught me that those commitments represented our best chance for peace in a hostile world. Every president since Truman has extended those commitments and believed in that policy. Not one thing has happened since to cause me to doubt it, either.

Ours was, then, a do-something Congress. Off the stump, Harry Truman agreed. Whatever his campaign protestations, President Truman appreciated the remarkably bipartisan statesmanship of our foreign policy. I certainly appreciated him. Of the six presidents with whom I served, Truman has a special place for me. Of unexceptional looks, his was an exceptional character. Everyone, Joe Stalin included, could measure it when he announced the Truman Doctrine and won from Congress Greek-Turk and Marshall Plan aid. Stalin and the world saw it, too, when Harry Truman later preserved Berlin's independence by airlift, fortified the United Nations in Korea, and served our Constitution by dismissing General Douglas MacArthur. The man had steel in his blood.

I recall the first time that I met him. Early in my first year in Congress, George Smathers got up a group of us new congressmen and went down to the White House. It was George's idea, so he laid out some issues that he thought would help the president with the next election. When George finished, Harry Truman pointed to a globe that he had sitting on his desk and said, "I'm not interested in forty-eight. I'm interested in that little globe. I'm going to do what I can to preserve it." I barely held back the tears to choke out, "Mr. President, I will do what I can to help you."

A very little thing that I could do happened in 1948. Harry Truman was running what everyone knew was a hopeless race to keep his job. The Republican nominee, Tom Dewey, was ready to preside over his funeral. Two renegade Democrats, Strom Thurmond of the Dixiecrat right wing and Henry Wallace of the Progressive left wing, were going to be the pallbearers. Begrudgingly nominated by a demoralized party, Truman did not have much going for him.

Not much except courage, tenacity, conviction, and a plain-spokenness that just made sense. That is all he had to offer, and offer it he did in his famous whistle-stop campaign tour of 1948. I joined the tour in Bonham, Texas, Sam Rayburn's hometown. Oklahoma's governor, Roy Turner; our Senate nominee, Robert S. Kerr; and I were the ones who rode with the president into Oklahoma. We each made a little talk at every stop on the line, but Harry Truman always had the last—and the best—words. The crowds got steadily larger and steadily warmer, and it began to dawn on us that the news of Mr. Truman's death (like Mark

Twain's) was greatly exaggerated. If Harry Truman could keep getting his message out, he could win this thing.

At least he could win it if he could get his train out of the station. It ran out of money in Oklahoma City. We each got on the phone and found Sooners who threw in enough to get the train out of Oklahoma City and down into Little Dixie, my part of the state. There, the crowds got even more enthusiastic. Fortified, Truman carried the tour across the nation. Tom Dewey ended up going to a funeral, all right, and Harry Truman went back to the White House.

My initial assignment to the Post Office Committee had one great virtue. The committee's workload was so light and my other duties were so inconsequential that I had plenty of time to educate myself. My school was the House chamber. It is where I learned how to be a congressman.

In my first term, I do not believe that I missed a single day of the House's proceedings. I was there when the chaplain opened the day's work with prayer. I was there when the Speaker's gavel sounded adjournment. In between, I stayed on the floor, because that is where I had wanted to be all my life.

Of course, every day hundreds of tourists pass through the House galleries, there to watch their representatives work for them. My initial impression was not much different from those of tourists: the chamber is a lovely sight. Measuring 139 feet by 92, the room seems to enclose much of the majesty of American history. I never entered it (not on my first day, nor on my last, nor in the thirty years in between) without feeling slightly awed. It is part of the House habit that I acquired instantly and never lost.

Sitting on the floor of that magnificent chamber gave me a daily education in the incredibly complex proceedings of the House. Because of its larger size and subsequent greater need for organizational formality than the Senate's, the House of Representatives works with a unique sense of tradition and incredibly complex rules. Codified, the rules of the House run to well over ten thousand, seemingly to match any past situation or imaginable future circumstance with a formal rule. Like the tourists, I was dumb-founded early on by the arcane exchanges between the members and the presiding officer. "I have an amendment on the desk." "Third reading. A motion to recommit is laid upon the table." "Without objection, it is so ordered." The tourists were not alone: to a freshman member, too, it sometimes seemed like a foreign language.

But I was in the House to learn its habit and I came swiftly to love its traditions, its procedures, and its language. It took me a while to master them—after about two years I had a firm working knowledge—but it did not take even a day to fall in love with them. They are the living, breathing anatomy of the House as an institution. Like the English common law, the House rules have grown from the soil of tradition.

Because of my speech training, I expected to hear some great oratory in the House. I quickly learned, though, that speech making was a much overrated part of a congressman's job. Men of great reputation sometimes never spoke on the floor. Illinois' Tom O'Brien was one. Representative of Chicago's massive Democratic machine, O'Brien always sat languidly on the floor or leaned against the back rail. I do not recall once hearing him address the House, and yet every member knew that Tom O'Brien's judgment could pass or could doom virtually any bill. That I learned from talking with my new colleagues. They could tell you which were the eagles and which were the sparrows.

I learned something else from them, too: how very impressive the membership was. Denigrating Congress long has been one of America's favorite sports. I learned that there were some bigots and fakers among the members and a few show horses, too, but most congressmen were truly workhorses. Quiet, unassuming, dedicated members who were unsung by the press and unknown to the average citizen—these were the great majority. To my awe of the House's chamber and my love for its traditions, I quickly added respect for its membership.

However, the most important thing that I learned in those early days of sitting attentively on the floor was that House members were individuals. I heard every speech delivered. I watched every vote cast. I talked with every group and every member I met. Within three months, I knew the name and face of every one of the 435 members. I knew that this one came from a district that usually elected the opposition and feared losing his seat. I knew that that one followed his committee chairman's every lead. I knew that this one needed union votes to keep his job. I knew that that one was so secure that he could vote his convictions on anything, and I knew what those convictions were. My first session was not halfway through before I could tell how 80 percent of them were going to vote on any question.

And I knew that the Democratic leadership needed to know just that.

Nothing could have prepared me for the great legislators I found serving as the Democratic leadership. For my first fifteen years (half of my total service), John McCormack and Sam Rayburn directed the House Democrats. Except for the brief interlude of Republican majorities after 1946 and Dwight Eisenhower's 1952 landslide, they directed the House of Representatives as well, John McCormack as majority leader and Sam Rayburn as Speaker. Neither I nor the Democrats nor the nation had ever seen such a team.

Chosen by the members of the majority party, the majority leader technically is not an officer of the House but of his political party. Nonetheless, it is inconceivable that the House could function without him. Working closely with committee chairmen, he helps define each session's legislative program. Through the year, he directs the House calendar. Chief spokesman for his party, he often closes debates on major bills. As his party's leader, he also works to assemble winning majorities behind those bills deemed important to the party. John McCormack did all those things, all for a long time, all with distinction.

Born in 1891 to a builder in Boston's Irish ghetto, John left school in 1904 to support the family when his father died. Working long hours at unskilled jobs, he went to school at night until he entered the Massachusetts bar when he was only twenty-one. A born politician, he served in the state constitutional convention in 1917 and went to the state legislature in 1920 as a Democrat, a progressive Democrat. For another fifty years, he championed liberal reforms for state and nation, though he shunned the term *liberal* in favor of the more old-fashioned term *progressive*.

In 1928, John went to Congress, where he made friends with Sam Rayburn and impressed Speaker John Nance Garner. A diligent worker in committees, John won a seat on the Ways and Means Committee in 1933 and served to bring FDR's New Deal alive. Three years later, he delivered vital New England votes for Sam Rayburn's successful bid for the majority leadership. In 1940, when Sam Rayburn became Speaker, John McCormack became majority leader.

Of formidable intellect and equipped with sharp analytical skills, he was long our party's best debater in Congress. Sam Rayburn told me more than once that he would rank John second only to Alben Barkley as a debater in the fifty years of his own service. In one session alone I saw him debate powerfully, knowledgeably, and effectively more than two hundred separate bills. His tall, gaunt figure striding the floor, his long finger jamming out his points, he was for decades the Democrats' most forceful champion and the Republicans' most feared foe.

As a statesman, John had a remarkably national orientation. Representing an urban district, he cared deeply about rural America. Time after time, he cast New England's only affirmative vote for farm legislation. Thoroughly northern and thoroughly unprejudiced, he earned the respect of southerners for his fairness and willingness to compromise. In 1944, 1952, and 1956, the Democratic party put him in charge of writing the platform of the national convention. Each time, he engineered civil-rights planks that kept the party's northern and southern wings united. Only in 1948, when he was not in that position, did the party split open in the Dixiecrat revolt.

As a man, John was a true gentleman. Seldom was he ever heard to speak critically of a colleague. He once said of Claire Hoffman, a most contemptible member, that he held him in minimal high regard. As a boy, John McCormack had sworn an oath of abstinence to his mother, and he not once tasted liquor in his life. His devotion to his beloved wife was legendary. Whatever else he was doing, John had dinner with her every night of their long married life. When Harriet McCormack finally died in a hospital room, John McCormack occupied the bed next to hers.

As a freshman congressman, I first met John McCormack as my party's whip. Thereafter, I was proud to call him my friend. Sam Rayburn became my friend, too, but Mr. Rayburn (no one of my generation called him anything but that or Mr. Sam) became far more than my friend. In my last letter to him, written after he had gone home to Bonham, Texas, to die, I wrote the only words that can express my feelings for him. "I love the Speaker as I have loved no man in my lifetime except my own father. He is the greatest man I ever knew."

I still remember the first time I ever saw him. He was giving a rousing Democratic campaign speech from a railroad car over in Denison, Texas, back in the 1920s. Elected to the House in 1912, he was already a famous congressman, and his fame and contributions grew steadily. His fingerprints were on the legislation that transformed American life; some of it had transformed my own. Until I was fifteen, I studied by a coal-oil lamp. More than any other man, it was Sam Rayburn who put electric lights and running water in the homes of Americans like me with the bills he pushed through Congress in the thirties.

He represented Texas's Fourth Congressional District, the one lying just across the Red River from Oklahoma's Third. I almost regarded him as my own congressman. My mother and her father were born in that district, and I had dozens of relatives still living there. One of Mr. Rayburn's brothers lived for a while in my own district. His home in Bonham was only six miles from the Oklahoma border.

I had made it a point to visit Mr. Rayburn in Bonham as soon as I had won my first primary. During the next few years, I returned often. We took to fishing together once in a while—Mr. Rayburn

*I first met John McCormack as my party's whip.*

*I love the Speaker as I have loved no man in my lifetime except my own father.*
Carl Albert with Sam Rayburn.

used to say that he would rather catch a two-inch fish than spend
two days playing golf—in Lake Texoma, which lapped across our
districts' lines. He bought his alfalfa down in Yuba, in my district,
and we would talk for hours, leaning against a truck.

Physically, he reminded me very much of my father. Both men
were about the same height, though Mr. Rayburn was a bit stock-
ier. Like my father, he tended to look you straight in the eye; like
him, too, he tended to talk very straight as well. Both men could
joke, but both took the world seriously.

Mr. Rayburn's entire life was the House of Representatives. Most people did not know that he had been married for a few months in the 1920s. His real wife was the House, his family its members. In just under fifty years of congressional service, he left the United States only once: to inspect the Panama Canal. Otherwise, his years revolved around Washington and Bonham, the twin foci of his life as a complete congressman.

No one who met him could escape the force of his character. Many disputed his politics; none doubted his integrity. He absolutely could not tolerate lying, even of the little white variety. For decades he was known as Mr. Democrat, yet his fairness toward the Republicans and his respect for their leaders was legendary. Hardly a single member of either party could not recount at least one kindness from his hands. The veterans could count dozens. We junior Democrats quickly learned of his kindness, indeed, his fondness. Particularly as he aged (he celebrated his sixty-third birthday on my fourth day in Congress), Sam Rayburn kept his eye out for promising junior Democrats. He once explained that young men kept him young watching their growth, and he was always looking for young Democrats who had the capacity to love the institution of the House of Representatives. He was especially interested in finding promising junior congressmen from his own part of the country. Sam Rayburn loved the people with honest dirt under their fingernails. The men and women who toiled in the cotton patches, cornfields, and peanut rows of the southwest and the Red River valley—these were the ones he called the real people. He looked unblinkingly for one who might represent them as well and as powerfully as he did.

I suppose that that is what first drew his attention to me. He knew me from our early talks, and I know that he respected my family's roots in the soil and my education at Oxford, both about equally. I nearly burst my buttons with pride when a friend told me how Mr. Rayburn had bragged on my maiden speech in Congress. It was a short defense of the working folks threatened by the viciously antilabor Hartley bill. People told me that Mr. Rayburn had pronounced it one of the best speeches he had ever heard by a freshman member.

But more than anything else, what drew Mr. Rayburn was my obvious enthrallment with Congress. Sitting on the floor day after day, listening to every speech delivered, watching every vote cast, talking with every member I could corner—these things I did not from ambition but out of love for the House. Sam Rayburn liked me for what I did; he liked me more for why I did it.

After a while, he would sometimes call me to the Speaker's dais and ask me how I expected a vote would come out. I would tell him, and I would usually be right, maybe within a half-dozen votes of the actual count. When he could not identify a particular congressman, he learned that he could ask me. I knew each one. Usually I could tell him what he wanted to know about the member. Generally, I could predict and explain the fellow's position on an upcoming vote.

Growing from my hunger for the House habit, it was these qualities, not the accident of geography, that first gained me entrée into Mr. Rayburn's inner circle. The occasion was the prize most cherished by every member, freshman and veteran alike: an invitation to join him at the Board of Education.

The Board of Education was an unofficial but not invisible institution of the House. At the end of each day's session, Mr. Rayburn liked to invite a select group of friends to join him to talk over politics and "strike a blow for liberty," as he and his friend Harry Truman called the evening's libations. When Sam Rayburn invited me to join the group, I knew that I was on my way.

The board met in Room H-118 in a place small (twelve by twenty feet) by Capitol standards. Once a House committee room, for decades it had been assigned to the Speaker for his own use. Over the years, Mr. Rayburn had furnished it to his personal tastes. An old Persian carpet covered the floor; framed political cartoons, signed photographs, and a few portraits covered the walls. Eight chairs, some straight backed, most overstuffed in leather, were scattered around Mr. Rayburn's big desk. A long black leather couch lined one wall. It was noted as the place where Harry Truman was sitting when the White House summoned him to give him the news that Franklin Roosevelt was dead and he was president.

In my first term, Mr. Rayburn invited me frequently; thereafter, I had a standing invitation. The usual group included Texans (Lyndon Johnson, Homer Thornberry, Frank Ikard, and the like), some of Mr. Rayburn's oldest friends (typically Gene Cox, Clinton Anderson, John McCormack, and Lew Deschler, the House parliamentarian), and a select group of promising youngsters (maybe Hale Boggs, Henry Jackson, Wilbur Mills, and usually Richard Bolling). Over drinks, we would talk some legislative business and listen to Mr. Rayburn's stories of Texas and of Congress. He listened, too, constantly judging men's characters and measuring the shifting moods of the House. Sam Rayburn consumed information, and the information that he gained in those evening sessions kept him in touch with the House. About seven o'clock, we would break up, almost always to Mr. Rayburn's last words, "Let me know if you hear anything."

The knowledge that Mr. Rayburn collected plus the character that he displayed gave him power far beyond a Speaker's institutional authority. Actually, the revolt against czar Joe Cannon's rules back in 1910 had stripped the Speakership of most of its formal authority. The power that Sam Rayburn exercised over the House was the power of his being Sam Rayburn. No Speaker of this century had had such respect. None had known better the mood of the chamber, and none had accumulated such a bankroll of personal favors granted and intimate kindnesses extended. It was a blessing to know him. It was a privilege to serve with him. It was my great good fortune to have him as my friend and my mentor.

I learned very early to trust his judgment. On important votes, I hardly needed it. Representing the same kind of people, we almost always thought alike on major issues. I honestly do not recall a single instance of his asking me to vote a certain way on any bill.

He knew that I would vote my convictions and that they were almost always one with his.

What I did take to heart was his counsel regarding my career in the House. Because of his influence, I won a seat on the Agriculture Committee in 1949. He knew that the assignment was good for me and good for our people. A little while later, a vacancy occurred on ways and means, the most prestigious and powerful committee in the House. Several members urged me to seek the position, but Sam Rayburn advised against it. He told me frankly that I could expect to be in Congress for a long time and that I had a bright career ahead of me. Assignment to a committee as controversial as ways and means, he said, would only complicate the career.

I remember that Lyndon Johnson urged me to ignore Mr. Rayburn's advice: go for the power. I trusted Mr. Rayburn's judgment instead. As usual, it was exactly correct; it always was. Even as a freshman congressman I had learned to appreciate his wisdom. The first time we talked in Washington, he told me what he had told hundreds of newcomers before me. He spoke about the importance of judgment and common sense, "the only kind of sense there is," he said. He told me to ignore the adage about freshmen being seen but not heard. He did, however, stress that any congressman had best be sure he had something worth saying when he took the floor. "There's a whole lot more men have talked themselves out of Congress than have talked themselves into it," he observed. Mostly, he stressed that a congressman should never forget his district. Answer every letter you get, he told me, particularly the ones handwritten in pencil on Big Chief tablet paper. He said when a person like that writes you, he really needs help. If you help him, he will never forget it, and he will be your friend for life.

I never forgot that advice.

I doubt that I even needed Mr. Rayburn's advice about the importance of keeping up with the home folks. I had wanted to go to

Congress so badly and my first election had been so close that I was determined to put Carl Albert's name before every voter in my district and keep it there. Besides, visiting with my friends in the courthouse, talking to school groups, eating campaign barbecue—these gave me as much pleasure as anything that happened in the capital.

In the earliest years, this was relatively easy. Congress usually adjourned in late summer, leaving the fall months free to return to the Third District before a new session convened in January. Through the year, I also made just as many trips home as possible. They were long railroad trips that a congressman paid for out of pocket back then because they were part of his job. Typically, I would pull into McAlester late Saturday, spend the weekend at home (Mary and I kept a residence there), and take out across the district on Monday morning. I would be gone all week before returning home for the weekend and hitting the road again the next Monday.

Typical was one long stay when I made it a point to visit every house on the east side of Ardmore. My poor returns there in 1946 had almost cost me my dream, and I was determined to win those people over. So I printed up some cards with my name and address, saying that I was their United States congressman. I parked my car at each block's end, walked both sides of the street, and then went on to the next block. When no one was home, I left a note: "Sorry I missed you. Please contact me if I can be of service." If someone answered my knock, I would chat a bit, often hearing that I was the only congressman they had ever seen, especially at their front door. I made it a point to get the name, address, and telephone number of anyone who showed interest in me. These started getting periodical letters. No one who got one ever forgot me after that.

I also tried to meet my constituents at their post offices. Cards, posters, and newspaper notices would announce that I would be at the post office in Howe or Tom or Smithville at a certain time. I met and kept in touch with a lot of voters that way. Usually, I would take with me a notebook to record their concerns or their needs. In addition to being a good way to make contact, I found it invaluable for helping with my constituents' problems with the federal bureaucracy. My post-office visits were especially important to the poor folks, who had nowhere to turn for help. It was my job as their congressman to help when I could. Sometimes it was my privilege, for these were times when I truly served them.

One came during the Korean War. One of my campaign helpers called Washington from the little town of LeFlore, Oklahoma. LeFlore is just about the most isolated town in the state, and it is one of the poorest. So small and so isolated is the place that there used to be only four telephones in the entire town. My friend was calling from one of them.

He told me that one of my constituents had come to see him. She had ridden in on a horse. She knew that he knew her congressman and maybe he could help her. She had lost three sons in World War II. Her only remaining boy was in the Marine Corps, stationed in San Francisco but under orders to be shipped to the Korean front. Someone had told her that the government could keep her boy out of the war, since he was her only surviving son. She wanted her boy home. "You gotta remember," the caller told me, "she came in here on a horse."

I was familiar with the sole-surviving-son rule from World War II, so I got on the phone and called the Navy Department. I got quite a runaround before some officer finally told me there was nothing he could do: the rule applied only to World War II. Besides, he added gratuitously, "this is just a police action. It's not important, like a war." I knew—and I told him—that it was a war to that woman and it was awfully important to her.

Dejected, I went over to the office of Congressman Carl Vinson. Mr. Vinson was a Georgia Democrat, the longest-serving member of the House and the unflinching chairman of the Armed Services Committee. Congressmen, presidents, admirals, and generals—all yielded to his authority. I told him the story. "Mr. Chairman," I ended, "the woman came to town on a horse." Carl Vinson raised his right arm. "By God!" he vowed, "the Navy's either got such a rule or they will have one before sundown." When I got back to my office, the secretary of the Navy was waiting on the telephone. He said that he had just held a staff meeting in which it was decided to reinstate the sole-surviving-son rule for the Korean War. Moreover, he had traced this marine's orders. The boy was on a ship off Japan; the moment it docked, the Navy would put him on a plane back home.

The boy came back. In fact, he came to see me and he was furious. His brothers had had the chance to fight for their country, he was a marine, and he wanted that chance, too. In marine-barracks language, he told me that he did not want any congressman to do anything for him.

"Son," I told him, "I didn't do anything for you. I did it for your mother."

Representing the Third District, I welcomed every opportunity to appear there for public occasions. In time, my staff would sometimes chide me for my determination. But to me, that was part of the House habit. On one occasion, I had promised that I would appear at a certain village, only to discover the roads blocked by a flood-swollen river. Luckily, a farmer lent me his plow horse, I forded the stream, and I met my obligation and my constituents. More than once I turned down appearing at a big national fund-raiser because I had agreed to give the commencement speech at some tiny high school. Those people of my district knew which was more important to me, and I did, too.

Gradually, I used those personal contacts to build up quite a file, about four thousand names in all. As my duties in Washington grew and became unavoidable, the file and the telephone allowed me to keep in touch. Three afternoons a week I would spend on the telephone to the people of my district. I would call about twenty different people scattered in twenty different towns. That way, I knew the next morning in twenty different coffee shops twenty conversations would begin with someone saying, "I talked to the congressman yesterday . . . ."

In no time I built up a network of listening posts throughout the district. In every community I had at least one dependable friend who could tell me who wanted what and who was mad at whom. Sometimes these were local politicians; sometimes they were just special friends. Probably the best I ever had was a waitress in a little café. In my very first campaign, I learned that she knew absolutely everything about everyone in the surrounding county. Thereafter my staff knew, even when I was majority leader and Speaker, to put Miss Virgie White through immediately when she called me. Years later she was on the Johnny Carson show and she really held her own.

One thing these listening posts helped me with was the treacherous factionalism that divided even the smallest community in Little Dixie. As long as I represented the area in Congress, I became ever more convinced that it really was true that everything down there was political except politics. That was personal. Congressional patronage was just one of the trouble spots, but always a big one. In those days, a congressman named every rural mail carrier and many postmasters in his district. Picking the wrong one was sure to stir up a lot of local enmity.

My allies were usually dependable counselors on how to antagonize the smallest number of people. Sometimes, though, even they could not fathom the depths of local feeling. I well remember one occasion when I appointed a woman the postmistress of some tiny hamlet. Overnight, every man in the community was complaining, declaring that I had passed over many needy men supporting families, men who had veteran's preference at that. I checked and made it a point to announce a visit to that post office. When I got there, I told them that the woman had a veteran's preference, too. She had lost her husband, who was killed in action in World War II, and was supporting a family. She was going to stay the postmistress. She did, and I doubt that I ever named a more conscientious or more deserving one.

However sensitive I believed a congressman had to be to public sentiment, I also believed that he had to be his own man, too. Of course, that involved much more than selecting a postmistress. It went right to the heart of my beliefs about the nature of representation. Just after my first election to Congress, I told a reporter how I looked at it. "There are two theories of how democratic government should operate," I said.

> One theory holds that a public servant should listen closely to his constituents and give 'em what they want. That's the simple old formula of "let the people rule."
>
> The other theory, and the one to which I subscribe, contemplates that a public servant should have a mind of his own. Listen to the people, sure; hear their arguments on all questions and weigh all sides. But have convictions of your own and act on them, even when they don't jibe with the popular wishes. You'll have to stand or fall on that basis.

Back at Oxford, that was called the Burkean theory of representation in honor of the great Edmund Burke's view that what a representative owed his constituents was his independent judgment. I doubt that many voters in Oklahoma's Third District had ever heard of Edmund Burke or his formulation of representative theory, but I know that they had a congressman who was willing to stand or fall on that basis.

For my part, I would not have wanted it under any other circumstance. As much as I loved being a congressman, I did not want to twist and turn with every momentary breeze. My constituents never expected me to. Because the Third District's voters knew and trusted me, they let me build a career of service. They knew that that career was more important than any vote I ever cast because they knew that my service embraced the best of their beliefs and the greatest of their needs.

Philosophically, few things trouble a congressman more than the tension suggested in his formal title. A United States representative must at once recognize the national interest of the entire United States; at the same time, he represents the special interests of his own district. I believe that it can be said of me that I resolved that tension. On nearly every major vote cast over thirty years, I was able to vote what my conscience understood to be the national interest. One reason that I could do that was that I was always very attentive to my district's special needs.

Most of those needs were economic. Oklahoma's Third District is the poorest district of one of the nation's poorest states, yet its people are independent. They do not reach for handouts, but they do deserve a fair shake. My job was to see that they got one. Very early on in my career, I got them one on something mighty important to them. It was peanuts.

Back in the 1930s, the New Deal's Agricultural Adjustment Act had sought to improve farm prices by slashing surplus production. For major cash crops—peanuts were one—national production quotas set in Washington trickled down to establish state and county quotas. Out of the county quotas, individual farm allotments were calculated on the basis of acreage planted to the crop the past five years.

The Second World War completely absorbed any problem of surplus production. Quotas vanished and allotments disappeared. In fact, the government called for vast expansion of production, and Oklahoma's farmers answered by planting worn-out cotton land in peanuts, peanuts planted, cultivated, and harvested with expensive new machinery. Peanut production quadrupled in two years and reached 240,000 acres, most of them in my district.

Then, in 1949, decreased demand at home and abroad met that increased production to upset the economic balance again. Once more, quotas and individual allotments would govern farmers' work and farmers' income. The national peanut quota was set at 1,610,000 acres. Except for Virginia and North Carolina (major peanut states with major power in Congress), every state's allotment would be cut severely. None would suffer like Oklahoma, where the very recent expansion would be lost in the calculation of average plantings over five years. By the law's formula, Oklahoma growers would be held to 60,000 acres, a sudden drop of 75 percent, ensuring sudden ruin for tens of thousands of our small farmers with equipment unsuited to any other crop. That was not peanuts.

As a very junior member of the House Agriculture Committee, I lacked the power that protected Virginia's and North Carolina's farmers. About all I had was the solace of knowing that the same thing was happening with other crops to other states. Cotton was most important. During the war, cotton production had shifted from Oklahoma and the old Confederacy to the irrigated fields of Arizona, New Mexico, and California. By the same calculations, New Mexico, for example, was set to lose about 80 percent of its cotton crop.

Except that New Mexico's new senator, Clinton Anderson, was not about to let it happen. Sitting on the Senate Agriculture Committee, which was headed by my old friend Elmer Thomas, Clinton Anderson pushed through a cotton bill that saved New Mexico's farmers by guaranteeing that each state could plant at least 70 percent of its average cotton acreage of the past *two* years. The Senate quickly passed the bill and sent it over to the House Agriculture Committee.

On a very cold night, I awoke in the middle of my sleep. What awakened me was a simple realization: what Clinton Anderson was doing for New Mexico, Carl Albert could do for Oklahoma. I could amend his cotton bill in the House committee to provide the same guarantee for peanuts. Working with Steve Pace of Georgia, a legislative genius and chairman of the price-support subcommittee, I presented the amendment and won committee approval on the crucial question by two votes. So amended, the bill passed the House and went to a conference committee headed by Senator Thomas. There it faced the inexplicable and unyielding opposition of Clinton Anderson. He was determined to strike that peanut amendment from the final act, and my own senator seemed willing to let him do it.

At that point, I called upon all I had yet learned of the House habit. And I demonstrated to my old friend just how much I had learned about politics since the spring night in 1927 when he had shown me the Capitol.

I got a membership list from the Oklahoma Peanut Growers Association, and I got on the phone to every member. I called every peanut processor and sheller in the state. I called every banker in every peanut-producing county in Oklahoma. I told each of them the same thing. I told them that Senator Thomas needed to be educated about just how important that peanut amendment was to Oklahoma. During the next three days, the senator received five thousand letters, telegrams, and phone calls—a pretty educational experience.

The next thing I knew, Elmer Thomas invited me, a very junior congressman, to meet with his Senate conferees. I told them the plain truth in a politician's language, "I can't get a peanut bill to pass alone, but Senator Anderson has a horse that will ride, and I want this peanut amendment to ride on it." Senator Thomas threw several hundred telegrams on the table and spoke even plainer: "There won't be any cotton bill until Carl Albert is satisfied on peanuts."

There was a cotton bill. Carl Albert was satisfied on peanuts. The little peanut farmers kept most of their acreage, and the people of the Third District could judge whether they had a congressman worth keeping.

Every two years the voters could decide whether to keep me. My good friend and fellow Oklahoma congressman Tom Steed for years told a story about how I approached those election times. One year I drew no opponent at all, but Tom reckoned that I would still find something to worry about. Sure enough, when Tom observed that I was lucky to have no race to run, I answered, "I know it looks that way, but my name won't be on the ballot this time. Did you ever think about what that might do to me two years from now?"

I guess that I did earn my reputation as a worrier, particularly in my early years. That was one reason that I was so determined to work my district year round. In 1952, when I found my most serious challenger, it all paid off.

Nineteen fifty-two was a good year to challenge any Democratic incumbent. The stalemated war in Korea had devastated Harry Truman's popularity and had cast a dark shadow over all officeholders. The 1950 census returns had registered a significant population loss for Oklahoma, enough to cost the state one House seat and require complete redistricting for every incumbent. The state legislature added two new counties, Johnston and Murray, to my district. Both were dependably Democratic (there were no other kind in that part of the state), but neither had ever cast a single vote for Carl Albert in a Democratic primary election.

Those circumstances called forth the challenge of a formidable rival. Kirksey Nix had the euphonic name that voters remembered. His background was deliciously humble. His father had died three months before his birth, leaving the widowed family an estate of one sorghum mill and a pack of hounds.

The old man also left a son who was a natural-born politician. After working his way through law school, Kirksey built up a lucrative practice defending hundreds of poor folks in workmen's-compensation cases. Not one client ever forgot him, and he never forgot one of them. He was legendary for his ability to recall the face, name, nickname, job, and kinfolks of thousands of voters. My hometown, McAlester, had sent him to the state senate and kept him there. By 1952, he was easily the strongest man in the Oklahoma Capitol, maybe the strongest in southeastern Oklahoma. When he launched his long-delayed challenge, I had cause for worry indeed.

His campaign never lacked for money. The story was that sixty thousand dollars stood behind it, every penny donated by a Hollywood fellow who had invested in some of Kirksey's oil interests, a fellow named John Wayne. Whatever the source, the money paid for billboards that plastered the district, unending radio time, and scores of well-orchestrated Nix rallies, the last with the obligatory string band. In stirring tones, my opponent rarely mentioned my name and never my record. Rather, he stuck to the tried-and-true formula of blasting the big shots and fat cats who allegedly stood behind me and between the people and their poor-boy champion, Kirksey Nix.

By that time, after three congressional terms, I had the record to match his rhetoric. My own campaign never mentioned the challenger; I ran for Carl Albert, not against anyone. We updated our original campaign tract to proclaim: "The Man Who Went from the Cotton Patch to Congress Has Made Good." Inside, we detailed the work that I had accomplished for the district and its people: peanut farmers, veterans, schoolchildren, workers, and Indians. My campaign organization (that is, my local friends) tacked up 9,000 posters and passed out 170,000 campaign cards. We also mailed the voters 66,199 letters, 40,000 of them handwritten by me.

When Congress recessed for summer campaigning, I hit the stump full time. Kirksey and I crisscrossed the district a dozen times, never meeting but always providing Little Dixie's electorate with the kind of campaign oratory that they just loved. According to him, that is what made the difference. Years later when he served on the bench of the Oklahoma Court of Criminal Appeals, he smilingly remembered that hot campaign of 1952. "For a while," he told a reporter, "I had Bug Tussle's pride treed up on his own well-worn stump. But in the last two weeks of the campaign, he laid the lash of that Biblical oratory on me. I don't know why folks call that guy 'little.' He's just wound up tight. When he talks, he commences to unwind, and before he shuts up, he's ten feet tall." Maybe so. I know that when the votes came in, I felt ten feet tall. I carried every county, including the new ones, and the district by a margin of two to one.

Thereafter, I never had a serious challenge for my seat. In fact, my friends in Washington came to tell two jokes on me. One was that I was the only congressman who did better in his elections than Nikita Khrushchev did in the Soviet Union's. The other was that I could always find something to worry about at election time.

Tom Steed was the one who most liked telling those jokes on me. In fact, Tom liked to tell almost any joke. Every morning he would greet his Capitol friends with a new joke, and if they did not laugh hard enough, Tom would tell them another and another until he got the volume of laughter he wanted.

That quality would have surprised many voters because Tom

Steed looked just like what he was: a former newspaperman steadily building up a record of quiet public service. We had known each other since I was in high school and Tom was covering some of my speech contests for a local paper. When I first ran for Congress, Tom Steed directed my campaign in the northern part of the Third District. Two years later, in 1948, Tom came to Congress, too, to start representing the Fourth District for thirty-two years. Over that time, he was quite a congressman, one who rose up the

*He was a first-class congressman, and I never had a better friend, in or out of Congress.* Carl Albert with Tom Steed.

ranks of the Appropriations Committee to direct its treasury, postal service, and general government subcommittee. In that capacity he supervised the appropriation of billions of dollars and did it with absolute integrity and professional expertise.

Of course he could be tough, as anyone who dealt with him knew. When some of his constituents got all riled up over some insignificant vote, Tom flew back to Oklahoma, walked into a protest meeting, stated his position, and walked out. As he left, he told the disgruntled that they would find the state flower (the mistletoe) pinned to the bottom of his coat.

He flew back to Washington as he always flew: first class. When a young reporter for Oklahoma City's *Daily Oklahoman* thought he could win favor with E. K. Gaylord, the paper's reactionary Republican publisher, with a story on Tom Steed's extravagance, Tom's answer was exactly right: "What the hell, I'm a first-class congressman." He *was* a first-class congressman, and I never had a better friend in or out of Congress.

In those early years, I developed other friendships that came to stretch over the years. Tom Steed is dead now, but Bill Natcher of Kentucky's Second District is still going strong, still in Congress, and still a model for any young member to emulate. He came to Congress in 1954 to fill an unexpired term and quickly impressed everyone. Like Tom Steed, he always did his work quietly. Like Tom Steed, he did it professionally. No one I ever served with was his equal as a complete congressman, for whatever the job demanded, Bill Natcher gave it, and gave it with no superior. Certainly no one ever can surpass his attendance: at this writing, Bill Natcher has not missed a single quorum call or a single recorded vote in more than thirty-four years of service. Always a member of the gym group, Bill has stayed fit and vigorous well into his seventies. I am told that he is still as well groomed as when I first saw him and that he still changes his starched white shirts three times daily. I know that no one ever equaled him in presiding over the Committee of the Whole House, the legislative device in which legislation is initially debated and amendments initially voted.

Everyone—every Republican, every Democrat, every northern liberal, every southern conservative—knew that he would preside with absolute fairness.

It is a wonder (maybe it is a comment) that few citizens outside central Kentucky or the United States House of Representatives even have heard Bill Natcher's name. One day they may, for Bill Natcher will leave Congress with a priceless contribution to our republic's history. Two contributions, really. One is a complete daily diary, now bound in forty-eight leather volumes, of Congress's work since 1954. No one in two hundred years of our history has done that. The other contribution is Bill Natcher's service that it records. No one in my lifetime has matched it.

Even as a young congressman I learned that many of my best colleagues—and, it seemed, my best friends—were like Tom Steed and Bill Natcher: hard-working, selfless men devoted to the House and oblivious of national publicity. Another of my very best friends was just that way, though not himself a House member. Lew Deschler was not a congressman, but the Congress could not have functioned without him. He was our parliamentarian and had been since Speaker Nicholas Longworth's day back in the 1920s. I guess that meant he was a Republican (most old-timers said he was), but no one could tell, for he was first and last the Speaker's invaluable right hand, dispensing seasoned advice to Republicans and Democrats alike. I first saw this large (six feet, four inches tall, 275 pounds) but almost painfully shy man do that for Sam Rayburn on parliamentary subjects at the Speaker's dais. In the Board of Education, I saw him do it, too, on political questions. In time, I was lucky enough to have him at my side when I was Speaker. When I was just a young congressman from Oklahoma, I was lucky to have him as a friend.

Steed, Natcher, Deschler—I am almost reluctant to list those names now because I made so many more friends in those days, and any list leaves out too many. Let me say only that these three are not a list but examples. Some of my closest friends in this life I made in the House. Like these, they made public service their career. Like them, they loved the House and did the countless little

*I was lucky enough to have him at my side when I was Speaker.* Carl Albert with Lew Deschler.

jobs that made it work. Like Tom Steed, Bill Natcher, and Lew Deschler, they blessed me with their friendship and honored me with their loyalty. And their name was legion.

I was just as lucky in the people who worked for me. It was only a few in the early days. In fact, I started as a congressman running an office with a pencil and one secretary. As my career advanced and as my responsibilities grew, I built a real staff. Most came to me from Oklahoma, a place I judged to be of undervalued talent. They were all talented. Charles Ward, for instance, left a small newspaper and started working for me on district problems in the 1950s. In no time he became a master at dealing with federal agencies. After I moved into the leadership, I was able to add bright young people to help with my legislative duties. Back home, I later had an office in the Federal Building in McAlester. I staffed it with Bill Anderson and Sara Lane. Bill is the one I had known as

Mook when we were both boys back in Bug Tussle. All of them shared the qualities that I had known forever in Bill and valued in all others: personal loyalty and a devotion to duty. Most of them stayed with me for years, and during those years they stayed with me from the time I got to the office, about 7:00 A.M., till the time I left it, seven or eight o'clock at night.

Mary sometimes kidded me that the staff and the job were my real family. She added that she had married a soldier and ended up with a politician. Being one put a whole lot of strain on my family, but Mary saw to it that it was an awfully good politician's family. In the early days, she campaigned right beside me. Despite her South Carolina ancestry, she quickly became thoroughly Oklahoman and revealed a priceless gift I had not imagined when she was a War Department secretary: Mary Albert almost never forgot the face or the name of a Third District voter.

Something awfully close to her own face reappeared in my life in the middle of my first term when she gave us a daughter, Mary Frances Albert. From birth, Mary Frances had her mother's perky face. When she learned to walk, it was with her mother's quick, toes-out stride. In no time, too, she displayed her mother's taste for humor and a strong streak of independence. If it had not been for her own mother, I might have thought that Mary Frances Albert was the most willful female on earth.

A son, David, was born in December 1954. He took after the Albert men: small, quick, curious about his world. Like Mary Frances, David turned out to be a fine student, too. In fact, the demands of their education largely defined where Mary and I would live. She and I both wanted those children to know that their father worked in Washington but that Oklahoma was their home. For as long as possible, that meant that we lived in a small Washington apartment (one bedroom, a kitchen with dinette) but kept our house in McAlester. Mary and the children would go there early every summer, and I would join them as soon as Congress adjourned. When fall came, Mary would go down to McAlester's neighborhood school, enroll Mary Frances, and keep house through the fall semester.

Only reluctantly did we have to give that up. Congressional sessions kept running longer each year, keeping me back in Washington, first through the summer and in time through much of the fall. But the turning point came when Mary Frances discovered that she could not take part in Brownie Scouts if she was not in Washington when the school year began and the troops were organized. Thereafter, we stayed in Washington for the entire school year, in time settling in an apartment on Cathedral Avenue so that the children could walk to school, Mary Frances to National Cathedral and David to St. Alban's.

Watching them grow up, I was often struck by how very much different their lives were from what I had known back in Bug Tussle. It was not just that they went to bigger schools and stayed out of the cotton patches, it was the whole atmosphere. Sometimes it was a big improvement. I remember in the 1960s, when civil rights was a major issue and a tough one for my folks in Little Dixie, Mary Frances announced at the dinner table one night that anyone who did not believe in civil rights should drop dead and she was willing to help them! She was as old as I was when the Ku Klux Klan was running rampant in Pittsburgh County.

Sometimes, though, it seemed a more mixed blessing. When I was a boy, every lad had a .22 rifle. With his father and his friends, he freely hunted the meadows and valleys near Bug Tussle. My own son wanted to hunt, and I bought him his own little rifle, which he learned to shoot. But I was a congressman, not a farmer or a coal miner, and I worked day and night at the Capitol, not in a field. What Papa and I could have done almost any day at home required David and me to take the time somewhere else. I remember when we finally could, how excited David was when we went down to Congressman Frank Boykin's big forest and private hunting preserve in Alabama. With the first blast of his shotgun, David brought down a huge tom turkey. When I bagged a goose, David was more impressed than if I had been on network news with the president. He insisted that we take mine back to Washington and have his mother cook it as our dinner. She did, and right in the middle of the preparation the phone rang and Mary stopped to

*With Mary and the children there, I always knew that whatever was cooking at home would be well done.*

answer it. Somebody at the Capitol was trying to reach me but, being polite, first asked Mary what she was doing. "Why, I'm cooking Carl's goose," she said.

Maybe so. But with Mary and my children there, I always knew that whatever was cooking at home would be well done.

Just as Speaker Champ Clark had said, as my constituents kept returning me, they helped me and them both. For me it granted the freedom to vote my convictions. I could be the only kind of representative that I wanted to be, the kind who gave his people the benefit of his judgment and his appreciation.

That was not the only benefit they got.

After my amendment had saved tens of thousands of peanut farmers, Alabama's Lister Hill had told me that I had just reelected myself to three more terms, that I did not have to do one thing more. But I was not in Congress to be reelected. I was there to serve. And I did. What we told the voters in the Nix campaign was true. I wrote amendments increasing Oklahoma's funds for twelve thousand students in the 4-H programs run by the Agriculture Department's Extension Service. I secured and increased monies for McAlester's naval ammunition depot, the city's largest employer. I wrestled through Congress the appropriations that brought Rural Electrification Administration power lines—and the modern world—to the people of my district's hills and valleys. I took on my constituents' problems with the federal bureaucracy, by our count, on more than thirty-five hundred occasions in the first six years alone. In one long battle, my work literally changed my constituents' lives and the entire face of my district and state.

Even in the 1950s the word *Oklahoma* still conjured up images of billowing dust and echoes of howling winds. The Dust Bowl lingered as an indelible part of the state's image and its collective memory. So dramatic was that disaster of the 1930s that it overshadowed the brutal history of floods during the 1940s, even though the latter caused more damage and drove more of our people off the land.

The droughts and the floods were opposite sides of the same

coin: the state's powerlessness to transform its environment so that it might serve people rather than destroy them. Water was the key to the difference. Stored, it would ease the pain of future droughts. Controlled, it would lessen possible floods. Harnessed, it would provide power for better lives. Channeled, it would provide cheap transportation for Oklahoma's producers and consumers. Altogether, Oklahoma's control of its water could lift the burden of poverty from the state.

As an Oklahoman I knew that. As an Oklahoma politician I learned just how hard the battle over water could be, and I also learned how sweet victory tasted.

My position on the Agriculture Committee put me in close contact with the Agricultural Stabilization and Conservation Service. A little-known federal agency, it did mighty big work building farm ponds throughout the nation. I saw to it that the ASCS built thousands in Oklahoma, thousands of tiny ponds that collectively made possible a prosperous cattle industry on land reclaimed from a miserly despot, King Cotton.

I also worked closely with two other agencies, the Soil Conservation Service and the Bureau of Reclamation. With the SCS, Oklahoma developed a model for upstream flood-control projects. The eleven experimental projects the SCS built on the Washita River inspired nationwide efforts resulting in hundreds of small lakes that gave other states the benefits first seen in my district, particularly in flood control, municipal water supply, and recreation. When the U.S. Army Corps of Engineers refused to recommend a small dam in Murray County, I turned to the Bureau of Reclamation; its regulations supported the project. The House Interior and Insular Affairs Committee authorized it, the House passed the bill, and the president signed it. The appropriation was soon forthcoming, and the lake was built.

My district's geographic location put me in the center of the two largest water basins in Oklahoma. Every drop of water that leaves Oklahoma makes its way out of the state in one of two river systems, the Arkansas or the Red. The Third District is the only Oklahoma congressional district that is part of both basins. The Red

River defines the district's southern border, the Arkansas part of its northern.

Before I entered Congress, the Flood Control Act of 1946 authorized major dam projects all over the nation. Those for the Arkansas River promised real benefits for northeastern Oklahoma. Those authorized for the Red River offered far less to southeastern Oklahoma. The dams to be constructed in Oklahoma were to be built only for the protection of lands in Arkansas and Louisiana. To keep the Red River from flooding in these states, the act called for three dams near the mouths of the Boggy, Kiamichi, and Little rivers just above where each emptied into the Red. The dams were purely for downstream flood control, almost all of it in Arkansas and Louisiana. In Oklahoma, they would back up floodwaters for miles, spreading the floods' damages. When the rains subsided, the waters would be released, leaving behind nothing but mud flats and mud holes. No recreation, hydroelectric power, irrigation, or navigation was ever contemplated.

One reason for those uneven benefits was political: both Arkansas and Louisiana had some awfully powerful men in Congress. Another was bureaucratic: the Soil Conservation Service and the Bureau of Reclamation each had its own methods, its own pet projects, its own constituencies. The U.S. Army Corps of Engineers had its own, too, and the three could rarely cooperate on any united effort, rarer still in a coordinated program for an entire river system or, in this case, a multiriver system. For both the political and the bureaucratic reasons, I knew that I had to find an ally, a man of both strength and vision, the two welded by unbreakable tenacity. Bob Kerr was that ally.

I had known Bob's brothers back at the University of Oklahoma and I had thought them two of the strongest men I had ever known, but Bob was even stronger than the two of them together. When he announced for the Senate in 1948, I knew instantly whom I was going to support.

As soon as he arrived in Washington, I knew that I had been right. The first bill that he introduced (S. 1576) was to create an interagency commission forcing the appropriate departments to coordinate a massive public-works program for the Arkansas, White, and Red basins. Its task was to bring to all three river systems "a comprehensive and coordinated plan or plans for the control, conservation, and utilization of the waters [and] . . . for conservation and development of the land areas of such area; for flood control, navigation, reclamation, agriculture purposes, power, recreation, fish, and wildlife."

I had been in Congress only two years, but the old veterans agreed with me: this was the broadest proposal for a public-works project they had ever seen. Soon those veterans were agreeing with me about Bob Kerr's strength. Kerr rammed the measure through the Senate as an amendment to the Flood Control Act of 1950, lost it in the House-Senate conference, and won it back when President Truman ordered the agencies to cooperate toward Kerr's end. Eighteen months after he reached Washington, Senator Kerr had an official Arkansas-White-Red Basins Interagency Committee. For the rest of his life, he rode that committee to reclaim Oklahoma's land, wood, and water—almost a holy trinity to Bob Kerr.

It solved my problems on the Red River. Emphasizing interagency cooperation and broad public purposes, its stacks of reports and recommendations gave me the ammunition to change the 1946 authorization in favor of a string of multipurpose dams bringing enormous benefit to southeastern Oklahoma. We built multipurpose dams on the Little River, and the Millwood, Pine Creek, Broken Bow, and Glover dams brought clean water and recreation, not mud flats, to the surrounding communities. The same came from new dams on the Kiamichi system at Hugo and Sardis.

Even the transformation of the Red River basin paled before the work done on the Arkansas. It was Kerr's obsession: a vast project for flood control, water use, recreation, hydroelectric power, even ocean-bound navigation. When completed in 1971, it did all that at a cost of $1.2 billion, making it the largest and most expensive project ever built by the Corps of Engineers. At the dedication ceremony, President Richard Nixon unveiled the marker that said it all:

Conceived in Dust
Cradled in Flood
Created by Men

Oklahoma's congressional delegation provided the men who did it. Armed with massive studies of the interagency committee, we fought battle after battle for the project, one of them within our own ranks. Mike Monroney left the House for the Senate in 1950 and took his opposition to the Arkansas project with him. An Oklahoma Citian, Monroney said of the eastern Oklahoma project: "You could pave the Arkansas cheaper than you could navigate it." By 1955, though, Senator Kerr and some eastern Sooner Democrats had sat Mike down and made a Christian out of him.

We still had to deal with President Eisenhower's opposition to new projects—"no new starts" was the slogan—and Chairman Clarence Cannon's tight grip on the House Appropriations Committee's purse strings. The latter was especially tough for me and Ed Edmondson, the Second District's congressman after 1953. We were not the only members having trouble with the smart but eccentric Cannon; dozens of authorized projects went unfinanced because Cannon refused to give them money.

Fortunately, he went too far, far enough to stir up a floor revolt to add money to Cannon's appropriations bills. Ed Edmondson and I were next to each other on the House floor when the revolt erupted, and we could tell it would be successful and that it was our best chance to take a giant first step on the Arkansas project.

"Where do you want to start?" Ed asked. I answered, "Eufaula," the site that lay on the line dividing our two districts. Thereupon, Ed offered a $900,000 amendment for new construction on the Arkansas River with $450,000 earmarked for Eufaula Dam and $450,000 earmarked for Dardanelle in Arkansas. The coalition held together on the floor of the House, and the entire package of new projects won House approval. Immediately after the adoption of the amendment, I ran to a telephone booth in the Democratic cloakroom of the House. I called Bob Kerr and told him what Ed had done. He said, "You don't mean it." I said, "Yes, I do, and it's in the bill and the bill is on its way to the Senate."

When the bill went to the Senate, Ed asked the senator if he was going to add some money to it. Senator Kerr answered, "Absolutely not. I am not going to change one comma. There is no going to be anything in the conference report that will enable the House to come back in disagreement. The amendment will be passed as it came to us from the House. It will never be changed." What the Senator had projected happened. The Senate adopted the amendment exactly as Ed had written it.

Both houses passed the bill, but Eisenhower vetoed it as too expensive. Cutting 2 percent off, we passed it again. Ike vetoed that one, too, but both houses overrode the veto. The president then refused to release the money—nobody said a project like this would be easy—and we turned to our delegation's one Republican, Page Belcher, for help. Page represented the Tulsa district, sat as ranking Republican on agriculture, and was invaluable to the administration in Congress. Page told the president that if he could not get that Arkansas River money released, he would not be in Congress much longer. The money came forth quickly, and the work began. There would be other fights, but none would be so hard and none would stop the progress.

It was going ahead full steam when Bob Kerr and I were out on the final campaign day before the 1962 election. After a round of speeches, all of which predicted the completion of the Arkansas navigation project, Bob Kerr and I drove down U.S. 59 to the Arkansas River. We drove onto the bridge that crossed the river, and Kerr stopped the car. As we both got out, Kerr talked about the river's future and said to me, "If anything should happen to me, I hope you will finish this project for me. You're the one person that I know can do it."

We climbed back in the car and drove on over to Spiro, where Kerr gave a ringing speech about Oklahoma, its rivers, and its future. Closing, he shouted, "Let's all sing 'Shall We Gather at the River?'" We must have sung it a dozen times, each with the fervor of a brush-arbor revival. We liked doing it so much that we did the same thing at Poteau, the stop that finished the day's campaign. The words were ringing in my ears when Bob Kerr and I shook hands and promised to meet in Washington when the 1963 session opened.

I never saw him again.

On January 1, 1963, I had just taken my seat at the Orange Bowl to watch Oklahoma play Alabama when I got the message that

*The man who had done the most to create that future.* Bob Kerr campaigning with his good friend Lyndon Johnson. Mrs. Kerr is on the left, and Carl Albert is beside her.

Senator Kerr had died unexpectedly at Bethesda Naval Hospital. I flew to Oklahoma City for Bob Kerr's funeral at the First Baptist Church, where he had taught Sunday school for twenty-five years. As his pastor said, a mighty oak tree had fallen, leaving a lonesome place against the sky.

We finished that project, though. With the other water projects, it did indeed transform Oklahoma's environment. It made unbearable dust and uncontrollable floods part of our history, a modern life part of our future.

By then the man who had done the most to create that future was gathered with the saints at the river that flows by the throne of God.

There is no better judge on earth—and no fairer jury—than a congressman's own colleagues. The other members could survey my record on my district's and state's behalf. It testified to the quality of my work, just as successive reelections forecast my long tenure. The flower of both was added respect, the most precious quality a congressman can have in Washington.

The fruit of that flower was my steadily increasing responsibility in the House. After my appointment to the Agriculture Committee, my colleagues later added me to the committee that oversaw the Library of Congress. It was a great assignment, for I came to enjoy its staff people and to love their work with the world's greatest library. In 1950, the Democratic leadership put me on a select committee to investigate lobbying activities. The Buchanan committee, named for its chairman, Frank Buchanan of Pennsylvania, did a thorough job publicizing the work that lobby organizations, particularly extremist groups, were doing to whip up grass-roots hysteria against Congress. Four years later, Mike Kirwan put me in charge of the speakers' bureau for his Democratic congressional committee. That was where I came to respect Mike immensely, for in spite of his second-grade education this son of an Ohio coal miner was a tough and resourceful congressman and campaigner.

Our work in 1954 helped contribute to the Democratic recapture of the Congress that year. Two years after the Republicans had ridden General Eisenhower's coattails to give them only their second control of both chambers since the Great Depression, we picked up seventeen House seats and two in the Senate to restore Democratic majorities on both sides of the Capitol. All of us Democratic congressmen celebrated. Among other things, the victory would increase our share of every House committee and put our senior men into their chairmanships. One of those senior men was Percy Priest of Nashville, Tennessee, due to move up to chairman of the House Committee on Interstate and Foreign Commerce.

That seemingly small fact became the most important single thing that happened during my entire tenure in Congress.

Percy had served four years as the Democrats' House whip. The term was of English origin. It derived from *whipper-in,* the title given the man assigned to keep the dogs close to the pack in hunts. As early as the 1770s, the parties in Parliament were designating their *whips,* charging them to mobilize their memberships on major votes. Both the term and the function reappeared in the American Congress. In the early years, various members served their parties in that role in a more or less haphazard fashion, often for a single floor fight only. In 1900 the position was institutionalized when the Democratic caucus voted to create the office of party whip. Oscar Underwood, the Alabamian who authored the initial resolution, thereupon won the floor leader's appointment to the job. Since then, the position's influence had grown, but one thing remained constant: the whip was appointed by the Democratic floor leader. When the party held the House majority, the whip thus became (with the Speaker and the majority leader) the third member of the leadership team.

Just after the 1954 election returns came in, Percy wrote Sam Rayburn, saying that no one congressman could do both the whip's and a major chairman's jobs. Of the two, he preferred the chairmanship of interstate and foreign commerce. Through December 1954 and January 1955, Washington was abuzz with rumors of whom the Democrats would name to the post. Wilbur

Mills of Arkansas and Hale Boggs of Louisiana, both young, established, and very outstanding members, were the betting favorites. No one mentioned Carl Albert, least of all Carl Albert.

On January 4, 1955, I was working in my Washington office. The Eighty-fourth Congress would convene the next day, but I had plenty of routine work to do. I was answering some mail from the Third District when my secretary stuck her head in the door and said that John McCormack wanted to see me right away. I remember wondering at the time what the Democratic floor leader might want with me, but since I had no idea, I just trotted down the hall, like any other young member summoned by Mr. McCormack.

When I got there, I was surprised to see Sam Rayburn—a very smiling Sam Rayburn—in the office. John McCormack got right to the point. Congress would convene in less than twenty-four hours, and he and Mr. Rayburn needed to name a new Democratic whip. They had been going down the list of Democratic members, John reading the names aloud. When he called off the name *Carl Albert,* Sam Rayburn stopped him. "That's it!" they both cried in unison. I was a champion orator and a Rhodes scholar-graduate of Oxford University, so I responded, "Who, me?" I thought to add: "I didn't even know I was in the running."

Then Sam Rayburn took over. "Son," he said, "you've been in the running since your first day here. Since you sat there on the floor every day and listened to every speech and watched every vote. Since you showed us that you loved the House of Representatives."

I do not even recall my response, but I do remember that Sam Rayburn looked at John McCormack and said, "We believe you have enough sense not to make people think you can drive them anywhere, but we think you have finesse enough to lead them part of the way." Then Sam Rayburn looked straight at me. He smiled and said, "Besides, I like the kind of dirt that grows under your fingernails."

Only minutes later, Mr. Rayburn, John McCormack, and I announced the news. Tall and thin John McCormack made the announcement. Then Sam Rayburn, only a little taller than I, spoke, as always, plainly. He did not say anything about the Red River dirt beneath my nails, but he did say something that made me mighty proud, something he would say again and again: "Carl has tact and energy, intelligence, education, and a sense of responsibility. And mind you, these things don't always come together. I've been watching House members since Woodrow Wilson's administration, and I can tell big timber from small brush."

*I can tell big timber from small brush.* No metaphor had pleased me so much since the McAlester High School yearbook had called me a little giant.

CHAPTER SIX

# *You Have to Plow with the Horses You Have*

$J$ust as Mr. Craighead had told us back in Bug Tussle, Speaker Champ Clark had known the House of Representatives. I had set out to master "the house habit," and I had done it. The voters kept returning me to Congress, and my career had prospered "as surely as the sparks fly upward." The old Speaker was just as correct when he described the responsibilities of my new job. The parties' whips, he had said, existed to serve as "the right hands of the two party leaders."

In my case, I was becoming the right hand of John McCormack, himself the strong right arm of Sam Rayburn. Hand, arm, and brain—we three were the team that gave our Democratic party its formal leadership in Congress.

That part of the job put me at the highest level of congressional leadership yet achieved by an Oklahoman. Sometimes it seemed that the home folks were even prouder of that than I was. One of them sent me a gift that we put on the wall of my new office. The fellow who sent it thought it a fitting token of my new job. It was a long, braided leather bullwhip.

It made a great wall hanging, but it was not a very appropriate symbol. No party whip would be caught dead using a bullwhip on his colleagues. Maybe that should read, "One who tried to use a bullwhip could end up dead." The House of Representatives is far too complex an institution for that, and the members are too independent, too. The whip's job, I already knew, was much too subtle to allow strong-arm tactics. The hand of the leadership could wield no bullwhip, for a big part of the whip's job was to know the membership and represent it in the highest councils of Congress. When Mr. Rayburn broke up meetings with instructions to "let me know if you hear anything," the whip was expected to do the most hearing and the most letting know.

So a great deal of my new job was just what I had been doing all along during my first eight years. I had to know each of the Democratic members, what made each of them tick, what made each of them vote. The major difference was one of purpose. No longer did I do it from my affection for the House and my curiosity about its members; now my purpose was tied to the highest demands of party leadership in Congress. I had to know what the largest numbers of Democrats would support. I had to know what instruments could increase those numbers, if necessary, one by one. I had to predict how scores of votes—major and minor, procedural and substantive—would turn out. I had to do all of that so that the Democratic leadership could define and could pass a legislative program.

Befitting the institutional significance of the whip's role, Congress gave him elaborate instruments, both formal and informal, to meet his obligations. Back in 1933, the new Democratic majority that was anxious to push through Franklin Roosevelt's New Deal had provided him a system of regional whips as his assistants. Originally fifteen in number, these since had been increased to eighteen. Congressmen from several states usually represented each region, and those members either elected their own regional whips or the delegations' deans appointed them. Each regional whip represented about a dozen or so Democratic members.

The regional-whip system was essential to our operations. Before major votes, we used it to conduct formal polls. I would have the regional whips consult every Democratic member and note their individual opinions ("yes," "no," "undecided") on formal, printed sheets. Armed with that information, we knew what was likely to happen even before a floor fight would begin. We knew

*It was a long, braided leather bullwhip.*

whether we had the votes to win. If not, we went to work to get them. One way could be to alter a bill just enough to convert a few opponents and pick up some undecideds. Scheduling was another tool. The regional whips were available for weekly attendance polls that let us know when each congressman would be away from the Capitol. That allowed us to set the week's calendar with the most critical votes coming when we could expect maximum support. When those days came, I often had the regional whips check their attendance polls against the first quorum call. If a member whom we had expected had not answered the call, I got on the phone and tracked him down. Just before the vote was to be taken, the regional whips, the Capitol switchboard, and I went to work again, calling every member's office and thereby getting our people on the floor in fifteen minutes' time.

On the really tough votes, the ones where we were close but just short, the whip had the hardest part of his job. I had to get those extra votes. Here I had few institutional devices to call upon. I might have his regional whip or an influential congressman approach a member. In special cases, I could get Mr. Rayburn to use his personal influence. Sometimes, I could call on our outside friends with interest and influence. But in almost every important case these were only aids; the real job of persuasion was the whip's personal job. The job was persuasion. And it was personal.

When people used to ask me about my duties, I sometimes joked that one aspect of my job (maintaining party discipline, the political scientists called it) reminded me of what one of my old Bug Tussle teachers had said about correcting the behavior of an unruly farm boy:

> You should appeal first to his honor,
> Then to his pride,
> Then to his conscience,
> Then to his hide.

The only trouble with that advice was that, aside from wall decorations, party whips did not have much of a way to appeal to an unruly congressman's hide. The folks that gave the fellow his job usually lived a long way from Washington. Once in Congress, he could stay and rise in the House without toeing any party line. No whip, no leader, no one could make a single member vote against his own wishes.

That is what made the whip's job of persuasion such a personal one. In the House of Representatives, if you could not get votes by persuasion, you could not get them at all. In my job, I did not twist a colleague's arm; I shook his hand.

I made sure to keep my friendships with veteran congressmen, and I worked very hard to make a friend of every new member that arrived. My position as whip really helped. I do not know how many times a young member came to me with a problem. I guess that I seemed the most approachable of the leadership team. Members in awe of the towering John McCormack or the legendary Sam Rayburn found it a lot easier to open up with me. I gave them a lot of advice, most, I hope, sound; some, I trust, taken. I also became something of their champion with the most powerful congressmen, men more likely to pay attention to the Democratic whip than to a young representative. In time, they learned that I was their friend and a friend who could help them. I might campaign in their district to tell their constituents how much we needed them in Washington. Or I might help pry one of their project's funds loose from the grip of Clarence Cannon, the money-squeezing chairman of Appropriations.

These favors did not guarantee a single member's vote on a single question, but they did assure that nearly every single time I needed to approach a colleague, I was approaching a friend. And friends are a lot easier to approach than colleagues.

So when the House leaders needed votes, they knew that their whip could approach his friends. I usually began by explaining the merits of the question—the whip had to know that and know it on almost every tough question. My usual closing was simple. "We really need you on this one," I might say, "and I don't see any reason why you can't go along with us." To be sure, those last words required that I know the member's district and its demands as well as he—just one more thing a party whip needed to know.

I kept the leather whip up on the wall. Help with personal favors, concerned counsel, a willing ear, attention to every detail, long and grueling workdays—these were the tools of my new job. They made the leadership's right hand a strong one.

The party that I was serving had a majority, but a bare one, in Congress. When we Democrats took control of the House and I began as whip in 1955, our majority was only twenty-nine seats. No whip and no leadership could expect to push through a controversial program on that thin majority. Any significant issue would open fissures that would doom the question and divide the party. On top of that, we were working with the first Republican president since the Great Depression.

As Allied supreme commander and general of the army, Dwight David Eisenhower easily had been America's favorite soldier in World War II. After the war, he was its most popular citizen. So popular was he that a few liberal members of my own party had toyed with the notion of drafting him to replace the "unelectable" Harry Truman in 1948. The idea went nowhere, but neither did Ike's popularity. In 1952, the Republicans nabbed him as their nominee, but only after Eisenhower had given up the notion of first entering the New Hampshire primary on *both* tickets.

No one seems to doubt that he could have won (in New Hampshire and nationally) on either ticket. That he could have done so testifies to his incredible popularity. That he once considered running on both tickets measures his equally incredible political naïveté. Ike came out of the small pre–World War II professional army. He was part of an officer corps that viewed elective politics with independence, if not scorn. The first ballot he cast was (presumably) for himself, but a landslide of voters voted as he did to propel him into the White House, where his popularity did not diminish.

Neither, it seemed to me, did his political acumen increase much. Like a later immensely popular president, Ronald Reagan, he knew very little about politics or its professional practitioners, particularly in the Congress. Like Reagan, he knew very little, either, about the complex issues of the time. Like Reagan's, Ike's staff and his aides by and large ran the government in his name. As in Reagan's case, that was often to the president's sorrow and the nation's misfortune.

In one respect, Eisenhower had it different from Reagan, and better, too, I think. In Congress, President Eisenhower found Democratic leaders who were willing to give the administration its chance. More than that, we were anxious to let it work. Eisenhower may have been a Republican and he may have been naïve, but we knew that he was the only president we had and that for just those reasons he needed all the help that we Democrats could give him. We gave it to him, often in greater measure than his own party members.

Ike had not been in office long before Sam Rayburn laid down the line that we Democrats would generally follow for the next eight years. First elected in 1912, Mr. Rayburn was one of the few congressmen to have experienced divided government at its worst: just after the Armistice, when a newly elected and vengeful Republican Congress had made war upon Democratic President Woodrow Wilson. That war had cost the nation any chance for international peace and domestic tranquility after the First World War. Sam Rayburn and the Democratic leadership were determined not to repeat the Republicans' mistake when it was our turn.

Eisenhower therefore faced a Democratic Congress that rejected the old notion that it was the duty of the opposition to oppose. Except for one circumstance: we were in no mood to countenance any Republican attempt to turn back the clock to the "good old days," the days before FDR's New Deal, the days without Social Security, minimum-wage laws, collective bargaining, and public power. If Eisenhower sought to consolidate and extend the New Deal's legacy of an activist government, he could count on friendly Democratic cooperation. If he were to try to unravel the New Deal's fabric, he could count on a determined Democratic opposition. As Mr. Rayburn said, "any jackass can kick a barn down, but it takes a good carpenter to build one." My party was

*. . . a Democratic Congress that rejected the old notion that it was the duty of the opposition to oppose.* Carl Albert at the signing of the first bill passed while he was serving as Democratic whip, 1955. Republican Floor Leader Joe Martin is at Carl Albert's right. Photograph by Abbie Rowe, courtesy National Park Service.

full of good carpenters, and we were not about to allow any jackass or general to undo our work.

Through the fifties, we proved as good as our word. On issue after issue, enough Democrats and I voted to support the president's position to save it from the opposition of the Republicans themselves. In fact, of the first 164 occasions in which Eisenhower's views became law, it was the Democrats who gave him his congressional majority 121 times. Thereafter it often remained Democratic votes that built Eisenhower's record and dragged his party kicking and screaming into the twentieth century.

In 1955, for example, one of my first major jobs was winning Democratic votes for Eisenhower's request to renew the Reciprocal Trade Agreements Act. After two generations of unflinching Republican protectionism, FDR and the New Deal Congress had laid that act as the foundation of American trade policy and the promoter of our expanding exports. When Ike proposed to extend it, I worked furiously to line up Democratic support. We won the critical vote by a margin of 206 to 199. It was 140 Democrats who saved the program from the Republicans, who voted 119 to 66 to oppose their own president and kick down the barn that sheltered America's commerce.

At times, we had to work as carpenters. Our overall approach to divided government was to give the administration much of the legislative initiative. We really had no choice. The decentralized committee structure in Congress, the internal divisions within the slim Democratic majority, the likelihood of presidential veto of any broadly ambitious program—all of these mitigated against trying to assemble an overall congressional program for the nation. Rather, our main effort was to take the administration's proposals, pass or improve the best ones, and defeat or replace the worst ones.

One example important to my other congressional duties involved agriculture. As whip, I continued to serve on the Agriculture Committee. That put me directly in the face of Eisenhower's one attempt to reverse the New Deal. The president raised in Kansas farm country was determined to get the government off the farmers' backs, or at least get its price supports out of their pockets. Since the 1930s, it had been Democratic policy to maintain rigid price supports at 90 percent of parity, a complicated formula that ensured farmers' relative purchasing power, if need be, through government purchases at the parity price. Eisenhower and his agriculture secretary, Ezra Taft Benson, were determined to end that with something they called flexible parity.

However they and their economists might define that, I saw its meaning every trip home. In the 1950s, nature cursed our farmers with drought, the marketplace tormented them with overproduction, and now the administration was ready to afflict them with an insensitive farm policy. It was measurable when my own state lost more farmers to the Republican farm policies of the 1950s than it had to the Dust Bowl of the 1930s.

It seemed every year that we had to fight again in our farmers' behalf the battle that Franklin Roosevelt had won back in 1933. Always the fight was close, for the administration generally held the allegiance of even the farm-state Republicans. In 1955, for instance, I put in countless hours polling members and lining up support—vote by vote in the end—to push through a rigid price-support law by a margin of just five votes, 206 to 201. A year later, I had to do it all over again, this time only to see the effort wasted with Eisenhower's veto.

On the whole, however, the Republican president and the Democratic leadership practiced, in the language of the day, a peaceful coexistence. More often than not, it was even a productive coexistence. Many of us appreciated Eisenhower's success in quieting the noisy right-wing demons of his own party, and he came to appreciate the cooperation that the loyal opposition was extending toward his program.

One token of his appreciation was more informal meetings with us at the White House. At one of them, I remember Eisenhower going over some routine business. As we were breaking up, he called Mr. Rayburn and me over.

"I wish you could do me a favor," he said to the Speaker.

"If I can, Mr. President," Mr. Rayburn answered.

"I remember from World War II how important information can be," Ike went on. "I wish you could get the appropriation for Radio Free Europe kicked up by several hundred million."

Mr. Rayburn asked me whether I could get the Democratic votes for it. I said we could. We did. And Radio Free Europe got its money.

That particular job was not too hard. Like Speaker Rayburn,

Majority Leader McCormack, and myself, most Democrats in Congress were anxious to acknowledge the president's leadership in foreign affairs. The Second World War had taught us all the need for strong executive leadership. The GOP's support of Harry Truman's tough decisions in the 1940s had established a pattern for bipartisanship. Already it was understood that party bickering ended at America's shores. We were determined only to affirm that.

In a series of international crises through the fifties, we did. For all of John Foster Dulles's campaign talk about "rolling back" communism and Richard Nixon's criticism of containment as "cowardly," President Eisenhower, as well as his secretary of state and vice president, followed closely the lines laid down in the Truman Doctrine. The major emphasis was upon refining and applying its terms. Here the president took the initiative, and the Congress unhesitatingly handed him its assent.

One historic example occurred right at the start of my service as Democratic whip. On New Year's Day 1955, Chiang Kai-shek predicted war "at any time" with the Red mainland. Communist leader Chou En-lai instantly agreed; war was "imminent" against Chiang's forces on Formosa and the surrounding island groups. Already Communist forces were moving on some islands and threatening others. America's commitment to "free peoples who are resisting attempted subjugation" was set to be tested, and the test likely would come somewhere in the waters between the mainland and Formosa. No one knew where, but when seemed soon.

In Washington, the crisis was played out against the recent and painful memory of Harry Truman's troubles with congressional Republicans over our Korean intervention. President Eisenhower wanted none of the criticism that Truman had taken for not consulting Congress before committing American forces, so he prepared a formal resolution, the Formosa Resolution, that gave congressional consent for any action he might take, including the use of troops, in the defense of Formosa, the Pescadores, or any other "closely related localities." The precise definition of the last was left to his own judgment. In one and two-thirds centuries of

American history, no executive had once asked Congress for such advance approval of an open-ended policy that could lead to war. Ike got it.

Mr. Rayburn pledged the support of the Democratic members. He, too, remembered Truman's experience in Korea, and when a few Democrats privately protested, he reminded them of how "the Republicans patted Truman on the back when he first went into Korea and kicked him in the pants afterward. We're not going to do that," he promised. We did not. In fact, our own leadership insisted that there be no debate at all on the resolution. There was none, and only one Democrat dared vote in opposition.

I had watched history made. I had seen the opposition party in one branch sign a blank check for a president to do what he wished, when and where and how he wished. I was not the only one who did not notice that we were also watching a precedent being set.

In 1956, American voters seemingly ratified the prevailing cooperation in Washington. Eisenhower won again, even increasing his large margin of 1952 while carrying all but seven states, all of those in the Deep South. At the same time, the electorate returned Democratic majorities to both houses of Congress. In fact, we Democrats got a bit more breathing room in extending our majority to 234 to 201, a gain of four seats. However predictable the outcome, historians noted that Eisenhower thereby became the first winning presidential candidate since 1848 whose party carried neither house in Congress, but then everyone knew that the general's famous battle jacket had no coattails at all.

Still, major figures in both parties were upset. Noting the congressional defeats, a few Republican leaders complained openly of Ike's inattention to the party's fortunes and his subsequent inability to transfer his personal popularity to the GOP. On the Democratic side, a number of prominent men—most northerners, most liberals, and most safely outside the arena of elective politics—complained even louder that the Democratic leadership of

Congress was no help at all to the party's presidential ambitions. A few even judged it a hindrance. Former New York Senator Herbert Lehman, for instance, moaned that

> the mistakes that really hurt were mistakes made in Congress. . . . The Democrats in Congress failed to make issues during the 18 months we were in control. On the contrary, almost everything the leadership did during that time was designed to prevent any controversial issue from being seriously joined or vigorously debated.

The upshot of those complaints was that a few weeks after the election the Democratic National Committee and party chairman Paul Butler announced creation of the Democratic Advisory Committee. Its purpose would be to define the Democratic party line. Twenty people, including such luminaries as Harry Truman, Eleanor Roosevelt, and Adlai Stevenson, would head the group to define the canon of Democratic orthodoxy. Butler also saw fit to include the Democratic leadership of the House and Senate. For us, that was Speaker Rayburn, Majority Leader McCormack, Mike Kirwan of the campaign committee, and myself, the party whip.

Since Congress was adjourned and I was back in Oklahoma, I got wind of this only when I received Butler's telegram inviting me to join the group that he presumptuously had announced. On the next day, I got a phone call from Bonham, Texas. Mr. Rayburn wanted to know if I had received a telegram from Butler. After I told him that I had, he asked me if I had responded yet. My answer was that I was waiting until I could confer with the Speaker and John to get their reaction. My wait was over. "Tell Butler you cannot, as a House leader, serve on such a council."

Each of us did just that. To the press we released a polite response signed by Mr. Rayburn and Lyndon Johnson, by now the Senate's majority leader. Although it graciously acknowledged our interest in "the help of any committee set up by the Democratic National Committee" and expressed a willingness to "consult with them at any time," we explicitly rejected any attempt to assert "outside" influence upon the two deliberative bodies. Our actions spoke even louder: each of us in both bodies' leadership refused to participate. As it turned out, only eight of the twenty did join. Shorn of any of the Democratic congressional leadership, the advisory committee limped along for a few more years, issuing pronouncements and manifestos that nearly everyone ignored.

The result was a major embarrassment for Paul Butler and, I suppose, the national committee. It should be said, however, that they should have known better. Anybody who understood the congressional leadership should have known better. Anyone who wants to understand the Democratic party or the American Congress of the late 1950s has to know better.

The congressional leadership was just that: the leaders of Congress. As Democrats, we supported our party's presidential nominee and worked for his success. I know that I spoke for Adlai Stevenson at every opportunity in both 1952 and 1956. Nonetheless, like Sam Rayburn, John McCormack, and (in the Senate) Lyndon Johnson, my job was not to put Governor Stevenson in the White House. Neither was it to see that his campaign promises or the pronouncements of some appointed advisory committee became law. Our job was to cultivate winning majorities in the two houses of Congress. Our Democratic party was the elected Democratic membership of Congress. The Democratic program was what it would approve. And as we say in Oklahoma, you have to plow with the horses you have.

What we had was 230 or so Democrats in the House. The exact number was just that number of individuals, and some of them were truly individuals, men of independent judgment and pride in that independence. A good whip had to know who they were and how to approach them, and know, too, that he would not often be successful. A large number, however, fell into one of three broad groups.

One was the congressmen, usually northern or eastern, who represented the last of the legendary big-city machines. Their ethnic and working-class constituencies still rolled up huge Democratic majorities that could be delivered with dependable regularity. Those close to the machines' inner councils thereby could count on making careers of Congress, as well as on the ability to make or break their colleagues' careers. Moreover, they tended to maintain alliances with other urban machine representatives on matters vital to their similar constituencies—labor and welfare issues, for example. Thus, Chicago's Tom O'Brien could sit silently on the House floor and with the slightest nod of his head decide the fate of many a bill; he did not have to say a word to do it. He did not even have to stand to show the votes that he carried around in his back pocket.

Another group of congressmen liked to stand and speak on the House floor and anywhere else they got the chance. The liberals were a small but vocal minority. Usually northern or western in origin and younger in age, the liberals shared a common belief in change. That generally meant taking the inherited Democratic agenda both deeper (increasing Social Security's responsibilities, for example) and broader (into black civil rights, for another). Men like Minnesota's Eugene McCarthy and Montana's Lee Metcalfe were tireless champions of both causes and much more, too. As a group, however, the liberal crowd never had anything like the discipline of the machine Democrats. Beyond common convictions, they lacked specific concentration. Moreover, many were mavericks, unwilling to scar their convictions with the branding iron of compromise, either with other groups or even one another.

Neither of these groups had anything like the significance that fell to the southerners. As I write this thirty years after the fact, I put them last. At the time I was my party's whip, they always came first.

One thing that always put them there was simple arithmetic. The South (by which I mean the old Confederacy plus the former slaveholding border states of Missouri, Kentucky, West Virginia, Maryland, and Oklahoma) was still pretty much the Solid South, at least in congressional elections. A very popular Republican like Eisenhower might turn voters' heads in isolated presidential races, but in congressional campaigns, the southerners went right on stamping that Democratic rooster, just as their daddies had done ever since Reconstruction. I do not know that the saying was true that they would have sent a yellow dog to Congress if he were on the Democratic ticket, but I do suspect that they would have kept him there if he were an incumbent.

Nowhere else, except in a few big cities, was the Democratic label as vital to success. For that reason, the sixteen southern states usually sent more Democrats to Congress than did the rest of the states combined. After 1954, for example, they gave us 134 of the 231 Democrats in the House. Nowhere else, not even in the big cities, was a Democratic congressman so secure from competition. For that reason, they stayed on and on. Those southern Democrats who were sitting when I became whip collectively had served 1,248 years, with very many more sure to come.

Although the South had not even a quarter of America's voting population, no minority had ever exercised such power in national affairs. Its hold upon so many Democratic seats was a hold upon the lever that governed the country. More than numbers was involved, though. While there were exceptions—I was one of many—most of those southern Democrats represented a powerful establishment, an interlocking network of landowners, financiers, industrialists, and professionals, all men of power, all men of white flesh. Over generations, that establishment had learned to pick outstanding young men of talent, men imbued with the establishment's views, and send them to Congress. It kept sending them back and watched them grow old as they voted the establishment's way and expressed the establishment's opinions.

Their soft southern drawl sheathed the cold steel of shared convictions. Its highest priority was to maintain that establishment. This meant to discourage voting by blacks and poor whites through poll taxes, literacy tests, and stiff registration laws. It meant maintaining states' rights to keep the federal bureaucrats out of Dixie. It meant minimal welfare laws to turn back the carpetbaggers. It meant harsh antilabor statutes to cast out union organizers. It meant miserly educational programs to ward off alien ideas. Most of all, it meant white supremacy.

Their numbers gave the southern Democrats influence; their common convictions gave them force. What gave them their power was the House's internal structure of authority. The mechanism that America had evolved to guide legislation turned out to be perfectly fitted to the southerners' interest in shaping it.

"Congress in committee," Professor Woodrow Wilson wrote long ago, "is Congress at work." So it remained. No president, no party panel, not even the Speaker and the formal leadership determine what Congress will and will not do. For that matter, neither does the mass of 435 members. The membership, contained entirely within the House walls and answerable only to independent districts, controls the House, but only as that membership is organized into committees. In most cases it is the committees that draft the bills the House will consider. The committees declare what form those bills will take. Often, the committees decide what changes the House can consider in them. The committees determine how long the House will debate. The committees' recommendations usually decide how the House will vote. Congress in committee *is* Congress at work. And Congress in committee was usually the southern Democrats in control. What made that so was the mechanism of committee assignment and the internal structure of committee influence.

Just as I had done back in 1947 when I boldly sought assignment to three prestigious committees, every person who first comes to Congress publicly indicates his committee preferences and privately prays for success. For a Democrat, those prayers and preferences are answered by the party's committee on committees. Between 1910 and my own Speakership, that consisted of the Democratic members who also sat on the Ways and Means Committee. When I went to Congress, six of the ten committee Democrats were senior southerners. By the time I became whip in 1955, it was eight of fifteen, and the same number sat at the decade's end.

Although the Ways and Means Democrats paid some attention to an individual's preference and more to achieving some claim to regional balance, the South's influence was visible in the assignments. A routine committee like Interior and Insular Affairs had in the mid-1950s only six southerners among its eighteen members. For a powerful committee like Armed Services, the proportion was fourteen southerners out of twenty-two.

Far more important even than assignment was the structure of power *within* each committee and thereby for the Congress as a whole. Like other men, all congressmen may be created equal, but in Washington, they do not stay that way. Committee chairmen separately could determine their committee's products; collectively they could decide the Congress's output. Their power was great and its source was singular. Congressmen became chairmen (and thus more equal than others) at the exact moment they had served on a committee longer than any other committee member. Seniority was its name. Southern domination was its effect.

Like so much else, the process dated to 1910, when the Democrats and some rebellious Republicans smashed the power of old Joe Cannon. Like most of his predecessors, Speaker Cannon had assigned committee memberships for both his own party (the Republicans) and the minority, too. He also had selected each committee chairman. In the revolt of 1910, the Democrats won the right to make their own committee assignments, giving it in time to the southern-dominated Ways and Means Democrats. That revolt also overturned the Speaker's power to name chairmen. Heretofore dictated by the whims of one man, chairmanships became the automatic reward of an unarguable process. They were the prizes of longevity.

For all of its apparent irrationality and injustice, the seniority system did have its virtues. It undeniably fostered stability by encouraging members to stick with their committees for their entire careers, and it guaranteed the committees experienced leadership. Because the process was automatic, it preserved Congress's independence from outside pressures, including lobbyists and the White House. Also, it unquestionably was the only way men like Bill Dawson and Adam Clayton Powell could have become chairmen. Despite Powell's later notoriety, the two were capable legislators. For a long time they were the only two blacks in Congress, but precisely because they were there for a long time, both rose to become committee chairmen, Dawson of Government Operations and Powell of Education and Labor.

More noticeable, though, and far more important, were the system's more typical beneficiaries. Because southern Democrats profited most from incumbency, they profited most from the seniority system. When I became whip, New England, the North Atlantic, the Midwest, and the West all combined to provide chairmen of only five committees: Illinois's Bill Dawson (Government Operations), California's Clair Engle (Interior and Insular Affairs), New York's Emmanuel Celler and Charles Buckley (Judiciary and Public Works, respectively), and Pennsylvania's Francis Walter (Un-American Activities.) Everywhere else I looked—across fifteen committees—there ruled a solid phalanx of southern chairmen:

Agriculture—Harold Cooley of North Carolina
Appropriations—Clarence Cannon of Missouri
Armed Services—Carl Vinson of Georgia
Banking and Currency—Brent Spence of Kentucky
District of Columbia—John McMillan of South Carolina
Education and Labor—Graham Barden of North Carolina
Foreign Affairs—James P. Richards of South Carolina
House Administration—Omar Burleson of Texas
Interstate and Foreign Commerce—Percy Priest of Tennessee
Rules—Howard Smith of Virginia
Veterans' Affairs—Olin Teague of Texas
Ways and Means—Jere Cooper of Tennessee

Surrounding them were the ranking members of the majority party. As heads of the chief subcommittees, these men controlled many of the separate pieces of major legislation. In full committee deliberations, their voices spoke louder than others in shaping those pieces into a whole. And because of the seniority system, those voices, too, usually had southern accents. Take, for example, my own committee, Agriculture. Ranking behind Chairman Cooley in order were the following in 1955: Bob Pogue of Texas; George Grant of Alabama; E. C. Gathings of Arkansas; John McMillan of South Carolina; Tom Abernathy of Mississippi; myself of Oklahoma; Watkins Abbitt of Virginia. Altogether, then, the South not only held fourteen of the twenty-one Democratic seats on that committee, but southerners occupied all of the top eight positions. It was the South, then, not Ezra Taft Benson, not Dwight Eisenhower, not the Democratic National Committee, and not some outside advisory group, that wrote America's agricultural legislation. It also was southern committee chairmen, none of these others, who decided what the Democratic House of Representatives would do.

There was not a weak man among the chairmen. All had learned from experience. All were capable. And yet I could not help but reflect upon how accidents of birth in the right part of the country, mixed with some early good fortune, had put them where they were.

Take Carl Vinson, for instance. After he helped me with my Marine and his mother, Vinson and I became close friends. I already knew he had served in the House longer than any current member except Mr. Rayburn (Vinson eventually established the record for continuous tenure: fifty years). I knew, too, that his colleagues admiringly called him the Swamp Fox in testimony to his canniness. In time, he told me how he had come to be in the House.

It seems that back in 1914, when I was just a boy down in Bug Tussle and Dwight Eisenhower was a cadet at West Point, Vinson had announced his candidacy for Congress from Georgia's Sixth District. He had the reputation for a fondness for alcohol, not unique to the district or to Georgia, but enough to cause a certain Baptist preacher to come out strongly against him. The fellow had enough of a following to swing the election, so young Mr. Vinson called on him.

The preacher came out on his front porch early one morning to find Carl Vinson there. He had slept the night on the porch so as not to miss him. The preacher was surprised to find the candidate there, but he swiftly buckled on his moral armor and went on the attack.

"It won't do you any good being here, 'cause I'm not about to be for you," he said. "Georgia cannot elect a man of your sorry morals to the House of Representatives. I will never support a man like you." Vinson's eyes misted a bit as he softly answered, "I didn't come here to ask you to vote for me. I came here to ask you to pray for me." The two went into the preacher's house, and one of them was converted. The preacher came out blazing for Carl Vinson for Congress. Vinson went to Congress, went on going to Congress, and went on drinking, too.

With no real opposition (after the preacher), Carl Vinson rose steadily up the ranks. He rose to head the Naval Affairs Committee and its successor, the Armed Services Committee. Utterly secure, he ran a committee with no tolerance at all for interference. Lyndon Johnson used to tell the story of when he had served with Vinson on Naval Affairs and once had tried to ask a question of an admiral who was testifying. The chairman slammed his gavel down and ruled the question out of order. Lyndon, no shrinking violet himself, got mad. Declaring that he had never once been allowed to speak, he shouted that "after three terms a fellow should be allowed to ask a simple question." "All right," Vinson gave in, "but just one."

Such was part of the power that seniority could give a man. But that was only a part. The bigger part was that Armed Services Chairman Carl Vinson largely made up the defense budget of the United States. Carl Vinson authorized to the penny what the army, the navy, the air force, and the marines would spend. With fellow Georgian Richard Russell of the Senate Armed Services Committee, Carl Vinson determined the exact location and allowable appropriation for every military base in every congressional district in the entire country. Seniority gave him that power. His great expertise, his awesome intelligence, his fierce willpower—these allowed him to make the most of it. Still, I never quite got over thinking how important that preacher's prayer had turned out to be.

That so many legislative committees sat firmly under southern domination explained a great deal of that one region's impact upon congressional affairs. Separately, powerful southerners determined many of the problems that Congress would address.

Each, in his special field, defined the allowable answers. At the heart of the South's powers, however, lay one very special committee, one designed to have no legislative authority at all. Nonetheless, skillful southerners had managed to transform it into the citadel of southern ascendency. It was the House Committee on Rules.

Before 1910, the Rules Committee had functioned as an indispensable arm of the House leadership. It was known as the Speaker's committee because the Speaker named its members, and, befitting its significance, he himself served as its chairman. Once again, however, the revolt against Speaker Cannon had born soured fruit. By barring the Speaker's service on the committee and declaring that its members would be appointed and its chairman selected like those of every other committee, the reformers had made the Rules Committee independent of Speaker Cannon's whims. They also had made it independent of any future Speaker's control.

Attempting to democratize power by dispersing it, the reformers had left it for some group outside the elected leadership to grab. The Rules Committee was the place to grab it, for that one committee sat right at the center of congressional power, not power over a single bill, but power over the entire process of legislating *all* bills. The metaphor commonly used to describe that power was to refer to the Rules Committee as the House's traffic light.

As the legislative committees sent finished bills down the road to consideration by the full House, each bill first pulled up at the Rules Committee. The committee would assign for each a rule that established the conditions for House debate. Commonly, the rule would fix the time limit for debate. In addition, it could specify the number and type of amendments that would be permitted from the floor. Some bills—tax legislation, most notably—usually received closed rules, which allowed no amendments and forced the members to vote up or down on the committee bill. Other bills received open rules, which permitted unlimited amendments. In yet other instances, the rule could specify precisely what amendments would be allowed. Sometimes it would specify the exact wording of the permissible amendments.

The power inherent to defining those different conditions was obvious, but the committee's power ran even deeper. It could refuse to issue any rule at all. When it did, the traffic light burned a steady red and the entire legislative process screeched to a halt. Without a rule, there could be no debate, there could be no amendments, there could be no consideration of the bill at all. Not, at least, without circumstances known to congressional scholars but hardly ever seen by House members.

Four procedures existed to move a bill beyond the Rules Committee's stoplight, but none had much potential. First, the bill could be placed on the Consent Calendar and thereby be called to the floor on the first and third Mondays of each month. A single objection (certain to come on any matter of importance) by even one of the 435 members would close that exit, however.

The second escape was the suspension-of-the-rules process, but it required a two-thirds vote for the bill's passage. No broad bill could press through that narrow tunnel.

A third alternative occurred once a week on Calendar Wednesday when committee chairmen could bypass the Rules Committee to put a bill before the House. That avenue, however, opened only as the Speaker went down the roll of committees in alphabetical order. Moreover, any bill so presented had to be disposed of in that one legislative day; otherwise, the process would begin again a week later. Thus, a chairman of Agriculture or Appropriations could cooperate with the Rules Committee to maintain the traffic jam of Ways and Means or Veterans' Affairs bill that sat idling behind him.

Finally, a bill's supporters could file a discharge petition to pull the bill from the Rules Committee and set it on the floor. All that took was for a majority of the members, 218, to sign the petition. At first glance this might seem a plausible deliverance, since any bill truly desired by the majority could reach the floor if that same majority merely signed a piece of paper. In fact, it probably was the easiest way to bypass an obstructionist traffic light. It was so easy that from 1923 to 1959, some 797 discharge petitions had been filed, but exactly one bill (the 1938 Wages and Hours Act) had made good the escape to become law under this—the easiest—alternative.

Even should a way be found to bypass the Rules Committee, get a bill to the floor, and pass it, the committee had yet another power, this time the power to erect an impassable barricade. If the Senate were to pass the same bill with as much as a single difference—one word more or less, one comma added or deleted—the difference would have to be resolved before sending it to the president. The mechanism was to send the bill to a conference committee, where House and Senate members would iron out the differences. Should a single member object to sending the bill to conference, the Rules Committee first had to approve the submission.

In practice, then, that one committee could serve not as a traffic light but as an execution chamber. That is exactly why every Speaker through Joe Cannon had insisted upon controlling the Rules Committee. When Cannon lost to the reformers, what was lost was the leadership's (and the membership's) right to control the House of Representatives. The people who won it were those brilliant practitioners of congressional politics. They were the southern Democrats.

As long ago as 1937, the southerners perfected the method of their control. Their conservative economic and social views made them the natural allies of equally conservative Republicans. Roosevelt's liberal programs made the two more compatible ideologically. Only FDR's early towering popularity helped hold the southerners to him. In 1937, that popularity was broken when Roosevelt attempted to "pack" the Supreme Court with a bill to increase the number of justices. The public uproar over the move, and Congress's defeat of the bill, signaled that the southern Democrats could safely side with the Republicans against their own president and their own House leaders. Led by Georgia's Gene Cox, a crude but crafty race baiter, they did just that. The three southern Democrats serving on the twelve-member Rules Com-

mittee began voting with the four Republican members to produce a seven-to-five majority that kept the New Deal at bay by
keeping its initiatives off the floor. It is estimated that this little
coalition of seven willful men killed more than twenty bills of
Democratic Presidents Franklin Roosevelt and Harry Truman.
One scholar, James Robinson, has counted exactly eighty-three occasions between 1947 and 1959 when the same coalition similarly
nullified the directions of the Democratic leadership of Congress.

The number would have been larger yet but for the extraordinary personal influence of Sam Rayburn. Mr. Rayburn got along
well with Joe Martin, the former Speaker who stayed on as the
GOP's floor leader. He got along even better with Gene Cox, who,
despite his ideological differences, almost worshiped the Speaker
and loved striking blows for liberty with him at the Board of Education. I do not know how many times a word uttered there by
Mr. Rayburn persuaded Martin or Cox to pressure one of their fol-
lowers into switching a swing vote or arranging a timely absence. I
do know that the number was large, and I know that Sam Rayburn
was the only man with enough personal prestige to pull it off.

That, though, was a consequence of Mr. Rayburn's personal
stature. His institutional power as Speaker over the Rules Committee was much less. In fact, it was almost nonexistent. Only
briefly did the House allow anyone power to bypass the committee. In 1949, on the opening day of the Eighty-first Congress, the
House amended its rules to allow a committee chairman to bring a
bill to the floor if the Rules Committee had not done so within
twenty-one days after receiving it. Only because of the twenty-
one-day rule was the House able to vote on such important legislation as the anti–poll tax bill, as well as on public-housing and
minimum-wage bills. Two years later, after the Republicans had
picked up twenty-nine seats in the 1950 elections, the rule lost to
a coalition of Republicans and southern Democrats. Both recognized the Rules Committee as the traffic light that protected their
minority's pedestrians. Neither was concerned with the traffic jam
that stalled the majority's vehicles.

The Democratic leadership thereupon had only the personal influence of Sam Rayburn to overcome the situation that became unendurable with two events in the 1950s. In 1959, Charles A. Halleck of Indiana engineered a coup that ousted Joe Martin as the Republicans' leader. Halleck won the post after criticizing Martin's "cronyism" toward the Democrats in general and Sam Rayburn in particular. A self-proclaimed "gut fighter," Halleck was not at all inclined to swing an occasional Republican vote on the Rules Committee to benefit the Democratic leadership.

By that time, we needed all the help we could get. In 1955, Howard W. Smith had ascended to the chairmanship of Rules. He was every bit as conservative as Gene Cox, but Judge Smith (he kept the title long after his early service in the Virginia judiciary) was infinitely smarter. In fact, with the possible exception of Sam Rayburn, Howard Smith was the smartest man and the most able legislator that I ever saw in Congress. And, as he often said, he was not serving in Congress to be some traffic cop.

Personally, the old judge was a living monument to Virginia gentility. I never once saw him lose his temper. His floor speeches were models of decorum. Always polite, his innate reserve parted just enough to display his friendliness toward every member. He was the kind who could drape an arm around your shoulder while his free hand was cutting out your heart. He knew the parliamentary rules better than any member and how to turn them to his advantage. When he was working on a bill, he knew as much about it as its authors and more about how to beat it. Most of all, he had a determination that you hardly ever see in people. To Howard Smith, being called a reactionary was no insult. To him, it was a badge of honor, testifying to his consuming faith. Reaction was his religion, and he was its prophet, its messiah, and its apostle, all rolled into one.

So reactionary and so talented was he that even Virginia's other legendary archconservative, Senator Harry Flood Byrd, recognized Howard Smith as his own superior. In the House, every conservative southern Democrat deferred to his leadership. Any

*With the possible exception of Sam Rayburn, Howard Smith was the smartest man and the most able legislator that I ever saw in Congress.*

bill that threatened their hidebound orthodoxy could count on Judge Smith direct their fight against it. He led it with all the brilliance of a Confederate general—and with more success.

First would come the assembly of the southern high command, the so-called southern caucus, in which the wily veterans of many a fight would gather in a private office. A typical collection might include Sidney Herlong of Florida, F. Edward Hebert of Louisiana, Graham Barden of North Carolina, Jim Richards of South Carolina, and Mississippi's William Colmer and John Bell Williams. Under the judge's leadership, the group would dissect the offending measure line by line, determining what was to be stricken and what was to be amended, how, and by whom. The strategy set, each participant became an emissary to the remaining southerners, marshaling Dixie's troops for battle. Meanwhile, Smith contacted Charlie Halleck to arrange for Republican reinforcements.

As the floor fight unfolded, Howard Smith became the field commander, a master in battle. A salvo of southern oratory might open the struggle, to be followed by brilliant parliamentary maneuvers to outflank and demoralize the opposition. Counterattacks were parried; brief reverses were met with instant tactical changes. Whatever the outcome, it could be said of Judge Smith, as it was said of General Lee, that even his adversaries respected him. Because I was often one of them, I knew that especially his adversaries respected him.

Of course, the judge had one legislative advantage for which Robert E. Lee had no military equivalent. After he became chairman of the Rules Committee, he was in a position to dictate the terms of battle and on occasion win it with a single mighty blow. Working with him on the committee was his faithful lieutenant, Bill Colmer. Bill lacked Smith's brilliance but gave him all the loyalty expected of an awestruck junior officer. In league with the four archconservative Republicans that Halleck put on the committee, Smith always had the easy option of a six-to-six vote on sending a bill to the full House—enough to keep it his prisoner, for release required a majority, at least seven. Even without employing that weapon, the mere threat of it could be enough to compel his foes to accept his views, in effect to surrender the substance of the fight just to get the bill out of committee. During my first term as whip, Howard Smith did exactly that with bills regarding housing, absentee voting, the doctors' draft, and the distribution of polio vaccine. With Colmer and Joe Martin's obstinate Republicans, he refused any compromise to bury outright a bill to provide aid to chronically depressed areas.

As it turned out, the aid bill was one of the items that Paul Butler and his advisory group wanted to place on the Democratic agenda. They were looking for issues that a Democratic nominee could use in the next presidential election. In the House leadership, we were looking not for issues but for laws. They wanted to make a record; we had to make policy.

And we had to plow with the horses we had.

In some circles, there was talk at the time that something had to be done to break the power of the House's southern Democrats. I knew quite well just how much power they had and just how difficult it was to work around. Still, I judged much of that talk to be unrealistic. In the first place, much of it was of the form of what Congress *should* be, entirely unmindful of what Congress in fact *was*. The power of the southern Democrats was a consequence of the internal structure of Congress, not its cause. To break their power would require the complete dismantling of much of that structure. That, in turn, would require the cooperation of precisely all those elements that had benefited from the structure. And nearly every powerful member had benefited from it; it was why they were powerful. Moreover, the experience of the last major reform of congressional procedures—the 1910 Cannon revolt—provided, at best, mixed lessons regarding the salutary effect of breaking up congressional power.

What really troubled me most was the implied (sometimes the explicit) claim that the southern Democrats were not "real" Democrats. This was not just because many outsiders looked upon me as a southerner, too, though many in the news media and the academy did. Neither was it because many southerners were my close friends, though they often were men whose friendships I valued and whose abilities I respected. No, what struck me was the arrogance of the claim that the men who gave us most of the Democratic membership of Congress were not Democrats. If they were not Democrats, who were? What gave any other group an exclusive claim to that title? There was none stronger than the fact that these men had been elected to office as Democrats and were judged by their own constituents every two years to be worthy Democrats. I could not help but notice that few of their journalistic and academic critics could offer the same credentials.

Ours was a diverse party of diverse viewpoints, but our diversity only mirrored that of the American people. No one group had a unique claim to the word *Democrat* any more than to the word *American*. As part of the party's congressional leadership, I never once forgot that.

Neither did I forget the limits to our leadership. Historically, the elected leadership of Congress had maintained its institutional authority by controlling the Rules Committee and the legislative committees, as well as by using the Democratic caucus to shape party policy. In the 1950s, the Rules Committee had become an independent fiefdom. Only on very important matters could Speaker Rayburn step in to direct a committee chairman's work, and even then his entrée was his enormous personal prestige. Sam Rayburn would not cheapen that currency by using it often. The party caucus that other Speakers had used to bind Democrats to a common position had withered to brief biennial assemblies to renominate our leadership team. Mr. Rayburn dared ask no more of it for fear that the party would split wide open.

If these were our limits, then dedication, sensitivity, and a spirit of cooperation became our tools. Because they had them, Sam Rayburn, a Baptist from Fannin County, Texas, and John McCormack, a Catholic from South Boston, worked together. They had a whip (this Methodist from Oklahoma) who worked with them. I was determined to do as much as possible to win as much support as possible on as many issues as possible. Knowing just what *was* possible, I was awfully proud of what we did.

Events at the decade's turn simultaneously highlighted and magnified both the leadership's limits and its possibilities. In 1958, Americans went to the polls amid a major recession, the second

Republican recession in five years. The effects were most severe in midwestern and northeastern industrial areas. The consequence was that those districts turned out Republican congressmen and replaced them with a corps of young, activist Democrats. Altogether, we picked up forty-eight seats, forty-three of them from those two regions. Two hundred eighty-two Democrats gave our party its largest majority since so many had come in with the Roosevelt landslide of 1936. Even more striking, for the first time since FDR the South provided less than half of the Democratic membership.

Many of the new members were beneficiaries of a rare organized effort by liberal Democrats to unite to increase their number and influence. A group led by Lee Metcalfe had provided some eighty northern and western candidates with free (and effective) campaign aids. As the grateful but confused newcomers reached Washington, the group followed up its work by providing orientation sessions, temporary office space, and experienced individual advice. I knew from my own experience as a freshman just how helpful that could be to a new member. I also knew that the veteran liberals had much to gain, too. Familiar with the House's ways, I was not too surprised at the outcome.

Toward the end of the 1959 session, six experienced liberals called a meeting of northern and western Democrats to discuss "imperative issues of concern." About forty came. One who was there described that initial meeting as having the air of an old-time revival. Member after member rose "to confess his own failure or frustration and to signify his own willingness to work for the common good." Other meetings followed. Soon the revival turned into an embryonic organized religion. Calling itself the Democratic Study Group (the title was deliberately neutral), the group selected Metcalfe chairman and surrounded him with capable, experienced assistants. Frank Thompson of New Jersey became secretary. Co-equal vice-chairmen were John Blatnik of Minnesota, Frank Coffin of Maine, William Green of Pennsylvania, and FDR's son James Roosevelt of California.

It was an impressive group. More impressive still was the river of activity that flowed from the DSG's small temporary office. To increase communication and build morale, it sponsored seminars conducted by outside experts. A steady stream of mimeographed papers provided issue analysis and explained congressional procedures, including such arcane practices as Calendar Wednesday. Seven task forces, each directed by knowledgeable members, worked on issues of common concern: civil rights, aid to education, depressed areas, housing and urban renewal, the farm problems, a higher minimum wage, and a medical care program under Social Security. For each, the task forces prepared thorough background papers and mapped legislative strategy. Meanwhile, the initial group of 40 had swollen to around 125, mostly western and northern Democrats—just about the same number, 133, that came to us from the South.

Through all of this, the DSG was careful to pledge its allegiance to the formal House leadership. On our side, my position as whip ruled out any personal participation. Responsible to the entire Democratic membership, I could no more be identified with its efforts than I could those of Judge Smith's informal but mighty southern caucus. Nonetheless, I fully appreciated the DSG's efforts and marveled at its ability to harness so many strong but heretofore free-spirited broncos. This was a group that could do some plowing.

It was also a group that could kick over the traces. Sam Rayburn was at the very peak of his influence and authority. Thus, the DSG emphasized its desire to help the Speaker by cooperating with his leadership. More revealing than its words was its reliance upon Richard Bolling.

Dick Bolling had represented the Kansas City district since 1948. An early member of Americans for Democratic Action (ADA), Dick was a steady champion of liberal causes. He also became something of a protégé of Speaker Rayburn. Perhaps Mr. Rayburn saw him as a bridge to the party's ADA types. Perhaps he believed that Dick's Alabama upbringing and newspaper and academic experience could combine with his liberal sentiments to make Dick sensitive to many party elements. Most likely, Sam

Rayburn saw in Dick Bolling what he had seen in Lyndon Johnson, Hale Boggs, and others (including me): here was a smart young congressman with a brilliant career that the Speaker could promote and shape. In any event, Dick became a regular at the Board of Education. It was natural that the DSG would turn to Dick as a link to the leadership and as a source of important counsel.

For his part, Mr. Rayburn appreciated the group's deference and steadily increased his reliance on Bolling. Publicly, he granted the DSG its office space (one of the Speaker's prerogatives) and told the press that these were "good boys" whose enthusiasm was a blessing. Privately, I learned from John Holton, the Speaker's administrative assistant, that Mr. Rayburn would pace the floor of his office, talking loudly to himself. He swore that if these smart young kids wanted to take him on, he would "tear them to pieces."

It was not Sam Rayburn they wanted to take on; it was the House's structure of power and its conservative consequences. Although the 1958 elections had changed vastly the complexion of the House since I had become whip, there had been virtually no change in its distribution of effective power. Only one southern chairman had been replaced by a nonsouthern beneficiary of seniority, that when Thomas E. Morgan of Pennsylvania ascended to the chairmanship of the Foreign Affairs Committee in place of South Carolina's Jim Richards. Any loss of southern influence there was more than offset by the change in two of our most vital committees. Ways and Means was now commanded by Wilbur Mills of Arkansas, a man just as southern as his predecessor, Jere Cooper, and even more capable. On Interstate and Foreign Commerce, Percy Priest had departed to turn over the chairmanship to Oren Harris of Arkansas, with John Bell Williams of Mississippi as ranking Democrat. Both were close to Howard Smith.

Smith's own influence had weakened none at all. As cagey as ever, he grew even more experienced as he continued to head the Rules Committee. That committee had kept exactly the same Democratic membership in exactly the same order of influence. The only difference after 1958 was that Charlie Halleck stacked the Republican side with four archconservatives. Hence the election of the most liberal Congress since the New Deal and the impressive creation of the Democratic Study Group made no difference at all in the House's decision-making process and little noticeable difference in its decisions. The difference was that Sam Rayburn, John McCormack, and I all found our jobs harder still. Two groups of nearly equal number but quite disparate power were pulling away in two different directions. Caught in the middle was the Democratic leadership, surrounded by questions that begged for answers and issues that cried out for Democratic peace when there was no peace.

And then presidential politics made the cries even louder.

In 1960, General Eisenhower was the grateful recipient of the GOP's anti-third-term slap at FDR. Without the popular Ike to run against, our party's prospects of returning to the White House were good. They were good enough to call forth a small swarm of Democratic contenders. Two of them were friends of mine from the House.

Jack Kennedy had entered the House with me and had gone on to the Senate with impressive election wins in 1952 and 1958. In between was his near capture of the vice-presidential nomination in '56. From that moment on, I knew that he had a national career ahead of him, a career pointed toward the presidency.

As a congressman, Lyndon Johnson had served only one term with me, and he had spent much of it campaigning for the Senate election of 1948. Upon reaching the other body, he soared to singular prominence. As its young majority leader, he made that office what it remains today. His influence in the Senate had but one equivalent: that of his mentor, Sam Rayburn, in the House. Around Mr. Rayburn, at least, Lyndon took no pains to conceal even loftier ambitions. I remember accompanying them on an airplane trip in 1956 when Lyndon Johnson begged the Speaker to help him get that year's presidential nomination. Mr. Rayburn sat embarrassed and silent, but both he and I knew that Lyndon's eye would never wander far from the main prize.

Both Jack Kennedy and Lyndon Johnson were my friends. Ei-

ther could have been (and both became) outstanding presidents.
In 1960, I admired Jack Kennedy for his vigor, his eloquence, and
his ability to organize an impressive nationwide campaign. Lyndon Johnson I respected for his masterful legislative expertise.
Their combination into one ticket was a formidable alliance that
made me awfully happy personally. It did result, though, in one
immediate discomfort politically.

Kennedy's Catholicism concerned me not at all, except that I
knew it would hurt him badly in my own state. As a young man I
had seen Al Smith fall victim to Oklahoma's militant Protestant-
ism, and I had not seen much happen since to convince me that
Sooner voters were ready to support a Catholic candidate. In the
campaign, I was mighty proud that one thing had changed. Back
in 1928, nearly every Oklahoma Democratic politician had made
rats' departures from Smith's sinking ship. In 1960, a good number of us came out squarely for John Kennedy and against religious bigotry. In more than sixty speeches and radio addresses, I
spoke earnestly of the need for Democratic leadership in the
White House, and I mixed reason with derision to take on intol-
erance directly. Our young governor, J. Howard Edmondson, willingly sacrificed his own shrinking popularity to tell Oklahomans
what they did not want to hear. I may never have been prouder of
Senator Robert S. Kerr than I was when he forthrightly addressed
a hostile crowd at an Oklahoma City rally. Engaged in a tough reelection fight himself, the man famed as Baptist Bob blasted the
ugly Know-Nothingness of bigotry to endorse boldly "a patriotic
Catholic Democrat for president."

In the end, our appeals did not turn the situation around.
Richard Nixon kept the state in the Republican column where Ike
twice had placed it. Kennedy carried only one congressional district, my Third. But then I already thought a lot of its voters' good
sense. Our efforts may not have been in vain, though. Since the
governor, the senator, and many more of us (including Jack
Kennedy) took on the issue squarely in 1960, Oklahomans have
elected one Catholic governor (Dewey Bartlett), two Catholic
senators (Bartlett and Don Nickles), and one Catholic congressman

(James Jones). That is testimony to what may have been the lasting effect of Kennedy's election for Oklahoma and America. It removed the unspoken, unholy religious test for public office.

In the context of the Congress and of 1960, John Kennedy's campaign and election had a different meaning. They triggered the hardest fight I ever saw in the House. At stake was the nature of the Democratic party and control of the legislative process. The battlefield was the House Committee on Rules.

Both houses had recessed for the national conventions and returned in August. Those last few hot days of the Eighty-sixth Congress were important to our party and our nominees, Senators Kennedy and Johnson. Both pledged their "full energies" to pushing a program through to final adoption. At its heart were three bills that had consumed most of the previous two years: an expanded housing program, federal aid to education, and a higher minimum wage. Each died a graceless death in the Rules Committee at the hands of Judge Smith and his gang of five. The postconvention session had been billed as "Kennedy's Congress," a demonstration of the Democrats' ability to "get the country moving again" behind an activist nominee and his running mate, a man chosen for his legislative legerdemain. Instead, it pointed to the paralysis that kept the Congress from moving at all. It turned out to be Howard Smith's Congress, not John Kennedy's and not the Democratic leadership's.

To the press and general public, the issue that Smith's power and obstinacy had raised was singular. Would the new Democratic president control the House or would a tough-minded reactionary from Broad Run, Virginia? To us in the leadership, that question was secondary to other, harder ones. Could we meet our obligations to the House and the nation with an independent and hostile Rules Committee? Could we intervene in the legislative process without upsetting its interlocking machinery of committees, seniority, and procedure? How could a Speaker from Texas and his allies (including this whip from Oklahoma) take on the southern Democrats in the very bastion of their strength? Could we discipline our largest single element without driving them to permanent estrangement? These were the questions with which we wrestled. And we, not the young fellows moving into the White House, were the ones who had to answer them.

We began on a Saturday, the last day of 1960. Sam Rayburn had summoned us to the Capitol early. In the Speaker's office, John McCormack, Dick Bolling, Lew Deschler (the House parliamentarian), a few Texas congressmen, and I met with Mr. Rayburn to consider the options. Doing nothing was not one. The dismal records of the postconvention session had forced the issue.

For some time, the DSG had been pushing one alternative: restoring the twenty-one-day rule. I knew Mr. Rayburn well enough to know that that would go nowhere. The Speaker had been unenthusiastic about the procedure when we had it and had made no effort to block its repeal. He was not about to take away Smith's power to bring legislation to the floor only to give it directly to the committee chairmen. By doing that, a twenty-one-day rule would only further weaken the Speakership.

A second possibility was to expand the committee by adding three members to it, one Republican and two Democrats. While preserving the traditional two-to-one formal party split, two moderate or liberal Democrats would break the informal six-to-six conservative coalition. Mr. Rayburn told us that he had given Howard Smith that option just that morning. But the old judge would have none of it. He was ready to fight any move to alter the committee's makeup and its ability to block any legislation that he felt would bring ruin to America—by building schoolrooms, for example.

One option remained. Bill Colmer, the ranking Democrat and Judge Smith's alter ego, had been removed from the committee once: in 1947, when we had lost four assignments to the new Republican majority. Although there was no requirement that a member be restored to a committee assignment when his party regained the majority, Colmer had pleaded with John McCormack to get the place back when we took control in 1949. John had agreed, out of his friendship with Colmer, and Mr. Rayburn reluctantly had gone along to restore him to Rules. Colmer's mossback sentiments made him the sixth vote of the obstructionists; the same sentiments now made him vulnerable again. With Jamie Whitten, Arthur Winstead, and John Bell Williams, Bill Colmer had been one of four Mississippi congressmen to campaign openly against their party's presidential ticket in favor of a slate of independent electors. Twice before—after Theodore Roosevelt's Bull Moose campaign of 1912 and Robert M. La Follette's Progressive candidacy in 1924—the GOP caucus had punished disloyal Republicans by stripping their seniority and removing them from choice committees. Now, Bill Colmer's party bolt gave us the same option: remove the Mississippian in favor of a moderate or liberal Democrat on rules.

Carefully, we explored every option on that December afternoon. I remember that Sam Rayburn listened closely and questioned probingly. Whatever his own thoughts were, he kept them to himself. All of us knew that the final decision would be his.

The president-elect found out the same thing. When John Kennedy met with the congressional leadership team, he began by ticking off some routine items of business. Quickly disposing of them, he drew himself up and solemnly announced, "Now, I'd like to talk about the Rules Committee." Sam Rayburn's hand slapped the table, sounding like a gunshot. "No, sir," he shouted. "That is House business, and the House of Representatives will decide that. The White House has no business there at all." Kennedy sat silently, as we all did. Awkwardly, he moved on to another topic. Sam Rayburn had made his point. Now he would make his decision. All of us—the president, the floor leader, and the whip— would have to live with it. The president's program and our control of Congress would live or die with it, too.

For all of his apparent simplicity, Sam Rayburn was the most complex man I ever knew. On much lesser problems, I had seen him mull for days, never speaking, but weighing every factor in his remarkable mind. This time, he did the same thing. Not one of us closest to him knew what he would do. What he did was to devise the most brilliant strategy of his long career.

On January 2, 1961, the Speaker met with a group of liberal Democrats. There would be no restored twenty-one-day rule, he said, and Judge Smith had refused the compromise of enlarging the committee. Under the circumstances, he had decided that there was only one recourse: he, Sam Rayburn, would recommend that the Democratic caucus remove William Colmer from the Rules Committee and replace him with a loyal Democrat.

Almost instantly the liberals (never known for their secret-keeping capacity) leaked the word to the press: Sam Rayburn was going to "purge" Colmer. Most of the press and the House members were stunned. I know I was. In 1949, Mr. Rayburn stoutly had refused to punish the bolting Dixiecrats, and he had done the same thing in 1956 when Adam Clayton Powell endorsed Eisenhower. Singling out Colmer, therefore, flew in the face of his own precedents, always a powerful factor to the Speaker. Moreover, it seemed certain to provoke the southerners to revolt.

It did provoke them—to compromise. Even Howard Smith offered one. He agreed to release five bills that the president-elect had declared critical. This time it was the Speaker who would have none of it. The offer itself affirmed the committee's supposed sovereignty. Besides, the new president might end up wanting a hearing on more than five bills. (He did. In three years he sent us 1,034 recommendations.) Judge Smith's compromise was no compromise at all; it was an instrument of surrender, and now it was Sam Rayburn who was determined to fight.

It was old Carl Vinson who offered the only compromise Mr. Rayburn would accept. Fearful of a bloody fight to purge Colmer and of its even bloodier consequences, the Swamp Fox made the Speaker an offer. If Mr. Rayburn would drop the purge notion, Vinson would get him enough southern Democratic votes to add three new members to the Rules Committee. That was exactly where Mr. Rayburn had started and, I suspect, exactly where he wanted it decided. The purge threat had served to make the expansion seem moderate and to flush out the critical support in advance. The fight would be on Sam Rayburn's terms. Vinson's offer meant that whatever its outcome, a twelve-member committee or one of fifteen, there would be no permanent division into embittered southern and antisouthern elements.

Our job was to win that fight, and we called on all the resources we had. I approached every member, listening and persuading. John McCormack did the same. Carl Vinson worked among the southerners to redeem his commitment. Our outside friends, labor unions and civil-rights groups most notably, contacted every member who would listen to them. Our greatest asset, however, was Sam Rayburn. Those few weeks seemed to take thirty years off his tired old body and fifty off his spirit. He monitored, directed, and coordinated all of our efforts. His stout frame, stepping lightly now, roamed the House hallways, where he cornered members and pressed his case. At least one heard it in language that no ambitious member could resist. "The question under discussion is a simple one," Sam Rayburn told the young fellow. "Are you for the Speaker or are you for that old man from Virginia?"

That old man from Virginia, who was two years younger than the rejuvenated Speaker, used all of his caginess, too. He had now an open alliance with the Republican leadership to block the expansion (the "packing," they called it) of the committee. While Charlie Halleck slammed into Republican guts, Judge Smith went his soft-spoken way. That way was to marshal all the forces of the southern establishment—the editors, the bankers, the manufacturers, the professional men—into a mighty force to save Dixie by denying Mr. Rayburn the southern votes he needed to win.

For his part, John Kennedy was publicly detached. At his first press conference, the new president observed that he hoped Mr. Rayburn would prevail, but he emphasized that "the responsibility rests with the members of the House. . . . I merely give my view as an interested citizen."

If that indicated that the president had learned the Speaker's short but forceful lesson in civics, his work behind the scenes showed only that he should have. His chief legislative aide, Larry O'Brien, started contacting members. "Let's win this one for Jack, Jackie, and little Caroline" was his appeal, not yet knowing how lightly those considerations lay upon a congressman's conscience.

Cabinet members, most notably Interior Secretary Stewart Udall, tried to pressure some. Before taking a cabinet seat, Udall had been a reform congressman, and he still could not resist attempting to remake the House, this time by threatening to eliminate the water projects of four wavering Democrats. Other than causing resentment, the results were negligible; all four ended up voting with Smith.

President Kennedy's one known attempt to involve himself had the same result. In the presence of an uncomfortable Mr. Rayburn, Kennedy called Harold Cooley, the dean of North Carolina's delegation. The new administration had been awfully good to that state, the president reasoned, in naming three of its Democrats (Luther Hodges, Charles Murphy, and James Webb) to top assignments (respectively, secretary of commerce, undersecretary of agriculture, and director of the National Aeronautics and Space Administration). Surely, the Tar Heel State could give him more help on the Rules Committee fight. In the end, it gave exactly one vote, Herb Bonner's, and he had been committed to Sam Rayburn before the call. After that vote came, Mr. Rayburn was exactly right when he observed that the White House "did not change a vote." He was right for the same reason that he had been right a few weeks earlier. This was House business.

The vote came on December 31, 1961. Precisely at noon, Sam Rayburn stepped up to the Speaker's dais, just as he had hundreds of times and other Speakers had for 172 years. For the first time ever, this Speaker entered to a standing ovation. The galleries were packed with what may have been the largest crowd in House history. The floor was filled with what was nearly the entire membership. After H. R. Gross, a Republican gadfly, demanded a quorum call, the long-awaited debate began and the long-awaited showdown unfolded. Would the rules for the Eighty-seventh Congress be amended to provide a fifteen-member House Committee on Rules?

Formal House speeches rarely change a single vote, and certainly none would on this question. What the two leading debaters offered was a special glimpse into their talents and their characters. Howard Smith's was the voice of sweet reason, gently but forcefully outlining the arguments against "packing." He repeated the solemn pledge that he had made, and unquestionably had honored, when he took over the committee. "I will cooperate with the Democratic leadership of the House of Representatives," he promised before adding, "just as long and just as far as my conscience will permit me."

At the qualification, the House erupted into laughter. The old judge paused in quiet dignity, let it subside, and then added in a voice as calm as the Virginia countryside and as cold as the outside air: "Some of these gentlemen who are laughing maybe do not understand what a conscience is. They are entitled to that code, and I think I am entitled to mine."

Sam Rayburn had the last word. He handed me the gavel and descended into the House well. His opening words captured his character and the source of his influence perfectly, just as Judge Smith's verbal stab had done for his own. "Whether you vote with me today or not," he began, "I want to say that I appreciate your uniform kindness and courtesy that has been displayed toward me."

The speeches finished, the clerk began the roll: "Abbitt, Abernathy, Adair, Addabbo, Addonizio . . . ." The first three answered no, the second two yes. "Albert . . . ." My vote tied it at three each. So it stayed through the roll call: the two sides even, then first one and then the other inching ahead by two or three. After the clerk reached Jim Wright of Texas, Sam Rayburn led by one, with only twelve votes left. The roll call complete, the clerk handed the Speaker the tally card. Mr. Rayburn did not even smile as he solemnly announced, "On this vote, there being 217 ayes and 212 noes, the resolution is adopted."

Two hundred seventeen to 212. By a margin of just five votes, Sam Rayburn had shown what respect, courtesy, and kindness could do when they were combined with nearly a half-century of legislative experience and brilliance. Howard Smith accepted his defeat gracelessly by refusing to provide the three new committee members with chairs. Only when one's constituents sent him a chair larger than the chairman's did he give in.

Howard Smith was a gentleman of conscience and a legislator of brilliance, but in the end he was just a mean old man.

Not until the House Judiciary Committee voted impeachment resolutions against Richard Nixon did I see a congressional vote as dramatic as the 1961 decision to expand the Rules Committee. Though it was hailed as a great victory for the Democratic leadership and President Kennedy, I recognized just what its limits were. The expected eight-to-seven liberal-conservative lineup only gave the leadership a chance to unstick Howard Smith's blazing red light; it did not put the light's controls in our hands. At best, that belonged to any one of the liberal eight. The loss of a single vote would restore Judge Smith's power of uncontrolled obstruction.

That is exactly what happened on the one domestic issue that the new president judged most important for 1961. At the time, America's schools were groaning from the pressure of the millions of school-age youngsters born to returning servicemen. Those numbers, coupled with inadequate salaries, had caused a severe shortage of teachers, a shortage of both quantity and quality. Bound to tax systems that dated to a simpler and cheaper past, the nation's fifty states and forty thousand school districts were stretched to their financial limits, and those limits were well short of the need.

Congress had not been unmindful of that need. With the added incentive to catch up with the Soviet Union's sputnik of the previous year, we created in 1958 the first specialized federal aid to education in modern times with the National Defense Education Act. In fact, one of my proudest moments as whip came when I persuaded Mr. Rayburn to put the bill on the floor. It was the session's last day and the bill's author, Carl Elliot, was desperate. Every time I asked Mr. Rayburn to call it up, he found some reason to put another matter ahead of it. Finally, I cornered him when there was absolutely nothing else pending, and the Speaker reluctantly called the bill up. He confided to me later that he still believed that school costs should be borne by local districts, but we had managed to open a modern era of educational financing.

In the 1960 session, both houses had passed a general school-aid bill. That bill had died, however, when Howard Smith's six-vote coalition stubbornly refused to submit our slightly different bill to a conference committee. The frustrating episode had given us one of our strongest arguments in favor of expansion. There could have been no better, for that willful band of six thereby had asserted its mastery over *both* the House *and* the Senate. With the final vote on expansion so close, that one episode well could have made the difference.

If so, the experience of 1961 was all the more frustrating. Understandably sensitive to lingering concerns for the separation of church and state, President Kennedy presented us with a school bill that deliberately forbade taxpayer assistance to religious and parochial schools. His own education message cited a "clear prohibition of the Constitution" against aiding such schools, and not even the Catholics' highest prelates could budge him. It may have been that *especially* the prelates could not budge him for when the bishops, archbishops, and cardinals of the National Catholic Welfare Conference vowed to oppose any federal aid that excluded their schools, the president had to refuse them rather than reopen the issue of his alleged subservience to the church.

In that form, the only form the president would sign, the Senate passed its bill in May. The House Education and Labor Committee dispatched ours to the Rules Committee in July. Judge Smith was ready for it. Declaring that the bill somehow would "complete the subjugation of the southern states," he put Bill Colmer in his pocket and lined up the new committee's five Republicans, who seemed more anxious to embarrass a Democratic president than to educate schoolchildren. Then he got the eighth and deciding vote.

Jim Delaney was a veteran Democrat representing the good Democratic Queens district of New York City. Its voters were working-class Catholics, stubborn in their convictions. Jim was just as good a Catholic and even more stubborn in his. If his faith's 12,700 schools, 5 million students, and 102,000 teachers could get not one penny of aid, then no one else would, either. And there was nothing we could do. I talked with him. The two other Catholics on the Rules Committee reasoned with him. Secretary of Health, Education, and Welfare Abraham Ribicoff pleaded with him. Twice, President Kennedy sat him down for long off-the-record sessions. Not one of us could move him. Jim Delaney voted his convictions, and the House Committee on Rules voted not to report the bill to the floor. It was by just the margin, eight to seven, that the expansion had led us to expect. Close, but we had the seven.

It stayed just that close all that year. John Kennedy himself had been elected president with the closest popular-vote lead in American history. Our party had dropped a net of twenty-two seats to the Republicans since 1958, making Kennedy the only president of the century to win the White House while his party was losing strength in Congress. Each of the twenty-two were Democratic liberals from the industrial North and East. Our five-vote victory in the Rules Committee fight had come only because twenty-two Republicans had had the guts to withstand Charlie Halleck's threats. Sixty-three southern Democrats (sixty-one of them from the old Confederacy) had stood with Howard Smith on that one.

What all of this meant was that President Kennedy and the Democratic leadership could expect nearly every vote to be a close one. Mrs. Kennedy could have been describing all of us when she said that her husband was "an idealist without illusions." As idealists, we wanted to get the country (and the Congress) moving again, but we had no illusions about how very hard that would be and how very close every vote would be. When, as whip, I had to line up the votes for something like emergency farm-price supports, I found it every bit as hard as it had been with Ike in the White House. With a Democratic president and a Democratic agriculture secretary backing the bill, we still won that one by just seven votes. Close.

Except for the president's initiatives in military spending and foreign affairs, most of them were just that way. A few we lost. Others we did not force, knowing that we would lose. Some of the ones that we won required all of the parliamentary skills we could muster.

The minimum-wage bill was typical of that, and of just how demanding and frustrating the whip's job could be. Kennedy had campaigned on a pledge to raise the minimum wage to $1.25 an hour while expanding its coverage. The proposal had been another one that Howard Smith's Rules Committee had buried in the dismal 1960 postconvention session. With the restructuring of the committee, we did get the bill to the House floor in 1961. And then the real fight began.

The opposition was ready for us with a substitute authored by Paul Kitchin, son of former floor leader Claude Kitchin and a committed North Carolina conservative Democrat, and William H. Ayers, a wily, chain-smoking Ohio Republican. On the face of it, the Kitchin-Ayres substitute was about as attractive as Kennedy's bill. It, too, offered a higher minimum wage, but $1.15 compared with $1.25. It, too, covered more workers, 1.3 million more, compared with 4.8 million. It was those differences that made it even more attractive than Kennedy's bill to tight-fisted Republicans and southern conservatives.

Back home in McAlester, I got a taste of that. It seemed that every time I walked into a store, the owner would pull me aside to protest a new minimum-wage law covering his employees. Quite often when I left, some of the clerks would follow me out on the sidewalk. Believe me, they knew the difference.

The problem in Washington was that the Republicans and the southern Democrats together held 302 seats. They had the votes to bury Kennedy's bill, and we had to work to resurrect it. In Sam Rayburn's office, he, John McCormack, Dick Bolling, Carl Vinson, James Roosevelt, and I met with Secretary of Labor Arthur Goldberg, several of his Labor Department's technical experts, and Larry O'Brien. Quickly we hammered out a new version of Kennedy's bill, one that we hoped could peel enough votes from the Kitchin-Ayres substitute that we could pass it. Observing how important the southern Democrats would be, O'Brien suggested that I personally present the new bill and lead the debate for it.

All night I studied the bill, pored over committee reports, and prepared my speech. Larry later wrote that I "made an absolutely brilliant presentation when the debate was held." Brilliant or not, we lost to Kitchin-Ayres, 186 to 185. I am told that when Larry broke the news to President Kennedy, the president stabbed a letter opener into his desk. I know what happened when Sam Rayburn and I identified three Democratic liberals who had sat in the House restaurant during the vote and seven others who had not bothered to leave their offices. We made a brilliant presentation.

In the end, we won, but we did it by parliamentary maneuver. The Senate passed a bill close to the president's original. Our conferees who carried the Kitchin-Ayres version to the conference committee had been carefully selected by Speaker Rayburn, whose powers included naming all conference members. They brought back for both houses' approval a bill very much like that which we had produced with Secretary Goldberg in Mr. Rayburn's office. Both houses passed it. It was a decent bill. But I had had to fight for the president—and the store clerks—every step of the way.

I know that the store clerks appreciated it, and I know that the president did, too. That fall, he came down to my Third District to the community of Big Cedar. The *Big* was entirely in the name, since it was but a highway intersection marked by four houses, a barn, and a filling station. But Senator Kerr lived nearby, and Bob Kerr was a man that John Kennedy had to have in the Senate if he was going to go anywhere in 1962.

So John Kennedy went to Big Cedar, dedicated a highway, gave a great speech, and spent the night at Kerr's ranch. The entire community showed up for the speech, though it was many times outnumbered by the friends of Kerr and me, as well as the Secret Service and the White House press corps. The president graciously spoke about the work that I had done for him and his New Frontier, and I was mighty proud of that. Some of the press even read it as a plug for me as the next majority leader once John McCormack moved up to Speaker upon Mr. Rayburn's retirement.

*The "Big" was entirely in the name.* President John Kennedy at Big Cedar, Oklahoma, 1961. On the platform, left to right: Congressmen Tom Steed, John Jarman, Ed Edmondson, Mike Monroney, and Carl Albert; President John F. Kennedy; Governor J. Howard Edmondson; Senator Robert S. Kerr; unidentified person; Methodist Bishop Angie Smith.

We knew that the Speaker had left Washington early to rest. We did not know that Sam Rayburn was dying.

Mr. Rayburn had never been sick a day in his life, but his life was seventy-nine years long. His sight failed him badly that year. His daily two-mile walks around the Capitol took him longer. What troubled him, though, was a gnawing pain in his lower back. Several Washington physicians tried to treat it. Nothing they could do made any difference. Sam Rayburn's own diagnosis was just as

*Now he can say in the language of the apostle Paul, 'I have fought the good fight.' Sam Rayburn's funeral, Bonham, Texas, 1961.*

plain as he was. "I've got lumbago," he said, "and no one's ever died of lumbago."

What he had was cancer, and several Rayburns had already died of that. In time, we learned that it had started as pancreatic cancer, a particularly vicious form because it does not appear on X-rays or in other tests until it has metastasized through the lymphatic system. Until then, it steadily gnawed away at him.

It was doing so that summer when, on June 12, the House of Representatives officially honored Mr. Rayburn. That date marked his sixteenth year and 273d day as its Speaker. On that day he had served more than twice as long as any other Speaker in House history, twice as long as the only man who could contest him for greatness in the office, Henry Clay. He spoke that day of his love for the House of Representatives. His dimming eyes wept as he spoke, too, of his gratitude to the people of his district for trusting him all those years.

At the end of August, it was to those people that he returned. Bonham, Texas, he had always said, was the kind of place "where people know when you're sick and they care when you die."

He did not expect to die. He kept telling everybody—himself, too, I suppose—that he would whip this lumbago and be back to the House he loved. He surely was not going to die in any hospital bed. No, Sam Rayburn said, when he died he wanted to have his boots on his feet and a gavel in his hand.

The doctors at Baylor University Medical Center put him in a bed. That is where he was when they finally found his cancer. By then, it was so far gone that they gave him a week to live, two at most. He lived six weeks more. I visited him once, but I hardly recognized him. Gone was the gleam of his eye, gone with most of the weight of his body. About all that was left was his fierce will. It, too, left him early on the morning of November 16, 1961. For his last two weeks, he had been at his home in Bonham, "where people know when you're sick and they care when you die."

In Sam Rayburn's case, many people cared. A 74-year-old country preacher from the Primitive Baptist Church performed the funeral service. His congregation, heretofore never larger than forty-five, was in the thousands and included three American presidents and the next one: Truman, Eisenhower, Kennedy, and Lyndon Johnson. The preacher pronounced the judgment that we all shared. "Our good friend," he said in Sam Rayburn's soft Texas accent, "made himself a servant, not of the classes but of all of the men and women and the boys and the girls and the children. . . . Now he can say in the language of the Apostle Paul, 'I have fought the good fight.'"

Surely some of us remembered and repeated to ourselves the words that Sam Rayburn had choked out in his own eulogy for his friend Alben Barkley: "God comfort his loved ones. God comfort me."

# CHAPTER SEVEN

# Congratulations, Mr. Majority Leader

$S$am Rayburn did not get his wish. He had not died with his boots on his feet and a gavel in his hand. But he had died as Speaker of the House of Representatives, and his death left vacant the Speaker's chair for the first time since William Bankhead's death put the gavel in Mr. Rayburn's hand. That had been back in 1940, before World War II, before the Cold War, before either Dwight Eisenhower or John Kennedy was involved in politics. Of the 435 House members serving at the time Mr. Rayburn died, only the most veteran members, 14 of them, had known a Democratic leadership other than John McCormack's and Sam Rayburn's.

Most of us had sensed that this would end in 1961; Mr. Rayburn would not be back. As the reality of the situation sank in, fifty or sixty members must have approached me; it was always at their initiative, and their message was always the same. "You've worked hard as whip," they said, "don't just sit here and be done out of what you're entitled to." A few even offered that I was entitled to the Speakership and could win it against seventy-year old John McCormack. Those always got the same answer, an answer that I meant as much as I had ever meant anything in my life: John McCormack had earned the Speakership; he had the qualities that would make him a great Speaker. Above all that, John McCormack was my friend. He and Mr. Rayburn had put me in the leadership. To oppose him for the post that was his due would be the act of an ingrate. It would never be the act of Carl Albert. But Carl Albert did know what his own due was. I believed that my six years as Democratic whip had prepared me to succeed John as majority leader. I believed that I could handle the job. I believed that I could win it in the Democratic caucus vote. And I knew that I wanted it.

After Mr. Rayburn's funeral on a Saturday, I returned to Mc-Alester. I already had planned to announce my candidacy for majority leader on the following Wednesday. On Sunday, however, I got quite a shock. Charles Ward, my administrative assistant, called me from Washington. He told me that Dick Bolling had just announced that he was running for majority leader. I knew Bolling well, and, as most members did, I respected him. I had seen how close he and Mr. Rayburn had become, especially in the Rules Committee fight, when Bolling had kept the liberals in line and twisted many an arm for the Speaker. I knew that he was esteemed by the party's most liberal interests outside Congress: the labor unions, the civil-rights groups, and the many reform clubs. I knew that he had a warm relationship with the New York and Washington political writers. I knew that his candidacy was no attack upon me, any more than mine would be upon him. I knew that outside the walls of Congress many people honestly believed that Dick Bolling would be the more forceful advocate of Democratic liberal programs. But I also knew that the decision was going to be made within the House walls.

Once I had confirmed Bolling's announcement by hearing it on national radio and reading it in the McAlester paper, I made my own press announcement by calling Bill Arbogast, the Associated Press's congressional correspondent. Then I called Western Union and dictated a simple telegram:

> I take this means of advising that I am making the race for majority leader of the House subject to the action of the Democratic caucus. I

will greatly appreciate your support and help. I would like to talk to you about the matter at your convenience.

Kindest regards
Carl Albert, M.C.
Third District, Oklahoma

The company billed me $399.99 to send that message to 269 individuals: a few friends and the entire Democratic membership of Congress. Then I started calling each of them personally, just as I had in making whip polls for the past six years. I started with the western states (I suppose because Bolling might have had an initial advantage there), and I started with my friends there.

As I was reaching for the phone to make another call, it rang for me. It was Bob Kerr, Oklahoma's senior senator and one of the Senate's richest men. He was ready to use his money to help Oklahoma, as he saw it, and that meant he would use it to help me. When he asked what help I needed, I told him that all I could use was a little help with the phones. Within the hour, three telephone workers installed a bank of telephones that covered most of the vacant space in my offices in the McAlester Federal Building. I do not know what it cost Kerr (I bet it was more than $399.99), but I trust that it ended up helping Oklahoma. I do know that I stayed at that phone bank for the next four days. By the first one's end, I had lined up endorsements from all but four or five western Democrats. Then I went to the other states.

While I was doing that, I began to take calls from members who had received my telegram. One of the first was from John Fogerty from Rhode Island. John told me that Mike Kirwan had contacted him and the two of them were going to go all out for me. Those two fighting Irishmen—fighting for me—meant a lot of votes from the big-city northern Democrats.

The next call was more of a mixed blessing. I picked up the receiver to hear the familiar voice of Adam Clayton Powell, Harlem's flamboyant black representative. "I'm for you a 100 percent," Adam vowed, "and I'm issuing a statement to the press." I thanked him even while wondering whether his endorsement would cost me more than it gained me. I really wondered after the phone rang again. It was Judge Howard Smith, and he wanted me to know that not only was he backing me, he wanted to work with the southerners on my behalf. I had to tell him, "I really appreciate that, Judge, but you need to know that Adam Clayton Powell just called me and he's going to put out a press release supporting me. I wouldn't want you to be embarrassed."

"Don't worry, Carl," the old judge chuckled, "I figure a guy's got to get a vote anywhere he can get it, and you still have mine." As always, Howard Smith was true to his word and a real pro. He helped get me a lot of votes where only he, certainly not Adam Clayton Powell, could have gotten them.

The rest I got myself. As I went through the states, my usual strategy was to contact each delegation's dean and work downward through the ranks of seniority. That way, I could meet any resistance within the delegation by mentioning the senior men who already had endorsed me. In a few cases where I was less certain of the veteran's attitudes, I reversed the process. I started with the younger members, the ones I had helped as whip. By the time I got to the top, I thereby was able to tell the old-timers that I already had most of their delegations behind me.

Either way, I never once mentioned Dick Bolling (or, for that matter, John Kennedy, the New Frontier, or any issue). I just asked my listeners for their support, and usually I got it. The people I was calling knew me, knew my talents, knew my habits, knew my record. If that would not earn me their support, nothing I could say about any transient issue would.

Nonetheless, the press tried to play the contest up as some sort of liberal-versus-conservative battle. The fact that Bolling and I had almost identical voting records made no difference. Neither did the fact that we both had supported President Kennedy's program in more than 90 percent of the 1961 roll-call votes. Some ignored that, too, to write it up as a struggle over the fate of Kennedy's program in the House.

For his part, the president knew better. Publicly, he never wavered from neutrality. Privately, he knew that the New Frontier could not lose between Bolling and me. Everyone knew his respect for Bolling, but to all who asked, he acknowledged his gratitude for my work on his program's behalf in the long session just ended. Meanwhile, I stayed at the phone bank, doing House business.

By the time I was through going down every state and every member, I had enough votes pledged to win the job when the caucus met in January. I went to Washington early and made an appointment to meet with John Kennedy. On a bright, crisp winter day, I walked into the Oval Office and shook the hand of the man whom I first had met fifteen years earlier, when Representative Kennedy had asked if I was the new congressman from Oklahoma who had been a Rhodes scholar. This time, when I released the same hand, I said, "Mr. President, I have enough votes pledged to make me the next majority leader of Congress." The president replied, "Congratulations, Mr. Majority Leader."

My election was a formality. On January 3, a week before the 1962 Congress convened, Dick Bolling made a short announcement to the press. "I am withdrawing from the race for leadership of the House," he said. "Developments of the last few days have convinced me that I don't have a chance to win."

At the party caucus to name our leadership slate, neither John McCormack nor I drew an opponent. That was expected for John, since the majority leader's elevation was an unbroken tradition in this century. My unanimous selection—it was Dick Bolling who made the motion for unanimity—was rarer, and for that reason I treasured it more. I thereby became the first majority leader in the twentieth century to win his party's initial caucus election without opposition. As the second session of the Eighty-seventh Congress opened, my selection as majority leader was announced and the House voted, as always, on straight party lines (248 to 166) to elect John McCormack its Speaker.

Our first order of business was to name our party's whip. The new Speaker and I were in complete agreement: my old job would pass to Hale Boggs. As majority leader, I made the announcement. Hale was a Louisianan of distinguished southern lineage. His grandfather had been a major general of the Confederacy, and Hale was a Tulane journalism and law-school graduate. Tall, striking, blessed with a melodious voice, he first went to Congress from the New Orleans district in 1941. Hale lost his reelection bid in 1943, joined the Navy, and came back in 1946 to retake his House seat. This time, he stayed in it. With a voting record that was liberal by southern standards, he earned a place on the Ways and Means Committee and steadily moved up its seniority ladder. Like me, he also became an early protégé of Sam Rayburn. The lonely bachelor loved eating dinner with Hale and his charming (and very astute) wife, Lindy, and played with their children, Barbara, Tommy, and Cokie. Lindy, though, was the one who best explained Mr. Rayburn's interest in Hale. "Mr. Sam," she said, "just liked smart southerners."

Hale was smart, and he profited from the Speaker's interest. In 1955, when Mr. Rayburn and John McCormack had picked me for whip, they also had created a new party post especially for Hale: deputy whip. When John and I both moved up one rung on the ladder, it was only natural that we reached down to pull Hale Boggs up one rung with us.

To the new Speaker, the new whip, and I fell the task of guiding a Democratic program through Congress. To help us, we had a Democratic president who already had created a remarkable liaison operation in the White House.

Prior to John Kennedy's administration, both Republican and Democratic presidents had dealt with the congressional majority in a haphazard fashion. White House legislative initiatives usually fell to the affected department for oversight; the Agriculture Department looked over farm bills, for example, or the Labor Department worked with Congress on minimum-wage proposals. Only on very special matters did the president or a top staff

*Hale was a Louisianan of distinguished southern lineage.*

assistant try to coordinate the legislative strategy on several diverse bills.

John Kennedy brought to congressional relations the same talent for organization that had won him nomination and election in 1960. Every proposal on every subject in every field passed through the White House and stayed under its steady eye. In charge of the operations was one of the ablest politicians and finest men I ever knew, Larry O'Brien. The son of Irish immigrants, Larry's entire life had been spent in Democratic politics. He had signed on with Kennedy for his first Senate campaign and stayed with him into the White House. There he had a first-rate staff of bright young men to help him. The president's other aides, particularly Theodore Sorensen, Kenny O'Donnell, and Pierre Salinger, also lent their considerable talents and energy to working directly with the congressional leadership.

Ready to join them were the other administrative officials. Sargent Shriver, the president's brother-in-law and choice as first director of the Peace Corps, practically moved into my Capitol office while we were working on the agency's creation. I never had seen a man as dedicated and energetic as Shriver was with the Peace Corps. I sometimes said that Kennedy's labor secretary, Arthur Goldberg, was better than any professional lobbyist in Washington. When Goldberg was working on a bill, he would come into my office with an informed count on where it stood, a carefully detailed legislative strategy to move it, and a thorough analysis of what it would take to pass it. More than once I suggested that we needed some of the members to make floor speeches on his bill's behalf. Agreeing, Goldberg would tick off the names of the most appropriate ones, reach into his briefcase, and pull out typed speeches—just in case they needed them.

Every Tuesday morning, the congressional relations people, affected White House officials, the president, and the vice-president met with us for breakfast at the White House. Speaker McCormack, Hale, and I represented the House; Mike Mansfield, who had won Vice President Johnson's old job as Senate majority leader, and Hubert Humphrey, the Senate's Democratic whip,

*John Kennedy brought to congressional relations the same talent for organization that had won him nomination and election in 1960.* President Kennedy with Senate Majority Leader Mike Mansfield, Senate Democratic Whip Hubert Humphrey, House Democratic Whip Hale Boggs, House Majority Leader Carl Albert, and Vice-President Lyndon Johnson.

came from the other body. Over a good American breakfast—ham, eggs, toast, juice, and coffee—we would go over the week's legislative business. The president always took the initiative, but we offered the benefit of the Speaker's long experience in congressional strategy, Hale's latest whip counts, and my knowledge of the status of the committees' work.

Another of our jobs was to help the White House people best

use the tools of influence available to them, all the while knowing just how limited those tools were. The president could pick up a few votes by the adroit use of his few patronage powers and the executive branch's control over certain federally financed projects. Campaign help (an endorsing speech before a member's constituents or just a picture of Representative X counseling with the president) could add a few more. A few members were susceptible to the flattery of presidential attention at formal dinners or public receptions. Added together, those were about all that the president had available.

On the other side, President Kennedy had some disadvantages, inescapable disadvantages, that neither he nor his liaison team nor the House leadership could ignore. Congressmen may be fond of White House attention and executive assistance, but they can be awfully resentful of White House pressure. Of course, it was often hard to draw the line between attention on one side and pressure on the other. A good general rule, though, was that the more powerful a congressman was, the more attention looked to him like pressure. Eight years of independence from a Republican White House only added to that tendency.

The circumstances of Kennedy's election did nothing to help. Whether they liked the president or did not, whether they believed in his programs or did not, the fact was that few congressmen owed him anything. The great bulk of Democratic members had run well ahead of Kennedy in their districts; his own contribution had been negative, sometimes powerfully so. The most powerful congressmen tended to come from safe, one-party Democratic districts in which any subsequent challenges would surface not in the general elections but in a party primary. In these future contests, there was little the president could offer them. Local business, commercial, and professional interests could offer a lot, but those were precisely the settled groups furthest removed from the New Frontier.

Finally, there was the inescapable power of simple arithmetic. In 1962 as in 1961, the nearly two-to-one formal party lineup ripped open on the stubborn rocks of southern regionalism. With nearly every Republican committed to opposing nearly every Democratic initiative, we would have to keep fifty to sixty southern Democrats with us in order to win—by five or six votes. After we lost five seats in the 1962 elections, even that arrangement would have us losing—by five or six votes. It was going to stay just that close.

Altogether then, the new leadership team, the president, and his staff had our work cut out for us. President Kennedy and we could not win on every fight. We could not always get the country moving again. But we did get Carl Albert moving quite a lot.

On some matters, it was easy to move the Congress with us. President Kennedy entered the White House after eight years of Republican devotion to tight defense budgets. American conventional forces had deteriorated steadily in favor of an overreliance on nuclear weaponry. Eisenhower had called it his New Look, while Secretary of Defense Charles Wilson had caught its appeal when he labeled it "a bigger bang for the buck." The problem was that it left the country with few military options short of the big bang. Threats to American interests could be met by either doing nothing or blowing up the globe. Those were pretty poor choices.

In 1962, we addressed that with overwhelming bipartisan support for the president's efforts to restore balance to our defense capacity and options to our military. Congress voted the funds to put one-half of our bombers on fifteen-minute alert, to increase our antiguerrilla forces by 150 percent, to add seventy-four ships to the active fleet, to bring our NATO forces to full strength, and to step up M-14 rifle procurements from 9,000 per month to 44,000. When added to the continuing buildup in strategic forces and delivery systems that Kennedy and Congress had inaugurated the year before, it meant an American military supremacy not seen since 1945.

In foreign affairs, too, Kennedy found a steady ally in Congress. The tradition of bipartisan support for presidential direction of foreign policy that dated to the Second World War and had been strengthened by the Cold War still held firm. An occasional congressman might speak out against some immediate action, and a few senators discovered that criticizing the president's foreign policy could get them before the television cameras. By and large, however, the powerful leaders of both houses agreed with nearly all of their members: the president made our foreign policy; we supported it.

Three stunning examples occurred in my first fall as majority leader. With Nikita Khrushchev rattling his missiles and threatening to end Allied occupation rights to West Berlin, President Kennedy turned to Congress to support his determination to keep the city and to keep it free. In October, we rushed through a resolution authorizing the president "to prevent by whatever means may be necessary, including the force of arms," any Soviet attempt to interfere with Western rights in Berlin.

Only a month earlier, we had used exactly the same words regarding Cuba. Fidel Castro's betrayal of any hopes for Cuban democracy, his steady barrage of anti-American harangues, his declaration to be a Marxist-Leninist, his thirst for Soviet aid and arms—all of these added to a mounting crisis. In September, we had passed an official resolution that authorized *any* presidential action to prevent the export of Castro's revolution or any "externally supported military capability endangering the security of the United States." As we had done for Eisenhower with Formosa, we did now for Kennedy with Berlin and Cuba. We signed a blank check authorizing the president to do whatever he wanted whenever and however he wanted. We did it with hardly a murmur of dissent.

In Cuba's case, the check came close to being honored in blood and nuclear ashes.

On a Monday afternoon in October, I was summoned to the White House to meet with the president at five o'clock. When I got there, I found the entire congressional leadership of both houses, including the Foreign Affairs and Armed Services committees' chairmen. The president got straight to the point. Only six days earlier, he had received incontrovertible evidence that the Soviet Union was installing nuclear-equipped ballistic missiles in Cuba. Continuing surveillance indicated the near-completion of the missile sites, and more Soviet nuclear hardware was crossing the ocean bound for Cuba. He would inform the nation by television of the situation and announce his decision to "quarantine" Cuba with a naval blockade to turn back the Soviet freighters while negotiating for removal of the existing installations. His speech would air in exactly two hours.

As we sat there talking on that autumn afternoon, American missile crews were already on maximum alert. Already troops were headed for Florida and Georgia to join five divisions poised to move on Cuba. One hundred eighty warships already surrounded the island. Already the Strategic Air Command had been dispersed to civilian landing fields to lessen its vulnerability. As we sat there conferring, America's B-52 bombers, their bellies engorged with atomic bombs, already were in the air. The instant one landed for fuel and a fresh crew, another climbed into the sky. In those circumstances, we leaders of Congress learned just what "whatever means may be necessary" meant.

The only dissent was in favor of stronger action. Richard Russell, chairman of the Senate Armed Services Committee, spoke first and most forcefully. He said that he could not live with himself if he did not state in the strongest possible terms that a quarantine was too weak a response. What we needed to do and do now was invade the island, destroy the missile sites, and get rid of Castro once and for all. President Kennedy listened calmly and offered his view that an invasion likely would trigger a nuclear war. If the blockade were unsuccessful, it might come to that. He hoped it would not, but he was ready if it did.

John Kennedy left us to prepare for the television address. As he did, he was obviously shaken by the criticism. Still, he knew that what I told him at the end was true. Any misgivings expressed in that room would be forgotten. He was our president. He would get our support. He did, and he proved to be right; we soon recognized that. Only later did we realize where the precedent pointed.

Cuba had been a moment of singular crisis. Powerful legislators had buried their differences with John Kennedy when we all might have been buried otherwise. A president could expect that, but he had to expect also that without such a crisis other differences would arise. They did in the House, and powerful legislators demonstrated just how much power they had.

Not many members had more power than Wilbur Mills. Part of it was due to his native Arkansas intellect, an intellect sharpened by Harvard schooling. More of it was due to his position. In 1943, at the beginning of only his third term, Mills had landed a seat on the Ways and Means Committee. Such a prized assignment was rare for one so new, but Wilbur Mills was another of those smart southerners that Sam Rayburn liked to help. The assignment surely helped Mills. In fact, it made his career. By 1957, he was chairman of Ways and Means, probably the most powerful committee in the House.

One reason for its power was its immediate jurisdiction. The one great power constitutionally assigned to the House alone is the power to initiate all revenue bills. Since the earliest days of the Republic, the responsibility for writing tax legislation had fallen to Ways and Means. From that power more followed, so that the Ways and Means Committee became a web of immense scope and power. Because America's first tariffs were *taxes* on imports, Ways and Means grabbed control of anything involving foreign trade. Because the Social Security System was financed by a payroll *tax,* Ways and Means assumed authority over anything touching it. Because the first federal welfare plan was incorporated in the 1935 Social Security Act, Ways and Means took over the nation's entire welfare system. And so it had been continued.

Despite its many responsibilities, Ways and Means had no subcommittees at all. Every title, every section, every paragraph, and every line of every bill on every subject was worked out by all fifteen members of the entire committee, with Wilbur Mills presiding. Its craftsmanship complete, its bills went to the Rules Committee, which traditionally assigned them closed rules, forbidding amendments from the House floor. The consequence was that the other 420 members could only approve or disapprove its bills; they could not change them.

The final element of Wilbur Mills's power was that he was Wilbur Mills. No one—no one in the House, no one in the Senate, no one in the Treasury Department—knew more about the incredibly complex tax code than this Democrat from tiny Kensett, Arkansas. So thorough was his knowledge and so complete his preparation that the members would often accord him a standing ovation when he presented a bill.

Such expertise had not come easily. One of the first bills that he had presented as chairman had come out of a divided committee and was beaten on the floor. Wilbur Mills never forgot his humiliation. From that day onward, he never produced a bill until he was certain it would pass. He was absolutely obsessed with having the overwhelming support of his committee, including the support of its ten Republican members, before producing a bill. He was determined to have the votes on the floor before presenting it. Until he was sure, his committee would conduct hearings, it would debate, it would work its way line by line. And it would do that on just one major bill at a time.

The Ways and Means Committee was, then, in a position to make or break much of John Kennedy's New Frontier. Sometimes it was Wilbur Mills who made it. In my first year as majority leader, the president's central legislative effort was a trade-expansion bill. Eight years of Republican inactivity had bequeathed America a stagnant economy at precisely the moment that the birth of Europe's Common Market threatened our markets abroad. By granting the president the authority to negotiate with the Europeans mutual tariff reductions ranging to 50 percent, the bill would get our exports and America moving again.

Larry O'Brien and I put everything we had behind that one. I must have talked with every Democratic member. I kept O'Brien's people informed of just where the administration might use just what influence. Between updates at our weekly breakfasts, the president threw himself into it with exceptional vigor. But the legislative craftsmanship was Wilbur Mills's. Patiently, he brought his committee to consensus behind the Kennedy bill. When the

White House and I had the floor votes, and the Speaker and I had the schedule set, he undraped the bill. Wilbur Mills got the members' applause that day, but it was all of us who won the key vote, 253 to 171.

One vote we did not even take testified to Mills's ability to break the New Frontier. Medicare, the payment of the elderly's hospital expenses under Social Security, had been a proposal of Senator Kennedy and a campaign promise of candidate Kennedy; now it was a White House bill of President Kennedy. Offered in 1961, the bill went to Ways and Means, where the chairman put it behind other bills. His committee started its hearings just before adjournment. In 1962, the hearings continued, with no end in sight.

I knew that what Wilbur Mills was after was not more information from more witnesses but a consensus on his committee. I knew, too, that he was not going to get it. Medicare was just too much for the ten Republicans and the eight southern Democrats. Because the president wanted the bill so badly, my advice was that he would have to get it from the Senate. If Medicare were attached to a Senate welfare bill, we could bring it to the House as a conference-committee report on our own welfare bill. What my strategy did not calculate was the influence in the other body of a man just as powerful and just as resourceful as Wilbur Mills. He was my own state's senior senator, Robert S. Kerr.

John Kennedy had known what he was doing when he came down to Big Cedar; it simply had not worked. Amid the championship Angus on Bob Kerr's ranch, the two had talked about Medicare, to no resolution. Kennedy wanted it; Kerr did not. As the president and his entourage were leaving, Kerr told me in tones as calm as they were confident, "He thinks he can beat me on this, but I'm gonna beat him."

I already knew that Bob Kerr was a man not likely to lose any fight that involved such immense determination. My only wonder was at his determination on this one issue, a determination on an issue that seemed to have nothing to do with his one great fixation, Oklahoma. After we got back to Washington, I found out why: Medicare touched the one matter that counted for even more to Bob Kerr. Riding in his car up Independence Avenue to the Capitol, the senator told me that he did not care one way or the other about Medicare, but his wife, Grayce Breene Kerr, was a Christian Scientist. Like her faith's other believers, Mrs. Kerr did not want Social Security paying for medicine, doctors, and hospitals.

Senator Kerr was going all out to beat the president for his wife and her church.

Beat him he did. In a masterful bit of maneuvering, Kerr won for the Christian Scientists by keeping Medicare out of the Senate welfare bill, fifty-two to forty-eight. There was no medicare amendment to the conference report. There was no vote on the House floor. And the hearings went on.

There were not many things more frustrating than something like that. One of them was dealing with Clarence Cannon. Cannon first came to the Congress back in the early 1900s as a secretary to Champ Clark. For a time, he served the House as its parliamentarian. In fact, his codification of House rules and procedures, *Cannon's Precedents,* stood for decades as the bible of the legislative process, or at least as its ten thousand commandments. In 1923, Clarence Cannon took Clark's old seat and in time rose to become chairman of the House Appropriations Committee.

Eighty-two years old when the 1962 session opened, Clarence Cannon was set in his ways. He knew the House procedures, and he knew the Constitution. He took very seriously that language of ARTICLE I, SECTION 7: "All Bills for raising Revenue shall originate in the House of Representatives; . . . ." Our power of the purse was one that he cherished. I came awfully close to being *his* power of the purse.

Cannon's equivalent in the other body was a lot like him. Carl Hayden also came to Congress in the early 1900s: as the voteless delegate of Arizona Territory. The state of Arizona sent him to the House when it entered the Union in 1912. In 1927, he went to the Senate. By 1962, when Carl Hayden was eighty-four, the Arizonan was the Senate's president pro tempore and head of the Appropriations Committee. He cherished his great power, including the constitutional power granted by the closing clause of ARTICLE I, SECTION 7: ". . . but the Senate may propose or concur with Amendments as on other Bills."

In 1962, these powerful and willful men each stood stubbornly on his respective constitutional clause. Caught in the middle was the entire United States government. Each house had passed appropriations bills but in different forms for different amounts. All of them had to go to a conference committee, its members including and chosen by Chairmen Cannon and Hayden. That was not the problem. The problem was where to have the meeting. Asserting the House's prerogative and his committee's responsibility, Clarence Cannon refused to meet on the Capitol's Senate side. Proclaiming the Senate's rights and his committee's authority, Carl Hayden refused to meet on the House side. For more than two months, each stood his ground. Two months was not long from the octogenarians' perspectives, but it was an awfully long time for us. Unless one of them would budge, the government would go out of business, unable to pay its bills or honor its payroll checks.

At the weekly leadership breakfast, President Kennedy would turn to us for some help out of the impasse. Declaring that Cannon would not even return his calls, the president dispatched me to have Cannon call him. I took him the message, and old Clarence Cannon responded like a shy adolescent. "Why, I'm just a little bitty congressman from Missouri," he said. "I'm not a big enough person to trouble the president of the United States with a phone call."

I tried a different strategy. I told Cannon that I needed to meet with him in a Capitol room to discuss some other business. When he showed up, Larry O'Brien and some of the White House people were waiting there to reason with him. I left them, and in a few minutes Clarence Cannon came storming out. "Damn you, Carl Albert," he roared. "This is too important for a bunch of damn kids in the White House." So much for the little-bitty-congressman bit.

I finally did find a way out. After poring over the building's blueprints, the Capitol architects found me the one place, Room 101 of the East Front extension, that could hold the conferees in a place exactly halfway between the Senate and the House wings. I took the drawings to Clarence Cannon, and he agreed to meet Carl Hayden on that neutral site. Each (literally) met the other halfway. So it was that the government was empowered to pay its bills.

It was not always that frustrating. As majority leader, I was working on legislation that did get America moving again. The president's bold initiatives to move the economy took us a lot of time, but it was paying off. The trade expansion bill was law by the end of 1962. In that year, we also completed the first major over-haul of the federal tax system since 1954, winning the decisive vote with only twenty-three to spare. A year later, we took up Kennedy's proposal to slash taxes across the board. With its cus-tomary thoroughness, Wilbur Mills's committee spent two months in hearings, another two in closed executive sessions, and four months drafting a bill. When everything was in place, the House passed it on September 25 by a comfortable margin of 271 to 155. Republican conservatives had howled that the bill's deliberate creation of a deficit was heretical and dangerous, but combined with our previous steps, the tax cut's stimulus sparked the longest and greatest sustained period of economic growth in the nation's history. National production soared, inflation remained minimal, unemployment virtually disappeared. The government's revenue rode with the economy, leaving John Kennedy just short of an overall budget surplus for his period in office.

I am proud to write these few sentences, and it is easy to do it; it was not nearly so easy to win some of the battles. Some we lost. Ways and Means continued to hold up Medicare through all of 1962, 1963, and 1964. Clarence Cannon and his foreign-aid sub-committee chairman, Otto Passman, cut billions off that necessary program. It was all we could do just to save it. We did not even try for a general aid-to-education bill. The need was great, but the continuing church-state controversy was greater.

These we could not turn around, but others we could. This happened when the majority leader was doing his job well, and it made his job fun. Particularly when it involved agriculture, it also was mighty important to this leader's district.

For all of his learning, John Kennedy knew almost nothing about agriculture and had to find an agriculture secretary who did. He first had leaned toward a recognized farm leader, a real, live practicing farmer. The president-elect had met with the fellow at his Georgetown residence, had interviewed him, and had become so bored that he actually fell asleep. He finally settled on Orville Freeman, the former governor of a farm state (Minnesota), deliverer of Kennedy's convention nomination speech, and a man who needed a job, for Freeman had lost his reelection contest in 1960.

In 1962, Secretary Freeman gave us a complicated new proposal to establish supply-management controls for milk and feed grains, including wheat and corn. I knew the vote would be close, and the harder I worked on it, the more certain I became. In the last days, I was fighting for it one vote at a time until I had every vote that it could get, including four members who intended to vote no but agreed to switch to aye if that would save it. As the House voted on June 21, I watched the count. It turned out to be 215 to 205 against us. A fifth switch would have saved it because Speaker McCormack would have voted to break the tie, but I could still be one short, so I spared the four to fight another day.

It came on September 20. The Senate's farm bill had secured supply management for wheat but not the other commodities. Our conferees brought that version back to us and gave me one last chance to turn it around. The odds were not good, though. Back in June, every Republican but one had voted against the bill. As the clerk went down the roll, it was obvious that the GOP was still determined to beat us. I just about gave up on it.

Steadily, the margin against us rose. At one point, it reached twenty-one. And then it began to drop, slowly but consistently. As the clerk read on, we climbed within seventeen, then sixteen, then fifteen, then fourteen. We had broken the momentum. We could turn it around. As more Democratic members filed into the House to vote, Hale Boggs and I grabbed them. "If you come with us," I pleaded, "we can win this thing." Speaker McCormack called a few northeasterners up to his chair and pressed the case to help us.

The margin kept dropping. It was eight, then seven, then six. With just a few more minutes, we could win it. I bought them by dispatching a few rank-and-file members into the House well. "Mr. Speaker," each asked in turn, "how am I recorded?" As the clerk patiently looked up each member's name and told the member what his own vote had been, I scurried around the floor, picking up a new vote here, gaining a switch there. Furious, the Republican leadership tried to cut us off. Charlie Halleck rose to shout out a point of order. "Members are asking how they are recorded," he declared, "for obvious purposes of delay." John McCormack overruled the objection. "The Chair cannot look into the minds of members and determine their motives," observed the old veteran of many a fight.

Finally, I had cornered every entering member and had persuaded three to switch their original votes. The clerk completed the long-delayed roll call and handed the Speaker the official tally. We had won by 202 to 197. This time, I had the three switches that were exactly what we needed.

During my first year in Congress, I got one of those letters that Sam Rayburn had told me about. It was from a poor fellow who wanted some help. It read, "We Okies expect you to uphold our interest in this nigger question."

It was an attitude not universal in my district and not unique to it, either. You could find it all over America. I had been raised among people who held it. Most of them had voted to send me to

Congress to be their representative. Theirs was a view centuries old; it was the custom of our daily lives; it was enshrined in the laws of our states and localities. What is remarkable is not its existence, not its expression, not its strength. What is remarkable is that my district, my state, and my nation have overcome it. It happened while I served in Congress, most of it while I served as majority leader.

In a sense, it began with Harry Truman, the Missouri courthouse politician who became the first president in this century to ask Congress for civil rights legislation. After the 1948 Democratic National Convention committed the party to a civil rights program, Harry Truman boldly made the commitment his own. It split the party and came to nothing legislatively, but it secured Harry Truman's election and his place in history.

However meager the immediate results, the issue, once raised, did not go away. In the most important constitutional case of this century, the United States Supreme Court, in the 1954 *Brown* case, unanimously forbade the racial segregation of students in American schools. Subsequent decisions steadily chipped away at segregation's foundation. In Montgomery, Alabama, a young minister, the Reverend Dr. Martin Luther King, Jr., took up the cause of a middle-aged seamstress, Mrs. Rosa Parks. In the streets of the Cradle of the Confederacy he forged the tactic, the passive resistance of nonviolent protest, that made her cause his people's cause as it blazed across the South and seared the nation's conscience.

Cautiously, almost painfully, Congress began to move. In 1957, we marginally strengthened black voting rights with the first civil rights act since Reconstruction. I remember that when it came up, I sought the advice of Sam Rayburn. Mr. Rayburn represented the same kind of people I did. In 1948, he had had to save his seat from a vicious demagogue by swearing his powerful opposition to any civil rights laws. But I still remember what Sam Rayburn told me that day in 1957. "Carl," he said, "under the Constitution, every man has the right to vote. You can defend the position before any audience in this country." That cleared it up for me immediately. Any other consideration slipped away, and I saw the issue in moral terms. On the decisive teller votes, I marched down the House aisle with the civil rights people. I voted for the act on final passage. I did the same thing three years later when Congress passed a second (though still weak) civil rights bill.

Still, the issue did not go away. By endorsing stronger action and dramatically securing Dr. King's release from a Georgia jail cell, John Kennedy won the overwhelming support of black voters and, only because of that, the presidency. But if black votes at the polls had made him president, southern votes in the Congress would decide his fate. For that reason, he (and we in the leadership) moved cautiously. In 1961, we worked on only one civil rights measure, an act to extend the Civil Rights Commission created in the 1957 law. Candidate Kennedy had roundly criticized the Eisenhower administration for failing to end discrimination in Federal Housing Administration loans by executive order—with "the stroke of a pen," he had said in 1960—but it was November 1962 before President Kennedy moved his own pen under such an order. Even as late as February 1963, Kennedy's eloquent message on civil rights led only to meek White House proposals to tighten existing laws and provide assistance for school districts that were integrating voluntarily. Nothing was said about the thousands of districts and entire states that still refused to integrate nine years after the *Brown* decision, and little was done to push the little that was proposed.

If political reasoning seemed to compel such a lack of vigor, events far removed from the Capitol moved to their own logic. In April of 1963, Dr. King took his cause to Birmingham, Alabama, the city that he described as "the most thoroughly segregated big city" in America. Mass demonstrations, many involving schoolchildren, followed. The city's police commissioner, Eugene ("Bull") Connor, met the children with fire hoses and attack dogs. Scores were injured, and 3,300 demonstrators were arrested and herded into pens. In early May, a bomb destroyed the church that Dr. King was using as his headquarters. Four little black girls, each clad in her Sunday-best dress of white, lay crushed beneath the rubble. More bombings followed. Eventually, and inevitably, some blacks put down their picket signs and picked up rocks. Spasms of rioting, looting, and terror threatened to tear the city apart. In other cities, from Cambridge, Massachusetts, to Cambridge, Maryland, mass protests in the streets marched a hot breath from violence.

Atop it all, Governor George Wallace finally got his chance to keep his campaign promise to "stand in the schoolhouse door." After long and tedious litigation, a federal court had ordered the University of Alabama to admit two black students. Deputy Attorney General Nicholas Katzenbach personally delivered and read the order at the Tuscaloosa campus. Standing before him was the cocky little governor, who melodramatically read his statement of defiance. Standing metaphorically behind the governor was the possibility of mob rioting, such as had injured hundreds a year before at the University of Mississippi. Standing literally (if somewhat distantly) behind Katzenbach were army troops already aboard helicopters at Fort Benning, Georgia. It was George Wallace who stood aside. Neither the spirit of defiance nor the prospect of violence budged at all.

Beginning in May, the president had talked in the leadership breakfasts about withdrawing his original meek proposal in favor of a real civil rights act, one with teeth like Bull Connor's dogs. He told us that his Justice Department already was working on just such a bill. On June 11, 1963, he told the nation. It was on the evening of George Wallace's stand in the schoolhouse door. It also was John Kennedy's finest hour. All of the eloquence that he always had displayed and all of the passion that he heretofore had withheld went into his speech. Observing that the events in Birmingham and elsewhere had "so increased the cries for equality that no city or state or legislative body can prudently choose to ignore them," the president outlined the legislation that he would submit, but he added that the nation faced not "a legal or legislative issue alone" but rather "a moral issue. It is as old as the Scriptures and is as clear as the American Constitution. . . . Those who do nothing are inviting shame as well as violence. Those who act boldly are recognizing right as well as reality." The moral issue was the nation's, but the legislative issue fell to the Congress. The time had come for us to act boldly.

Most people recall the events that surrounded our deliberations. The president, his brother (Attorney General Robert Kennedy), and his entire administration seized every public forum to urge the bill's passage. Dozens of labor unions, church groups, and reform bodies mobilized their moral energies and mounted lobbying campaigns. In the summer, a quarter of a million people marched on Washington as a human petition for civil rights. Gathered around the reflecting pool of the Lincoln Memorial, they were stirred by Dr. King's great "I Have a Dream" speech, and they left most of the country ready to make that dream come true.

To the congressional leadership fell the undramatic task of turning the dream into a law. In the nature of things, we would have to do it first in the House of Representatives. Submitted directly to the Senate, the bill would fall into the clutches of Mississippi's James Eastland and his fellow southerners on the judiciary committee, the unhappy hunting ground of civil rights. Because Senate rules allowed a bill already passed by the House to bypass committee assignment and go directly to the floor, we would have to produce the bill for them.

On our side, we were lucky. The House Judiciary Committee was one of the few not headed by a southerner. Emmanuel Celler was chairman of the committee. For forty-one years he had represented an ethnically diverse and intensely liberal Brooklyn district. There may have been no firmer friend of civil rights in the House of Representatives.

Working closely with Speaker McCormack and me, Manny Celler made his first decision. It turned out to be the most important (if unpublicized) decision in the long legislative battle to come. That decision—not a passionate speech, not a massive march—made the 1964 Civil Rights Act. It was Celler's designation of the subcommittee that would take up the bill.

The Judiciary Committee's original work on the bill, including its initial drafting, would fall to the subcommittee of Manny Celler's choice. That was one of his prerogatives as a committee chairman. Unlike those of most legislative committees, Judiciary's subcommittees were designated by number, not by narrow and hard lines of jurisdiction. Celler therefore was free to choose any of five subcommittees. His choice was Subcommittee 5, the only one not headed by a southerner or a southern sympathizer. Its chairman was Manny Celler himself, and its Democratic membership included some of the most enlightened members of the House: Pete Rodino of New Jersey, Byron Rogers of Colorado, Harold Donohue of Massachusetts, Herman Toll of Pennsylvania, Robert Kastenmeier of Wisconsin, and Jack Brooks, a Texan who was one of the strongest and most determined men in the House. Heading the subcommittee's four Republicans was William McCulloch of tiny Piqua, Ohio. McCulloch was the full committee's ranking Republican and a man respected on both sides of the aisle. Much of that respect flowed from his absolute devotion to principle.

Manny Celler's subcommittee took up President Kennedy's bill and proceeded to rewrite it. Its symbolic heart, Title II, remained the same. In one strike the bill outlawed discrimination in public accommodations, forbidding the awful system of whites-only practices in privately owned facilities that served the general public. Everywhere else, the subcommittee improved the bill by strengthening it. It added a new section outlawing employment discrimination. It fortified Title III by empowering the attorney general to initiate suits to desegregate public facilities and to intervene in suits brought by citizens seeking equal protection of the laws. Kennedy's bill had sought a four-year extension of the Civil Rights Commission; the subcommittee went all the way and made the commission permanent. The president had sought the discretionary power to deny federal funds to discriminatory programs; Manny Celler's subcommittee gave him no choice: it *required* their denial. All in all, it was Subcommittee 5 of Manny Celler's House Judiciary Committee that made John Kennedy's civil rights bill.

It was the job of the House leadership to sell it, and the first person we had to sell it to was the president.

John Kennedy feared that a bill too strong would never pass the full House or the Senate. In fact, he had dispatched his brother the attorney general to testify in the subcommittee against most of its changes. When the subcommittee went ahead anyway, he called us to the White House. Speaker McCormack, Chairman Celler, and I went, along with several rank-and-file members of the full committee. Bill McCulloch, Charlie Halleck, and a few others represented the GOP. Late into the night we argued with the president for the subcommittee's version. It was the right thing to do, it was the right time to do it, and we believed we could pass it. Judging the House's mood, I figured we could get as many as 140 or 150 Democratic votes for final passage. If the Republicans could get us even half of theirs, we would win it. Halleck and McCulloch said they could do that and declared they would. It was our bill that we took out of the White House that night, and it was our bill that the full Judiciary Committee overwhelmingly reported to the House of Representatives.

First, though, it would have to go before Judge Smith's Rules Committee. Knowing what to expect, Manny Celler was preparing a discharge petition the day he submitted the bill, November 20, 1963. The next day, President Kennedy left for Dallas.

I had first heard of Kennedy's trip from Lyndon Johnson; I thought it a bad idea. Dallas had become something of the capital of right-wing extremists, some of whom recently had heckled and assaulted United Nations Ambassador Adlai Stevenson. But the thing that struck me when Johnson told me about it was LBJ's mood.

Lyndon Johnson had left the power and the action of being Senate majority leader for the vice-presidency. Apparently he had believed that he could use the vice-president's constitutional role as the Senate's presiding officer to make himself John Kennedy's chief of Congress. He and Mike Mansfield had cooked up a scheme to make him head of the Senate's Democratic conference, but his former colleagues would have nothing of it since it jeopardized their independence from the executive branch. Johnson thereby was left with the empty honor of the vice-presidency. I suspect that he soon agreed with one of his predecessors' view of their job.

The vice-presidency, Texas's John Nance Garner had said, is "not worth a bucket of warm spit."

While he served as vice-president, Lyndon Johnson seemed a changed man. Usually active, assertive, even aggressive, he meekly went about his duties. He publicly spoke for the president's policies; he headed a few committees and boards. I saw him most frequently at the weekly leadership breakfasts. Lyndon Johnson, a man once hailed as a legislative magician, rarely spoke except to answer a question. His answers usually were short, and frequently they sounded detached. Otherwise, he sat passively, his face drawn, his eyes wandering.

That is what made so memorable an evening in the fall of 1963. Mary and I were leaving an after-work press-club reception when a long, black limousine pulled up to the curb. It was the vice-president's official car. Its darkened window dropped, and Lyndon Johnson leaned out to invite Mary and me over to his northwest Washington residence for dinner with him and Lady Bird. We piled in and had a fine meal: corn bread, black-eyed peas, and peach ice cream. Afterwards, Johnson and I sat out on his patio. I had not seen him so animated or so enthusiastic in years. He told me about a private poll he had commissioned down in Texas. It looked like John Kennedy could not carry Texas in 1964; the president would have to visit the state to rally his troops. What accounted for his exhilaration, though, was his belief that he was getting another chance to do something important. If John Kennedy was going to Texas, he would need Lyndon Johnson.

On the morning of Thursday, November 21, President Kennedy had a meeting with the Democratic leadership of the House and Senate in the Cabinet Room just before he was going to leave for Texas. When the meeting was over, he asked me to come into the Oval Office with him to discuss a legislative matter. While we were talking, his helicopter flew up and landed near the Rose Garden, just south of the East Wing of the White House. He turned around and watched the helicopter as it was stopping, then turned to me and said good-bye. He left the Oval Office for the helicopter, boarded it, and departed for Andrews Air Force Base. I was the last person to visit with him in the White House.

On Friday, November 22, I was eating lunch in the Congressional Hotel when Lydia Vacin, a secretary for the House Agriculture Committee, ran up to me. She said television had just carried the news that the president had been shot in Dallas; no one knew his condition. I rushed over to my office and learned that Ted Sorensen, President Kennedy's top aide, was calling me. I picked up the phone and he told me the president was dead. I walked into my inner office, closed the door, and turned out the lights. I railed against the madness of the assassination. I said over and over that he never should have gone. Standing in the darkness, I wished I could cry.

That night I accompanied a group of Lyndon Johnson's oldest House friends to Andrews Air Force Base. *Air Force One* rolled up, and a military guard removed a coffin. When Johnson got out, he joined us, and we drove over to the Executive Office Building. Through a little side door, we went into the White House. Nobody had said much of anything by the time we broke up an hour or so later. No one had to.

The whole country needed Lyndon Johnson.

Almost instantly Lyndon Johnson became once again a changed man. All the energy, all the ambition, all the talent that had frustrated him so in the vice-presidency now drove him, even consumed him. My phone never seemed to stop ringing. It was the president, not a secretary, not an aide. Lyndon Johnson wanted action, and he wanted it now.

In the few weeks left to 1963, I learned just how much I had ahead of me with Lyndon Johnson beside me, behind me, and seemingly all over me. The hard work that we had been doing on civil rights had put more routine bills in jeopardy. At the time of Kennedy's murder, we had passed only one of twelve general appropriations bills. Johnson drove us to get the others through, and he never let up. Finally, we were down to the last one. It was

*The whole country needed Lyndon Johnson.* Carl Albert with Lyndon Johnson at the White House, December, 1963.

the foreign aid bill, and I never had seen a bill so hopeless. After months of wrangling, each house had passed a bill and we finally had gotten a conference report acceptable to House and Senate negotiators. But Clarence Cannon, chairman of Appropriations, opposed it; Otto Passman, chairman of the Foreign Aid subcommittee, opposed it; Charlie Halleck and the entire Republican leadership opposed it.

The immediate problem was that the conference bill was lodged in the Rules Committee, awaiting dispatch to the floor. Sure, Howard Smith opposed it, and the Republican committeemen literally had taken their opposition with them when they left Washington to return to their homes. I could not really blame them, though. Several Democrats on Rules had done the same, and for good reason: it was December 23, only a few hours before Christmas, and this one bill was preventing the end of what was already the fifth-longest session in American history. When some Democrats and all the Republicans left, we were one vote short of the quorum necessary to get the bill out of Rules.

Even had we wanted to do so (and we did not), Lyndon Johnson was not about to let us end without getting the money to run a foreign aid program. Thus, I spent the night of December 23 at the White House. The president, the Speaker, and I moved into the Oval Office and worked the phones, trying to find that one vote for a quorum on rules. We could not even locate most of its members; those we did find were neither happy nor cooperative. It was 2:00 A.M. before I reached our last possibility, Bill Colmer. He was in a Mississippi hospital tending to his sick wife. I did not waste time arguing the bill's merits because I knew that it had none for Bill Colmer. What I said was, "Bill, we need you, your party needs you, and President Johnson needs you. We all need you to give us a quorum."

Bill Colmer left his ailing wife's bed, boarded a plane, flew through a blizzard, and reached Washington that night. At 7:00 A.M. the next day, he voted not to discharge the bill, but his presence gave us a quorum to take the bill to the House. The House passed it, and we voted adjournment on December 29. Gene Mc-

*With Lyndon Johnson beside me, behind me, seemingly all over me.*

Carthy joked that Sam Rayburn had died before teaching John McCormack and me how to adjourn Congress, but we finally managed that. What we were learning was how to deal with Lyndon Johnson.

Right from the start I learned that I was working with a man utterly consumed with politics. Lyndon Johnson ate, drank, breathed, and lived politics every minute of every day. He must have fallen asleep by counting votes. I never saw a man so obsessed with anything as Lyndon Johnson was with politics, especially its legislative expression. I can remember visiting him down at his ranch and trying to make some small talk. "Those are some fine-looking cattle," I might say, and Johnson would not miss a beat. "Yeah," he would answer. "That old bull over there looks just like Chairman So-and-So. What do you think we can do to move such-and-such a bill out of his committee?"

That total absorption found expression in his matchless gift for one-on-one persuasion of legislators. When he was a senator, he was famed for The Treatment, and as president he used it just as Rowland Evans and Robert Novak had described it:

> He moved in close, his face a scant millimeter from his target, his eyes widening and narrowing, his eyebrows rising and falling. From his pocket poured clippings, memos, statistics. Mimicry, humor, and the genius of analogy made The Treatment an almost hypnotic experience and rendered the target stunned and helpless.

But Lyndon Johnson was neither a hypnotist nor a magician. He was a consummate politician who made it his business to know what mattered to whom and why. Through individual contact and hard bargaining, he knew just what each congressman needed. And that is why he usually got for himself exactly what he wanted.

In 1964, he got a big chunk of it when we finished action on John Kennedy's two chief proposals of 1963. Although it had taken Wilbur Mills's Ways and Means Committee eight months to produce a tax-cut bill, it took only eight weeks for the Senate to pass it and the president to sign it once the session opened.

In even less time we got a civil rights bill to the Senate. Howard Smith used all of his legislative skills to delay it in his Rules Committee, but he no longer had the power to block it entirely. Manny Celler had gone ahead and filed his discharge petition, and its signers steadily climbed toward 218. Dick Bolling, committee member and fearless student of parliamentary procedure, kept the heat on Smith by finding an obscure procedure to make the committee meet over the chairman's objections. Recognizing the inevitable, Judge Smith allowed his committee to vote a rule on January 30. All five Republicans honored Charlie Halleck's commitment, and with the six nonsouthern Democrats, the committee voted eleven to four to release the bill.

The old judge assembled about sixty southern Democrats that same afternoon to plan a strategy, but Howard Smith's long night had passed. Manny Celler and Bill McCulloch handled the floor debate brilliantly. They hurled scores of emasculating amendments back into Smith's face. The one successful amendment of substance involved the subcommittee's outlawing of employment discrimination on the basis of race, color, religion, or national origin. To those forbidden categories the House added another: sex. Thus, the bill became a landmark in the cause of women's rights as well as black rights. It was an odd fate, for the amendment's purpose had been either to damn the bill as unenforceable or defeat it as too strong. Never before had its author made such a blunder—or such a contribution. That author was Representative Howard Worth Smith of Virginia.

So amended, the bill won overwhelmingly, 290 to 130. We got 152 Democratic votes, losing only 4 outside the South (and getting 11 there). The Republicans honored Charlie Halleck and their country by going for the bill 138 to 34.

Two White House aides who watched the final vote went out in the hall to congratulate themselves. As they stood there celebrating, a pay telephone began ringing in a nearby booth. Curious, one of them answered it. The caller was Lyndon Johnson. All he said was, "All right, you fellows, get on over there to the Senate because we've got it through the House, and now we've got the big job of getting it through the Senate."

It was a big job. Only after a three-month southern filibuster did the Senate vote, seventy-one to twenty-nine, to shut off debate. The margin was just four above the two-thirds needed. Its battle of words lost, the South lost the war, seventy-three to twenty-seven, on final passage. That vote came on June 19, 1964, exactly one year to the day after John Kennedy had submitted his bill. It had been a much longer time coming.

Presidents Kennedy and Johnson deserved all the credit they got. Manny Celler and Bill McCulloch deserved far more credit than they received. Dick Bolling deserved far more than the public ever knew. I guess I deserve some credit, too. I finally had answered that old letter wanting me to do something about the race question.

By 1964's end, Lyndon Johnson and the Congress had passed most of John Kennedy's program, but not all. Federal aid to education still tossed around the rocks of religious controversy. After Bob Kerr's untimely death in 1963, the Senate attached a Medicare amendment to the next year's Social Security bill. Wilbur Mills killed it in conference because he knew that it could not have gotten through ways and means and feared it would not pass the House.

In one stunning particular, we had gone far beyond Kennedy's public agenda. With Walter Heller, chairman of his Council of Economic Advisers, President Kennedy had talked privately about making poverty a vague campaign issue in 1964 and introducing antipoverty legislation after the election and after the tax-cut and civil rights bills had been cleared. On the evening of November 23, Lyndon Johnson's first full day as president, Heller had told Johnson of those plans. Lyndon Johnson had jumped all over the poverty issue. "Go ahead," he had told Heller. "Give it the highest priority. Push ahead full tilt."

"Push ahead full tilt" was exactly what Lyndon Johnson himself had done. During the Christmas holidays of 1963, he had put his staff to work on framing antipoverty legislation, not campaign speeches, and for 1964, not down the road. In his January State of the Union message, the new president was ready to swear that "this administration, here and now, declares unconditional war on poverty in America." The legislative expression of that was the Economic Opportunity Act of 1964. The president built a national consensus for the measure with dramatic televised tours of poverty regions and persuasive personal appeals to groups ranging from the Daughters of the American Revolution to the Socialist party. Sargent Shriver, his designated commander of the war as director of the proposed Office of Economic Opportunity, moved into my office again to help direct the congressional fight. Knowing the significance of southern Democratic votes, we assigned the bill not to education and labor's chairman, Adam Clayton Powell, but to a respected Georgian, Phil Landrum. The work that Landrum, Hale Boggs, and I put in with the southerners paid off on August 8. We got exactly the two-thirds southern Democratic support that I had figured would be our maximum, as 60 southern Democrats voted with 144 nonsoutherners and 22 Republicans to give us a comfortable 226-to-185 majority. Hale and I called the president just after the vote and I confessed my surprise at winning that easily. He thanked us, and I got ready to push ahead full tilt again and immediately.

Congress had recessed for the Republican National Convention in July, and I had taken a brief but singular vacation. Mary and David and I decided to drive up to Canada to get away. For the only time ever, I told no one on my staff even where I was going. I wanted this occasion to be a real getaway, so I made sure that no one on earth could find me. Or so I thought.

We went up to Quebec, where we visited with Paul Bouchard, a Rhodes scholar who had gone up to Oxford with me in 1931. After a nice dinner with Paul, David and I were watching Canadian television in our room. Right in the middle of the news, an announcer broke in with a bulletin: "The Royal Canadian Mounted Police is endeavoring to locate Congressman Carl Albert. He is believed to be in Canada and driving a 1964 Thunderbird, Oklahoma license PB 827. Anyone knowing the whereabouts of Carl Albert will please immediately notify the Royal Canadian Mounted Police." David looked at me like he expected Sergeant Preston to bust down the door any minute. I hurried to a phone and called the Mounties, wondering why I was a wanted man. The fellow I asked laughed. "Sir," he answered, "you're not wanted by us. Your President Johnson is the one who wants you." It figured. The president had put the FBI, the RCMP, and the White House switchboard to work finding me. It had taken them several hours, but they had done it. The president wanted me to direct his own convention's platform committee, and he wanted me to start now.

It turned out to be a pretty good job. It was a sign of how rapidly and how tightly Lyndon Johnson had seized the fallen reins of leadership that we produced a platform exactly to his liking. In fact, the only dispute involved a minority that wanted an extreme civil rights plank that was sure to touch off a bloody floor fight. Manny Celler, whom I had put on the drafting subcommittee because of his responsible leadership for civil rights, took care of that. Like the entire platform, the final plank was a testimony to Democratic unity behind a progressive yet realistic program.

That was a mighty big asset in the 1964 election. At San Francisco's Cow Palace, a fractious Republican National Convention had chosen as its candidate a man regarded as neither progressive nor realistic. Barry Goldwater had built a reputation as a conservative ideologue. He welcomed hardly any major advance of the past third of a century, not Social Security of the 1930s, not public housing of the 1940s, not his own party's moderation of the 1950s, not even civil rights of the 1960s. In hundreds of speeches, a syndicated column, and a widely read book, Goldwater also had revealed a disquieting tendency to shoot from the lip. He wanted to call nuclear weapons "nukes," apparently to make them seem friendlier. At a moment of international crisis, he had offered the discomforting advice of "lobbing a few into the men's room of the Kremlin." All of this had made Goldwater something of a hero to every right-wing extremist group in the country, and the candidate had not shunned their sweaty embrace. On the contrary, he had bellowed at San Francisco that "extremism in the defense of liberty is no vice; moderation in the pursuit of justice is no virtue."

By the time of our own convention, Republicans everywhere had displayed his picture: steel-gray hair; square, set jaw; black lensless glasses. The last eliminated the photographer's glare but did nothing to improve the Arizonan's peculiar vision. Beneath it ran the 1964 slogan: "In your heart you know he's right."

In Atlantic City, we Democrats had our fun with candidate Goldwater. Hubert Humphrey's speech accepting the vice-presidential nomination ran through the litany of recent reforms backed by our party. Each, he added, was embraced by the vast majority of

Americans. Soon the crowd was chanting with him the line that followed: "But not Senator Goldwater." I made my own contribution to Democratic humor when I said of the opposition's slogan, "In your heart you know he's right—too far right."

Our good spirits continued right through Election Day. Lyndon Johnson carried all but six states (five in the Deep South, plus Goldwater's home state) in rolling up 61 percent of the popular vote, a new national record. All across the country Democrats owed their elections to him, or, perhaps, to Barry Goldwater. That was surely the case in Congress, where we added two seats to our already substantial Senate majority and another thirty-eight in the House. In both chambers the Democratic party held its largest advantage since the Roosevelt landslide of 1936. The tide that Lyndon Johnson had mounted in 1963 was rolling along. In 1965 it reached flood proportions, crested, and fell.

When the 1965 Congress had completed its work, President Johnson gave me a present that I promptly put on my office wall. Today it is one of the few souvenirs of those days that I display in my office at the Federal Building in McAlester, Oklahoma. It is a framed set of fountain pens, each bearing the title of a separate bill. At the bottom is a plaque engraved with what must have been dictated by the president. Who but Lyndon Johnson would say "With these fifty pens, President Lyndon B. Johnson signed into law the foundations of the Great Society which were passed by the historic and fabulous first session of the 89th Congress"?

"The historic and fabulous first session of the 89th Congress" was indeed the most remarkable Congress of my generation. In its 293-day session, it passed the bills that completed the Democratic agenda that had been stalled since the 1930s, bills that established Lyndon Johnson's reputation, bills that defined national priorities into the 1980s and beyond. Since I had become party whip, I had become accustomed to settling for half a loaf; sometimes I had gotten the crumbs. In 1965, we got the whole loaf with the meat, the condiments, and the beverages thrown in to give us a real legislative feast.

It was the House's leadership that made sure we got it, and we made sure we got it by the end of the session's first day. After the election, Speaker McCormack, Hale Boggs, and I resolved to make the most of our majority. We knew that thirty-eight new Democrats would not automatically change the decisions of Congress, not unless the decision-making process changed. That is what we set out to do. We told the president and he was more than sympathetic, but he recognized that these were House matters. This was our fight, and it was the leadership of the House that won it.

One change gave us more leverage over the Rules Committee. Having made the 1961 expansion permanent in 1963, we now added a twenty-one-day rule. Unlike that of 1949, this one took some of the committee's power and gave it directly to the Speaker, not other chairmen. The Speaker gained the discretionary power (not the obligation) to recognize *any* member of a committee who wanted to call up a bill on the floor if the Rules Commitee had not reported it favorably within twenty-one days. In addition, we eliminated outright the Rules Committee's power over the submission of bills to the House-Senate conference committees.

The other change involved the critical Ways and Means Committee. For years the committee's membership had been frozen at fifteen majority members and ten minority members, regardless of the party ratio in Congress. In 1965, we insisted that the overall ratio (more than 2:1) prevail on that vital committee. The result was that the GOP slipped to eight seats and we went to seventeen. With one vacancy otherwise, we then added three moderate-to-liberal members: Richard Fulton of Tennessee, Phil Landrum of Georgia, and Charles Vanik of Ohio. Down the road was the promise of a more representative Congress, since the seventeen Democratic members would continue to make our committee assignments.

Without those changes—entirely conceived and executed by the House leadership—that framed gift on my wall would hold very few pens. It was on that day by those deeds that we made it possible for the Congress to have a "historic and fabulous" session.

The president was ready to make the most of those opportunities. The drive that I had seen in 1963 and 1964 only increased in 1965. Lyndon Johnson had the big majority that every Democratic president since Roosevelt had wanted and needed. He had the House leadership and internal structure that even Roosevelt had lost, he had the momentum of a national mandate of record proportions, and he had the sense to know that he must use them all while he still had them. Use them he did with 469 legislative proposals. At the session's end, we had approved 323 of them, giving Lyndon Johnson a batting average of .689. No president since FDR had won nearly so much; none since LBJ has, either.

Many of them he won only because of our internal reforms. If Lyndon Johnson had had to deal with Howard Smith's old Rules Committee and Wilbur Mills's old ways and means, he would have gone down swinging. As it was, the changes engineered by the House leadership allowed the president to set a record. In many cases, that record also was indebted to the long labor of unsung congressmen. Take Medicare, for example. Presidents John Kennedy and Lyndon Johnson both had fought hard for the bill, but the original idea belonged to neither president. Back in the 1950s, Representative Aime J. Forand of Rhode Island had introduced the first bill to pay the elderly's hospital expenses under Social Security; that was essentially the bill that President Johnson sent us in 1965. What the leadership had done ensured that Congress would pass it.

Even before those changes, the election results already guaranteed there would be some health-care legislation for the elderly that year. Even the Republicans and the American Medical Association knew it, so they aimed to defeat Medicare with something called Eldercare. Unlike the Forand proposal for compulsory hospital coverage, theirs would pay only the elderly's doctor bills through voluntary contributions. The battle would be fought in Wilbur Mills's Ways and Means Committee, and our changes in that committee won it. In a brilliant maneuver dictated by the altered memberships of both his committee and of the House, Wilbur Mills outflanked the opposition by coupling its alternative to Representative Forand's original idea. The compulsory payroll tax of Social Security financed the elderly's hospital costs; voluntary supplementary coverage (at a cost of three dollars monthly) would cover the participants' doctor bills.

The same principle applied to the landmark Elementary and Secondary Education Act of 1965. For years, general aid to education had stalled because of the church-state issue. Lyndon Johnson and the White House finally found a way around it, but it was the way that had been blazed by Representative Cleveland Bailey of West Virginia. Back in the 1950s, Congressman Bailey had put through Congress a number of specialized aid-to-education bills. Because heavy federal employment at untaxed federal facilities took money away from local school boards while it put children in their classrooms, the Bailey Acts distributed money in proportion to the federal impact upon enrollments. From that precedent came the 1965 proposal. Since the government was waging a war on poverty, general education aid could be made available to any school (public or sectarian) impacted by large numbers of poor students. So conceived, the bill passed handily.

Another example is the 1965 immigration-law reform. Back in the 1920s, the Republicans had pushed through an act placing a tight lid on the total number of immigrants allowed in the United States. Worse, the act had adopted the notorious national-origins system of quotas. Seeking to freeze the nation's racial mix as it had stood before the influx of southern and eastern Europeans, the act had assigned each nation a quota of allowable immigrants on the basis of that nation's proportional contribution to the American population *of 1890*. In 1965, we got rid of that once and for all. Lyndon Johnson signed our bill before the Statue of Liberty, but the bill he signed was essentially the one that John McCormack and Manny Celler had called for in their maiden speeches in Congress, both delivered before Lyndon Johnson was old enough to serve there.

That is not to say that the president deserved no credit and made no contribution. Manny Celler lived to put the bill through his Judiciary Committee, and John McCormack lived to sign it as Speaker, but when its time came, Lyndon Johnson was behind the bill all the way. His Justice Department prepared the detailed "blue books" that went to every member and persuasively made the case for reform. His press office recorded messages in forty languages and distributed them to 250 radio stations to stir up popular support. And it was Lyndon Johnson himself who sat down and reasoned with the chairman of the House Judicial Subcommittee on Immigration, Michael Feighan. It was The Treatment that finally washed away Feighan's objections and made the bill possible.

On other bills, too, the White House's influence was undeniable. The Voting Rights Act of 1965, the one law that has most revolutionized American politics in my lifetime because it made southern politicians answerable to millions of black voters, was described by the press as Johnson's hurry-up answer to Martin Luther King's march in Selma, Alabama. Though that march dramatized the need, the fact was that the president, the Justice Department, and the congressional leadership were preparing to write and pass a voting-rights bill before a single marcher ever set foot on Edmund Pettus Bridge. This simply was an act whose time had come.

The same story stands behind almost all the pens that rest in that maple case in my office. Their time had come. We were no rubber-stamp Congress blindly catering to the president's ego. Lyndon Johnson was harvesting the work of those who had gone before him. He could do it because we stood by him. We knew our part, and we did it; he did his better than any president in my lifetime.

Until Vietnam.

Before the Eighty-ninth Congress, before the Johnson landslide, on August 4, 1964, President Johnson asked me to stay after our regular leadership breakfast to go over some other business. We had just begun talking pleasantly when the president received a phone call. His mood changed abruptly. He said to the caller, "They have?" He silently took the answer, then he shouted into the phone: "Now, I'll tell you what I want. I not only want those patrol boats destroyed, I want everything at that harbor destroyed,

I want the whole damn works destroyed. I want to give them a real dose." With that, he slammed the receiver down. Awkwardly, we finished our business without another word on the subject of the call.

Not until that evening, when I was called to be at the White House at seven o'clock. Joining me were six other congressmen and seven senators. Collectively, it was the entire bipartisan leadership of Congress and the Foreign Relations and Armed Services committees. With the president were Secretary of State Dean Rusk, Secretary of Defense Robert McNamara, Central Intelligence Agency Director John A. McCone, and General Earl Wheeler, chairman of the Joint Chiefs of Staff. Clearly, this was no routine assembly, a judgment confirmed by the president's opening words: "Some of our boys are floating around in the water."

Quickly, the administration's leaders outlined the circumstances that had brought us there. McNamara explained the morning's phone call when he told us that for the second time in as many days, North Vietnamese patrol boats had attacked an American naval vessel routinely patrolling waters forty to sixty miles at sea in the Gulf of Tonkin. Rusk ran through the immediate diplomatic background and sketched the responses already unfolding. McCone gave us the intelligence estimates regarding the involved North Vietnamese forces, and Wheeler read the message that he had dispatched to the commanders of our men serving as advisers in South Vietnam. After some general discussion, President Johnson told us his purpose—and ours.

He had prepared a resolution, based directly on the Formosa, Berlin, and Cuban resolutions, that he would present to Congress the next day. The resolution authorized the responses already made (as he read it, American planes were warming their engines for a retaliatory strike) and much else besides. In language used before, it generally empowered the president "to take all necessary steps, including the use of armed force" to assist any allied nation of Southeast Asia "in defense of its freedom." Explicitly, it expressed congressional approval and support for the president's "determination . . . to take all necessary measures to repel any armed attack against the forces of the United States and to prevent further aggression." From the entire assembly there was not one word of opposition. Each of us praised his resolve; each of us predicted overwhelming congressional approval. We departed with Senator George Aiken's comment, "By the time you send it up, there won't be anything for us to do but support you."

Lyndon Johnson sent it up and we did. The resolution cleared Thomas Morgan's House Foreign Affairs Committee without debate and without opposition. On August 7, Morgan presented it to the full House. No one spoke against it, and I was one of those to speak for it. "The president has asked us as representatives of the American people for our support," I said. "It is now time for all of us to join together as a nation firmly united behind our Commander-in-Chief and to express our complete confidence in him and in his leadership." In the House, we all did. The vote was 416 to 0. It had taken us just forty minutes.

Behind those minutes were years of experience. Not once since the sobering episode of Woodrow Wilson's Versailles treaty had an American president sought the support of Congress for his foreign policy and failed to get it. The world's bloodiest war had followed that failure. Since that war, both parties in both houses had stood united behind the critical policy decisions of four presidents. Both parties had acknowledged the chief executive's primacy in foreign policy, and every time America had stood united behind the president, peace had prevailed. Both Eisenhower and Kennedy had committed us to maintain the independence of South Vietnam. Every commitment we had made everywhere we had honored, and peace was the product. In an American election year, with a president and a candidate I knew to cherish peace, with the American flag under armed assault, this was no time to forget those lessons. When we voted that resolution, we were not making a military decision at all but a decision of the highest politics, and we made it with that past before us.

Few doubted our choice. Before the episode, opinion polls recorded that two-thirds of the American people cared little or not at all about Vietnam. After it, 85 percent expressed their approval of what we and the president had done. Otherwise, the immediate political effect was to defuse recent Republican charges that we were letting down our guard in Vietnam and to add to Lyndon Johnson's majorities. Compared to Barry Goldwater's rhetoric, President Johnson's acts were reasoned and responsible, firm but unthreatening. When he told a campaign crowd in my own district that "we don't want our American boys to do the fighting for the Asian boys," all of us—the president, the crowd, and I—believed that what we were doing was the one thing that could keep American boys out of the fighting. We believed because it always had in the past. This time it did not.

In South Vietnam we were setting our feet firmly upon an unstable slope that dropped to chaos. Following the military's 1963 overthrow and murder of Premier Ngo Dinh Diem, a series of governments, each more inept than its predecessor, came and went. Determined to take advantage, the Vietcong and North Vietnamese came and fought. Poorly led and demoralized, South Vietnam's army rarely stood to fight back, never successfully. The emboldened Communist forces even struck at American targets. In November 1963, they shelled our air base at Bien Hoa, destroying five planes and leaving four Americans dead. At Christmas, they bombed a Saigon hotel that housed both military and civilian personnel, killing several. On February 6, 1964, they assaulted a military outpost at Pleiku, killing nine of our soldiers.

Never before had a Communist force dared directly provoke a power such as the United States. Never before had there been such a power. In the mid-1960s, the United States produced half the world's wealth. Eleven of our states outproduced the entire Soviet Union; California alone outproduced Red China. A few good American counties generated more economic might than did all of North Vietnam. No one—not the Vietcong, not North Vietnam, not Red China, not the Soviet Union, not the entire Communist block—could match the military resources of the United States. Intelligently and carefully brought to bear, those resources surely would end the aggression. The military leaders told us it could be done with air power alone. Having seen the devastation that ruined Japan even before Hiroshima, I wanted to believe them. Lyndon Johnson did, too.

Two hours after the Pleiku attack, the president ordered a series of retaliatory raids directed at specific North Vietnamese targets. Two days later, those raids became a sustained and graduating air war that eventually would drop on North Vietnam more tons of high-explosive bombs than had fallen on Japan or on Germany or on all military targets in the history of warfare. It would not be enough.

By the summer of 1965, that was already clear. The Vietcong and the North Vietnamese had not cowered from American might, they had taunted it by stepping up the pressure of their attacks. Our military saw the bloody consequences and the certain outcome: the imminent collapse of South Vietnam.

On July 27, the congressional leadership met again with President Johnson to discuss the situation. With him were all of his top aides, both military and civilian, as well as our ambassador to South Vietnam, Henry Cabot Lodge. The collection told me how important the meeting was. Again the president's opening words told us why. The situation in Vietnam, he said, was critical. The Communists had rejected his recent calls for peace. The only change was that South Vietnam's army was nearing disintegration. General William C. Westmoreland had requested a real commitment of American power, manpower, for a land war. The general also had declared that South Vietnam could be saved only if the United States military shed its role as advisers and "put its finger in the dike" by taking charge of the war in the south.

Calmly, Lyndon Johnson described for us five possible responses to the dire situation. One was to destroy North Vietnam utterly and totally by unleashing the full might of America's war power. A second was just as extreme: we could walk away. The third was to cling to the status quo—as he put it, "hope Lodge can pull a rabbit out of the hat." Not even Ambassador Lodge smiled at that or at the fourth option: to proclaim a national emergency, call up the reserves, and declare war. His last option was to increase draft calls to meet Westmoreland's immediate requests, seek supplemental appropriations to pay the bill, and trust that that measured commitment would be enough. If not, we could always add to it.

Not one person in that room believed either one, two, or three was even an option. The experience of China's intervention in the Korean War made the first a potential disaster that no one would risk again. The experience of appeasing Hitler at Munich ruled out the second, a point that John McCormack particularly stressed. The evaluation of Lodge and Westmoreland made the third a thinly disguised version of two; it was appeasement on the install-ment plan. No one in that room doubted that Lyndon Johnson's only real alternatives were either the fourth or the last. We all could tell—his tone, his words, even the ordering gave it away—that the last was his strong preference. Perhaps it was already his decision. Without dissent, we each agreed to back him. No one wanted another Korea or Munich, but no one wanted to declare war in Vietnam. No one thought it necessary; no one thought it prudent; no one wanted a third-rate Communist state to stop our progress toward a Great Society.

A few days later, President Johnson announced that he was sending 50,000 American boys immediately to Vietnam, toward a year-end total of 175,000. Moreover, he would grant General Westmoreland whatever additional numbers were necessary to do the job that was now our job. He did not say that we were going to war. We did not know that we were—on the installment plan.

The overwhelming majority of Americans supported that deci-sion. I think they did so for the same reason I did: we had the experience of the past, and we had confidence in our capacity to shape the future. But we could not have foreseen or even have imagined how that future would unfold.

We could not know how little the material might of the world's greatest industrial power would affect events in the jungles of Vietnam. We could not tell that the government we were backing there would waste the lives of our men (and its own, too) with ceaseless scheming and unbounded corruption. We could not imagine that the military superiority of the United States could not break the will of an insignificant state equipped with no navy, no air force, and a peasant army. We could not envision an on-again, off-again war. We could not foresee that the enemy would use negotiations as its military weapon. We could not imagine an enemy ready to die faster than our weapons could kill. We could not foresee that one escalation would beget another and the sum of them all would be the most divisive national experience since the Civil War. We could not know that this war might be lost but not lost before it had provoked a constitutional crisis in our own country. I do not know what any of us—the president, the leadership, the American people—would have done had we foreseen the unforeseeable. I know only that we were all summoned to honorable purposes, not to prophecy.

Most of Vietnam's worst effects lay down a long, twisting, and bloody road. One, however, surfaced immediately. After our commitment was made, the Great Society's momentum broke and then retreated. I could see it as early as the 1966 session, and I saw it up close. We had declared a war on poverty, not on Vietnam. While fighting the undeclared war, we had to finance the declared one.

Knowing it would be too little, the Democratic leadership got an antipoverty authorization of $1.75 billion, every penny that could be gotten through the Appropriations Committee or the House. Events showed just how close we had cut it, for when we put the bill on the House floor, the Republicans moved to strike the enacting clause, thereby killing the bill and eliminating any funds at all. They carried the motion 128 to 118 on a teller vote. Hurriedly, I called for a roll-call vote and rounded up every Democratic vote I could find to save the program. We did, 259 to 157. Still, I doubted that it even would have come to that only twelve months earlier.

Because we had the numbers, we won that one, and many others besides. For all of our difficulties, the two sessions of the Eighty-ninth Congress proved what we could do with a decent number of Democrats. A Harris Poll showed what the public thought of that: 71 percent gave the Congress a favorable rating, 4 percentage points above Lyndon Johnson's best rating and 36 points above our own rating in 1963. Our major accomplishments—Medicare, aid to education, tax reform, and voting rights—earned favorable ratings of 82, 90, 92, and 95 percent respectively. Never in my lifetime had Congress been so highly regarded, and rightly so. On that record we should have swept the 1966 congressional elections. But we were not judged on that record. The poll came before Vietnam was nightly bad news; before war spending began to overheat the economy and send inflation soaring; before the terrible summer riots in Chicago, Atlanta, Cleveland, and New York City; before the disruptive demonstrations on college campuses. The congressional elections came after those, and they gave the Republicans forty-seven new seats. That broke the back of the Great Society right there.

A restored Republican–southern Democrat coalition immediately repealed the measures that had made possible the 1965 burst of congressional energy. Its members ended our twenty-one-day rule, thereby weakening the leadership's control of House business. They restored the old fifteen-to-ten split on ways and means, thereby giving the coalition control over important decisions. Thus fortified, they proceeded to turn back new initiatives and reduce old ones to sepulchers haunted with dead promises of what might have been.

Symbolically, the end came on July 20, 1967, when we debated House Resolution 749, the Rat Extermination and Control Act of 1967. All of the fun that we Democrats had poked at candidate Goldwater came back at us as Republicans hooted about a "civil-rats" act and jested at the notion of "throwing money down a rat hole." Their chief fun maker, Joel Broyhill of Virginia, urged that "the 'rat smart thing' for us to do is to vote down this rat bill 'rat now.'" And they did, 207 to 176. That afternoon, I told Barefoot Sanders, President Johnson's top legislative assistant, that no new programs should even be sent to the House thereafter. All we could get him were the bare essentials, and we could not always get those.

In a few months, I had seen Lyndon Johnson move from a symbol of national unity to a source of national division. Vietnam literally was consuming and destroying him. At our leadership meetings he would go over the war again and again, and in time it became an intensely personal matter. I remember that at one of those in February 1968 he made the wounded comment, almost enraged, almost tearful, that "nobody says anything about Ho Chi Minh. Ho has a great image. But they call me a murderer."

Vietnam consumed him politically as well. Campaigning on a peace platform, my old friend from the House Agriculture Committee, Gene McCarthy, came within a few thousand votes of beating him in the New Hampshire primary. Days after that vote, Robert Kennedy announced his own candidacy, it, too, demanding an end in Vietnam.

By the end of March 1968, I knew just how hopeless his situation had become. On March 28, I gave a rousing partisan speech before a strangely somber crowd at the South Carolina Democratic Convention. I understood the quiet only afterwards when the state chairman told me that Lyndon Johnson could not carry even one of the state's six congressional districts in a Democratic primary. McCarthy or Kennedy would get every district in South Carolina, one of the nation's most conservative states. The next day, I went to New York City to help Representative John Murphy's campaign. The professionals there told me that Johnson would finish third in New York, one of the nation's most liberal states.

For those reasons, I probably was the least surprised man in America when Lyndon Johnson called me two days later, on March 31, 1968. I knew that he had a major television address scheduled only a few hours later, but President Johnson wanted to tell me personally: he was withdrawing from the presidential race. Soon it would all be over for him.

It was left to our convention to decide on a candidate, and the president was leaving me with one last mighty responsibility: I was to be chairman of the 1968 Democratic National Convention, scheduled for Chicago, Illinois, at the end of August.

That is when it is always hottest in Chicago.

It was hot. It is odd, but one of the things I remember most

*When it is always hottest in Chicago.* Carl Albert at the 1968 Democratic National Convention.

clearly about that convention was the air conditioning. It blew straight at the rostrum, hurling chilly blasts at the presiding officer. That was I, and within minutes of going to the platform, I developed a cold that first became laryngitis and then impaired my hearing. I was coming down with that when I addressed the convention upon my formal election as its permanent chairman. I said: "Our actions here will be viewed around the world. We will be judged by our decorum. We can make this convention a showcase of democracy or a shambles of discord. We might even make it lively and spirited." I never uttered a grander understatement. It was plenty lively and spirited, but no one can convince me that it was a shambles.

Discord there was, in abundance. Johnson's withdrawal had not ended our party's division. Robert Kennedy's assassination had added to the strife, as had the earlier murder of Martin Luther King. Thousands of antiwar protesters, ill barbered, ill clothed, and ill tempered, descended on the city, determined to close the proceedings in the name of peace. They were ill housed, too, and when they met Mayor Richard Daley's policemen in the city's parks (some of which were under the Vietcong flag), riots resulted. All of that the television cameras picked up, and most of the nation saw it.

We in the convention hall were among the few who did not. Inside the hall, we had our own discord. A sizable body of delegates was there in Gene McCarthy's name. These had no chance. Others, originally selected as Kennedy delegates, had no candidate. Both were determined to have their way on the one issue, Vietnam, that united them and gave them moral fire, the moral fire that, like the religious zealots', would be quenched with no compromise. So intense was their hatred of the war that they placed its ending, or even the opportunity to denounce it, above the convention's real purposes.

The unavoidable result transcended liveliness and spiritedness. Every attempt to transact orderly business (no easy task, at best, with more than five thousand delegates and alternates plus packed galleries plus wandering newshounds) ran headlong into all of the bitterness, all of the divisions, and all of the frustrations that our assembly only mirrored. If the result looking confusing to a politically inexperienced television viewer, I can only say that it looked and sounded awfully confusing to the presiding officer up there on the rostrum. Confusing, yes, but I got the job done. The job was not to entertain a television audience, it was to see that every view was heard in an orderly fashion. It was. Our second day was given over completely to the platform and debate on it. In past conventions, the tradition was that minority views on individual planks were granted thirty minutes of debating time. Knowing the significance of the issue, I got those rules amended to grant two full hours of orderly, informed debate on the Vietnam plank. Amid the millions of angry words over Vietnam, those were two rare hours of structured and responsible debate.

We had to select a candidate, and we did. Hubert Humphrey deserved our nomination. For sixteen years he had been a fighting liberal in the United States Senate, the kind of liberal who early advanced the issues to which the nation later came. It was Hubert Humphrey, for instance, who had first committed the Democratic party to the cause of black civil rights when he carried the minority civil rights plank to the floor and won back in 1948. It was the same Hubert Humphrey who later guided the 1964 Civil Rights Act through the Senate's dangerous shoals. In Hubert Humphrey we also had the one Democrat who stood a realistic chance of winning the election. Robert Kennedy might have done it, but he was gone; Gene McCarthy never could have. Hubert Humphrey, starting so far back, came as close as he could get to winning it, and given a few more days or a couple of breaks, he would have won it.

Humphrey did get one break. Since the advent of saturated network coverage of convention proceedings, one of a convention's functions has been to present its nominee in prime time, before the maximum television audience, for what will be his most important single address. For all the comments about disorder, anyone who turned on a television at exactly 9:00 P.M., eastern standard time, saw Hubert Humphrey speak his opening sentence, not some riot. I thought of that four years later when a hand-picked, stacked convention nominated George McGovern and put him on the air at 3:00 A.M., thereby gaining the insomniacs' votes but (judging from the count) few others.

There is one last contrast I can mention. People commented about the businesslike efficiency of the Republicans' earlier convention in Miami, the convention that nominated Richard Nixon and Spiro Agnew. Few remember that outside its doors the police killed three rioters and shot five others. In Chicago we had an open convention, chose a strong candidate, and gave him our best possible sendoff. And no one was killed. We did not laugh as often as we had in 1964. When the Chicago convention ended, I went home and to bed. I was sick and I was tired. And I was not one bit ashamed.

# CHAPTER EIGHT

# What Happened to Ernie Albert's Boy

It was a hard winter back home in January 1971, especially hard for the old folks, especially the ones without good heaters and decent houses. One of those was an elderly fellow named Walter Johns, a veteran of the First World War and a retired miner. One night in early January, his gas heater ignited his leaky frame house, and it burned to the ground. Destroyed with his house was everything the old man owned: his clothes (except what he was wearing), his furniture, even his glass eye that he had set beside the bed. He stayed the night in the only shelter he could find from the winter's cold, the Pittsburg County Jail.

The next morning he came by his congressman's office. Sara Lane was working there, and she told me later how Walter Johns had tried to cover his empty eye socket with his smoke-blackened hand. He did not want to embarrass her any, but he thought that maybe she could get him some help, maybe a little money, maybe just another glass eye from the Veterans Administration. He told her how he had fought in the first big war and how his son had fought in the second one. The boy had been killed in action, and the government had sent Walter Johns a form letter of condolence and an insurance check for his boy's life. He told her that he had sent the check back, wrapped in a hand-written note on ruled paper. The note thanked the government but explained that his boy was not for sale.

Sara Lane got hold of the nearest VA office and called some McAlester folks who pitched in to help out my constituent, Mr. Johns. Very grateful, he thanked her, apologized for troubling her, and told her why he had called on my office first. "I used to mine coal with Ernie Albert," he said, "and I just knew that Ernie Albert's boy would help me."

Sara later told me that she answered Mr. Johns with a smile moistened by tears and asked him, "Don't you know what happened to Ernie Albert's boy?" Mr. Johns said no. All he knew was that I was the son of a man who had dug out a living with him, underground in the coal mines.

Three days later, on January 21, 1971, Ernie Albert's boy took the oath as forty-sixth Speaker of the United States House of Representatives.

The man I was succeeding had been my leader, my mentor, and my friend for a quarter-century. John McCormack is little remembered now. For more than twenty years, he had labored in the living shadow of the legendary Sam Rayburn. Even as Speaker, McCormack's steady work was lost to the glare of President Kennedy's glamour and President Johnson's energy. By the time of Richard Nixon's presidency, most Americans outside Congress thought of Speaker John McCormack (if at all) as a feeble old man, a sepulchral figure sitting behind the president at his annual State of the Union addresses.

Inside Congress, we knew better. Yes, John was old (he finally achieved the Speakership at age seventy, after thirty-four years of congressional service), but Speaker John McCormack kept all the intellectual tenacity and physical vigor of men not half his age. Anybody who thought him a doddering old man never saw him in debate or ran up against his towering will. In his seventy-third and seventy-fourth years, he presided firmly over the Eighty-ninth Congress and its burst of legislative energies. In the Ninetieth Congress, John kept the Great Society alive, his few defeats sharing but one cause, or maybe forty-seven causes: the exact number of Democrats replaced in the 1966 elections. In the first years of

Ernie Albert in 1947, the year of his death and Carl Albert's first year in Congress.

his presidency, Richard Nixon learned that the thin man behind him on the television screens was no lightweight. Like a Democratic rooster, John McCormack's age just made him tough.

Nonetheless, he was a product of another time. The Congress that John McCormack first entered in 1928 was nearly as far removed from that over which he presided as was Henry Clay's or Joe Cannon's. It grew more diverse as he remained constant. It grew unruly as he remained gentle. It got younger as he grew older. Every ambitious member expected his appearance at every evening fund-raiser, but John McCormack kept his evenings private, sharing them only with his beloved Harriet. Reformers hoped to open an avenue for themselves into the leadership's narrow ranks by creating a policy council after Mr. Rayburn's death. John gave them their answer at his first press conference: "A policy council is out." It stayed out, and they did, too. Excluded from John McCormack's narrow circle of old friends and committee chairmen, the reformers called for breaking up the seniority system. John answered that with the same thing that Sam Rayburn had said every two years at every organizational caucus: the seniority system was not going to be disturbed.

First singly, then collectively, first privately then publicly, some of the brightest young men in Congress moved to challenge John McCormack's ways, even his power. Dick Bolling, Sam Rayburn's young liberal protégé, disappeared from our informal gatherings. In two widely discussed books (*House Out of Order,* 1965, and *Power in the House,* 1968) Bolling openly questioned the Speaker's ability. In 1969, Arizona's able young congressman, Morris Udall, mounted a rare and open attack. At our organizational caucus, Udall challenged John's reelection as Speaker. It did not get very far—John won in the caucus by a 178–58 vote—but even to have a contest was almost unheard of.

Of course, the public heard of it, and some heard the continuing rumbles of discontent that periodically reverberated through the Capitol's marble halls. In December 1969, for example, Speaker McCormack met with Democrats serving on the Education and Labor Committee; the members were complaining about his handling of an antipoverty bill. John McCormack, who had been pushing "progressive" legislation for decades, patiently tried to counsel the young members on the need for patience. They would have none of it. "Look," 37-year-old Bill Clay exploded, "I'm not interested in what you did before I was born." John kept his own counsel, patience, and closed the meeting by saying, "I think some of you want to run the House." New Jersey's Frank Thompson retorted, "That's perfectly true. Some of us do."

But John McCormack, not Bill Clay, not Frank Thompson, ran the House. I believed he ran it well, very well considering what he was running up against. I knew that neither Mo Udall, Dick Bolling, Bill Clay, Frank Thompson nor any of his young critics could ever depose him. They (and I) knew that there was only one member who might beat John McCormack out of the Speakership, and we all knew who he was. His name was Carl Albert.

Few approached me openly about it, I suppose because they knew my position. As majority leader, I was John McCormack's ally and supporter. As a man, I was his friend. As a congressman who had worked with him for decades, I regarded him the world's chief legislator. I knew John McCormack as well as I knew any man in the House, and I respected him more than any other. If it took Carl Albert to defeat him, nobody would.

Those circumstances weighed not at all on my conscience, but they weighed heavily upon my time. The social obligations that accompanied the Speakership fell to me to fulfill. More importantly, I became the intermediary between the established leadership and the young reformers. The former never doubted my loyalty; the latter always expected my sympathy. Both were correct, and because they were, I became the conciliator working behind the scenes to maintain public harmony while carefully weighing and quietly promoting the allowable measures of change.

A small change (small at the time, central for the future) came in 1969, when I persuaded John McCormack to reawaken the Democratic caucus. Back in Woodrow Wilson's presidency, the caucus of all Democratic members had been the instrument of party discipline and the tool of party governance. Leaders like Oscar Underwood and Jack Garner had convened it regularly and directed it to party positions binding upon all Democratic members. In time, though, it had withered to nothing, nothing except biennial assemblies to ratify committee assignments and our leadership slate. Sam Rayburn had distrusted the caucus as much as he had feared its potential for opening bloody regional wounds. John McCormack fully shared that distrust, but he reluctantly agreed to call caucus meetings monthly after January 1969 to allow both the leadership and the rank and file to discuss party strategies. For a while, there was a lot more discussion than strategy, but the caucus had been reborn.

One of its first substantive decisions was to appoint in March 1970, a committee on organization, study, and review. Headed by Julia Butler Hansen, a very capable congresswoman from Washington, the committee would meet regularly during the next four years. I helped Mrs. Hansen select its members, like her, careful to build a committee representative of our party's many interests and elements. In the critical caucus meeting that defined its responsibilities, I took the floor to speak directly for explicitly including study of the one institution of the House that, "if valid, can stand the test of study." Over the united protest of the southern chairmen, we charged the Hansen committee to examine the heretofore unstudied (and untouchable) seniority system.

In that same year, I worked quietly on behalf of the first act to modernize congressional procedures since the La Follette-Monroney Act, passed in the year of my first election. A complex bill that generated enemies with every complexity, the new proposal had been tossed around for years. Finally, Dick Bolling and I got the votes to take it out of the Rules Committee and to the floor. Once there, I used every single lever I had available to add the one amendment that towered over every complexity in the existing bill: it was the amendment to provide for recorded votes on amendments to any bill thereafter considered in the committee of the whole. That amendment may look small now, but it ended the practice of a member's concealing his position on critical votes by marching past tellers, who announced the totals without recording a single individual's vote. We carried that amendment and the entire bill, the Legislative Reorganization Act of 1970, and every member knew what he had won: a major step toward opening our deliberations to public scrutiny.

Each change was a step, but only a step, toward internal changes impossible to foretell at the time, impossible to contemplate only a few years earlier. I gladly let others lay claim to making the footprints, and I never let a single one fall on the toes of my friend the Speaker. Even had I wanted to (and I did not), I knew better. John McCormack could accept changes, but he was not going to let anyone walk over him.

Like the country preacher who prayed that God would tell him when it was time to retire before He told the congregation, John had the faith to stay in the Speaker's chair rather than let anyone run him out of it. John himself decided when it was time to walk away. That was toward the end of the 1970 session. Announcing his retirement, he fielded a few press questions. His personal choice as successor? His answer was as decided as his own career. He was endorsing Carl Albert for Speaker and nobody else for any other job. I liked that.

In January 1971, John McCormack left the Capitol that he first had entered as a young man in 1928. On his last day in Congress, his other friends and I spoke of his many contributions and long leadership. His last words from the podium were these: "Next to God and Mrs. McCormack, I love the House of Representatives best." With that he walked away, the failing Mrs. McCormack at his side, and he left us that he might spend all of his time as he always had spent his private time: at Harriet McCormack's side. To her death and beyond, to his own, John McCormack kept his pride and his dignity. The first Speaker in more than a century to step down voluntarily, he knew when God wanted him to retire. I liked that, too.

With Sam Rayburn's death, I had mounted a vigorous campaign for the majority leadership. With John McCormack's retirement, I needed none for the Speakership. Within days, nearly every state's delegation endorsed my election. Nearly every powerful and respected member added his individual voice. One had the soft Arkansas accent of the one member powerful and respected enough even to mount a serious challenge. "If you're campaigning to be Speaker," Wilbur Mills said, "forget it. You've got it sewed up." He was right—Wilbur Mills always knew how to count votes—and only a last-minute and half-hearted challenge from Michigan's John Conyers denied unanimity to my caucus nomination. I won it 220 to 20, the latter, like Conyers's candidacy, a symbolic protest to the caucus participation of Mississippi's all-white and thoroughly segregationist delegation. Shortly thereafter the entire

Carl Albert presiding as forty-sixth Speaker of the United States House of Representatives.

House elected me its forty-sixth Speaker. I accepted the office from the same dais where I had watched John McCormack and Sam Rayburn preside, the same dais from which Champ Clark was speaking when I was Ernie and Leona Albert's boy in Mr. Craighead's class at Bug Tussle.

There to share it with me were many of the people who had put me there, people who had shaped my biography. There was Bill Anderson, Mook, my earliest playmate in Bug Tussle. At his side was Lottie Ross, the first-grade teacher who taught me how to read. Mary, David, and Mary Frances were at my side. Working her way through some of my McAlester High and University of Oklahoma classmates, Sara Lane whispered Walter Johns's story to me. Political supporters dating to my very first campaign congratulated me. Sitting before me were 434 members of Congress, 32 of whom had seen me enter Congress in 1947, when Sam Rayburn's secretary had thought me a page. It was to all those members that I directed the last line of my brief acceptance speech. "The biography of this Congress," I said, "will shape the legislative history of the seventies." Even as I spoke the biography of that Congress was changing, and those changes, which only accelerated through the 1970s, would largely shape my Speakership.

Of course, Congress is a living institution, one constantly changing. Nonetheless, it seemed to me in my six years as Speaker that I was watching more changes in that body's inner makeup than had occurred in any in so short a time since the Civil War. There were reasons for it. The black migration from the rural South to the urban North became complete in the early seventies. In northern city after city and district after district, blacks overwhelmed the old majorities of immigrant stock who long had sustained the urban machines. Many of the machines' veteran spokesmen left Congress, their places often taken by young, ambitious black members.

Down South a long-delayed revolution was smashing the white conservative Democratic stranglehold on power. The 1965 Voting Rights Act directly enfranchised millions of black voters, who took their ballots and their demands to Democratic primary boxes. Indirectly, the same law, with the national party's other commitments to black equality, helped drive southern whites finally out of the party of the Confederacy and into the party of the union, not Abraham Lincoln's Union but Richard Nixon's union of political, economic, and social conservatives. It seemed that every election brought news that first this southern state then that one, first this district then that one, was sending to Washington its first Republican congressman since Reconstruction. They took the places of the old Solid South, the southern establishment, which had figured so decisively during most of my own earlier tenure. Other establishment types wisely retired or lost their seats to young Democratic challengers, challengers elected with black votes and therefore even more different from the old Dixiecrats than were the new southern Republicans. Already (in 1966) black votes had defeated the old South's formidable champion, Howard Smith. Every year, others joined him in the graveyard of the white man's Democracy.

Smith's defeat had another explanation, too. In the mid-1960s, the federal courts directed that every district in every state be apportioned strictly on the basis of "substantial numerical equality." District lines were redrawn, adding to the political influence of cities and suburbs at the cost of farms and small towns. The kind of voters (college-educated white suburbanites) who helped retire Howard Smith did the same for others, North and South, East and West.

By 1972 yet another change had altered the national electorate with other effects upon the collective biography of Congress. In that year, eighteen-year-olds, heretofore young enough to fight but usually not old enough to vote, went to the polls throughout the nation. When the 1971 session passed the resolution that made it possible, I pronounced it to be akin to the abolition of slavery and the removal of property, racial, and gender qualifications for voting: it was another step in "perfecting our democracy." Thereafter, the new faces in Congress confirmed my expectations that new voters would demand new representatives.

New voters—something of a new electorate—is what I saw as Speaker. What I had to deal with was a new Congress that that electorate summoned forth. As early as 1973, the start of my second term as Speaker, fully half the members of Congress had begun their service after 1966. Representing new voters, they brought new experiences with them. Unlike my own generation, few of them had reached political maturity during Franklin Roosevelt's New Deal, when my party had assembled a coalition of the dispossessed around the bread-and-butter issues of the Depression. Few had followed either the bitter debates before Pearl Harbor or Harry Truman's refashioning of American military and foreign policy in the cold years that began the Cold War. Many had not even marched to John Kennedy's New Frontier or helped Lyndon Johnson push its borders outward to the furthest reaches of social change. For many of them, the defining global experience of their own political orientation was Vietnam, not Munich. The domestic concerns that moved them involved inflation and the environment, not unemployment and civil rights.

Despite all of those differences, the overall quality of Congress changed not at all, except possibly to improve it. We added two additional black women as members, but representatives like Barbara Jordan and Yvonne Burke would have added luster to any assembly. Pat Schroeder was every bit as outstanding as any male veteran, even as good as any of the few women with whom I already had served, women like Margaret Chase Smith, Martha Griffiths, Leonor Sullivan, Katherine St. George, or Julia Hansen. Other minorities, too, finally took their rightful places in Congress, adding both to its diversity and its distinction. Spark Matsunaga, Patsy Mink, and Norman Mineta followed the indomitable Daniel Inouye as outstanding members of Oriental ancestry. Henry Gonzales, Kika de la Garza, and Ed Roybal rose to the top as Hispanic members.

Representatives like these flew right in the face of the prevailing stereotype of Congress. During my first twenty-four years of service, I already had seen the Congress either attacked or ridiculed by nearly every pundit. As Speaker, I knew that most Americans still regarded it as a somber, cumbersome, unappealing body of anonymous men and women, mostly old. They blindly plodded along, insensitive to pressing problems and content to idle while others made progress and headlines. If that were ever true, it was not while I served in Congress, and it was never less so than when I was its Speaker of the House of Representatives. Most of the criticism of Congress overlooked that last word. Its members are representatives, not merely in title but in fact. The altered electorate and the transformed membership only made us more representative. What we represented was a nation of diversity, a nation divided by interest, philosophy, and values on every important issue of the day. Some criticized us for never speaking firmly and decidedly in a single voice, and we did not, for we spoke the many voices of the American people. We were their representatives and what we represented was the collective judgment of the American people.

Our forefathers had meant it to be that way. Originally, the Constitution had made members of the House the only federal officials directly elected by the people. Senators were to be chosen (and were well into the twentieth century) by the state legislatures. The president and vice-president were selected by the Electoral College, which was intended to be a body of independent electors of superior judgment. Judges and cabinet officers were presidential appointees, the former for life. For all the evolution of America's constitutional forms and its political practices, senators, judges, cabinet officials, even the president and vice-president— all still may be appointed to office. Only the members of the House of Representatives hold their seats exclusively by the ballots of the American people, ballots cast every two years in 435 separate districts, not one just like another.

None of those 435 members, not even their Speaker, pretended to represent the entire nation or labored under the illusions that he either could or should. Our Constitution cast us as a deliberative body. Our selection guaranteed that our deliberations would represent all of the conflict, all of the contention, even all of the confusion of the American people. Nearly two centuries of experience had shaped our procedures purposely to forestall hasty action without full consideration of all of the needs and all of the interests of all of the people. Some regarded this as plodding, but neither our forefathers nor political philosophers ever listed speed and efficiency among the virtues of a representative assembly. They were right. Not one weighty issue is ever amenable to overnight solution. Hasty action too often exchanges new dilemmas for old. Too often, today's unsolvable problem arises from yesterday's ill-considered solution.

As Speaker, I understood that. I understood, too, just what responsibilities my position involved. First, I was spokesman for the entire House of Representatives, including the Republicans and the Democrats, the conservatives and the liberals, the young and the old, the ambitious and the satisfied. Speaker for all, I first must listen to all, particularly regarding the institutional business of our assembly. There was nothing so sacred about our procedures, however old and however entrenched, that they could not be altered to make us more representative. There was, though, something sacred about our assembly's power, within the framework of American government, and it must always be defended. The speed and efficiency our forefathers had sought in the executive branch had to be balanced by the deliberativeness they had vested in our own. Defending that balance transcended defense of the House of Representatives, for that defense was of nothing less than the United States Constitution.

As Speaker, I also was leader of my party in the House. Because I was destined to be the first Speaker in modern times to serve entirely with the opposition in the presidency, it was a mighty responsibility, since I occupied the highest elected position of any Democrat in the country. I took that job seriously, but it was more than my natural modesty that allowed me to see its limits. I had no claim to speak for Democratic senators, governors, mayors, or presidential candidates. Every day's headlines showed me they could speak for themselves. Within the ranks of the House, the Speaker had exactly one vote in the Democratic caucus and, by custom, rarely one on the floor. The transformations of the late 1960s and early 1970s broke up old Democratic blocs and replaced them with temporary coalitions, reforming with every new bill, sometimes with every new amendment. Unchanged was the fact that no Speaker since Joe Cannon had had any real power over legislation. That fell to the chairmen of 20 standing committees and 138 subcommittees, each with power independent of the Speaker.

I was that Speaker, but I was also Carl Albert. When I took the Speaker's chair, I took the prize toward which I had directed my entire life. I knew what put me there. I was there because I worked hard, because I was loyal to my friends, because I tolerated differences, because I practiced conciliation, because I wanted the possible, not the ideal, because I sought compromise, not headlines. For better or worse, what had made me Speaker would have to make my Speakership, too.

I understood the Congress. I understood my job. I understood myself. Richard Nixon I never understood.

I had known Richard Nixon since that day back in 1947 when we were both freshmen congressmen and he was the first Republican member I met. From that day onward, I never found him anything but friendly personally. After he went to the Senate, even after he became vice-president, I never saw him anywhere without his coming over, calling me Carl, and chatting a bit.

Politically, I appreciated his abilities early on. I sensed that only Lyndon Johnson may have been more consumed with politics or in greater command of its strategies. In Nixon's case, however, that command early was tied to the lowest form of partisan tactics. I regarded his House work on the Un-American Activities Committee, particularly his crude use of the Alger Hiss affair, as partisan demagoguery incidentally clothed in fact, with only the outer trappings distinguishing it from Joseph McCarthy's tactics in the Senate. I knew that leading Democrats never forgave him for the Red-baiting campaign that beat Helen Gahagan Douglas in the Senate campaign of 1950. His charge of "treason" against high Democratic officials during the Eisenhower campaign of 1952 earned him the undying enmity of both Harry Truman and Sam Rayburn. The earthy former president thereafter always referred to Nixon as "a snaky-eyed son of a bitch." Nixon's name never came up at Sam Rayburn's Board of Education without the Speaker's saying that he, Mr. Rayburn, had looked out over the House into more than three thousand faces in his day and Richard Nixon's was the only one that would have looked more in place in a prison.

From time to time, Nixon watchers (a sizable, somewhat masochistic band, particularly in the press) pretended to have discovered a "new Nixon." Theodore H. White was absolutely sure that a more statesmanlike Nixon had emerged during the campaign that he chronicled in *The Making of the President, 1960*. White was equally sure of the same thing when he wrote *The Making of the President, 1968*. After that campaign, editorial cartoonist Herblock even granted Nixon's caricature a free shave to distinguish the dignified campaigner and chief executive from the crude, unshaven partisan of past drawings. An able public speaker, Richard Nixon could deliver statesmanlike addresses. Men who heard them and then engaged him in friendly conversation over political strategy understandably came away impressed. Maybe their fault was not in judging the new Nixon so uncritically but in thinking of the old Nixon so simplistically.

The Richard Nixon I knew—old, new, or otherwise—was anything but simple. He remained a brilliant political strategist. After the debacle of the Goldwater campaign, when some Republicans had suggested disbanding the party, Richard Nixon did more than any man to restore it to respectability two years later and to power two years after that. No Republican since Lincoln had done more for his party. Neither had any Republican since Lincoln won the White House after suffering such bitter personal defeats, in Nixon's case the 1960 presidential race and the California gubernatorial campaign of 1962 that seemed to have ended his career permanently. In the White House, he stayed just as friendly. I was still Carl, just like always, but even so, he could show a streak of vindictiveness, even meanness. In formal meetings with the congressional leadership, he often would bring up some small slight of years past. The give and take that we professional politicians accepted as the routine stuff of politics apparently was intensely

*I knew that Richard Nixon saw politics as a personal battle.*

personal to Richard Nixon. When he would attack Adlai Stevenson for some unremembered remark or President Truman for some forgotten misdeed, I knew that Richard Nixon saw politics as a personal battle, a series of interwoven and unending crises. For that reason, Richard Nixon was a man incapable of either forgiving or forgetting.

What united this personal Nixon with the public Nixon was the same thing that bound in one the partisan Nixon to the statesmanlike Nixon, the old Nixon to the new Nixon. From his very first race in 1946 through every campaign to follow, Richard Nixon had been a master of negative campaigning. He had run best when he had something to run against. Without it, he had never won. In his earliest races, he had to manufacture his enemies: Jerry Voorhis, the incumbent Democratic congressman he ousted in 1946 by identifying him with socialists and Communists; Helen Douglas, whom he made his victim as the "pink lady" of 1950; and the entire Democratic party, which he portrayed as leading to "ultimate national suicide" in 1952. In 1968, circumstances conspired to produce Richard Nixon's enemies for him: an endless war in Asia, race riots and antiwar protests in America. In no case was there either an old Nixon or a new Nixon. There was only Richard Nixon, a complex man who needed, publicly and privately, enemies to campaign against. Finally winning the White House, he had to govern for the first time in his political career, and he needed something to govern against. It was the United States Congress.

Though he had served in both houses, Nixon was accustomed to running against Congress. Particularly as Ike's vice-president, he had campaigned against what he perceived as its excesses in the midterm elections of the fifties. More than anything else, it was the same tactic, generously donated to countless Republican candidates, that allowed his political resurrection with the midterm elections of 1966. As president, he attacked Congress with a rare vigor. Presidential news conferences and television speeches scored us for our delay in ratifying his proposals and our dispatch in passing our own. The latter often met his veto, usually on pretended grounds of economy. In January of 1970 he even took the unprecedented step of vetoing a bill—a $19.7 billion labor-health, education, and welfare appropriation—on television, melodramatically signing the veto beneath the glare of camera lights before a nationwide audience.

What the cameras did not record and the audience did not see was the pattern of the administration's dealing with Congress. The president met rarely with the Democratic majority leadership, and he often left even the Republican leaders blind to his intents and purposes. Even they complained that as many as eighty calls from Republican congressmen daily went unanswered by the White House. Nixon's aides, most inexperienced, all ambitious, many arrogant, made no effort to understand Congress except to deride it. The same administration that castigated us for our delays routinely followed stirring presidential messages with weeks of inactivity during which it provided no detailed proposals for our deliberations. By 1971, the new legislative liaison director, Clark MacGregor, was wearing a button: "I Care About Congress." No one else in the White House wore one, and neither MacGregor nor the attitude lasted long.

Meanwhile, the rhetorical attacks upon Congress continued, reaching a frenzy in the 1970 elections. Vice-President Spiro Agnew fired the first blast during a national campaign tour in September. As the Senate's presiding officer, the vice-president and I shared many responsibilities, and I thought that I had come to know him well: a quiet, modest, genteel, and honest man. During that campaign, however, he revealed a surprising talent for invective unheard since the old Nixon of the early fifties. It was Agnew who set the election's shrill tenor by reducing every issue to one: "Will America be led by a president elected by a majority of the American people, or will we be intimidated and blackmailed into following the path dictated by a disruptive, radical, and militant minority—the pampered prodigies of the radical liberals in the United States Senate?" Unstated was the assumption that radical liberals also infested the House and pampered our own prodigies. Unacknowledged was the fact that these same senators and representatives themselves had been elected by a majority of the American people, while this particular president had won a three-cornered contest against Hubert Humphrey and George Wallace with less than 44 percent of the vote.

By mid-October, that president had thrown himself directly into the elections. Attacking "permissiveness," "terrorism," and "crime," he attempted to identify his congressional opposition with all that was abhorrent in national affairs, with nothing that was at issue in any race. The Election Eve commercial that was broadcast nationally closed it all with a voice-over of deep concern: "Support men who will vote for the president, not against him. Bring an end to the wave of violence in America." On Election Night, the administration could count the scalps of two senators. We added a net of nine Democrats to the House and eleven governorships. Whatever those results said about the president's tactics, they testified to the common sense and basic decency of the American people. The entire episode both completed two years of unprecedented executive-legislative discord and introduced my greatest challenge when I became Speaker two months later. I presided over the House that was elected in that campaign and served with the president who had conducted it. Demographic, electoral, and membership changes already were transforming the House. I would have to complete that transformation if we were to face that president.

The transformation began in the January 1971 organizational caucuses, in which my party first began to assemble its leadership team. My fellow Democrats named me their candidate for the Speakership. John McCormack's retirement and my own elevation opened a slot, majority leader, and it was opened to an intense competition that registered the changes already moving the House. Hale Boggs had served right below me since 1955, when Sam Rayburn and John McCormack appointed me whip and gave him the new post of deputy whip. In 1962, John and I named him our own whip. As the man most experienced in our leadership councils, he figured to have no more trouble winning the majority leadership than I had had when I eventually won it unanimously. Arguably, he might have had even less trouble, for Hale was a southerner born and bred, and he had worked well and closely with the northern big-city Democrats. Since the 1930s, that coalition had dominated our party councils. In 1971, it did not.

A small army of determined challengers aggressively contested Hale's election. Their number, and their bases of support, testified to the recent changes within the party. Mo Udall represented a rising number of young, ambitious members who were united by a faith in liberal issues and a dislike of the House's crusty ways. Bernie Sisk, a Californian of Texas birth, hoped to assemble a new coalition of the South and the West in place of the fading southern-northern machine combine. Jim O'Hara of Michigan sought to go entirely outside the House's internal structure of power to build a candidacy on the external power of organized labor. Ohio's Wayne

Hays, chairman of the House Administration Committee, went just the other way. That chairmanship gave him his only power, but great power it was, for Hays had turned the heretofore clerical job into an emperorship with oversight into every member's allowances and perquisites.

Though I could have worked with any of those men as my majority leader (except maybe Hays, whom no one could work with in any capacity), Hale was my own favorite. I made no effort to help him, since I could think of no worse way to enter my Speakership than to antagonize so many different groups. I let Hale Boggs make his own fight, and he won it, though it took him two ballots to secure his majority by a margin of only twenty-five votes. The press pronounced it a victory for the House's old ways of a simple regional coalition, but its old ways would not even have seen such a fight.

The press overlooked the most important election in that caucus. With the revitalization of the caucus as an ongoing party mechanism, its elected chairman became a member of the informal House leadership. Dan Rostenkowski, a big-talking, big-living former car salesman turned agent of Mayor Richard Daley's big Chicago machine, was that chairman. I thought he was my friend, though hardly my brainiest one. At the 1968 convention, I had done him what I thought was a favor when I handed him the gavel to preside briefly and ceremoniously over the delegates assembled in his hometown. I had forgotten the whole incident by the time the story began to circulate that big Dan Rostenkowski had wrestled the gavel out of the hands of little Carl Albert because only big Dan Rostenkowski could bring order to that convention. If that were so, no one had told me about it at the time. But it was pretty plain who was telling it later.

Maybe Dan was busy telling that story in the days just after John McCormack announced his retirement. I do not know. But I do know that as state delegation after delegation lined up behind me for Speaker, one state was conspicuously absent: Illinois. Mel Price, one of my oldest friends from there, could not understand

Illinois's delay, and he offered to call a state caucus to learn why. Afterwards, Mel told me straight out that the entire delegation of Illinois was for me to a man, except one: Dan Rostenkowski, who refused to issue an endorsement of the only candidate groomed for the job or even seeking it.

By the time the Democratic caucus met to approve my nomination, enough of my friends shared enough of my wonder about Rostenkowski's attitude and sense to do something about it. They had come together to oust Rostenkowski as caucus chairman in favor of a man loyal to me—at least to a man with enough brains to climb on board a bandwagon while it was roaring out of the station. Olin ("Tiger") Teague, was that man, and he was a dandy. Born in Woodward, Oklahoma, Teague got his nickname on the football fields of Texas and the battlefields of Europe. His adopted state sent him to Congress in 1947, and he had risen to become chairman of veterans' affairs. Though intensely conservative in his voting, Tiger had not a single enemy, liberal or otherwise, in the House. When the time came to vote on caucus chairman, someone put Tiger's name in nomination. The surprised Teague marched forward with his own ballot held high, showing it already marked with Rostenkowski's name. The even more surprised Dan Rostenkowski watched it become one of the 91 votes he received, compared to 155 for Tiger. Still surprised, the loser told the press, "I got my brains beat out." I was not surprised at all.

A few days later, Hale Boggs came by my office to complete our leadership slate. It was still the tradition that the majority leader appointed the party whip, subject only to the Speaker's veto. Hale wanted to give the job to the man who had sat with him on ways and means, Dan Rostenkowski. He got the Speaker's veto instead. Hale did get a list of ten names, any one of which I would accept as whip. One of those was Tip O'Neill's.

Tip had been around Congress since 1953, when he took the seat John Kennedy left to go to the Senate. Big and gregarious, his earliest attribute seemed to be his laziness. He was what we called a "Tuesday-Thursday congressman," one who spent four days a

*Tip had become a protégé of John McCormack.* Thomas P. O'Neill, Carl Albert, and John McCormack.

week back home and three on House business. When I was appointed whip myself, Tip had come by, had spun a few stories, and had told me that he would not have the job; it took too much work. Nonetheless, Tip had become a protégé of John McCormack, who eventually got him a seat on the Rules Committee. In 1970, Tip still ranked behind Chairman Bill Colmer and three other Democrats on the committee, and he had no other basis of power. But he had started to work a little harder, he had friends all over the House, and his New England district and liberal orthodoxy represented important elements in the party. When Hale suggested that Tip's appointment would please John McCormack, I agreed.

To help him, we also selected two others to become deputy whips. John McFall was Hale's choice. One of Hale's eighteen regional assistants, John represented an agricultural district in California. His selection thereby broadened the Southwest–New England regional axis that had dominated Democratic House affairs since Sam Rayburn and John McCormack had become Speaker and majority leader back in 1940. My addition was a midwesterner, Indiana's John Brademas. Representing the South Bend area, John already had established his mark as education's most articulate champion in the House. Besides, he had two personal qualities that I much admired. One was tenacity—he had won his seat in 1958 only after suffering two earlier defeats. The other was brains—John Brademas had been a Rhodes scholar and had had an outstanding record at Oxford. He belonged on our team.

Carl Albert, Hale Boggs, Tiger Teague, Tip O'Neill, John McFall, and John Brademas—that was the Democratic leadership team that had taken shape by mid-January of 1971. Among us, we represented every region of our country and every element of our party. We were men of diverse viewpoints and diverse talents. If we had to, we could take on the men, all so similar and all so ambitious, sitting in the White House. Not one of us ached to do it. For myself, I would have preferred the nonconfrontational relations that President Eisenhower and Speaker Rayburn had conducted in the 1950s. But if Richard Nixon wanted to make Congress his enemy, we had the talent to make it a contest.

We certainly had the issues.

As a boy, I had been taught down in Oklahoma's Little Dixie that there was a difference between Democrats and Republicans. My folks and I belonged to the party that cared about average, working Americans. Republicans spoke for the wealthy—belonged to them, some said. At best, they might let prosperity trickle down to the little people; at worst, they would keep it for themselves; at a minimum, they just did not care about the common folks.

As a student of government in two universities and as a congressman, I learned that things were not always that simple. There were quite a few rich and insensitive Democrats and there were plenty of hardworking and generous Republicans. Nonetheless, what I kept seeing never did erase that first impression. The common, average, working American man or woman was more likely to get a better shake from the party of Jefferson and Jackson than from the party of Coolidge and Hoover. I know that the party that controlled both houses of Congress was ready to give them better than the party of Nixon and Agnew.

We already had given them a sustained prosperity never before achieved in this century. The stock market reached a record level; bank deposits did, too. Personal income climbed to a figure never before seen in the world. Unemployment dropped out of sight as the rate (3.4 percent) that stood at 1969's beginning met the economists' definition of full employment. Even though much of President Johnson's Great Society went underfinanced, the rising tide of prosperity raised many of the poor to a better life and gave all the promise of a better future.

It was Vietnam that bled the Great Society of its funds, and it was Vietnam's costs that explained the one sour economic note of the late sixties: inflation. Candidate Nixon had made much of the issue—inflation, not Vietnam's expense—in the 1968 campaign, and President Nixon was determined to do something about it. It was the same thing that Republicans usually offered: economic policies that promised to exchange inflation for recession.

He could not even do that.

We got the recession, all right. At the touch of his misguided wand, Nixon magically transformed the prosperity that was his presidency's inheritance into the first full-blown recession since that last Republican president's, back in 1958. Steadily, the economy's production slipped below its capacity. At the end of Nixon's first year in office, the gap between performance and potential was $25 billion annually and growing. Through 1970, national production actually declined. In 1971, it rose, but only by 3 percent, enough for the president to declare a recovery, even though it was a recession by any measure other than his own dismal record.

The cost of that recession fell disproportionately on working Americans. The lucky ones suffered a decline in real wages, the first decline since the 1930s. The unlucky ones had no wages at all, for the unemployment rolls grew with every presidential pronouncement of prosperity. By 1971's end, the unemployment rate was 80 percent above what it had been at Nixon's inauguration. The percentage difference obscured the human cost: two and one-half million Americans who had lost their jobs, plus another half-million uncounted because they had given up on finding any work at all. Even that number left untold the price paid by the neediest: those in central cities, sixty of which were declared to be depressed (compared to six in 1969); black teenagers, who suffered from an unconscionable unemployment rate pegged at 44.9 percent; returning Vietnam veterans, 375,000 of whom came back to an America that had no jobs for them.

Knowing where Nixon was leading us, I knew that it was the job of the Democratic Ninety-second Congress to lead us out. I knew also that it was the job of the entire Congress, not just its House Speaker, to do it. Senate Majority Leader Mike Mansfield and I began to meet regularly with the press, a practice rare since the days of Sam Rayburn and Lyndon Johnson, to reveal the dismal economic record that lay beneath the administration's slick public relations. While our young reformers berated the seniority system, I worked quietly and realistically to include the committee chairmen in a united and effective legislative leadership. For the first time since the New Deal, the Speaker and appropriate chairmen also met with the press to discuss our own legislative initiatives to replace the executive's inactivity. They got the publicity, which was fine with me, since they, not I, would have to craft our bills and get them through their committees. Behind the scenes, I met with those same chairmen, the rest of our formal leadership, and leaders of every one of the House's many new factions. We coordinated our bills (another innovation), planned our calendar, and mobilized every vote we could get. We could not always get enough, for no one said that the House's collective judgment should be the same as the Speaker's judgment; least of all did this Speaker even think it. Nonetheless, we did get bills written, we did get them out of committee, we did take them to the floor, we did pass them, and we did send them to Richard Nixon. He vetoed them, twenty of them in the Ninety-second Congress alone.

Most of the twenty were bills that had taken months to fashion and to pass, bills that would have primed the economy's dry pump and eased the recession's worst immediate burdens. One of the most disheartening for me was H.R. 15417, a $30.5 billion appropriation for desperately needed employment and welfare programs. Declaring that it was too expensive by $1.8 billion, the president wiped out the work of months and the hope of millions with a stroke of a pen. Seeking compromise, we passed it again at the same level but authorized the president to withhold up to $1.3 billion if he wished. This time, it died without a pen's stroke as President Nixon pocket-vetoed the entire act. So it went: Appalachian regional development, economic-opportunity amendments, promotion of family medicine, expansion of public works and employment, medical care for veterans, rehabilitation for the handicapped, assistance to the elderly, aid to schools—every one of them terribly needed, every one of them tragically vetoed.

For each one, Richard Nixon offered the same set of tired excuses: the bill was inflationary because it cost too much; the economy could not afford it because the debt was too high. The congressional leadership knew better. Though such bills did exceed the administration's niggardly requests, we also were cutting its requests in other areas. On balance, we appropriated each year less total money than the president had requested. The issue was not the level of spending but the form of spending, and the president did not have a monopoly on the wisdom of setting those priorities. Was the economy too small and the debt too large? The

Nixon recession was what was shrinking the economy. That recession cost the Treasury $50 billion in reduced tax collections over the life of the Ninety-second Congress, enough money to have erased the entire federal deficit of fiscal year 1971 and most of it for fiscal year 1972. Instead, the Treasury was hemorrhaging with billions of dollars ($10 billion in 1972 alone) flowing out unproductively in unemployment compensation and welfare payments.

That is what gave Congress the issue to take on the White House. What gave it the reason was the fact that the avowed object of the president's policies and his vetoes was the war against inflation. Soaring unemployment was costing the economy twenty million man-days lost per year, a cruel draft to enlist unwilling soldiers in that war, and it was a war that inflation was winning anyway. The cost of living rose steadily, right along with the unemployment rolls, a paradox never before thought possible in an industrialized nation. One other thing rose with them, and its rise resolved the paradox. Between 1971 and 1973, corporate profits shot up 36.3 percent. That money went straight to those who owned corporate stock, and half of all corporate shock was owned by less than 1 percent of the American population. The net result of unemployment or wage declines for the working people and healthy dividend checks for the well-heeled was a silent transfer of income unprecedented in American history: $10 billion a year moved from the pockets of the poor to the bank accounts of the wealthy.

Maybe the folks back in Pittsburg County, Oklahoma, had a point when they talked about the difference between Democrats and Republicans.

As Speaker of the House, I never believed that the difference was all that simple. Neither did I believe that the effect, however real, of the president's policies, however misguided, were all that deliberate. Nixon and his advisers just believed in something that did not exist. Their policies would have worked in Adam Smith's eighteenth-century world of small producers competing for buyers in an unfettered marketplace in which an invisible hand set prices fairly and automatically. But that world was as dead as Adam

Smith. The marketplace was fettered, not by government, but by giant corporations that dominated every segment of the economy to palsy the hand of free competition. Thus, policies born in illusion matured to enrich the comfortable few and torment the hardworking many.

The latter were the ones the president called the "silent majority," the ones he thought of as "the forgotten Americans." If his economic policies forgot them, his social views tried to pander to them. Years after the Supreme Court had outlawed state-written prayers in public classrooms, the president and his allies piously demanded a constitutional amendment to restore the practice. As the federal courts were following out the logic of the 1954 *Brown* decision to include the transporting of students as one tool to integrate schools, they raised a howl of protest against "busing" and again demanded a constitutional amendment to deny the practice.

For me, those issues went to something far more important than an appropriations bill or an economic index. What was at stake was what had brought me to Washington, not as a new congressman in 1947, but as a high school senior twenty years earlier. It was the Constitution of the United States. If I would let the committees handle our legislation, on that matter the Speaker had to speak out, forcibly, directly, and immediately. I did. When Louisiana's Joe Waggoner tried to use the Democratic caucus to support his antibusing bill this particular member rose to answer him. My answer hardly used the word *busing* at all, for that was not the issue. Not even civil rights was the issue. The issue was the U.S. Constitution, the separation of powers, the subversion of the independent judiciary. On that basis, maybe by that speech, we voted the thing down on May 17, 1972, the eighteenth anniversary of the *Brown* decision.

I also had spoken six months earlier, that time on the House floor. Over the stout opposition of Manny Celler, an outright majority of our members had signed a discharge petition to bring a school-prayer amendment before the House. The petition's success pointed to an easy victory, not for school prayer but for those who would tamper with our heritage of constitutional govern-ment in the momentary heat of public passion. I closed the debate with the same thoughts, almost the same words, I had expressed back when I was a college freshman orating on our Bill of Rights: "Any interference by any official at any level is a violation of free-dom of religion. I am not prepared to let the hand of government of any level, of any degree, to be placed on any man's altar."

We beat that amendment by a handful of votes. I understand that House veterans, both Republicans and Democrats, still talk about that speech, pronouncing it one of the few that ever changed a vote's outcome. I do not know about that, but I do know that I kept and treasured a letter thanking me for "standing twenty feet tall" in turning back a step that would have "cut the artery of our freedoms." What made it special was that it was from Herschel Hobbs, pastor of Oklahoma's largest Baptist church. I was even prouder—not for myself, but for them—of the church leaders and Christian worshipers from all over my Third District who wrote or called in their support. I always understood that there is a lot of common sense in the common people.

If the president wanted a confrontation with the Congress over the Constitution, I never doubted our need to join the fight or our ability to win it. If he chose to fight us over his sorry economic record, I knew that we had the common people on our side. What happened, though, was that many of my colleagues chose to en-gage him in another war. It was the war in Vietnam.

Even at the time of the Gulf of Tonkin Resolution and Lyndon Johnson's subsequent injection of American power, I had had no great enthusiasm for the Vietnam War. The thing that I had seized with most optimism was the military's 1964 and 1965 assurances that the thing was winnable with neither great expense nor long fighting. It was not long before I learned that that prediction never changed. However dismal the reports from Vietnam, the military never tired of the prediction of imminent victory. It was a rare moment of candor when General Earl Wheeler, Johnson's chairman of the Joint Chiefs of Staff, interrupted his rosy forecasts to the congressional leaders to speak of the conflict as "this miserable war."

It was miserable, miserable for all of us. It dragged on and on with no end in sight. Even after our negotiators sat down in Paris with North Vietnam and Vietcong representatives, the war went on until it tore at the fabric of American society. In the process, it helped drive Lyndon Johnson from the presidency and put Richard Nixon into it. Though he had talked as a candidate of a "secret plan" to end the war, Nixon turned out to have no secret at all, at least none except for the secret bombing of Cambodia that he launched (and covered up) in 1969. Publicly, he did announce a policy and gave it a label: "Vietnamization." Masters of coining new words to mask old errors, the White House officials actually were offering what the French had tried back in the early fifties under the name *jaunissement.* Translated literally as "yellowing," the French policy was to force upon the Vietnamese the combat manpower requirements for the war. Cynics referred to it as "changing the color of the corpses." It did do that but little else. Defeated and exhausted, the French had left Vietnam to its fate in 1954.

Years later it was Richard Nixon's fate to try to get America out, not defeated and before it was exhausted. That meant ending the steady escalation and the perpetual quest for tomorrow's victory in favor of an orderly withdrawal of American ground forces, their places taken by an American-trained, America-financed, and American-armed South Vietnamese army. It also meant extending the war to include enemy sanctuaries in Vietnam's neighbors. Constant was the commitment that was ours since Harry Truman's day: the United States would do everything within its power to maintain an independent and anti-Communist government in Vietnam. Vietnamization was, at last, recognition of the limits of our power.

Under the miserable circumstances of that miserable war, I felt it was the best that the president, and the country, could do. Precipitate withdrawal of all our forces and all our power would not end the war, not even our involvement. The killing would continue, doubtlessly through the ranks of both South Vietnam's soldiers and its civilians. The certain collapse of its government to a Communist foe would involve us in a moral indictment for the murder of a government that we had conceived and birthed. It also would be the repudiation of a policy that generally had preserved the world's peace through the maturity of my generation. Starting down another road, the American feet fleeing from Vietnam would wear a path to no certain end and none not filled with potentially greater perils. That was what gave Vietnam a significance too great for easy solution, that and thirty thousand American deaths already.

One was Allie Brannon's boy's.

Allie was a Bug Tussle girl, born in the community in a house that still stood. I had known her all her life and her husband, Roy, for forty years of his. Allie worked in a garment plant in McAlester, and Roy farmed at Bug Tussle in sight of the house where Allie was born. I used to go by and talk with them about the old-timers when I was home from Washington. As my leadership duties became heavier, I did not have much of a chance to do it, though, because I just did not have the time. In 1969, I made the time. In their front yard I talked with Allie and Roy, not about the old folks but the young ones, especially their son. He had been a Bug Tussle boy, too, had gone to the same little two-room school as I, and had gone to Vietnam. Now he was dead. Vietnam was personal to people like Allie and Roy Brannon. It was to me, too. And it was a miserable war.

Its politics could be just as miserable. The people wanted out, the president wanted out, and Congress wanted to help. Between 1966 and 1972, Congress voted 145 times on Vietnam. Right up until the very end, it gave two presidents everything they wanted. To Lyndon Johnson it gave the authority to commit our forces and the money to equip them. To Richard Nixon, it gave support for Vietnamization and the money to execute it. With each vote, though, the politics became more miserable.

Over in the Senate, a large and growing number felt that the president was moving too slowly to withdraw, too rapidly to spread the conflict. Because the Constitution bestows only upon the Senate the power to approve or reject all treaties, the other body has always given great weight to its responsibilities in foreign affairs. The evolution of modern politics—the centrality of foreign policy, the televising of Senate hearings, the use of the Senate as the launch pad of presidential aspirants—has also served to make foreign affairs more important to the Senate than to the House. Vietnam was a nasty and divisive issue, one that raised incomparable public passion. Their six-year terms and statewide constituencies gave senators the opportunity to speak out on that issue without immediate fear of electoral retribution. Year by year, they spoke louder and louder.

By 1969, what had been the lone voice of Mike Mansfield's early protest was joined by influential senators—William Fulbright, Frank Church, Gene McCarthy, Ted Kennedy, John Sherman Cooper, and others. Starting in that year, the Senate began to debate amendments to foreign-affairs and military bills that would restrict the president's policies around Vietnam and hasten his withdrawal from it. By 1971, the first year of my Speakership, the Senate twice passed the so-called Mansfield amendment, attaching it once to the draft-extension bill and again to the defense-procurement bill. In each form, it would have compelled the withdrawal of all American combat forces in Indochina within six months, pending only North Vietnam's release of our prisoners of war.

On both those occasions and others, a large majority in the House rejected the Senate's amendments. My chamber was more inclined to give the president a free hand in the war, the withdrawal, and the negotiations going on in Paris with the Communists. Unlike the situation in the Senate, where the Foreign Relations Committee was a center of dissent, our Foreign Affairs Committee and our most influential members in the field tended to back Nixon's policies. Subject to elections every two years in districts small enough that any one issue could tip the balance, we knew that the public was fed up with the war but was gagging on the antiwar movement of students and chronic critics.

Vietnam was, then, no easier a question for public policy than for military strategy. Any attempt to make it simple was misguided from the start. To try to make it a partisan issue or an issue that divided the Congress from the president was worse than wrong, it was stupid. An extreme antiwar position, one demanding immediate, unconditional withdrawal, would divide my party, paralyze the House, and hand Richard Nixon the one political issue that he could dominate. Some wanted to do just that.

A minor but frustrating example of this involved the reborn Democratic caucus. When I had persuaded John McCormack to restore it, I had hoped it would become a party tool in which the leadership and membership could reach consensus for effective legislating. As Speaker, I learned that it too easily became a target of a righteous antiwar minority who sought to turn the caucus into a forum of protest. New York's Bella Abzug, for one, took the floor at every early meeting to urge this or that motion against the war. Sometimes she just wanted a chance to denounce it. Undeterred by her motions' one-sided defeats, Bella would be back at the next caucus with another motion and another speech.

Congressmen can be a patient lot, but after awhile enough Democrats began boycotting Bella's tirades that most meetings adjourned without a quorum. On one notable occasion, I had wanted to use the caucus to discuss overall federal spending, but Bella got the floor first, began another speech, and continued as more than half the membership sullenly walked out. Shorn of a quorum, that caucus adjourned with no discussion of spending, no discussion of anything, just Bella Abzug's speech. Eventually, Tiger Teague and I amended the caucus rules to permit the chairman (Tiger) to set a definite agenda and give the Speaker and majority leader the floor at any point. Even if the war issue thereby lost its power to kill the caucus, it always stood ready to disrupt it.

It could do the same thing—and did—to something much bigger than the House Democratic caucus: the national Democratic party. By 1972, Richard Nixon's economic record had made him exceedingly vulnerable, but a gaggle of presidential aspirants chose to squawk most loudly on the war. Moderate views went unheard in favor of denunciation of the war's "immorality" and the need for a "new politics" to end it. Mobilizing a determined minority, George McGovern demonstrated that minority's power in a divided field of a divided party seeking to govern a divided country.

George had worked with me on Agriculture's wheat subcommittee when he served in the House. I thought him a man of unbending character and burning idealism. In the Senate, he turned both against the Vietnam War. After the 1968 convention, he had used them to rewrite the Democrats' party rules to require the open participation so esteemed in the new politics. During the campaign season, he used those rules to pile up delegate support out of all proportion to his popular appeal. I remember that Oklahoma County, a conservative county in a conservative state, sent a solid McGovern bloc to our state convention. The same thing happened enough other times in enough other states to give McGovern a first-ballot victory in 1972's national convention.

Of course, his election campaign was a disaster from the start, with one mistake following another. All were irrelevant, though, compared to the original mistake: America was not going to oust a president promising (and apparently delivering) "peace with honor" in favor of a candidate said to be willing to "crawl to Hanoi." The election returns showed that, as Richard Nixon—arguably the most vulnerable sitting president since Herbert Hoover—ran up a record popular-vote margin and swept forty-nine of the fifty states. He did it in classic Nixon style by running against George McGovern, against the "peace-at-any-price" crowd that he always put at his opponent's back. It was unlike 1970 because Richard Nixon had not had to run against Congress. Just as well for him; he could not have beaten it. Though we lost a few Democratic seats in the House (most to redistricting's toll on incumbents), we still had 243 Democrats to 192 Republicans. We actually picked up two Senate seats to give us a 57-to-43 split in the other body.

Richard Nixon had the majority of votes that always had eluded him, even in 1968; we had the same majority that we always had. The war in Vietnam had elected him again. The people of America had elected us, too. He took his election as a mandate, and his self-perceived mandate became our unavoidable challenge. In little time, the resulting clash became the greatest constitutional crisis of the century. When it came, we already had our house in order.

The entire Democratic House leadership worked hard to keep that majority in the face of the Nixon landslide. I campaigned all over the country for Democratic candidates, and the other leaders did, too. In early October, a month before the election, one of them jokingly asked me if I wanted to join him on a campaign swing. "No," I told Hale Boggs, "I went there last year, so I think I'll let you make this trip to Alaska."

Hale went up with Nick Begich to campaign for Nick's reelection to Alaska's one congressional seat. On Monday night, October 17, I was resting up from one of my own campaign trips when the phone rang. It was the White House, wanting me to call Lindy Boggs. Hale's plane, with him, Nick, and two others aboard, was missing in the Alaska bush, somewhere between Portage Pass and Juneau, where the plane was last heard from twelve minutes after takeoff.

That was the hardest phone call I ever made. I told Lindy the news. All she said, in her soft Louisiana accent, was, "Oh, Cahl." Though the air force and others searched for that plane to the limit of human endurance, no one ever found it. We had lost our majority leader, and I had lost a good friend, colleague, and ally. The House had lost the man destined to be its Speaker, but Louisiana's loss was tempered when Mrs. Corinne ("Lindy") Boggs won the seat after it was declared officially vacant.

It was a shame that Hale did not live even a few months longer. He and I were the first Speaker and majority leader team born in the twentieth century. When the Ninety-third Congress convened the next January, we began the process that finally brought the House of Representatives fully into that century. When that Congress adjourned two years later, it had effected more reforms of its own procedures than had any Congress since the Cannon revolt, maybe more than in the intervening thirty Congresses combined.

Most of those reforms had been a long time coming. Nonetheless, the press and the pundits still expressed surprise at how swiftly and thoroughly each prevailed. They looked for explanations and found them everywhere. Some credited the new membership elected in 1972, though we had only sixty-eight freshmen in that class, just above average for a post–World War II Congress. Of those, only twenty-six were Democrats, and they did not make much difference in the body that sponsored most of the changes, the Democratic caucus. Other credited the Democratic Study Group, which had grown steadily to include nearly two-thirds of the Democratic membership. Despite its numbers, the DSG lost on every reform proposal that lacked the leadership's support. Within that leadership, Hale's successor as majority leader, Tip O'Neill, got a lot of the credit, and Tip took it, too. Outside the leadership, Dick Bolling, a brilliant student of Congress and a longtime press favorite, got acclaim for realizing reforms that he long had championed. Amid that praise, Dick told one of Ralph Nader's investigators that he was happy to get it and happier to see those reforms finally accomplished, but he added that there would not have been "one iota of reform if it had not been for Carl Albert. Anytime I've needed help on reform, he's always been right there."

I was right there, right there to help, right there to support, but not right there to grab the credit. I looked at it as Sam Rayburn had taught me: "You can accomplish almost anything as long as you don't mind who gets the credit." Others got the credit, but what I accomplished was a set of reforms that made the House more open to public scrutiny, more sensitive to members' needs, more amenable to its elected leadership, and more capable of meeting its responsibilities.

In early 1973, we went a long way toward each of those goals. Our vehicle was the Democratic caucus. Though long rusting, it was still the one carriage open to the entire Democratic majority. Earlier I had persuaded John McCormack to pull it out of storage. In 1973 and after, I saw to it that it became the engine pulling the entire House into its modern era.

It began with our very first caucus meetings in 1973. In January, the caucus approved the recommendations of Julia Hansen's committee to elect all chairmen automatically and to do it by secret ballot. The decision capped at least fifteen years' effort to break the hold of seniority and came after an angry debate, a debate in which many of yesterday's young reformers came forward as that day's champions of seniority. The anger outlasted the decision. In fact, a day later a second caucus meeting attempted to repeal the new rules. It might have done so except for my speech welcoming and embracing the change. The repeal effort failed, and the seniority system—for sixty-two years the single path to committee domination—died that day. Its beneficiaries still held their power (every chairman won election handily), but they knew that their power sprang not from their personal longevity but from their colleagues' institutional voice: the Democratic caucus.

That same caucus meeting agreed to place the Speaker, majority leader, and caucus chairman on our party's committee on committees. Since 1911, that committee—the committee that targeted every young member's entire career—had consisted of the Democrats sitting on ways and means. Putting us there both strengthened us as leaders and gave us a new way to lead. For the first time, we could control directly and successfully a chairman's attempts to fill his committee with members of like mind—like *his* mind. Louisiana's F. Edward Hebert, for instance, long had refused to add a black to his Armed Services Committee. In 1973, he begrudgingly agreed to accept a black member, any black member except California's Ron Dellums. He would not consider at all Patricia Schroeder, an outstanding new member for whom I had campaigned in 1972 in her first race for any office. Once enlarged, the new Democratic committee on committees put two new members on armed services. One was Ron Dellums; the other was Pat Schroeder. With their selection, both learned something about power and its ends. Eddie Hebert did, too.

In the case of one committee, the Rules Committee, I needed no educating at all. I already knew about that committee's power and its use. I knew that no Speaker since Joe Cannon had controlled it.

I knew that not even Sam Rayburn's expansion of it in 1961 had broken its power. Finally, I knew that I was going to control that committee, not for the exaltation of Carl Albert, not even for the power of the Speakership, but for the rights of the entire House membership, too often frustrated by that obstinate committee. Sitting on my party's committee on committees placed me in a position to do it. Three vacancies gave me the opportunity. All three were taken by men entirely loyal to the elected leadership: Gillis Long of Louisiana, Morgan Murphy of Illinois, and Clem McSpadden, a new member from Oklahoma.

The new Rules Committee retained its old prerogatives, and I wanted it that way. When the House subsequently considered giving the Speaker the arbitrary power to bypass the committee and put bills directly on the floor, I led the fight that beat it by a three-to-one margin. The House needed a traffic cop, but it did not need a despot. Never again would this cop signal a steady halt to frustrate the House's majority.

In each of these cases, the Democratic caucus effected the changes, since each of them applied only to the party's way of doing business. While the press and pundits looked around for people to credit, I had the quiet satisfaction of knowing that the same caucus that was a worthless instrument for most of my majority leadership was moving the entire majority party behind my Speakership. In other cases, it moved the entire House by sponsoring the very reforms I knew to be long overdue.

At the recommendation of the Democratic caucus, the House voted in early 1973 to speed the flow of legislative business by adding two days per month to clear noncontroversial bills and by giving the Speaker the power, subject to majority vote, to convene the House before noon, a hoary but inefficient tradition. More importantly, the caucus's recommendation became the House's policy to open to the public nearly all committee hearings and markup sessions (in which bills were assembled), all frequently done heretofore behind closed doors. The same source finally established a procedure to allow amendment of tax bills, a practice unknown— and thoroughly undemocratic—since the 1930s. Caucus recommendations also established a subcommittee bill of rights, which sapped the authority of tyrannical chairmen, opened legislative power to the young and able, and protected the minority's rights.

Because I had my way and because the time was right, we did all of those things and did them all in a few months in 1973. If I had had my way, we would have done even more. We would have remade what was at the very heart not only of our procedures but of our products: the standing-committee system.

Not since 1946 had anyone dared address the committee structure. The redefinition of committee lines in that distant year may have made sense, considering the Congress's old responsibilities, but by the 1970s it made less sense and still less with every passing year. Some committees, Ways and Means most noticeably, steadily had acquired awesome power, power that in the case of Ways and Means drained the energies of its 25 members and frustrated its 410 nonmembers. Other committees served no important function at all. Still others had established jurisdiction over items ill fitted to their expertise. Banking and Currency, for instance, had authority over urban mass-transit legislation, though no one knew just what that had to do with either banking or currency. Finally, new issues unforeseeable in the 1946 committee organization lay completely beyond its structure; sometimes, they lay all over its structure. Energy legislation, unknown in the cheap-oil years, potentially fell within the jurisdiction of eighty-three committees and subcommittees.

None of these problems was new. What was new was a determination to do something about them, even if that something disrupted our traditional ways of doing business so that we could get our business done. Securing the Democratic caucus's approval for a study committee on committee realignment, I added the warm support of the Republican leadership, got a million-dollar appropriation to finance its work, and named a committee of outstanding members to make recommendations. At its head I placed Richard Bolling.

Bolling's committee held six months of hearings and spent seventeen days drafting its recommendations, every one of those days open to the public. On one of them, I testified to the need for complete restructuring, thereby becoming the first Speaker to appear before a congressional committee in more than a century. When it was all over, the committee had a sensible and far-reaching set of proposals. They were sensible because they balanced committee workloads, because they rationalized jurisdictional assignments, and because they adopted the House's committee structure to the nation's modern needs. They were far reaching because they transformed every committee they touched and because they touched twenty of the twenty-one standing committees. Veterans' Affairs would see no change, but three (Internal Security, Merchant Marine and Fisheries, and Post Office and Civil Service) would be abolished. Each of the remainder would have altered responsibilities, sometimes dramatically so.

It was, of course, those features that accounted for the stubborn opposition to the proposals. Members serving on committees slated to lose responsibilities—and Ways and Means was to be the big loser—rallied all of the influence that those same responsibilities gave them. Liberals heretofore intent upon remaking the House suddenly became advocates of tradition when changing that tradition would cost them their hard-won influence. Outside lobbyists, comfortably tied to the existing structure, rallied to defend those ties. The result was the otherwise inexplicable alliance of such strange bedfellows as the DSG, organized business, and organized labor in a single mighty bloc. What explained it was that politics is not about issues, it is about people, and those people had a lot to lose.

They did not lose it. Dick Bolling and I did. After a bitter debate, the caucus voted narrowly to refer his committee's proposal to the continuing Hansen committee. The latter reported a set of procedural reforms—many valuable, none affecting committee responsibilities—that the caucus sent to the entire House. All won but all fell short of readying the House for the twenty-first century. However, we had brought it squarely into the twentieth.

One final way that we had done it came back in February of

1973. At the same caucus that affirmed the election of chairmen and approved the appointment of the Bolling committee, we voted to establish a Democratic House steering and policy committee. An agent of the caucus, it was firmly under the control of the leadership. The majority leader, the caucus chairman, the whip and his deputies, joined me on the committee, with other members elected regionally. In addition, I appointed enough other members to make it the Speaker's committee. By 1974's end, that committee had taken from our Ways and Means members the role of our party committee on committees, filling every Democratic assignment to every committee except one, Rules, which the Speaker alone would fill.

As great as the procedural authority of the new steering and policy committee was, its policy powers were even more important. For the first time since Joe Cannon's one-man rule, it gave the majority party a means to recommend legislation and coordinate its passage. Cannon had done it himself, as a tyrannical czar, and his rule had created a revolt.

No one ever confused Carl Albert with Joe Cannon or with a czar, but without an "Albert revolt," I had created and now directed something bigger than any one man and more important, too. I also had seen to it that the Democratic caucus functioned for the first time since the 1920s. For the first time since 1911, the elected House leadership controlled committee assignments and the flow of bills through the Rules Committee. For the first time in too long, we all shared our power with each other and did our work in full public view.

A lot of people got and deserved a lot of credit for all of that. When I looked at it, I remembered some of Sam Rayburn's talks back at the old Board of Education. Mr. Rayburn reminisced often about how weak the office of the Speakership was for many years, his first years there, years before he became Mr. Democrat and bigger than the office. In less than four years, I had seen the Speaker's institutional authority grow to transcend even Sam Rayburn's personal influence. Mr. Rayburn could not have foreseen it, but he was right: you can accomplish almost anything as long as you do not mind who gets the credit.

"The U.S. is facing a constitutional crisis. That branch of Government that most closely represents the people is not yet broken, but it is bent and in danger of snapping." Those two sentences opened the cover article of *Time* magazine's issue as the Ninety-third Congress convened on January 3, 1973. In the article, congressmen, political scientists, and others described the impending death of an independent Congress. One senator spoke openly of the tendency toward an "Executive Monarchy." An esteemed professor saw the Congress "sliding down a razor blade, with no way to pull back." *Time*'s own congressional correspondent, Neil McNeil, speculated that it would soon be necessary "to stuff a congressman and stick him in the Smithsonian in among other extinct species, so that future generations will know what a congressman looked like."

Down Pennsylvania Avenue a mile from Capitol Hill, no one was worrying about the executive's future. Richard Nixon was beginning his second term determined to reform his house, too. He had interrupted the celebration of his reelection to request letters of resignation from each of the top 2,000 officers in the executive branch. Not all were accepted, but enough were to put Nixon loyalists in charge of such heretofore semi-independent agencies as the Internal Revenue Service, the Federal Bureau of Investigation, and the Central Intelligence Agency. Unmindful of federal statutes, the president was reorganizing his cabinet by creating a super cabinet of three cabinet officers who assumed White House offices and White House titles to direct the nation's domestic affairs. Equally unmindful of statute, Nixon established a super super cabinet of three to manage the nation's foreign affairs. Not one of the new positions, unknown to law, required Senate confirmation. In the privacy of the Oval Office, men like H. R. Haldeman, John Erlichman, Maurice Stans, John Mitchell, Charles Colson, and John Dean looked with delight to four more years. Rarely did they mention a "third-rate burglary" that had occurred in June. Always, hidden tape recorders whirred along.

Politically, things seemed to be breaking well for the president, too. Exactly one week after his second inauguration, Paris negotiators formally signed an agreement that he declared secured "peace with honor" in Vietnam. In February, the first of our prisoners of war returned from Hanoi. Soon, the American military left South Vietnam but left its government with massive stockpiles of sophisticated arms and in control of 75 percent of its territory and 85 percent of its population. That government also had Richard Nixon's entirely personal "absolute assurance" of "swift and severe retaliatory action" should Hanoi renew the fighting.

No wonder the president was ready to renew his own fight with Congress.

With Indochina seemingly gone as a political issue, the president defined the contest in economic terms. Its initial skirmish involved his proposed budget, the budget of a president who had his hands in its pockets and his eyes on the ground. The hands squeezed pennies tightly, especially those devoted to domestic social needs. The eyes saw only inflation's shadow, and the president was determined to escape it. What he was still determined to do helped transform a budgetary squabble into a constitutional contest.

No one could deny that inflation's shadow was real, and no one in the Congress ignored the problem. No one could. After a modest price increase of 3.4 percent over 1972, the cost of living shot up 8.8 percent in 1973—three and one-half times the self-serving estimate of that year's budget. Food costs alone soared 30 percent, meaning that the needy, as usual, paid the heaviest price. Responding to the challenge, Congress regularly had given the president the power and tools that only the executive could use. Some this executive misused; others he used not at all. Over a four-year span, the president devised his own "game plans." Seven of them. Phase One price controls, followed by Phase Two, Phase Three, and Phase Four, all punctuated by two separate price freezes, always the talk about holding down spending. Not one of them worked.

At least, not one of them worked economically. Politically, their very failure worked to the president's advantage. They gave him the false ammunition of congressional spending and congressional irresponsibility that the White House daily fired off in televised newscasts and occasional somber speeches. They gave him an issue to rally support for his own spending priorities. They gave a basis to the charge that Congress was a bent branch in danger of snapping. Most of all, they gave the president the excuse to veto any spending bill he did not like, even if what he disliked was not the dollar sum but the program himself. And veto he did. After our 1972 adjournment, the president refused to sign twelve appropriations bills. Through 1973, his veto came steadily forth.

I thought it was all bad economics. I thought it was bad politics, too. Too often stung by a hostile president, even Republican members were backing away from Nixon's policies and failing to support his legislative requests. Enough stayed loyal that we could not override his vetoes (he won eight straight override attempts in 1973), but neither could we prevent them.

Bad economics is one thing, and bad politics is another, but the upshot of it all was worse. Even if he signed our bills, the president often refused to spend the money. "Impoundment," he called it, and that was more than economically bad, it was constitutionally evil.

Of course, Nixon was not the first president to impound congressionally appropriated money. The process dated to Thomas Jefferson, who refused to spend fifty thousand dollars that Congress had given him to purchase gunboats for the Mississippi River after the Louisiana Purchase made them unnecessary. Subsequent executives also had impounded funds, and the Antideficiency Act of 1905 gave them explicit but narrowly prescribed authority to do so. Under that law, a president could decline to spend appropriations in "some extraordinary emergency or [under] unusual circumstances which could not be anticipated at the time of making such apportionment." Within those bounds, twentieth-century presidents often impounded limited amounts of funds for limited times, always after consultation with Congress.

Richard Nixon's impoundments had none of those features. First, the sums were vast, an average of $1 billion per year. Second, the impoundments were permanent. Third, not once did he consult Congress in advance. Finally, the impoundments rested not upon even the pretense of an extraordinary emergency or unusual circumstance. The circumstance and the emergency both were the arrogant claim of the president's unrestrained right to refuse to spend lawfully appropriated monies, a right that Nixon labeled "absolutely clear." The intent was to repeal or gut social programs that dated to the Great Society and the New Frontier, even to the New Deal. The effect was to assert the executive's sole right to define public priorities, and that he could not do. It was absolutely clear.

The Constitution explicitly reserves for Congress the duty and the power to finance all national programs through "appropriations made by Law." The Constitution explicitly charges the chief executive to see to it that "the Laws be faithfully executed." Both principles grow out of the soil of colonial experience, when American assemblies had learned that only their jealously guarded power of the purse could defend their prerogatives, and their citizens' liberties, from executive despotism however asserted, whether in the name of the king or even (presumably) by the need to fight inflation.

Thus, when Richard Nixon responded to our override of his veto of a $6 billion appropriation for rural sewage treatment by simply refusing to spend the $6 billion, what was at stake was more important than country sewage and more priceless than $6 billion. When he refused to spend "appropriations made by Law" for highway construction—though that law explicitly denied any right to impoundment—he simultaneously asserted a monarch's prerogative and denied a president's responsibility to see that the laws were "faithfully executed." When he and his spokesmen proclaimed a policy to veto any appropriation passed by 535 elected members of two houses of Congress should one man disagree with its level or purposes and then to impound the money if Congress overrode that veto, he proclaimed the intent to flee the shadow of inflation by casting a pall upon the Constitution. It was absolutely clear.

The federal courts agreed. In twenty-one lawsuits, twenty-one decisions voided specific impoundments as illegal. Constitutional scholars agreed. One, William Rehnquist, the future chief justice whom Nixon himself judged qualified to appoint initially to the Supreme Court, wrote that Nixon's broad claim of an inherent presidential authority of impoundment was "supported by neither reason nor precedent." Civic groups agreed. Those as diverse as the United Auto Workers, the National Association of Home Builders, and the American Nurses Association protested the president's policy. Even conservatives agreed. Our Appropriations Committee chairman, George Mahon, and the Senate's Sam Ervin, neither some wild-eyed spender, prepared bills to overturn the impoundments and conserve Congress's constitutional heritage.

My job as Speaker was to get some bill that we could pass. Although I never wavered from the constitutional issue involved, I also knew that what we confronted was not a theory but a circumstance. The difficulty of getting a bill through both houses was part of the circumstance; the president's likely veto was another. The hardest was to address the illegitimate issue of impoundment while also dealing with an undeniable reality. The whole method of congressional appropriations lacked expertise, coordination, and direction. That lack, which had existed since George Washington, gave a gloss of apparent legitimacy to Nixon's claim of executive power. His counselor, John Erlichman, had a point when he declared that the problem with congressional control of spending was that "the right hand does not know what the left hand is doing. The fingers of the right hand do not even know what the other fingers of the right hand are doing." If we had to strengthen our constitutional hand against the president, we would have to strengthen the budgetary hand, too.

We did it by using all of the reforms that we had set in place. At our very first meeting of the steering and policy committee, I appointed Dick Bolling to head a task force on the question of impoundments. Dick had the help of John Barrier, an able professional staff man who worked for the full committee. Periodic meetings both kept the caucus informed of our progress and allowed the members to make contributions. Chairman George Mahon put his Appropriations Committee to drafting a workable bill for budgetary reform. With Mike Mansfield, I worked to keep the public informed and to get a Senate bill as close to ours as possible.

All the pieces came together in the Budget and Impoundment Act of 1973. A very complex bill, it brought order to our appropriations process. An overall budget ceiling provided a framework within which separate appropriations must fit. New budget committees in each house would reconcile separate appropriation bills and revenue bills. The new Congressional Budget Office would give us the expertise to correct White House figures. Altogether, the budget provisions of the bill finally rationalized the entire method of congressional spending by allowing us to build a comprehensive budget from the ground up rather than cheese-paring one from the top down.

They also rendered impotent the threat of a presidential veto. A president who criticized so loudly our "irresponsible" and "inefficient" ways had to sign that bill, even though it contained a separate title carefully restricting the same president's impoundments. Dick Bolling successfully joined the two in the Rules Committee, where he had the help of my three new men. Firm yet realistic, we did not forbid all impoundments under all circumstances. Instead, we provided a mechanism whereby the president would have to justify all future impoundments to the Congress. Final authority to maintain or to release the impoundments would rest firmly where the Founding Fathers had placed it: in the United States Congress. Agreeing to the bill, President Nixon tacitly bowed to the principle.

It was one of the sweetest victories of my Speakership. The victory was not mine over Richard Nixon nor even Congress's over the president. It was a victory of principle, sweetened because in winning we had acted responsibly. We were responsible to our own new procedures. We were responsible to the need to get our budget-making process in order. We were responsible to the tradition that linked the assemblies, first of noblemen, then of businessmen, and finally of common men through the ages. The executive's demands for money met again its check and its balance in the representatives' power to give money and determine its use. We had affirmed what kings had learned to their sorrow and humanity's gain since they first had turned to those assemblies for money to fight their wars.

We affirmed it again when President Nixon needed money to fight his own war.

Though President Nixon pronounced the Paris Agreements a peace with honor, they created a peace that never was in a war that would not go away. American combat troops left Vietnam, but they left hostile armies itching for battle all over Indochina. In South Vietnam itself, government and Communist forces fought for momentary advantages while each prepared for a major offensive. In neighboring Cambodia, brought into the war by Nixon's "incursion" of 1970, the government controlled only the capital. Communist armies surrounded the city and threatened to overrun it. After publicly hinting that the United States might return again to Vietnam, the president unleashed American airpower over Cambodia. Doomed to fail, the renewed bombing had one inescapable consequence. It raised again the president's claim to make war with neither congressional consultation nor consent.

It was not the first time, not even for Richard Nixon. During each of the three preceding springs, the president had widened and intensified the war in peace's name. The Cambodian invasion of 1970 had been followed by 1971's cover for South Vietnam's invasion of Laos and the American mining of Haiphong Harbor in 1973. In not one instance had the president even seen fit to inform the Congress or its leaders. In each instance, the Senate had responded with efforts to end the war by cutting off funds for it; each of those efforts had died in the House. Not one had even come within fifty votes of passing.

This time it was different. There were no negotiations to disrupt. There were no departing American troops to protect. There was only a nation sick of the war and a Congress tired of having no voice in it. In 1973, Congress raised its voice. In the House, ours was magnified by the new reforms that we had assembled. Under my direction, the Steering and Policy Committee voted overwhelmingly (eighteen to three) to join the Senate in cutting off funds for the bombing. We took the resolution to the full Democratic caucus, which voted also overwhelmingly to put the party on record. Legislative leaders and I agreed to put the issue in the form of an amendment to a military-appropriations bill. Because of 1970's requirement of recorded votes on such amendments, no one had a place to hide. On May 10, the House of Representatives passed the amendment to deny the president the money to make war in or over Cambodia by a vote of 219 to 188. Joining the majority were thirty-five Republicans, who refused to follow their president even one more bloody step. Unable to veto the measure without simultaneously vetoing all military spending, President Nixon signed it into law. In the same way, six other amendments became laws of the Ninety-third Congress and collectively erected an impassable legal barrier against any American military or paramilitary operations in, over, or off the shores of Cambodia, Laos, North Vietnam, or South Vietnam. The last still had what was left of $350 billion in American tax money spent there over the years—spent along with the lives of 57,000 of our young men. If that could not guarantee South Vietnam's independence, nothing we could do later would, either. It would be no mistake to waste not another dollar nor another life there.

There had been mistakes, many of them, and in Congress we had learned from them. The same Constitution that created our offices and gave us our power of the purse also gave us another exclusive prerogative: only the Congress could declare war. We had not declared one in Vietnam, but we had fought one. We had accepted uncritically the president's judgment—several presidents' judgments—until we had been trapped. Handing the commander in chief the power to put our forces in harm's way, we had lost any practical power to keep them and us out of war. In Vietnam we did not regain it until those forces had left the war. In the future, we would have to assert that power first. The man who made it possible was Clem Zablocki.

Outside Congress and the Fourth Congressional District in Wisconsin, few people ever heard of Clem Zablocki. Sixty years old when the Ninety-third Congress convened, Clem had come to Congress in 1949. He worked quietly but effectively on our Foreign Affairs Committee. In time, he ranked behind only Chairman Tom Morgan and headed the subcommittee on national security policy and scientific developments. There, he did the hard and unpublicized work that made possible the Peace Corps and the United States Disarmament and Arms Control Agency. I got to know him well when President Johnson sent Clem and me to represent the United States at a conference in the Philippines in 1966. We both took our wives along, and Mary, Blanche Zablocki, Clem, and I became fast friends.

In 1970 at the time of the Cambodia invasion, Clem came by my office. We both had supported every step taken in Vietnam to that point, but in 1970 I agreed with him that the widening of the war drove home the need for more congressional involvement. That day, I gave him a promise that I kept for three years: I would back his efforts to secure appropriate legislation to that end.

Through the summer of 1970, Clem's subcommittee held hearings and finally produced a joint resolution. The full committee reported it favorably, and it passed the House but died when the Senate failed to act. In 1971, he started all over. This time, differently worded resolutions passed both houses but could not find agreement in a conference committee. Undaunted, Clem Zablocki started fresh again in 1973. Again he held extensive hearings, and this time he produced a new resolution, one much stronger than the earlier versions. It passed the House. A similar version passed the Senate. Senate and House conferees agreed to a compromise, and it passed both houses handily. It was the War Powers Act.

The law acknowledged the modern president's powers in a world far removed from the eighteenth-century world of the Constitution, but it also reasserted and redefined Congress's obligations and prerogatives. Essentially, it set a sixty-day limit on the presidential commitment of American forces to combat. After that time, a president must either justify their use and secure a joint congressional resolution of approval or withdraw them. No president's hands would be tied in an emergency, but neither would Congress be powerless to do anything but silently acquiesce.

Richard Nixon would have none of it. Declaring the act both dangerous and unconstitutional, he gave it his ninth veto in ten months.

Clem Zablocki did not give up, nor did I. I knew, though, how hard an override would be. It would take a two-thirds majority, always hard, and harder still on something this controversial. We did not have a two-thirds Democratic majority in the House, and we could not expect much Republican help. Many of our Democrats were conservatives unwilling to buck a conservative president on a diplomatic issue. Others were liberals, several of whom had voted against the bill on original passage on the grounds that even sixty days was too long. This override would be the hardest yet, hard enough that I twice put off the vote.

On November 7, 1973, I finally put the question to the House. Clem and Phil Burton, a Californian who was my informal liaison with the doctrinaire liberals, had found six liberals who had voted against the bill but were approachable to switching their votes for an override. We all three approached them. My pitch was simple. "Look," I said, "Nixon has beaten us on eight straight override attempts. If you go with us, we can win on this one, and it's the biggest one of all." Each of the six agreed to stand aside while the vote was taken. If we needed them, they would vote with us. We needed them, and we got them. We repassed the bill, 284 to 135. Because of the six, we won by a four-vote margin. The Senate overrode that same day, 75 to 18.

After three years' work, Clem Zablocki had brought Congress's war-making power into the post–World War II world. As it turned out, the hardest work of all was probably done on the last day. I had not chosen it at random. A few days earlier, President Richard

Nixon had fired one of his employees, a lawyer named Archibald Cox. That made it easier to pass the War Powers Act. It also elevated a third-rate burglary into a first-rate constitutional crisis.

At the time, back in June of 1972, I thought it was a third-rate burglary, too. When the *Washington Post* first reported the Watergate break-in, I put it aside as a silly criminal act that would go no further than the district courts. Even as the newspapers began to develop the story and attach it to the White House, the only thing that aroused the slightest interest in me was that James W. McCord, one of the burglars, was said to have once lived in Waurika, Oklahoma, a friendly little town in my district.

Only in late 1972 did I begin to suspect that the Watergate affair might involve more than an isolated legal problem. One morning, Larry O'Brien, the Democratic National Committee's chairman, called and told me that there were some financial implications. Money, considerable sums of it, apparently had financed the burglars, and some of that money had been laundered in Mexico. If so, Congress might need to act. I contacted Wright Patman, chairman of the Banking and Currency Committee, and asked him to look into the matter. He did, and Republicans on the committee and elsewhere howled that we were playing politics. Wright went on along anyway, ignoring those complaints and assembling boxes of evidence. The Ninety-second Congress adjourned before he could do much with them, so Chairman Patman sealed the boxes and sent them over to the Senate. He sent them to Senator Sam Ervin.

Senator Sam. In his committee's long investigations of early 1973, America made him a folk hero, an old country lawyer with a face designed by a cartoonist. Gradually, America learned what we in Congress knew about the senator: behind that country-lawyer facade was a Harvard Law School education; behind those jowls and self-propelled eyebrows was the mind of a first-rate constitutional scholar. Gradually, too, America learned something about the break-in, more about the White House, but not enough about the president. Every passing day brought new revelations. Beneath Watergate's tip was a chilling iceberg of misdeeds, venality, and outright stupidity. Watching it all, I, too, began to wonder, in Senator Howard Baker's phase, "how much did the president know and when did he know it?" Like most, my expectation (maybe my hope) was that he had known too little too late.

Right in the middle of the Ervin hearings, the press began to report another story. This one I followed with more than passing interest. Vice-President Spiro Agnew was under investigation by a Baltimore grand jury. United States attorneys were preparing charges of fraud, bribery, and other crimes.

On September 25, Gerald Ford and Leslie Arends, the Republicans' House leader and whip, respectively, asked whether I could see the vice-president. They also asked whether I had received a call from Attorney General Elliot Richardson. I had not, but the question told me why the vice-president wanted to see me: it had to involve that investigation.

It did. Agnew came by and handed me a letter. It asked for a congressional inquiry into the allegations against him and cited as precedent such an investigation requested and given Vice-President John C. Calhoun more than 150 years earlier. We talked alone for a while, and he complained bitterly about the Justice Department's handling of the case. He added that top White House officials were pressuring him to resign, and he gave every indication that he never would.

Agnew's request was a bolt from skies grayed by the Watergate investigations. To this day I do not understand why he wanted it, but I knew instantly that the House must not involve itself in a nearly completed criminal investigation before the federal courts. I talked with Peter Rodino, chairman of our Judiciary Committee, and he agreed. He also offered to check the Calhoun precedent and report to me the next morning. When he did, he confirmed my suspicion that the cases were not at all similar. That morning, I gave the whole story to the entire House leadership, and I gave them my decision: I would steer the House of Representatives clear of the impending clash between the judicial and executive branches. Whatever Spiro Agnew's intent, he would not put the legislative branch in the breach with him.

Two weeks later, I got a second letter from Agnew. It was a copy of one informing the secretary of state that he was resigning his office. He thereby traded the vice-presidency of the United States for a suspended sentence on a single charge of income-tax evasion. As part of the deal, the Justice Department published the charges and evidence against him. Uncontested by Agnew, they documented years of sleazy kickbacks that ran straight into the vice-president's office, where Spiro Agnew had collected envelopes of cash from crooked contractors, slimy characters as crooked as he.

I was glad to see him go, but it meant a big difference in my own life. The country had no vice-president, and I was Speaker of the House. In the presidential-succession sequence, I was next in line. Carl Albert was now the one heartbeat away. For all I cared, it could have been a thousand. I worried neither that I would get the job nor that I could do it. The biggest difference for me was entirely personal: the Secret Service invaded my Washington apartment.

For invaders, they were a nice-enough occupation army. Their leader, Gil Parachos, was a fine fellow. His agents accompanied me everywhere. At home, they installed a hot line by my bed to connect me directly to the White House in the event of a national emergency. It rang two or three times, never with any news of great substance but always with an ominous sound. The agents also drew the drapes carefully whenever I was home, explaining that I made a fine target for snipers. Mary threw them open as soon as I left in the morning because she was not particularly worried about snipers. The agents also offered to help Mary carry out the garbage, but she would not allow it. Maybe they feared a bomb in the Dumpster. I do not know. I do know that they X-rayed everything that entered our little apartment.

Because there were no vacant rooms around us, the Secret Service's headquarters was a van parked in the back alley. One of our neighbors returned from abroad unaware of what had happened, noticed the van, observed it, and consulted the apartment manager. A bunch of hippies had set up in the alley, he protested, and they were probably dope dealers, too, since men and women entered and left the van at all hours. Other tenants stopped Mary and told her how glad they were to have the Secret Service there; they never had felt so safe.

I was ready to get back to normal as quickly as possible. President Nixon was, too. On the afternoon of Agnew's resignation, the president summoned Mike Mansfield and me to the White House. The Twenty-fifth Amendment provided that the president would fill a vacancy in the vice-presidency by nomination, subject to confirmation by both houses. Clearly anxious to get a vice-president as quickly as possible, Nixon told us that he would ask Republican leaders at all levels for suggestions. He also said he would welcome any advice we had to offer. I thought it just a courtesy, but Mike gave him two names: Secretary of State William Rogers and a former senator from Kentucky, John Sherman Cooper. I said that since Mike had offered some choices, I knew the one who would be the easiest to confirm. "Who is it? Jerry Ford?" the president asked. "Yes sir," I answered.

Of course, House Minority Leader Gerald R. Ford was his choice, and a fine one. Although the House (unlike the Senate) had never before confirmed a presidential appointee for any office, I knew that I would assign the task to Pete Rodino's Judiciary Committee. That committee had worked on the Twenty-fifth Amendment and had general responsibility for constitutional issues. Besides, I knew that Pete's committee would conduct an impartial inquiry into the candidate's fitness, not his politics. Quite a few members, especially the younger ones, were busy advising me that we Democrats could and should block any nominee who might run against us in 1976. I thought that was nonsense. The House had a unique responsibility to the Constitution, not to my party's advantage. I knew that Pete and his committee shared that. Sure enough, the Judiciary Committee began a thorough and diligent consideration of Ford's nomination. Just ten days into it, the entire picture changed; in fact, it exploded.

On October 20, President Nixon ordered Attorney General Elliot

Richardson to fire Special Prosecutor Archibald Cox. Charged with investigating Watergate and related crimes, Cox was seeking a court order to compel the president to hand over some of the famous White House tapes for evidence. For that reason, Nixon wanted him fired, and Richardson refused to do it. So did his deputy, William Ruckleshaus. Both resigned instead. Finally, Solicitor General Robert Bork executed the order and fired Cox.

Never did I see such a spontaneous emotional eruption as the rage that greeted Nixon's "Saturday Night Massacre." Cartons of telegrams and telephone messages awaited me at my office on Monday. Resolutions of impeachment virtually rained on the House floor. I had no doubt that if one were to be called up, it would be voted through instantly.

To that point, I carefully had kept the House clear of any investigation of the president. Everyone knew that the House of Representatives alone held the constitutional power of impeachment. Any investigation, whatever its focus, would raise the shadow of that singular but ultimate sword. After the departure of the three top justice officials, all apparent victims of the president's need to conceal evidence, there was no choice. Impeachment was a possibility. Its consideration was the House's duty. How to manage it responsibly required the Speaker's decision.

I never got more unsolicited or more foolish advice. Some told me that we should strike back at the White House with our power of the purse: slash its appropriations. Otherwise sensible people saw a chance to forestall Ford's confirmation, impeach and remove Nixon, and hand the presidency to the next in line, me. Many wanted to set up a select committee to handle impeachment. Some of those wanted me to fill it with our most outstanding members; others wanted me to pack it with Nixon haters. Both pointed to precedent: the one presidential impeachment in America's history, that of Andrew Johnson, had been handled not by a standing committee but by a select committee.

I had not asked for any advice. I did not put it to a vote. I cannot even claim even to have listened very politely to such suggestions. No decision I could ever make would be more significant for my

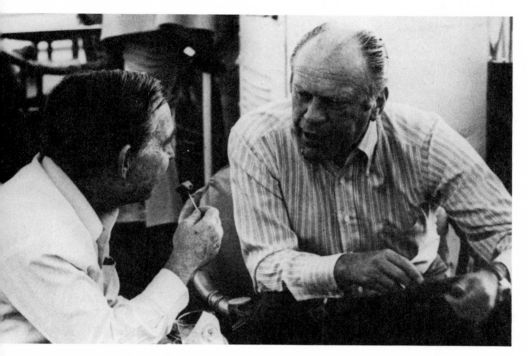

*I knew the one who would be easiest to confirm.* Carl Albert with President Jerry Ford.

country. In an impeachment inquiry, two institutions would be judged, not one. We would examine the president, and the American people would examine us. I did not know what we would learn about the president, but I never doubted what the people would learn about their House of Representatives.

On Monday afternoon, October 22, 1973, I announced that I would refer all impeachment resolutions (there were twenty-five at the time) to the House Committee on the Judiciary. Whatever its eventual decision, no one could claim it rigged. Judiciary was a standing committee, most of its members serving for many years, all of them there when impeachment was just a word in civics

*That was Peter Rodino.* Mary Albert, Carl Albert, and Judiciary Committee Chairman Peter Rodino at the grave of Winston Churchill, in 1976.

texts. Probably not one American in a hundred could name even one of its members. They were neither particularly powerful nor prominent. By tradition, all were lawyers, but otherwise they were quite average members, average in age, average in experience, representatives of both sexes and every section, race, religion, and viewpoint in the country. I thought the average committee, if called upon to do an important job, would do it right.

Like the average committee, judiciary's most important member was its chairman, in practice the committee's most senior man. In this case, that was Peter Rodino. New to the chairmanship in 1973, he long had labored behind the famed Manny Celler. He was a quiet man of quiet talents. I suppose he was about average for a chairman. He always went about his work modestly but thoroughly, paying due regard to his committee's members and the House's traditions.

I never claimed to be much more than an average Speaker, either. I had neither sought nor received publicity. I was not a national celebrity daily before the cameras. I did not run the House, I only respected it. My job was to let Pete Rodino and his thirty-seven committee members do their job. My job was to let the House of Representatives do its work its way.

I had been in Congress nearly thirty years. For all of them, I had heard the criticism of that way: the slowness of our deliberations, the inefficiency of our procedures, the authority of our anonymous old men, the mediocrity of our members. Quite recently the critics had grown louder. The president should make decisions because all we could do was debate. The White House had to act swiftly because we took too long. The bright young men gathered there had to be loyal to the president because we were too divided. The executive branch knew what to do with power, but our branch was bent, in danger of snapping.

After clearing Ford's confirmation as vice-president, Chairman Peter Rodino and the Committee on the Judiciary of the United States House of Representatives took up a resolution of inquiry into the impeachment of President Richard M. Nixon. In the light of day, the American people would judge us all.

Yes, we were slow. Committee hearings and debates consumed nine full months. But because we were slow, we ensured that every view was aired and examined, every piece of evidence weighed and measured. Yes, we were inefficient. But because we were, we were thorough. Yes, we were divided. The thirty-seven committee members were individually loyal to no one man but were collectively bound to the U.S. Constitution and its faith in deliberative government. But no, Peter Rodino proved not to be just an anonymous old man. He became a celebrity, but only because he acted true to the House's ways. And no, his committee members proved not to be mediocrities. When Americans watched members like Barbara Jordan, Paul Sarbanes, Jack Brooks, Elizabeth Holtzman, and others wrestle publicly with their own consciences and their nation's future, America was watching representative government work. They were all average members working in a way long derided, but those people and that process worked just as well as I had expected and as the Founding Fathers had intended. Because they did, they assembled the evidence, and they debated and approved the resolutions that caused Richard Nixon to ask me to meet him in the Executive Office Building on a Thursday night in August.

With me were Senators Mike Mansfield, Hugh Scott, and James Eastland, along with John Rhodes, the new House minority leader. Collectively, we were the leaders of the Congress that the president had battled, ridiculed, and ignored over five and one-half years. There was no enmity that evening. As president, Richard Nixon told us that he would announce his resignation the next day, August 9, 1974. As a man, he talked about his inclination to stay on and fight it out, about how his family wanted him to do so, but he knew that the outcome was certain and that the country would be torn apart. Then he thanked us collectively for our support and asked us to extend it to his successor. He turned to one of us for his last words. The man who twenty-seven years earlier had asked me if I was the same Carl Albert who had won a speech contest in 1928 put his arm around my shoulders. "We've always been friends," Dick Nixon said. I could not help but be touched by it. He had been my friend, my first Republican friend in Congress. He could have been a great president, for his instincts were sure and his insights were sharp, but he was a flawed man who confused personal power with constitutional processes. His departure was not the defeat of his person but the triumph of that process.

It did not end all of our problems. The deficit still mounted. The recession worsened. Inflation increased. An old war in Indochina neared its tragic end. A new one might erupt in the Middle East at any time. My own problems did not end either. Until Nelson Rockefeller was confirmed as vice-president, I was once more next in line. The Secret Service parked its van in the alley again, installed another hot line, and started drawing my drapes. To get away, I sometimes went over to the Library of Congress and worked on some old hobbies—genealogy and translating Miguel de Cervantes's *Don Quixote.* That may have been where I encountered the diary of Frederick Muhlenberg, the first Speaker of the House. Reading it, I realized just how little America had changed since its first congressmen had ridden their horses over muddy trails to that first Congress. "The coffers are empty, the taxes almost unendurable, the people in bad humor, the money discredited," Muhlenberg had written. But he had written, too, of what was even more enduring: "However, the present Congress, believe me, consists of honest, brave, and wise men. Let us once more take cheer and be steadfast, rely on God and our own strength, and endure courageously, then we shall be sure of reaching our goals."

Like every Congress since Frederick Muhlenberg's, mine kept reaching for its goals. Like every Congress before mine (and assuredly after), we never grasped them, for it is the unending act of reaching that animates American government. Though inevitable, the process could be awfully frustrating. Our new president, Gerald Ford, was a good man and one of my best friends in Congress. He was an honest man, a decent man, a modest man. We all had smiled at his line (uttered when he became Nixon's vice-president) that he was "a Ford, not a Lincoln." But Jerry Ford also could be a stubborn man, stubborn enough to make me question whether this particular Ford was a Henry or an Edsel.

Even more tenaciously than Nixon, he clung to the determination to fight inflation by fighting Congress over the budget. A barrage of vetoes shattered the peace of our brief honeymoon. Neither the president nor the Congress won the economic fight. Only inflation did.

Politically, we won a big victory in 1974's election. Watergate had tarnished every Republican's candidacy, and Jerry Ford's premature pardon of Nixon did nothing to help them. The result was that eighty new Democrats won election to Congress in 1974, the largest turnover in membership since the New Deal. Nearly all had Nixon and Ford to thank and no one else. They certainly showed little gratitude to veteran House leaders.

Because they comprised more than a quarter of all House Democrats, the members of the Class of '74 had a lot of muscle. Sometimes they had more muscle than heart or brains. They showed the strength of the first (and, in my view, the absence of the second and third) at our organizational caucus. Three veteran committee chairmen lost their positions in a flood of freshman, anti-establishment votes. My own vote lost, too, but not as much as did Eddie Hebert, Bob Pogue, and Wright Patman. Hebert could be a pain in the neck, but I thought he deserved another term leading Armed Services. The freshmen and some others thought he had had one too many already. Pogue was a fine chairman of Agriculture, but he had goaded the professional liberals too often. Patman's loss of Banking and Currency's chairmanship pained me most. For twenty-three terms, Wright Patman had been a fighting congressman, fighting for farmers and poor people and black people. His only sin was his age, eighty-one when the Ninety-fourth Congress convened. And that was a sin to the young newcomers, who booted him out, unmindful of the fact that their own presence was ultimately traceable to those boxes of evidence that Wright Patman had assembled and given to Sam Ervin.

As Speaker, I tried to be the leader of this group that refused to be led. They wanted to build a record, not a policy, and they had the votes to pass bills that I knew Jerry Ford would have to veto. He did, but they did not have the votes to override them. The consequence too often was neither a record nor a policy. It was just frustration.

Not always, though. It was the big freshman bloc that made possible my final piece of congressional reform. In late 1976, John Brademas brought David Obey by my office. Dave was a comparatively young member himself (then forty-two, he had come to Congress in 1969), and we talked about the need for a revised code of ethics for House members. I thought it a great idea, got a resolution passed to establish the House Commission on Admin-

With Bob Pogue, George Mahon, and Wright Patman.

istrative Review, and put David Obey in charge of it. The commission did an excellent job. Its eventual fruit (harvested just after my retirement) was a comprehensive code requiring public disclosure of members' financial records, limiting their income earned outside the House, and abolishing unofficial accounts. With that piece set to be placed, I knew that I could leave a Congress remade under my Speakership, a Congress more open and more democratic but a Congress just as solid as Frederick Muhlenberg's.

I liked that aspect of my job. I liked, too, some of its perquisites.

*A Speaker has many ceremonial duties here and abroad.* Carl Albert in China with John Rhodes, George Bush, and Deng Xiaoping.

As leader of the legislative branch of American government, a Speaker has many ceremonial duties here and abroad. I had loved to travel since my boyhood, and I had not had such fine experiences since my Oxford days. Asked to represent the United States, I visited the Soviet Union and had long personal talks with Leonid Brezhnev. In China, I walked along the Great Wall and met Communist party leaders (there were no other kinds of leaders) at every level. No trip thrilled me more—nor, I think, meant more to America—than the one that took me back to England in 1976. I was there not as an Oxford student to receive an education but as my country's chief legislator, there to receive the physical symbol of America's inheritance from Britain. To honor our bicentennial of independence, our mother country was lending us one of four surviving original copies of the Magna Charta. The charter of liberties that English barons had forced upon King John was the tip of the taproot that had flowered into our own Declaration of Independence and U.S. Constitution.

Its loan to America symbolized the completion of a long journey unforeseeable at Runnymede in 1215. I felt that it symbolized also the completion of a long personal journey that I had begun

*Now I was back in England once more to accept its gift for America but also for me.* Carl Albert with Queen Elizabeth II in 1976, when Britain loaned a copy of the Magna Charta to the United States in honor of the bicentennial of independence.

about seven hundred years later. At Bug Tussle School, I had dreamed of being a congressman, even a Speaker. At McAlester High School, I had studied the Constitution and won a trip to England and elsewhere. At the University of Oklahoma, I had orated on our Bill of Rights and had won a Rhodes scholarship and a trip back to England. As a young congressman, I had been given the chance for leadership, and for more than twenty years, I had met its demands. I had done all I ever dreamed of. I had done the best I could to defend the heritage of constitutional liberty that reached back to the Magna Charta. Now I was back in England once more to accept its gift for America but also for me. I returned, my long journey complete.

A few weeks later, I announced my retirement as Speaker of the House of Representatives and member of Congress from the Third Congressional District of Oklahoma. Already (ten years earlier) I had had one major heart attack. My doctors told me that my heart just would not take too much more. I was still young enough and still healthy enough to enjoy many years with my family and friends. A lot of those friends were in Congress, and several tried to talk me out of it, but they were friends enough to know just how determined Carl Albert could be once his mind was set.

People who did not know me quite so well made me some generous offers. For handsome salaries, I could have served on the boards of dozens of corporations and associations. I knew what they wanted. They wanted me to represent them in Washington, where I would lobby my old friends in Congress. That would amount to selling myself and the Speakership of the United States Congress. Ernie Albert's boy was not for sale. So I took my unspent campaign funds of thirty years' service (seven thousand dollars) and gave two thousand dollars to the Democratic Campaign Committee and five thousand dollars to the University of Oklahoma. I turned the Washington jobs down and went back to a little community called Bug Tussle, near the town of McAlester in Pittsburg County, Oklahoma.

It was the kind of place where nobody's boy was for sale.

# Where No Man Wears a Crown

In 1947, Mary and I packed everything we owned in a two-door Pontiac and drove to Washington. Thirty years later, we drove back to Oklahoma. We owned more, much of which we would have to ship, and we had two children, too. We had a Thunderbird, not a Pontiac, but the fact remained that Carl Albert was driving. I still am.

Since I had been home as much as possible over those thirty years, I knew that McAlester had changed a lot. No longer is it the booming industrial city that my parents knew, nor is it the metropolis that had so frightened a kid from country schools, but neither is it what it had been in the mid-1940s: a declining regional trade center slowly drying up with the hinterland about it. Its population has grown—grown bigger, not less friendly. The federal ammunition depot is still its major employer, but it employs more people. It has been blessed with its share (but no more than its fair share) of government projects that keep the town healthy. One fact is constant here, too: McAlester is my hometown.

The town takes a lot of pride in that. Grand Avenue, where I heard some of my first political "speakings," has been renamed Carl Albert Parkway. Amid the gas stations and fast-food franchises that line the new highway bypass, a bright blue water tower proclaims "McAlester—The Home of Carl Albert." A fine regional medical complex has revitalized the northeast part of town. One of its features is the Carl Albert Mental Health Center. So far, I have not had need of its services, but I do occasionally fill my car's tank at Carl Albert Texaco.

Down the street is the federal courthouse, renamed the Carl Albert Federal Building and United States Courthouse. At the corner of its site, there is a nice bust of Carl Albert with some awfully nice words about him; the people of McAlester put that up. The Oklahoma Historical Society put up a big granite slab several blocks away. There's not much there now, a few vacant lots and some rusting rails where the Katy Railroad once carried cars filled with coal from the Bohlen mines. The marker explains that this quite undistinguished site is the birthplace of Carl Albert, member of Congress, 1947 to 1977, and Speaker of the House of Representatives, 1971 to 1977. I guess those things strike visitors who call on me, and maybe they impress the town's occasional tourist.

One who is not impressed at all is Kathryn Marie Albert. Katie is the daughter of David and his wife, Elizabeth, and she is my favorite visitor. A bright girl of three, she must have gotten her red hair from me. When her parents bring her down from Oklahoma City, she pays no attention at all to the bust of Carl Albert at the Federal Building. Instead, she runs to my office and heads straight for a file cabinet's bottom drawer, the one that I have marked "Katie's Drawer." She knows that inside there will always be a little gift, and she gives me back a big smile.

Katie calls me Grandpa. When I walk down Carl Albert Parkway, nobody calls me Mr. Speaker. I am just plain Carl to them. I always say the best sound to a politician's ear is that of his own name. Most of the time, I know the person who stops me—know his parents, even grandparents, too— and we have a nice conversation. That pleases me more than any marker I ever saw.

I work nearly every day in McAlester. Back when I was majority leader, Congress passed a law to give retired Speakers benefits similar to those extended to retired presidents, so I have an office in Carl Albert Federal Building on Carl Albert Parkway. The government lets me hire a small staff, and for years Sara Lane and Lois

Washington have helped me with my papers, my visitors, and my obligations.

As I have grown older, one or both of them drive me to occasional events held in my honor. I am still surprised at how often these occur, and I am always proud. A very special one came a few years ago when Oklahoma put my portrait in its capitol rotunda. Charles Banks Wilson, an artist from Miami, Oklahoma, painted the portrait, as he already had done for the few Oklahomans honored there: Sequoyah, Jim Thorpe, Bob Kerr, and (later) Angie Debo. For mine, he chose to portray me in movement, stepping out of a background. That background is his reproduction of an old photograph of the Bug Tussle student body of 1914, when I was a first grader standing in the front row and dreaming of going to Congress. I was proud to be in Oklahoma City for its unveiling; I was prouder still that every living person in that painting was there, too, and I saw that they were individually introduced on the occasion that honored them.

I live now among many of them. When we returned home, Mary and I sold the house that we had kept all those years as our McAlester home. We bought the house next to my sister Kathryn's. My two surviving brothers, Earl and Noal (Budge), live in the area, too, but Kathryn and I always tease them that we are the lucky ones because they do not live in Bug Tussle; we do. In fact, my sister and I live on a piece of land that Papa farmed when we were all kids growing up in an unpainted frame house. Just down the hill from me is the very bottomland where he grew the cotton that I so dreaded to pick every year. That land is covered by water now, the water of Lake Eufaula. About ten miles northeast stands the Eufaula Dam, which created that lake.

It must be the lake that accounts for the remarkable fact that the Bug Tussle community has more people now than at any time in its history. Some of them are old-timers, folks like Kathryn and me and Manes Craighead and Bill Anderson, pals from my boyhood. More of them are newcomers, drawn by Lake Eufaula's recreation and Bug Tussle's simple country living. Quite a few live, like me, on the lake's shores, their homes backing to the waters that are there because of the dam. Every night a lot of them like to sit on their back porches and look out over the lake toward Eufaula Dam. A few know that this neighbor was one of those who helped build that dam conceived in dust, cradled in flood, and created by men. As for me, I prefer to sit on my front porch, where I can look over the hills and meadows of the old Bug Tussle community. God created those.

If I walk just a bit, I can be at the old Bug Tussle School. It is not a school any longer. Its enrollment fell below the state-required level in 1968 and it had to close. One of my saddest days was that one. I spoke at the closing, and my friends thought it would be nice if I were the one to padlock the school on its last day. I could not do it. Carrying a lunch bucket and red primer, I had walked through that same door into a world of learning and achievement. I would not be the one to lock it behind me.

Over in McAlester, the high school that I entered as a scared country kid in overalls and brogans stayed in use until recently. The old building still stands on a hill a block from my office, but the kids now go to a modern building a few miles away. Every once in a while, I have given a speech to those kids, and I find that it is just as rewarding to be in the new building as in the old. From time to time, I tutor some of those kids, helping them with their grammar or their Spanish or getting them ready for a college-entrance examination. It is partial repayment of a debt that I owe their parents and grandparents.

The University of Oklahoma has had me teach, too. Just after I retired, I offered a course on politics and congressional leadership. The young students seemed to enjoy it. Maybe one or two will one day profit from it as I did from Cortez Ewing's lectures back in the twenties and early thirties. Dr. Ewing's lectures still stand as the university's greatest gift to me, but there have been others. One has been to honor me with the creation of the Carl Albert Congressional Research Center. The only academic facility in America devoted to the study of its legislative branch, the center attracts top graduate students from all over the country and brings them

Carl Albert, from the painting in the Oklahoma Statehouse rotunda by Charles Banks Wilson.

together with outstanding scholars and major congressional figures. The center also maintains an archive filled with the papers of several congressmen from Oklahoma and elsewhere. Mine are there, all two million pages of them, the mountain of paper that records my public life and makes possible this book. From time to time, I like to visit the center and talk with the bright young people there. I am asked to give them an occasional speech, and I am always pleased to do so. In fact, I give a lot of speeches. Mary sometimes kids me that the soldier she married became a politician and turned out to be a speech maker. I just remind her that I started out a speech maker and it is what made everything else possible.

Some speeches I give before my earliest audience: the people of McAlester. They are not the same people, but I am not a high school kid, either. I do, however, sometimes use thoughts and phrases that I had even then. On July 4, 1985, I did that. I spoke at McAlester's First Baptist Church to commemorate our Declaration of Independence. I told them how, nine years earlier, I had given another speech in Washington as Speaker of the House when I welcomed England's queen and accepted her nation's gift: the loan of the Magna Charta. On that day in 1985, I was not the Speaker. I was just Carl, and I spoke the words I had used as a student orator. They were words about how our balance of powers and our Bill of Rights "distinguish Americans from the subject races of the world. They are the things that make of America a land where all are kings, but no man dares to wear a crown." The difference this time was that I had a lifetime's experience to affirm that. The constant was that I was once more in McAlester, Oklahoma, one of those places where no man wears a crown.

Lest I be tempted to forget that, I remember well one speech I gave. It was at a little country school and I was mighty glad to get its invitation. I talked to a bunch of elementary kids, and I told them about when I was a boy back in Bug Tussle School. Congressman Charlie Carter had told us all about Congress, had told us that one of us might one day become a congressman. Hoping to inspire them, I told them the same thing.

In a way it worked. I finished, and a little towheaded boy came up to me.

"Mister," he said, "that sure was inspiring."

Pleased, I asked him just what words I had said that he found so inspiring—I would have to use them again.

He answered, "It wasn't anything you said. It was watching you. I was thinking if a little shrimp like you can grow up to be a congressman, I can grow up to be president of the United States."

In this country, with that attitude, he can.

Some of my speeches are not that much fun. The people I knew as a boy are old now, and many are dying. Too often, I am asked to speak at their funerals. I spoke at one just a few months ago, that of Joe Thomas. It was at a little black church. I talked about how long I had known Joe. I talked about how we had been boys together back in Bug Tussle. I told about the day we both had started school, about how we had walked together to Kyle Tennant's meadow, how when we had gotten there, how I had angled off to the left and Joe and the other black kids had turned right. I told Joe's family and friends what I had thought about segregation back then: that it was unfair, unhuman, un-Christian. I told them how happy I was that Joe Thomas and I had lived long enough to see it end and how glad I was that Joe's grandchildren would have a better chance. I told them that I was thankful they had given me the chance to help make that true.

Then I went home.

# Index